Navigating Today's Environment:

The Directors' and O~~ Guide to Restructt~~

D1215869

John Wm. ("Jack") Butler, Jr – Consulting Editor
Skadden, Arps, Slate, Meagher & Flom LLP

Published by Globe White Page Ltd

GLOBE
WHITE PAGE

Navigating Today's Environment:
The Directors' and Officers' Guide to Restructuring

Consulting editor John Wm. ("Jack") Butler, Jr
Skadden, Arps, Slate, Meagher & Flom LLP

Editor Nigel Page

Chief production editor and sub-editor Matt Rowan

Assistant to consulting editor Sarah Baker
Skadden, Arps, Slate, Meagher & Flom LLP

Publisher Tim Dempsey

Publishing directors Tony Harriss, Nigel Page

Printing and binding R.R. Donnelley & Sons Company

Distribution manager Amanda Green

Navigating Today's Environment:
The Directors' and Officers' Guide to Restructuring
is published by:
Globe White Page Ltd
New Hibernia House
Winchester Walk
London Bridge
London SE1 9AG
United Kingdom
Tel +44 (0) 20 7234 0606
Fax +44 (0) 20 7234 0808
Email info@globewhitepage.com
Web www.navigatingtodaysenvironment.com

Published 2010
ISBN 978-1-905773-08-4

Navigating Today's Environment: The Directors' and Officers' Guide to Restructuring
© Globe White Page Ltd

Front-cover artwork
©iStockphoto.com/Paulo Ferreira

www.globewhitepage.com

Contents

Navigating Today's Environment:
The Directors' and Officers' Guide to Restructuring

Contents

Contents

Navigating Today's Environment: Introduction and acknowledgments

John Wm ("Jack") Butler Jr,
Consulting Editor
Skadden, Arps, Slate, Meagher &
Flom LLP

In my experience, the men and women who lead public companies understand their duties of loyalty and care to their companies and work diligently to fulfill these responsibilities in good faith. Most have come into their leadership roles in the boardroom and executive suite with a track record of business success that has distinguished themselves from their peers. They are opportunists who are keenly focused and interested in furthering the success of their business enterprises and increasing returns to their stockholders. And without apology, they are capitalists who desire to be well compensated for their contributions to their companies.

Yet the wealth of experience and good intentions present in most boardrooms does not necessarily translate into an immediate ability to anticipate and effectively manage rapid change in a company's circumstances. During my career, I have had the privilege of working with boards and senior management teams on transformational restructurings in the airline, automotive, energy, healthcare, manufacturing, media and telecommunications, retail and utilities industries. These mandates have come from such diverse companies as Comdisco, FPA Medical Management, Rite Aid, Service Merchandise, Sprint Nextel and Xerox. They have taken me to US Airways' headquarters on one of the first commercial flights after 9/11, to the Enron executive suite on Thanksgiving weekend in 2001, to the Kmart Corporation boardroom during New Year's week in 2002, and to Delphi's world headquarters in Michigan on a weekly basis for almost five years to participate in the realignment of the automotive industry that culminated in the Chrysler, Delphi, Ford and GM restructurings.

In each of these situations and thousands of others, directors and officers are confronted with unanticipated challenges to their company's business model, strategic vision, liquidity and even survival. While there are always notable exceptions, these men and women are often forced to operate outside their comfort zones to make risk assessments and pursue strategic paths previously uncharted in their professional lives. While not often expressed, I believe that, because of their unfamiliarity with the terrain they are navigating, many of these leaders are concerned about the degree to which they must rely on external experts for guidance. And while they always make the business decisions, I believe that their degree of reliance on others more experienced in change management and corporate restructuring (whether their fellow directors or managers or outside advisors) represents a level of *de facto* delegation that is troublesome to them.

A resource guide for directors and officers

Navigating Today's Environment is a resource guide for US officers and directors, as well as those who are interested in and follow the management and corporate governance of US companies. Much of the knowledge and experience conveyed in these pages is relevant to leaders of public and private companies of all sizes, whether small-cap, middle-market or Fortune 1000. And directors and officers of non-US domiciled companies should also find this book informative, although they will need to adapt these lessons to the legal and regulatory frameworks of their own domicile.

Navigating Today's Environment was written to promote corporate governance best practices by supplementing directors' and officers' prior experiences with specific knowledge about how to manage companies that are undergoing rapid change and/or are at risk of becoming, or have already become, distressed business enterprises. Like most "self-help" books, it is best consumed before it is needed, since one of the greatest contributions directors and officers can make to their company and their stakeholders is to detect and mitigate distress at its earliest stages.

Unlike many other professional books, *Navigating Today's Environment* was created as a series of conversations with the leading financial advisors, investment bankers, investors, lawyers and turnaround managers in the restructuring community.

I believed from the outset of this endeavor that directors and officers would be benefited most by exposure to the leading voices of the restructuring world, rather than a treatise prepared by a single author or organization.

As Consulting Editor, I was afforded complete autonomy to establish the content of this book and to invite the contributors who have lent their experiences and imperatives to these pages. While a few of my friends and colleagues were not able to participate, I am grateful to the many authors who have contributed their voices, knowledge and judgment. The content in this book reflects their individual views, and those views are not presented as those of their firms, other contributors or the editors.

Forty-five "conversations"

Grouped into seven sections, *Navigating Today's Environment* consists of 45 separate "conversations" with the leading restructuring voices of our generation.

We begin with observations from my fellow members in the inaugural class of the *Turnaround, Restructuring and Distressed Investing Industry Hall of Fame*. Dom DiNapoli, Larry Marsiello, Henry Miller and Bill Repko each provide unique perspectives on the crucial role that directors play in preventing corporate freefall and keeping companies afloat in turbulent times. Wilbur Ross shares his investor sensibilities in a practical guide for directors of distressed companies, Professor Edward Altman explains why liquidity, profitability and (lack of) leverage are the most influential determinatives of a company's long-term success, and Harvey Miller reflects on

planning effective restructurings through the looking glass of 50 years of reorganizations.

Following a primer on corporate governance, including the role and influence of government and activist shareholders, we turn to enterprise risk assessment. Cogent and methodical risk assessment is clearly one of the most important tasks undertaken by boards of directors and senior management teams. We focus on risk examinations that include understanding the impact of liquidity and derivatives on the corporate enterprise, maintaining effective internal controls, refinancing the looming "wall of debt", and differentiating between strategic decision-making and "desperation" transactions.

We then examine the full range of restructuring tools in the corporate arsenal such as debt buybacks, exchange offers, asset dispositions, negotiations and refinancings with lenders, and various claims adjustment and corporate restructuring alternatives available under federal and state law (ranging from state law assignments for the benefit of creditors to receiverships to prearranged and traditional bankruptcy reorganizations). These restructuring strategies are evaluated in the context of how they may be influenced by the trading of a company's debt claims and securities and how, why and when creditors may credit bid their debt for control of the company in a change-of-control transaction.

In our "Special Focus Forum", we explore what directors should be prepared to consider when a spinoff fails, how transfers made in business transactions can be avoided subsequently through federal and state "fraudulent" transfer statutes, executive compensation "best practices", managing global enterprise value across international borders, and emerging practices in the selection of boards of directors when companies are restructured. Because distressed situations require specialized resources, CEOs and other leading executives representing turnaround firms, communication specialists, claims agents and independent asset advisory firms each explain their organizations' roles and value proposition for distressed companies.

Navigating Today's Environment concludes with closing reflections about whether the US Chapter 11 reorganization system should be reformed, and about how directors and officers should be prepared to protect companies from the boom and bust cycle by "finding, facing and fixing" operational, structural, competitive and macroeconomic problems.

Navigating the "new normal"

The task facing directors and officers in today's "new normal" is especially challenging. From 1960 to 2007, directors and officers managed their companies in an economy where real GDP rose an average of 3.4 per cent each year, and the Dow Jones Industrial Average rose from 618.04 to 14,279.96. Following the recession that began in December, 2007 and technically ended in the third quarter of 2009, real GDP is forecast to rise an average of only 2.6 per cent per year over the next decade through 2020. The Dow Jones, after falling to a low of 6,547.05 in March 2009 and recovering to 11,205.03 in April 2010, declined back to the mid-9000 range in July, 2010. From 2007 to 2010, US government spending surged from $2.728 trillion to $3.720 trillion per year (from an inflation-adjusted $674 billion in 1960) as the US deficit surged to more than 10 per cent of GDP — about twice the prior high over the last 50 years.

One of the most compelling features of the "new normal" is sustained volatility, which implies continuing wide swings in market performance, asset values, consumer confidence and spending, and availability and cost of capital. Another feature is increased regulation. For example, the Dodd-Frank Wall Street Reform and Consumer Protection Act of 2010 features unprecedented federal oversight of corporate governance, including shareholder "say on pay" on executive compensation, independence requirements for board compensation committees and their consultants, executive compensation disclosures and clawbacks, disclosure of employee and director hedging, elimination of broker discretionary voting, and proxy access by shareholders. New regulatory schemes for financial institutions, including changes in capital requirements and the regulation of hedge funds, may have unintended collateral consequences on the availability, form and cost of capital.

How do companies manage themselves in the new normal? In 2008, near the beginning of the recent recession, my colleagues and I distributed a client letter in which we suggested that directors and senior management of all companies, regardless of size or domicile, should consider the need for risk reviews, focusing particularly on liquidity and capital resources, in order to navigate through what appeared to us to be "the perfect liquidity and capital storm of declining operating cash flow, fixed (or increasing) costs and limited availability of new credit and equity capital and/or the withdrawal of existing credit". We believed that directors and officers might best fulfill their duties to stakeholders, and their constituency expectations, during those troubled times by focusing primarily on building a liquidity bridge across an abyss of then-unknown depth and duration. Fortunately, this difficult message, communicated through many channels, resonated with most officers and directors, who effectively guided their companies through the recession by creating and maintaining expansive liquidity bridges, albeit often at the cost of other economic opportunities.

The bar has been raised

Post-recession, in the new normal, I believe the corporate governance bar has been raised and the challenges facing directors and officers are more nuanced and complex in a global marketplace that is experiencing de-globalization, de-leveraging and re-regulation. Recently, my colleagues and I supplemented our earlier viewpoint in our 2010 *Skadden Insights* publication. We suggested that, looking forward, directors and officers should continue to assess potential liquidity and capital risks while also focusing on opportunities presented within their companies, across their sectors and in regional, national and global economies, including those created during the recession. Among these opportunities are potentially undervalued companies and/or assets (including over-leveraged investments that holders desire or need to monetize), industry consolidation, emerging technologies, demand arising from new public mandates, and new capital structures and channels. These capital conduits are being fueled by over $3 trillion in cash on the balance sheets of US corporations, which represents the largest asset class in the US.

I believe that assessing the "risk-reward" ratio of potential corporate opportunities while maintaining diligent and effective risk oversight will be tremendously challenging to US corporations in the near-term. While directors and officers generally understand that these assessments should be made through the prism of current economic conditions and near-, intermediate- and long-term prospects, they should exercise caution in this high-volatility environment (while avoiding paralysis and the failure to maximize business enterprise value).

And as before, directors and officers have to contend not only with the unintended collateral consequences of their actions and inactions, but also with "event risks" (eg, the impact of Icelandic volcanic ash on the global economy, natural and man-made environmental disasters like Hurricane Katrina and the Deepwater Horizon failure in the Gulf of Mexico, and global terrorism since we cannot rely on bombs not going off in the shoes of airline passengers or vehicles driven into Times Square). While these events cannot be precisely forecast in advance, what is known is that event risks occur — and that their impact on a corporate enterprise can be mitigated to some extent by careful planning.

Directors and officers will also need to take into account unfamiliar features of the new normal. These include stricter but inconsistent government regulation, government actions to increase revenues (including through substantially higher direct and indirect taxes), continued high "real" unemployment (which translates into nearly one in five US workers unemployed or under-employed), materially reduced consumer spending and investment, a weaker US dollar, and increasing economic pressure on state and local governments — caused in part by unfunded federal mandates — that will likely result in municipal insolvencies and disruption in the municipal bond market.

But is this time really different?

While I believe that directors and officers must be prepared to navigate the new normal, I also think it is essential for corporate leaders to maintain their composure by not over-reacting to the current environment. Instead, their companies will be best served by directors and officers using their wealth of experience and expanding their knowledge base in order to make informed judgments that benefit their stakeholders.

Last year, Princeton University Press published a serious book by Carmen N Reinhart, an economist at the University of Maryland, and Kenneth S Rogoff, an international chess grandmaster, former chief economist of the International Monetary Fund and current Harvard professor. Their book, *This Time Is Different*, reconstructs hundreds of financial crises from 66 countries over the last 800 years. Their thesis is that the recent recession is not a novel catastrophe, but rather a re-run of our human experience. But I think that their work also teaches another important lesson: throughout history, very smart people can, and, unfortunately, often do, make very poor business decisions. So whether the current environment truly represents a new normal, or instead the latest sequel in the Reinhart-Rogoff economic passion play, officers and directors need to be well prepared and well grounded to meet the demands of this post-recession environment.

In this period of gradual recovery and serious continuing challenges in the global economy, companies should continue to examine their liquidity and capital needs and sources, while also factoring in the risk of potential future financial distress. But they must also remain sharply focused on maximizing shareholder value by pursuing the corporate opportunities that they have identified, including those created during the recent recession and its aftermath.

Acknowledgments

The premise of *Navigating Today's Environment* — that a book of conversations could be crafted from the leading voices of the US restructuring community to engage and inform directors and officers of US corporations — would never have become reality without the support of many people, including all of the contributing authors whose names and profiles are located at the back of this book. Equally important was the support, patience and collaboration of the publisher and editorial team at Globe White Page Ltd, including, especially, Tim Dempsey, Nigel Page and Matt Rowan. I am also very grateful for the contributions of my colleague, Sarah Baker, who worked alongside me to consider every word on these pages.

Our publication team gave a great deal of thought to the distribution scheme for *Navigating Today's Environment*. I am grateful to the publisher and to RR Donnelley for their agreement to distribute the softcover edition to the Lead Independent Director, CEO and CFO of the Fortune 1000. This was underwritten in part by our headline sponsors, FTI Consulting Inc and Rothschild Inc, without whom this book would not have been published. Our endeavor has also benefited greatly from the participation of the American Bankruptcy Institute and the Turnaround Management Association, two of the pre-eminent professional associations in the corporate restructuring world. The ABI and TMA not only contributed editorial content but have also provided additional distribution channels for the book. In addition, the hardcover edition of *Navigating Today's Environment* is being distributed through commercial channels in participation with Beard Group. I have always admired Chris Beard's vision as a publisher, editor and reporter in the restructuring community and his involvement in this project is welcomed and appreciated.

Finally, I am grateful for the support of my law firm and my family. Both understand my long-standing commitment to helping companies and their investors successfully execute complex business reorganizations, as well as my particular focus on helping directors and officers navigate their companies through distressed situations. Both have afforded me the time and opportunity to pursue my vision of this book. I hope that the thoughtful conversations awaiting the reader in these pages will help facilitate corporate preparedness and will provide helpful strategies for *Navigating Today's Environment*.

Turnaround, Restructuring, and Distressed Investing Industry Hall of Fame Contributors

The role of the board in preventing corporate freefall

Dominic DiNapoli, Executive Vice President and Chief Operating Officer, FTI Consulting Inc

If fall is the season of cooling temperatures, then the autumn of 2008 should be remembered as the "deep freeze". In a three-week period beginning in September 2008, eight renowned financial institutions teetered or fell. And like dominos dropping, they brought the US financial system to its knees and sent the global economy into a tailspin. Lehman Brothers filed for bankruptcy. Fannie Mae and Freddie Mac were seized by the federal government, as was AIG, effectively, in the form of an $85 billion bailout. Washington Mutual and Merrill Lynch, both on the verge of collapse, were forced to sell themselves hastily to larger rivals.

All of these firms had top-notch talent, many decades of history, and well-respected businesses and brands. All had relatively diversified and accomplished boards, although some would argue they were skewed toward an older generation of executives. They were also publicly traded on the New York Stock Exchange, which requires the boards of its listed companies to assign a committee to regularly review major financial risks and assess steps management has taken to address those risks. The most obvious question that lingers in the aftermath of the deep freeze is: "Where were the boards?" This question is particularly pertinent in light of the many subsequent revelations of dubious business practices within other financial institutions.

Where were the boards?
A major responsibility of the board of directors is to ensure the viability and sustainability of the firm. When a board's fiduciary role is largely assumed by US Treasury Department officials, how can the performance of those directors be seen as anything other than inadequate? Some say that these institutions were faced with sudden and unmanageable conditions created by an unfathomably complex and interconnected financial system; they were victims of an inherently flawed system that could be leveled by a few weak links. Many point out that this crisis was unprecedented.

And while this may be true to a degree, this argument overlooks the fact that we were warned about the potential of such a meltdown back in 1998. The collapse of Long-Term Capital Management (LTCM) demonstrated all too clearly that complex financial institutions pose serious systemic risks that require laser-focused oversight by managers and directors.

In the case of LTCM, the directors did not adequately understand the complexity of the firm's derivative-based trading models and the extent of leverage employed until it was too late. The firm's collapse forced a massive bailout by other banks and investment houses under supervision of the Federal Reserve.

So what did boards learn from the Long-Term Capital incident? Since 1998, have boards of financial institutions become more engaged in the businesses they are appointed to oversee? The deep freeze of 2008 would challenge a "yes" answer to this question.

Moreover, between 1998 and 2008, we had the monumental failures of Enron, HealthSouth and Worldcom, among others. In March 2004, the *CPA*

Journal cited 'passive, non-independent, rubber-stamping boards of directors' as the most significant transgressor in the governance lapses that led to the scandals in the early part of the decade. The result was the Sarbanes-Oxley legislation, which famously mandated new rules of board independence, management accountability, reporting standards, and other safeguards. Most experts agree that Sarbanes-Oxley did bring about some substantive governance improvements. A December 2008 Business Roundtable survey of member CEOs, for example, revealed that 90 per cent of member company boards were at least 80 per cent independent. Yet, we still had notable failures of corporate governance in 2008, prompting one commentator in *The Wall Street Journal* (October 14, 2008) to ask: 'Were they lulled into complacency by their CEOs? Or did they lack the insight to see that their firms had placed themselves in great peril if there were major disruptions in financial markets? Or were they looking at computer models rather than applying the judgment they were selected to make?'

There is the key word: what exactly is this thing called judgment? And what kind of judgment will be expected from directors and boards at the close of such a tumultuous decade?

The rubber stamp has left the boardroom

The quaint perception of a director goes something like this: he/she attends four meetings a year, listens carefully to presentations, sits on a committee, and collects the fee. Most directors generally do not second-guess management, at least not openly. On the CEO's part, he thinks of the board as his advisors, a handful as his confidants, and one or two as his friends. When he is having a tough time with his Asian subsidiary, he might call one of his directors with relevant experience and ask for advice. The following week, he might call a different director just to chat about whatever is on his mind.

Today, there is nothing quaint about directorship. For the past two decades, and most notably since Sarbanes-Oxley, the formality of board roles, discussions, and interactions with management has increased dramatically. More than ever, directorship today requires a substantial commitment of personal time and mental energy. Even retired executives can no longer afford the time and focus to sit on five or six boards, as they might have done in the past.

Today's directors know their role will be active, business matters before them will be urgent, and their decision-making may be highly scrutinized. Shareholders pay directors (yes, your fee is their money) to watch over their investment, so a director's responsibility is to bring an independent perspective to enterprise strategy and risk, and to ensure that management is executing strategy and managing risk suitably. Today, particularly in light of the deep freeze, wise boards govern with the knowledge that the worst can happen.

Unfortunately, this increased sensitivity in boardrooms coincides with a general decline in the operational experience of the average corporate director. In June 2009, *Harvard Business Review* disclosed new research that found only 20 per cent of directors today can be categorized as "experienced CEOs", a dramatic decrease from 53 per cent in 2000. The Business Roundtable survey mentioned earlier reveals that 36 per cent of actively working CEOs serve only on the board of the company they are managing, and 76 per cent serve on only one additional board. With hands-on management experience harder to find in boardrooms today, it is clear that boards are less equipped to navigate operational declines and other business adversity than in the past.

In a weak economic environment, pressure on directors intensifies due to the possibility of a company entering the ominously named "zone of insolvency". When a company approaches insolvency, a murky term generally meaning it cannot meet its ordinary debt obligations as they come due, directors' primary fiduciary duties shift from shareholders to creditors, and the legal protections normally afforded directors under the business judgment rule become less clear. This greatly alters the dynamic of an already urgent situation. It is extremely difficult to maintain the confidence of senior lenders, who tend to be less patient, more demanding, and more likely to request removal of incumbent management and/or appoint a chief restructuring officer. Effective control of the company by its creditors entails a loss of management prerogative and a potential increase in legal liability for boards and directors.

Amid such increased scrutiny, criticism, second-guessing and potential liability, what is a board to do? The key here is vigilance. This quality must become the new reality in boardrooms. Directors need to make sure their eyes and minds are wide open from their first day on the job, and I have two recommendations for doing just that. First, learn the business as if you will have to manage it someday…because you might. Second, assume you are only getting partial information.

Learn the business as if you will have to manage it some day

Generally, boards are most helpful when focusing on the forest through the trees. But it is necessary to study the trees on occasion, too. In the wake of the Enron and Worldcom scandals, 25 per cent of CEOs surveyed by Yale School of Management in 2002 said their board did not appreciate the complexity of the business they oversaw. This is troubling, since in the event of a restructuring, a board needs to take a more active, and knowledgeable, role in challenging the turnaround plans of management.

Reading relevant publications, following trends and asking the right questions are some of the ways directors can keep abreast of the company and its market dynamics. However, vigilance is not just about information; it is also about interaction. Directors should get out and talk to people.

Companies with particularly complex business models or capital structures often come with a steep learning curve for directors. Still, one of the most effective ways for a board to learn the business and the marketplace is by studying the competition. What are your company's relative strengths and weaknesses compared to key competitors? Are competitors positioning their companies or their products differently? Are competitors seen as better equipped to serve changing needs? How many customers are being lost to competitors, and why?

Let us look more closely at this last question. In such a scenario, a common response from management is that a particular competitor is simply "buying the business", or lowering prices in a way that is unsustainable.

However, a wise board understands that any competitor gaining market share is a threat, whatever the reason or rationale. As a director accountable to shareholders, you are obligated to investigate or request management to investigate. For example, you might request a presentation from the relevant managers at the next quarterly meeting. The point here is that directors should not rely solely on management presentations, internal information packets or trade publications to learn about the business.

Assume you are only getting partial information

I often encourage directors to approach their responsibilities and attend meetings and management presentations with an "assumption of selectivity". In other words, directors should assume that management is providing them with information selectively, or withholding certain

intelligence, purposefully or inadvertently. This is not to suggest that senior management are in the habit of dissembling or deception, but that a CEO will use his judgment as to what qualifies as worthy of board discussion. Enron's Ken Lay, for example, decided not to share with his board that whistle-blower Sherron Watkins had raised major questions about financial irregularities.

Boards that assume they are getting partial information ask a lot more questions and make a lot more requests. This greater board vigilance may put the CEO on his back foot and affect the level of trust around the room, but the alternative is governance in the dark. Boards have to work at creating a delicate balance, because a CEO who does not believe his board to be in his corner is also problematic. In the September 2002 issue of *Harvard Business Review*, governance expert Jeffrey Sonnenfeld wrote: 'What kind of CEO waits until the night before the board meeting to dump on the directors a phonebook-size report that includes, buried in a thicket of sub-clauses and footnotes, the news that earnings are off for the second consecutive quarter? This is surely not a CEO who trusts his or her board.'

Board vigilance may create tension with management, but it should be seen as healthy tension. It may feel like opposition to management, but it should be seen as loyal opposition. The dynamics of checks and balances should serve to foster a sense of mutual respect. And respect, along with trust and candor, are essential ingredients of healthy corporate governance.

When a company's performance begins to seriously decline, directors must make a point of becoming even more vigilant and engaged. Even if the declines are incremental, the board must respond with urgency. I have seen many boards squander the "luxury" of time by assuming that matters will naturally stabilize or that one weak quarter is no cause for action.

Businesses can unravel at lightning speed; there is absolutely no excuse to "wait and see". Even if the business will not deteriorate quickly, the speed with which the board intervenes can make the difference between what we call a soft landing (restructuring as the culmination of thoughtful strategy) and a freefall (a sudden, unanticipated bankruptcy).

So when there are signs of trouble, how exactly can a board exercise its duties to ensure the best possible outcome? At the first sign of performance weakness, boards should answer the following four questions:

Do we have the right management team for the task at hand?

The CEO is the single most important factor determining the success of a company. That is why the first question boards must answer is whether the current CEO and his team are right for the job, assuming a protracted decline in performance. The CEO's challenge, in most cases, is to demonstrate agility and the decisiveness necessary to lead the company through the difficult times.

Boards should avoid snap judgments here. Some CEOs can make the shift, which helps to preserve continuity in leadership, always helpful when navigating a tough environment. From my experience, however, a majority of CEOs perform better in good times than in bad.

Sometimes a CEO's sales and marketing orientation, which has allowed him to exploit the up cycle, works against him in an adverse environment. According to a survey conducted in 2003 by Seton Hall University, 87 per cent of CEOs and financial professionals believe that management's inability to change is one of the three primary reasons that companies fail. "Terminal euphoria" is a common syndrome of incumbent management.

To help in the assessment of management, it is important for boards to understand and keep in mind the nature of performance decline. If the broad marketplace is declining, then the key question is whether the CEO is willing and able to hunker down and retrench. It is this type of assessment that boards of major homebuilders, for example, should have been making in early 2007 when it was clear that the housing market was in steady decline. In a weakening market, companies need to aggressively reduce the overhead cost base that was built up during the growth cycle. The CEO must demonstrate a survivalist temperament. For example, is his highest priority fixed on maintaining liquidity and monitoring cash flow? Can he institute and enforce an aggressive action plan to cut costs and hoard cash? Is he ready to furlough or lay off employees, stretch out vendor payments and/or re-negotiate contracts?

If performance decline is unique to the company, however, then the issue is likely one of core business strategy or execution. Here the mantra is "First, direction; then, traction". Is the CEO's core strategy flawed and is he willing and able to change direction? Is the new strategy demonstrating traction and evident in operating results?

The ousting of Fritz Henderson from General Motors in December 2009 was a decision based not on his ability to retrench or fix the balance sheet, which by the time of his departure had grown to a record $42 billion in cash. Instead, Henderson was reportedly removed based on his perceived unwillingness and inability to shift strategic direction, particularly whether or not to sell Vauxhall/Opel, the company's European division, according to many reports. Fair or not, Henderson was unable to lose the "old GM" label. One source was quoted in the *Financial Times* (on December 1, 2009) as saying: 'I don't think anyone thought his tenure was a disaster. This is just a killer board.'

Do we have the right strategic plan?

Most distressed companies face critical challenges beyond the balance sheet. Recapitalization is important for quickly shoring up finances, but it does little to ensure demand for the company's products and services, long-term cash flows, and operational sustainability. While reducing overhead costs is important, particularly during a period of broad market decline, directors and management must acknowledge that you cannot cut your way to a long-term turnaround. Equal focus must be placed on deeper strategic or structural problems in the core business.

In formal strategic planning, typically the board relies on management to perform the SWOT analysis, conduct the market research, present the competitive intelligence, and define the strategic commitments. However, boards should use caution and not rely exclusively on management's "spin" on the market opportunity. Invariably, there will be loyalty to legacy businesses and practices, so boards need to ask detailed questions, challenge assumptions, and perhaps recommend outside consultants and advisors to help guide the planning process.

Directors also need to make sure that management's focus does not wander away from the core business. Think twice if management immediately presents a strategic vision focused on launching new products or entering new markets, in the belief that revenue growth will solve underlying strategic or operational weaknesses. Directors should ensure that the strategic plan is built on a genuine and unassailable competitive advantage. Without a competitive advantage as the foundation of any new strategy, an operational turnaround will be virtually doomed.

As I mentioned earlier, once the direction is agreed, the next step is to assess traction over time. Changing strategic direction is not easy. It may involve selling off non-core businesses, increasing R&D investments, or retrenching from certain markets. It may involve shuttering factories, reducing headcount, or dissolving brands. Whatever the requisite changes, directors and management must work together to make sure that disruptions are productive, not destructive. The goal is to implement the changes and make traction before conditions worsen and formal restructuring talks are required.

Let us revisit General Motors as an illustration of how difficult it can be to shift strategic direction and escape a flawed business model, particularly in the manufacturing sector. By now, the automaker's legacy costs, labor union dependencies, and lack of organizational agility are legendary. For decades, the company's cost base was deemed to be unsustainable, yet management displayed a bewildering inability to take dramatic action or commit to new strategic directions. GM's market share dropped from 46 per cent of the US automotive market in the 1950s to a 19 per cent share just as it filed bankruptcy in June 2009. As I mentioned earlier, operational turnaround is virtually impossible without an authentic competitive advantage. In June 2009, could anyone have identified GM's unique competitive advantage?

According to recently published research by Harvard Business School, the long and steady decline of General Motors was caused by management's inability to continue doing the three things that had made the company so successful in earlier days: first, pay close attention to what is happening in customers' lives in the context of the larger environment; second, keep an equally close eye on the competition; third, understand how a company's structure and culture relate to its strategy.

Customers. Competition. Culture. These are the three levers that MBA candidates study in Strategic Planning 101. This was not about the need for balance sheet re-engineering. It had everything to do with core business strategy. It is astonishing that a company whose early success was defined by strategic insight could lose that discipline in such a momentous fashion.

A company's genuine competitive advantage must be the ballast that will strengthen the core business over time. A troubled company's end-game, its future condition following a successful turnaround, must be driven by customers and markets, not financial engineering or capital structure. For what features will the market pay a

premium? Which product or quality can the market get nowhere else? Is your brand peerless? Do you dominate your fastest-growing markets? The strategic plan must leverage your competitive advantage to produce a unique market opportunity, and that opportunity will generally be the company's only hope for improving performance over time.

Have we protected our access to capital?

Directors do not need to pore over balance sheets, but they do need to direct management to ensure sufficient liquidity to sustain the business in a worst-case scenario. This can take a variety of forms, including new debt, an equity capital raise, or other funding strategies. Troubled companies often attract, and sometimes resort to, unconventional and even predatory sources of capital. Directors should work with management to ensure that all financing options are assessed for their likely impact on a potential long-term restructuring process.

Directors must be familiar with the company's long-term liquidity situation, including debt maturities and covenants. Liquidity is an all-encompassing priority, and so directors must work with management to anticipate possible risks and sensitivities. They must also understand the availability of additional capital sources, such as tapping equity markets or obtaining refinancing from major lenders. It is not uncommon for management's relationships with major lenders to become strained or fatigued during difficult times.

Often, directors are reluctant to engage with key shareholders directly, but there is little evidence that such direct exchanges are unproductive. Risk Metrics, the proxy advisory firm, recently studied board-shareholder dialogue at eight of the largest US corporations, where directors generally meet with large investors at least once annually. The firm found that despite a wide variety of formats, the outcome of these interactions, as reported by both sides, was positive. In fact, most shareholders in the study predicted – and welcomed – more frequent exchanges in the wake of the financial crisis of 2008.

Should we hire an outside advisor?

To answer this question, directors must collectively decide to what extent they feel comfortable with the information they are receiving from management and other sources. As a board, are you asking every question a shareholder would ask? Are you comfortable with the quality and thoroughness of the answers to those questions? From my experience, the answer to both of these questions is often no.

If the board is at all hesitant about the quality of information provided, it should bring in an outside advisor to provide another opinion. Frequently, incumbent management will resist, particularly if they have never experienced a restructuring. They may raise the issue of cost, stating that advisory fees could further weaken the company's financial position. The board should turn such protests on their head, citing the potentially catastrophic costs of acting on incomplete or unreliable information. Investing in a second opinion is a sound investment when the viability of the company is at stake.

An outside advisor brings objectivity, credibility and a wealth of experience in similar situations that can be extremely reassuring throughout the decision-making process. An advisor can also more effectively negotiate with banks and creditors, who will typically become increasingly antagonistic, particularly when dealing with a management team that has already disappointed them repeatedly. A third-party advisor can often help mitigate any negative sentiment and level the playing field for a more thoughtful negotiating process.

There are countless real world examples of scenarios that would have ended up quite differently if it were not for outside advice. I have personally been involved in many of them, including a major North American automotive supplier, where my team and I were brought in to assist in a debt restructuring contemplated by management's business plan. Based on our review of the plan and its assumptions, significant changes were made to the final operational plan presented to the board.

The company seemed to have been in a perpetual restructuring mode. In 2002, its North American business experienced its first annual loss in a decade, resulting in a 4 per cent workforce reduction, a share price drop to a 40-year low, and elimination of its dividend for the first time since the Great Depression. The following year, the company's performance worsened despite a widespread product recall by its top competitor; management had tried raising prices to capitalize on the shortage but this move backfired and their market share slid even further.

From a capital structure perspective, they were caught in a trap. Liquidity had dwindled. It was impossible for them to meet their ordinary debt obligations while also investing in the types of activities required to enable an operational turnaround. Upon taking over the process, we were able to stop the bleeding by restructuring billions in debt, renegotiating bank loans and covenants, and adding a new line of credit.

From a strategic perspective, we advised the company to explore commodity-hedging strategies, exit certain North American product categories, and shift a variety of support services to an off-shore model, among other actions. The company struggled to cut costs and shift strategy, particularly given its unionized workforce, but ultimately won concessions from its labor unions to shed jobs and close factories. These changes were difficult, even painful, but the company was able to avoid bankruptcy, sustain operations, and generate value for its shareholders over the long term. If they had not sought an outside opinion, they most certainly would have suffered through one of the largest bankruptcies in US history at that time.

Disaster cannot always be avoided, but it can be managed

It is impossible to simplify the responsibilities of directors into four simple questions, especially when discussing an imminent restructuring or bankruptcy scenario. But when a company begins to show distinct signs of weakness, there is no time to learn on the job. By maintaining an aggressive and proactive posture, practicing wide-eyed vigilance every day, and focusing on these four questions at the first sign of trouble, boards will be in the best possible position to avoid the types of freefall collapses we have seen in recent years.

No matter how vital your company appears to be today, adversity or disaster can sometimes strike quickly, and directors and managers may find themselves standing on a precipice in what seems like a brief moment. With billions in shareholder and creditor value hanging in the balance, the last thing stakeholders want to hear from the board is "we didn't know". The truth is that you have been amply forewarned that any company could be out on that ledge in fairly short order. So what are you doing today to prepare for that eventuality?

The views expressed here are those of the author and not necessarily of the other professionals at FTI Consulting Inc.

2

How to spot the warning signs and stay on top of corporate distress

Henry S Miller, Chairman, Managing Director and Co-Founder, Miller Buckfire & Co

As a veteran of the restructuring industry, I have attended hundreds of client board meetings and have learned that many directors and officers have an "investment grade" mindset and are thus slow to recognize and react to the indications of distress.

The board of a healthy company owes a duty of care primarily to its shareholders and is responsible for setting the strategic direction of the company. This responsibility involves the task of hiring and supervising the management team, which then executes the strategic vision through the day-to-day operation of the company. While I am not advocating a drastic change in the roles and responsibilities of directors and officers, I believe both groups need to be increasingly mindful of warning signs that may be the precursors of serious problems. An uncertain economic environment and the potentially severe results of inaction are such that directors and officers must proactively consider low-probability, high-consequence outcomes sooner and more decisively than has commonly been the case.

There are instances where the onset of distress is both sudden and catastrophic (Lehman Brothers, for example), but more often there are numerous signs pointing to pending trouble (GM comes to mind). I once met a famous New York decorator at a dinner party, and I asked him how he was able to convince his customers to pay such high prices for his products. He laughed and explained that when he sells someone a pillow, he invoices them in the first month for the fabric, the second month for the embroidery, the third month for the trim, the fourth month for the stuffing and the fifth month for the shipping; without realizing it, the client has paid $4,000 for a pillow.

Directors and officers should take care they do not pay a far higher price for distress by being inattentive to its presence. It is easy to create/accept an explanation for a few months of lagging sales or lower profitability without considering what may be a larger-scale or more fundamental problem that requires increased scrutiny and a more drastic solution.

The flashing red signal of liquidity

One of the key costs of either a lack of attention to (or ignoring of) a company's ongoing challenges is the potential for a liquidity crisis. I have often been called by directors and officers who are unsure if they will be able to make their next payroll. One might ask how a company, especially a large one, can find itself literally running out of money. Behind every liquidity crisis there is usually a series of seemingly "normal" or "customary" decisions and opportunities missed that slowly but inexorably deplete the company's cash. Kmart is an example of such a situation.

The impact of a liquidity crisis cannot be overstated. Companies in distress seek additional time and options, both of which are limited if the business cannot fund ongoing operations with either cash on hand or availability under a revolving line of credit. Out-of-court restructuring options, such as amendments, debt-for-debt or debt-for-equity exchanges and refinancings, etc, cannot generally be executed in less than three months, and often take six to nine months. A company running out of money may have no option but to "hand over the keys" to its creditors or file for Chapter 11.

One of the common reasons why directors cannot foresee liquidity issues is their lack of detailed knowledge about their company's cash management systems. The directors may be told that the company has $500 million of cash on its balance sheet, but where this cash resides can be as important as how much of it there is. As an example, retailers have cash in their stores, but the treasurer cannot pay bills with that money. Another example is a company with large international operations where cash cannot be repatriated easily due to regulatory, tax or legal restrictions. If management cannot quickly and concisely answer questions about its cash availability, how quickly the cash can be accessed, and at what cost, then directors should immediately take a closer look at the company's cash management system as well as its financial managers! "We don't manage the company that way" is not an acceptable answer.

Scrutinize management information
As signs of distress begin to percolate, directors should scrutinize the information and ideas presented by management, who may wish to minimize the problems in the hope that they will self-correct. For example, consider a company whose sales are down in the first half of the year and improve markedly in the second half. It may be tempting to cheer the prompt turnaround, but unfortunately sometimes the "cure" is worse than the disease. Management may have taken allowances and discounts on volumes that are not achievable but in the interim appear to be a solution to lagging sales. However, pulling forward future sales will ultimately make the crisis more swift and severe. And yes, the distress will indeed appear sudden at that point, but only because a temporary fix was used to paper over a serious problem.

Similarly, management suggestions that appear to be "quick fixes", such as non-core asset sales and capital market transactions (sale-leasebacks, refinancings, etc), should be examined with care by directors. We recently represented a client who owned an asset that represented a major operational advantage over its competitors. In an effort to meet debt-service and capital-expenditure requirements, the management team asked the board of directors to approve the sale of the asset. The request was clearly an attempt to avoid the underlying problem, which was the company's inability to service its ongoing cash interest obligations while funding an overly ambitious capital expenditure plan. Regrettably, the directors approved management's request and shortly thereafter the company faced a serious liquidity crunch with decreased operational flexibility as a result of the sale.

A second reason for heightened scrutiny is that selling a business for an EBITDA multiple lower than the multiple of debt to EBITDA actually worsens the problem. This, of course, is exacerbated by any debt or security agreement that requires asset sale proceeds be used exclusively to pay down debt rather than retained as working capital.

In order to avoid being unprepared and surprised, it is the directors' responsibility to ask the difficult questions and make sure they are receiving clear and unambiguous answers supported by proper data and analysis. Unquestioned trust of management is not an appropriate rule of thumb. Additional attention should also be directed to the company's information technology systems and controls to ensure that reliable information is available in a timely fashion. Poor systems and controls can be just as disastrous as a management team in denial. If it takes months to compile data or if the information is of questionable accuracy, it may be impossible to identify the problems, much less move swiftly to address them. This is especially true if the company is highly decentralized by design and/or the product of a series of acquisitions (a "roll-up", for example), which often masks underlying weaknesses during the "good times", but raises serious issues when business is soft or in decline.

Early awareness
If directors and officers are able to recognize the signs of distress at an early stage, the company will maximize its available operational and financial options. Early awareness provides the time necessary to conduct a comprehensive review of the company's business(es) and implement required operational changes such as cost-cutting programs, working capital adjustments and a review of capital expenditures. More transformative adjustments should also be evaluated, including revising benefits packages, negotiating union concessions, closing factories and scaling down or exiting certain non-core business lines. While these changes can be

burdensome to stakeholders and necessitate layoffs or reductions in force, the focus should be on re-establishing the operational health of the business to complement any prospective financial restructuring.

From a financial perspective, the early detection of distress has a number of significant benefits. Firstly, companies can proactively approach their key creditors with a proposal that provides the business with additional time and flexibility. For example, if its lenders are informed that the company is likely to violate a financial covenant in the near term, they will be more inclined to work to reach a consensual solution than if the company had waited until after the violation to begin the dialogue. Restructurings are situations where it is often less painful to ask for permission than to beg for forgiveness. In addition, companies may be able to avoid aggressive creditors who typically buy into capital structures after companies are deeply distressed, with the intent of influencing the restructuring process or, worse, mounting a takeover. Early recognition also maximizes the company's chances of accessing the capital markets other than through debtor-in-possession (DIP) financings, which are available only in Chapter 11. As a result, even if creditors are unwilling to work to reach a mutually acceptable solution, the company may be able to secure third-party capital to refinance the existing creditors' debt.

Beware of the pitfalls

It should be noted that while creditor-led and capital-market solutions are attractive, directors should be wary of certain pitfalls. First, there is no such thing as a financial solution to an operational problem. If the company is suffering from a protracted industry-wide downturn or severe operational difficulties, no amount of new financing will by itself solve these problems. Indeed, very few lenders or investors are likely to agree to throw good money after bad or put capital at risk when the business itself is not performing. All attempts to the contrary notwithstanding, it is extremely difficult to borrow your way back to prosperity.

Second, a director should evaluate the alternatives the company may be required to give up. For instance, does it have to grant a security interest to lenders on previously unencumbered assets, or cede cash dominion? While a near-term transaction may seem to provide additional time and breathing space, pricing terms and structural features can actually limit the company's future

options without addressing the underlying reasons for distress.

Third, the mere availability of alternatives is not a guarantee of success. Directors and officers must have one or more contingency plans ("Plan B") in the event of an unsuccessful outcome. One of our recent engagements was working for a high-tech business with a significant debt load as a result of a leveraged buyout. The company's operating performance indicated weakness for multiple quarters, while its directors and officers pursued a first lien financing using a "basket" in their credit agreement. The financing was meant to bridge the company to an IPO that was expected to pay down a large portion of that first lien debt. The future of the business depended on both of the transactions occurring and the company did not have a viable backup plan. After months of negotiations with potential financing sources, it became evident that both transactions would be unsuccessful. Moreover, during that time the company's operating performance continued to decline and it was faced with a severe liquidity crunch. Further inquiry revealed that the company had been channel stuffing during the first half of the year to make up for weakening demand, which further constrained its liquidity.

This crisis could have been avoided through an honest assessment of the business's prospects and by planning for other options in the event that the financing transactions failed.

How to manage a restructuring

Even if directors and officers are attentive to the signs of distress, there are a number of circumstances that will require a company to undertake a comprehensive restructuring. The question that follows is how directors and officers are affected as a result. While the change is one of degree rather than kind, it is not an insignificant one. They will find there are increasing demands on their time and that their actions — past, present and prospective — will be under intense scrutiny from the shareholders, creditors, employees, customers, suppliers and, in the event of a bankruptcy, the court. There will be suggestions from all sides as to the actions the company should be considering — some helpful, many not, and most skewed to favor the source of the recommendation. Suffice it to say, directors and officers will not be lonely (though for the wrong reasons) throughout the process, whether in court or out of court.

Company officials should have realistic expectations about the length of time necessary to effect a restructuring. It may seem paradoxical that you can be short of time for an extended period, but this can assuredly be the case during a restructuring. The steps in the process can be spoken of in days and weeks, but the process itself customarily takes months and even years. Negotiations with multiple parties are complex and protracted, and court-supervised negotiations often take longer.

Call in the advisors

Once the decision to pursue a comprehensive restructuring has been made, directors and officers ought to assess the merits of engaging restructuring experts to help guide them through the course of action. The company should expect to have its outside corporate counsel introduce his/her restructuring partner(s) and should consider engaging either or both a turnaround advisor and financial advisor.

Turnaround advisors can be vital when companies face the prospect of a full-scale restructuring. The factors that have led to the current financial and operational position are likely to worsen as distress becomes more acute, and a turnaround advisor can add much-needed "boots on the ground". Additionally, the company's existing finance staff may be unfamiliar with the 13-week cash-flow forecasts and other essential financial reporting requirements that creditors demand in a restructuring, and may well lack the experience of dealing with hostile creditors.

Regardless, these tasks are a major distraction from the daily management of the business, particularly at a time when attention to the business is increasingly important. Turnaround advisors are accustomed to producing the information that both the company and its creditors will need in order to evaluate the alternatives. Getting these basic steps right can go a long way toward effecting a successful restructuring transaction.

Financial advisors also play an essential role in restructurings. Most immediately, they will shield the company from excessive questions and due-diligence requests from its creditors and their advisors, and help develop an orderly process for providing information. This should provide a welcome respite for directors and officers, as they will likely have already realized that creditors can be overly burdensome, while in the meantime their friendly bank calling officer has been replaced by a hard-nosed work-out professional.

In the early months, the financial advisor will work with management and the turnaround advisor to develop the company's new business plan, while simultaneously facilitating diligence for creditors and their advisors. The business plan is the basis of the company's negotiations with its creditors and is a fundamental component of the valuation and debt-capacity analyses, which underpin the actual reorganization. Most importantly, the financial advisor will work with directors and officers to assess the company's strategic alternatives and will lead negotiations with the stakeholders.

When choosing a financial advisor, the company should seek a firm that understands both the fundamental financial analyses and the strategic approach necessary to lead a company successfully through a restructuring. Just as important, the firm must be able to provide a full team of experienced restructuring bankers (not just M&A or coverage bankers who have recently been converted to restructuring work as a result of a slow M&A market).

Finally, both turnaround and financial advisors can provide a helpful "reset" in the relationship between the company and its stakeholders. Though not intentionally, the company may have previously delivered forecasts that proved to be overly optimistic, and its projections (and the company itself) may have lost credibility in the eyes of its creditors. The knowledge that the forecasts have been reviewed and "blessed" by a turnaround and/or financial advisor can help alleviate these concerns. Creditors with experience in corporate distress will have often encountered these advisors in other situations, and will view them, if not with enthusiasm, then at least with a level of professional respect.

Similarly, negotiations with the creditors may have become strained or contaminated and an advisor can immediately help ease tensions and begin rebuilding these relationships. The initial diligence period for the company's advisor (and likely, at this point, the creditors' advisors) can serve as an important cooling-off period. Both sides should use the time to analyze and agree upon the salient facts of the situation, not negotiate the restructuring transaction. This should allow officers to focus on the business while their advisors acclimate themselves and their counterparts to the company.

Developing a business plan

At its core, restructuring is a process of determining a company's value (marking it to market) and then negotiating an agreement among the creditors (and hopefully, though not always, "old" equity) on the amount and form of their recovery. The first step in this procedure is the development of the company's long-term business plan. Directors and officers should expect this to be an iterative process since the prospects of the business will depend on the operational and strategic decisions made in the short and intermediate term, and in turn these decisions will be dictated and possibly limited by the trajectory of the business.

Business plans are typically expected to be three to five years in length and represent a detailed, bottom-up model of the business that can be defended, explained and achieved. It is imperative that the plan be prepared correctly the first time because further revisions during negotiations will be viewed with extreme skepticism, as creditors suspect that the company is "goal seeking" to a desired outcome. This is especially true when talks on valuation and debt capacity are underway. Furthermore, revisions will call into question the validity of the original business plan. The credibility that the company worked so hard to build throughout the process will be at risk, and further negotiations will likely be more contentious and strained.

Due to the importance of the business plan in restructuring negotiations, directors need to understand and scrutinize the methodologies and assumptions that drive the projections. While it is management's responsibility to prepare the plan, directors should be ready to be as critical of it as the creditors will be; soft-pedaling concerns or doubts at this point will leave the company ill-prepared for likely challenges. Directors should attempt to anticipate how various creditor constituencies will interpret the business plan, and help prepare the company to address legitimate questions and concerns.

Valuing the restructured company

After development of the long-term business plan, the company and its advisors will likely shift their attention to the valuation of the post-reorganization business, which is one of the most contentious yet essential components of a restructuring.

Directors and officers are typically familiar with the concept of valuation in terms of buying and selling assets, or more generally in M&A situations. Such valuations are often supported by third-party guidance and/or fairness opinions. In those cases, directors and officers are usually focused on avoiding either overpaying or not generating enough consideration for the assets, and

generally the valuation disparities between the buyer's and the seller's bid/ask are not substantial.

While the academic exercise of valuing a business is similar in both healthy and distressed companies, the relative importance of the process is dramatically different. In a restructuring, the valuation takes on strategic and tactical significance. It impacts the form of restructuring (sale v reorganization, third-party v standalone, going concern v liquidation), the method of execution (in-court v out-of-court) and the approach to negotiations with the company's creditors.

Out-of-the-money creditors will find any and all reasons to argue for a higher valuation. Simultaneously, in-the-money creditors will make a case for a lower valuation, as they are hesitant to have their recovery diluted by other creditors. At some juncture, a court may make the final decision as to the "winning" argument, after notice to all interested parties and, possibly, a lengthy evidentiary hearing. This divergence of opinion and its potential impact on the outcome is precisely why valuation is a cornerstone of most restructuring cases.

As a result of the creditor influence on the restructuring process, directors and officers should understand that the company's valuation may not always be "intellectually pure" in an academic sense. However, they should ensure that the valuation analysis and conclusions follow customary market norms and the academic literature. In bankruptcy proceedings, the valuation is subject to determination by judges who occasionally substitute their own interpretation for the conclusions of the company's advisors if they feel the financial advisor has strayed from accepted valuation standards or even if they want to provide a recovery to certain parties.

Directors and officers must understand the valuation's implications for creditors and ensure that the methodologies and the resulting conclusions have been properly developed and are supported by data, facts and credible and realistic assumptions. Ideally, the company's valuation will be unassailable, so as to avoid what could be a long and expensive contested confirmation hearing where creditors can challenge the company's assumptions and the reorganization plan that derives from them.

How much debt do you want?

A corollary to valuation is the determination of a company's debt capacity, meaning the aggregate amount of post-reorganization debt that a restructured company can realistically support. Upon emergence, the company will be re-entering the "real world" and the amount of leverage and cost of debt capital will strongly influence its future chances of success. This too is a topic that will be intensively negotiated between the company and its creditors and may not have an "intellectually pure" result.

As a practical matter, our inclination is to push for as little debt post-restructuring as possible, so as to avoid future distress if business plan projections are missed or if economic conditions are less buoyant than expected. At the very least, we strenuously argue that companies should not emerge with more debt than their peer group competitors.

Many, if not most, restructurings depend on achieving concessions from labor, landlords, suppliers, customers, financial creditors, etc. These parties will renegotiate their contracts (willingly or unwillingly) and facilitate the operational turnaround so long as there is both an equitable shared sacrifice and the company actually fixes its capital structure by reducing leverage and having available sufficient liquidity. Directors and officers should recognize that future negotiations with these constituents will be extremely difficult if the company has to re-engage because it did not "fix" its balance sheet the first time around. For example, we represented a tier two automotive supplier in a situation where concessions were requested to help the company complete an out-of-court restructuring. Contrary to our advice, the restructuring left the company with too much leverage, and when it went back for additional concessions a mere 18 months later, the request was rejected and it was forced to liquidate. On the other hand, we advised one of the largest tier one suppliers, which cut net debt to 0.6 times EBITDA, retained $1 billion-plus of cash and had access to over $1 billion in lines of credit. That company is viable and successful today, some three years after the restructuring was completed — despite continuing hardship in the auto industry and a still-weak economy.

Unfortunately, our desire to keep a client's leverage as low as possible post-restructuring is not universally shared. Many creditors prefer to receive their recovery in the form of debt, as opposed to equity; they are prepared to tolerate more leverage than may be prudent on the premise that they are more comfortable as lenders than as equity investors. This is doubly true in the case of

collateralized loan obligations, which are frequent holders of senior debt and are generally prohibited from owning equity by their investment mandate. This is yet another example of a component of the restructuring process where directors and officers should expect and be prepared for pushback. The advisors should be directed to take a tough line to preserve financial flexibility because many companies, especially those that are in distress because of operational challenges, may not recover as fast as they initially believed. The holding period of creditors who receive either new debt or equity in the restructuring may be decidedly short term, meaning they will sell very quickly. That may suit their fund rate-of-return targets, but leave the company with the residual effects of a still over-leveraged balance sheet.

Never watch sausages — or restructurings — being made

The company's valuation and debt capacity are the building blocks upon which the restructuring negotiations are based and the following question must be addressed: "How does one distribute value among parties who all demand more?"

The starting point for negotiations will be the company's proposed restructuring plan. Unless there is unusual hostility among the interested parties or there are operational problems or fraud endangering long-term viability, the company has the statutory right to propose the restructuring plan (period of exclusivity) for a minimum of four months and usually for the entire bankruptcy. While many might expect value to be distributed according to a legally established waterfall determined by seniority of claim, the Bankruptcy Code does not speak to the allocation of value except in the case of liquidation. As such, most restructurings, both in and out of court, are a product of arduous and time-consuming negotiations that, as mentioned earlier, may not lead to an "intellectually pure" result. Parties will use all means available to exert leverage in the negotiations and many restructurings require creative solutions to reach a conclusion that everyone, including, if applicable, the court, can support.

There is an old quote about laws and sausages that says, "you should never watch them being made". It could be argued that this also applies to restructuring negotiations. Directors and officers should allow their advisors to lead the talks with their counterparts, who represent the other interested parties. Generally, directors are not actively involved in negotiations, although sub-committees may be formed to assist the company's advisors, if appropriate. What is imperative is that directors and officers make the time and effort necessary to keep apprised of the status of negotiations and to provide guidance and make decisions when necessary.

While the company's advisors are largely responsible for the valuation report, debt-capacity analysis and restructuring negotiations (with guidance from directors), there will be a number of occasions in the process when directors will be asked to make difficult decisions. We cannot explore all of those points here, but some representative examples include: a) whether the company would maximize value for its creditors by putting itself up for sale; b) determining the highest and best value when there are competing restructuring plans; and c) how to react when management has aligned itself with a third party. In each of these cases, directors will benefit from seeking independent assessments from both legal and financial advisors.

The significance of liquidity

The steps we have outlined in the restructuring process rarely occur sequentially; rather, they take place in parallel based on a number of factors, the most important of which is the company's current and projected liquidity. As mentioned earlier, lack of liquidity can precipitate a restructuring earlier than was expected (or when not believed to be necessary at all) and will have a significant impact throughout the process. A company with limited liquidity and without access to new/additional sources of capital may not have the time to address its operational challenges before creating a long-term business plan. While counter-intuitive, the companies that are able to navigate a financial restructuring and put themselves in a position for future success usually share a similar trait: they have sufficient liquidity and are not forced to take value-damaging actions in order to survive.

The significance of liquidity has never been more pronounced than it has in the recent past, with directors routinely asking why their companies could not borrow as they have historically. The temporary shutdown of the capital markets should act as a warning to directors and officers to keep a keen eye on current and projected liquidity. This is especially true when a company is in financial distress, because the availability of liquidity to fund a restructuring will maximize options and limit negative outcomes. Waiting and hoping that the problem or markets will self-correct will lead to more difficult negotiations with the parties-in-interest and possibly to liquidation.

Conclusion

For most directors, confronting distress is not an enjoyable experience, nor was it on the radar screen when they joined the board. Dealing with distress is time-consuming, contentious and may carry financial and reputational risks. As they say, "S—t happens."

Board members need to be astute enough (if for no other reason than self preservation) to ensure that management provides extensive and clear financial and operational information, and, where appropriate, seeks outside advice. To the extent business conditions continue to deteriorate, directors must be prepared to move swiftly and decisively to stay in front of the company's problems, thereby avoiding the risks and consequences of a more adverse outcome than was necessary or otherwise achievable.

3

From hangover to recovery?
The thoughts of a turnaround lender

Lawrence A Marsiello,
Special Advisor, Pine Brook
Road Partners LLC

Economists, government officials, business leaders and other pundits continue to debate the root causes of the recent financial crisis. Much effort has been expended attempting to explain the complexity and interdependence of these causes, with each expert placing different emphasis on the particular stress points. At this time, it is fair to say that additional time and effort is needed to reach a durable consensus.

In analyzing what happened, it is helpful to look at some of the prime suspects.

Sub-prime mortgages and the over-extended consumer

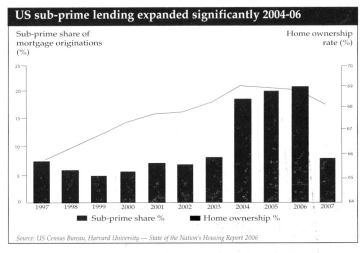

US sub-prime lending expanded significantly 2004-06

Sub-prime share of mortgage originations (%)

Home ownership rate (%)

■ Sub-prime share %   ■ Home ownership %

Source: US Census Bureau, Harvard University — State of the Nation's Housing Report 2006

The term sub-prime refers to borrowers with weak credit histories and a greater propensity to default on debt obligations. In the period preceding the crisis, we witnessed significant growth in the sub-prime mortgage market driven by the following:

• Relaxation of underwriting standards, as demonstrated by weaker debt-to-income ratios and the absence of income verifications — the so-called "liar's mortgage".
• Wide use of introductory "teaser" interest rates and the adjustable-rate mortgage.
• Predatory lending practices.
• Low or zero downpayments.
• Wide use of home equity loans to repay ballooning credit card debt and other household expenditures.[1]

Although the social goal of increased home ownership across the US

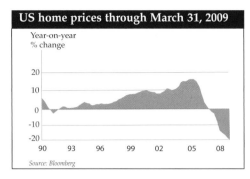

US home prices through March 31, 2009

Year-on-year
% change

Source: Bloomberg

population was attained, the resulting mortgage and consumer-related debt proved unsustainable. This asset bubble was dependent upon the continuation of three primary conditions:

• Increasing personal income driven by overall employment levels.
• Increasing residential real estate values.
• An endless supply of easy mortgage money or liquidity, driving both new home construction and the refinancing of existing mortgages.

Meanwhile, market participants (banks and investors) also placed significant faith in the historical fact that since the depression of the 1930s, the US had never experienced a significant nationwide fall in housing values. Past declines were largely in the "margins" of regional and local markets.

These circumstances left the consumer over-extended and housing values inflated.

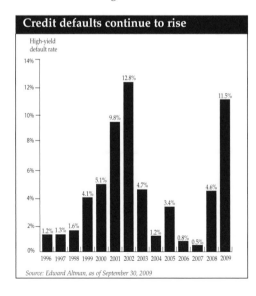

Credit defaults continue to rise

High-yield
default rate

Source: Edward Altman, as of September 30, 2009

Leveraged finance and the over-extended corporate borrower

The excessive use of debt, or leverage, by corporations prior to 2008 eventually led to an abrupt increase in the number of defaults for high-yield bonds. In 2005, and through the first half of 2007, many corporate finance practitioners complained about the extraordinary level of market liquidity, as well as reduced returns for the risk taken. There was just too much money chasing too few deals. The debt-financed price for corporate assets was bid up to levels that were too high, given the underlying risk.

For a given middle-market mergers and acquisitions transaction, we witnessed multiples of senior debt to EBITDA rise within the space of just a year, from a range of three to four times to as high as six to seven times. This increased debt level was driven by increased liquidity availability and not a fundamental improvement in operating cash-flow or earnings. For each successive leveraged transaction, we saw loan covenants, collateral and structural protections diminish. The terms "covenant-lite loans" and "PIK toggle" (the borrower has the option to repay principal and interest in new debt in lieu of cash) entered our vocabulary. We witnessed sponsor equity contributions decline to as low as 20 to 25 per cent of total capitalization. Clearly, the risk pendulum had swung too far. Market participants, in chasing dwindling returns and inflated valuations, closed their eyes to risk concerns, resulting in yet another asset bubble.

Securitizations and syndications spread risk

The easy money, or excessive liquidity, that flowed into the consumer mortgage and leverage finance markets was partly fostered, in my view, by the structural separation of entities that originated debt from those that held debt for investment purposes — the rise of the shadow banking system. The game was that if we could originate debt instruments which could be sold to others, at a gain, then the credit or default risk of the underlying instrument insidiously morphed into a secondary consideration. The originator, post sale, did not have any financial "skin in the game" other than some reputational risk. The "originate to distribute" model dislodged the earlier one of "originate and hold"; financial institutions made more profits from originating and selling assets than holding assets on the balance sheet for spread purposes. As market liquidity grew, the ultimate buyers of debt instruments clamored for paper in spite of lower yields, relaxed terms and structural protections. Within financial institutions, highly incentive-driven capital market groups (distrubutors of risk) of major Wall Street banks became increasingly influential profit generators, driving earnings, returns and bonus pools.

Untested financial innovations
Prior to 2008, inventive financial instruments were growing in popularity, including the bundling of sub-prime mortgages into mortgage-backed securities (MBSs), or leveraged loans into collateralized debt obligations (CDOs) and collateralized loan obligations (CLOs), for sale to investors — a type of securitization. We also saw the rapid rise of the credit-default swap (CDS) market, a form of risk insurance.

The distribution of these new instruments spread risk throughout the global banking system. Advocates believed this spread of risk made the entire financial system more resilient to risk of loss, and at the time only a few pundits openly disagreed. But these new products were highly complex and not "cycle tested". For any given MBS, CDO, CLO or CDS transaction, the true risks —be they credit, operational or related to liquidity — were underestimated and mispriced. The stage was set for a systemic correction.[2]

The party ended poorly
From 2003 to 2007, market participants ranging from financial institutions to investors, regulators and rating agencies viewed the world as a safe place — one with an extremely low risk of loss and awash with cheap liquidity. Eventually, the demand-supply imbalances drove up the value of financial assets. The consequences of these forces became brutally clear to many, starting in the summer of 2007. In the flight to safety that followed, diversification, market-neutral strategies and risk controls all failed to perform as expected.

Government bailouts to the rescue
In the fourth quarter of 2008, following the Lehman Brothers bankruptcy, the credit markets just froze. This unexpected backup left financial institutions with unsold inventories, vulnerable to loss on previously originated leveraged loans, mortgages and securities. Financial institutions reacted defensively by severely curtailing the supply of credit. Distrust and skepticism were rampant. The unthinkable had happened. Subsequently, the losses destroyed the capital bases and solvency of powerful institutions — AIG, CIT, Citibank, Fannie

Mae, Freddie Mac, GE Capital, GMAC and Merrill Lynch. The financial carnage was global. In the UK, for instance, HBOS, Northern Rock and Royal Bank of Scotland in effect failed, requiring government intervention.

Through an alphabet of various stimulus programs, the US government and Federal Reserve Bank propped up teetering financial institutions via the Troubled Asset Relief Program (TARP) and the Commercial Paper Funding Facility, among others. Nevertheless, significant wealth destruction occurred, suppressing consumer spending and business investment. All the market participants experienced a severe hangover. The billions of dollars spent as part of the bailout of the financial markets accelerated the level of US national debt — more than $12 trillion at the time of this writing,[3] the highest in history. The country is running up so much debt, so rapidly, that investors in US Treasury securities, particularly the Chinese, are worried that these dollar-denominated reserves may eventually be devalued. The longer-term impact upon financial markets is unavoidable: interest rates will eventually rise, though by how much remains a matter of political debate.

A sustainable recovery or another asset bubble?
A complete global financial meltdown was averted by aggressive and co-ordinated intervention by central banks and governments. The much-feared deflation in asset values had, for now, been halted and reversed. Broadly speaking, by the third quarter of 2009 market participants were feeling better. In conjunction with improving credit availability and rising equity markets, many analysts upgraded their outlooks for economic growth. The recession was declared over, with forecasters attempting to gauge the shape and strength of the recovery. My forward view, with the typical disclaimer, sees an uneven, anemic upturn — a soft, W-shaped recovery with a bias to the upside, and not the strong V-bounce that we have experienced in past recovery periods. Here is why.

Consumer spending days are over
Employment drives consumption, and the outlook for jobs is bleak and likely to deteriorate. Meanwhile, anybody who has not already lost their job is nervous that they might. The typical American now realizes that "savings" come from spending less, not in the form of home price appreciation, a new credit card or a ballooning stock portfolio. The consumer has seen the

precipice of financial ruin and the insecurity is converting a nation of confident spenders into frugal savers.

On the mortgage front, one in seven US households are either behind in payments or in foreclosure, according to new data from the Mortgage Bankers Association. That is up from one in ten a year before.[4]

At the root of the problem is the relaxed mortgage practices of 2003-2007, but since then the problem has been compounded by rising unemployment — the so-called jobless recovery: unemployment levels reached 10.2 per cent in October 2009, the highest since 1982, and were poised to go even higher.[5] US consumers, who represent approximately 70 per cent of GDP, are having difficulty balancing their checkbooks, and the result is a trend towards household de-leveraging. It is hard to see how retail demand and revenues will gain any momentum any time soon.

A stubborn housing market persists

The excess inventory of unoccupied homes prevents a rebound in residential construction and spending on related durable goods. Sales and starts of new construction have fallen 75 and 80 per cent respectively.[6] The good news is that the inventory of existing unsold homes listed for sale has declined, but a couple of things need to be placed in perspective. First, househunters are clearly incentivized by the first-time buyer's federal tax credit, and in my view this credit is artificial since it is a politically driven stimulus. Second, home prices continue to fall: on a regional and annualized basis, the median price declined in the West (15.1 per cent), the South (7.6 per cent), the Northeast (7.0 per cent) and the Midwest (1.0 per cent).[7] Clearly, personal net worth is still declining. With the home being the consumer's largest asset, the fall in home values will depress future spending.

Anemic growth on the corporate front

The outlook for a weak economic recovery, largely driven by a tapped-out consumer, leaves leveraged companies vulnerable. True, recent earnings reports have shown several bright spots, but upon closer examination, earnings generation has been largely driven by aggressive cost cutting and conservative inventory management; executives lack confidence in top-line revenue growth. Bear in mind, one company's expense cut or job cut is another company's revenue loss.

There is no clear reason why corporate earnings and cash flow should not remain anemic. The

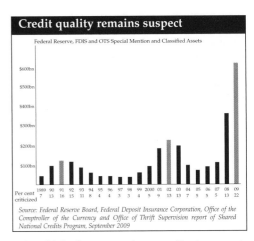

Credit quality remains suspect

Federal Reserve, FDIS and OTS Special Mention and Classified Assets

Source: Federal Reserve Board, Federal Deposit Insurance Corporation, Office of the Comptroller of the Currency and Office of Thrift Supervision report of Shared National Credits Program, September 2009

writer thinks that companies struggling to generate top-line operating earnings represent a secular shift, and not a temporary cyclical occurrence.

The state of the capital markets

Today's capital markets players are far more conservative and defensive compared to the 2006-07 boom years. The capacity of the markets has been reduced by two primary developments. First, financial institutions — in reaction to nagging credit losses, heightened regulatory scrutiny and investor concerns — have significantly tightened credit screens and increased pricing requirements. Today, management teams in these institutions are greatly concerned about solvency and capital adequacy as they work through credit-quality issues.

Second, the capacity of the secondary market or shadow banking system that fueled the "originate to distribute" model is significantly reduced. There are far fewer buyers of risk. For example, many hedge funds were forced to shrink or close during the 2008-09 period as fear-driven investors issued redemption notices. It is estimated that hedge fund industry-wide capital shrunk by as much as 33 per cent.

Moreover, many collateralized loan obligations have severely reduced their appetite for new loans or just closed their doors. Today, what capacity does exist is demanding tighter terms and higher pricing.

The refinancing challenge

This leads the writer to contend that leveraged companies with capitalizations of the 2005-07 vintage may face a difficult challenge in refinancing as these debts approach maturity. The credit market today is far more lender-driven than it was in the boom.

If fundamentals do not change, a leveraged

Illustrative middle-market leveraged transaction

	2007	2009
Senior debt as a multiple of EBITDA	3.5x – 4.5x	2.0x – 2.5x
Total debt to EBITDA	5.0x – 5.75x	3.0x – 3.25x
Equity as % of total capitalization	25% - 35%	45% - 50%
Amortization of term debt	1% per annum With a Balloon Payment in year 5 or 7	50% Debt Repayment within 3 years
Covenants	Covenant lite	Restrictive covenant basket

company struggling to generate earnings/cash flow and facing a refinancing needs to de-lever. This may occur through some combination of increased equity, asset sales, bankruptcy, or debt-equity exchanges — a painful and costly process.

Jump through the refinancing hoop

Given the enormous liquidity that governments around the world have pumped into capital markets, no one should be surprised that credit conditions finally started to thaw in the second quarter of 2009. As you can see from the graph alongside, credit spreads for leveraged loans dramatically improved. The market continues to benefit from a highly accommodating general interest-rate environment, as demonstrated by the historically low three-month LIBOR. For loan agreements, LIBOR serves as the refinance base index rate, and although it is practically zero, lenders are currently enjoying historically wide spreads over the base rates.

Many companies, according to JP Morgan, tapped the high-yield market to refinance leveraged loans. This market priced $116 billion of new debt through September 2009. Clearly, many companies that had otherwise defaulted successfully refinanced.

Two observations on the improved market conditions. First, available credit is highly company-specific and significantly weighted toward lower-risk situations. Second, the market recovery remains rather fragile.

Fixed-income investors (buyers of debt originated by banks) are highly aware that ultra-low interest rates, along with a scarcity of quality loans, may have pushed asset values to unreasonable levels.[8] The current market is long on anxiety: participants remain fearful that we may see a near-term correction or pullback.

As mentioned, high-yield bond default rates,

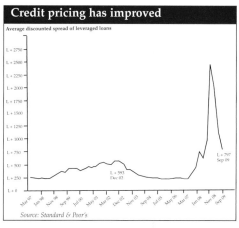

Credit pricing has improved

Average discounted spread of leveraged loans

Source: Standard & Poor's

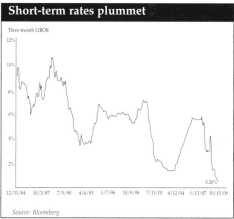

Short-term rates plummet

Three-month LIBOR

Source: Bloomberg

considered a lagging economic indicator, continue to rise, even if predictions have recently been lowered, with Moody's Investor Services expecting the global rate of default to peak at 12 per cent, down from 16 per cent.

The lower forecast is significantly influenced by a narrowing of bond spreads and the reopening of the high-yield bond market.[9] On the leverage-loan front, commercial banks have, for the most part, continued to originate loans for resale into a pre-arranged or "club" market, mitigating potential balance sheet exposure.

Upcoming wall of maturities

The leverage-loan and high-yield bond markets remain receptive to good companies with poor capitalization via refinancings, purchasing debt below par and pushing out maturities. Through ultra-low interest rates, the US government and the Federal Reserve have created a window to accommodate refinancing activities.

As we look forward, the wall of maturities coming to market, mostly in 2013 and 2014, becomes greater and greater. The largest threat to refinancing these maturities remains the Federal Reserve raising interest rates to control inflationary pressures or prop up the value of the dollar. Further upward pressure on rates results from the federal government refinancing the record level of national debt.

Higher interest rates would prevent borrowers from qualifying for refinancing, regardless of whether credit capacity exists. Given the current accommodating interest-rate environment, excess market liquidity and a comparatively light maturity schedule, a leveraging company would be well advised to seize the long-term benefits of refinancing before the wall of maturities materializes in 2013-14.

Another threat is the health of our banking system. Banks remain the primary originators of leveraged loans and the underwriters of high-yield securities. If they find themselves shoring up capital bases eroded by credit losses, one may expect a different attitude to originating new credit risks, along with a need for higher spreads over base index rates (cost of credit). It is no longer unthinkable that we could have an environment of tighter credit capacity, where access divides companies into the "haves" and the "have-nots", dramatically affecting the competitive landscape of many industries. Credit availability is proving to be a company's critical competitive advantage.

The writer is not an economic forecaster, but the evidence supports a potential scenario where the consumer is a saver, capital markets are less borrower-friendly, corporate earnings and cash-flow growth are depressed, and general interest rates are elevated.

If only some of the discussed market conditions

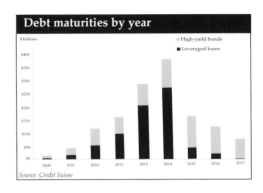

Debt maturities by year

Source: Credit Suisse

prevail, expect a prolonged period of increased corporate defaults. The capacity of the credit markets may prove inadequate to absorb, at any price, the upcoming wall of leverage-loan and high-yield bond maturities.

What you know and when you know it really matters

For a leveraged company operating in uncertain and volatile conditions, a brief timeline separates liquidity from insolvency. Most troubled situations might have been avoided if directors and managers had possessed timely and relevant information on what was going on, both within and, just as importantly, outside the company. Such details include performance metrics on critical operations; customer satisfaction; vendor relations; competitor behavior; industry dynamics; employee morale and skills; and government regulations. A dashboard of information allows managers to identify variances in expectations that require attention and to take action to remedy the issue well before operating cash flow is impacted. The key to success is to measure the right things. Poor information systems allow a progressively weakening situation to go undetected until it is too late to fix.

The development of a frequently updated management dashboard can assist executives and boards in anticipating opportunities, as well as threats; financial reporting systems alone are not sufficient since they generally measure what has happened in the past. A well-constructed dashboard is predictive: it measures a limited number of critical success factors and models what has to go right for a company to succeed. It allows executives to ask the right questions early; to analyze and debate facts and complexities; to evaluate strategic trade-offs and consequences; and finally to act with conviction. In my view, the speed of informed decisions is critical to managing in uncertain times. Early intervention may involve the sale of an underperforming business, a significant downsizing, a major refinancing or a vital acquisition – actions taken while the company remains well regarded by banks and capital markets.

One of my favorite examples of this type of forward thinking in action comes from the Ford Motor Company. In 2006, in an unexpected and controversial move, Ford borrowed approximately $24 billion by mortgaging all its assets, including the famous "blue oval" logo. Two years later, both GM and Chrysler filed for bankruptcy, desperately needing a taxpayer bailout, while Ford ditched its request for government support and at the same time launched a campaign trumpeting its self-reliance. It gained hard-fought market share and avoided the bureaucratic burdens of government oversight. Many analysts contend that having ample liquidity, when credit markets froze and light-vehicle sales evaporated, served as Ford's competitive advantage. The company's story supports the time-tested adage in finance: "borrow when you don't need the money".

A sharp focus on liquidity

Liquidity availability is a key component of a leveraged company's dashboard. By liquidity, I mean cash on hand as well as access to reliable, committed credit facilities. It is astonishing how often directors and executives are unaware of their company's liquidity position.

As turnaround experts well know, businesses do not fail due to operating losses, asset write-downs, poor working-capital management and the like; they fail due to an unanticipated lack of cash and credit. Regardless of the severity of a given company's situation, from a simple covenant relief to a complicated debt-equity exchange, liquidity remains a prerequisite. Let us discuss two techniques to manage liquidity levels.

A rigorous liquidity management process is essential for a leveraged company, and significantly differs from traditional financial accounting, which often, and inadvertently, masks changes in liquidity. As a consequence, boards and management may be misled by a myopic reliance upon financial statements as the sole indicator of financial health.

For a leveraged company, a dwindling liquidity position will be a sign that something else requires the management's attention. Sales and margins may be softening; operating expenses may be out of alignment with revenues; plant utilization could be slipping or working capital backing up. A comprehensive, rolling 12-month cash-flow forecasting process gives boards and managers an early alert on liquidity slippages, with ample time to apply a remedy using a broad array of tactical short-term solutions.

Intensive care

For more intense liquidity situations, a rolling 13-week cash-flow forecast is another useful tool from the turnaround manager's bailiwick. This forecast captures all cash receipts and disbursements, line by line, and helps management to make decisions affecting overall liquidity on a weekly or even daily basis. Any variance between actual and forecast liquidity requires urgent management remedial action, and this tool helps a company to maintain liquidity while a deeper solution is being sought.

Know your banker

Today, a debt-dependent company needs to be particularly sensitive to the health of its lending banks, as well as monitoring conditions in the secondary loan and credit-default swap markets. With these insights, boards and managements will be able to evaluate continuously the availability, reliability and cost of credit. The transition to a lending environment more centered on capital markets comes through the interplay between originating banks, secondary market participants and the utilization of risk-transferring techniques such as credit default swaps. The market dynamics are as follows:

• Banks, as arranging agents and lenders, continue utilizing "originate to distribute" techniques. A bank's credit appetite is influenced by its ability to sell, for a profit, credit exposure to other banks and into the secondary markets.
• The capacity of the bank syndication and secondary markets permits banks not only to underwrite new credit facilities but to exit deteriorating situations, at a loss, rather than enter a prolonged and costly work-out — a type of risk transfer.
• The growth and standardization of the credit-default swap market has given both banks and secondary market players another means of tailoring exposure and transferring credit risks, influencing subsequent lender decisions and behavior.

It is essential for boards and managements to establish data-gathering processes to capture real-time, changing capital market dynamics. This can have an impact on a leveraged company's credit availability, and the reliability of credit providers in satisfying company requests.

The credit crisis of 2007-09 shows that boards and management need to continually evaluate the financial health of a leveraged company's primary lenders, as this will significantly influence their ability and willingness both to lend and to modify the terms and covenants of existing credit agreements.

In the third quarter of 2009, the Federal Deposit Insurance Corporation (FDIC) reported a 3 per cent, or $210 billion, decline in total loan balances — the largest fall since data collection began in 1984.[10] This was driven by a combination of reduced loan demand and more restrictive bank lending practices, even though the market offers lenders historically wide spreads and sound protections. With both bank failures and "problem" banks on the rise, even a minor request such as a covenant waiver or resetting may encounter an obstinate and illogical response.

Consensus building within a diverse lending group can prove highly frustrating. The agenda may not be the health of the leveraged borrower but the financial health of the lenders.

The secondary loan market matters

In traditional loan syndications, a bank at the inception of the credit facility sells down the loan at par value to other banks. In contrast, the secondary loan market is dominated by alternative investment firms accustomed to active trading in public bonds and equities such as hedge funds. Today, these secondary market players frequently purchase leveraged distress loans at various discounts to par value. The impact of the purchase discount risk adjusts the effective yield on the bond or loan, reflecting the increased probability of default. This development represents a game changer. The secondary market trading activity in distressed loans often changes the lending group's behavior and motivation towards a given borrower, since each secondary lender may have a different cost basis, return expectation and risk tolerance.

Further complexities arise since secondary market players manage their portfolios by frequently trading in and out of a given loan or bond position. In a situation where we have a good company with poor capitalization, a secondary market player's motivation may be to "lend to own" via a prepackaged bankruptcy and/or a debt-equity exchange.

The trading at a discount of a leveraged company's loans and/or bonds simply reflects the economic realities of a weakening situation. In effect, the market is aligning the value of a company's debt to match the perceived expectations. This is the function of the distressed debt market. As a consequence, the continual changing composition of the lending group makes consensus building a daunting task. The board and management of a leveraged company are urged to secure the proper business and legal talent to deal with the exponentially increased level of difficulties and complexities.

Credit-default swaps — another predictor

In its simplest form, a credit-default swap is a contract under which the buyer pays a premium for in effect insuring a bond or loan against payment default. The seller of the swap receives the premium in monthly payments. If the bond or loan defaults, the seller has to pay the agreed amount to the buyer of the swap.

The CDS is frequently compared to insurance, but there are differences. Here are two:

• Buyers of a CDS contract need not own the bond or loan. They are free to purchase multiple contracts which gain value if the underlying bond or loan trades at an increasing discounted value to par. We have seen situations where the outstanding monetary value of swaps grows to a multiple of the referenced security.
• The seller need not be a regulated entity. Often, the seller is the buyer's "counterparty", which means that if the loan or bond defaults, the CDS buyer turns to the counterparty for payment. In effect, the CDS transfers the default risk from the issuer to the contracted counterparty. The risk of counterparty default and capital adequacy became a burning issue in the 2008 government bailout of AIG.

A leveraged company needs to be aware of CDS hedging activities taking place in its outstanding public bonds and/or loans. CDS market activity is highly predictive, reflecting the market's forward sentiment on default risk. In many situations, increased CDS hedging activities and rising premiums often precede an eventual downgrading on the part of credit-rating agencies.

Following the 2008 crisis, the swap market is showing signs of maturity, with the formation of a central clearing house and standardization replacing arcane customization. These developments assure the continued proliferation of

CDSs as a risk-hedging tool by not only sophisticated hedge funds but all types of traditional debt holders.[11] In distressed situations, creditor behavior is often affected by hedging activities. For example, the value of the CDS contract rises, offsetting or mitigating the default risk of a loan or bond. The board and management of a leveraged company are well advised to monitor swap activity in their outstanding public bonds and loans, as yet another reliable predictor of capital market sentiment and lender behavior.

In closing

As an economy, we are continuing to navigate in uncharted waters. The writer embraces the sentiment that we face massive uncertainty. The major unknown for GDP is how much the consumer spends and saves. If the savings rate is high, the economy will suffer; if the savings rate is modest, the economy will likely experience anemic growth. Given the enormous loss of wealth and the jobless recovery, one can expect the consumer to save, continuing to de-lever. Unfortunately, making a highly confident prediction remains speculative for the time being.

The other major issue is the fear of government fiscal policy combating near-term deflation, eventually leading to long-term inflation. Here the question is, will the Federal Reserve boost overall interest rates and withdraw market liquidity to temper inflationary pressures, in the face of sluggish growth and stubborn unemployment?

Numerous other wildcards include the dollar's continued role as a global reserve currency, in view of its persistent weakness; the financial health of US banks along with the capacity of the shadow banking system; the fiscal deficit; the Treasury's ability to finance our ballooning national debt; and the fragile health of other national economies, especially in southern Europe.

Given the mountain of uncertainties, it is a strategic imperative for a leveraged company to maintain ample liquidity to absorb anticipated as well as unexpected shocks. Predictive indicators of business performance, along with a sophisticated liquidity-forecasting model, can heighten management's sensitivity to expected opportunities as well as threats.

In addition, the 2008 crisis taught us to maintain a level of liquidity reflecting the "unexpected". How much of a liquidity cushion remains judgmental and influenced by the dynamics of the specific situation, but the chance of the unexpected occurring needs to be incorporated into a management team's forward thinking, subject to timely and continual re-evaluation. In many ways it assures the survival of a leveraged company as it navigates toward more stable times.

4

Know your exit game plan first: Effective strategies in restructuring

William Repko,
Senior Managing Director,
Corporate Advisory Business,
and Co-Head of the
Restructuring Practice at
Evercore Partners Inc

Future readers of the chapters in this book must do so with some perspective. It is impossible to judge even the modest restructuring successes achieved in 2008 and 2009 without considering the environment in which we operated.

My perspective has been shaped by over 30 years at JP Morgan and its predecessor institutions, during which time business cycles have generated numerous structural, economic and financial challenges. Some of these were of our own making and were important learning experiences. Others were external, affecting the economy and us in various ways, and were learning experiences as well.

In response to a series of credit events in the late 1970s, the bank built and rolled out a risk-taking and measurement system. Over the years, as experience taught us new lessons, the system was recalibrated and grew in sophistication. I had the good fortune to be a part of that process and, on occasion, was granted the authority to operate the system as an approving credit officer and as part of a team who understood that risk taking is a collaborative exercise… and will forever be imperfect.

With that as the backdrop, I have been a keen observer of efforts to understand, communicate and repair elements of the infrastructure that is a foundation of our capitalist society. As I write this, I would give good grades for understanding the root causes of a financial crisis, failing grades on communicating them (the only thing more destructive to value than a bear market in the economy is a bull market in politics, and I much prefer scholarly analysis to talking heads), and an incomplete grade on repair.

Risk taking

Capitalism requires taking risk. I once asked a lecture group to raise their hands to signify whether they were "distressed investors". All raised their hands. I followed up and asked how many had gone beyond financial or statistical analysis and met with management to formulate a view on what was behind the numbers and whether that particular management had the ability to execute its plan. A smaller number raised their hands. I told them they were the distressed "investors" in the room; the rest were speculators.

Speculation is of course a form of risk taking, as is gambling. In that case, the risk taker must assess his or her willingness to put value on the line with low odds of success (including zero) for what could be a high rate of return. Or alternatively, an informed risk taker might make a well-researched "bet" for a return that is more certain, and more likely lower.

Risk taking in the most recent past had a fundamental flaw: the confusion between logical and mathematical constructs of equality and identity. In constructing the over-collateralization percentage in mortgage securitization pools involving "low doc" borrowers or those with low credit scores, the structure was generally based on statistics that extrapolated long-term loss histories for conforming mortgages (pretty much akin to the odds of drawing the inside straight). These securities were created and rated on the basis of "if" this was the result. However, the reality was that the structure held only if the assumptions were valid. What was missing in the risk equation was the question: 'What if not?'

The most important lesson is that risk is risky.

Forgiveness and the right to reorganize

It is axiomatic in the turnaround business that one has to embrace change and this has been confirmed by virtually every restructuring I have observed over the past 30 years. There are fundamental aspects of the US system for reorganizing companies that are even more important now as we recover from recent events.

In Charles Dickens' vision of debtors' prisons, as Little Dorrit was told: 'Anyone can go in… but it is not everyone who can go out.' In my early days of being a work-out banker, I viewed this as a fitting result to not being able to live up to "I promise to pay". But this version of the roach motel gave way to a more mature view of restructuring as we practice it in the US, especially after watching the post-insolvency value destruction that occurs in other parts of the world.

The Bankruptcy Code has an important and fundamental premise: the borrower has the right to reorganize. And one of the key tenets of the code is the exclusivity granted to the debtor and its management to reorganize by proposing and soliciting votes on a plan to exit bankruptcy and provide recoveries to the various constituents. The philosopher in me says that the framers of the Bankruptcy Code built rehabilitation into it out of a sense of fairness, recognizing that mistakes can and do occur. Those mistakes — innocent of fraudulent behavior, for that is dealt with separately and harshly — and the people who make them should be forgiven. Importantly, though, the consequences are put into stark relief via the absolute priority rule.

This notion of forgiveness through our bankruptcy process has intrigued me throughout my career. It is at the heart of the unique entrepreneurial spirit that exists in the US. Take a chance, invent a product, start a business, take it public, get rich. How many times have we heard of successful business leaders who have tried multiple times to make it, failed and tried again, and maybe failed again, before finally making it? The debtors' prison does not foster that spirit; the ability to be rehabilitated and reorganized does.

The best of the bad options

I do not recall who coined this gem, but it has often been said that once a company reaches the restructuring department, there are no good options available; just the best of the bad ones.

Often, maybe mostly, management and perhaps the board are consumed by avoiding bad options, or at least what are perceived as bad options. On many levels, acknowledgment that a restructuring is required means recognizing mistakes have been made — too much leverage, a bet on a product or strategy that did not work, a legal issue gone awry — which makes recognition hard. At other times, especially recently, the environment creates issues that overtake even a well-conceived business strategy, and most certainly a badly conceived or badly executed one.

To tie these issues together, once restructuring becomes a legitimate answer, the analysis and preparation of options must focus on the value that is available, or could be available under sets of circumstances including a potential business insolvency. This analysis guides the decision-making throughout the options evaluation and seeks answers for questions as fundamental as: 'How much value is there and where is it?'

No one should be confused about what is being said here; preservation of options can often be the most expensive strategy. Before making the decision on which ones to preserve, the options must be identified and risk assessed. Various scenario short-form names are often developed but usually seem to settle on Plans A, B and C, although D, E and even F surface on occasion.

Know how you will get out

A core feature of this process is to assess the several options with one overriding outcome in mind: before you go "in", you have to know how you will get "out" of the restructuring, whether it is accomplished out of court or using a bankruptcy filing.

Another core feature of any options analysis is funding. Whatever scenario is being investigated, always ask: 'How much will it cost and how will you pay for it?' Many corporate problems are brought to the surface by a deterioration in liquidity as markets and analysts assess a company's relative risk and capital providers wind down exposures or eliminate them entirely. So in an environment of scarce or expensive capital, how and where to fund the business becomes especially important.

The goal of maximizing value in a corporate finance restructuring is often problematic, and at the very least it is somewhat counter-intuitive. The changed economic environment has resulted in impaired operating performance, while credit markets have abandoned marginal borrowers, and markets overall have traded down values, resulting in a lethal combination of bad operating results and unwieldy balance sheets.

But, as has often been said: 'There's always a pony in there somewhere.'

Our system responds to the thought that often a business goes through tough times and needs a little time to sort things out. What this means to me is that the preservation of value should be thought of in a broad context. For example, operating performance can be improved in many ways, organically and/or through various enhancement methods, such as cost reductions, divesting underachieving or poor-fit businesses, or redeployment of capital to operations showing better returns.

Avoiding Chapter 11

Most often, and always in the initial stages of a restructuring discussion, "the optimum fix" is considered to be avoidance of a formal Chapter 11 proceeding — Plan A. It can be accomplished in many ways, such as an out-of-court exchange offer for a company's existing securities. This once-ubiquitous technique has become more prominent lately, particularly as capital markets closed or became otherwise unavailable to businesses. An exchange offer is an effective way to deal with over-leveraged capital structures or simply to induce stakeholders to trade an unsecured position for a more secured security, albeit with lower principal and/or coupon terms.

Another solution is refinancing, or, as has become increasingly popular recently, the transaction known as "amend and extend". Increasingly, capital providers are willing to give challenged companies more runway to address capital-structure deficiencies. I have had the recent experience of telling a CEO — who had gradually accepted the need to execute a complicated exchange offer in order to capture a significant discount in the company's debt securities — that paying off the debt at par was also a legitimate strategy, as the credit markets would welcome new issues to repay near-term maturities.

Planning the plans

In considering Plan A, B or C scenarios, there are several important questions to address. How do we accomplish this from a business and a legal perspective? Can we actually accomplish this? When should we, or must we, get this done? External forces may have a big influence on timing,

which should never be allowed to come as a surprise.

One of the important aspects of this planning is carrying out a comprehensive review of key documents. First, what are the financial and/or other interests of the important constituents? Also, what exactly can be implemented across a broad spectrum of choices? (For example, what are the company's legal rights?) And, importantly, what are the other parties' legal rights? Put another way, as a plan is developed, what can others do to stop or delay it?

An additional function of this inquiry is the sequencing of decision-making. Selecting a particular course of action in order to facilitate Plan A, for example, might eliminate a course required to preserve value in Plan C. That is essential to know and understand, especially as duress increases; choosing an unpleasant action in order to achieve a better result, and being able to explain it in rational terms, is more than just good decision-making — it tends to settle the situation down, improve the dialogue and add confidence to a chaotic situation. It does require that hard questions are asked, motivations understood and biases checked at the door.

The answers to this inquiry have the added benefit of avoiding both unintended consequences and business cases that turn out to be futile because of potential economic, legal or financial barriers.

Incidentally, part of the analysis centers on need — do we need a certain group to agree or can they be ignored? For example, if Plan A involves an exchange offer for a series of company securities, how important are the potential holdouts? This topic is especially interesting depending on the strategy employed — a coercive transaction or one strictly designed to appeal to a creditor's economic interest. If the former, the discussion quickly turns (sometimes at the direction of the creditors) to the preparation of a prepackaged Chapter 11 to avoid the cost of potential holdouts and a divergence of economic interest that defeats the purpose.

"Need to" is also a factor in electing other potential options where an analysis of what liabilities can, and should, be compromised causes often stark choices. In the General Motors Section 363 sale in 2009, for example, liabilities represented by warranty claims were not compromised. Could they perhaps have been left behind in "oldco"? Maybe, but as a practical matter it would create issues for repeat buyers, leading to loss of revenues; the trade-off was intuitively obvious.

Some choices are obvious and easy to define,

others not so. But in the planning, each is important to consider in its own way.

Stay within the law of intended consequences

Often, an important creditor will have a view of what a restructuring should offer. Sometimes that view is an educated one, assisted by an expert. Occasionally, however, it is not and that can make for very bad decisions and inject a risk into the planning process that goes beyond external factors and what they might do to defeat a plan. Uninformed thinking goes out of the realm of the law of intended consequences. There are many things a company should not do and those will be identified and dismissed as appropriate. But lenders are not always so well placed and understanding what levers can be pulled is important in assessing valuation preservation.

Communication about this among the parties is a solution, and it is useful to level expectations in a non-confrontational way.

When theory became stark reality

It is too soon to tell how financing markets will change given the impact of the Great Recession, as it is being called. It is clear that adjustments in risk assessment will occur. Markets, such as the leveraged loan market, which incurred losses beyond multiple standard deviations, will recover and capital will be provided to creditworthy borrowers. How the regulatory environment will change is unknown and will be important to measure. The maturities over the next four years will result in more restructuring discussions versus refinancing discussions than in years past, which may slow market recovery but will not stop it.

Nevertheless, this was not the environment in the last part of 2008. Financing markets were closed, risk capital had become unavailable, and suddenly restructuring had a potential outcome that was an existential threat. At no time in recent memory was this an eventuality that had to be seriously considered. Liquidation was always an analysis performed for a theoretical outcome, but in the fourth quarter of 2008 it became a real and likely eventuality.

In several cases, Plan A had been constructed, and an alternative in case Plan A failed was well under way — an organized bankruptcy, using accelerated-process theories: either prepackaged procedures or what eventually became an expedited Section 363 sale. The unavailability of risk capital in the form of debtor in possession

financing, however, created a real chance that the normal operating requirements of a business (wages and salaries, to start) could not be funded.

This created a desperate third option. Under Plan C, known as "go dark", most components of a business would shut down, employees be sent home, and creditors likely receive no recovery. It is unclear in this situation whether it is possible to resuscitate certain businesses.

Fortunately, through innovative uses of financing technologies and high coupons (LyondellBasell) or government policy imperatives (General Motors), two large enterprises avoided this outcome. But until capital markets are restored completely, forward planning must at least consider the unavailability of financing — not just in amounts sufficient to operate the business in a "normal" way, but at all. As noted earlier, options analysis gravitates to the best of the bad outcomes, and if outside financing is not available, accommodations with existing creditors will move up the spectrum of options.

Seizing the opportunity for change

So far, this discussion has focused on the financial aspects of restructuring. There are occasions when it is imperative to go beyond this and into the realm of crisis management. Crisis management can also spill over into the need to do something more significant.

Perhaps the most notable illustration of this recently was provided by the General Motors bankruptcy in June 2009. Through the Section 363 sale process, the company was able to initiate one of the most comprehensive industrial restructurings of all time, involving four brands, multiple manufacturing facilities and thousands of dealers. In addition, the United Auto Workers union agreed to sweeping reforms in how the company operated, in effect changing labor from a fixed cost to a variable one.

Make the best of the situation

In years past, operational restructuring was accomplished under the aegis of an extended stay in Chapter 11, appropriately funded and executed in a measured way. The 2005 changes to the Bankruptcy Code and the recent short-duration bankruptcies potentially give rise to a changed solution, one in which the legal and financial restructuring is completed quickly but the industrial changes must be made over a longer period.

This is a unique opportunity to think outside

the box. It does make the cost equation different, but the ability to shed unprofitable brands or businesses that exist as a matter of inertia ("we can turn this around…") is an investment decision. Properly structured and communicated, it can accelerate value recovery in ways that may not be available except through restructuring.

The key point here, however, is to ensure this option is flagged up in businesses where operational attributes can be modified to increase or unlock value.

5

Memo from your investors: A practical guide for the boards of directors of distressed companies

Wilbur L Ross, Chairman and CEO, WL Ross & Co LLC, and Chairman, Invesco Private Capital

Executives and directors of companies approaching the zone of insolvency are besieged by lawyers, investment bankers, accountants and turnaround advisors, all eager to take charge of the process. The corporate insiders usually have little or no experience of such matters and often have no one to turn to for practical advice on what they should do, other than to bring in the hired guns. Here are a few thoughts that may be useful to consider.

The board should first figure out just how they got into trouble. Management will typically blame it on external factors such as economic recession, foreign competition, the labor unions, etc, but is that really the reason or did the people in charge simply get it wrong? The question is important because one of the major decisions for the board is how much to rely on existing management to bring the business through the work-out.

A second test of management should be to have them quickly prepare a plan to maximize liquidity and a program for turning the company around. It never ceases to amaze me when existing management claim that it will take six months or even a year to develop a turnaround plan. If they are not sufficiently knowledgeable about the operations or not sufficiently hands-on to meet these challenges quickly, perhaps it is necessary to replace them with a turnaround team.

I advise against accepting a plan that basically assumes the original strategy and tactics were correct but just needed more time to come to fruition. This type of denial means management is unlikely to succeed, and is very likely to cause warfare with the creditors. My experience is that in 70 per cent of successful reorganizations, much of the "C" level of management is changed. It is hard to imagine that the chief executive officer, chief operating officer and chief financial officer all got everything right but the business failed. More often, we find either that the financial controls and/or treasury management practices were weak — or, if they were strong, that they were overridden or ignored by a CEO or COO with a dominating personality.

Where did it all go wrong?

It is crucial for the board to figure out where the breakdown occurred. One of my favorite truisms is that, "you cannot fix a problem unless you have identified that it is a problem." Another favorite is, "if you can't measure it, then you can't manage it." These analytical exercises are not about witch hunts, but rather rational decision-making by the board.

Let us say the board decides the CFO is the weakest link. This does not absolve the CEO from blame because, after all, he or she either picked the CFO or at least allowed the CFO to remain. But the question then arises of how to fill this hole. Three immediate possibilities emerge: first, promote the existing controller or treasurer; second, recruit a new CFO from outside — a somewhat time-consuming and difficult process because not every candidate will take the risk of joining a company verging on insolvency; third, retain a temporary team of outsiders and leave the post vacant. This last option is potentially a quicker solution, but their agenda may or may not be consistent with the board's thinking and it just postpones the need to find a permanent CFO.

Choosing a new CEO

If it seems the CEO is the real problem, it may be that the COO or CFO could be promoted. If neither seems qualified and there is no other internal candidate, the board has yet another reason to dismiss the CEO: running the company into insolvency and failing to have a real succession plan constitute two major management failures.

When a new CEO is to be brought in from the outside, several characteristics are paramount. The newcomer's management strengths should match the predecessor's weaknesses; if they do, it will accelerate the recovery timetable. In most cases, it is also best for the new CEO to come from the same industry; an outsider, however gifted, will need a number of months, often six to 12, to understand the sector and the company, and this is a dangerously long lag in a semi-insolvent situation. We have found that in these circumstances, someone who has either just been passed over for CEO at his present firm, or is a number two of the same age or older than his CEO, may be a strong candidate. In terms of experience, someone who has come up through line operating functions is much more likely to be able to fix a business than someone who has come up the staff ladder.

The line-up of advisors

Once the management structure is in place, retaining expert bankruptcy counsel will give the board the technical expertise it needs. Depending on the complexity of the capital structure and the potential for divestiture of some or all of the business units, the board will likely need to retain investment banking advisors as well. Depending on just how badly the company is bleeding, it may need turnaround advisors, either instead of or in addition to financial advisors.

It is handy, but not essential, if the non-legal professionals have some bankruptcy experience, but the major objective should be to fill in weaknesses in the management team, and it may be that more than one such group is needed. In general, the mindset should be to bring out of the process a company that has offloaded its weakest and/or non-strategic components, and to use some combination of the resulting proceeds plus equity to de-leverage the emerging business. Most likely

the board will need debtor-in-possession financing from day one and possibly third-party financing as it exits the bankruptcy proceedings.

Beware of the pitfalls

There are a couple of frequently made mistakes to avoid. Some boards are so eager to get out of bankruptcy quickly that they agree to what I would call a patch job. They fail to take on the fights needed to deal with the pension, healthcare or wage issues that are strangling the business. Alternatively, in order to make a quick deal, they agree to leave too much debt. Worse yet, they commit to an overly optimistic business plan. Any of those errors could well result in a repeat bankruptcy, which is referred to as Chapter 22. Believe it or not, these really do happen.

The other strategy would be to wallow in bankruptcy for as long as possible, which usually happens if the board adopts a very passive attitude, hires an army of insolvency professionals and hands the keys over to them. This approach can be problematic. Many bankruptcy professionals have strong personalities and may have conflicting views about the right restructuring path. Without an equally forceful client to mediate such dissension, the process can easily get out of control and lead to endless, even mindless, litigation. Because bankruptcy is ultimately a court-driven process, it is inherently easy to slow down and inherently hard to speed up. In the absence of a strong client, litigation can easily replace negotiation. One is also tempted to note that because professional retentions mainly involve time-based compensation, they do not necessarily have the same sense of urgency that a civilian might have.

The compensation question

Compensation is one of the trickiest issues for the board to decide. It is routine for management to insist upon being paid "stay bonuses", to encourage their continuity of service. Recent bankruptcy rule changes have made these less egregious than before, but there are still legitimate questions for the board to ask. First, is it really reasonable to believe that everyone in senior management at a failed enterprise is a hot candidate to be recruited away? Second, would the loss of each one be that damaging to the company?

Compensation of professionals is equally tricky. Many are now seeking "success bonuses" in addition to their time-based fees. It is hard to argue with the concept that particularly meritorious work deserves extra compensation, but the questions arise as to how you define success and how you allocate the rewards among the professionals. Many will seek a success fee based simply on the fact that a plan of reorganization is approved and implemented. This does not seem to me to be a high enough hurdle for a bonus since the vast majority of cases do result in an approved plan of reorganization. A better system might relate more specifically to factors under each one's control. These might be items such as the speed of confirmation of a plan, or the total trading value created in the plan, or achievement of certain capital ratios, or some combination of the above.

There even are issues in the basic compensation of professionals. There have been numerous cases in which the fees of the equity committee or unsecured creditors committee, or both, exceeded the recoveries achieved by those constituencies. This makes little sense to me because in those cases the direct cost of these professionals decreased the aggregate recovery of the estate without accomplishing a reallocation to their constituencies. To the extent that the out-of-the-money constituencies delayed the case or engaged in fruitless litigation, they further detracted from the recoveries of more senior but still impaired creditors because the lawyers for the in-the-money constituencies also spent money defending the litigation.

Bankruptcy professionals are naturally unwilling to contest each other's fees because they fear tit-for-tat, but I believe the board of the bankrupt company should actively monitor all fees. It is, after all, the use of the debtor's funds that is the issue, so the board should be concerned. In a number of cases, judges have become sufficiently upset with runaway fees that they have appointed specialists to examine them and make recommendations to the court. This generally results in reductions, although it also brings in a new fee-seeking party. But how could an outsider brought in late in the process be a better evaluator of the professionals than the board, which has been involved throughout?

Monitor the stakeholders
The next challenge for the board and for management is to keep track of the changing identity of the stakeholders. Because most equity investors are relatively passive, institutions regularly buy and sell shares and creditor claims in solvent companies without affecting board or management decisions. Distressed investors,

however, are a rather different breed. They tend to be both activists and highly skilled at using bankruptcy technicalities to their advantage, and to the disadvantage of other stakeholders. As the proceedings advance, an increasing percentage of creditor claims will flow into such hands. There may also be a rapid turnover of the claims, depending on how the case is going. It is important, therefore, for the insiders to have a view on which type of claimant has a legitimate economic stake that should be respected by the debtor, and which are simply out-of-the-money opportunists trying to divert value from valid claimants. The board is in as good a position as anyone to try to make the playing field fair.

Inside information
The turnover of creditor claims raises another nagging issue: misuse of insider information. Most courts do approve of processes, particularly so-called "information walls", that permit even members of official committees to trade if the parties making investment decisions are isolated from those participating in the committee deliberations. But the reality is that if something material is disclosed at a committee meeting, there is an almost instantaneous change in the prices of the securities. This makes one wonder how well the confidentiality and information walls are being respected.

Even more troubling is the lack of disclosure of changes in the securities holdings of committee members. In a normal company, officers and directors must disclose promptly any changes in their ownership. I believe that since committee membership entails similar fiduciary responsibilities, companies and courts should require prompt disclosure of portfolio transactions by committee members. Similarly, it is not unusual for a committee member to divest his or her entire position and resign, again with little or no disclosure of the price and date of sale and with little or no effort by the issuer to make sure there were no improprieties. I would urge directors to request the court to adopt much more effective defenses against trading on inside information.

As if to add another layer of complexity, some large, discount-price buyers of creditor claims may not want to serve on the committee because they do not want any trading restrictions. This presents a huge difficulty because it means that reaching agreement with the committee may not ensure success in terms of the creditors voting to approve the plan.

For these reasons, I believe that boards should insist on a more level information playing field.

There is also the question of how much time a director should spend on meetings during a bankruptcy. I believe that the meetings should be more frequent when the company is in trouble than when it is healthy; the legal overlay and complexity of constituencies alone mitigate in favor of more, rather than less, board involvement. So does the point that, typically, no annual meetings are held during bankruptcy and therefore the board is literally self-perpetuating.

Whenever the business plan is revised, I believe that it should be released publicly at the same time as it is presented to the committee. Similarly, when debtors propose a plan of reorganization to a committee, the plan should be made public, as should the committee's response. Removing the shroud of secrecy would make membership on committees by major stakeholders less complicated, would improve decision-making and would address the problem of trading on inside information. Disclosure of what is going on with a troubled company should be even more fulsome than with a healthy one, because the stakes are higher and the potential for abuse is more severe.

When takeovers loom

Mergers and acquisitions are a hot topic in many boardrooms as insolvency approaches. Some boards seem determined not to be taken over by a strategic acquirer or an investment fund, on the basis that it is the wrong time to be sold when the business is doing badly. The reality is that control will change hands as unduly burdensome debt is turned to equity. The only question in my mind is whether or not the value of the estate is maximized by a formal sale in bankruptcy. In general, boards can extract a premium in return for turning over control of a healthy company, but that may or may not be true of a bankrupt one. The way to find out is to pursue the parallel paths of a standalone restructuring and a sale of the company and to present the result to the relevant constituencies. They are the parties that should really make the decision because they are the economic stakeholders.

This issue should be decided, in my opinion, by the affected stakeholders and not just the board. If the stakeholders prefer the standalone plan to the acquisition, they should have the right to make that choice, but it is only by running both paths simultaneously that a fully informed decision can be made. Along the way, it may be that a predatory fund or strategic investor accumulates claims to position itself to take over the company, or at least to have a major voice in takeover decisions. There is relatively little the board can do about such tactics, but if it does adopt a liberal policy of communication, at least it can ensure that predators pay a fair price.

Other bankruptcy practitioners might have very different, even stridently different, views. Nonetheless, I hope that directors and executives of future first-time Chapter 11 filers will be able to draw on this discussion to make a strong contribution to the successful restructuring of their distressed company.

6

Managing in the "new normal": A self-help corporate governance program for directors and officers

John Wm ("Jack") Butler Jr,

with Peter Allan Atkins and

J Eric Ivester, Partners,

Skadden, Arps, Slate, Meagher &

Flom LLP

The recession that began in December, 2007 and technically ended in the third quarter of 2009, and its aftermath, represent the most economically tumultuous period since the Great Depression. Multiple economic forces combined to create a perfect liquidity and capital storm of declining operating cash flow, fixed or increasing costs, limited availability of new credit and equity capital, and the withdrawal of existing credit. The 2007-09 recession has left in its wake a changed economic environment that has been labeled the "new normal" — an environment that features sustained volatility and continuing wide swings in market performance, asset values, consumer confidence and spending, and availability and cost of capital. The recent economic crisis may have hit financial institutions the hardest, but non-financial corporations and small businesses were also affected.

In the recession's wake, directors and officers are expected by their stakeholders to effectively manage their companies in a global marketplace that is experiencing de-globalization, de-leveraging and re-regulation. In today's "new normal" this is especially challenging as they not only continue to assess potential liquidity and capital risks but also focus on internal and external opportunities created during the recession. At the same time, consumers, investors, the government and other stakeholders have reported a loss of confidence in directors and officers of corporations, often blaming them for the economic crisis. These constituencies posit that directors and officers were slow to assess and respond to the risk profiles of their own corporations, which exacerbated out-of-control systemic risk leading to the global recession. This loss of confidence and trust has resulted in more government regulation and intervention in the day-to-day business affairs of corporations in the US and other countries.

The Dodd-Frank Act

The centerpiece of the federal government's efforts to restore public confidence in the financial system and curb perceived abuses in corporate boardrooms and executive suites is the Dodd-Frank Act. The Act, which is over 2,300 pages and impacts almost every aspect of the US financial services industry, also gives the federal government the authority to regulate certain aspects of corporate governance.

The underlying premise of the corporate governance provisions in the Act is that the federal government must intervene in the traditionally state-governed area of corporate oversight because the current system is inadequate and prone to abuse. While stopping short of repealing the deferential business judgment rule, the Act requires enhanced disclosure of executive compensation and the independence of members of, and advisors to, board compensation committees, gives shareholders the right to a periodic "say on pay" vote on executive compensation, and authorizes the Securities and Exchange Commission to adopt rules giving nominating shareholders access to a company's proxy. In addition to these new corporate governance mandates, the Act's sweeping new regulatory scheme addressing oversight and systemic risk, financial institutions, capital markets and consumer protection will likely create unintended consequences and "event risks" for non-financial companies. These event risks must be effectively anticipated and mitigated by directors and officers.

As stewards of business, it is incumbent upon officers and directors to rebuild the confidence and trust of their diverse constituencies if they are to navigate their corporations in today's environment. Directors and officers pursuing corporate governance "best practices" should reflect upon and beyond the fiduciary duties they owe to their various constituencies and how these duties and the expectations of these constituencies are affected in volatile times of economic distress and recovery.

Recognizing how their fiduciary duties and constituency expectations are affected by economic distress will enable officers and directors to effectively assess enterprise risk and proactively respond to changing economic conditions in the future.

In addition to responding to the mandate of the Dodd-Frank Act, directors and officers should carefully consider developing and publicly committing to their own set of principles of conduct to demonstrate that comprehensive board oversight of corporate risk can help facilitate a transparent and stable economic system.

Fiduciary duties: back to basics

Under most state corporate laws — including Delaware, where most corporations are organized — directors and officers owe fiduciary duties of loyalty (including good faith) and care. In most states, while a corporation is solvent, directors' and officers' fiduciary duties are owed exclusively to the corporation and its shareholders.

The duty of loyalty requires directors and officers to act solely on the basis of what they honestly believe to be in the best interests of the corporation and its shareholders, without regard to personal or private interests or motivations, financial or otherwise. The duty of care requires directors and officers to act with the care an ordinarily prudent person would exercise under the same or similar circumstances. More particularly, the duty of care requires directors and officers to be informed of all reasonably available material information prior to making business decisions, including available alternatives, and to act in a deliberative manner. Applying these principles, directors and officers are expected to exercise informed, disinterested and good-faith business judgment in connection with affirmatively dealing with material business risks. In discharging these duties, directors and officers are entitled to rely on the advice of the corporation's management and outside experts, as long as they are reasonably believed to be knowledgeable/expert in their respective fields and there is no known reason not to rely on the information.

In their decision-making with respect to most business decisions, including affirmative decisions regarding dealing with risk matters, the law presumes that directors and officers have discharged their fiduciary duties in accordance with the standards described above. Unless this presumption is rebutted, directors and officers are protected from personal liability if a business decision ultimately proves unwise or unsuccessful. This rebuttable presumption is often referred to as the business judgment rule.

The business judgment rule insulates directors and officers from judicial second-guessing in light of the availability of new information and the clarity of hindsight. When a business decision is evaluated after the fact, directors and officers may not be held personally liable for any negative consequences flowing from the decision, even if the decision was wrong or risky, as long as the decision-making process was rational and employed in a good-faith effort to advance corporate interests.

As applied to affirmative decisions regarding risk-taking, the business judgment rule protects directors and officers and their decisions unless a shareholder can meet the burden of proof that the decision was made in breach of their fiduciary duties or was simply irrational.

Under Delaware law, which many states follow, the fiduciary duty of directors and officers does not extend, however, to an obligation to ferret out or monitor business risk (as opposed to a duty to monitor risk with respect to fraud or criminal misconduct). The distinction between affirmative risk-taking decisions and inaction with respect to business risk is important in identifying the sources of pressure on directors and officers to engage in business risk oversight in the "new normal" environment.

Fiduciary duties and corporate insolvency

Senior management and directors are expected to make business decisions with their various fiduciary duties in mind. However, this obligation is never more apparent than in times of economic crisis and distress. When dealing with a distressed company, basic corporate governance principles still apply; which is to say, directors and officers are expected to exercise informed, disinterested and good-faith business judgment for the benefit of the corporation and its shareholders. The fundamental nature of their fiduciary duties does not change when the company is insolvent or approaching insolvency, and directors and officers are still protected by the business judgment rule.

When a corporation becomes insolvent, however, it is fair to say that directors' and officers' fiduciary duties expand and include a larger community of interests, including creditors. As a practical matter, once a corporation becomes insolvent, officers and directors must manage the company to maximize its value for the benefit of its creditors as well as its shareholders. This duty runs to all corporate stakeholders, not to any particular groups or to any particular individuals. Consequently, once a corporation becomes insolvent, the directors and officers must focus on maximizing the value of the enterprise, rather than attempting to maximize recoveries for any one particular constituency.

One of the more daunting challenges facing directors and officers of a distressed company is determining whether the company is insolvent in the first instance. Deterioration of a business is often a gradual process, so it is not always clear whether a corporation is insolvent. For that reason, courts refer to the "zone of insolvency" or the "vicinity of insolvency" to more accurately depict the reality facing troubled companies and their directors and officers.

Courts have held that directors' and officers' fiduciary duties expand before bankruptcy or equitable insolvency when the corporation is in the zone or vicinity of insolvency. There is no universally accepted definition of the zone of insolvency. As such, directors and officers of a distressed company should consider their company to be in the zone of insolvency — and their fiduciary duties correspondingly expanded to include stakeholders other than conventional shareholders — when the company's current financial situation causes them to seriously consider whether it is in fact insolvent.

Breach of fiduciary duty

The idea behind the zone of insolvency was first articulated by the Delaware courts in 1991 in the case of *Credit Lyonnais Bank Nederland NV v Pathe Communications Corp*. Therein, the court explained that officers and directors of solvent corporations

entering the zone of insolvency may find that the most efficient and fair business decisions diverge from those choices that are the most beneficial to the corporation's shareholders.

Certain factions interpreted this language to mean that directors and officers of companies in the zone of insolvency owed fiduciary duties to creditors as well as shareholders of the corporation. The practical effect of this interpretation was that creditors could directly sue board members for alleged breaches of fiduciary duties. That interpretation became a sword in the hands of creditors, which for a period of time was wielded to great effect.

Over the past few years, Delaware courts have blunted the sword wielded by creditor constituencies against directors and officers of companies in the zone of insolvency. Indeed, the courts have explained that *Credit Lyonnais* was never intended to expose directors and officers to attacks by recalcitrant creditor bodies. Rather, it was intended to shield board members and management of companies in the zone of insolvency from attacks brought by disgruntled shareholders for making business decisions with other corporate stakeholders in mind.

Courts have noted that while fiduciary duties expand to include creditors, as well as shareholders, when a company is in the zone of insolvency, this does not give rise to independent causes of action by creditors against directors or officers for breach of fiduciary duty.

Even though the fiduciary duties owed by directors and officers of an insolvent company do not change, the same cannot be said for the potential beneficiary of any recovery received as a result of a breach of fiduciary duty.

For instance, under Delaware law, a claim against directors or officers alleging a breach of fiduciary duties owed to a solvent corporation may be brought by the corporation or through a shareholder derivative suit. A derivative action is brought on behalf of the company because it is the corporation that suffered the harm as a result of the breach of fiduciary duties. For that reason, the recovery ultimately goes to the corporation.

Shareholders of a solvent corporation typically have standing to enforce claims on behalf of the corporation through a derivative suit, because they are the intended beneficiaries of a corporation's growth and any increase in the value of its assets.

When a company is insolvent, creditors may bring such claims through a creditor derivative suit. This is because creditors, and not the shareholders, are the likely beneficiaries of any increase in the value of an insolvent company. As is the case with shareholder derivative suits, the insolvent company is the beneficiary of any monetary recovery.

Practical application to responding to the needs of a distressed company

In times of economic uncertainty, particularly while a company is in danger of entering the zone of insolvency, directors and officers are called upon to promptly and accurately gauge the extent of the corporation's troubles and to formulate an appropriate plan of action. More often than not, the emphasis will be on the state of the company's liquidity at the present time and in the near future.

In order to respond effectively under these circumstances, directors and senior management should engage in a comprehensive review of the corporation's finances and business plan. In conducting this review, directors and officers should consider, among other things, the following:

• Identifying and implementing cost-reduction and other cash-conservation measures.
• Establishing a program for monitoring the key indicators of the company's performance, with prompt reporting to the board of material variances and their potential consequences.
• A "stress test" of the company's business plan against downside scenarios.
• Paying particular attention to assumptions regarding key contributors to operating cash flow (the contributors will vary depending on the type of business).
• Identifying and evaluating risk issues related to the increasingly globally interconnected nature of many businesses.
• Determining what capital expenditures in the company's existing plan are "essential" and what commitments can or should be deferred or are discretionary.
• Re-examining the sources of liquidity and capital underlying the current business/operating plan, and assessing the extent to which they should be considered reliable going forward. In particular, the accessibility, and risks to accessibility, of the company's short- and long-term liquidity resources should be assessed. The board should also consider contingency planning for access to alternative sources of liquidity and capital beyond the company's traditional sources.
• Reviewing debt agreements and the company's other material agreements against the current business plan, and downside scenarios, to evaluate

potential compliance issues with respect to covenants and agreements.
• Communications planning, internally and externally, on a contingency basis, should circumstances develop to the point where special communications to the company's various constituencies are warranted.
• Whether and how to respond to misinformation and rumors that may be having an immediate impact on the company's stock price.
• Reviewing the company's current disclosures and continuing to oversee them going forward, in light of the company's financial position and risk profile under current and developing conditions.
• Evaluating the appropriate frequency of board and senior management meetings in order to devote the time necessary to understanding the issues facing the company, the options available to it and the risks of each, and then properly and contemporaneously documenting the efforts of the board and senior management.

Generally a comprehensive review of this type will necessitate the involvement of outside experts. Outside advisors familiar with these types of risk review can assist officers and directors in defining the scope of the review, the most efficient process for conducting it, the extent to which the review should be documented and any disclosure obligations under the law.

Looking ahead: enterprise risk assessment

Now that the tailwinds of the 2007-09 recession are beginning to subside, directors and officers are turning their attention from liquidity risk issues to the assessment of other business risks. Specifically, they are starting to assess what enterprise risk management measures should be implemented or enhanced to better serve the interests of their corporations and their stakeholders.

The needs of different businesses vary greatly. For that reason, enterprise risk assessment is best characterized as a fluid concept, incapable of precise definition. The Committee of Sponsoring Organizations of the Treadway Commission, an expert in the area of risk management, describes enterprise risk management as the process by which corporations balance risk with their overall business plan; improve risk response decisions; reduce losses in connection with risk; identify and manage risk across a family of inter-related companies; define and realize new business opportunities; and improve the overall allocation of capital.

The core concept to glean from this broad

description is that a corporation that effectively identifies and manages risk as part of its overall business plan is better placed to identify problems and make the necessary adjustments earlier, thus neutralizing looming threats before they get out of hand, and positioning itself to reap the rewards of a successful risk strategy.

The importance of enterprise risk assessment

While conducting comprehensive enterprise risk assessments may not be necessary in order to fully comply with fiduciary duties, the failure to conduct such assessments may result in other "real world" consequences.

In July 2009, the Securities and Exchange Commission proposed new rules relating to executive compensation and corporate governance disclosure. Therein, the agency acknowledged the role that risk and the adequacy of risk oversight played in the recent market crisis. The new rules, which became effective on February 28, 2010, require companies to include enhanced and new disclosures in their proxy statements to shareholders.

Specifically, the new rules require disclosures about a board's leadership structure, its role in the risk management process, and how a company's compensation policies and practices generally create incentives that affect the company's risk profile.

Certain of the new corporate governance provisions in the Dodd-Frank Act will also require directors and officers to consider these issues, including new disclosure requirements relating to the relationship between executive compensation and financial performance.

Risk assessment is not a new concept. In the wake of the Enron scandal, Congress enacted the Sarbanes-Oxley 404 requirement that companies assess the effectiveness of their internal controls over financial reporting. Congress also required senior officers to certify the accuracy of the corporation's financial reporting.

Furthermore, the New York Stock Exchange requires that listed companies have an audit committee to discuss the company's risk assessment and management guidelines and policies. As part of this policy, listed companies are expected to identify their major financial risk exposures and the processes by which management seeks to control such exposures.

In addition to these legal and regulatory requirements, directors and officers should be concerned with the public's perception of how

seriously corporations are treating risk assessment and management going forward. Notably, investors, the media and the government perceive the failure to proactively assess and manage risk as a prime catalyst for the recent economic crisis. Intensely scrutinizing, anticipating and disclosing material risk will help boards and their corporations to reaffirm their commitment to responsible corporate oversight and re-establish relationships of trust and confidence with their diverse stakeholders.

Board review of risk governance issues

As boards are turning their attention to formulating and implementing risk assessment policies and procedures, it is important to note that there is not a "one size fits all" approach to identifying and managing risk. Every business is different and has its own unique set of circumstances that will have to be considered.

As a guide to assist boards in fulfilling their risk oversight role, the Blue Ribbon Commission on Risk Governance of the National Association of Corporate Directors released a report in October 2009 entitled "Risk Governance: Balancing Risk and Reward". The Commission believes that, as a general rule, the full board should have primary responsibility for risk oversight, with its standing committees supporting the board by addressing the risks inherent in their respective oversight areas.

Boards should review the report and the following recommended principles as they work (together with management and their advisors) to achieve their risk oversight objectives:

- Understand the company's key drivers of success.
- Assess risks in the company's strategy.
- Define the role of the full board and its standing committees with regard to risk oversight.
- Consider whether the company's risk management system, including people and processes, is appropriate and has sufficient resources.
- Work with management to understand and agree on the types and format of risk information that the board requires.
- Encourage a dynamic and constructive risk dialogue between management and the board, including a willingness to challenge assumptions.
- Closely monitor the potential risks in the company's culture and its incentive structure.
- Monitor critical alignments of strategy, risk, controls, compliance, incentives and people.
- Consider emerging and inter-related risks.

- Periodically assess the board's risk oversight processes.

In addition to reviewing these principles, a board should take into consideration best practices and industry standards for risk management programs. The integrated framework issued by the Committee of Sponsoring Organizations of the Treadway Commission is widely accepted, and boards should be aware of its approach to oversight of enterprise risk. The board's oversight role is a critical step in establishing the appropriate company-specific risk management program. In the current economic climate, boards and managements should work together to establish an acceptable risk level that produces the greatest opportunity for reward.

The critical elements and basic principles of oversight

While the wisdom of increasing government intervention in the day-to-day affairs of corporations through the Dodd-Frank Act and other legislative initiatives may be open to debate, the imperative for directors and officers to demonstrate that vigilant, independent and honest oversight can be relied upon as the driving force of corporate governance is not. One approach to addressing these concerns at the board level is to develop and publicly adopt a set of voluntary principles of conduct.

A voluntary program that would enable directors and officers to demonstrate their commitment to responsible risk management and corporate governance would need to include certain critical elements in order to be successful. First, an agreed-upon set of basic principles of oversight needs to be formulated. These principles would reflect focused and real commitment to comprehensive board oversight of corporate affairs, including self-evaluation of compliance to reinforce quality oversight and support credibility. Next, broad and demonstrable support for the program among directors of public companies is critical. Without widespread support, it will be difficult — near impossible — for corporate boards to staunch their very public detractors and convey their commitment to more stringent, self-imposed oversight guidelines.

The most important of the elements listed above are the basic principles of oversight, which must adequately address the public's concerns about past failures of corporate governance practices, particularly with regard to risk assessment and management, while maintaining the board's autonomy and role as overseer of the business. With these goals in mind, directors and officers should develop basic principles of oversight with regard to identification of key corporate areas requiring board oversight; formulation and implementation of a process for performing board oversight; and ensuring that the oversight process is transparent and inclusive in a meaningful way.

First, the basic principles of oversight would require a board to identify and publicly disclose all key areas that are appropriate for board oversight. The board should generally oversee and otherwise be involved in: (1) financial systems, controls and reporting; (2) disclosure controls and reporting; (3) operations of material business segments; (4) identifying and understanding material risks inherent in and taken by the company, and evaluating the efficacy of the company's risk-management programs; (5) evaluating key management strengths, weaknesses and performance; (6) establishing and monitoring compensation policies and practices; (7) succession planning; (8) nominating and governance policies and practices; (9) health, safety and environmental policies and practices; (10) tax policies and practices; (11) diversity policies and practices; (12) asset-protection policies and practices; (13) public/government affairs policies and practices; (14) privacy/data protection policies and practices; (15) corporate sustainability and reporting; and (16) other material company-specific areas appropriate for board-level oversight.

Next, the board should identify, implement and disclose a responsible framework for performing quality board oversight. This framework should include, among other things: a majority of, and in many cases exclusively, independent, disinterested directors performing the oversight function; identification of desired/required director experience and skills for the particular oversight area; use of outside advisors, consultants or specialists at the sole discretion of the board or committee performing the oversight function; direct interaction with and support from appropriate company personnel; and, in some cases, attendance of directors at educational seminars or programs to obtain or enhance relevant knowledge.

The basic principles should also mandate that a board will solicit and evaluate commentary from its company's shareholders and employees as to additional areas that should be the subject of board oversight and improvements to the board's framework for performing quality oversight. Ideally, a board will annually evaluate whether it has fully satisfied each of the foregoing mandates and report its findings publicly.

This call for action is little more than a simple and straightforward set of principles that represents a clear commitment to responsible oversight in a very public way. Key areas of oversight designated by a board will be disclosed to the public. If the corporation's employees and shareholders believe the scope of the board's oversight is too narrow, they will be able to voice their concerns as part of the oversight process.

By voluntarily subscribing to these principles, a board will be publicly committing to oversee the business and affairs of its company thoughtfully, carefully, comprehensively and proactively. Moreover, the board will be sending a clear message that its business and affairs are to be conducted legally and ethically.

Having done so, directors are likely to be highly motivated to act in accordance with their public commitment, even though they are voluntarily accepting a higher standard of conduct than is required as a matter of fiduciary duty under state law.

Conclusion

As senior management and directors continue to navigate through improving but uncertain economic conditions, they should concentrate on reaffirming their commitment to responsible corporate oversight in order to regain the confidence and trust of their many stakeholders. In order to do so, directors and officers should pay particular attention to periodic business enterprise risk assessments and what actions should be taken in order to implement effective reviews. As part of this process, directors and officers need to be cognizant not only of their fiduciary duties, and how those duties may come into play in situations where their companies experience stress and even financial distress, but also the expectations, demands and requirements of all relevant constituencies focused on the roles of directors and management in identifying, overseeing and managing company risk, particularly in the "new normal" environment.

Directors and officers of a company experiencing rapidly changing circumstances must devote the time necessary to understanding the issues facing the company, the options available to the company, and the risks of each. Board members should obtain and rely on reports prepared by management and outside advisors. Directors and officers should actively participate in board discussions by asking probing questions and by exercising independent judgment. They should also recognize and be prepared to deal with disclosure requirements that may apply to business enterprise risk reviews and their adoption of a voluntary set of principles of corporate governance conduct.

In charting their course, directors and officers need to be acutely aware of the consequences of failure to meet the expectations, demands and requirements of their relevant constituencies. For example, allegations of ignoring "red flags" regarding business risks can lead to questions as to the adequacy of a company's disclosure, including with respect to risk factors and as to compliance with company risk oversight policies. Moreover, the spotlight on director conduct as a governance matter and in the media has become increasingly bright, and notoriety individually as a director or as a member of a board spotlighted as failing to monitor risk is obviously harmful in and of itself. And increased shareholder activism, particularly with respect to the election of directors, is a practical reminder that the record and reputation of directors is more important than ever.

Portions of this article appeared originally in client letters and Skadden Insights 2009 and 2010, and were published by Peter Allan Atkins on the Harvard Law School Forum on Corporate Governance and Financial Regulation.

7

Avoiding Chapter 22: Why post-emergence liquidity, profitability and leverage make all the difference

Edward Altman,

Max L Heine Professor of Finance at the Stern School of Business, New York University, and Director of the Credit and Fixed Income Research Program at the NYU Salomon Center,

co-authored with

T Kant and T Rottanaruengyot

More than 40 years ago, this author published an article (Altman, 1968) on how fundamental financial data and equity market values could be combined to effectively predict whether firms would go bankrupt in the US. That resulting Z-Score model has become an established tool for assessing the creditworthiness of manufacturing firms throughout the world and is used by scholars and practitioners in a variety of ways, including credit and debt analysis, investment decisions, default probability and M&A screens. It is also used by advisors and managers themselves in executing a financial turnaround of distressed companies.

The predictive indicators used in the original article have been expanded to uniquely assess the health of corporate industrial entities as they emerge from the Chapter 11 bankruptcy process, and to examine the likelihood of whether the debtor will have to file for bankruptcy again — the so-called "Chapter 22" phenomenon.

Chapter 11 bankruptcy reorganization

Over the years, in addition to the issue of the overall effectiveness of Chapter 11 in the US, there has been constant debate on whether the process provides the right balance between reorganizing economically viable firms and liquidating non-viable companies under Chapter 7. For those companies that do attempt a reorganization, seeking temporary protection from creditors while an improved operational plan and financial structure are put in place, there are several ways in which one might evaluate its success.

The first requirement of a restructuring is that the company can emerge from the process as a going concern. A further test is to assess the post-bankruptcy results of the entity in terms of its operating and/or its stock market performance. While this performance may be compared to other firms in the same industry or to some market index, it is clear that if the firm is forced to seek another distressed restructuring relatively soon after emerging, the process has not been a success at all. The most extreme instance of a failed Chapter 11 is that the company files for bankruptcy again — Chapter 22. (Hotchkiss, 1992; Altman, 1993).

Studies of post-bankruptcy performance have found that while many firms restructure without the need for further remedial action, a striking number of cases require another restructuring through a private work-out or a second (or third) bankruptcy. For example, Edith Hotchkiss (1995) found that 32 per cent of a sample of large companies that had emerged as a public entity restructured again through a private or court-determined restructuring, while LoPucki and Whitford (1993), in their study of larger Chapter 11 filings, found that 32 per cent filed again within four years of emerging. While some companies come out of the process still holding too much debt, most cite operating problems as the primary reason for the second filing.

As we will show, the troubling incidence of subsequent failures has accrued despite requirements — under the Bankruptcy Code enacted in 1978,

Table I

Academic studies of post-bankruptcy performance
This table lists a number of existing studies related to the performance of firms emerging from Chapter 11

Ability to Meet	Operating Performance	Cash-Flow Projections	Stock Performance	Sample
Hotchkiss (1995)	√	√		197 firms emerging by 1989
Hotchkiss & Mooradian (2004)	√		√	620 firms emerging by 2004
Maksimovic & Phillips (1998)	√			Plant-level data for 302 manufacturing firms in Chapter 11, 1978-1989
Alderson & Betker (1999)	√			89 firms emerging from Chapter 11, 1983-1993
Hotchkiss & Mooradian (1997)	√			288 firms defaulting on public debt 1980-1993 (166 reorganized in Chapter 11)
McHugh, Michel & Shaked (1998)		√		35 firms emerging from Chapter 11, 1990-1994
Betker, Ferris & Lawless (1999)		√		69 firms emerging from Chapter 11, 1984-1994
Aggarwal, Altman & Eberhart (1999)			√	131 firms emerging from Chapter 11, 1980-1993
Goyal, Kahl & Torous (2002)			√	Firms distressed between 1980 and 1983; 35 firms in first year after resolution of distress to 25 firms five years after
Lee & Cunney (2004)			√	111 firms emerging from Chapter 11, 1988-2005

Source: Updated from Altman & Hotchkiss (2005)

and amended in 2005 (Bankruptcy Abuse Prevention and Consumer Protection Act) — that in order for a reorganization plan to be confirmed, the court must make an independent finding that it is feasible and further reorganization is not likely or needed; specifically, that the plan 'is not likely to be followed by the liquidation or the need for further financial reorganization of the debtor or any successors of the debtor under the plan'. In reality, however, unless there is convincing opposing evidence presented by interested parties, the bankruptcy court has little choice but to sanction the plan as presented.

The purpose of this study is not to debate the merits of Chapter 11, especially since the Bankruptcy Code was substantially modified in 2005. The purpose is to analyze whether one can predict, with a reasonable degree of accuracy, which firms emerging from bankruptcy are more likely to suffer subsequent problems and file again under Chapter 22. In other words, can advisors, analysts, investors and debtors — indeed, the court system itself — avoid as much as possible the Chapter 22 phenomenon?

Post-bankruptcy performance
A relatively high proportion of larger companies that attempt to reorganize under Chapter 11 do emerge as independent going concerns. At the same time, for public firms of all sizes, only between 26 and 45 per cent (depending upon the year) emerged over the period 1990-2002 with their

reorganization plans confirmed by the courts, and these statistics include many companies with multiple filings for various subsidiaries of the same group. For those firms that had their plans confirmed, about 44 per cent emerged as publicly registered companies.

The most important factors in coming out of the process successfully are the firm's size and its ability to secure debtor-in-possession financing.

Stuart Gilson (1997) found that leverage remained high after both out-of-court restructurings and Chapter 11 reorganizations, although it was considerably more elevated in the former. In a study of 58 out-of-court cases and 51 firms that went through the Chapter 11 process between 1980 and 1989, he found that the median ratio of long-term debt (face value) to the sum of long-term debt and common shareholders' equity (market value) was 0.64 for firms in out-of-court restructurings and 0.47 for those in Chapter 11. Hence, significant remaining debt on the balance sheets of reorganized firms could contribute to their refiling not too long after emergence. He also found that as much as 25 per cent of his total sample had to file for bankruptcy or restructure their debt again.

Heron, Lie and Rodgers (2006) came to a similar conclusion in that while the 172 firms they studied for the period 1990-2004 had substantially reduced their debt burden in "fresh start" Chapter 11 reorganizations, they still emerged with higher debt ratios than was typical in their respective industries.

Studies that have examined the post-bankruptcy performance of firms registered as public companies can be found in Table I. Several of these studies assessed profitability and cash flows relative to comparable firms in similar industries. The eye-catching result was that more than two-thirds of those emerged firms underperformed industry peers for up to five years following bankruptcy, and in some studies (eg, Hotchkiss 1995) as many as 40 per cent continued to experience operating losses in the three years after emergence. McHugh *et al* (1998) shows that projections provided by the bankruptcy reorganization plan for two-time filers (Chapter 22s) prior to their emergence from their first Chapter 11 are typically overstated, and these overstatements are more pronounced than for single filers.

On the other hand, the experience of larger firms does show improved post-bankruptcy performance and one study, by Eberhart, Aggarwal

Table II

Chapter 22s and 33s in the United States 1984-2009

Year	Number of Chapter 22s	Number of Chapter 33s
1984	2	0
1985	2	0
1986	4	0
1987	1	0
1988	5	0
1989	4	0
1990	10	0
1991	9	0
1992	6	0
1993	8	0
1994	5	0
1995	9	0
1996	12	2
1997	5	0
1998	2	1
1999	10	0
2000	12	1
2001	17	2
2002	11	0
2003	17	1
2004	6	0
2005	9	1
2006	4	0
2007	8	1
2008	19	0
2009	18	1
Totals	215	10

Source: The Bankruptcy Yearbook & Almanac, Boston: New Generation Research and Altman and Hotchkiss Corporate Financial Distress and Bankruptcy, J. Wiley, Hoboken, NJ (2006)

and Altman (1999), shows excess stock market returns in the 200 days following emergence for those firms that came out of the process between 1980 and 1993 with publicly listed equity. While such positive performance seems to be cyclical, with poorer outcomes in the mid-to-late 1990s, a number of firms enjoyed spectacular returns after the surge in bankruptcies in 2001-2002. Lee and Cunney (2004) found that investing in formerly bankrupt firms' equities between 1988 and 2003 (sample of 111 firms) resulted in a positive average 85 per cent relative to the performance of the S&P

Table IIIa

2008 Chapter 22s: size and duration
This table lists the actual firms that filed for bankruptcy protection a second time in 2008.

Company	Bankruptcy Date	Assets	Confirm Date	Time Between Confirmation and Second Filing	Public/ Private
Aloha Airlines Inc (2004)	12/30/04	$100,000,000	11/26/05	2 years, 4 months	Private
Aloha Airlines Inc (2008)	03/20/08	$215,850,000			Private
ATA Holdings Corp (2004)	10/26/04	$869,987,000	01/31/06	1 year, 1 month	Public
ATA Airlines Inc (2008)	04/02/08	$100,000,000			Private
Bally Total Fitness Holding (2007)	07/31/07	$396,771,000	09/17/07	1 year, 3 months	Public
Bally Total Fitness Holding (2008)	12/03/08	$1,376,000,000			Public
Dan River Inc (2004)	03/31/04	$466,479,000	01/18/05	3 years, 3 months	Public
Dan River Inc (2008)	04/20/08	$50,000,000			Private
DESA Holdings Corp (2005)	06/08/02	$132,500,000	04/01/05	3 years, 9 months	Public
DESA LLC (DHP Holdings II) (2008)	12/29/08	$233,896,000			Private
Friedman's Inc (2005)	01/14/05	$447,883,000	11/28/05	2 years, 2 months	Public
Friedman's Inc (2008)	01/28/08	$245,787,000			Private
Gemini Air Cargo (2006)	03/15/06	$59,363,216	07/21/06	2 years, 0 months	Private
Gemini Air Cargo (2008)	06/18/08	$100,000,000			Private
Indesso International (2000)	11/17/00	$165,846,000	01/11/02	6 years, 6 months	Public
Continental AFA Dispensing (2008)	08/07/08	$18,000,000			Private
Intermet Corp (2004)	09/29/04	$686,684,000	09/25/05	2 years, 11 months	Public
Intermet Corp (2008)	08/12/08	$50,000,000			Private
KB Toys Inc (2004)	01/14/04	$507,000,000	08/18/05	3 years, 4 months	Private
KB Toys Inc (2008)	12/11/08	$100,000,001			Private

Continued overleaf

500 Index in the first 12 months after emergence. The volatility of these returns was extremely high, however, with only 50 per cent of the stocks outperforming, although the excellence of many firms in the 2003-2005 period prompted one investment bank, Jefferies & Co, to create an index of post-bankruptcy equity performance, the Jefferies Re-Org Index (SM).

A few additional studies show fairly positive post-bankruptcy performance. Alderson and Betker (1999) examined a sample of 89 firms emerging between 1983 and 1993 and computed the five-year annualized return earned by the reorganized company, relative to the value that would have been received in liquidation and invested in alternative assets. Where the liquidation value was not available from the plan, the authors used the plan's estimated market value at emergence. They found that the reorganized firms' annualized returns were not significantly different from those on the S&P 500 Index.

From a sample of 288 firms that defaulted on public debt, most of whom went bankrupt, Hotchkiss and Mooradian (1997) found that while 32 per cent experienced negative operating performance in the year following emergence if there were no outside "vulture" investors directly involved with significant ownership, only about 12 per cent had the same negative experience when a "vulture" was actively involved in the restructuring.

Subsequent distressed restructurings

As noted earlier, roughly one-third of firms emerging as a publicly registered company go through some form of distressed restructuring again, including filing for a second (or third, or even more) bankruptcy. Table II shows the number of Chapter 22s and 33s from 1984 to 2009. Including 19 in 2008 (the highest single annual total in our sample) and 18 in 2009, there have been 215 Chapter 22s and ten Chapter 33s (see Table X for the list of Chapter 33s). In a sample of about 60 Chapter 22s, all the second filings took place within nine

Table IIIa (continued)

2008 Chapter 22s: size and duration

Company	Bankruptcy Date	Assets	Confirm Date	Time Between Confirmation and Second Filing	Public/ Private
Key Plastics LLC (2000)	03/23/00	$388,490,000	04/02/01	7 years, 8 months	Public
Key Plastics LLC (2008)	12/15/08	$100,000,001	01/29/09		Public
Leiner Health Products Inc (2002)	02/28/02	$353,137,000	04/15/02	5 years, 11 months	Public
Leiner Health Products Inc (2008)	03/10/08	$378,618,000	10/15/08		Public
Mattress Discounters Corp (2002)	10/23/02	$105,746,000	03/04/03	5 years, 6 months	Public
Mattress Discounters Corp (2008)	09/10/08	$16,922,316			Private
Penn Specialty Chemicals Inc (2001)	07/09/01	$83,260,620	07/19/02	6 years, 5 months	Private
Penn Specialty Chemicals Inc (2008)	12/17/08	$1,000,001			Private
Polar Molecular Corp (2008)	01/11/08	$400,001,500	05/19/08	6 years, 3 months	Private
Polar Molecular Corp (2008)	08/04/08	$1,500			Private
Polaroid Corp (2001)	10/12/01	$2,043,000,000	11/18/03	5 years, 1 month	Public
Polaroid Corp (2008)	12/18/08	$250,000,000			Private
Steakhouse Partners (2002)	02/15/02	$45,390,000	12/19/03	4 years, 5 months	Public
Steakhouse Partners (2008)	05/15/08	$17,750,000			Public
US Wireless Data Inc (2004)	03/26/04	$13,963,000	12/27/04	3 years, 3 months	Public
StarVox Communications Inc (2008)	03/26/08	$4,865,000			Public
Sun Country Airlines Inc (2002)	03/12/02	$ 55,200,000	12/19/03	4 years, 10 months	Private
Sun Country Airlines Inc (2008)	10/06/08	$9,923,642			Private

Average time between emergence and second filing: 4 years and 6 months

Source: New Generation Research, Boston, MA and NYU Salomon Center Bankruptcy Database

years of the firm emerging from its first Chapter 11 and a surprisingly large proportion (92 per cent) happened within five years.

For example, among the "class of 2008" Chapter 22s, 12 of the 19 filed within five years and 15 within six (Table IIIa). The average time between the first emergence and the second filing was four years and six months. In 2009, ten of the 18 filed again within five years and the average time between the first emergence and second filing was four years and five months (Table IIIb). Usually, but not always, the amount of assets in Chapter 22 firms is greater at the time of the first filing, since one of the strategies found in most bankruptcy reorganizations is the selling of assets to improve operations or to provide much-needed liquidity.

It is interesting to observe that Chapter 22 cases are still prominent now, even though the outright sale of a bankrupt firm during the reorganization period has become quite a common occurrence under the revised code of 2005. Time will tell if the Chapter 22 phenomenon will decrease somewhat as the older reorganizations are flushed from the system. What we are now observing, however, is that many of the larger Chapter 11 filings involve "prepackaged" agreements, which usually only attempt to "fix" the capital structure problems of the distressed company. Among these cases, more Chapter 22s might be expected.

Avoiding Chapter 22

To predict the performance of firms emerging from Chapter 11 bankruptcy reorganization, we utilize the Z-Score model, which was first developed for testing the credit scoring of emerging-market firms and then applied in the US, primarily for manufacturers but for other industrial groups, too.

The logic behind this methodology is that if a model has proved credible and is accepted by academics and practitioners as a way of predicting corporate distress, it might also be effective in assessing the future health of firms emerging from bankruptcy reorganization, especially if the result you are trying to predict (avoid) is a second filing.

Table IIIb

2009 Chapter 22s: size and duration
This table lists the actual firms that filed for bankruptcy protection a second or third time in 2009

Company	Bankruptcy Date	Assets	Confirm Date	Time Between Confirmation and Second Filing	Public/ Private
Bruno's Inc (1998)	02/02/98	$791,430,000	12/30/99	8 years, 2 months	Public
Bruno's Supermarkets LLC (2009)	02/05/09	$100,000,001	09/25/09		Private
Eagle Geophysical Inc (1999)	09/29/99	$273,200,000			Public
Eagle Geophysical Inc (2009)	05/31/09	$6.526.394	n/a	n/a	Public
Spiegel Inc (2003)	03/17/03	$1,889,580,000	05/25/05	4 years, 1 month	Public
Eddie Bauer Holdings Inc (2009)	06/17/09	$596,920,000			Public
eNucleus Inc (2001)	05/10/01	$2,505,930	11/06/03		Public
eNucleus Inc (2009)	07/25/09	$500		5 years, 8 months	Public
Filene's Basement Corp (1999)	08/23/99	$202,700,000	10/23/00		Public
Filene's Basement, Inc (2009)	05/04/09	$79,967,643	01/26/10	8 years, 7 months	Private
FIRSTPLUS Financial Grp Inc (1999)	03/05/99	$2,447,206,000	04/07/00		Public
FIRSTPLUS Financial Grp Inc (2009)	06/23/09	$19,620,935		9 years, 2 months	Public
Foamex International Inc (2005)	09/19/05	$645,710,000	02/01/07		Public
Foamex International Inc (2009)	02/18/09	$430,550,000		2 years, 0 months	Public
Fortunoff Fine Jewelry & Silverware, LLC (2008)	02/04/08	$267,624,000			Private
Fortunoff Holdings LLC (2009)	02/05/09	$154,698,000	n/a	n/a	Private
Goody's Family Clothing Inc (2008)	06/09/08	$313,000,000	10/07/08		Private
Goody's LLC (2009)	01/13/09	$206,000,000		0 years, 3 months	Private
Hayes Lemmerz Int'l Inc (2001)	12/05/01	$2,811,100,000	05/12/03		Public
Hayes Lemmerz Int'l Inc (2009)	05/11/09	$1,096,200,000	11/03/09	6 years, 0 months	Public

Continued overleaf

Firms need to be public entities since one of the variables, the market value of equity/total liabilities (X4 in Table IV), requires the availability of publicly traded equity. In order to make the model more robust across all industrial groupings, as well as for privately owned companies, the Z-Score model was adapted (see Table V): note that it now has four variables, not five as in the original model; the Sales/Total Tangible Assets variable is removed and the coefficients re-estimated.

To give the model more meaning, the idea of a bond-rating-equivalent (BRE) of the Z-Score has been developed. Table VI shows the Z-Score model and its BREs based on data from 1996, chosen as an appropriate year for our subsequent empirical tests. The equation used in the calculations was modified by adding a constant term of 3.25 so as to scale the scores to a "D" rating equal to zero (0.0). Firms with Z-Scores above zero have BREs in the non-bankrupt zones (AAA to CCC-).

We will now explore the results of applying the Z-Score model to two samples of firms that emerged from bankruptcy. One sample consists of

Table IV

Z-Score component definitions and weightings
This table shows the original Z-Score model's variables and co-efficients

Variable	Definition	Weighting factor
X_1	Working capital / Total Assets	1.2
X_2	Retained earnings / Total Assets	1.4
X_3	EBIT / Total Assets	3.3
X_4	Market value of equity / Book value of total liabilities	0.6
X_5	Sales / Total assets	1.0

Source: Altman & Hotchkiss (2006) and Altman (1968)

Chapter 22s or 33s, the other represents those companies that emerged from Chapter 11 and did not file a second time.

Since both categories comprise companies that have undergone an extensive restructuring, usually

Table IIIb (continued)

2009 Chapter 22s: size and duration

Company	Bankruptcy Date	Assets	Confirm Date	Time Between Confirmation and Second Filing	Public/ Private
Holley Performance Inc (2008)	02/11/08	$111,997,000	03/19/08		Public
Holley Performance Inc (2009)	09/28/09	$46,426,943		1 year, 6 months	Public
JL French Automotive Inc (2006)	02/10/06	$366,681,000	06/21/06		Public
JL French Automotive Inc (2009)	07/13/09	$100,000,000	09/03/09	3 years, 1 month	Private
Meridian Automotive Inc (2005)	04/26/05	$530,000,000	12/06/06		Private
Meridian Automotive Inc (2009)	08/07/09	$25,593,104		2 years, 8 months	Private
Penn Traffic Company (1999)	03/01/99	$1,563,590,000	05/27/99		Public
Penn Traffic Company (2003)	05/30/03	$806,370,000	03/17/05		Public
Penn Traffic Company (2009)	11/18/09	$193,714,000		4 years, 8 months	Public
Pliant Corp (2006)	01/03/06	$777,092,000	06/23/06		Public
Pliant Corp (2009)	02/11/09	$675,979,000	10/06/09	2 years, 8 months	Public
Silicon Graphics Inc (2006)	05/08/06	$452,145,000	09/19/06		Public
Silicon Graphics Inc (2009)	04/01/09	$415,195,000	11/10/09	2 years, 7 months	Public
Trump Hotels and Casino Resorts Inc (2004)	11/21/04	$2,031,433,000	04/04/05	3 years, 10 months	Public
Trump Entertainment Resorts Inc. (2009)	02/17/09	$2,231,211,000			Public
Ultra Stores Inc (2002)	03/07/01	$76,060,000	12/03/01		Private
Ultra Stores Inc (2009)	04/09/09	$63,850,350	07/28/09	7 years, 4 months	Private

Average time between emergence and second filing: 4 years and 5 months

Source: New Generation Research, Boston, MA and NYU Salomon Center Bankruptcy Database

Table V

Z"-Score model for manufacturers, non-manufacturer industrials and emerging market credits
This table shows a modification to the original Z-Score model. It is known as the Z"-Score mode.

Z"	$= 6.56X1 + 3.26X2 + 6.72X3 + 1.05X4$
X1	= $\underline{\text{Current assets – current liabilities}}$ Total assets
X2	= $\underline{\text{Retained earnings}}$ Total assets
X3	= $\underline{\text{Earnings before interest and taxes}}$ Total Assets
X4	= $\underline{\text{Book value of equity}}$ Total liabilities

Source: Altman and Hotchkiss (2006)

Table VI

US bond rating equivalents based on Z"-Score model (*Sample size in parentheses*)
This table shows the standardized Z"-Score model and the bond rating equivalents for the resulting scores
$Z" = 3.25 + 6.56X1 + 3.26X2 + 6.72X3 + 1.05X4$

Rating	Average 1996 Z"-Score
AAA/AA+	8.15 (8)
AA/AA-	7.16 (33)
A+	6.85 (24)
A	6.65 (42)
A-	6.40 (38)
BBB+	6.25 (38)
BBB	5.85 (59)
BBB-	5.65 (52)
BB+	5.25 (34)
BB	4.95 (25)
BB-	4.75 (65)
B+	4.50 (78)
B	4.15 (115)
B-	3.75 (95)
CCC+	3.20 (23)
CCC	2.50 (10)
CCC-	1.75 (6)
CC/D	0.00(14)

Source: Compustat, Company Filings and S&P

of both their operations and their capital structures, one might expect that their financial profiles upon emergence would resemble a going-concern, non-bankrupt entity. If, however, the model is effective in detecting future problems, we should find the

Table VIIa

Z"-Scores for Chapter 11s

This table lists a sample of firms and their Z"-Scores that emerged from bankruptcy and did not file for bankruptcy protection a second time

Chapter 11 Company name	Effective date	Z"-Score after emergence	Bond rating equivalent	Z"-Score 1-year post	Bond rating equivalent
1 Boonton Electronics	11/18/94	7.67	AAA/AA+	7.63	AA
2 CAI Wireless Systems Inc	10/14/98	2.12	CCC-	n/a	n/a
3 Cherokee Corp	06/01/93	4.00	B	2.09	CCC-
4 Consolidated Hydro Inc	11/07/97	3.90	B-	4.81	BB-
5 El Paso Electronic	02/12/96	4.36	B+	4.75	BB-
6 Elsinore Corporation	02/28/97	3.65	B-	4.18	B
7 Emcor	10/03/94	4.03	B	4.38	B+
8 Emerson Radio	08/09/94	5.42	BB+	4.08	B
9 Fansteel Inc	12/22/03	0.72	D	2.67	CCC
10 Flagstar Companies Inc	01/07/98	2.90	CCC+	(0.44)	D
11 Gantos	03/07/95	6.58	A	6.17	BBB+
12 Gentek Inc	10/07/03	4.51	B+	2.19	CCC
13 Grant Geophysical	09/30/97	4.49	B+	4.14	B
14 Harnischfeger Industries Inc	07/13/01	5.70	BBB-	5.30	BB+
15 Hayes Lemmerz International	05/12/03	4.38	B+	0.18	CC/D
16 Heartland Wireless Inc	04/05/99	6.11	BBB+	5.01	BB
17 Hexcel Corporation	01/12/95	4.83	BB-	4.45	B+
18 Hvide Marine Inc	12/15/99	3.69	B-	3.64	B-
19 Imperial Sugar Co TX	08/29/01	3.98	B	5.00	BB
20 Kaiser Group International Inc	12/18/00	6.94	A+	4.23	B
21 Kash N' Karry	12/12/94	4.20	B	4.60	B+
22 Kitty Hawk Inc	09/30/02	6.19	BBB+	7.39	AA
23 Krystal Company	04/22/97	3.46	CCC+	9.41	AAA
24 Laidlaw Inc	02/28/03	4.40	B+	5.55	BBB-
25 Loehmann's Holdings Inc DE	10/31/00	5.48	BBB-	6.24	BBB+
26 Loewen Group Int'l Inc	01/02/02	3.09	CCC+	3.62	B-
27 Lone Star Industries	03/01/94	5.16	BB+	6.19	BBB+
28 Magellan Health Services Inc	10/08/03	4.96	BB	7.89	AAA/AA+
29 NRG Energy	11/24/03	3.75	B-	1.22	CCC-
30 Paragon Trade Brands Inc	01/28/00	5.72	BBB-	n/a	n/a
31 Pathmark Stores Inc	09/18/00	4.12	B	2.47	CCC
32 Peregrine Systems Inc	07/18/03	4.28	B	3.47	CCC+
33 Petroleum Geo Services ASA	10/21/03	4.32	B	5.48	BBB-
34 Phone Tel	11/18/99	3.54	B-	4.30	B
35 Polymre Group Inc	01/03/03	2.35	CCC	2.09	CCC-
36 Redback Networks Inc	12/22/03	6.56	A	6.19	BBB+
37 Safety Components Int'l	10/11/00	6.13	BBB+	5.13	BB+
38 Southern Mineral Corp	08/01/00	5.38	BB+	n/a	n/a
39 Stage Stores Inc NV	08/24/01	9.98	AAA	11.78	AAA
40 Sterling Chemicals Inc	12/19/02	4.98	BB	3.58	B-
41 Stratosphere Corporation	10/04/98	8.16	AAA	8.56	AAA
42 Telemundo	07/20/94	5.00	BB	4.98	BB
43 Teletrac Inc	09/15/99	3.82	B-	2.54	CCC
44 Vista Eyecare Inc	05/31/01	3.41	CCC+	3.34	CCC+
45 Warnaco Group Inc	01/16/03	4.27	B	4.62	B+
Number of Bankruptcies		45		42	
Average Z Score		4.73	B+	4.65	B+
Median Z Score		4.38		4.53	
Standard Deviation		1.63		2.55	

Source: Author's compilation from Capital IQ data.

average Z-Score values of the Chapter 22 group will be significantly worse than among the Chapter 11s.

In our samples, the effective confirmation dates of the bankruptcy reorganization plans for the 45 Chapter 11s was between 1993 and 2003 (Table VIIa). These companies were chosen mainly according to data availability for calculating the Z-Score distress-prediction. Our objective was to assemble a reasonably large representative sample of industrial firms that had filed for bankruptcy and emerged as publicly held firms with post-bankruptcy financial data available during roughly

Table VIIb

Z"-Scores for Chapter 22s

This table lists a sample of firms that filed for bankruptcy protection at least two times, and their Z"-Scores just after emergence and a year later

Chapter 22 Company name	Effective date	Z"-Score after emergence	Bond rating equivalent	Z"-Score 1-year post	Bond rating equivalent	Re-filing date	Period between emergence and second filing: years, months, days
1 American Banknote	11/21/00	0.34	D	0.35	D	04/08/05	4, 4, 18
2 Ames Dept Stores	12/18/92	4.74	BB-	6.31	BBB+	08/20/01	8, 8, 2
3 Anacomp	06/04/96	3.72	B-	2.93	CCC+	10/19/01	5, 4, 15
4 Anchor Glass	11/25/97	3.62	B-	3.73	B	04/15/02	4, 4, 21
5 Anchor Glass	08/09/02	3.61	B-	4.05	B	08/08/05	2, 11, 30
6 ATA Holdings	01/31/06	3.18	CCC+	3.40	CCC+	04/02/08	2, 2, 2
7 Brendle's	12/20/93	6.65	A	6.60	A	04/16/96	2, 3, 27
8 Coho Energy	03/21/00	1.71	CCC-	(3.27)	D	02/24/03	2, 11, 3
9 Eagle Food Centers	07/10/00	2.49	CCC	3.45	CCC+	03/25/04	3, 8, 15
10 Edison Brothers	09/26/97	4.19	B	2.85	CCC	03/09/99	1, 5, 11
11 Galey & Lord	02/10/04	(0.66)	D	0.28	D	03/05/04	0, 0, 24
12 Grand Union Co	05/31/95	2.81	CCC	1.90	CCC-	06/24/98	3, 0, 24
13 Grand Union Co	08/05/98	3.41	CCC+	0.76	D	10/03/00	2, 1, 28
14 Harvard Industries	08/10/92	2.38	CCC	1.10	CCC-	05/08/97	4, 8, 28
15 Harvard Industries	10/15/98	1.21	CCC-	0.80	D	01/16/02	3, 3, 1
16 Heartland Wireless	03/15/99	3.87	B-	5.25	BB+	09/05/03	4, 5, 21
17 Homeland Holding	07/16/96	4.73	BB-	4.18	B	08/01/01	5, 0, 16
18 Ithaca Industries	12/16/96	7.21	AA/AA-	6.86	A+	05/09/00	3, 4, 23
19 Lamonts Apparels	12/18/97	2.83	CCC	2.16	CCC	01/04/00	2, 0, 17
20 McleodUSA	04/18/02	(2.77)	D	3.42	CCC+	12/16/05	3, 7, 28
21 Memorex Telex	02/07/92	(0.49)	D	1.37	CCC-	02/11/94	2, 0, 4
22 Memorex Telex	03/14/94	0.62	D	(1.30)	D	10/15/96	2, 7, 1
23 Payless Cashways	12/02/97	5.19	BB+	5.64	BBB-	06/04/01	3, 6, 2
24 Penn Traffic Co	05/27/99	4.39	B+	3.73	B-	03/17/05	5, 9, 18
25 Pillowtex	05/02/02	2.78	CCC	n/a	n/a	07/30/03	1, 2, 28
26 Planet Hollywood	01/21/00	(8.24)	D	(6.77)	D	10/19/01	1, 8, 28,
27 Rymer Foods	04/07/93	4.44	B+	4.14	B	07/08/97	4, 3, 1
28 Salant	07/30/93	6.52	A-	5.80	BBB	12/29/98	5, 4, 29
29 Smith Corona	02/28/97	5.36	BB+	3.92	B-	05/23/00	3, 2, 25
30 Solo Serve	07/06/95	2.98	CCC+	1.50	CCC-	01/20/99	3, 6, 14
31 Steakhouse Ptnrs	12/19/03	1.41	CCC-	1.19	CCC-	05/15/08	4, 4, 26
32 Todays Man	12/12/97	7.24	AA-	9.12	AAA	05/06/04	6, 4, 24
33 Tokheim	10/09/00	3.90	B-	(0.57)	D	11/21/02	2, 1, 12
34 Trans World Air	08/11/93	(1.33)	D	1.98	CCC-	06/30/95	1, 10, 19
35 Trans World Air	08/04/95	3.05	CCC+	2.09	CCC-	01/10/01	5, 5, 6
36 Trism	12/09/99	(2.06)	D	(1.02)	D	12/18/01	2, 0, 9
37 United Merchants	08/16/91	(1.51)	D	0.63	D	02/22/96	4, 6, 6
38 US Airways Group	03/18/03	2.63	CCC	1 84	CCC-	09/16/05	2, 5, 29
39 USG	04/23/93	3.48	CCC+	3.82	B-	06/25/01	8, 2, 2
40 Westmoreland Coal	12/22/94	2.18	CCC	(4.36)	D	12/23/96	2, 0, 1
41 Wherehouse	12/16/96	7.59	AA/AA-	7.95	AA+	01/20/03	6, 1, 4
Number of bankruptcies		**41**		**40**		**Average**	**3,4,16**
Average Z-Score		**2.67**	**CCC**	**2.45**	**CCC**		
Median Z-Score		**3.05**		**2.51**			
Standard deviation		**3.06**		**3.18**			

Source: Author's comilation from Capital IQ data

the same data period as our Chapter 22 sample. Our data source is New Generation Research.

For the 41 Chapter 22 firms in Table VIIb, the effective date of emergence from their first bankruptcy ranged between 1993 and 2006 (only two were after 2003). Five were Chapter 33s, so they appear twice in the sample. The average time between emergence and the second filing was three years, four and a half months, and the range was from one year and ten months (TWA) to eight years and eight months (Ames Department Stores). While the number of Chapter 22s sampled is about

Table VIII

Difference in means test between Chapter 22 and Chapter 11 results
The table shows the difference of Z"-Score means test between Chapter 11 firms that did not file for bankruptcy a second time, and those that did file at least twice (Chapter 22s)

	Z"-Score after emergence	Z"-Score One-year post emergence
Chapter 11 Mean (Chapter 11 Standard Deviation)	4.73 (1.63)	4.65 (2.55)
Chapter 22 Mean (Chapter 22 Standard Deviation)	2.67 (3.05)	2.45 (3.18)
t-test(*)	3.84(**)	3.60(**)

*Significant at .01 level, **significant at .10 level.
Source: Author's calculations from firms listed in Tables VIIa and VIIb, Capital IQ

30 per cent of the total Chapter 22s since 1993, they represent a cross-section of industrial companies.

Post-bankruptcy distress-prediction results
We can see from Table VIIa that the average Z-Score for our sample of single-filers, based on data from their first financial statement following their emergence from Chapter 11, was 4.73, with a bond rating equivalent of B+ (see Table VI). The B+ BRE is consistent with our observations over time that almost all firms emerging with bonds outstanding have a bond rating usually in the single-B to double-B range, rarely higher. For our Chapter 22 sample, the average Z-Score was much worse at 2.67, with a BRE of CCC (Table VIIb). The

differential between the Chapter 11s and 22s stayed similar when the data took in an additional one year beyond the date of emergence (4.65 vs 2.45). Indeed, the Chapter 22s average scores dipped by 0.08 one year after the first financial period, consistent with deteriorating conditions as the firm moved towards its second filing.

For the sample of Chapter 22s, nine of the 41 firms actually had a financial profile (BRE) near the date of emergence consistent with a "D" (default) rating, and only 16 had a BRE better than CCC. Most of these firms showed early-warning signs of distress. In the Chapter 11 sample, only one firm (Fansteel) had a Z-Score consistent with a "D".

Significance test
To examine the statistical significance of our average results for the two samples, we performed a "difference of means" test, indicated in Table VIII. The t-test (statistical hypothesis) between a mean of 4.73 (Chapter 11s) and 2.67 (Chapter 22s) was significantly different at the .01 level (t-test = 3.84) both at the point nearest the emergence date and also one year later (t=3.60). So, it is clear that those firms that eventually filed again had a much worse financial profile just after emerging from bankruptcy than did those firms that remained going concerns for at least five years.

Why can't firms restructure successfully?
It now remains to observe whether there were specific warning signs, in addition to the composite Z-score, on the impending fate of these two groups of enterprises. To accomplish this, we analyze the four individual indicators that comprise the model: corporate liquidity, solvency, profitability and leverage. The results are quite revealing.

Table IX

Difference in means and tests of specific performance and risk levels: Chapter 22 firms vs Chapter 11s
This table shows the mean values for the four variables in the Z"-Score model and the difference in means tests between Chapter 11 and Chapter 22 firms

Variable	Chapter 11 sample	Standard error	Chapter 22 sample	Standard error	Difference in means test (t-test)	P-value
X1 = Working Capital/TA	0.15	0.16	0.09	0.28	1.24	0.22
X2= Retained Earnings/TA	(0.09)	0.22	(0.22)	0.39	1.88**	0.06**
X3= EBIT/TA	0.01	0.07	(0.07)	0.19	2.49*	0.02*
X4= Book Equity/Total Liabilities	0.74	1.08	0.27	0.39	2.71*	0.01*

*Significant at .01 level, **significant at .10 level.
Source: Author's calculations from firms listed in Tables VII(a) and VII(b), Capital IQ

Table X: Chapter 33s

Chapter 33 is the unofficial name given to companies that have filed for Chapter 11 reorganization for a third time. Below is a historical listing of companies in this category

Company	Bankruptcy Date	Confirm Date	Assets ($ millions)
Anchor Glass Container Corp (2005)	08/08/05	04/18/06	657
Anchor Glass Container Corp (2002)	04/15/02	08/09/02	536
Anchor Glass Container Corp (1996)	09/13/96	11/25/97	1,208
Grand Union Co (2000)	10/03/00	10/08/02	1,089
Grand Union Co (1998)	06/24/98	08/05/02	1,061
Grand Union Co (1995)	01/25/95	05/31/95	1,394
Harvard Industries Inc (2002)	01/16/02	02/26/04	277
Harvard Industries Inc (1997)	05/08/97	10/15/98	618
Harvard Industries Inc (1991)	04/11/91	08/10/92	533
Levitz Home Furnishings Inc (2005)	11/08/07	unknown	178
Levitz Home Furnishings Inc (1997)	10/11/05	12/15/05	245
PLVTZ Inc (Levitz Furniture) (2007)	09/05/97	pending	934
Memorex Telex Corp (1996)	10/15/96	10/09/98	268
Memorex Telex NV (1994)	02/11/94	03/14/94	1,139
Memorex Telex NV (1992)	01/06/92	02/07/92	1,643
Salant Corp (1998)	12/29/98	04/16/99	233
Salant Corp (1990)	06/27/90	07/30/93	333
Salant Corpn (1985)	02/22/85	05/19/97	95
Samuels Jewelers Inc (2003)	08/04/03	03/30/04	48
Barry's Jewelers, Inc. (1997)	05/11/97	12/22/98	146
Barry's Jewelers Inc (1992)	02/26/92	06/19/92	158
The Penn Traffic Co (1999)	03/01/99	05/27/99	1,563
The Penn Traffic Co (2003)	05/30/03	03/17/05	606
The Penn Traffic Co (2009)	11/18/09	unknown	184
Trans World Airlines (2001)	01/10/01	06/18/02	2,137
Trans World Airlines (1995)	06/30/95	08/04/95	2,495
Trans World Airlines (1992)	01/31/92	08/11/93	2,864
United Mechanics & Manufacturers (1996)	02/22/96	04/19/97	27
United Mechanics & Manufacturers (1990)	11/02/90	08/16/91	224
United Mechanics & Manufacturers (1977)	07/01/77	unknown	unknown

Source: The 2008 Bankruptcy Yearbook & Almanac, New Generation Research, Boston, MA 2009

We conclude from the values shown in Table IX that the Chapter 22 sample was inferior in all four dimensions and that, in particular, measures of profitability and leverage were significantly different between the two groups. While we could argue that a reorganization plan might eventually lead to an improvement in profitability, there does not appear to be any excuse for being over-leveraged. Indeed, the equity/total liability ratio of Chapter 22 firms was only 0.27, vs 0.74 for the Chapter 11 firms.

To put it differently, the leverage of firms that failed again was almost three times greater than for those that emerged and remained solvent. The Chapter 22 sample had almost four times as much liability as equity ($3.70 of debt to every dollar of equity), while the Chapter 11 firms had about $1.35

of debt to every dollar of equity. The prescription for successful reorganizations is clear: emerging firms must not overload the balance sheet with debt.

Table IX also shows that the average working capital to total assets of Chapter 22 firms was 0.09, against 0.15 for Chapter 11 firms. The retained earnings to total assets for Chapter 22s was a negative 0.22, vs a negative 0.09 for 11s, and the EBIT/TA for the Chapter 22s was a negative 0.07, against a positive 0.01.

Implications and conclusions

Using the Z-Score model, we have found that those firms filing a subsequent bankruptcy petition had a significantly worse financial profile than those emerging as going concerns and continuing on down that path. Indeed, the average financial profiles and bond ratings of firms in the Chapter 22 sample, on emerging from their first bankruptcy, were not that much better than those of companies in default.

We believe that a credible distress-prediction model can be an important indicator of the future success of firms emerging from bankruptcy, and could even be used as an independent technique by a court in assessing the viability of a reorganization plan. It could also be used by those responsible for devising the plan, especially if in identifying signs of continuing distress, they can make further modifications. Another potential benefit may be felt by creditors of the "old" company, in the sense they can assess the value of the new package of securities, including equity, offered in the plan. Finally, professional turnaround specialists can use this early-warning technique to assess the likelihood of their efforts succeeding.

This article is an updated version of the original published in the Journal of Applied Corporate Finance (Volume 21, Number 3, Summer 2009), a Morgan Stanley publication.

8

Planning effective restructurings through the looking glass of 50 years of bankruptcy and reorganization

Harvey R Miller,

Senior Partner,

Weil, Gotshal & Manges LLP

What, after all, is bankruptcy? It is a substantive and procedural process, intended to resolve claims to the assets of a debtor that is unable to satisfy its obligations and that may be insufficient to satisfy all legitimate claims. From that basic premise, bankruptcy has expanded in scope and size to include a variety of third parties with different objectives propelled by the hope of financial gains. It is an ever-changing process fueled by economic cycles, tempered by political objectives and, sometimes, the actual intervention of government to protect national interests. It fluctuates through stages of protection of debtors to the enforcement of creditors' rights, often depending on how one construes the "plain meaning" rule. In a retroactive overview of 50 years, there are cycles favoring debtors, other times creditors, and sometimes encouraging purchasers and, finally, furthering governmental objectives.

I start with the 1960s as the beginning of modern bankruptcy practice. It was the Age of Aquarius and individual and sexual freedom, but bankruptcy was not a part of the public consciousness or considered as one of the legal and strategic options for distressed debtor enterprises. The results of the railroad reorganizations of the last part of the 19th century that had leached into the 20th century, and the fallout of the Great Depression of the 1930s, had largely dissipated. It was a much simpler world. Most businesses were privately owned. They operated on the foundation of long-term relationships, customer and vendor loyalty, and prudence. In most situations, you could actually determine the value of a business by reviewing its financial statements. Wall Street was laboring under post-Depression protective legislation such as the Securities Act of 1933 and its related statutes. The SEC and various national securities exchanges actively regulated the financial markets. There were no highly esoteric, incomprehensible securities being created, packaged and sold. There were restrictions on financial engineering intended to hide liabilities as off-balance sheet items. Auditors actually audited companies and economists were contained within their academic precincts. The inventions of the PC, BlackBerries and iPhones were a long way off.

Bankruptcy was considered a sub-stratum of commercial law — a small, arcane, undesirable practice area inhabited, allegedly, by somewhat shady groups accused of feeding off the carcasses of failures. Most elite law schools did not offer a bankruptcy course. Major law and accounting firms shunned the bankruptcy arena. Individuals and businesses, public and private, strived to avoid the stigma of bankruptcy. Federal courts were considered too formalistic to assist in business cases. Debtor/creditor issues were resolved through the medium of common law compositions or in state courts through receiverships and assignments for the benefit of creditors.

Notwithstanding the enactment of the 1938 Chandler Act amending the Bankruptcy Act of 1898, federal bankruptcy proceedings, generally, were limited to liquidations to provide access to the avoidance powers of the Bankruptcy Act.

Strange days

Bankruptcy professionals represented a small and parochial group of attorneys and accountants. Active trade creditor associations functioned as forums to facilitate expeditious and efficient solutions for private business failures. There were no turnaround experts, distressed debt traders, hedge funds, restructuring officers, specialized bankruptcy financial advisors or the like. Defaulting debtors were considered outcasts. Contractual rights of secured creditors reigned supreme. The bankruptcy court was a strange place. There were no judges. Rather, bankruptcy cases were filed in the United States District Court and referred to and administered by referees in bankruptcy, who were appointed by the district court for five-year terms and served as support personnel. They exercised such authority as was referred to them by the district court. Referees did not have law clerks and very little in the way of facilities. There were no national bankruptcy law reports.

The courts relied on two treatises: *Remington on Bankruptcy* and *Collier on Bankruptcy*. Eventually, *Remington* faded and *Collier* became the leading treatise under the editorial leadership of Professor Lawrence P King of the NYU Law School. King was very clever: he edited *Collier* so that it could be cited for any proposition. *Collier* became the *Pepper v Litton* of legal publications. There was no centralized bankruptcy court filing system or a general docket in a district in which there was more than one referee in bankruptcy. In some districts there were part-time referees who presided over bankruptcy cases two or three days a week and otherwise privately practiced law.

The go-go years begin

In addition, bankruptcy, despite its stigma, was considered something akin to public service. Embedded in bankruptcy proceedings was the spirit of economy mandating that bankruptcy professionals be compensated at rates less than those prevailing in the private sector. Consequently, it was not considered to be a very desirable practice area. It was very localized. New York bankruptcy professionals were not welcome in New Jersey or Connecticut, and Manhattan bankruptcy professionals crossed the East River to Brooklyn with great trepidation, as Brooklyn bankruptcy professionals likewise did when crossing to Manhattan.

However, as the 1960s progressed, something was happening in the United States. Economic change was in the air. Wall Street was shaking off the shackles of the Depression and World War II-related restraints. The go-go years were beginning. "Going public", as presented by Wall Street dealers, caught the imagination of businessmen. It provided capital for growing businesses to expand. To accommodate the expanding economy, financial markets began to grow. Volumes on the NYSE at last exceeded 5 million shares a day. Access to credit became more liberal and the use of leverage became seductive. Businesses and the economy became more credit-intensive and, naturally, because financial discipline did not grow at the same pace, this led to over-leveraging and failures. This is an integral element of capitalism, otherwise known as creative destruction. That danger and its reality spurred the thinking that there had to be ways to constructively deal with failure.

The genesis of Chapter 11

Some professionals began to investigate the options and possibilities of alleviating the consequences of failure, as well as the rights and protections to which debtors might be entitled. The Chandler Act had codified debtor relief provisions as Chapter 10 and 11. Chapter 10 provided a very detailed, comprehensive scheme for corporate reorganization, primarily directed at public corporations. It mandated appointment of one or more trustees and strict imposition of the "Absolute Priority Rule". Chapter 10 proceedings were to be presided over by a United States district judge with the heavy involvement of the SEC as a party. It was not attractive to distressed debtors and its use was discouraged. In contrast, Chapter 11, as enacted, was limited to voluntary cases and initially to small businesses that needed to make arrangements with their unsecured creditors to relieve oppressive debts.

However, by the 1960s, Chapter 11 no longer required application of the absolute priority rule and did not mandate appointment of a trustee. Rather, it provided that a debtor could continue to operate and manage its business and assets as a "debtor in possession". Although the recognition of the debtor in possession concept was not uniform throughout the United States, it became the norm for Chapter 11 cases filed in the Southern District of New York. In addition, and very importantly, a Chapter 11 debtor had the exclusive right to file a plan of arrangement for so long as the Chapter 11 case was pending. This represented a tactical weapon of significant potential, as the alternative to a plan of arrangement would be liquidation and the loss of the going concern value of the business and its assets to the detriment of the creditors.

These features — plus a growing appreciation by professionals that bankruptcy courts in Chapter 11 cases might liberally construe the bankruptcy law beyond its original intent to (a) enjoin secured creditors from exercising remedial rights for extended periods of time; (b) enjoin all unsecured creditors and others from taking any actions against the debtor and its property (both of which led to the automatic stay); (c) construe rejection and assumption of executory contracts, including collective bargaining agreements and unexpired leases to favor debtors in possession or trustees; and (d) allow dilution of equity interests as part of a Chapter 11 plan — were very attractive.

Gathering momentum

The threat of SEC action to force conversion of Chapter 11 cases to cases under Chapter 10 became less of a problem as the Supreme Court beat back the SEC in a series of decisions that tipped the scale decidedly in favor of Chapter 11. In 1960, there were 715 reorganization and arrangement cases filed in the United States. In 1970, there were 1,422 such cases filed. In 1975, the first billion-dollar Chapter 11 case was commenced by the WT Grant Company. WT Grant was an NYSE-listed corporation that had once been considered the Tiffany of retailing. Its liabilities included $640 million to a syndicate of banks. The big time had arrived for debtors! After the enactment of the 1978 Bankruptcy Reform Act, in 1980 and 1990, respectively, there were 6,348 and 20,783 reorganization cases filed in the United States.

The 1980s through 2000 — the age of the debtors

The enactment of the Bankruptcy Code essentially fused former Chapters 10 and 11 into the Code's business reorganization chapter. Under that chapter, which allowed relaxation of the Absolute Priority Rule, a plan of reorganization could affect all creditors, secured and unsecured, as well as equity interest holders. The Bankruptcy Code was intended to provide a level playing field for debtors and creditors by balancing the needs of the economic stakeholders in the interests of the rehabilitation and reorganization of a distressed business. Its enactment was actively and unanimously supported by all major constituencies, including the financial community, unsecured creditor associations, stockholders' organizations and the bankruptcy judiciary. It

evidenced the mutually agreed principle that the reorganization paradigm was better than liquidation because it preserved going concern value, protected industries and jobs and, generally, projected greater recoveries for impaired creditors.

Chapter 11 reorganizations had entered the mainstream of commercial life in the United States. Over-leveraging, excessive real property financings and other investments, the loss of competitor status as the global economy began to take hold, as well as fraud and other causes, resulted in a sharp increase in the volume and size of the assets and liabilities of cases filed under Chapter 11 — and, not to be forgotten, the expanded demand for professionals and the increase in potential fees.

The leveraged buyout mania of the 1980s led to Chapter 11 cases filed by Federated Department Stores, RH Macy & Co, Trans World Airlines, Southland Corp, Global Marine, National Gypsum Corp and, in part, Drexel Burnham and Olympia & York, among others. Massive toxic tort litigation precipitated Chapter 11 cases by the Johns Manville enterprise, AH Robins, and a host of major American businesses that were tainted by some connection to asbestos, some of which continue to this very day. Pension and labor issues, and, sometimes, environmental issues, caused the demise of LTV, Bethlehem Steel Corporation, Allis-Chalmers and numerous rust-belt entities, as well as a host of airlines including Braniff, Continental, Pan American, Eastern, United, Delta, Northwest and US Air, as well as a large number of smaller airlines. Some of the airline cases went on to become classic Chapter 22s and, in the case of TWA, a final Chapter 33. In 1987, a massive state court judgment ($11-plus billion) caused Texaco Inc to commence the then largest Chapter 11 case in history.

It was the zenith of the age of the debtor. The consensus was that Chapter 11 actually worked, despite the wailing cries and criticism coming from certain academics. The size and scope of cases filed under Chapter 11 continued to increase. As the 20th century drew to a close, the financial and credit markets continued to expand. The lessons of the past were ignored, or, perhaps more appropriately, it became evident that there is no institutional memory.

A new century begins

The 21st century began with a series of major cases precipitated by claims of fraud and other misdeeds, including Enron, Global Crossing and WorldCom and the dot-com fiasco. The first decade of the 21st century ended with even larger, more complex, difficult and novel cases initiated under Chapter 11, including Lehman Brothers ($600 billion), LyondellBasell (chemical companies) and General Growth Properties (shopping center REIT), among others, as the world slipped into a deep economic morass. A morass that caused the federal government to become a major player in the bankruptcy arena, as it endorsed and financed the use of Chapter 11 to resolve the distress of General Motors, Chrysler and Delphi Corp, and injected billions of dollars into various entities to stave off bankruptcy.

But something was occurring during the 1980s and 1990s and into the 21st century that would dramatically change bankruptcy reorganization. Prior to the mid 1990s, the bankruptcy law was amended, perhaps, once or twice in a decade. It took over five years to pass the Bankruptcy Reform Act of 1978. However, for the past 15 or more years, there has rarely been a session of Congress in which there has not been some attempt, in some way, shape or form, to amend the bankruptcy law. Each amendment made to the Bankruptcy Code starting in 1984 and through 2005 has tilted the proverbial level playing field against the debtor, as special interest legislation was enacted. Each clawback amendment, and particularly the 2005 amendments under the absurd title of the Bankruptcy Abuse Prevention and Consumer Protection Act (BAPCPA), has clawed back debtor protections both for individuals and businesses, and reduced the efficacy of the Bankruptcy Code as a vehicle to rehabilitate businesses, preserve jobs, serve the public good and provide a fresh start to debtors.

Defining events

In that context, what are the major defining events of the past 50 years? There are at least six, other than the work of the National Bankruptcy Commission of 1970 and the enactment of the Bankruptcy Reform Act of 1978, that have been seminal in the evolution of bankruptcy laws and practice:

- **The enhancement and elevation of the bankruptcy court** as a part of the 1978 Reform Act, and the appointment of the best and the brightest to the bankruptcy bench. Judges of high intellectual powers, discretion, independence, dedication and objectivity. Judges willing to be bold in the discharge of their duties, despite being woefully under-compensated.
- **The trading of claims**. Debt became a salable commodity long before the enactment of the Bankruptcy Reform Act. But it was also to be the crucible for a radical change in business bankruptcies. In the 1980s, distressed debt traders began to emerge from the caves of Wall Street. They began to disrupt the basic fabric of bankruptcy reorganizations that were premised upon longstanding relationships between the debtor and its creditors. The year 1991 was a watershed year for business bankruptcies. The amendment of Bankruptcy Rule 3001 to facilitate the free trading of claims marked the end of the debtor/creditor relationships that facilitated reorganization cases. Distressed debt traders and funds, sometimes referred to as "vulture funds", were motivated by different objectives. They sought to buy low, sell high and, in many cases, did not have any real concern as to whether the debtor would be reorganized or rehabilitated.

Claims trading made a casino out of bankruptcy. As a traders' market, it has become a freestanding industry. Hordes of business school graduates are employed by firms dealing in distressed debt trading to analyze value and create programs to buy and sell claims against debtors. The traders took over and have continued to dominate reorganization cases, reducing the debtor in many instances to a conduit. It has given rise to *ad hoc* committees, associations of similarly situated creditors (mostly traders) and the domination of statutory creditors' committees.

- **The worlds of finance and business have changed**. During the age of the debtor, the predominant creditor groups were unsecured. They were contained within the four corners of the Bankruptcy Code. The code was enacted in the context that reorganizations would principally deal with unsecured creditor claimants. Over the last ten years, the importance of the unsecured creditor constituency has diminished significantly. Business is conducted in a completely different fashion than it was in 1978 and in the 1980s. At long last, institutional creditors found the Uniform Commercial Code.

Essentially, all major financing is done on a secured basis. Generally, all of a debtor's assets are subjected to liens and encumbrances. The result has been that debtors do not have unencumbered assets with which to support a Chapter 11 administration. It is the odd case today in which the major outstanding debt is unsecured. As a consequence, a debtor in possession may only look to the existing secured creditor group for debtor in possession financing. The ability to prime existing secured creditors is almost non-existent. This has enabled secured creditors to impose onerous and oppressive provisions on debtors in possession that include roll-ups, excessive interest and often precipitate dismemberment and sale of the debtor's business and assets. It has also substantially increased the cost of administration.

In addition, the world has become much smaller and much more integrated. Global competition and pressures impact mightily on the ability to reorganize. Supply chains have contracted, limiting competition among suppliers and raising the costs of operations. Control of financial assets has consolidated in fewer institutions. The creation of SPEs as vehicles to avoid bankruptcy expanded, albeit probably in vain.

• **Debtor in possession financing**. Under the prior Bankruptcy Act, there was virtually no post-petition financing in reorganization or arrangement cases. Section 364 of the Bankruptcy Code served as the catalyst for banks to finally realize that debtor in possession financing was a good, profitable and essentially low-risk business. It did not really take hold until the mid 1980s, but it spread like wildfire and was a major factor in the increased use of bankruptcy by distressed businesses. Initially, debtor in possession financing was unsecured but entitled to the highest administrative expense status. Then debtor in possession loans got so large that the lenders began to syndicate them. This added another facet to the reorganization process, as the marketing of the debtor in possession loan slowly but surely required that the borrower be subjected to more rigorous obligations and, ultimately, to the collateralization of debtor in possession loans to enhance the syndication process.

• **Prepackaged or pre-arranged Chapter 11 reorganizations**. The recognition that the Bankruptcy Code would accommodate a pre-packaged or prearranged Chapter 11 plan that could short-circuit the time and oversight of the bankruptcy court was feverishly adopted by creditors and debtors. Chapter 11 plans were presented to bankruptcy courts on an expedited basis, with the requisite acceptances and the agreement of all parties that the confirmation standards of Section 1129 of the Bankruptcy Code had been satisfied. In the absence of opposition, bankruptcy courts freely confirmed these plans. Unfortunately, they led to a high level of recidivism that, in turn, gave ammunition to the academic critics of Chapter 11 to accuse the court and debtors of failing to discharge their responsibilities.

• **Emergence of the "Section 363 option"**. In the casino-like atmosphere that began to dominate the business bankruptcy arena, the desires and objectives of the debt traders to realize their objectives of big recoveries or faster ownership, and the criticisms of academics, led to the use of Section 363 for debtors to sell all or substantially all of the assets of a debtor's business shortly after the commencement of a business bankruptcy case. As the economy began to sputter in 2007, Section 363 became more and more attractive. It (a) accelerated recoveries by secured creditors; (b) provided the purchaser with the assets and properties free and clear of claims and liens of any kind; (c) offered injunctive protection; and (d) gave virtual finality if the sale was quickly consummated. To effect such sales, which can provide for an ongoing business and secure employment, an almost formalized process has developed known as the "stalking horse". Section 363 sales predominated business bankruptcy cases through the final years of the first decade of the 21st century.

Evolution in focus

The Chapter 11 scenario that evolved during the 50 years to 2010 is materially different from that which was contemplated in the mid 1960s and by the Bankruptcy Reform Act of 1978. In today's world, a debtor is essentially a captive of its secured creditors, the designated chief restructuring officer, and the trading market. Secured creditors have become *de facto* creditors in possession. The creditor constituencies often change on a daily basis as claims freely trade. If collateral security is reasonably liquid, a quick sale may be the result. The role of the debtor has retreated to something akin to that of the 1960s.

Esoteric, virtually incomprehensible securities represent the backbone of much of the credit markets. Derivatives, the time bomb that exploded in 2007 and 2008, have continued to command the attention of the world, as the plight of Greece and others illustrates. Through the expert, efficient and effective efforts of a well-financed lobby, the financial community has caused the Bankruptcy Code to be riddled with provisions that protect derivatives and more. These safe-harbor provisions place derivatives beyond the jurisdiction of the bankruptcy court and the discretion of the bankruptcy judge. They are representative of a growing wave that seeks more and more to contract the power of the bankruptcy court and the discretion of bankruptcy judges.

The objective of rehabilitation, once tempered

by the need for protecting creditor recoveries, is now more than offset by the demand for expeditious maximization of creditor recoveries. These two objectives may be in eternal conflict and negatively affect the probability of rehabilitation.

The Bankruptcy Code has been, and continues to be, subject to criticism for being too debtor-protective and invasive of contractual rights. Some believe that the reorganization paradigm is dead and that bankruptcy reorganizations no longer preserve going concern values. They argue that going concern values have been achieved through bankruptcy sales such as those under Section 363. However, those contentions were all made in the context of the robust economy and easy credit of 2003-2007, an economy that was built on shifting sands.

Bankruptcy is a pervasive part of our economy. Its growth has attracted all manner of entities, businesses, governments and others.

Bankruptcy has moved to the front pages of our newspapers and to the internet and is covered by many, many blogs. It is a constant subject in the halls of Congress. Managers and management teams spend an inordinate amount of time studying bankruptcy in high-priced seminars and in the halls of the most prestigious business schools. Hedge funds, private equity funds and other financial institutions are aggressively recruiting self-styled bankruptcy experts.

While bankruptcy may be here to stay, it is not the same bankruptcy reorganization process that flourished in the 1980s, 1990s and early 2000s. The question is whether that is all bad. Is it wrong to have a secured-creditor-oriented process and defer to contractual rights? Is Chapter 11 serving a useful purpose? Have the volume and efficacy of Section 363 sales demonstrated that the objective of bankruptcy should be a prompt disposition of viable assets and businesses that might be continued by a purchaser, with the balance of the bankruptcy simply being to pursue winding up and liquidating the affairs of the debtor? Is there a need for Chapter 11? Has the debtor in possession concept outlived its need?

There is an abundance of work-out specialists, turnaround managers, valuation experts, compensation experts, other business specialists and professionals that have been rooted in the fertility of the bankruptcy law. It has made many of us more than comfortable. For better or worse, bankruptcy is a part of the public consciousness, the commercial lexicon and legal and strategic plans. It has graduated from being an aberrational possibility. It is a reality.

Determining the proper use of bankruptcy

But, we need to determine what is the proper use of bankruptcy in connection with the failure or distress of business entities and, indeed, for individuals, including sensitive interconnected financial institutions. Is there an alternative to Chapter 11 that would be more efficacious and protective of the interests that need to be served? How should bankruptcy laws integrate with global systems? Is bankruptcy a means to deal with "too big to fail?"

Chairman Ben Bernanke of the Federal Reserve wrote to Congress that on the basis of the Lehman case, bankruptcy proceedings are inadequate to deal with the failure of large financial institutions. The Treasury and the FDIC have submitted proposed "resolution authority" proposals that would relegate failed financial institutions to, in effect, administrative provisions within the star chamber of the FDIC. The underlying premise is that you can trust the government to do the right thing. An interesting concept! I suggest interested parties read the Examiner's report filed on March 11, 2010 in the Lehman case and its conclusions regarding the responsibility, or lack thereof, on the part of the regulators and government that aggravated the financial crisis of 2008 and the demise of Lehman.

The world that existed in 1978 is long gone. We face a global economy with a different dynamic and vastly different financing techniques and pressures, economic policies, as well as ever-present political issues. What is the bankruptcy law that will properly balance the needs of stakeholders as well as global interests? The challenge is monumental. Looking ahead, our profession must resolutely focus on working in the best interests of a feasible and effective bankruptcy law that will serve the objectives of fairly dealing with economic distress and failure, and assist in the appropriate deployment of the assets of a failed business.

This article is adapted from Mr Miller's keynote address to the American College of Bankruptcy at the US Supreme Court on the occasion of the induction of its 21st class on March 12, 2010.

Corporate Governance

9

Making critical decisions and monitoring performance during a restructuring: A field-guide for boards

DeLain E Gray, Senior Managing Director and Practice Leader, and Randall S Eisenberg, Senior Managing Director, at the Corporate Finance Practice in **FTI Consulting Inc**

Serving on the board of a public company has always brought with it a certain amount of pressure and scrutiny. After the past decade of corporate collapses, accounting scandals and regulatory reforms, the pressure on boards to make decisions that withstand scrutiny seems to be at an all-time high. This is particularly true when boards are faced with decisions that can materially impact enterprise value. The knowledge that enterprise value can virtually disappear overnight, whether from accounting fraud (Enron), weak risk management (Lehman Brothers), or broken business models (General Motors), places directors in a new reality fraught with risk, even for companies boasting decades of long-term stability.

Now imagine that your company's performance has taken a turn for the worse and the company has entered a restructuring process, or even a formal bankruptcy proceeding. Imagine the frequency and intensity of decisions facing the board as the company looks to stem the bleeding, secure additional capital, quickly sell off non-core assets to raise cash, close factories, or appoint a new CEO. The impacts and implications of these restructuring-based decisions are exponentially more significant than decision-making during ordinary business cycles. Imagine if every decision you make as a director may determine whether or not the company survives and can be questioned, often publicly, by other interested parties. This is the reality of directorship during a corporate restructuring.

Critical decision-making

While board-level decision-making typically focuses on long-term strategic and financial issues, during a restructuring directors quickly become engaged in many decisions that will impact day-to-day operational matters, as well as preservation and/or recovery of enterprise value. They are required to make many more decisions than in the past, and will need to make them in a fast-paced, even chaotic environment and often with imperfect information.

When serving on a board during a restructuring, the risks to the enterprise are no longer theoretical but are already showing up on the income statement and in the cash flows. Boards must have detailed, real-time information about the state of the business in order to make decisions that will best protect shareholders and stakeholders. While the potential impact of decisions can never be known with certainty, directors need to feel confident that they are following a well-reasoned decision-making process with the optimal knowledge, understanding and perspective to make the best possible decisions during uncertain times.

Adopting a clear framework for decision-making and performance monitoring can help to dramatically increase this level of confidence, and reduce the stress that directors will experience throughout the turnaround process. There are certain key elements of an effective decision-making process during a restructuring or turnaround, and a monitoring framework that can be adopted by boards of directors to keep up to speed in the often rapidly changing dynamics of a company in the midst of a turnaround. Before these elements are discussed in more detail, let us review three primary ways in which board decisions are fundamentally altered during a restructuring scenario.

The impact of restructuring on board decision-making

The impact of decisions on the company and its constituents, and the environment in which decisions are made, are different during a turnaround. Decisions can have a much broader impact on employees and other constituents, and are more prone to "Monday morning quarterbacking" by others. Below we have highlighted three distinct factors that board members must recognize when engaged in decision-making during a restructuring.

Decisions involve significant trauma and cultural tension

Understanding the power of a company's culture cannot be over-emphasized. Either explicitly or implicitly, culture embodies the firm-wide values, behaviors and incentives that have guided the company to its present state, so this same culture often becomes extremely vulnerable or potentially counter-productive to effecting a restructuring. Actions taken during a restructuring are mission-critical, transformative and often dramatic, so even the most well-established corporate culture is bound to become damaged, or even undone altogether.

Cultural impacts are often the most traumatic to the organization during a restructuring, as culture serves as the glue that holds employees together. When an established culture is forced to change, it can have significant consequences on collaboration, staff retention and productivity, so the board must be highly attuned to cultural risks as part of the decision-making process.

Most restructuring scenarios require a shift of operational focus away from growth and toward efficiency and profitability, often culminating in dramatic actions such as the implementation of aggressive cost-cutting campaigns and major headcount reductions. This shift is likely to challenge the distinct sense of culture that unites the enterprise. And while some may dismiss cultural issues as less important than more tangible operational issues, the value of the right culture to achieving better performance is well documented.

A positive corporate culture helps to drive sales, quality of service, productivity and reputation. In fact, many large corporations invest years in developing their reputation as an "employer of choice", yet changes to the core culture during a restructuring can damage their employer brand, often irreparably. When the restoration of profitability takes precedence over all other concerns, the employer image can quickly shift from that of a caretaker to that of a survivalist, breeding anxiety and fracturing loyalty across the workforce. Often a dramatic change in culture is required, so management must walk a fine line by making changes but not alienating or losing that portion of the culture that is core to the business going forward.

Workers in the automotive, steelmaking and other heavy manufacturing industries have notably experienced this kind of trauma in recent years; the employer-provided safety nets they had come to depend on have been removed. Restructuring efforts have resulted in widespread offshoring of jobs, elimination of defined-benefit retirement plans, and the dismissal of the concept of lifetime employment. Cultural change and fundamentally new ways of both thinking and managing became essential to save and revitalize these businesses.

Decisions will often impact a broader group of constituents

Under normal circumstances, a board's primary focus is to maximize shareholder returns. Decisions made during good times do not usually have far-reaching adverse impact, and they certainly do not directly affect other constituents to the same degree as when a company is involved in a restructuring. Once a company has entered a turnaround or restructuring, board decision-making is complicated by the need to balance the concerns of a much broader array of constituents. While shareholders remain important, the needs and demands of creditors must also be considered. Moreover, the expanding number of constituents often has needs that are in conflict with each other.

Improving cash flows may necessitate obtaining significant concessions from labor unions, or the need for additional runway to effect the turnaround may require lenders to waive potential loan covenant violations. Directors need to acknowledge upfront that it will be impossible to make decisions that please everyone. Many decisions are bound to alienate one or more constituents. For example, headcount reductions, pay cuts and benefit cuts may help to safeguard enterprise value, but may compromise culture and retention within the employee base. This type of challenge, where certain constituents' needs are diametrically opposed to one another, requires the board to remain objective and adopt a sound and rational decision-making process.

Decisions are made in a fish-bowl

The third unique challenge for decision-making during a restructuring, specifically during an in-court proceeding, is transparency. With court oversight of a restructuring, board decisions and their outcomes ultimately become part of the public record and are often highly scrutinized. And given the often high-profile nature of bankruptcy proceedings, even information not on the public record often eventually leaks into the public domain.

The transparency of the process creates significant tension. A large number of stakeholders now have access to details of the company's current financial situation and will have a say in certain actions taken by the company. The entire restructuring plan can often unfold in the public spotlight, which can spur certain parties to jockey for position in the public eye. For example, bondholders may publicly question the rationale behind decisions made by the board.

A framework for decision-making during a restructuring scenario

Given the unusual circumstances which demand greater director involvement during a restructuring, a board must ensure the process for decision-making is sound and can stand up to scrutiny; a restructuring is an extraordinary situation, so "ordinary" procedures must be supplemented and refined.

The board must stay attuned to the financial and operational condition of the company, which is likely to change more rapidly and severely than during ordinary times. This almost always leads to increased frequency of board meetings and calls. Reporting will become more thorough. Board members will request more information and should be prepared to ask questions of management to ensure they fully understand the company's evolving situation. Directors will be faced with more complex decisions (and on a more regular basis) than before. They will often also have much less time to decide on the appropriate course of action.

Given the pace and intensity of a restructuring process, it is helpful for boards to approach each key decision via a consistent and thorough evaluation process before taking action.

Six-step framework
1. Have an accurate assessment of the company's current operations and viability.
2. Review a well-balanced assessment of the factors impacting the decision and the anticipated results from its implementation.
3. Objectively assess and challenge management's recommendations.
4. Understand all of the alternatives.
5. Where appropriate, seek input from other constituents.
6. Seek advice from outside advisors when their expertise and experience provide unique insights for the board to consider.

Through adhering to the following six-step decision-making framework, directors should feel confident that, despite the anxieties involved, decisions are being made using a sound decision-making process.

1. Have an accurate assessment of the company's current operations and viability
A company's situation can change rapidly during a restructuring. The resignation of a senior manager, the emergence of an activist investor, or a sudden drop in sales due to waning customer confidence are examples of events that can change the game and complicate the best-laid plans. Every time the board is convened to discuss and decide on next steps or new initiatives, management should provide the most up-to-date data reflecting the company's operations and financial condition. This highlights the critical need for a robust performance-monitoring process that will be discussed in the next section.

It is also important that decisions are not made in an operational or financial vacuum, but always in the context of creating a viable entity and a successful restructuring plan. Therefore, in advance of any key decision, the board must also review the status to date of the restructuring plan and how the decision made will help to achieve this plan, and similarly, what the impact will be if a decision is delayed or not made in the direction management has recommended. Is the plan on track? Which milestones have been missed? Which milestones have been achieved early? During a restructuring, financial and operational metrics must always be evaluated in the context of the larger plan. A 5 per cent quarterly increase in sales might reflect progress, but what does it mean if the restructuring plan calls for a 10 per cent increase?

Questions to ask include:
• Does the information presented by management reflect the most current view of the company's financial and operational status?
• What does this information say about the status of the restructuring efforts?
• Is performance meeting or exceeding expectations according to the plan?

2. Review a well-balanced assessment of the factors impacting the decision and the anticipated results from its implementation

Decision-making during a restructuring involves a dangerous paradox. While the complexity of decisions rises dramatically, these same decisions must often be made in a compressed timeframe. This magnifies the risk of decision-making considerably and requires a thoughtful and well-balanced evaluation of the factors that should be considered by the board. Directors must clearly understand the rationale for each decision, including a review that weighs the likelihood of success against the potential risks of its implementation. A review of pros and cons should also be facilitated by management, allowing ample time for questions and evaluation. It is important that board meetings during these critical times are not cut short, but should be structured to ensure that board members have an opportunity to have all of their questions answered.

While boards and management will feel pressured to act quickly to reassure stakeholders of progress, a key decision must not be rushed when a company's survival is at stake. As much as possible, boards should set timelines for board meetings and clear expectations of what is expected from management in advance of each meeting. Management should provide the relevant supporting data in advance of board discussions to ensure sufficient time for course corrections or alternatives to be explored before final decisions are required. Similarly, if certain directors express reservations about authorizing big decisions, their hesitation should be respected. The board should feel free to request additional information if needed and schedule further discussion at a later time. Often, boards will reconvene later so that board members can contemplate the decision at hand.

Questions to ask include:
• How time-critical is this decision? What is the latest date by which a final decision must be made?
• Have we reserved sufficient time for discussion and debate?
• Do I fully understand the impact of the decision on the company's ability to achieve the turnaround objectives?
• Do I as a board member clearly understand the views of various board members and have I weighed them carefully in reaching my own view?

3. Objectively assess and challenge management's recommendations

Decision-making during a restructuring is a collaborative process between management and directors. Given that management has a more comprehensive view of day-to-day operations and the potential implications of certain actions, the board should always request that management present its formal recommendation with a detailed rationale for which course of action to take at each key milestone in the restructuring process. Management should accompany this recommendation with a thorough analysis of risks and alternatives.

It is then the board's responsibility to weigh this recommendation against the objectives and priorities of the overall restructuring plan as well as its obligations to its constituents. The board may choose to accept or reject management's recommendation, but regardless of the final decision, listening carefully to management's insight and analysis will be a valuable exercise.

Since the board is accountable to stakeholders, it is essential that it stays in control of the process. A restructuring is often a public event, so a board's involvement (or lack thereof) is visible and can be scrutinized at every turn. The public record should show that the board has thoroughly reviewed and authorized every key decision during the process.

Questions to ask include:
• What is management's specific recommendation on this issue?
• Was management's analysis thorough in arriving at their recommendation?
• What are the viable alternatives, and the risks and benefits of each?
• Is this recommendation in the best interest of the stakeholders?

4. Understand all of the alternatives

As part of performing its own due diligence and making a final decision, the board must consider all viable alternatives, and their advantages and disadvantages. While some alternatives will be dismissed, the board needs to have considered all of the options available to feel confident that they have executed sound business judgment. Where possible, the impact of each alternative should be quantified and depicted in a way that enables board members to understand how each alternative could impact the success of the restructuring.

Questions to ask include:
• Has the board considered all viable alternatives?
• Does the board understand how each alternative could impact the company's overall restructuring plan?
• What are the risks to each alternative?
• How will constituents react to each alternative? How would this reaction impact the company and the outcome of the restructuring plan?

5. Where appropriate, seek input from other constituents

As mentioned earlier, boards are responsible to a broad array of constituents during a restructuring situation. Therefore, the board must avoid having tunnel vision when considering the impact of its decisions. It is extremely valuable for directors to actively solicit input from all key stakeholders – lenders, shareholders, customers, suppliers, employees and other relevant constituents. Every decision has the potential to impact every stakeholder, positively or negatively, so these potential impacts must be clearly understood by the board as part of the decision-making process. Shuttle diplomacy becomes important. Often, outside advisors to the company can help the board understand the various constituents' perspectives and how best to seek input, address concerns and obtain support as needed.

Questions to ask include:
• How is this decision likely to impact our key stakeholders (lenders and bondholders, shareholders, customers, suppliers, employees, retirees)?
• How will the government/regulatory agencies react?
• What actions could various stakeholders take if opposed to the decision? How would the company address those actions?
• How will this decision be played out in the media?

6. Seek advice from outside advisors when their expertise and experience provide unique insights for the board to consider

Boards and management teams can obtain valuable insights from outside advisors experienced in similar situations. Unlike most directors and managers, financial and legal advisors spend their entire careers working on complex restructurings and turnarounds, so their expertise is based on hands-on, real-world experience in a wide variety of scenarios. Boards can learn from their experiences of both success and failure. Given their vast and varied experience, advisors bring both historical context as well as current knowledge of the financial and legal environment.

Equally important, advisors often bring deep knowledge of the key stakeholders themselves. For example, they may already have sat across the table from your company's major lenders on multiple occasions. They may have experience negotiating with stakeholders on opposing sides and so can bring a significant degree of goodwill to the negotiations, which is often essential to the completion of a company's restructuring. In addition, advisors well respected in their field can often help to validate the board's decisions in the eyes of stakeholders.

Questions to ask include:
• Should management seek input from its outside advisors on this decision?
• What is the advisor's experience with similar decisions in similar situations?
• Does the advisor have direct experience with our stakeholders? Can the advisor predict how these stakeholders will react or respond to the decision?

Performance monitoring in a restructuring

The framework above will help to ensure that directors make decisions with sound business judgment and the highest level of confidence. For this framework to be effective, it is essential that board members carefully monitor the impact of these decisions and the company's overall performance (and anticipated performance) while in the midst of a turnaround. Boards must create a continuous feedback loop that will show how the restructuring plan is progressing based on key decisions and milestones along the way.

The board's monitoring of the company's performance and operations takes on heightened importance during a restructuring since the rapidly changing situation often requires the board to be informed and in a position to make decisions at very short notice. Close monitoring of ongoing performance will help to ensure decisions are made by a fully apprised board.

The board should request that management institute a monitoring and reporting process to provide frequent and thorough updates on the performance of the company and progress of the restructuring efforts. The breadth and depth of information to be monitored will depend in part on the company's specific situation, but in general we recommend that monitoring spans across four areas.

Overall state of restructuring efforts

The monitoring should include an assessment of how well the restructuring process is achieving planned objectives and milestones, including a general sense of timing and next steps in the process. If and when certain goals are not reached within the planned timeframe, management should explain why and how this will affect the next steps in the process. If at any time the company's ability to achieve a predetermined milestone is at risk, the board must be sufficiently knowledgeable to understand the implications to the plan and take corrective action as necessary. It is helpful for boards to establish timelines, even if modified frequently, to clarify expectations and create accountability.

Liquidity

Liquidity, or cash flow, is the lifeblood of any business. During a restructuring, the state of liquidity is among the most critical metrics to be monitored by management. The board should ask management to provide liquidity forecasts on a regular basis, with detailed explanations of variances from forecast. These forecasts should include a combination of both numerical forecasts and management commentary so that the board clearly understands the assumptions on which the forecast is based, as well as any upcoming liquidity issues and risks, such as pending debt maturities or vendor payments. In the context of this forecast, management should also provide detailed updates of its ongoing actions to preserve and manage cash. If liquidity is running short, the board should have a clear understanding of what actions can be taken to preserve liquidity, as well as the impact and status of implementing remedial liquidity generation measures.

Operational performance

Apart from the liquidity forecast, the board should also receive concise reports, or financial dashboards, detailing key operational data and trends for the business. Flash report data must be directionally correct and should reflect a broadly accurate picture of the company's performance. It should also include key productivity and profitability metrics – both specific to the company and compared to industry statistics.

A more detailed monthly operational report should be submitted to the board as well, including analysis of variances between budget and actual performance. A set of financial projections and assumptions should have been submitted to the board during the restructuring process, and these projections should be periodically revisited and revised as changes in circumstances warrant. The board should keep in mind that budget projections are only useful if they reflect current circumstances and reasonable expectations of performance. Timely and insightful operational reporting not only ensures the board remains fully up to speed on both current and future performance, but also allows the board to stay abreast of the progress of the turnaround and raise important questions when performance deviates materially from recent trends and/or budgets.

Stakeholder sentiment

Management should regularly update the board on the general state of relations with key stakeholders, including reactions and responses to actions the company has taken. A restructuring scenario can be volatile and negotiations with and among financial stakeholders can quickly become confrontational and disruptive. A particularly antagonistic party can significantly alter the outcome of the restructuring, so directors must be kept informed about any difficulties that may arise. Advance notice of potentially hostile behavior allows management and directors to prepare not only their response, but also how the development will be communicated to public and internal audiences as necessary. Specifically, the board should stay apprised of each significant stakeholder's current position and sources of leverage, as well as the likelihood that they will use that leverage.

In addition, management should assess and report on each stakeholder's general sentiment toward the management team and the board. Some stakeholders may become increasingly frustrated and aggressive as the restructuring process evolves, while others may become more willing to compromise or even complacent. Such developments can have major consequences on the outcome of the restructuring and should be discussed in detail with the board regularly.

Management should also provide updates on

other stakeholder groups, such as customer sentiment, employee morale, and supplier relations. Working with sales, marketing, human resources, and other corporate functions as necessary, management should strive to provide updates on how these stakeholders perceive the progress of the restructuring, and how these perceptions may be affecting their behaviors. If sentiment appears to be increasingly negative, then management should recommend a specific course of action to improve relations.

Maximizing the likelihood of a successful restructuring
Serving on a board during a restructuring is a major challenge in any director's career. Executing a successful turnaround requires dramatic changes inside the company, and such changes can bring enormous levels of pressure, scrutiny and criticism. Reputations of not just companies but also individuals can be made or broken. A restructuring is not an easy process for anyone, especially not for the board of directors.

However, as we have described above, wise boards know that establishing rigorous protocols for decision-making and reporting during such a tumultuous period can bring greater structure and accountability to the process, as well as increasing directors' confidence and comfort levels. Strong process management by itself cannot fix a broken company, but it can help minimize chaos and maximize the likelihood that the board will successfully guide the company to achieve its objectives.

The opinions, facts, and conclusions contained herein are those of the authors or the sources cited and not those of FTI Consulting, Inc. The information contained herein is of a general nature and is not intended to address the circumstances of any particular individual, entity, or transaction. No one should act on such information without appropriate professional advice after a thorough examination of the particular situation.

10

Restructuring under a microscope: Cautionary tales for directors and officers in "distressed land"

Harvey R Miller, Senior Partner,
Weil, Gotshal & Manges LLP

You are the chairman and chief executive of a Delaware public company that manufactures and sells healthcare products. The company's common stock has been delisted and, from time to time, trades at approximately $10 per share. You were appointed to the board of directors and to be chief executive officer at the insistence of the preferred shareholders. Prior to your appointment, the company's operations were deteriorating and its future was dubious. The intent of the preferred shareholders was that you should lead a turnaround of the operations and find an exit transaction that will enable them to realize a recovery on their investment. The other four directors consist of three independent directors and the chief financial officer. You have developed a business strategy that was approved by the board and is in the process of implementation.

After ten months of stabilization and signs of improvement, you are presented with a merger opportunity. After review, you have presented the proposed opportunity to the board of directors. The proposed merger transaction will result in a very substantial recovery for the preferred shareholders and will not impair any creditor obligations. However, it will leave no value for holders of common shares.

Although it has been generally recognized by the healthcare industry and financial markets that the company was open for sale proposals, there have been no comparable offers or proposed transactions. According to the company's financial advisors, the merger purchase offer is very attractive and, from a financial statement perspective, fair. The advisors have recommended acceptance.

A question of duty

The board of directors may have an easy decision to make. There is one potential problem. The company, under your leadership and your business plan, has been steadily improving. It has adequate financing for the next year provided that there is no change in the financial markets and operations that might cause a loan covenant breach. You and the board of directors are faced with the issue of immediate realization of a fair sale price for the company, but the sale will eradicate the interests of common shareholders. If the sale offer is rejected and the company's improvement ceases or declines, preferred shareholders and creditors may be seriously impaired. News of the proposed M&A transaction has leaked out. Certain common shareholders have told you that they will oppose any sale that will eradicate their interests. What action should you and the board take?

It is generally accepted that the fiduciary duties of directors of a solvent company — the duties of loyalty, care and good faith — run to the shareholders. Generally, however, once a company enters the zone of insolvency, director fiduciary duties are to the company and not to any particular constituency. Actions taken in the best interests of the company will benefit its residual stakeholders. In the context of the zone of insolvency, a director has to take into account all the interests of the company's economic stakeholders. However, in contrast to shareholders, creditors are protected by their contractual or other arrangements with the company.

As a result, when considering transformative transactions such as a merger, which may alter or shift where the residual ownership of the company lies, it is not at all obvious which stakeholders' interests should be given greater weight. In an age of increased transparency and economic turbulence, directors and officers of distressed companies may be called upon to choose from restructuring options that may limit creditor recoveries and dilute or eradicate equity interests. Financial distress is often played in the context of a zero sum game — that is to say, there may not be enough value to satisfy debts and liabilities or to extend to equity interests. Because of the enhanced transparency and increased stakeholder participation, the acts of a board or other governing body and the management will be carefully scrutinized, particularly by "out of the money" creditors and equity interest holders. Directors must be aware of the scope of their fiduciary responsibilities in considering substantive and strategic options to alleviate or resolve distress.

Your company has been steadily improving — but for how long? You now find yourself at a crossroads, where diverging options result in a different constituency potentially emerging as the company's residual stakeholder and the beneficiary of the proposed merger. One option is certain to wipe out the common shareholders but will satisfy creditors in whole and provide the preferred shareholders (who were responsible for your appointment) with the opportunity to substantially recover their investment. The other option may result in potential value for the company's common shareholders — but this option is less certain, and if unsuccessful, may leave the company's creditors impaired. Implementation of the latter option might result in claims by preferred shareholders and possibly creditors against you and the other directors for malfeasance and breach of fiduciary duties to the company if it proves unsuccessful. You have been advised of the generally applicable principles of law as derived from Delaware corporate law. Which option should the board adopt?

The importance of process

Process, due deliberation and judgment must be the mantra of directors and officers who pursue restructuring solutions — particularly when these fiduciaries may have relationships to certain stakeholders whose interests may be in conflict with those of the company. For example, directors and officers having personal relationships with investors may find themselves pressured to pursue sales or other restructurings that may be advantageous to such investors. To avoid potential liability in these circumstances, directors and officers should proceed with heightened caution. The sale or restructuring of a distressed company, while "cashing out" some stakeholders, may limit or deny recoveries to other groups. Those groups may, in turn, question whether the directors and the company's officers have acted disinterestedly and solely in the best interests of the company. All actions must therefore be based upon a comprehensive record of mature consideration and deliberation as to the interests of the company that need to be served in the particular circumstances of financial distress and the applicable duties of care and loyalty imposed on all directors.

Process is critical in building such a record to support the exercise of business judgment. It may provide directors and officers with the insulation needed to survive assertions of potential claims and litigation by adversely affected creditors or shareholders.

The MIG case

The case of Metromedia International Group Inc (MIG) illustrates the importance of process. In February 2003, when a new chairman of the board was appointed, the company faced "a severe liquidity crisis". To generate cash flow, the chairman's strategy included selling several of MIG's subsidiaries. The strategy was successful, as reported:

'Following its August 2005 $212 million sale of ZAO PeterStar, a fixed-line telephone provider based in St Petersburg, Russia, [MIG] has operated free of any substantial long-term or secured debt. Additionally, [the] resurgent performance [of its subsidiary, Magticom] in the past three years has generated sizable free cash flow and EBITDA. [MIG]'s common stock, which traded at 3 cents per share in February 2003, has experienced a more than fifty-fold increase in value.'

In 2006, this success attracted a group of investors to propose a sale of Magticom, MIG's principal asset and the Republic of Georgia's leading mobile phone provider. According to MIG's board: 'The consideration offered for [MIG]'s 50.1% interest in Magticom far exceeded that of any previous unsolicited offer and represented an objectively fair valuation of the asset.'

There was only one problem. As a "sale of all or substantially all" the assets of the company, MIG was required to hold a shareholder meeting and solicit the vote of the company's common shareholders. MIG was not able to hold such a meeting, however, because it was not current in its filings with the SEC as required by the Sarbanes-Oxley Act of 2002. On the advice of counsel, the board concluded 'that the federal securities laws barred it from calling a meeting or soliciting proxies, and thus prevented a vote of the common shareholders' to approve the sale. Nonetheless, the board viewed the sale as being in the best interests of the company and its economic stakeholders.

Finding itself in an unusual position due to 'this combination of burgeoning financial results and delinquent reporting', the board sought an alternative strategy for approving the sale. This strategy involved executing the sale agreement and then seeking court approval of the sale pursuant to Section 363(b) of the Bankruptcy Code, followed post-sale by a plan of reorganization. To ensure approval, MIG negotiated a "lock-up" agreement with the holders of roughly 80 per cent of the company's preferred shares. During the course of negotiations, the preferred shareholders were provided — subject to confidentiality agreements — with a sizable amount of non-public information regarding MIG's financial condition in order to value their interests. In those negotiations, preferred shareholders were also able to exert their bargaining power to guarantee a highly favorable treatment for the preferred shares in the transaction.

Under the proposed transaction, MIG granted preferred shareholders a vote — and, therefore, bargaining power — that they would not otherwise have under the terms of the preferred shareholders' certificate of designation, thus depriving common shareholders of the exclusive voting right that they would otherwise have outside bankruptcy. When MIG publicly announced its intention to consummate the sale under Section 363(b) of the Bankruptcy Code, two common shareholders that owned a substantial amount of common stock sued the board of directors in the Delaware Chancery Court, seeking to enjoin MIG from executing the sale agreement and the lock-up agreement.

An inequitable course of action

The Delaware court found the board's decision to circumvent the need for common shareholder approval to sell Magticom by using the bankruptcy process to be inequitable for two reasons. First, the

court found it to be an 'an abuse of the bankruptcy process for a robust and healthy corporation, encumbered by virtually no debt, to seek out the vast and extraordinary relief a bankruptcy court is capable of providing'. The board's decision to place the company in Chapter 11 therefore 'inequitably abridged the justified expectations of the common stockholders'. Second, the Delaware court was deeply concerned about the unwarranted disenfranchisement of the company's true residual owners — the common shareholders — that would result if the company consummated the sale of Magticom through the bankruptcy process.

Under MIG's organizational documents, the common shareholders were the only constituency entitled to vote on a fundamental change of the company's form, such as the sale of substantially all the company's assets. Preferred shareholders, in turn, were entitled to appoint two representatives to the board of directors if the company failed to pay dividends for six consecutive quarters, and were entitled to a liquidation preference but not the power to authorize the proposed sale. The board's bankruptcy solution warped this arrangement. It expanded the rights of preferred shareholders and relegated common shareholders 'to the status of sideline objectors in bankruptcy court', irrespective of the fairness of the purchase price. The bankruptcy solution deprived the shareholders of the bargaining leverage implicit in the right to approve or reject the proposed sale.

The primary interests protected by the bankruptcy process are those of creditors. Because of this simple fact, the Bankruptcy Code does not contemplate a freestanding right to vote by the holders of common equity. Were such a vote available, the legal rights of the creditors to the remaining assets of the entity would take a subsidiary position to the interests of the residual owners who, at least where a company is insolvent, no longer have any identifiable financial interest to protect.

Accordingly, the Delaware court entered an order 'prohibiting the corporation and its directors from making any agreement to sell all or substantially all of the assets that is not conditioned upon the approval of the corporation's common stockholders'. With respect to the requirement of Sarbanes-Oxley, the court's order 'expressly contemplate[d] that [MIG would] promptly seek exemptive relief broad enough to permit it to comply with the order's requirement of a stockholder vote'.

Perhaps if the MIG board had obtained the

support of a percentage of its common shareholders as well as the preferred classes — indeed, if MIG had reached out to the two objectors that were substantial holders of common stock — the sale of Magticom might not have been derailed. In this respect, MIG's case is illustrative of how certain constituencies may act — not only how courts may react — when directors undertake decisions affecting or determining the interests of the residual stakeholders of a company, or otherwise deprive such stakeholders of their statutory rights. The disenfranchisement of a shareholder class entitled to vote on any major transaction is a significant action. Failure to employ the correct process and analysis might give rise to potential claims of breach of fiduciary duties with attendant personal liability.

Beware the conflicting demands of private equity
It is typical for private equity sponsors to cause the appointment of directors in their portfolio companies as a means of monitoring and protecting their investments. This involvement of investors in company governance, and particularly in the sale of distressed assets, has dramatically increased the potential conflicts of interest that directors and officers face when making material decisions, such as when evaluating the sale of a company (or of substantially all its assets).

As the masters of the policies and affairs of a company, directors are charged with fiduciary duties in the discharge of their respective obligations. State statutes and the common law of the state of incorporation generally govern these fiduciary duties. As over 850,000 businesses have elected to be incorporated under the laws of Delaware, the Delaware statutes and court decisions construing those statutes generally establish norms and governing principles for company management. In Delaware (and most other states), the primary fiduciary duties owed to the company are the duties of loyalty and care.

The duty of loyalty requires that directors abstain from any actions that could be detrimental to the company and its shareholders, or that are intended to benefit the director's own interests or the interests of a third party. The duty of care mandates that directors and officers exercise 'that degree of care which a person of ordinary prudence would exercise under the same or similar circumstances' (*Meyers vs Moody,* 1982). This duty incorporates an obligation for directors to, among other things, inform themselves 'prior to making a

business decision, of all material information reasonably available to them', including a responsibility to consider alternatives and obtain professional advice where appropriate (*Aronson vs Lewis,* 1984). The duties encompass the obligation that fiduciaries also act in good faith.

The business judgment rule
In discharging their fiduciary duties, directors, generally, have the protection of the business judgment rule. This, if properly invoked, insulates directors in their decision-making. The rule 'is a presumption that in making a business decision the directors of a corporation acted on an informed basis, in good faith and in the honest belief that the action taken was in the best interests of the company' (*In re Trados Incorporated Shareholder Litigation,* 2009). The party challenging the directors' decision bears the burden of rebutting the presumption. The essence of the rule is based on the proposition that, in the absence of clear grounds for rebutting the rule's presumption, a court should not micromanage or second-guess the business decisions of a board of directors. If the presumption is rebutted, then the burden of proving the fairness of the proposed action shifts to the directors.

The business judgment rule mandates that courts focus on process, not content, when evaluating the decisions made by the directors of a company. As the Delaware Chancery Court noted in *In re Caremark Int'l Inc Derivative Litig*, the evaluation of a director's discharge of fiduciary duties can never be appropriately judicially determined by reference to the content of the board decision that leads to a corporate loss, apart from consideration of the good faith or rationality of the process employed. That is, whether a judge or jury — considering the matter after the fact — believes a decision substantively wrong, or degrees of wrong extending through "stupid" to "egregious" or "irrational", provides no ground for director liability, so long as the court determines that the process employed was either rational or employed in a good-faith effort to advance corporate interests.

To employ a different rule — one that permitted an "objective" evaluation of the decision — would expose directors to substantive second-guessing by ill-equipped judges or juries, which would, in the long run, be injurious to investor interests. Thus, the business judgment rule is process-oriented and informed by a deep respect for all good-faith board decisions.

Although it is originated in common law, the rule has been adopted, with some variation, in every state. For the protection of the business judgment rule to hold, however, a director or officer must be able to demonstrate that he or she is disinterested in the transaction. As more and more directors and officers have relationships with outside investors, such as private equity firms or hedge funds, such disinterestedness may become stretched. Accordingly, it will be crucial to approach any restructuring transactions with a sharp focus on process and the creation of a clear record of deliberation as regards the impact on all stakeholders of the company as a result of the proposed transaction.

Focus on Trados Inc

A Delaware Chancery Court case is illustrative. In *In re Trados Inc Shareholder Litig*, Trados Inc, a German software company, moved to the United States and became a Delaware company in March 2000 with the intent of ultimately becoming a public company. Trados accepted investments from venture capital firms in exchange for preferred stock and the right to place representatives on the board of directors. Of the board's seven members, besides the CEO, four were designees of this preferred shareholder group, while two others were representatives of the company's employees.

By April 2004, the company's under-performance prompted the board to form a special "mergers and acquisitions committee" — comprised of three board members from the preferred shareholder constituency — to explore a sale of the company. Of the two board members who represented Trados's employees, one was appointed president, the other CEO. The CEO's charge was 'to grow the company profitably or sell it'. At the time, 'the Company was losing money and had little cash to fund continuing operations'. The directors decided that the 'fair market value of Trados's common stock was $0.10 per share'.

By the fourth quarter of 2004, circumstances for Trados had changed for the better. The company 'was well financed and experiencing improved performance' under the leadership of the CEO, who at the February 2, 2005 board meeting 'presented positive financial results from the fourth quarter of 2004, including record revenue and profit from operations'. It appeared that a sale of the company was no longer critical. Nevertheless, directors persisted in pursuing that objective. As one member of the board reported to his constituency of preferred shareholders, the company's performance was improving, but '[the CEO's] mission is to architect an M&A event as

soon as practicable.' The obvious objective of the preferred shareholders was to execute a sale and reap a large recovery on their investment.

A review of the board's members is indicative of the incentives behind the board's persistence. A majority of the members were designees of the preferred shareholders:

• **David Scanlan**: designee and partner in preferred shareholder Wachovia Capital Partners LLC.
• **Lisa Stone**: designee, director and employee of Rowan Entities Limited and Rowan Nominees Limited RR, transferees of the preferred stock held by Hg Investment Managers Limited, of which Stone was also a director and employee.
• **Sameer Gandhi**: designee and partner in several preferred shareholder entities known as Sequoia.
• **Joseph Prang**: designee of Sequoia and owner of Mentor Capital Group, another holder of preferred shares.

The preferred shareholders represented venture capital firms that had made substantial investments in Trados in 2000, when the goal was to take the company public. Four years later, these firms were looking to recapture their investments and, if possible, a significant profit, based upon the preferred stock's high liquidation preference of $57.9 million. That preference explains why Trados rejected the initial $40 million offer made in August 2004 by an interested party, SDL plc, which would ultimately acquire Trados for $60 million.

The only apparent obstacle to the board's pursuit of the SDL merger was that the company's executive officers did not have the same incentives as the preferred shareholders and they might not vote in favor of a sale. As reported: '[In] July 2004, Scanlan (as a preferred shareholder and director) expressed concern that the executive officers of the Company might not have sufficient incentives to remain with the Company or pursue a potential acquisition of the Company, due to the high liquidation preference of the Company's preferred stock.'

The preferred shareholders recognized that they needed to align the interests of the executive officers more closely with their own if a successful sale was to be effected. 'This led to the December 2004 board approval [of a] graduated compensation scale for the Company's management based on the price obtained for the Company in acquisition.' The result was to incentivize the officers to seek and approve a sale of the company that would benefit the preferred shareholders.

Accordingly, when the deal was struck to sell Trados to SDL for $60 million, $7.8 million was allocated for the executive officers and management, with the balance going to the preferred shareholders in partial satisfaction of their $57.9 million liquidation preference. In that context, the Chancery Court described the sale: 'In contrast, the common stockholders received nothing as a result of the merger, and lost the ability to ever receive anything of value in the future for their ownership interest in Trados. It would not stretch reason to say that this is the worst possible outcome for the common stockholders. The common stockholders would certainly be no worse off had the merger not occurred.'

Clearly the interests of the preferred shareholders and common shareholders diverged. Common shareholders promptly sued the directors for allegedly breaching their fiduciary duties to shareholders. The Delaware Chancery Court denied the directors' motion to dismiss, noting that it is a settled point of Delaware law that where the interests of common and preferred shareholders diverge, 'generally it will be the duty of the board, where discretionary judgment is to be exercised, to prefer the interests of common stock — as the good faith judgment of the board sees them to be — to the interests created by the special rights, preferences, etc, of preferred stock, where there is a conflict.'

Inability to exercise independent judgment

Of greater interest to directors and officers, however, was the court's finding that the plaintiffs had 'alleged facts sufficient to demonstrate that at least a majority of the members of Trados's seven-member board were unable to exercise independent and disinterested business judgment in deciding whether to approve the merger [because of these relationships to preferred shareholders]'. As the court noted, ordinarily '[directors] of Delaware corporations are protected in their decision-making by the business judgment rule, which "is a presumption that in making a business decision the directors of a corporation acted on an informed basis, in good faith and in the honest belief that the action taken was in the best interests of the company".' The common shareholder plaintiffs in Trados, however, alleged two facts that 'support[ed] a reasonable inference that Scanlan, Stone, Gandhi, and Prang, the four board designees of preferred stockholders, were

interested in the decision to pursue the merger with SDL, which had the effect of triggering the large liquidation preference of the preferred stockholders and resulted in no consideration to the common stockholders for their common shares'.

First, each of the four challenged directors had been designated by a holder of a significant number of preferred shares. The court acknowledged that 'this, alone, may not be enough to rebut the presumption of the business judgment rule', (but nonetheless cited a recent case involving such association with shareholders 'which, in their institutional capacities, are both alleged to have had a direct financial interest in this transaction'). In addition to being their board designees, however, 'Scanlan, Stone, Gandhi, and Prang each had an ownership or employment relationship with an entity that owned Trados preferred stock'. While it is unclear whether merely being a designee of these entities would have yielded the same result, the court held that '[the] allegations of the ownership and other relationships of each of Scanlan, Stone, Gandhi and Prang to preferred stockholders, combined with the fact that each was a board designee of one of these entities, [was] sufficient to rebut the business judgment presumption with respect to the decision to approve the merger with SDL.'

The above combination of facts, compounded by the plausible argument that the SDL merger was no longer necessary, made Trados an extreme example of directors' failure to recognize the interests of all of the economic stakeholders and thereby lose the protection of the business judgment rule. Nevertheless it is worth noting that the directors did not lose this battle because the decision to go forward with the merger was a bad one; the quality of the decision to sell had nothing to do with the fairness of the sale. The directors lost because of the context in which that decision was made — in other words, because nobody reviewing the record could reasonably conclude that the directors were anything but acutely interested in the outcome of the SDL merger and the board had not adopted a process that would insulate the integrity of its decision and be compliant with the duty of loyalty.

The establishment of a special committee to review and decide whether to approve this or any transaction may have produced a different result for the company. As the case discussed below will demonstrate, however, even measures such as those may not be sufficient to cleanse an already tarnished record.

Fiduciaries in Chapter 11

Once a company is in Chapter 11, the need for directors and officers to establish a clear record to dismiss any doubt as to their disinterestedness is accentuated. A company in Chapter 11 will be subject to a variety of divergent interests — not only among creditors and shareholders, but even divergent interests within different creditor groups. These types of conflict are common in restructuring and bankruptcy cases. When particular stakeholders appoint one of their chosen people to positions on boards or as officers of companies that ultimately commence Chapter 11 cases, those directors and officers will inevitably face heightened scrutiny.

One remarkable example of this is the battle of competing reorganization plans that took place in the Chapter 11 cases of Coram Healthcare Corporation and Coram Inc (collectively, Coram). The battle over reorganization plans was waged primarily between Coram, through its chief executive officer, a major venture capital firm as an investor, and an Equity Interest Holders Committee that was appointed by the court two months after the commencement of the Chapter 11 case. Among the noteworthy members of this committee were Samstock, a Delaware limited liability company devoted to investments, whose president was the noted investor Samuel Zell. Samstock had purchased 450,000 common shares of Coram at an average price per share of $1.146 pre-petition, and an additional 2,050,000 shares post-Chapter 11 at an average price per share of 8.4 cents.

Coram filed its first joint plan of reorganization (POR) along with its Chapter 11 petitions on August 8, 2000 (*In re Coram Healthcare Corp*, 2004). The POR essentially proposed to give certain noteholders, and others, total ownership of the company, wiping out Zell and the other equity holders. The POR provided for (i) cancellation of all existing shareholder interests; (ii) the issuance of new shares of common stock, representing 100 per cent of the reorganized debtors' equity, to the noteholders, who collectively held 100 per cent of the debtors' outstanding unsecured notes; and (iii) payment of $2 million to unsecured creditors.

The equity committee opposed the first POR, and at the confirmation hearing it was revealed that the CEO was also employed as a consultant for one of the major noteholders and had been receiving compensation of approximately $1 million a year from that noteholder, in addition to his salary as CEO of Coram. The court concluded that 'this employment created a conflict of interest which tainted the Debtors' restructuring efforts.' Confirmation was denied by a bench decision because the court was 'unable to find that the Debtors had proposed their POR in good faith in accordance with Section 1129(a)(3) [good faith] of the Code'.

Back to the drawing board

The court sent the parties back to the drawing board. In an effort to overcome the lack of good faith, Coram proceeded to establish a 'special committee of independent directors to review the Debtors' affairs and propose a new [POR]'. This committee retained an expert 'to perform an impartial investigation', after which Coram proposed a second POR, under which (i) noteholders, again, would receive all the reorganized debtors' equity, and (ii) shareholders would share $10 million if they accepted the POR.

For Zell, with ownership of 2,500,000 shares at an average price per share of less than 8 cents, the second POR represented a material return on his investment. Nevertheless, the equity committee opposed the second POR. After seven days of confirmation hearings in November and December 2001, the court again denied confirmation, finding in its published opinion that the employment relationship between [the CEO] and [the noteholder] had not changed since the first confirmation hearings. Accordingly, [the court] again held that it 'could not conclude that the Debtors' Second Plan satisfied the [good faith] requirements of Section 1129(a)(3)'.

As a result, on January 18, 2002, the United States Trustee in Delaware filed a motion for the appointment of a Chapter 11 trustee 'to oversee the Debtors' operations and to facilitate the reorganization process'. The court granted the motion. On March 7, 2002, the court approved the appointment of Arlin M Adams, a retired Third Circuit judge, as trustee. With the appointment of a Chapter 11 trustee, Coram lost its exclusive right to file and solicit acceptances of a POR. Accordingly, in December 2002, the equity committee filed its proposed POR under which the common shareholders would retain ownership of the reorganized debtors. The court's response was to defer consideration of the equity committee's POR until the Chapter 11 trustee had been given reasonable time to assume his duties and have an opportunity to consider the proposal of a POR.

The instructive irony in this battle over the integrity of Coram's CEO was that the appointed CEO was an excellent choice. He had turned the business around and was uniformly applauded by all parties. Indeed, the Chapter 11 trustee filed a motion seeking to extend his employment, in which the trustee provided an impartial positive assessment of the CEO's performance. The trustee had 'independently examined the actions undertaken by [the CEO] as the Debtors' chief executive officer' and found 'that [the CEO] has operated the company profitably and efficiently'. Specifically, the trustee found that '[under the CEO], notwithstanding being in these bankruptcy proceedings, the Debtors have experienced positive operating margins and EBITDA, reduced cost of services, reduced operating costs, improved inventory management, improved information systems, improved management tools, and maintained a stable cash position with no net borrowing to fund post-petition operations.'

Nevertheless, the CEO suffered from a severe lack of disinterestedness because of his contemporaneous employment by a dominant noteholder with obligations to give the interests of the noteholders priority — a conflict that could not be glossed over, as there would be continual doubt as to which master the CEO was serving. The dismissal of the CEO or the appointment of an independent fiduciary — ie, a Chapter 11 trustee — were the only alternatives.

Coram illustrates the degree to which an officer or a board's potential lack of disinterestedness may undermine any of the protections ordinarily available to a company's directors. It is also noteworthy that the court could not rely upon Coram's second POR, which had the benefit of a special committee, due to the process employed and the ineffectual conduct of the engaged expert.

Directors are typically protected when relying in good faith on the advice of such special committees or the company's professional advisors, such as attorneys, auditors or financial advisors — provided that the special committee and such professionals have acted appropriately and comprehensively. Reliance on outside advisors establishes a record of due deliberation and must establish that the decisions made were based upon independent evaluation free of any bias or loyalty to a particular constituency within the company.

For directors and officers with ties to outside investors, such as the Coram CEO, it is essential to establish a process that includes reliance on outside, independent advisers, or on special independent committees when considering restructuring solutions that may wipe out a particular group of stakeholders.

But as Coram demonstrates, in these circumstances, any appearance of impropriety may render any reliance upon such experts futile. There can be no suspicion whatsoever that the advisors whose opinions are relied upon were "bought" for the purpose of consummating the proposed transaction.

The trustee's POR confirmed

Despite the Chapter 11 trustee's validation of the CEO's skill, and Coram's reliance on a special committee and expert for its second POR, Coram never regained control of the reorganization process. On May 2, 2003, the Chapter 11 trustee filed a POR. This provided for, among other things, cancellation of shareholders' equity for a pro rata distribution of approximately $40 million plus interests in litigation claims against the directors and others, and issuance of all equity in the reorganized debtors to the noteholders. It also (i) included a settlement with the noteholders of the estate's claims — including derivative claims — against them arising from their relationship with Coram's CEO; and (ii) preserved the estate's claims against the CEO and Coram's outside directors for the benefit of Coram's shareholders.

While the outcome of the case came down to a contest between the trustee's and the equity committee's PORs, the court ultimately confirmed the trustee's plan for several reasons, including the support of Coram's creditors who favored it by 'substantial margins'.

Nevertheless, Coram's shareholders fared considerably better than they would have under either of Coram's proposed PORs, catapulting from an initial proposal of $0 under the first POR, to $10 million under the second, and then $40 million plus interests in litigation claims against the directors and others under the trustee's POR. Thus, as a result of their persistence and their ability to exploit the lack of good faith and breach of fiduciary duties of the directors, the shareholders were ultimately able to reap a substantial recovery.

Summing up

The word fiduciary, from the Latin *fides*, implies a reliance based on faith and trust. For directors and officers to maintain their viability as fiduciaries, it is imperative for them to instill and maintain the trust of the stakeholders, especially when interests among constituencies diverge. Moreover, in a corporate environment permeated with private equity funds, distressed debt traders and other activist investors, directors and officers will frequently hold relationships with particular stakeholders in a company that may result in conflicts that impair governance. Faith is fragile, and easily tainted by any indication of impropriety or self-interested behavior. No degree of skill or qualification on the part of a director or officer can remedy a loss of faith on the part of stakeholders or courts — even where an officer's skills translate into positive results for the company.

Directors and officers with ties to any one stakeholder should therefore be continually focused on process when deliberating over transactions as material as a sale of the company, or any other material restructuring. Their deliberations should include a meticulous documentation of their analysis of the impact that a transaction may have on different constituencies. The documentation should include fairness opinions and third-party valuations, board minutes and related documentation — keeping in mind that all will be reviewed in hindsight.

Above all, private equity and other similar investment groups, if they install their own appointees as directors and officers, should develop and implement safeguards to insulate such appointees from undue influence. Certainly, any employment relationship with a particular investor, as existed in Coram, may be incurable, particularly if not disclosed. If a relationship must exist, full disclosure must be made and, if possible, appropriate consents from board members and other stakeholders should be obtained so that these parties will be on notice of the relationship.

If a particularly significant transaction is on the horizon — one that is more likely to result in litigation by disaffected stakeholders — a special committee of truly independent directors should be created to bolster the presumption of the business judgment rule.

Directors should not be misled, however, into thinking that the degree of protection offered by the business judgment rule changes depending on the size or significance of the transaction. As one recent decision by the Delaware Chancery Court confirms: 'Delaware law simply does not support this distinction. A business decision made by a majority of disinterested, independent board members is entitled to the deferential business judgment rule regardless of whether it is an isolated transaction or part of a larger transformative strategy'(*In re Dow Chemical Company Derivative Litigation*, 2010).

Ultimately, courts will find it difficult to question truly independent directors. If their decisions and actions are to be safeguarded from the growing threat of litigation in the turbulent world of a distressed economy and an aggressive plaintiff's bar, directors, like Caesar's wife, must be above suspicion and compliant with their duties of care and loyalty.

The author gratefully acknowledges the enormous contribution made to this chapter by Maurice Horwitz

Revisiting traditional notions of governance, fiduciary duty and the zone of insolvency from the creditors' perspectives

Keith J Shapiro,
Co-Chair of the
Business Reorganization and
Bankruptcy Practice,
Greenberg Traurig LLP

Recent economic turmoil has resulted in increased attention being paid to the fiduciary duties of directors and officers when a corporation is facing insolvency. This attention is coming from many interested parties, but it is particularly marked among creditors of struggling corporations.

It is well established that directors and officers owe their corporations and shareholders the duties of due care, loyalty and good faith. When a company is financially healthy, any breach of these duties may give rise to a derivative lawsuit by a shareholder against the director or officer on behalf of the corporation. Creditors typically lack standing to assert derivative claims; their rights stem instead from their contractual relationship with the corporation, so their opportunity to protect themselves comes during the negotiation process.

As a company approaches insolvency or even the zone of insolvency, however, the fiduciary duties may extend to the creditors. In recent years, courts have expanded (and subsequently retracted) the reach of directors' and officers' duties in the zone of insolvency. The duties in this zone vary from jurisdiction to jurisdiction and have been the subject of considerable litigation and uncertainty over the past decade, but it is still generally understood that they may be owed to creditors, as well as the corporation, when the company is operating in the zone of insolvency and when it is actually insolvent. Additionally, in bankruptcy cases, although not a classic derivative claim, creditor committees are sometimes authorized by the bankruptcy court to bring "breach of fiduciary" actions against directors and officers in the name of Chapter 11 debtors.

As the case law has evolved in this area, so have the views of creditors, who are now very familiar with the concept of fiduciary duties and have closely followed litigation regarding the circumstances in which these duties can extend to allow them a recovery from negligent or disloyal directors and officers. As more and more corporations have reached insolvency over the past several years, creditors have increasingly sought to collect some of their losses by asserting claims against officers and directors.

What are the duties owed by directors and officers?

As outlined above, creditors are becoming increasingly well versed in the minutiae of the three fiduciary duties owed to the corporation and its shareholders. The duty of care requires that directors and officers act with the care an ordinarily prudent person in a like position would exercise under the circumstances. The duty of loyalty requires them to put the interests of the corporation above their own personal interests. This is often the focus of breach of duty litigation, as shareholders (or creditors) look for instances in which directors and officers have conflicts of interest or engage in self-dealing.

The duty of good faith requires that directors and officers deliberate on risks to the corporation and do not demonstrate an intentional indifference to a risk of harm.

Creditor assertions of breach of fiduciary duty claims tend to arise out of three classic situations: self-dealing or insider preferences; a failure to minimize losses when it is clear that risk is not warranted; and decision-making without reasonably adequate information.

Shareholder and creditor lawsuits often center on the duty of loyalty rather than the duty of care because the "business judgment rule" serves to protect a board of directors' business decision so long as that decision was made on a fully informed basis, without self-interest, in good faith, and in the honest belief that it was taken in the best interests of the corporation and its stockholders (or, when in the zone of insolvency, creditors). It is much easier for a creditor to withstand a motion to dismiss if it can show a clear conflict of interest or self-dealing, because courts have generally been supportive of directors' business decisions.

Another fact pattern that creditors have attempted to take advantage of arises under a theory of liability known as "deepening insolvency". This has largely been rejected by courts, but may still be a viable basis for a creditor action in untested jurisdictions. Under the theory, liability is imposed against directors and officers for fraudulently or negligently prolonging the life of a corporation, and thereby increasing its debt and exposure to creditors.

What is the zone of insolvency?

Even more than the precise contours of the fiduciary duties, creditors are sometimes focused on the evaluation of when a corporation becomes insolvent and when it enters that hazy period of the zone of insolvency. Because creditors' fiduciary rights are triggered upon entrance, creditors are aggressively arguing for an expansive definition of the zone.

Unfortunately for directors and officers, there is no readily accepted definition. Additionally, the odds are against them in the early stages of a court case. A plaintiff-friendly standard is employed by courts in evaluating attacks on pleadings, which means creditors benefit from the ambiguity in the

definition of the zone. Creditors are therefore focusing their initial arguments on "proving" the corporation is either insolvent or in the zone of insolvency so the court will grant them standing to make their breach of duty arguments.

While courts may ultimately find against the creditors, getting past the pleading stage will give them discovery, opening the directors and officers up to extensive litigation costs and the risk of adverse verdicts.

Because creditors are so focused on expanding the definition of the zone, it is important for directors and officers to be similarly focused on the definitions employed by courts in assessing when a company is insolvent. There are three financial tests commonly used for this assessment:

• The balance sheet test, which asks whether the value of the assets or the enterprise value of the corporation exceeds the liabilities.
• The cash flow test, which asks whether the corporation has sufficient cash flow to meet its fixed financial obligations as they become due.
• The "unreasonably small capital" test, which asks whether the corporation has sufficient capital to obtain or support financing for future operations.

Courts vary in which of these they use, and will generally look at multiple tests to get a full understanding of the corporation's financial picture.

While these three tests are used to assess a corporation's solvency, there is no "bright line" test for when it enters the zone of insolvency. The determination of whether a corporation is or was in the zone will generally turn on a fact-intensive inquiry into whether the directors and officers could, at the time of the alleged breach, have reasonably foreseen that the corporation would become insolvent.

Additionally, a court will commonly be employing these legal tests with the benefit of hindsight, which means they are of little practical use to officers and directors in the midst of a financial crisis. It is therefore advisable for directors to act defensively and look beyond book values when assessing the financial strength of their corporation.

The balance sheet test does not actually focus on the asset value reflected on the balance sheet, but rather looks to the fair valuation of those assets. Thus, certain balance sheet items that are based on historical values, such as goodwill, may have very little fair valuation at the point when the company is approaching insolvency. In such cases, those book values should not be used by directors and officers as the basis for their insolvency assessments.

It is easy for directors and officers to engage in denial as warning signs pop up, or to simply want to continue business as usual in the face of concerns. But it is important to remember that the creditors' goal is to make it to the discovery stage, where they will have the opportunity to catalog each and every breached financial covenant and each and every concern raised at a board meeting. At the first sign of financial instability, it is prudent for directors and officers to behave as though the corporation is in the zone and to consider the entire body of interests. This includes staying informed of all factors relevant to any of the corporation's major transactions, seeking the advice of reliable third party professionals, especially with regard to accounting and finance issues, and considering all options to preserve value.

Does entering the zone of insolvency create new fiduciary duties on the part of the directors and officers?

More than anything else, creditors are keeping apprised of the fast-changing case law that governs the fiduciary duties of directors and officers in the zone of insolvency. The initial wave of litigation stemmed from the now-infamous *Credit Lyonnais* decision by the influential Delaware courts. *Credit Lyonnais* held that 'at least where a corporation is operating in the vicinity of insolvency, a board of directors is not merely the agent of the residue risk bearers, but owes its duty to the corporate enterprise'. (*Credit Lyonnais Bank Nederland NV v Pathe Communications Corp*, No 12150, 1991 WL 277613, at *34 [Del Ch Dec 30, 1991].) This 'duty to the corporate enterprise' meant the board 'had an obligation to the community interest that sustained the corporation, to exercise judgment in an informed, good faith effort to maximize the corporation's long-term wealth creating capacity'. Thus, *Credit Lyonnais* introduced the idea that the 'vicinity of insolvency' could be a trigger for fiduciary obligations owed directly to creditors themselves.

Naturally creditors took this ruling and ran with it. A series of lawsuits were filed in bankruptcy cases, alleging that directors and officers had breached fiduciary duties they owed to creditors when the corporation was operating in the zone of insolvency. These cases focused on all of the issues discussed above, including arguments as to when the corporation entered the zone and which duties may have been breached in this zone.

For example, in *In re Hechinger Investment Co of*

Delaware, a creditors' committee sought to claim for alleged breaches of fiduciary duty by the directors and controlling shareholders in connection with a pre-bankruptcy leveraged buyout (274 BR 71 [D Del 2002]). The court dismissed the breach of fiduciary duty claims against the shareholders but permitted the claim against the directors to go forward, citing the 'duty to the corporate enterprise' laid out in *Credit Lyonnais* (*Id* 89-90).

In a similar, though somewhat more troubling decision, the bankruptcy court in *In re Healthco Intern Inc*, interpreting Delaware law, permitted a breach of fiduciary duty claim by a Chapter 7 trustee against directors for approving a pre-bankruptcy leveraged buyout (208 BR 288 [Bankr D Mass 1997]). While the court was dealing with a direct claim by the trustee on behalf of the bankrupt corporation, it nonetheless found that 'when a transaction renders a corporation insolvent, or brings it to the brink of insolvency, the rights of creditors become paramount'.

The premise of *Credit Lyonnais* may not have been as broad as these later cases interpreted it, however, as its primary rationale seemed to be that directors and officers should be mindful of the differing interests of creditors and shareholders, but that their duties ultimately went to the 'corporate enterprise'. While this was taken by many observers (and many litigious creditors) to mean that the fiduciary duties of directors and officers extend to creditors when in the vicinity of insolvency, it was never clear that this was the intended reach of the case.

No blank check

Indeed, creditors are beginning to realize that zone of insolvency fiduciary duty litigation may not be the blank check that some had initially assumed, as the Delaware courts have scaled back the reach of *Credit Lyonnais* significantly in recent years. In *Production Resources Group LLC v NCT Group Inc*, the court expressed doubt that the *Credit Lyonnais* opinion went so far as to permit a creditor to bring a direct action for breach of fiduciary duties (863 A2d 772, 788 [Del Ch 2004]). It reasoned that the opinion simply stood for the proposition that directors and officers could take into account the interests of the entire corporate enterprise, including the creditors.

Interestingly, the court seemed to take the position that *Credit Lyonnais* was actually a decision intended to help directors faced with derivative suits from shareholders: 'In other words, *Credit Lyonnais* provided a shield to directors from stockholders who claimed that the directors had a duty to undertake extreme risk so long as the company would not technically breach any legal obligations. By providing directors with this shield, creditors would derive a clear benefit because directors, it can be presumed, generally take seriously the company's duty to pay its bills as a first priority.' (*Production Resources Group LLC*, 863 A2d at 788.) Although the court did not rule out the possibility of a direct fiduciary duty claim by a creditor, it noted that directors would be protected from derivative claims by creditors in the same manner that they are protected from shareholder derivative claims — via the business judgment rule, which allowed directors to 'legitimately take into account the interests of creditors [and others who might be considered a part of the community of interests] in making decisions on behalf of an ailing company' (*Id*).

Delaware moved further still from the idea that the directors and officers owe fiduciary duties to creditors in *Trenwick America Lit Trust v Ernst & Young*, stating: 'The incantation of the word insolvency, or even more amorphously the words, zone of insolvency, should not declare open season on corporate fiduciaries. Directors are expected to seek profit for stockholders, even at the risk of failure' (906 A2d 168 [Del Ch 2006], *judgment aff'd*, 931 A2d 438 [Del 2007]).

Finally, in 2007, Delaware flatly rejected the notion that corporate actions in the zone of insolvency could result in a direct claim by creditors against the directors and officers. In *North American Catholic Educ Programming Found Inc v Gheewalla*, the court concluded that directors of a Delaware corporation operating in the zone owe their fiduciary duties to the *corporation and its shareholders*, and not to its creditors (930 A2d 92 [Del 2007]). The court went further, finding that those duties continue to be owed to the corporation itself even when it is *actually* insolvent. However, in the case of an insolvent corporation (and perhaps one in the zone), creditors, as economic stakeholders in the corporate enterprise, have standing to pursue derivative claims for directors' breaches of fiduciary duty to the corporation.

The court reasoned that 'the need for providing directors with definitive guidance compels us to hold that no direct claim for breach of fiduciary duties may be asserted by the creditors of a solvent corporation that is operating in the zone of insolvency. When a solvent corporation is navigating in the zone of insolvency, the focus for Delaware directors does not change: directors must

continue to discharge their fiduciary duties to the corporation and their shareholders' (*Gheewalla*, 930 A2d at 101).

With regard to directors of insolvent corporations, the court saw the inherent uncertainty in dealing with the conflicting interests of creditors and shareholders and found: 'To recognize a new right for creditors to bring direct fiduciary claims against those directors would create a conflict between those directors' duty to maximize the value of the insolvent corporation for the benefit of all of those having an interest in it, and the newly recognized direct fiduciary duty to individual creditors. Directors of insolvent corporations must retain the freedom to engage in vigorous, good faith negotiations with individual creditors for the benefit of the corporation' (*Gheewalla*, 930 A2d at 103).

Where are creditors going from here?
Gheewalla represented an important turn in the zone of insolvency saga, but it did not remove directors and officers from the sights of recovery-starved creditors. Under *Gheewalla*, creditors of a completely insolvent corporation certainly have standing to prosecute derivative claims against directors, and creditors of a corporation that is merely in the zone arguably have standing. In response, creditors of Delaware corporations have been forced to refocus and prioritize their resources on litigation determining when a corporation becomes insolvent and which parties have the right to pursue the derivative claims.

Despite *Gheewalla*, it appears these cases will continue unabated as creditors seek to recover, even on a derivative basis, some of their money from the officers and directors of the bankrupt corporation. These suits will raise a host of other issues, including disputes over the proper mechanics of a creditor derivative claim. *Gheewalla* did not cite any cases as examples of these claims, so it is not clear how such an action would play out.

There are several procedural requirements for a shareholder derivative suit, such as the precondition that shareholders make a demand on the corporation to bring the claim itself. Without guidance on whether similar requirements would be part of a creditor derivative suit or who could join in such an action, litigation will inevitably ensue.

Additionally, creditors have not lost their ability to assert other direct claims against the bankrupt corporation. The *Gheewalla* court specifically noted that creditors have other non-fiduciary protections, such as covenants, liens, the implied covenant of good faith, and the law of fraudulent conveyance. These protections allow creditors direct claims against a corporation for breach of contract and fraud, as well as for fraudulent transfers. It is likely that as the ability of creditors to pursue fiduciary duty claims against directors and officers diminishes, the amount of fraudulent conveyance litigation against them will increase.

If there is a chance a corporation may be in the zone of insolvency, directors and officers should be mindful that certain corporate actions could be viewed later as fraudulent conveyances. This is because when a company is insolvent or under-capitalized, transactions that yield less than a reasonably equivalent value can be attacked as fraudulent even where there is no fraudulent intent. Creditors have focused in particular on dividends, affiliate guaranties, asset transfers between affiliates, assets sold in private sales by owners under financial distress, and executive compensation.

Moreover, should an insolvent corporation file for Chapter 11 bankruptcy protection, the company becomes a debtor in possession, which means that its fiduciary duties run to all parties with an interest in the estate, including creditors. In Chapter 11, the duty of care expands to include a duty to preserve the property of the estate for the benefit of creditors and to refrain from any action that might damage the estate or hinder the reorganization. The duty of loyalty expands to include maximizing the value of the estate, in addition to the state common law duty to refrain from engaging in self-dealing or opportunistic behavior.

Finally, while Delaware has been the leading jurisdiction for fiduciary duty litigation, each state must interpret its own corporate law to determine whether creditors have standing to pursue fiduciary claims. Recent cases suggest that other states are still following Delaware's lead in this area. California, for example, recently ruled that directors of either an insolvent corporation or a corporation in the zone of insolvency clearly do not owe fiduciary duties to creditors. (*Berg & Berg Enterprises LLC v Boyle, et al*, 178 Cal App 4th 1020 [Cal App 2009].)

Together with the *Gheewalla* decision, *Berg* suggests the law may finally be moving towards clarity on a director's fiduciary duties to a corporation's constituents when the corporation is insolvent or in the zone. Nonetheless, directors and officers should be wary when dealing with non-Delaware law as many jurisdictions have not assessed the law in this area post-*Gheewalla*.

Conclusion

The trend in the case law in this area is clearly away from creditors having rights separate and distinct from the rights of the corporation itself. It appears that the Delaware courts have finally settled on a consistent position that fiduciary duties of directors and officers run primarily to the corporation and not to the creditors directly.

The current creditor response to this roadblock seems to be to focus on insolvency arguments so that they can achieve derivative standing to challenge the actions of directors and officers.

Clearly, and irrespective of the developing case law, creditors of struggling companies continue to remain laser-focused on directors and officers (and, perhaps more importantly, on the corporation's directors' and officers' liability policies) as a backstop source of recovery. It is vital, then, that directors and officers remain vigilant in monitoring their corporation's level of solvency, and wary when the corporation is operating in the zone of insolvency.

The author wishes to thank his Greenberg Traurig colleagues Beth Sickelka, Collin Williams and Professor G Ray Warner for their thoughtful input into this article.

12

Fiduciary duties: Timing considerations in equitizing excess debt

James F Conlan, Co-Chairman, Corporate Reorganization and Bankruptcy Group, and Jessica CK Boelter, Associate, Corporate Reorganization and Bankruptcy Group.

Sidley Austin LLP

Even as the US and the global economy return to growth mode after the recession of 2007-09, de-leveraging will likely continue for many years. The reason is straightforward: the sizing and pricing of the funded debt of many companies, on which their balance sheets were built, simply no longer exist. Consequently, many may need to "equitize" excess debt.

Brief history

Leading up to 2007, the sizing (as a multiple of EBITDA) of funded debt available in the capital markets to companies expanded significantly, while the pricing spread over LIBOR of such debt declined significantly. This expanded the market value of equity, as companies could grow return on equity by leveraging at sizing and pricing levels that were extremely favorable. Terms also loosened as lenders competed for loans by reducing covenants.

The parties lending in this highly leveraged, low-priced and covenant-lite environment included traditional institutions and also newer players in the debt markets (including senior debt markets). In addition to large commercial banks, hedge funds, private equity firms and other investment funds began appearing in the line-up of parties holding senior loan indebtedness. These new entrants changed the dynamic of corporate debt facilities: gone are the days of financial institutions holding loans from their inception to maturity; the new parties often have different motivations and exit strategies. They were, in most cases, more highly leveraged than traditional commercial banks, so they could make an adequate return with thinner pricing on loans. Moreover, the mechanisms and liquidity that existed in a robust capital markets system allowed them to focus on the market value of the paper in the near term, rather than long-term credit quality.

For many companies, an uncomfortable level of leverage became difficult to avoid. If the business failed to lever up, it would produce a return on equity that was poor relative to rivals, and the potential consequence of that included being purchased by a competitor or private equity sponsor that would lever it up anyway.

What next?

The board and management of well-run companies with substantial EBITDA, but with levels and pricing of funded debt that are likely unsustainable, must skillfully navigate the deleveraging waters to build a sustainable balance sheet. The sizing, pricing and covenants of their debt are likely unavailable in the market, so there is little or no ability to refinance the balance sheet on terms that work. Efforts to obtain waivers, or an extension of maturities, from existing lenders are often fruitless. Rather, senior lenders sometimes view defaults as an opportunity to "price up" to market and rinse off junior creditors and equity holders who are "out of the money" at post-recession sizing and pricing levels. So faced with maturities or the prospect of default in the not so distant future, the board and management will ask, "what then and what now?"

Although the situation may appear sustainable for several months or even years, the corporation may be confronted in the short term with a decision such as whether to make a principal or interest payment on junior debt when it is suspected that such debt may well be equitized or extinguished in a future restructuring. Assuming the company has the liquidity to pay (and the payment is permitted under its covenant-lite debt documents), the board may at first blush conclude it should do so. But, is this the best answer? Should the company make principal and/or interest payments to junior debt holders who may be partly or completely out of the money? Does the board have a "duty" to preserve value for the benefit of "in the money" creditors? Or does it have a duty to avoid the payment default in the hope that in the future the corporation can regain value and flexibility for junior creditors and equity, including via changes in the capital markets? Is the question one of duty or of what is the most appropriate?

These and similar questions have forced over-leveraged companies to consider whether it is best to take steps to equitize excess debt in advance (and, in some cases, well in advance) of scheduled maturity or future defaults. We will provide a framework for the board when evaluating these "timing" questions, and we will also explore the legal options and their attendant risks.

Fiduciary duties of the board of directors

With increasing frequency, courts have recognized that the fiduciary duties of a board of directors expand in scope as the corporation's financial condition changes from solvent to the zone of insolvency to insolvent. As we all know, solvency is an elusive concept. For example, at what earnings projection level and at what multiple of earnings should assets be valued?

In a solvent corporation, it is widely recognized that fiduciary duties require the directors to act in the best interests of the company and its shareholders. However, when the business begins to operate in the vicinity of insolvency, the rules become more complex.

It is generally accepted that when a corporation is clearly insolvent, its directors owe fiduciary duties to the creditors. In essence, when a corporation is insolvent, the directors are operating a business whose equitable owners are no longer shareholders but creditors. As residual claimants to an inadequate pool of assets, creditors become exposed to substantial risk as the insolvent entity goes forward, given that poor decisions by management may further erode the value of the remaining assets, thus leaving the corporation with even less capital to satisfy its debts in an ultimate dissolution. Under these circumstances, the elimination of the stockholders' interests in the firm and the increased risk to creditor recoveries is said to justify imposing fiduciary obligations towards the creditors.

There is a developing body of law, however, that suggests directors begin to owe duties to the 'community of interests that a corporation represents' (namely, both shareholders and creditors) when it is merely in the zone or vicinity of insolvency. Directors of highly leveraged companies often find themselves within this gray area. Although the business may be able, in the immediate term, to pay its debts as they become due (one test of solvency), it may also be faced with the probability that it will not be able to do so with maturities and defaults closing in and no clear exit in sight.

When are highly leveraged corporations insolvent or in the zone of insolvency?

Determining whether a corporation is insolvent, or merely in the zone of insolvency, is vital. Courts have generally rejected the argument that insolvency occurs only if a bankruptcy filing is imminent. Instead, they have held that the fiduciary duties to creditors arise upon "insolvency in fact". Two definitions of insolvency have been used by the courts: "equity" and "balance sheet". Under the equity definition, a corporation is insolvent when it is unable to pay its debts as they become due in the ordinary course of business. Under the balance sheet definition, insolvency occurs when liabilities exceed the reasonable market value of assets held. The "zone of insolvency" theory further complicates this issue.

In general, whether a highly leveraged corporation is insolvent or in the zone of insolvency must be evaluated on a case-by-case basis, but this judgment is not straightforward. For example, while a business with a high leverage to EBITDA ratio may in the short term have adequate liquidity to pay its debts as they become due, its liabilities may exceed its assets, rendering it insolvent on a balance sheet basis. Alternatively, if the corporation is facing impending maturities or defaults, whether it can indeed pay its debts as they become due may be questionable. Directors and officers who are in this gray area should be aware that there may be room for argument that the corporation is insolvent or within the zone of insolvency.

Once in that zone, the decision-making must shift so that the board is considering the corporation's "community of interests", which includes both creditors and shareholders.

The standard of conduct in the zone of insolvency

Directors of a corporation in the zone of insolvency must recognize that they are no longer merely agents of the shareholders. They also need to understand that actions taken during periods of financial distress will not only have a bearing on the eventual success or failure of the corporation, but may also be the focus of intense judicial scrutiny. Personal liability may result if the directors neglect their obligations to the entire "community of interests" or engage in overly risky transactions for the sole benefit of stockholders.

In general, the nature of the fiduciary duties owed to creditors is the same as those owed to shareholders: directors are required to act in the best interests of the corporation. Specifically, they must fulfill two primary obligations — duty of care and duty of loyalty— and in doing so they may rely on the business judgment rule. Under this, the standard of care owed to creditors is not any greater than that owed to shareholders — that of an ordinarily prudent person. Similarly, the duty of loyalty will be satisfied so long as business decisions are made by disinterested and independent directors in the good-faith exercise of their business judgment.

Case law indicates that in determining whether the duty of care has been met, courts will look for a record establishing that 'directors have informed themselves prior to making a business decision of all material information reasonably available to them'. This done, the directors must act with 'requisite care in the discharge of their duties' when making the decision. Procedural safeguards – such as numerous and extensive meetings, active discussion and deliberation, and consultation with professionals (lawyers, investment bankers, accountants) and experts – help establish such a record and are viewed favorably by the courts.

Directors also owe a duty of loyalty to the corporation. This requires that they act in good faith and in the honest belief that the action taken is in the best interests of the company. Stated differently, the duty of loyalty mandates that the best interests of the corporation take precedence over any interest that is possessed by a director but not shared by investors generally. In essence, the director must not benefit personally at the expense of others, and specific acts and transactions that go against the duty of loyalty include self-dealing transactions, excessive compensation, corporate waste, personal use of corporate assets, and use of corporate funds to perpetuate control. This duty also prohibits the usurping of corporate opportunities by directors.

The business judgment rule is often described as the most important protection available to corporate fiduciaries. It basically creates a judicial presumption that business decisions are made by disinterested directors on an informed basis and in the best interests of the company. This presumption protects any decision taken in good faith and that 'can be attributed to any rational business purpose'. Courts will refrain from second-guessing the wisdom of the decision itself.

In determining if a director is entitled to the protection of the business judgment rule, courts usually examine the following factors: (a) whether the director made a decision after making a reasonable effort to inform himself or herself of the relevant facts; (b) whether the director reasonably believed the action taken was in the best interests of the corporation and its community of interests; and (c) whether the director was disinterested.

Options and risks in a highly leveraged corporation

Each decision by the board of a highly leveraged company should be viewed through the prism of potential litigation by either shareholders or creditors. If the corporation will more likely than not need to address its indebtedness (de-leverage) at some point in the future through a restructuring, the risk of successful creditor litigation related to earlier action or inaction may be greater.

The junior debt payment

If the decision is whether to make the payment to junior creditors, the first, and most obvious, option is to make the payment. This strategy would of course avoid a default under the debt instrument at issue and likely cross-defaults or cross-acceleration under the corporation's other debt instruments. In addition, making the payment would maintain harmony among the stakeholders for the near term while the corporation assesses the changing economic and capital markets environment. Given this strategic breathing space, the business might ultimately find itself in a better position to maximize value for stakeholders.

But, although this option is tempting, is it the most appropriate from a fiduciary duty standpoint?

Is it the most likely to maximize value for stakeholders? The answer to the latter should drive the answer to the former. As discussed above, the corporation's debt level, pricing and covenant package may not be available under current or even foreseeable market conditions. Although the company may have the liquidity to make the impending payment, a debt-for-equity restructuring or Chapter 11 restructuring may be probable in the future. If the junior debt will likely be equitized or even extinguished in a restructuring, by making the payment now the company will in effect be remitting value to junior debt holders that arguably should be preserved for senior creditors in the capital structure. Due to the litigation risk, the board should inform itself of the options and prospects for amortizing and/or refinancing the corporation's indebtedness (discussed below). In addition, the board may wish to explore restructuring alternatives to address excess debt that the company may be unable to refinance or amortize.

Pre-emptive de-leveraging

As part of the exploration of de-leveraging, the corporation may look into a straightforward exchange of junior debt for equity. These offers have many advantages if they work. They can be quick and there is minimal business disruption because there is no court process. In addition, exchange offers typically present a low risk of litigation because they are, by definition, consensual.

There are, however, substantial hurdles, including the following: (1) if the company is publicly traded, exchange rules may require shareholder approval if equity will be diluted by more than 20 per cent; (2) the agreement of all the exchanging debt holders is required; (3) provisions in the company's senior debt documents must permit (not prohibit) the offer and exchange.

If an exchange offer is not possible, the board may instead consider options to extinguish or convert excess debt with court assistance. This type of restructuring may take several forms. For example, the corporation may consider a prepackaged or prenegotiated Chapter 11 filing if the company believes it can garner the support of at least two thirds in amount and more than one half in number (ie, less than 100 per cent) of voting debt holders who will be impaired under the plan of reorganization. Prepackaged or prenegotiated Chapter 11 cases have many of the same advantages as exchange offers and the added

benefit of allowing the requisite majority of debt holders to force any holdouts from the exchange offer to come along.

As a practical matter, "pre-emptive debt equitization" is likely to take the form of an exchange offer or a prepackaged or prearranged Chapter 11, because it is unlikely that a traditional Chapter 11 with its attendant risks will be justified in order to address, pre-emptively, what appears to be excess debt. That said, even unsuccessful efforts to achieve an exchange offer — and if that fails a prepackaged or prearranged Chapter 11 — should fill the time between a maturity or default that is on the horizon, and a maturity or default that is on top of the company. That time and effort will not have been wasted because the pre-emptive debt equitization efforts should benefit the corporation in achieving a more consensual resolution in a traditional Chapter 11 should the pre-emptive efforts fail. Moreover, the fact that the board is exploring all alternatives on a fully informed basis should leave the board in a better position regardless of the outcome.

Conclusion

For a variety of reasons, economic models did not predict what began to happen in early 2007 and accelerated through 2007 and 2008. Sizing contracted to levels far below historical norms, and pricing spreads expanded to levels far beyond historical norms. While sizing and pricing have returned to more favorable levels, it is unlikely they will return to the levels seen in early 2007.

As a result, many large companies will have to de-leverage. In most cases, the best approach will be pre-emptive exploration of options to equitize excess debt. Those options will include exchange offers, and if that cannot be achieved, a prepackaged or prearranged Chapter 11.

In weighing the available options, directors must be aware of their fiduciary duties, and more particularly, how those duties change when a corporation is insolvent or teetering on the edge of insolvency. The constituencies to whom the directors' duties are owed may have grown to include a larger community of interests. As such, directors should review all available information about the proposed transaction and engage outside experts to help them choose a prudent course of action to better insulate themselves from potential liability.

13

Driving restructuring: The US government takes a lead role in bankruptcy

John J Rapisardi,
Co-Chairman of the Financial
Restructuring Department,
**Cadwalader, Wickersham
& Taft LLP**

Until very recently, the American government has seldom played a key role in major bankruptcy cases. The United States Trustee program appears in every bankruptcy case and is charged with promoting the efficiency and integrity of the process, including enforcing bankruptcy laws and providing oversight, and US attorneys often appear on behalf of the Internal Revenue Service or Environmental Protection Agency in large bankruptcies. However, while these agencies often help to shape plans of reorganization or liquidation, they seldom, if ever, drive the case toward a particular outcome. Historically, the US government has also played a limited role in corporate restructurings.

Prior to 2008, the government had helped to bail out a handful of corporate entities, including: the Penn Central Railroad in the early 1970s (culminating in a reorganization through bankruptcy), Chrysler in the early 1980s, and the Savings and Loans bailouts of the late 1980s and early 1990s. In the early 2000s, in the aftermath of the terrorist attacks of 2001, Congress approved a Loan Guarantee Program of up to $10 billion, under the Air Transportation Safety and System Stabilization Act, to help support the nation's airlines.

The government intervenes

However, starting with the failure of Bear Stearns in the spring of 2008, the Bush administration took an active role in protecting significant financial entities. The Federal Reserve Bank of New York provided $30 billion in financing to safeguard JP Morgan Chase against certain of Bear's toxic assets and to facilitate JP Morgan's purchase of the bank when Bear's collapse was imminent. In early September 2008, Congress placed Fannie Mae and Freddie Mac under the conservatorship of the Federal Housing Finance Agency and began investing the first portion of hundreds of billions of dollars to support the housing finance entities.

Shortly thereafter, Lehman Brothers filed for bankruptcy when the government failed to provide any funding to enable survival. But the next month, as the stock market collapsed, Congress approved the Emergency Economic Stabilization Act of 2008 (EESA), creating the Troubled Asset Relief Program (TARP) through which the US Treasury was authorized to invest up to $700 billion in troubled assets. Since then, a number of schemes have been created through TARP, including the Term Asset-Based Securities Loan Facility (TALF); the Capital Purchase Program — where the Treasury bought preferred stock in a number of purportedly healthy banks; the Community Banking Program; direct loans to Citibank, AIG, Bank of America and other large banks; and, most notably, the Automotive Industry Financing Program, through which the Treasury invested in General Motors, the General Motors Acceptance Corporation (GMAC), Chrysler and Chrysler Financial.

The Bush administration made initial loans to GM, Chrysler and Chrysler Financial in December 2008 and January 2009. As a condition of these loans, the Treasury required that GM and Chrysler propose viable plans for restructuring. After reviewing those plans, the Obama administration deemed both proposals flawed and, as a condition of further funding, pushed the companies to consider more aggressive steps.

In a speech to the nation on March 30, 2009, President Obama expressed the government's rationale for this decision: 'We cannot continue to excuse poor decisions. We cannot make the survival of our auto industry dependent on an unending flow of taxpayer dollars. These companies — and this industry — must ultimately stand on their own, not as wards of the state... And that's why the federal government provided General Motors and Chrysler with emergency loans to prevent their sudden collapse at the end of last year — only on the condition that they would develop plans to restructure.' From that date, GM and Chrysler worked aggressively to do just that. They co-ordinated with their only available source of funding: the US Treasury.

The auto manufacturers

For more than a century, the American automakers provided employment to countless individuals, served as the foundation for communities across the US, and defined America's industrial identity. Over the course of its storied existence, the sector weathered many storms, often in challenging economic climates. However, the global economic crisis that began in late 2007 pushed the American automakers to the brink of collapse, threatening not only their own survival but also the livelihood of hundreds of thousands of American workers, the future of innumerable suppliers and dealers, and ultimately, the American economy as a whole.

Amid rising gas prices, falling consumer demand and nearly frozen capital markets, Chrysler and General Motors struggled to keep pace with their leaner, more cost-efficient foreign competitors. The companies were saddled with high labor and legacy union costs and, given the expected sales volumes, were operating well above required capacity. Despite efforts to trim operations and conserve cash, the liquidity problems facing Chrysler and GM continued to grow as consumer demand spiraled downward and financial forecasts depicted an increasingly grim future for the automakers. In response, the automakers approached the US government for a bailout in the fall of 2008. In late December that same year, the outgoing Bush administration granted Chrysler and GM $17.4 billion in loans to keep them afloat long enough for the Obama administration to determine the best course of action.

In turn, the Obama administration created the Presidential Task Force on the Auto Industry, a cabinet-level group led by the Treasury Secretary, Timothy Geithner, and National Economic Council Director, Lawrence Summers. Ron Bloom, a former investment banker at Lazard and official for the United Steelworkers of America, served as the Treasury's senior advisor on the auto industry. A team of distinguished individuals from the private sector was tasked with implementing the policies of the task force, with Steven Rattner, a former investment banker at Quadrangle Group, leading the team and Harry Wilson, a former hedge fund manager at Silver Point Capital, and Matthew Feldman, a former restructuring partner at Willkie Farr & Gallagher, serving as senior members. In addition to providing direct loans to Chrysler and GM, the government, through the task force, implemented various programs to support and stabilize the domestic automotive industry, including providing credit support for receivables issued by certain companies and support for customer warranties.

GM and Chrysler approached the government for additional assistance starting in late 2008. The Treasury lent them $15.4 billion and $3 billion respectively in January 2009, on the condition that both submitted proposals setting forth their plans to restructure and achieve long-term viability. Once these proposals had been received, however, it was determined that neither would accomplish meaningful progress toward long-term viability. On March 30, 2009, President Obama announced that the auto task force had rejected Chrysler's and GM's proposals, and stated that the government's continued assistance was conditional upon each automaker effectuating a successful restructuring, or otherwise filing for bankruptcy protection, within the government's stated timeframe: May 1, 2009 for Chrysler, and June 1, 2009 for GM.

The President described how serious the situation was when he stated: 'It will come as no surprise that some Americans who have suffered most during this recession have been those in the auto industry and those working for companies that support it. Over the past year, our auto industry has shed over 400,000 jobs... We cannot, and must not, and we will not let our auto industry simply vanish.'

In the days and weeks that followed the President's remarks, the auto task force, Chrysler, GM and their respective teams of advisors continued extensive due diligence on the possibility of an out-of-court restructuring.

However, as the likelihood of this being accomplished faded, the auto task force became increasingly concerned about Chrysler and GM's ability to survive a bankruptcy. Given the uncertainties associated with a traditional Chapter 11 — including the length of time it could take the automakers to emerge from bankruptcy, if at all — serious questions were raised as to whether consumer confidence could withstand the vagaries of the process.

To address this contingency, the auto task force developed a strategy for the fastest track through Chapter 11. It was a plan that would become the driving force behind the Chrysler and GM bankruptcy cases — one in which each company would sell substantially all of its core operational assets to a new entity that would continue the tradition of manufacturing American automobiles, albeit on a smaller, more streamlined scale. President Obama described it as a 'quick rinse' for GM and Chrysler through the bankruptcy courts.

To that end, and in an effort to garner the critical support of their respective stakeholders, the automakers began negotiating in earnest on the contours of the contemplated asset sales.

Chrysler

On April 30, 2009 — after Chrysler had failed to obtain the backing it needed from secured lenders to achieve a consensual restructuring within the government's timeframe — President Obama described the company's economic situation as promising. He also spoke of 'a partnership that will give Chrysler a chance not only to survive, but to thrive in a global auto industry'. Following up on preliminary negotiations that had taken place prior to the provision of government funding, Chrysler had worked to negotiate a strategic alliance with Fiat SpA, an Italian automaker with expertise in smaller, more fuel-efficient vehicles. In addition, it had actively sought a new collective bargaining relationship with the United Auto Workers (UAW) union to establish a fresh wage structure as well as a new voluntary employees' benefit association (VEBA) structure to fund legacy healthcare obligations to retirees.

On that same day, April 30, Chrysler and 24 of its affiliates filed for Chapter 11 protection in the Southern District of New York. The filing marked the first bankruptcy by a major US automobile manufacturer, but President Obama gave an assurance that the process would be 'quick' and 'controlled'.

Shortly thereafter, Chrysler sought the bankruptcy court's approval to sell substantially all of its assets to New Chrysler, a newly created company that would be owned by Fiat, the governments of the Unites States and Canada, and a VEBA controlled by the UAW. In exchange, to create a new VEBA structure that would ensure UAW workers manned New Chrysler's factories, the US Treasury and Canada agreed to lend New Chrysler $2 billion, which would be used to purchase Chrysler's assets, and Fiat agreed to provide new technology and new management for the creation of smaller, more fuel-efficient vehicles.

Although Chrysler had secured the consent of most of its key constituents prior to filing for bankruptcy, it faced strong opposition from the outset of the case, receiving over 300 objections to the proposed asset sale. Bankruptcy Judge Arthur J Gonzalez conducted a three-day evidentiary hearing on Chrysler's sale motion from May 27 through May 29, with 16 witnesses and over 40 hours of testimony. The objecting parties — most notably certain Indiana pension funds holding a small amount of Chrysler's secured debt — argued, among other things, that the proposed sale constituted an illegal *sub rosa* plan of reorganization and violated the absolute priority rule because the sale gave value to unsecured creditors (for example, the UAW through the VEBA's receipt of an ownership interest in New Chrysler) without paying off Chrysler's secured debt in full. Additionally, certain tort and consumer victims objected to Chrysler's effort to sell the assets free and clear of personal injury and wrongful death claims, including claims relating to successor liability, asserting that such claims were not 'interests in property' as required by Section 363(f) of the Bankruptcy Code. Finally, a group of Chrysler dealers objected to the sale on the grounds that it was a *sub rosa* plan.

Late in the evening on May 31, 2009, just hours before General Motors filed for bankruptcy, Judge Gonzalez entered an opinion granting Chrysler's motion to sell substantially all of its assets and dismissing virtually all of the objections. Judge Gonzalez held that 'approval of the debtor's proposed sale of assets is necessary to preserve some portion of the going concern value of the Chrysler business and to maximize the value of the debtor's estates'. The Bankruptcy Court stayed the sale for several days to permit appeals and a number of parties did so, including the Indiana funds. Pursuant to 28 United States Code Section 157, the Second Circuit Court of Appeals heard the appeal on direct review, rather than having the district court for the Southern District of New York hear it first.

After nearly two hours of oral argument, the Second Circuit, in a seldom if ever-seen action, ruled from the bench and upheld the bankruptcy court's ruling in all respects. However, it did not issue a written opinion until nearly two months later, on August 5, 2009.

Following the ruling from the bench, the Indiana funds moved for a stay pending appeal from the US Supreme Court, which, after granting a brief stay to consider the issues, unanimously terminated the stay on June 8. The Chrysler sale closed on June 9, 2009, exactly 42 days after Chrysler had filed for bankruptcy.

General Motors

As the Chrysler bankruptcy reached its crescendo, GM was operating on a parallel track. In May 2009, the company worked to restructure through an out-of-court bond exchange offer. The offer came up far short.

Having failed to obtain the requisite number of tenders, GM and three of its affiliates filed for Chapter 11 protection in the Southern District of New York on June 1, 2009, becoming the second-largest industrial bankruptcy behind WorldCom's filing in 2002. Shortly thereafter, GM sought the bankruptcy court's approval to sell substantially all of its assets to New GM, a newly created entity that would be owned by the governments of the United States and Canada, and by a VEBA controlled by the UAW.

Later that same day, President Obama told the nation that the recent success of Chrysler's asset sale was evidence that a 'surgical bankruptcy' was indeed possible. In addressing concerns on the contemplated ownership of New GM, he stated that the government had 'no interest in running [New] GM' and that its ownership of 'large stakes in private companies' was necessary for the 'simple and compelling reason that [such companies'] survival and the success of our overall economy depend on it'.

Objectors to the proposed sale included a group of GM bondholders speaking for approximately 0.01 per cent of GM's total $27 billion bond debt, a *pro se* litigant holding approximately $5 million in GM bonds, and various tort, consumer and asbestos victims. Bankruptcy Judge Robert E Gerber conducted a three-day evidentiary hearing, from June 29 through July 1, during which the objecting parties raised arguments similar to those aired in *Chrysler* —arguing, among other things,

that the government's pre-petition loans to GM should be recharacterized as equity, or alternatively, subject to equitable subordination.

On July 5, Judge Gerber issued an opinion granting GM's motion to sell substantially all of its assets to New GM. Following the Chrysler decision, he held: '*Chrysler* is not distinguishable in any legally cognizable respect. On this issue, it is not just that the court feels that it should follow *Chrysler*. It must follow *Chrysler*. The Second Circuit's *Chrysler* affirmance, even if reduced solely to affirmance of the judgment, is controlling authority.'

The bankruptcy court again stayed the effectiveness of the sale order for several days to permit appeals. Several parties requested that the district court extend the stay but it declined to do so, and on July 10, 2009, the GM sale closed — a mere 41 days after the company had filed for Chapter 11 protection.

Analysis of Chrysler and GM sale opinions

Although the facts of Chrysler's and GM's bankruptcy cases are extraordinary, the law arising from such cases is, in large part, an extension of well-established precedent in the Second Circuit and the Southern District of New York. Set out below is a summary of the key issues from the Chrysler and GM sale opinions.

The sale did not constitute an impermissible 'sub rosa' plan

Creditors in both cases objected that the proposed sales constituted an improper *sub rosa* plan of reorganization. An asset sale pursuant to Section 363 of the Bankruptcy Code may be objectionable if, for example, the proposed transaction dictates the terms of a future plan, places restrictions on parties' ability to exercise confirmation rights, such as voting on a future plan, or distributes the proceeds among different classes of creditors. The Second Circuit held that the Chrysler sale did not constitute an impermissible *sub rosa* plan 'because it [did] not specifically "dictate" or "arrange" *ex ante*, by contract the terms of any subsequent plan'. Further, it dismissed the Indiana funds' contention that the sale of substantially all assets was dispositive on the *sub rosa* question, stating that the 'size of the transaction, and the residuum of corporate assets, is, under our precedent, just one consideration for the exercise of discretion by the bankruptcy judges, along with an open-ended list of other salient factors'.

The court also rejected the argument that the proposed sale violated the absolute priority rule, holding that the Chrysler deal in no way upset the priority between creditors, and affirmed Judge Gonzalez's findings that 'not one penny of value of the debtor's assets is going to anyone other than the [secured creditors]'.

Similarly, Judge Gerber held that the GM sale did not amount to a *sub rosa* plan, finding that the proposal did not attempt to dictate or restructure the rights of GM's creditors. Rather, in the bankruptcy court's opinion, the sale 'merely brings in value' and GM's creditors 'will thereafter share in that value pursuant to a Chapter 11 plan subject to confirmation by the court'.

A debtor may sell free and clear of future claims

On this issue, in the Chrysler case, the Second Circuit affirmed the decision of the bankruptcy court but declined to 'delineate the scope of the bankruptcy court's authority to extinguish future claims, until such time as we are presented with an actual claim for injury… that is cognizable under state successor liability law'. The Second Circuit upheld Judge Gonzalez's ruling that 'tort claims are interests in property such that they are extinguished by a free and clear sale under Section 363(f)(5) and are therefore extinguished by the [sale]'.

In the GM case, Judge Gerber considered the applicable case law on successor liability and noted that while national law was split in this area, the case law in the Second Circuit and the Southern District of New York was not. Citing principles of *stare decisis* and the fact that the 'claims sought to be preserved here are identical to those in *Chrysler*', he held that GM could sell its assets free and clear of successor liability claims.

Aftermath of the Chrysler and GM sale opinions

In December 2009, the Supreme Court granted the Indiana funds' petition for writ of certiorari, and citing *United States v. Munsingwear Inc, 340 US 36 (1950)*, vacated the Second Circuit Court of Appeal's judgment in *Chrysler* and remanded the case to the Second Circuit with instructions to dismiss the appeal as moot, which it did in January 2010.

At the time of writing, the GM sale remained subject to several appeals. On April 13, 2010, the district court for the Southern District of New York ruled on the first of these, denying a request from certain tort claimants to hold that the sale was not made free and clear of those claims. The district court dismissed the appeal as moot. Subsequently, the district court for the Southern District of New

York affirmed the sale over the appeal of a *pro se* GM bondholder on April 27, 2010.

Delphi

As in GM and Chrysler, the auto task force played a significant role in the sale of the assets of Delphi, a key supplier to GM. This was a move that would ensure the continued flow of essential parts to global automakers, particularly to GM, and facilitate Delphi's emergence from bankruptcy.

Delphi had filed for Chapter 11 protection in 2005 amidst rising labor and raw material costs, but the case languished for several years. In January 2008, the bankruptcy court for the Southern District of New York confirmed a plan of reorganization filed by Delphi and its affiliated debtors. Then, however, investors backed out of a commitment to provide the exit financing necessary for the implementation of the plan.

With the company's ability to reorganize — and, consequently, to provide an uninterrupted supply of critical parts to GM — in serious jeopardy, it focused on crafting an amended plan of reorganization centered on the sale of substantially all of its assets.

During the spring of 2009, the auto task force worked closely with Delphi, counsel for GM and an interested third party to structure a transaction in which assets vital to GM's operations would be sold directly to GM, and certain other assets would be sold to the interested third party.

After the bankruptcy court mandated that Delphi test this proposed sale against competing offers through a public auction, the company's post-petition lenders proposed a sale pursuant to which the lenders would credit bid for Delphi's assets and GM would acquire substantially the same assets as contemplated under the first proposal presented to the court.

Ultimately, the bid submitted by Delphi's post-petition lenders prevailed. On July 30, 2009, the bankruptcy court approved the company's request to amend its plan and consummate the sale, and GM, with financing provided by the Treasury, acquired key assets from Delphi that ensured the continued production of automobiles.

GMAC and Chrysler Financial Services

GM formed GMAC in 1919 as its automotive finance subsidiary, and Chrysler formed the Chrysler Credit Corporation, the predecessor to Chrysler Financial Services, in 1964. Over many decades, these companies fueled the sales, both wholesale and retail, of GM and Chrysler's vehicles and were critical to the business operations of the auto manufacturers. But as the industry declined in 2008 and 2009, they, like their parent companies, were suffering from the contraction in the capital markets.

GMAC

In December 2008, attempting to obtain relief from the considerable constraints on its operations, GMAC sought approval from the Federal Reserve to convert into a bank holding company. On December 24, 2008, the application was approved and GMAC became eligible for TARP assistance. As a result, the US government invested $5 billion in the company in exchange for certain preferred stock and warrants. GMAC raised another $2 billion by converting into equity $750 million of the existing equity held by GM and Cerberus Capital Management, the private equity firm, in GMAC, and conducting a rights offering through which GM purchased $884 million and investors led by Cerberus purchased $366 million of the new equity.

Pursuant to the Obama administration's Supervisory Capital Assessment Program, GMAC underwent a "stress test" that required it to raise $13.1 billion of new capital by November 9, 2009. Unable to achieve this through third-party sources, GMAC received $7.5 billion from the Treasury on May 21, 2009 and an additional $3.8 billion on December 30, 2009. To date, the company has received $17.2 billion in TARP support. By converting certain preferred equity into common stock, the Treasury acquired a 56.3 per cent interest in GMAC's common equity. It also appointed two directors to GMAC's nine-member board.

Chrysler Financial Services

In January 2009, Chrysler Financial obtained a TARP loan in the principal amount of $1.5 billion — funds that were designated for consumer financing in auto transactions. There were various challenges to the company's continued viability, among them that $20.4 billion of conduit financing was scheduled to terminate in July 2009. Given the subsequent recognition that Chrysler could not survive as a standalone entity and needed to pursue a business alliance with Fiat, it became apparent that Chrysler Financial would be unable to continue as a separate financial services company without a substantial capital infusion.

In late April 2009, to ensure continued auto financing for its parent company and its customers, Chrysler Financial agreed in principle to conduct an orderly transition of Chrysler's automotive floorplan financing to GMAC. On May 1, 2009, Chrysler Financial announced that it would no longer provide wholesale or retail financing to the debtor's dealers and customers. On May 14, 2009, Chrysler received bankruptcy court approval for the transition.

Chrysler Financial repaid its TARP loan in July 2009 with funds raised through an AAA-rated TALF securitization. At present, it is engaged in providing consumer financing and dealer insurance products, and also services its $26 billion portfolio. GMAC has become the preferred provider of consumer and dealer financing for Chrysler and, of course, GM. As its current capitalization exceeds historical industry averages, it is now positioned to pursue funding from third-party sources.

CIT Group

To provide struggling banks and financial institutions with much-needed stability and liquidity, the Treasury instituted the Capital Purchase Program (CPP), pursuant to TARP, in October 2008 and began investing in a number of financial organizations. Under the CPP, created with the goal of shoring up the balance sheets of supposedly healthy banks, the Treasury has invested approximately $204 billion in around 700 recipients. In exchange, it has received preferred stock and warrants in each.

In December 2008, as part of this program, the Treasury invested $2.3 billion in CIT Group, a major provider of middle-market and small business lending. Despite this infusion of capital, CIT struggled through the first half of 2009 and was forced to contemplate ways to restructure and ensure its survival. In the summer of 2009, the company launched an exchange offer coupled with a proposed prepackaged bankruptcy if it failed to secure the necessary consents for a consensual exchange. After the offer failed, CIT filed for the prepackaged bankruptcy in the Southern District of New York on November 1, 2010 — and emerged from bankruptcy on December 8, 2010.

Under the plan of reorganization, the Treasury received little recovery for its preferred stock and warrants. Specifically, it received 60-day contingent value rights that would have provided recoveries to the Treasury and other preferred shareholders only in the event that the value of CIT's post-bankruptcy equity was, 60 days after emergence, trading at a high enough price.

After 60 days, CIT's stock price had not sufficiently increased, and the contingent value rights provided no recovery. Despite this, the Treasury did not challenge the proposed plan in bankruptcy or otherwise litigate its claim.

Conclusion

The government's role in the GM and Chrysler bankruptcies, as well as the restructuring of a number of other entities, has been controversial. Nevertheless, the successful outcomes with both automakers have demonstrated that the government can be a key player in bankruptcies. However, these bankruptcies presented unique circumstances that may not be seen again in the near future. Indeed, the government has returned to its typical low profile, and has not taken a major role in any pending bankruptcy (most notably CIT). Moreover, it is working aggressively to unwind many of the investments of the 2008-09 period.

For example, Chrysler Financial repaid its TARP loan in 2009, and GM repaid its government loans in 2010. GM also plans to implement an initial public offering and redeem the government's preferred and common equity investments in the very near term. AIG, Bank of America, Citibank and other large banks have paid back, or are working to pay back, much of their loans; and the government has sold many of the warrants that it received during some of the restructuring transactions. Perhaps the age of government intervention in corporate restructurings is coming to a close.

Douglas S Mintz and Leslie W Chervokas, Special Counsel in Cadwalader's Financial Restructuring Department, and Audrey J Aden and Joseph V Zujkowski, associates in the firm's Financial Restructuring Department, assisted in the preparation of this article.

14

White-collar crime: The law enforcement agenda

John K Carroll, Partner, White Collar Crime and Regulatory Enforcement, and Richard Marmaro, Partner, Litigation, SEC Enforcement and White Collar Criminal Defense.

Skadden, Arps, Slate, Meagher & Flom LLP

The reckoning is upon us. As the financial markets develop more confidence and continue their recovery, the Department of Justice (DOJ) and Securities and Exchange Commission (SEC) should be concluding some of their investigations into the causes of the 2007-09 financial crisis. In a speech on August 5, 2009, Robert Khuzami, the director of the SEC's enforcement division, acknowledged that not 'every loss suffered in the credit crisis was a fraud or nondisclosure appropriately addressed by an SEC enforcement action. There was a great deal of inappropriate risk-taking, lack of understanding and poor decision-making that falls short of actionable misconduct. But where there was fraud and wrongdoing and investors suffered, we will take action.'

Following several years of complex investigations, the DOJ and the SEC must now strike that balance. We anticipate that they will take a hard line and actions that attempt to apportion blame for the crisis.

At the same time, we expect that the DOJ and the SEC will find themselves under the microscope. It is hard to overstate the effect of the Madoff scandal on the public's confidence in whether financial regulators are up to the task of policing the markets. The process of restoring that confidence faced a serious setback with the March 2010 release of the bankruptcy examiner's report on Lehman Brothers. The report details how the SEC and Federal Reserve Bank were embedded within the company, had access to its books and records and yet failed to detect that Lehman was engaged in questionable accounting practices. Further, a series of high-profile losses in criminal trials has raised questions about the DOJ.

Both the DOJ and the SEC have reacted to these criticisms by instituting structural and policy changes. Now the law enforcement agencies will be looking over their shoulders as they pursue their prosecutorial and regulatory agendas.

Both the culmination of the credit crisis investigations and the institutional criticism of the DOJ and SEC lead us to expect that we are migrating to an environment of aggressive law enforcement. The enforcers will look for corporate executives to blame and will try to prove to Congress and the public that they are up to the task of policing sophisticated financial markets.

The government's reaction to the sub-prime loan crisis

The collapse of the sub-prime mortgage industry triggered home foreclosures across the United States and was a cause of the international banking crisis and the global recession. While Wall Street executives have made a convenient target for criticism, there is plenty of blame to go around.

Some lenders may have pushed complex products on unsophisticated borrowers, only to shift the risk to holders of collateralized debt obligations (sub-prime loans packaged and sold on the secondary market by investment banks). But some borrowers may have falsified loan applications (some of which required little income verification) and home appraisals to manipulate loan-to-value ratios. Meanwhile the federal government, seeking to expand homeownership, facilitated the making of loans to less qualified borrowers by pressuring banks to lower underwriting standards. And regulatory agencies, particularly the SEC, did not provide adequate oversight of the market for complicated credit derivatives, including mortgage-backed securities.

In moving forward, law makers and regulators have instituted a number of reforms, including prohibitions on deceptive sub-prime mortgage practices, more stringent income-verification requirements for home loans, and increased scrutiny of credit rating agencies (which had overrated the quality of mortgage-backed securities). And still more measures are in the works.

Looking backward, law enforcement has been searching for someone to hold responsible for what happened. To that end, the DOJ and SEC have opened dozens of investigations into practices relating to sub-prime lending and mortgage securities. So far, however, only a small number of cases have been filed against corporations and senior executives, perhaps because of the nature of the sub-prime business, the complexity of the financial instruments at issue, and the part played by macro-economic factors in the industry meltdown.[1]

For example, sub-prime lenders, by their very nature, made loans to less creditworthy individuals — those who could not get loans from more traditional lenders. Public companies engaged in sub-prime lending generally made extensive disclosures on the credit characteristics of their borrowers, the nature of their loan products, and the general risks facing their businesses and the industry. Moreover, the credit characteristics of their borrowers did not materially change; rather, the world around them changed. A dramatic decline in real estate values floored many borrowers, particularly those who had adjustable-rate mortgages.

The scope of lenders' disclosures, as well as the external market factors that worked to bring down the entire industry, present hurdles to law enforcement in mounting cases based on an alleged failure to disclose the inherent risks.

But when those agencies burrow into high-priority issues, criminal prosecutions and SEC actions are likely to follow. And the financial crisis is no exception, as evidenced by the highly publicized action brought by the SEC against banking giant Goldman Sachs in April 2010. Goldman was charged with failing to disclose that the hedge fund that helped select sub-prime mortgage-backed securities to form one of the bank's collateralized debt obligation (CDO) products had shorted those securities, essentially betting that they would default. We expect that law enforcement will continue to attack the financial crisis on a broad front, taking in disclosure and accounting issues, as well as insider trading.[2]

Prosecutions: failures and successes
The DOJ's first effort to prosecute individuals for credit-crisis crimes was *United States v Cioffi*. There, the DOJ charged two former Bear Stearns employees, who managed a hedge fund portfolio including collateralized debt obligations, with conspiracy to commit securities and wire fraud. The government's case hinged on emails between the employees that arguably suggested a negative outlook on the collateralized-debt market, which the government alleged was concealed from investors. In November 2009, a jury acquitted both defendants of all charges. Several jurors commented after the trial that the government had failed to prove its case beyond reasonable doubt. As reported in *The Wall Street Journal* on November 12, 2009, one juror remarked: 'Just because you're the captain of a ship and it gets hit doesn't mean you should be blamed.'

No doubt the perfect storm of external, macro-economic factors that overwhelmed the sub-prime industry will be an oft-repeated theme in defense of industry players.

Other prosecutions and enforcement actions have been more successful. In February 2010, the SEC announced that State Street Bank and Trust Company would pay in excess of $300 million in fines because it led investors to believe it was operating a diversified money market portfolio, when in fact it was almost entirely invested in sub-prime products.

Similarly, in April 2009, the SEC entered into a $2.5 million settlement with Michael Strauss, former CEO of the sub-prime lending company American Home Mortgage Investment Corporation. The SEC alleged that Strauss and the company's former CFO and controller had intentionally committed several accounting improprieties, including mis-stating loan reserves to turn a loss into a profit.

In May 2009, the SEC brought fraud charges against several entities and individuals who operated the Reserve Primary Fund, for failing to disclose the money market fund's sensitivity to the performance of the now-defunct Lehman Brothers. The SEC's primary goal in bringing the action was to secure a liquidation plan that would permit unpaid investors to tap into a $3.5 billion pot, set aside by the Reserve to cover the cost of litigating cases brought against the Reserve and officers and directors of Reserve entities. That plan was approved by a judge in the Southern District of New York in November 2009.

On April 16, 2010, the SEC filed securities fraud charges against Goldman Sachs & Co for making material mis-statements and omissions in connection with a sub-prime mortgage product that Goldman structured and marketed to investors. Among other things, the SEC alleged that Goldman failed to inform investors that hedge fund Paulson & Co Inc played a role in the portfolio selection process, and that Paulson's economic interests were adverse to the portfolio's investors. On July 15, 2010, the SEC announced that it had reached an agreement with Goldman to settle the charges. Specifically, Goldman agreed to pay a penalty of $550 million. Of that amount, $250 million will be distributed to investors, and $300 million will be paid to the US Treasury. The settlement is subject to approval by the Hon Barbara S Jones, United States District Court Judge for the Southern District of New York. If approved, the $550 million settlement will be the largest penalty ever assessed by the SEC against a financial services firm.

We expect that the pace of prosecutions and SEC civil actions will pick up as law enforcement continues to dig its heels into the financial crisis and improves its understanding of the nature of the sub-prime industry.

The FCPA: prohibitions and penalties

The Foreign Corrupt Practices Act (FCPA) prohibits bribes to foreign officials and requires companies to implement accounting procedures in compliance with the Act. In general, a corporation or person cannot pay money or anything "of value" to a "foreign official" to garner favor from a foreign government. The regulatory framework also requires companies to implement certain accounting procedures prescribed by statute to track any potentially problematic payments.

In recent years, the government has shown an increased commitment to prosecuting FCPA violations — a trend we expect to continue — with companies facing the largest assessment of criminal and civil penalties ever imposed under the Act. For example, BAE Systems, a defense contractor, pled guilty in March 2010 to making false statements concerning its FCPA compliance. A federal judge imposed, among other things, a $400 million

criminal fine on the company. (Only two other fines outpaced BAE's: Siemens AG's $800 million settlement with the SEC in 2008, and Kellogg Brown & Root and Halliburton's settlement with the SEC and DOJ in 2009 for $579 million.)

In April 2010, a federal court approved civil SEC and criminal DOJ FCPA settlements with Daimler AG, including criminal fines totaling $93.6 million and civil disgorgement of $91.4 million. Daimler itself was not charged with anti-bribery violations, and resolved the DOJ's investigation by means of a two-year deferred prosecution agreement based on books and records charges.

The DOJ also ushered in 2010 in dramatic fashion with its largest single FCPA prosecution of individuals. On January 18, through co-ordinated warrant executions in Las Vegas and Miami, the FBI arrested 22 individuals alleged to have participated in a conspiracy to secure a contract to outfit the Georgian presidential guard with weapons.

As these cases indicate, penalties for FCPA violations can be severe. Companies face a $100 per day fine for violating the accounting and reporting requirements, and a $2 million per violation fine for falling foul of the bribery prohibitions. Individual officers face a fine of up to $250,000 and five years in prison per violation. Moreover, companies are in line for significant non-monetary sanctions under the statute, including the loss of their export license and ability to contract with the government.

How companies and executives can minimize FCPA exposure

With the increased law enforcement focus and potential exposure in the millions, companies and executives must navigate FCPA issues carefully. The voluntary implementation of rigorous compliance and oversight procedures can help prevent FCPA violations, and go a long way toward demonstrating a company's good faith.

Seeking legal advice prior to making any potentially suspect payments will also protect a company and its executives. The Act permits certain types of payments, such as those made to facilitate 'routine governmental action', those that are 'lawful under the written laws and regulations of the foreign' country, and ones that are 'reasonable and bona fide expenditure[s]... directly related to (A) the promotion, demonstration, or explanation of products or services; or (B) the execution or performance of a contract with a foreign government or agency thereof'.

Determining if a particular payment is permissible can often be tricky, and experienced counsel can help guide a company through these issues. Should clarification still be needed on the applicability of the FCPA to a payment, questions can be submitted to the DOJ, which must provide a response within 30 days of receiving all pertinent information.

A company should also consider self-reporting, as both the DOJ and SEC maintain that they look favorably on businesses that take a proactive approach to potential FCPA violations. With respect to DOJ investigations, voluntary reports will reduce a company's "culpability score" under the Federal Sentencing Guidelines. Additionally, the DOJ will enter into Deferred Prosecution Agreements (DPAs — discussed in more detail in the next section), which provide co-operating companies with assurances that the government will hold back on prosecuting FCPA violations under certain terms and conditions.

Self-reporting companies have effectively limited their FCPA exposure. For example, Helmerich & Payne Inc voluntarily disclosed 50 illegal payments made to officials in Latin American countries in order to import and export equipment without necessary government approvals. The company paid a $1 million fine to the DOJ and also agreed to disgorge $375,000 to the SEC. Similarly, UTStarcom Inc voluntarily disclosed $7 million in payments to Asian government officials and third parties; it was separately fined $1.5 million by the DOJ and SEC. Both companies agreed to implement "forward looking" compliance procedures, which the SEC considered in accepting the settlements.

Following the credit crisis, regulators have committed themselves to promoting orderly and efficient global markets as a means of minimizing the scale of any future downturn. As part of this, we expect the SEC and DOJ to continue extending their reach into cross-border cases, including FCPA actions.[3] Accordingly, companies and their executives should be particularly mindful of the pitfalls of doing business abroad, and of their obligation to ensure compliance with the Act.

SEC co-operation initiative

On January 13, 2010, the SEC introduced a new policy to foster co-operation by individuals and entities subject to investigation and possible enforcement action. In doing so, it hopes to follow other authorities, like the DOJ, who trade leniency for witness information as a way of increasing their ability to understand the nature and scope of suspected unlawful activity in an organization and to ferret out culpable senior executives.

Framework for assessing co-operation by individuals

The Policy Statement Concerning Cooperation by Individuals in its Investigations and Related Enforcement Actions, contained in the Enforcement Manual at Section 6.1.1, is the SEC's first statement of a standard for evaluating individual co-operation. With the caveat that there will need to be a 'case-by-case analysis of specific circumstances', the manual lays out four factors that the SEC will consider in crediting individual co-operation:

• **Assistance provided by the co-operator in an investigation or enforcement action**. Here the SEC will assess the value of an individual's co-operation, including its timeliness, whether it has resulted in substantial assistance to an investigation, and the truthfulness, completeness and reliability of the information.
• **Importance of the underlying matter in which the individual co-operated**. Under consideration here will be whether the violation relates to an SEC enforcement priority, the age and duration of the misconduct, and the isolated or repetitive nature of violations.
• **The societal interest in holding the individual accountable for his or her wrongdoing**.
• **The co-operator's history of lawfulness and acceptance of responsibility for past misconduct, as well as the person's ability to commit additional violations**. The latter inquiry includes whether the individual is a licensed securities professional, accountant or attorney, or an associated person of a regulated entity.

Framework for assessing co-operation by companies

The updated Enforcement Manual retains the SEC's framework for evaluating co-operation by companies, first announced in the 2001 Seaboard Report. The manual, however, clarifies this report by articulating four broad factors that the SEC will consider when assessing an entity's co-operation:

• **Self-policing prior to the discovery of misconduct**, including establishing effective compliance procedures and an appropriate tone at the top.
• **Self-reporting of misconduct upon discovery**, including a thorough review of the nature, extent and origins of the misconduct.
• **Remediation**, including dismissing or disciplining wrongdoers, improving internal controls, and compensating people adversely affected.

- **Co-operation with law enforcement**, including providing SEC staff with all relevant information on the underlying violation and remediation.

While compliance on these fronts can result in reduced charges or no enforcement action, they are only general guidelines and the SEC will exercise discretion in assessing the facts and circumstances of an investigation or action on a case-by-case basis.

Co-operation tools available to the SEC

One of the widely reported deficiencies of the Seaboard Report was its failure to describe any specific mechanisms by which the SEC would secure and reward co-operation. Section 6.2 of the updated Enforcement Manual addresses this void by defining various tools available to both individuals and entities:

- **Co-operation agreements**. SEC staff agree to recommend to the Commission that an individual or company receive co-operation credit or settlement terms in exchange for substantial assistance in an investigation or action.
- **Deferred Prosecution Agreements**. In a DPA, the SEC agrees to forgo enforcement action and in exchange the individual or company undertakes to: (i) co-operate truthfully and fully in the Commission's investigation and related enforcement actions, including producing all relevant non-privileged documents, responding to inquiries, appearing for interviews, testifying at trials and other proceedings, and waiving territorial limits on service of process; (ii) enter into a long-term tolling agreement; (iii) comply with express prohibitions or undertakings during the period of deferred prosecution; and (iv), under certain circumstances, admit or not contest underlying facts that would permit the Commission to establish a violation of the securities laws. Generally, DPAs also require individuals or companies to make disgorgement or penalty payments.

The term of a DPA will not normally exceed five years. If it is violated, SEC staff may recommend an enforcement action without limitation, and may use any admissions of fact in that action.

The Deputy Director of the Enforcement Division indicated recently that he expects DPAs to be 'relatively unusual', and that co-operation agreements will be the customary tool.

- **Non-prosecution agreements**. In limited circumstances, the SEC will enter into an NPA,

agreeing not to pursue an enforcement action. In exchange, the individual or company undertakes to: (i) co-operate truthfully and fully in the Commission's investigation and related actions, including producing all relevant non-privileged documents, responding to inquiries, appearing for interviews, testifying at trials and other proceedings, and waiving territorial limits on service of process; and (ii), under certain circumstances, comply with express undertakings. NPAs may also require disgorgement or penalty payments. If the NPA is violated, the SEC staff may recommend an enforcement action without limitation, and any statements or information provided by the co-operating individual or company may be used by the Commission.

- **Proffer agreements**. The SEC will use proffers to assess the probable value of co-operation. Generally, these are facilitated by written agreements that provide that the Commission may not use proffered statements against an individual in subsequent proceedings. The Commission may, however, use proffered information to generate leads or discover additional evidence, to impeach a person who later testifies inconsistently, or to refer an individual to appropriate authorities in a prosecution for perjury, false statements or obstruction of justice.
- **Oral assurances**. Where adequately developed evidence indicates an individual or company has not violated the federal securities laws in such a way as to warrant an enforcement action, assistant directors may, with the consent of a supervisor at or above the level of associate director, orally inform the individual or company that the SEC does not anticipate recommending an action.
- **Immunity requests**. In appropriate cases, to facilitate co-operation that will substantially assist in the enforcement of the federal securities laws, the staff may seek immunity orders or letters, which prevent the use of statements or information, directly or indirectly, against the individual in any criminal case except for perjury, false statements or obstruction of justice prosecutions. But the SEC will not be barred from using immunized testimony or information in a civil enforcement action.

The Commission has delegated authority to make immunity requests to the director of enforcement. As a procedural matter, absent exigent circumstances, the staff will complete a DOJ witness immunity request form prior to requesting authorization to seek an order. The form (i) documents the basis for the request, (ii) assists senior leadership at the SEC and the DOJ in evaluating the request, and (iii) serves as the formal mechanism for requesting immunity upon submission to the DOJ.

SEC staff will generally seek a proffer demonstrating the likelihood of substantial assistance prior to seeking approval to request an immunity order or letter from the DOJ. Generally, they will not seek authorization for an immunity request early in an investigation, when the role of co-operating individuals and the benefits of their co-operation are unclear.

Impact of the SEC's initiative

While it is far too early to make a judgment on the likely success of the program, it does address the opacity and limitations of the SEC's previous co-operation policy, holding out the strong probability of settlement, deferred prosecution or no action under appropriate circumstances. But the burdens of co-operating may prove very weighty.

Because the Commission's initiative requires greater disclosure of the details of the co-operation process, there is the prospect of heightened exposure to civil litigation and adverse publicity. DPAs, for example, will be available to the public upon request and may contain admissions of fact. Indeed, the Deputy Director of the Enforcement Division has said that while the SEC will consider case by case whether it is appropriate to require factual admissions in DPAs, an agreement entered into on a "neither admit nor deny" basis would be unique.

Additionally, admissions or agreements not to contest relevant facts will be considered appropriate for licensed and regulated individuals, such as attorneys, accountants and registered broker-dealers. Thus, would-be co-operators must consider the risk that formal co-operation will be leveraged by litigants in private suits.

Also to be borne in mind, though, are the consequences of failing to co-operate after being specifically asked to do so by the SEC. The Deputy Director of the Enforcement Division has said that if the Commission seeks co-operation from an individual or company that it believes is in a position to provide substantial assistance, and that individual or company refuses, the SEC will bring an enforcement action and seek the fullest sanction allowed under the law.

Although the new guidelines provide more formalized incentives for co-operating with the SEC, the scenarios above illustrate the importance of weighing up all the options.

Recent developments in prosecutorial misconduct

The loss in the Cioffi case was not the only recent, high-profile setback for the DOJ. In December 2009, for example, a District Court judge dismissed criminal charges against former Broadcom executives accused of backdating stock options. The executives had been indicted for securities fraud in connection with options grants made to employees between 1998 and 2005. Following an internal investigation, Broadcom restated its earnings by $2.2 billion in what the DOJ called the 'largest stock options backdating case in history'.

The government indicted former Broadcom CEO Henry Nicholas and former CFO William Ruehle. The trial of Ruehle, which was severed from that of Nicholas, never made it to the jury. Instead, the District Court ruled that because the 'government intimidated and improperly influenced the three witnesses critical to Mr Ruehle's defense,' the defendant was denied his constitutional right to a fair trial. (The SEC announced in February 2010 that, in light of the District Court's order, it would no longer pursue an enforcement action against Nicholas, Ruehle and two other Broadcom executives.)

The Broadcom case was one among several tossed or reversed by federal judges as a result of prosecutorial misconduct. In August 2009, the Ninth Circuit Court of Appeals reversed the conviction of Brocade's former CEO, who was also charged with backdating stock options, finding that the prosecutor had improperly made a false statement of material fact to the jury during the closing argument. In remanding the case for a new trial, the Ninth Circuit admonished: 'Deliberate false statements by those privileged to represent the United States harm the trial process and the integrity of our prosecutorial system. We do not lightly tolerate a prosecutor asserting as a fact to the jury something known to be untrue." (*United States v Reyes*.)

In April 2009, the conviction of Alaska Senator Ted Stevens on public corruption charges was overturned by a District Court judge, who found that the government had failed to turn over potentially exculpatory evidence to the defense team. The judge went one step further, appointing a special prosecutor to determine whether the attorneys prosecuting the case had violated any laws. Various forms of misconduct, including witness tampering and discovery violations, were also cited in a case brought against five Blackwater Worldwide security guards (*United States v Slough*), a Montana environmental case (*United States v WR*

Grace), and a healthcare case in Miami (*United States v Shaygan*).

The Department of Justice responds

A recurrent theme in these misconduct cases is the improper collection, disclosure and use of discovery by federal prosecutors. The District Court's order dismissing the Broadcom case, for example, described how the government (i) caused a key prosecution witness to lose her job with her new employer; (ii) conducted 26 "grueling interrogation[s]" during which the witness was warned that her co-operation arrangement required her to testify to facts contradicted by her earlier statements; and (iii) required her to admit facts unsupported by the record. In the Brocade case, the prosecutor took a statement made by one witness and falsely attributed it to an entire department within Brocade in order to establish an essential element of the government's case.

Meanwhile, the Shaygan case involved multiple violations of *United States v Brady* (requiring the prosecution to disclose exculpatory evidence to the defense) and *Giglio v United States* (requiring the prosecution to disclose agreements with cooperating witnesses), as well as the improper, clandestine recording of conversations between government witnesses and members of the defense team.

Against the backdrop of these and other abuses, United States Attorney General Eric Holder issued several public statements in 2009 regarding the professional standards of federal prosecutors. In the wake of the Senator Stevens debacle, Holder announced that: 'The [DOJ] must always ensure that any case in which it is involved is handled fairly and consistent with its commitment to justice.'

To this end, the DOJ formed a working group 'to explore the department's policies, practices and training related to criminal case management and discovery'. The group's recommendations were incorporated into three memoranda issued in January 2010 by Deputy Attorney General David Ogden (the Ogden Memoranda).

The Ogden Memoranda establish certain guidelines to ensure that prosecutors fulfill their discovery obligations in future cases and reiterate the DOJ's policy that such obligations exceed constitutional dictates, requiring prosecutors to 'take a broad view of materiality and [to] err on the side of disclosing exculpatory and impeaching evidence'.

Among the specific directives contained in the memoranda, US Attorney Offices have had to develop or update discovery policies to reflect local rules and precedent specific to their respective jurisdictions. These local policies should address such issues as timing of discovery disclosures, disclosure of reports of interviews with testifying and non-testifying witnesses, disclosure of agent notes, storage and review of case-related communications, email, and disclosures in excess of the requirements set forth in *Brady*, *Giglio*, the Jencks Act, and Federal Rules of Criminal Procedure 16 and 26.2.

The Ogden Memoranda also underscore the DOJ's policy that all potentially exculpatory and impeachment material should be obtained from each member of the prosecution team, including state and federal law-enforcement and government officials involved in the investigation of a criminal case. The memoranda describe in detail eight different types of data that should be reviewed to ensure timely disclosure. This information includes, among other things, files of DOJ law-enforcement agencies, confidential statements made by testifying and non-testifying witnesses, documents and evidence gathered by parallel authorities, like the SEC, and information obtained by prosecutors and agents during witness interviews. Regarding the latter, the guidelines encourage prosecutors to be particularly attuned to a witness's conflicting statements given over the course of multiple interviews, which may give rise to a duty to disclose.

The memoranda also caution that prosecutors are solely responsible for any discovery violations and are singularly entrusted with the responsibility of determining when disclosures are appropriate. Prosecutors are encouraged to provide broad and early discovery consistent with any countervailing considerations, such as witness protection and privacy, protection of privileged information, preserving the integrity of an ongoing investigation, and other "strategic considerations" that are likely to result in a "just" result.

Room for reform in the Office of Professional Responsibility

The Ogden Memoranda do not squarely respond to critics who argue that government overreaching is the result of a "take no prisoners" approach to criminal prosecution, especially in high-stakes cases, which is facilitated by the relative immunity from discipline that prosecutors enjoy.

Prosecutors must answer to state disciplinary bodies and federal judges, who have the power to issue sanctions, but one scholar has noted that state agencies are unwilling to pursue misconduct allegations for fear of interfering with a federal investigation or proceeding, and judges routinely refer such allegations to the DOJ.[4]

Moreover, state bars and federal judges have declined to discipline prosecutors for failing to follow internal DOJ guidelines on the grounds that the agency's policies expressly disclaim any legal effect.[5]

The DOJ, for its part, maintains an Office of Professional Responsibility (OPR), which is charged with investigating allegations of prosecutorial misconduct. Per the OPR's analytical framework, misconduct occurs when an attorney has 'violated or disregarded an applicable obligation or standard with the requisite scienter'. An OPR report on an investigation into a prosecutor's conduct will contain conclusions about whether an attorney intentionally or recklessly violated an applicable obligation or standard, or, conversely, exercised poor judgment, made a mistake or acted appropriately.

A review of the OPR's website demonstrates how reluctantly the office exercises this oversight function. The last OPR annual report, containing 'statistical information on activities, significant policy changes and developments, and summaries of cases completed during the fiscal year', was uploaded in 2007. The last report on the investigation of an attorney was uploaded in January 2009, and relates to an investigation completed in July 2008. This dearth of information has been attributed to the DOJ's practice, under the previous administration, of keeping disciplinary investigations and outcomes private 'to avoid embarrassing the prosecutor'.[6]

Consequently, any disciplining of federal prosecutors has occurred behind a curtain of secrecy, and government attorneys have operated largely without fear that their actions will be publicly scrutinized. In the absence of a move toward greater transparency at the OPR, federal prosecutors can continue to push the limits of their ethical obligations.

The scathing opinions issued in the recent misconduct cases, however, may signal a willingness on the part of judges to fill the void by exercising their authority to regulate attorney conduct and by holding prosecutors to the highest standards.

The District Court judge in the Shaygan case observed: 'It is the responsibility of the United States Attorney and his senior staff to create a culture where "win at any costs" prosecution is not permitted.' He further advised that 'the courts of the United States must let it be known that when substantial abuses occur, sanctions will be imposed to make the risk of non-compliance too costly.'[7] The judge who presided over the Stevens case suggested in his ruling that he might institute a practice of reminding prosecutors of their *Brady* obligations at the start of each case, and urged other federal judges to do the same.

Conclusion

Law enforcement has much to prove. The regulatory effectiveness of the SEC, and the ability of the DOJ to prosecute high-profile white-collar crime, have been called into question. We expect that law enforcement will respond aggressively on a number of prosecutorial fronts in an attempt to land hard blows on players involved in the financial crisis, and to assign blame for the causes of that crisis. While some may question how frequently those blows will land, in the light of recent experiences we believe that officers and directors, and the companies and stakeholders they are responsible to, are best served by maintaining corporate governance best practices and appropriate compliance and internal audit programs.

15

Strategies for addressing shareholder activism and communications

David F Heroy and
Michael F DeFranco, Partners,
Baker & McKenzie LLP

Board members of public companies that experience escalating economic problems can find themselves in an extremely challenging position. Often, a distressed company has an equally distressed stock price, and that can spark the discontent and opportunism of shareholder activists, as well as attracting the interest of suitors.

Activists can not only draw upon a playbook of "conventional" strategies — proxy fights and derivative suits, for example — but they can also gain additional leverage against the company and other constituencies through events that inevitably occur as a result of corporate distress. Their actions can run the gamut from simply obtaining a larger equity stake, made possible by distressed stock prices, to challenging management in the public forum of a bankruptcy case.

Determining potential responses to shareholder activities may depend on the level of financial distress at the company. Boards must also consider their duties to other constituencies and how these groups might be impacted by actions taken in response to the activism of shareholders.

The conventional activist strategies

Typically, activists seeking to influence board and management behavior begin by looking at a range of strategies that have been successfully employed in corporate contests for years, regardless of financial distress. These strategies often begin with a public relations campaign. For example, an activist first acquires a sizeable equity stake in the company and then engages the media, citing the acquisition as a springboard for transformative change, such as a management overhaul, a fundamental change in corporate strategy or sale. The disclosure rules of the Securities and Exchange Commission (SEC) will play a part in how this publicity affects the company. For example, Rule 14a-8 of the SEC's proxy rules addresses when a company must include a shareholder's proposal in its proxy statement and identify the proposal in its form of proxy when there is an annual or special meeting of shareholders. In a more aggressive campaign, activists could seek an inspection of the company's books and records under state law. They may even commence a proxy fight, often demanding a change in the corporate governance structure by eliminating a staggered board of directors, or seeking to replace certain or all of the board members directly.

In pursuing such measures, activists may hope to secure the informal support of other like-minded activists who either are or would become shareholders in the company. In doing so, they often take care to avoid any formal understandings (or the appearance of any understandings) with other stockholders. Such an agreement could lead to the participants being deemed a "group" under SEC rules or a shareholder rights plan maintained by the company.

Under Section 13(d) of the Securities Exchange Act, and related rules, for example, any shareholder or group of shareholders that acquires more than 5 per cent of the voting stock of an SEC-registered company must publicly disclose such stakes, including its intentions with regard to the company and its management. In addition, "group" status may have unintended consequences under state law, corporate organizational documents or contractual agreements, such as triggering change-of-control provisions or shareholder rights plans.

Standard responses to activism strategies

Most boards anticipate shareholder activism and are prepared to respond to an aggressive, unwanted activist that does not have the best interests of the company or its shareholders in mind. These boards know their company's major stockholders and monitor SEC filings and other sources so they are aware of potential activism or unusual trading in their stock. Additionally, they review the company's structural defenses to determine their effectiveness if faced by activist campaigns.

Directors and officers should consider whether the company's organizational documents place appropriate limitations on the ability of the activist to take actions directly without the involvement of the company's board of directors. Specifically, they should review the documents and ask whether they: (i) preclude actions by written consent of shareholders, (ii) limit the ability of activists to call special meetings of shareholders, or (iii) include "advance notice by-laws" in connection with shareholder board nominations and other shareholder proposals at an annual meeting.

Further steps to be considered include adoption of a shareholder rights plan that would be triggered upon an activist (or "group" of activists) acquiring a threshold number of shares, or structuring the company's debt instruments to prevent transfers that could create unwanted leverage.

Most directors are positioned to take action quickly should an activist go on the attack.

Once a campaign is launched against the company, the first step is to identify the activist and discern its ultimate intentions. If a public relations offensive appears likely, a counter-communications strategy is usually considered so that the board and management can publish their side of the story. This involves contacting other shareholders, either directly or through strategic use of media, and explaining the company's present and proposed course of action for navigating through financial distress.

Special attention is paid to counteracting complaints expected to be lodged by a particular activist, while asserting why the strategy of management, not the activist, is in the best pecuniary interests of the shareholders.

Companies should also explore whether they can take any actions to slow down the activist before momentum builds. For example, they should check that the activist has complied with all SEC disclosure, anti-trust and other regulatory requirements in acquiring its stake in the company — and take advantage of any discrepancies in order to buy time.

Shareholder activism in times of distress

Financial distress, including actual or threatened insolvency, provides fertile ground for activists, who can be expected to use the company's problems as a sword against the board and management to supplement their standard strategies.

However, a board can draw upon strategies of its own — a work-out, restructuring or even a bankruptcy filing, for example — to counteract the activists.

How financial distress can enhance shareholder activism

Insolvency and liquidity issues are distracting for managers and employees as emergencies arise often weekly or even daily. Significant diversion of resources, increased out-of-pocket expenses for professionals, loss of personnel and threats to morale can be expected.

When a company experiences this upheaval, directors must take special care not to forget shareholders, even though internal pressures may appear to make their concerns a low priority. In an environment that is ripe for activism, shareholder communication is paramount. Inattentiveness sends exactly the wrong message because the absence of communication can provoke activism that could otherwise be avoided.

Increased creditor influence, real or perceived, is also inevitable in times of financial distress, and shareholders may be more intent on activism if they feel they will receive less value as a result of management focusing on creditors.

In deciding what course of action to take in the face of shareholder activism, directors must also be mindful of their fiduciary duties, including the possible expansion of these duties to include creditors as the company approaches insolvency. This shift may generate increased shareholder activism as (i) the case for protection of the pecuniary interests of the shareholders becomes more difficult to maintain, and (ii) institutional creditors militate for strategies that generate cash immediately, such as asset sales, which could mean sacrificing opportunities for growth and returns on investments, to the detriment of shareholders.

Even worse from the perspective of shareholders, creditors may try to bargain for the "upside" of the business as part of a restructuring, potentially taking all of the future equity value to which the common shareholders might otherwise be entitled — at a time when value is, perhaps temporarily, at an all-time low.

Increased creditor influence can thus cause apprehension among shareholders regarding the future of their investment, leading directly to a reduction in the share price. That in turn makes it easier for activists to accrue a large stake and win over shareholders otherwise beholden to the current board and management, thus acting as a catalyst for increased activism.

Directors must therefore take care to balance the interests of both shareholders and creditors and understand how responses to activism will be perceived by both parties. If equity value is adversely affected by actions taken to appease creditors, a well-crafted communications strategy could comfort shareholders by highlighting the point that the ultimate goal of the board and managers continues to be increasing enterprise value for the benefit of all.

If the company continues to lose value or approaches default on its debt obligations, holding the line against shareholder activism can become increasingly difficult as creditors' interests carry greater relative weight.

Concessions to creditors are often warranted as the exercise of remedies that could be catastrophic to enterprise value and ongoing operations becomes more realistic, but shareholders will often not have all the information and may lose faith in the board and management when concessions are announced. They can also be in denial as to the prospects of a turnaround and view the whole exercise as creditor manipulation or a desire on the part of the managers to walk away, further inflaming the activists. This underscores the need for well-drafted communications.

Additional aspects of activism created by distress

Additional, enhanced shareholder activism may arise in other unexpected ways if the company continues to lose value, including: (i) the purchase of debt by activists at a discount to increase leverage; (ii) the frustration of work-out alternatives; and (iii) distressed investors targeting the company for acquisition.

Activists purchasing debt. This is a common strategy among aggressive, sophisticated shareholder activists. By purchasing debt, they put themselves in the position of being a counterparty with whom the company must negotiate in the event that it wishes to amend debt terms or seek waivers or forbearances. These negotiations can be used as a lever to require the company to take various actions typically sought by shareholder activists, such as cutting costs, changing management, selling assets or operations and using the proceeds to repay the activists (who will likely have purchased the debt at a discount), and possibly engaging in a process to sell itself.

In addition to putting themselves in the "pre-bankruptcy" position of being able to negotiate with the company, activists purchasing debt gain certain protections if the company were to enter the bankruptcy process, such as being able to hedge their total recovery.

Potential frustration of work-out alternatives. A voluntary work-out or sale of assets may be seen by management and creditors as the best alternative for all constituencies. Shareholders, however, can represent a major obstacle. In most cases, their consent will be required for any out-of-court debt restructuring and for significant sales of assets. Because creditors have a right to full payment that is superior to any shareholder recovery, they rarely agree to accept partial payment without shareholders giving up significant rights or being sufficiently diluted by new equity provided to creditors in the transaction. In addition, the existence of diverse and numerous shareholders may make it impractical to obtain consents, even in the absence of any meaningful activism. Shareholders who have seen a significant drop in share price may be inclined simply to ride it out instead of fixing their losses by accepting whatever minimal value the creditor is willing to provide to obtain their consent for an out-of-court work-out or sale, with all of the proceeds provided to creditors.

Additionally, if out-of-court work-out documentation contains typical releases for directors and officers, shareholders may deny consent solely to frustrate managers they see as being the cause of their losses.

In a distressed environment, directors should communicate sooner rather than later so that shareholders are adequately prepared to approve an out-of-court solution. If consent is still not forthcoming, however, insolvency proceedings can be used to circumvent shareholder consent requirements.

Increased opportunity for hostile acquisition. If the company's share price has fallen to a level where a large equity position can be purchased for relatively little in comparison to the size of the company's assets, so-called "vultures" (aggressive distressed buyers) may enter the fray, seeking an opportunity to make extraordinary returns. These investors may discount the notion of fiduciary duties to creditors and seek to leverage management to take advantage of creditors as captive investors. The "vultures" are more likely to pursue the strategy of buying debt at a discount at all levels of the capital structure so as to block alternative plans for the company. Disenfranchised shareholders can often join these investors in the belief that they see something management does not. Thus, the distressed investor may be able to obtain a measure of effective control of the capital structure with a relatively minor purchase.

Options for responding to activism in times of distress

The obvious, and best, option is to restore financial health as soon as possible. Having the time to accomplish that is the challenge. A realistic strategy for returning enterprise value to an indisputable level of solvency, while maintaining the relative positions of creditor and shareholder constituencies throughout the process, is to forge a standstill to allow a new business strategy to be implemented. This approach, while often best for everyone, can also be impossible to implement due to market conditions, liquidity concerns or the belief of creditors or shareholders that their respective remedies will present a better alternative for their distinct interests.

If adequate restructuring or forbearance agreements cannot be obtained, then the next best defense against both creditors and shareholders may be a Chapter 11 bankruptcy filing. Given the increase in leverage of creditors and shareholder activists, the board and management may be left in the unenviable position of being unable to satisfy anyone while owing fiduciary duties to everyone.

The company may be in default or on the verge of default, raising the spectre of creditor remedies that could be harmful to enterprise value. Further, the longer the distress has continued, the more likely it is that shareholder activists will have gained traction towards change. Faced with the differing interests and demands of shareholders and creditors, the board cannot simply pit one side against the other, as they can rarely be reconciled. Nor can the board simply walk away from its

fiduciary obligations. Filing a bankruptcy case under Chapter 11 is often the result, in order to preserve the control of the board and management over operations, and permit the modification of shareholder rights without consent. However, a bankruptcy filing is not the end of the road for shareholder activists, as it just creates a different platform for them.

Shareholder activism in bankruptcy

The filing of a bankruptcy case fundamentally alters the roles and responsibilities of directors. In a Chapter 11 case, the current board and management continue to operate the business as a debtor in possession (DIP) and generally cannot be displaced without proof of fraud or gross mismanagement, which is rare. The shift in fiduciary duties is indisputable, expanding to cover all holders of debt and equity in the company's bankruptcy estate, with due recognition of the priority of creditors over shareholders.

Activism in bankruptcy can typically include: (i) appearance and participation in bankruptcy court proceedings; (ii) appointment of an official committee of equity security holders; (iii) replacement of the board and management through a shareholder meeting or proxy fight; and, in rare cases, (iv) proposal of a shareholder plan of reorganization in competition with the plans of the company or its creditors.

Appearance by shareholders as parties-in-interest

The Bankruptcy Code generally provides that any party-in-interest may be heard on any issue, including an investor with as little as one worthless share. Nevertheless, common bankruptcy practice is that a party-in-interest's voice is only as strong as the value of its interest in the outcome of the proceeding. Bankruptcy courts generally do not allow individual shareholders to influence the course of a case, or to require the debtor to expend funds protecting non-economic shareholder rights, in the absence of solvency.

Appointment of an official committee of equity holders

The Bankruptcy Code provides for the mandatory appointment of an official committee representing unsecured creditors, paid for by the Chapter 11 debtor's bankruptcy estate. Shareholders can request the establishment of a similar committee to represent equity, but this is not mandatory and appointments are only made under certain specified circumstances. Nevertheless, activist shareholders often pursue this route in bankruptcy cases because the cost of an official equity committee is borne by the debtor's estate. In addition, the voice of an official committee is far more influential in a bankruptcy court than that of a lone shareholder.

The legal requirements for equity committee appointments include: (i) the existence of a diverse shareholder constituency that cannot afford to participate individually and is not otherwise adequately represented; (ii) that the debtor company is not hopelessly insolvent, such that shareholders arguably have a real economic interest at stake; (iii) the bankruptcy case is large and complex; (iv) the stock is widely held and actively traded; and (v) the costs of the appointment are outweighed by the benefits.

The first step an activist will pursue in this regard is to make a request to the Office of the United States Trustee, which has authority to appoint an equity committee without input from the bankruptcy court. This is typically accomplished through a formal letter, inexpensive to prepare, that sets out the basis for appointment. The US Trustee will forward this letter to the debtor company and creditors' committee with an opportunity to respond and then make a determination.

At this point, boards can assess whether it would be worthwhile to have an official shareholders' committee appointed. This decision will require balancing factors unique to every case. To be sure, a shareholder committee appointment can add cost to the bankruptcy proceedings and create an influential voice in court that could be adverse to the board and management. On the other hand, boards may believe that creating a separate, official voice for equity will lessen the tensions between the interests of creditors and shareholders. They may also believe that an influential shareholders' committee would be an effective ally.

Even if the US Trustee decides not to appoint a committee, the activist shareholders may file a motion with the bankruptcy court seeking to overrule the Trustee's discretion. Bankruptcy courts often defer to the Trustee, but in certain cases may direct the appointment of a shareholder committee themselves — although, like the US Trustee, they tend to be hesitant to impose additional professional fees and costs on an already expensive process, regardless of the facts.

If a committee is appointed, a debtor's board

and management are often best served by ensuring that the shareholders with the greatest stakes participate, in order to avoid the leverage of a committee being placed in the hands of small, perhaps only retail investors. Boards should take care to communicate regularly with the large shareholders in an attempt to maintain them as allies, especially because public company debtors often discontinue making SEC filings and other reporting obligations, as these can be expensive and provide little value to the bankruptcy estate as a whole.

It cannot be overlooked that committee representation can provide shareholders with a vehicle to challenge valuation of the bankrupt debtor, in order to show value for equity at the debtor's expense. This is the core issue of a bankruptcy case that can be extraordinarily expensive to litigate. Merely by raising the prospect of a dispute, an official shareholders' committee can often extract additional value for the otherwise junior interests of equity. Conversely, the support (or lack thereof) of the equity committee could make or break the debtor company's reorganization. Therefore, the board must look into ways of reaching compromises and avoiding unnecessary litigation. Again, this requires communication both generally and with the largest shareholders (subject to securities laws that govern inside information) — early and often.

Shareholder meetings and proxy solicitations

Activist shareholders that are unable to obtain an official committee appointment but are convinced of potential solvency may continue to participate in a Chapter 11 case by other means. For example, they can seek to compel a shareholder meeting of the bankrupt debtor under applicable state law, threatening a proxy fight to replace board members. Importantly, the filing of a bankruptcy case does not cut off these rights automatically. Upon receiving notice of this tactic, however, the debtor can request that the bankruptcy court enjoin the staging of a shareholder meeting on the basis that it will impede the restructuring or impose costs on the debtor without providing any value to legitimate stakeholders.

The legal rules in this area are uncertain because bankruptcy courts have often permitted shareholder meetings for certain purposes, but occasionally prevented meetings designed to effectuate board and management changes or otherwise determine the strategy of the debtor, especially on the eve of the resolution of a case.

This is an understandable judicial reaction, as the board and management are the representatives of the entire bankruptcy estate, and courts often believe that the debtor in possession's actions should not be controlled by a single class of interest-holders that is potentially (and perhaps likely) "out of the money".

Appointment of a bankruptcy trustee

Appointment of a trustee in bankruptcy is the only statutory method for replacing a debtor's management. As a technical legal matter, it may be sought by any party-in-interest in the bankruptcy estate, including shareholders in a woefully insolvent company.

The appointment must be sought by motion in the bankruptcy court, supported by evidence, and involves litigation that can be very expensive and time-consuming. The standards for such evidence, mainly proof of fraud and gross mismanagement, are very high and hard to prove. Given the high legal costs and judicial reluctance to replace management, trustee appointments are rare.

Nevertheless, the remedy can be sought by disgruntled shareholders, either as a weapon to leverage against the board and creditors, or even to obtain leverage where none might otherwise exist. The remedy, moreover, is potentially far more potent in the hands of official shareholders' committees, both because they are more influential and because the costs of the proceeding would be borne by the bankrupt debtor's estate, not the shareholders.

Reorganization plans

At the beginning of a bankruptcy case, only the debtor company has the exclusive right to file a plan of reorganization, which, if approved by the bankruptcy court, can effect a restructuring of the debt and equity of the company. This "exclusivity" ends 120 days after filing of the case, unless extended by the bankruptcy court.

Extensions happen routinely so long as progress towards reorganization is being made or other operational or bankruptcy concerns make the earlier filing of a plan infeasible. In 2006, however, Congress limited the discretion of bankruptcy judges by forbidding extensions beyond 18 months from the date of filing. If the bankruptcy court refuses to extend the deadline, or if the 18-month limit is reached, any party-in-interest may file a plan of reorganization, submit it to the vote of interest-holders and seek approval from the bankruptcy court. Although the debtor may object, its consent is not necessary, and a plan may be imposed.

Shareholders that see value in sponsoring reorganization plans can use this tactic, either by waiting until exclusivity expires, or by seeking to shorten its extension. This, too, is an expensive litigation tactic that can be much more effectively advanced by an official shareholders' committee. In fact, it is typically used by official committees to propose alternative resolutions to the bankruptcy case that would provide an enhanced return to the shareholders.

Conclusion

Directors of companies in economic distress should anticipate and be prepared to manage shareholder activism. Boards should be mindful not only of the public relations aspect of activism, but also their fiduciary duties to all constituencies as they decide how to respond. Before shareholders mobilize, companies can put in place structural defenses in organizational documents and anticipate tactics by frequent communication throughout the process, including the duration of any bankruptcy case that is filed. Properly prepared, boards will be able to make well-informed decisions so as to reach an optimal restructuring solution for all constituencies, despite the potentially disruptive threats from shareholder activism.

Editorial assistance was provided by Andrew PR McDermott, Ethan F Ostrow and Lawrence P Vonckx.

Enterprise Risk Assessment

16

Preserving and recovering value in illiquid times

Duffield Meyercord, Partner of
Carl Marks Advisory Group
LLC and Carl Marks Healthcare
Partners LLC,

writing on behalf of the

**Turnaround Management
Association**

Even before the extreme economic downturn of 2007-09, the "classic" turnaround had fallen out of fashion as lenders, investors and other constituents began to look to transactions as the primary means of addressing the challenges facing troubled companies.

The meteoric rise of hedge funds, and their impact upon the amount of liquidity available, fueled the wave of leveraged deals that crested in 2007 and 2008. The aggressive, transaction-oriented perspective of many funds was dramatically different to the credit-focused underwriting process followed by many lenders.

However, despite such philosophical differences in how to finance a company, the competition led historically conservative institutions to fund deals with progressively more leverage than ever before, based upon underlying operating assumptions that ultimately proved invalid as the global economy experienced a sudden and severely protracted softening (both in terms of decreased demand and greater margin pressure).

In the wake of the downturn, lender confidence in corporate restructuring was at an unprecedented low. Lenders saw historic failures of peer institutions that called into question their own business practices and job security. With an unprecedented ability to identify when the economic recovery would start, many made the decision to call outstanding loans. The result was an industry-wide hesitation to provide additional capital to corporations. Before the financial crisis, global companies were issuing about $30 billion of debt a month to fund operations; by the first quarter of 2009, the number was approximately $2 billion.

Although the credit markets have begun to improve from the severity and size of the recent economic turmoil, lenders are likely to remain conservative with lending strategies for the foreseeable future. While it is too early to tell what the long-term effects will be, institutional lenders appear to have taken on board the lessons of the economic downturn and have now curtailed lending to over-leveraged companies.

Kick the can down the road

In the aftermath of the downturn, borrowers learned that the inflated enterprise and asset valuations that had fueled growth over the preceding five years were now obstacles to providing the liquidity needed to effect true operational fixes. Risk-adverse lenders felt they had no sense of real valuations or understanding of how the slowing economy would affect their chances of being repaid. In fact, many lenders had never seen anything like the 2008 collapse of credit and felt that they were facing potentially catastrophic losses, putting their institutions and careers in jeopardy. To many, the idea of increasing exposure by funding a turnaround made no sense. Instead, they pushed for quick sales or liquidations to recover as much value as possible immediately, or to amend existing credit facilities by extending terms without writing down debt to true value, waiting for borrower revenue growth to return and save the situation. This latter "kick the can down the road" mentality became an easy way for a given lender to postpone one credit problem for another. This mentality continues to be prevalent in 2010 as investors push to employ cash — the largest asset class in the US — which is otherwise earning historically low returns.

Turnaround practitioners' vital tool used to fund operational revivals, liquidity, continues to be elusive for operational restructurings. As a result, distressed companies are forced to make changes around the margins to reduce cash burn, with the hope of waiting out the business cycle. Generally, this does not constitute real change or establish a true basis for restoration of value, but rather pushes the hard decisions to some time in the future. To preserve value for that future change, lenders, investors and borrowers must be willing to make the hard decisions required to establish a long-term sustainable corporate capital structure. This was made even more difficult than in the past as the credit boom left many companies with highly complex capital structures with vastly different points of view.

Restructurings move out of reach

Beyond the lessons of the economic downturn, the fundamental shift in the capital structures of many companies has affected their ability to avoid distressed transactions.

The blurred distinctions between and within the ranks of senior and junior stakeholders improved deal flow and access to capital during the bull market times of the mid 2000s. But in distressed situations, unraveling the complex tranches of debt that were created is complicated. This makes obtaining support for an operational restructuring difficult, as various holders across a variety of levels of seniority are concerned about collateral deteriorating. The result is a standstill among lenders in competing tranches, and sometimes within the same tranches.

The emergence of hedge funds, private equity funds and high net worth individuals as critical lenders has changed the rules of engagement for corporate officers when structuring a reorganization plan. Historically, lenders have been institutional banks without expertise or interest in managing an equity position in a company. Increasingly, as banks build stronger relationships with advisory firms that can help them run portfolio companies, and alternative investment vehicles look for ways to generate returns, more debt holders are willing to convert their debt positions into equity positions in corporations.

How officers can make a difference

The willingness to convert troubled debt into equity via a balance sheet restructuring has made standalone operational restructurings less desirable for lenders as they lose faith in management and prefer to dictate the process themselves. Despite the challenges, however, corporate officers can do a number of things to make a difference in maximizing enterprise value and increasing the chances of a successful reorganization.

A key principle in achieving a restructuring in an illiquid capital market is to engage the lenders early to discuss possible options. They will be more willing to consider restructuring alternatives prior to defaults such as missed payments or repeated covenant violations. The occurrence of either shifts influence to the lenders in dictating the restructuring process.

The importance of the business plan

To win the goodwill of lenders, companies need to begin by developing a credible, well-constructed restructuring plan, demonstrating both that management understands the current problems and has a road map for addressing them. Lenders will need a plan of this quality to persuade internal constituents that the restructuring is the best solution. In the aftermath of the recent economic turbulence, lending decisions are being made by top management committees, well beyond the one or two individuals who might know the company intimately.

A good plan will help the lender to "sell" the reorganization to internal decision-makers and so must take into consideration the probability of access to new capital, rapid changes that can be made to the business, overall market and consumer trends, and an exit strategy for the equity holders and lenders.

With liquidity tight, corporate officers must present compelling reasons why their company is worth saving, especially if additional capital is required. Prolonged restructurings will likely not be supported, as lenders fear increased exposure could be damaging to their organizations and individual careers.

The development of a restructuring plan must focus on achieving three primary goals: (i) implementation of operational changes to reduce cash burn and/or improve profitability; (ii) the raising of immediate additional liquidity to fund the required changes; and (iii) the defining of a timeline for when the process will be appropriately reflected in the company's financial performance.

Without all these, the likelihood of obtaining support for the plan will be diminished.

The plan must be precise

Management must also clearly articulate the steps it intends to take to put the company back on course for long-term profitability and growth. The plan must show a route to EBITDA results that are sufficiently improved to justify the financial risk to be underwritten by the stakeholders, and it must be rooted in facts and based upon credible assumptions.

A danger that must be avoided is presenting a business plan that is overly optimistic, particularly where management feels pressure to produce a compelling story to prevent liquidation. The risk being run here is that stakeholders will doubt the viability of the restructuring process and management's ability to solve the problems.

Each element of the plan to improve EBITDA and cash flow must be specific, with successful implementation being perceived as highly probable. In a tight capital market, an initiative to reduce costs by consolidating plants, for example, is much more likely to succeed than a new, untried revenue-generating initiative. That kind of clarity will be more attractive to key stakeholders and the chances of securing their support will increase dramatically.

Valuations based on EBITDA multiples are normally below historical norms during tight capital markets. However, many stakeholders try to maintain the viability of a company until the economy starts to rebound, on the expectation that valuation multiples will recover over time. Even in the case of a liquidation or sale strategy, the process will take time to complete and new financing might be required to reach the endpoint. Therefore, a set of reasonably achievable projections is important.

A company must also adjust its cost structure to be cash-flow positive or, at the very worst, cash-flow neutral, to ensure preservation of value. A pivotal document in obtaining support for an operational restructuring is a forecast for weekly cash requirements, 13 weeks at a minimum, supported by a detailed analysis of past, present and future needs. This will provide comfort to lenders and other key constituents as to what can be reasonably expected from the company in the near term. Material deviations from historical run rates must be clearly explained or will not be credible in the eyes of a lender.

The 13-week cash forecast needs to show the sustainability of the business excluding any additional infusions of capital. A self-sustaining cash-flow positive company will have more options when negotiating with stakeholders with the goal of avoiding an abrupt distressed transaction. If a company is cash-flow negative, immediate action will be required to ensure survival. Immediate cost-cutting tactics will have to be put in place, such as headcount reductions, stock rationalization, customer rationalization (eliminating low-margin purchasers) and more restrictive spending policies.

A significant opportunity for cost savings is evaluating which employees' positions can be eliminated or downsized immediately. In bullish economic cycles, management teams can swell beyond necessary levels, so possibilities often exist to flatten an organization and make the structure more efficient and cost-effective. However, care must be taken to retain the most important employees; sufficient talent must be kept in place to implement the proposed operational restructuring. Stay bonuses or other individually structured financial arrangements might be required between the company and key personnel to ensure loyalty through the process.

Financial forecasts

To support a restructuring and hold off a forced liquidation, lender groups will also likely require forecast financial statements for at least the next 12 months, and sometimes longer. These forecasts should be constructed by establishing budgets for each reporting unit and eventually consolidating them into a single balance sheet, income statement and cash-flow statement.

During any type of restructuring, the company must anticipate reporting results to the lender group and must avoid missing projections. In creating a positive view of the business, it is better to meet or exceed conservative forecasts than to fall short of overly optimistic projections. There needs to be some balance, though, in the sense that the projections must also imbue the lenders with enough optimism to warrant supporting a turnaround plan.

In a restructuring where the lender community has extended a lifeline to continue operations, management will be benchmarked against their financial projections. These will be used to establish covenants that, if not satisfied in future periods, will ultimately trigger defaults. Penalties for breaching covenants could be a charge of one time fees, increases to the effective interest rate, or a worst-case scenario of a forced distressed transaction by the lenders.

To ensure a forecast can be achieved, it must derive from detailed data. For example, payroll should be built by employee and clear assumptions must be made for hourly rates. Additionally, input pricing should be computed based on realistic cost assumptions.

Budgets demand dedication

A common problem among financially distressed companies is a lack of dedication to a structured budgeting process. Holding management and employees to periodic (weekly, monthly, quarterly) budgets creates accountability that helps instill a culture of achievement. When corporate performance is consistently measured against agreed budgets, there are often incremental benefits in terms of improved reporting, quicker closing of monthly financials, and more rigorous financial analysis. This is achieved by ensuring that department heads are responsible for the departmental budgets, and then linking the job security and financial rewards of employees to the company's ability to achieve the annual forecast. In many cases, achieving the results is not a matter of preference, but survival.

Corporate officers should also look to the balance sheet as a source of additional internal liquidity, because opportunities to generate cash or slow down cash outflow may be found in assessing the payment terms received from vendors and provided to customers. Understanding the value of a company relative to its suppliers, and looking at alternative sourcing options, can be effective tools in reducing cash burn. Successfully negotiating better terms with suppliers and customers offers a way of creating working capital from the existing business structure and helping the company to maximize enterprise value.

It may also be that cash burn can be significantly decreased through stock and customer rationalization efforts in which only the most profitable inventories and purchasers survive the cut. Inflated inventory levels are often symptomatic of a poorly functioning supply chain that can damage profitability. By reducing the costs related to product returns and managing slow-moving stock, a company can achieve savings in many different areas of the business.

Large capital projects must also be carefully evaluated. In distressed companies, a surprising number of projects have been approved and received heavy investment without an appropriate cost-benefit analysis. When assessing the future cash requirements of a company, carefully study capital projects that are either in progress or about to commence.

Winning over the stakeholders

Key stakeholders have much less patience than they had in the past for working with management through an operational restructuring. The experience of lenders in the illiquid markets of 2008 and 2009 has made them much more aggressive in handling distressed companies. In addition, media scrutiny of the bailouts and failures of many financial institutions has made lenders far more risk-adverse. They are now more inclined to encourage an abrupt distressed transaction, as a way of preventing further deterioration in their loan portfolios.

While finding a lender that is willing to support a company-led reorganization is not impossible, tight capital markets and the lessons of previous economic contractions mean management has to work much harder. Often, companies are left with two options: additional funding from their current stakeholder groups, or surviving without additional funds.

Management must understand the concerns of the important constituents and have a believable plan to solve these problems. A believable plan is fact based and relies heavily on restructuring initiatives that are highly likely to succeed (cost reductions, elimination of unprofitable customers/products, etc). Lenders will be unwilling to support a plan that has too much operating risk. In an illiquid capital market, failure to convince constituents that a solution exists significantly increases the risk that an abrupt distressed transaction will be their preference instead of an organized restructuring.

Turn to the turnaround experts

Turnaround professionals are a helpful resource in the process of obtaining stakeholder confidence. Tensions run high between key stakeholders and management in distressed companies and this often creates an environment of uneasiness and distrust that can undermine a company's future. Turnaround professionals can broker negotiations and will be well versed in the challenges that lie ahead. They can also provide support to the management team and help vet management's short- and long-term business plan. More specifically, they can provide advice on what concessions and support from employees, suppliers and customers are sellable and effective. Turnaround professionals can help management evaluate initiatives from both cash and business improvement perspectives and help establish regular communication programs with key constituents and their advisors.

Successful corporate reorganizations are achieved in times of tight liquidity by the relentless effort, on the part of management, to build stakeholder confidence. A seasoned turnaround professional can be vital in assisting this process.

17

Liquidity provides optionality: An approach for boards during a liquidity crisis

Adrian Frankum,
Senior Managing Director,
Armen Emrikian and
James Guglielmo,
Managing Directors,
FTI Consulting Inc

In October 2005, Delphi Corporation filed for bankruptcy with more than $1.5 billion in cash and $2 billion in available liquidity under its debtor in possession credit facility. This amount represented substantial liquidity for the car parts company, providing management with the time and the ability to design and effect a comprehensive restructuring plan, maintain its customers and manage its supply base. Management also had the time to proceed through a complex series of negotiations with both its constituents and potential investors to arrive at a consensual arrangement that was expected to provide substantial recoveries to its shareholders. A deal came within hours of being consummated in April 2008.

Unfortunately, unprecedented negative changes in the capital markets, a deep recession, government actions and the decline of automotive production volumes to levels not seen since the 1960s subsequently forced the company into a severe liquidity situation and impaired asset values. The luxury of time was gone. The board no longer had the option of waiting for improved operating results, values or offers and was forced to choose among more limited alternatives with reduced recoveries to most creditors.

The importance of liquidity

Almost all restructurings involve some current or future liquidity concerns. Liquidity issues are generally a symptom of more fundamental problems, but this is one case where treating the symptom as well as the cause applies. Liquidity is the lifeblood of a company. Without it, circumstances rapidly degenerate and, as was shown by the Delphi case, options for maximizing values and recoveries evaporate.

In particular, without sufficient liquidity, a company may be faced with the following challenges:

- Pressure from the secured creditors to take action; these constituents could foreclose on their collateral.
- Trade vendors eliminating lines of credit.
- Ineffective performance and turnover in the employee base.
- Downward pressures on revenues as customers fear deeper problems and seek alternatives to the company's products and services.
- Ultimately, deepening liquidity strains could force the company into a quick sale or liquidation of its assets, resulting in severe impairment to stakeholder values.

Given this, it is vital during a restructuring that boards take an active role in monitoring current and future expected liquidity positions, and provide direction and guidance to management.

A two-pronged approach to liquidity enhancement

It is tempting for a company in financial distress to focus on external sources of capital when attempts are being made to resolve liquidity issues.

Management and the board may feel that, if successful, this approach may allow the company to maintain its current strategy and avoid the disruption that would result from more aggressive actions.

The problem with this is that valuable time and cash will likely be lost while pursuing what is often a lengthy and sometimes unfruitful process.

In fact, companies often find that financing is readily available when they do not need it and much more difficult to obtain when they are experiencing operating difficulties. To the extent that a board has concerns about its company's future liquidity position at a time when capital is available, consideration should be given to building a "war chest" for potential future use.

Ford Motor Company employed such a strategy in 2006, when it levered up its balance sheet and raised over $12 billion in incremental liquidity. This action provided Ford with the breathing room to allow it to restructure its operations on its own terms and avoid the bankruptcy filings that befell the other two "big three" US automakers.

Once a liquidity crisis has struck, boards and their management teams are typically more successful if their approach to improving liquidity involves both aggressive internal actions and the exploration of external solutions. Internally, there must be a focus on instilling a "cash first" mentality throughout the company, often to the detriment of revenue, income and previous strategies.

A comprehensive liquidity-improvement plan must be produced by management and vetted by the board. The board should require management to provide liquidity projections and should have an understanding of the assumptions and risks associated with these forecasts.

There should be frequent updates from management, including progress against milestones, budget to actual results and updated projections, so that the board understands whether things are going according to plan or whether corrective action needs to be taken.

While the internal cash-conservation measures are progressing, the board should also require that management provide recommendations on both traditional and non-traditional sources of external liquidity.

These should be carefully considered by the board to ensure all reasonable sources are being evaluated and that those being pursued are properly prioritized and make sense given available resources and the likelihood of success.

Board reporting and the establishment of an effective cash management infrastructure

Given that most boards are composed of at least some external members who do not participate in the day-to-day management of the company, and that even internal board members may be somewhat removed from the cash management function, it is essential that timely, comprehensive reporting be provided to the board to allow it to fulfill its duties.

Contrary to systems used in non-distressed situations, most companies entering into a restructuring do not possess the reporting infrastructure or processes necessary to properly monitor and control liquidity. A financial advisor with extensive experience in managing liquidity can be an invaluable resource in establishing such a system.

In general, liquidity management for distressed companies can be divided into three categories: 13-week cash-flow projections, daily cash-balance monitoring, and a liquidity-improvement plan.

13-week cash-flow projections

Most practitioners use a 13-week cash-flow forecast that projects receipts and disbursements directly. When applicable, these projections will often incorporate a borrowing base forecast to give a comprehensive view of both expected future cash and liquidity.

Properly constructed and maintained, the 13-week forecast provides advance warning of impending liquidity events. Combined with regular and frequent cash meetings, staffed by appropriate personnel, to monitor receipts and approve disbursements, the forecast becomes a powerful cash management tool and helps to ensure that the company stays aligned with its liquidity goals. Sales, purchasing, operations and financial personnel should all participate in the development of the 13-week projections to ensure a robust forecast — and to ensure that function managers are aware of targets and can be held accountable for them. Budget to actual results should be prepared weekly and significant variances from the forecast explained and taken into account in refining the projections.

Finally, consideration should be given to producing these projections by region, legal entity or business unit to offer a better insight into cash usage, or the impact of specific jurisdictional matters that may prevent the repatriation or movement of cash, such as European director liability issues or limitations on paying dividends from China.

Daily cash-balance monitoring

This should be established in a manner consistent with company operations — for example, by account, legal entity or country, etc. It is critical to understand the actual cash balances, where they are located and any impediments to the use or transfer of cash. This is important both in managing disbursements and in planning a future liquidity strategy.

For example, monies located in countries that restrict the withdrawal of cash should not be relied upon to fund cash shortfalls in other regions. Similarly, funds held in accounts located at a secured lender may become unavailable under certain circumstances, such as the occurrence of a default.

A clear view of cash balances — their location and associated risks and restrictions — is critical to a strong cash management system in a tight liquidity environment. They should be reconciled on a weekly basis with the 13-week cash-flow forecast.

Liquidity-improvement plan

This document captures the company's strategy for enhancing liquidity both through internal actions and external sources. The anticipated impact of internal measures should be incorporated into the 13-week cash-flow projections once the timing and results are fairly certain. In addition, the liquidity-improvement plan should incorporate milestones against which progress can be tracked, and contingency arrangements to mitigate liquidity shortfalls should the company not achieve its plan.

Internal liquidity-improvement actions

While available liquidity-enhancement measures will vary between industries, and companies, a number of key areas are applicable to most distressed situations:

Working capital

An analysis of accounts receivable will often bring to light opportunities for more effective collection efforts, including enticing customers to pay earlier through the use of discounts, a prioritized approach to collecting past due amounts, and the use of alternative collection methods. Similarly, accounts payable can often be stretched, effectively allowing the company to use its suppliers' balance sheets to support operations. Suppliers can also sometimes be consolidated, providing the company with additional leverage in negotiating favorable terms or pricing.

It may also be a good idea to limit employee access to alternative methods of buying goods and services, such as company-issued purchasing cards. Employees can sidestep the liquidity-management process through non-standard payment methods, potentially harming cash flow through unapproved or unexpected purchases.

The careful management of inventory is another key aspect of working-capital improvements. Inventory should be analyzed for slow-moving and excess goods, and consideration should be given to liquidating items that will not be used in the near term. Safety stock and min-max levels should also be revisited to encourage use of on-hand items, reducing unnecessary cash purchases.

Purchasing levels must be based on realistic demand forecasts to avoid excess inventory throughout the production line and an unwarranted accumulation of finished product. Slow-moving items should be purchased in small quantities, even if the per-unit costs are higher, as overall liquidity will often be enhanced. The company should also look to apply all available vendor credits to minimize cash disbursements.

For boards of seasonal businesses, or businesses in industries coming out of a slump in production, it is important to be aware that increased volumes require higher amounts of working capital, tying up liquidity on the balance sheet. This drop in liquidity is typically not fully offset by increased availability of asset-backed loans, as a result of borrowing base restrictions.

Cost-reduction efforts

In good times, companies tend to accumulate costs and, once distressed, often find that their cost base is inflated relative to current revenues. Regardless of whether this misalignment is due to a failed growth plan, lax cost controls or falling volumes, the biggest liquidity improvements during restructurings typically result from cost-reduction efforts.

Some of the most significant costs at almost all companies are wages and benefits. Depending on the location — the US versus Europe, for example — and composition — union versus non-union — of the workforces, headcount rationalization can be one of the most meaningful liquidity-enhancement measures taken by a distressed company. Employee and labor expense must be sized appropriately relative to business volumes. A consolidation of shifts, for example, may be an appropriate way to scale back hourly labor. Alternatively, reducing the hours worked per week, eliminating overtime and/or implementing temporary layoffs will reduce weekly payroll expense and potentially induce attrition.

The company should also look at contract employees and outside services and determine if the current structure is cost effective or if it would be better off with company employees performing those roles. Particularly at the middle management level, staff can be asked to take on additional responsibilities that were previously outside their job descriptions, allowing the company to reduce what is often a fairly high-cost and overstaffed area.

Consideration should also be given to minimizing non-critical employee benefits. Healthcare benefits can be reassessed to increase the employee cost-sharing component and discretionary perks such as a 401-k match can be suspended. Furthermore, defined-benefit pension and post-retirement healthcare plans should be evaluated to determine the impact of freezing or terminating them.

While it is expected, and to some extent desired, that a rationalization of hours and benefits will result in some level of attrition, a retention plan may be necessary to help ensure that key employees remain in their current role. To improve effectiveness, these plans should be based on metrics such as EBITDA, cash flows or permanent cost-saving targets to align the interests of staff with those of the company.

An analysis of other fixed and semi-fixed cash costs is also advisable. Reductions in facilities costs and travel charges, as well as the outsourcing of IT and back-office functions, are examples of areas that may offer cash-conservation opportunities.

Negotiation of over-market contracts

Aggressive negotiation for payment relief on over-market contracts is important in preserving, and potentially enhancing, liquidity. If the restructuring involves reorganization through the bankruptcy courts, then the company will have the ability to reject contracts that are not to its liking. Even in the absence of a filing, the company should pursue negotiations with the aim of reducing contractual expenditures in the near term. Mortgages on properties where the underlying asset value is well below the liability being carried are ideal targets. Leases signed during better real estate markets can also present opportunities for reductions. Similarly, property taxes and insurance payments based on historical asset values, which may have since deteriorated, are often overlooked as sources of new liquidity. Successful renegotiation of commodity and labor contracts can also improve a company's future cash flows.

Capital expenditures, under-utilized assets and restructuring costs

Officers and directors of distressed companies should critically examine all new capital projects, except for those with exceptionally short payback periods. Maintenance capital expenditures can also often be deferred, but not indefinitely since such outlays are often necessary for the continuation of existing business operations or may have health and safety matters associated with them. While many will argue that deferring capital expenditures will impair the company's long-term prospects, the priority is to secure the company's ability to continue operating in the short term.

Similarly, the monetization of under-utilized or idle assets is a viable method of bringing in cash. It is important to focus not on the book gain or loss of the transaction, but rather on the amount of incremental liquidity. It does not matter what the company originally paid for the asset.

One counter-intuitive aspect of a restructuring is that it is sometimes better to refrain from cutting certain costs if the upfront charges of doing so will harm liquidity in the short term. For example, it is not uncommon for workers in certain European countries to be paid a lump sum amount equal to multiple years of their salary upon layoff. When this cannot be mitigated by negotiating with the employee to pay the severance over time, it may well be better to forgo the layoff until the company has stabilized.

Divestiture of businesses

Often, restructurings require management to reconsider long-held beliefs on the composition and strategy of the company. Each business in the group should be thoroughly evaluated to determine whether it is a drag on liquidity. As part of this process, it is important to ensure that inter-company and/or inter-business transactions are reflected as if on an arm's-length basis. Whether because of stale allocations, tax strategies or internal politics, it is not uncommon to find transactions that do not reflect market prices or actual costs.

Consideration must also be given to the impact on these transactions if one or more of the company's businesses are divested. For example, certain fixed costs that were shared between a number of businesses might have to be borne by a smaller operations base after divestiture.

The effect on working capital and other cash flows must also be neutralized in this analysis if some operations are acting as an "internal bank" to others through abnormal terms on inter-company sales, below-market loans, etc.

For businesses that are found to be currently detrimental to cash flow, and possibly those non-core operations that are not, management should realistically assess their potential. For each business, management should provide a recommendation to the board as to whether or not it should be divested or otherwise shut down. While this assessment cannot be based solely on liquidity, it can often bring to light a better understanding of where cash flows are being generated within the company, as well as opportunities for liquidity improvement both from ceasing operations that are not cash-flow positive and from the sale of operations.

External sources of liquidity

In times of economic distress, it is important that management and the board think beyond the "usual suspects" when exploring external sources of liquidity. While established lenders and, possibly, equity participants are an integral part of any search for funding, governments and customers have recently provided funding where more traditional sources would not.

The pursuit of both internal and external sources improves the odds of controlling a liquidity crisis. The liquidity-management infrastructure and "self help" measures that a company establishes internally can be important in persuading external sources to provide funds. Before releasing any money, these parties will want to know that management has a handle on the liquidity issues, has a plan to address them and is in control of the situation.

Traditional external sources

In a distressed situation, often the most likely sources of external funding are existing stakeholders. By virtue of their previous decisions, these parties are already "in bed" with the company and will likely be affected by the outcome of the restructuring. They will generally be seeking a solution that provides the best outcome possible for themselves and, as a result, may be more flexible and co-operative than parties that are making an initial investment decision. Another advantage of working with current stakeholders is speed. Time-consuming processes such as due diligence should be greatly reduced as a result of the stakeholders' familiarity with the company.

That said, new investors can present advantages as well. They make decisions with an understanding of the company's current financial health and typically do not have "investor fatigue" or an axe to grind. In addition, many of these organizations specialize in, and are comfortable with, distressed situations.

Secured lenders. A good place to start is with the company's existing secured lenders. While banks are sometimes viewed as the enemy, distressed companies can often establish a co-operative working relationship with them. Commencing discussions with these parties to understand their views and concerns is a first step in establishing an external funding plan.

The type of collateral that supports the loan will significantly influence the behavior of secured lenders. Somewhat counter-intuitively, a company may actually have more leverage in negotiating with its lenders when it is underwater and the collateral is not easily liquidated. In such circumstances, lenders may be more willing to restructure the debt to ease covenants, reduce or defer interest and amortization payments, and extend maturities.

A lender in an over-secured position, while possessing better negotiating leverage, may also be willing to work with the company in the hope of avoiding the bad publicity associated with foreclosure and of retaining the lending relationship in the future. In such circumstances, it may be possible to obtain incremental liquidity through such items as changes to advance rates on working capital based loans, or additional borrowings on significantly over-secured positions or unencumbered assets.

Regardless of the reason for co-operation, however, management must be able to demonstrate that the lenders' collateral will not be diminished during the restructuring and that recoveries are likely to be better with lender support.

If lenders are not comfortable on this last point, it is unlikely they will provide accommodations to the company and, as seen in a number of large retail cases in 2008 and 2009, may opt to take aggressive action in seeking to recover the value of their collateral.

Management and the board should be aware that any debt accommodation is likely to have significant costs. Apart from amendment fees, increases in interest rates, possible equity incentives, professional fees and the like, a greater level of scrutiny by the lenders will undoubtedly arise. They will want additional clarity on the company's financial performance and its progress with liquidity and operating improvements. They will almost certainly look for a robust cash management, monitoring and reporting process and may insist that the company attempt to sell certain assets to pay down the loan or take other specified actions. Finally, lenders may stipulate that the company's financial advisor be acceptable to them and, in more extreme cases, may require the company to install a chief restructuring officer to help ensure that it remains on track with its restructuring plan and has the resources on hand to address unexpected issues.

Other options. While the secured lenders may be "first on the scene" in a distressed situation, other options can be available to companies during a restructuring. In instances where the collateral value of pledged assets significantly exceeds the amount of first lien debt, an existing or new lender may be willing to provide a commitment in exchange for a second lien on the company's collateral. Accounts receivable (AR) securitizations, to the extent such assets are not otherwise encumbered, may be an option for certain companies where collection issues are minimal and advance rates and interest rates are favorable to what would be available under a traditional asset-based loan.

For companies whose restructuring plan includes engaging in bankruptcy proceedings, additional liquidity can sometimes be found on a secured basis through debtor in possession financing. DIP loans provide the lender with a super priority claim, which allows for greater assurance of a full recovery. DIP loans can be provided by new lenders. However, the company's existing secured lenders will often be willing to roll their pre-petition secured claims into a DIP facility in exchange for incremental borrowings so that, among other things, they can enjoy the protections afforded by the super priority status.

Companies may also explore opportunities to restructure their balance sheet through an exchange offer, which involves the conversion of debt, typically high interest-bearing, to either lower-interest secured debt (to the extent excess collateral exists) or more commonly to equity or some sort of equity instrument. This approach is often used with unsecured bondholders, who may couple this exchange offer with an infusion of cash to protect potential recovery. However, some senior lenders may also be willing to engage in exchange offers.

In over-leveraged situations, exchange offers can often provide the required relief to a company

through the reduction of interest and principal payments. An unusual example of an exchange offer came in 2008, when Vertis and American Color Graphics, two of the largest printing and pre-media companies in North America, filed prepackaged Chapter 11 cases concurrently and merged, exchanging their bonds for an aggregate of $550 million in new notes and substantially all of the new equity of the merged group. This plan had very little impact on business operations, as all trade vendors were paid in the ordinary course. The consensual prepackaged restructuring allowed the combined company to reduce debt obligations by approximately $1 billion. The de-leveraged company emerged with a $250 million senior secured revolving credit exit facility and approximately $400 million of funded term-loan debt.

To the extent that a company is closely held, it may also be possible to convince the existing equity owners to infuse additional monies. The ability to accomplish this, however, is subject to numerous factors, including:

- Whether the ownership group believes that the company is being impacted by temporary market issues or, if not, whether it can be turned around.
- The leverage that equity has relative to existing lenders. For example, in a highly leveraged company with poor collateral, lenders may be more willing to provide an accommodation to resolve liquidity issues.
- The ability of the equity group to provide additional liquidity.

If existing equity holders are unwilling or unable to provide additional capital, new equity investors may also be sought. Such investment, if available, will likely come at the cost of control.

Regardless of the source of new equity funding, such an infusion will generally be viewed as an additional cushion by existing lenders and can be very beneficial in securing accommodations from them.

Non-traditional external funding sources

The type and extent of non-traditional funding available to a company will be dictated by its own circumstances, the industry in which it operates and, possibly, the political climate. Examples of non-traditional sources include customers and government entities.

When a company falls into financial distress, its customers are likely to be concerned with continuity of supply. While the maintenance of the customer base is a critical issue for any distressed enterprise, it can present an opportunity in industries where the products being manufactured are highly specialized and subject to long qualification periods. In such circumstances, a supplier may be able to negotiate accommodations with its customers that help to enhance its liquidity position. These accommodations can include a reduction in payment terms in order to obtain a one-time improvement in working capital, an infusion of funds by the customer to keep the ailing supplier operating, or payments to support the wind-down and resourcing of unprofitable products.

Such actions are common in the auto industry, where long lead times, qualification and safety issues often prevent rapid resourcing of products. The Delphi-General Motors relationship offers one of the most well-publicized examples of this, with GM ultimately providing billions of dollars to Delphi through direct funding, assumption of liabilities and other mechanisms to ensure that Delphi emerged from its restructuring as a viable entity. American Axle, which was on the cusp of bankruptcy for several years, was able to avoid a filing partly as a result of obtaining liquidity support from its largest customer, GM.

Governments can also be a significant source of external funding for companies. Though it is questionable whether this will occur in the future, perhaps the most spectacular example of this was the US government's actions during 2008 and 2009 when it provided enormous amounts of liquidity to the country's financial institutions and automotive industry, through such programs as TARP, to prevent a meltdown of the global financial infrastructure and a country-wide disruption to the US manufacturing base. Such actions were replicated in many areas of the world.

On a smaller and more common scale, government support can be found locally through tax and other incentives. For example, a company may be able to negotiate a real estate tax abatement or even some type of financial support to modernize facilities, in return for a commitment not to move or close local operations.

On a federal level, companies should seek to take advantage of recent programs that allow companies meeting certain criteria to recoup taxes paid in the past.

Other government opportunities also exist. Many companies, for example, have materially enhanced liquidity through negotiating deferrals of required pension funding payments with the Internal Revenue Service, giving them the breathing room to stabilize their businesses.

Conclusion

Rapidly taking action to generate sufficient liquidity is one of the hallmarks of successful restructurings. Without adequate liquidity, options erode and companies can quickly deteriorate as customers, suppliers, lenders and other stakeholders all seek to protect themselves. In a distressed situation, the monitoring and management of liquidity becomes paramount and boards need to have a much more detailed understanding of the company's current and future liquidity position, risks and options.

Boards often provide critical guidance to management and need additional infrastructure to support their decision-making. Chief among the requirements are cash-flow projections based on credible receipts and disbursements, and a detailed liquidity-improvement plan.

These items are essential to achieving success under the two-pronged approach to improving liquidity: the pursuit of both internal measures and external funding.

The views expressed herein are those of the authors and are not necessarily the views of FTI Consulting Inc and its other professionals.

18

When cash is king: Understanding cash requirements for distressed companies and maintaining effective management and reporting systems

Ralph S Tuliano,
President and Executive
Managing Director,
Thomas J Allison,
Executive Vice President and
Senior Managing Director, and
Melissa Kibler Knoll,
Senior Managing Director.
**Mesirow Financial
Consulting LLC**

'Everything that can be counted does not necessarily count; everything that counts cannot necessarily be counted' (Albert Einstein)

One might be surprised, upon reading a series of Einstein's quotations, at how well his advice applies to those charged with leading a distressed company. Understanding what is important and knowing how to measure it are key ingredients in a successful restructuring.

In terms of what counts, never has the saying "Cash is King" been more true. Particularly amid the fallout from the economic crisis, cash management can no longer be business as usual for the company experiencing financial difficulties.

It is critical that executives have the knowledge necessary to identify and address impending cash shortages in time to avoid a crisis. This is a process that will drive decisions on everything from the human elements, such as staffing levels, to the ability of the company to survive a restructuring. As such, the mandate for implementing an effective cash management system needs to come from the top.

We will address the new perspective that must be applied, key success factors in cash forecasting, and the likely cash requirements during a restructuring.

Not business as usual: managing cash in a distressed company

'We cannot solve our problems with the same thinking we used when we created them'
'Intellectuals solve problems, geniuses prevent them' (Albert Einstein)

Rather than earnings per share or other accrual metrics, what matters in a distressed situation is cash. It gives a company increased flexibility. It provides options for addressing operational problems, and reduces the leverage of creditors in negotiating the terms of a financial restructuring. In short, it allows offensive rather than defensive strategies. While earnings are necessarily one of the principal measures in judging a company's long-term performance and shareholder value, cash is the barometer of success for businesses operating near or within the zone of insolvency.

So a deeper understanding of this valuable asset is vital. A company must shift from a monthly or quarterly outlook to one that is much more frequent – weekly for the near term, daily if in the throes of a liquidity crisis. Information must be more timely than typical accounting data, and detailed enough to enable a true understanding of the various sources and uses of cash. Only then will management be able to identify the true causes of a company's problems, whether underperforming products or divisions, bloated cost structures, competitive pressures, over-leverage, inadequate working-capital management or any number of other culprits. Armed with this data on the underlying causes of strained liquidity, officers and directors can be proactive in preventing a crisis.

Communication is another differentiator in distressed situations. Internally, companies must look beyond traditional reporting lines. All the organization's leaders must be involved in order to ensure the changes in both process and mindset that are required to implement an effective cash forecast. Additionally, top management across the various functional, operational and geographic areas must confer regularly to re-examine spending decisions and balance priorities so as to achieve the broader corporate goals.

External communication also has to be enhanced in a restructuring. Lack of reliable information on cash and liquidity is often the first concern voiced by lenders and other creditor groups. They will expect a 13-week cash-flow forecast, as well as regular reports of actual results and explanations of variances from the forecast.

Providing reasonable projections, quickly addressing issues that are identified, and eliminating surprises are key factors in establishing management's credibility with lenders and other creditors. In the case of an in-court restructuring, these and other, longer-term cash forecasts will be utilized by the parties to determine the size of the post-petition debtor-in-possession (DIP) financing. Often, they will also be the basis for certain covenants governing the use of that DIP financing or cash collateral.

The evolution of bankruptcy law and practice, as well as the constrained credit environment, has resulted in DIP agreements that frequently contain milestones requiring filing of a plan of reorganization or sale of the company by a certain date. A debtor's cash-flow forecast plays significantly in negotiating the length of the "runway" that lenders are willing to provide.

Many companies, particularly large public ones, do not have accounting systems that easily accommodate this new view of a cash position. In the next section, we address how to create one.

Cash forecasting: implementing an effective management and reporting system

'A man should look for what is, and not for what he thinks should be'

'I never think of the future — it comes soon enough'
(Albert Einstein)

The priority of any cash management and reporting system should be to give executives the information

---

Case in point

A large public company focuses on earnings instead of cash. It views this as the dominant measure of success and rewards its management team for maximizing reported profits. Cash flow is not something that has been of historic concern, since debt financing has been readily available over its entire history.

When the economy takes a drastic turn for the worse, however, the company finds its traditional sources of funding have contracted or disappeared. Suddenly, the market takes notice of the company's liquidity issues. While it appears to have valuable assets, it is cash poor and cannot monetize the assets as quickly as it wants. Management and the board, no longer in control of their fate, suddenly realize that reported earnings cannot save them.

---

needed to diagnose challenges to liquidity and to implement solutions. We often find clients are surprised by the problems exposed and the opportunities revealed once a thorough forecasting process has been put in place. Whether due to decentralized cash controls, compartmentalized management, historic focus or a combination of other factors, traditional financial reporting tools often fail to provide the depth of information needed for decision-making in a restructuring, and sometimes mask the real issues. As such, the leadership of a distressed company may need to abandon preconceived notions when undertaking the cash forecasting process. We will, therefore, have to depart from Einstein's view about the value of considering the future. Clearly, he had in mind neither the huge challenges facing the officers and directors of a troubled company, nor the expectations of its demanding creditor constituents.

Managing change
In many situations the treasury group may already have its own cash forecasting system, which needs to be understood in terms of the process for its preparation, its accuracy and its usefulness to management. The focus can then shift to designing a new forecast that builds on or enhances the existing one. It is often advisable to run the new and old systems in parallel during implementation, to allow adequate testing and modification and to obtain "buy-in" from the treasury staff, who will ultimately be responsible for preparing the cash forecast and related reporting.

Top management also need to be aware that there may well be tension among and within various internal functions, as changes to "business as usual" are required to prepare an effective forecast. Finance often has responsibility for long-term earnings projections, operations for business forecasts, and treasury for short-term cash management — and all of these areas will have to co-ordinate. Further, the information technology group may resist the reporting changes needed to extract new data in a different manner.

These various departments will frequently have been downsized and may already be overtaxed, so it is essential that the leaders of a distressed company acknowledge this dynamic and emphasize the importance of the cash forecasting process to the success of the restructuring. Creating accountability within each of the different functions is a key to obtaining co-operation; people pay attention to what is measured. If the cash forecast is regularly utilized in decision-making and explanations are required for variances, then more care will be taken in its preparation and more effort expended in meeting it.

Assessing the data

Achieving a sustainable cash forecasting process entails having data that is timely, accessible, detailed, relevant and reliable. The first step is determining what historical financial data is available to the business through its traditional accounting and treasury functions, and what kind of projections are generated by existing budgeting and forecasting efforts. Often this information is produced on a monthly, quarterly or annual basis, so it is important to understand the sources of the data and thus the company's ability to extract or create it on a more frequent basis.

The level of detail is also important. Can revenue, collections and margins be tracked by customer, product, division, geographic region, or some other significant category? Can payments be classified by the type of operating expenditure (payroll, inventory purchases, rent, utilities, etc) or capital expenditure, instead of just as "accounts payable"?

We typically hope the answer to these questions is yes, as it provides for a much more robust cash management process. However, the time and cost that may be required in obtaining such depth of insight must also be weighed against its benefit, and we have encountered situations where using more aggregated data is the right choice.

The forecast is generally implemented using a

Case in point

A technology company is losing market share to better-capitalized competitors. With billions of dollars of bond debt soon to fall due, it must execute a balance sheet restructuring while simultaneously investing scarce resources in new technologies to reverse the loss of its customer base. Paramount in this process is the effective management of its precious cash, which has never been a focal point for the business in its long history.

By using many of the techniques outlined in this chapter, the company was able to preserve its liquidity, invest in its business and achieve a successful restructuring without a bankruptcy filing.

---

cash-flow "model" and will be most efficient if prepared, populated and updated electronically. As such, knowledge of a company's underlying information-technology and accounting systems is also required.

With a basic understanding of the available data, the next step is identifying the critical metrics and their drivers, and analyzing related trends. This process starts not with crunching numbers, however, but with knowing the business. How are the operations managed? What internal and external factors have the most significant impact on the company's cash position? What data is available on which factors to use in developing the forecast assumptions? Who within the company has the strongest sense of the marketplace and the company's performance in certain areas? The best cash forecasting processes combine accessible data with individuals who know how to interpret that data.

Preparing the forecast

As noted above, cash forecasts used by a troubled company typically provide a rolling projection for at least 13 weeks, often adding monthly projections for another three to nine months. There tend to be two approaches to establishing the basis for a cash forecast — (a) extrapolation of longer-range projections and (b) historical run rate — and which one is used will depend on their reliability for a given metric. For example, historical run rates may be appropriate for fixed expenses or for segments of the business that are fairly static. Changes in demand, however, will often require that revenue and collection estimates rely more on projections.

In either case, one must carefully consider the

Drivers in cash-flow forecasting

Revenue/receipts — price, volume, growth, seasonality, billing cycle, accounts receivable, sales outstanding, bad debts.

Cost of sales/gross margin — product/ materials, inventory purchases, direct labor, overheads, inventory balances, inventory turns, terms/days payable outstanding.

Payroll and benefits — headcount, wages, bonuses, commissions, payroll taxes, healthcare costs.

Operating expenses — sales, general and administrative (SG&A), occupancy, locations, fixed vs variable, percentage of sales, terms/ days payable outstanding.

Taxes — income tax rates, refunds.

Capital expenditures — maintenance level, acquisitions and dispositions.

Financing — revolver, borrowing base, debt service, letters of credit, interest, fees, refinancing.

Cash on hand — minimum levels, float, historical variability.

timing of collections and payments, rather than relying on a traditional profit-and-loss view of the business. Revenue and expense must be translated into receipts and disbursements.

There is often a time difference between recognizing revenue and collecting receivables. Expenses, such as insurance, may be recognized monthly but paid quarterly or annually. Further, the validity of a weekly forecast requires more thought than simply dividing a monthly forecast amount by four. The timing of significant monthly or bi-monthly payments, such as rent and payroll, must be considered, and irregular cash items like pension contributions need to be captured. Other non-operating receipts and payments must also be incorporated, including capital expenditures, asset sales and financing items.

The "translation" process described above requires that the balance sheet be considered in addition to the income statement. Fluctuations in working capital can often have a big impact on overall cash balances. At a more practical level, however, any lender looking at the cash forecast will immediately turn to the page where the borrowing base and revolver level are forecast for an asset-based loan.

Another assumption that should be evaluated carefully is the minimum cash balance. A business

may have significant in-transit receipts or disbursements that have not cleared. Others may need to maintain cash-on-hand, such as a retailer holding cash in its stores. The variability in historical receipts and disbursements, as well as one-time cash needs, must be considered, in addition to requirements under any credit agreements.

Reporting and updating the forecast

A distressed company should anticipate that both the internal and external users of the cash forecast will expect reporting on a weekly basis and an explanation of variances. In general, variances should be tracked weekly and cumulatively and explanations should be provided for each discrete item, indicating the underlying cause and whether it is a matter of timing or a permanent difference.

Additionally, it is advisable to measure and report against both book and bank cash balances. Reporting at a book level is a better gauge of how the business is performing; reporting at a bank level, however, is more important to understanding how much cash will be available for use.

A discussion of reporting must also lead to consideration of the timing for results measurement and the issuance of updated forecasts. It is helpful if this question is addressed early in the process. We find it best to measure progress against the original forecast for the entire 13-week period to allow for a thorough assessment of both accuracy and inputs.

An equally important goal, however, is to have a projection that presents the most accurate picture possible of a company's cash horizon. While a rolling cash forecast necessarily adds on another week each period, a significant number of permanent differences may entail periodic updates to the entire forecast, perhaps as often as monthly. Just as a business might set its annual budget at the beginning of a year but later do an updated forecast based on actual results and revised expectations, so should a cash forecast incorporate that feature.

Actual results can be compared to both the original and updated forecasts. Dual comparisons will put a "stake in the ground" in terms of reliability and accountability, while at the same time ensuring that the most up-to-date information on the cash position is available to decision-makers.

Scenario analysis is another important concept. We often field questions on how "conservative" people should be when preparing forecasts, and the best answer is to try to be as reasonable as possible. While it is true that banks and creditors are far more forgiving of an upside surprise, large variances from a short-term cash forecast tend not to convey an impression of management outperforming but rather one of a lack of knowledge of their own business. That said, assessing downside scenarios for a company's cash position can be an important part of prudent contingency planning.

A cash forecast will never be exactly right; a forecast is by its nature an estimate. However, it can certainly be more than informative about the direction and drivers of a company's liquidity. The key to achieving this is to elevate the process far above the level of being just a box that needs ticking on a list of things requested by the parties in a restructuring.

Liquidity management: understanding the inventory of cash requirements for distressed companies

'The only reason for time is so that everything doesn't happen at once'
'You have to learn the rules of the game. And then you have to play better than anyone else' (Albert Einstein)

Liquidity management extends beyond preparing a good cash forecast to using that information to make meaningful changes. A forecast provides the roadmap out of distress, identifying the obstacles ahead and giving the company the time to make any necessary detours or to choose a new route.

Maximizing cash
Instituting measures to reduce expenditure and maximize cash should be foremost in the minds of officers and directors in a troubled company. This does not mean the long term should always be sacrificed for the short term; it does mean ensuring that the company lives to fight another day. Expenditures should be prioritized in terms of rate of return and payback, and non-critical spending may need to be deferred. This is the time to eliminate waste and over-capacity and to consolidate support functions.

On occasion, this process will entail renegotiating or terminating contracts and commitments. A distressed business may find itself re-evaluating the merits of paying discounted cash settlements today to avoid future obligations, such as buying out a lease for an unused facility. Alternatively, it may seek to preserve cash now at the expense of higher costs in the future, such as stopping work on a capital project that will have significant start-up costs if subsequently resumed.

In addition to expense reductions, working-capital management can contribute greatly to liquidity. Negotiating longer vendor terms, eliminating excess or obsolete inventory, and aggressively pursuing customer collections will all help.

To make a real difference in maximizing cash, senior management should continually re-evaluate significant expenditures and commitments. The CFO and other decision-makers must be aware of the levers that can be pulled when flexibility is needed, because circumstances can change quickly in a restructuring. Spending authority should be reconsidered, with a bias towards decision-making at a more senior and centralized level.

One mechanism that we have used to institute spending discipline is a commitment review committee, which includes the heads of operations, customer service, information technology, sales, marketing and supply chain management, as well as the CFO. It meets once or twice a week to review and approve, defer or decline all non-payroll operating and capital expenditures over a certain threshold. The objectives include the following:

• Improve liquidity by deferring or eliminating cash spending, as appropriate. In particular, enable the deferral of non-critical cash spending during the determination of business strategy and implementation of any recapitalization transactions.
• Increase organizational focus and controls around cash usage through enhanced executive oversight.
• Achieve stronger alignment between cash spending and strategic priorities.
• Balance the needs of the business units in spending decisions.
• Impact cost structure and improve profitability through reduced spending.
• Achieve indirect spending reductions through greater employee awareness of spending discipline and a decrease in requests submitted.

Understanding cash requirements in bankruptcy
Our clients quickly become adept at dealing with the liquidity constraints endemic among distressed companies: reduced profitability, strained credit facilities and decreased credit terms. They are often surprised, however, by the additional cash requirements that accompany a bankruptcy filing.

A successful bankruptcy process starts with a thorough planning process, in which one of the primary goals is to retain sufficient operating cash for the post-filing period. As discussed above, the preparation of the cash forecast and negotiations of the DIP facility are vital to this process. However, certain cash management techniques should be considered prior to the filing as well.

A central feature of bankruptcy in the US is the automatic stay, which stops creditors from pursuing collection from a debtor after a petition has been filed. The flipside of the automatic stay, however, is that the debtor is prevented from paying any debts incurred pre-petition in the absence of court authority. While it is typical for debtors to seek, and judges to grant, authority to pay those amounts that would otherwise result in harm to the debtor, such as payments to employees or critical vendors, that approval is neither certain nor immediate. As such, a company preparing to file bankruptcy should consider adjusting the timing of the filing or making advance payments for items including: employee payroll, expense reimbursements and payroll taxes; insurance premiums and retirement benefit contributions; single-source vendors; and essential service providers. The bankruptcy law requires that a company's legal and financial professionals do not have any unpaid fees at the time the petition is filed, and the length of time taken to obtain court approval for payment of fees post-petition also makes advance retainers customary.

A company's largest unsecured creditors are most likely to be chosen by the United States Trustee to serve as members of the official committee of unsecured creditors, which will represent that class's interests in the bankruptcy proceedings. As such, companies should be aware of how their payment decisions pre-petition will affect the composition of the constituents who will be most influential in their reorganization.

The automatic stay can result in a significant one-time cash benefit as the business no longer has to pay its pre-petition debts currently. However, an offsetting impact is often experienced when a company's vendors institute requirements for cash on delivery (COD) or cash in advance (CIA). The United States Trustee also imposes certain fees based on disbursement levels that must be paid quarterly during the bankruptcy. Another key ingredient in a successful bankruptcy is having competent attorneys and advisors, and the debtor is responsible for payment of its own professionals and those of certain creditors. The amount and timing of all of these payments must be estimated for cash-planning purposes.

In what might be viewed as adding insult to injury, the 2005 Bankruptcy Abuse Prevention and Consumer Protection Act (BAPCPA) substantially increased some of the cash requirements a debtor will face. These include the following:

- Sellers of goods received by the debtor in the ordinary course of business within 20 days before bankruptcy have 'administrative claim' status. All such claims must be paid in full in order to confirm a plan of reorganization, and creditors may appeal for earlier payment. More than any other, this provision has significantly increased the cash burden on a reorganizing debtor.
- Suppliers may demand return of goods received 45 days or fewer before bankruptcy.
- Each employee may be entitled to a 'priority' claim of up to $10,950 for unpaid wages and benefits.
- Utilities are entitled to a deposit as assurance for payment for continued service after a bankruptcy. For debtors with big utility expenses, such as heavy manufacturers, this provision can be particularly onerous.
- Retention plans that compensate key employees for staying with the debtor for a certain period have been significantly restricted, but a company may obtain approval for incentive plans with appropriate targets.

What one quickly learns is that a company must have a lot of cash and manage it well in order to undertake a restructuring, particularly in a bankruptcy proceeding.

Conclusion

'Concern for man and his fate must always form the chief interest of all technical endeavors. Never forget this in the midst of your diagrams and equations'
'If you can't explain it simply, you don't understand it well enough' (Albert Einstein)

To return to our theme — cash is king — one of the worst decisions officers and directors of a troubled company can make is to persist with traditional cash management philosophies. A proactive approach should include an enhanced focus on preserving cash and improved tools for forecasting and reporting the cash position. These actions are essential in providing the resources that the leadership needs in order to do what is right for all those whose fates are interconnected with the company's — employees, customers, suppliers and capital providers.

Knowing how to manage cash and doing it well will not necessarily ensure success for a distressed company, but not doing so will certainly engender failure.

19

Derivatives after Lehman: Assessing your company's risk profile

Mark A McDermott and
John W Osborn, Partners,
**Skadden, Arps, Slate,
Meagher & Flom LLP**

In September 2008, Lehman Brothers Holdings and many of its affiliates commenced insolvency proceedings around the world. In the wake of the company's collapse, its estate representatives, creditors and other parties-in-interest have been left to unwind more than one million open derivatives trades. Due to the complexity of these products, the insolvency proceedings have generated, and will continue to generate, litigations that may lead to important new precedents in several areas.

Overview of lessons from Lehman

A number of important lessons can already be gleaned from Lehman's collapse and the recent bankruptcies of other companies that utilized derivatives and structured products. These lessons, in turn, can assist directors and senior management in formulating guiding principles for their own use of, and reliance on, these complex instruments by: (i) conducting a top-down, risk-adjusted assessment of their exposure; (ii) increasing awareness within their organizations of the workings of these instruments and the ramifications when trouble strikes; and (iii) developing internal best practices and other checks for managing the risks.

The lessons, and related observations, include the following. First, many derivatives transactions are so complex that it is easy not to fully appreciate the risks and the ramifications of using them. As a result, when a counterparty becomes troubled, events may play out in a manner that is not in keeping with the general understanding of many business people, or in a way that may actually frustrate the parties' commercial expectations. Second, derivatives can significantly reduce a party's options, especially those of the troubled counterparty. Indeed, the so-called derivatives "safe harbors" of the US Bankruptcy Code were designed largely to protect non-debtor counterparties, while reducing or eliminating the ability of debtor counterparties to avail themselves of the usual protections of the bankruptcy law.

Third, when a company finds itself in choppy waters, events related to its derivatives transactions tend to move with alarming speed. Accordingly, the boards and senior management of troubled companies and their counterparties will not usually have weeks to develop contingency plans or to make risk-adjusted assessments of their options. Rather, they may have only days — perhaps hours — in which to react. This is partly because under many derivatives contracts, counterparties mark the values of the positions daily; margin calls must be met within one or two days; and counterparties frequently have considerable discretion determining the amounts of their margin calls. These features underscore the need for boards to be well acquainted with their company's positions and exposure long before trouble develops.

Fourth, while most derivatives transactions further legitimate and entirely proper business aims, they can and have been abused — to the detriment, embarrassment and exposure of businesses and the individuals who use them. In this regard, the single most important guiding principle is to go beyond a narrow assessment of whether a particular transaction technically complies with the letter of the law or governing accounting principles, and to analyze whether it is implementing a legitimate aim; whether it looks and feels fair and proper; whether it has substance to it rather than merely form; and whether it is the kind of thing that would lead to embarrassment if described on the front page of *The Wall Street Journal*. From Enron, to Global Crossing, to Lehman, this fundamental principle seems to have been lost all too often among some of the country's brightest businessmen and women.

A series of examples of the principles from the Lehman bankruptcy and other recent cases are discussed below. These examples are not exhaustive. Indeed, the law remains very unsettled, due in no small part to the fact that the derivatives-related provisions of the Bankruptcy Code were overhauled in 2005, and then changed yet again in 2006. These provisions have not been fully tested in the courts. Accordingly, the Lehman bankruptcy court and others will be unraveling these matters for years to come.

Lehman repo 105

The first example comes from Lehman, and illustrates the guiding principle that something that is technically right as an accounting matter could actually be all wrong from a broader business perspective.

Prior to its collapse, Lehman relied heavily on repurchase agreements to finance its operations. Of course, there is nothing inherently wrong about the use of repurchase agreements. On the contrary, they may be the most prevalent form of short-term financing, involving trillions of dollars of transactions each day. Indeed, they are essential to the smooth functioning of the US economy, including the financing of Treasury obligations.

Under a repurchase agreement, a seller agrees to sell certain financial instruments, with a simultaneous agreement to buy back equivalent instruments at some future time at a price equal to the sales price plus an interest factor. The term of these arrangements can be very short — including a single day. While the assets contractually are "sold", repurchase agreements are, in substance, secured financing arrangements: the funds obtained from the buyer at the time of sale serve as a short-term loan that must be repaid on the date the seller has to repurchase the assets and pay the interest factor.

From a legal standpoint, there are some published court decisions that characterize repurchase agreements as sales, but there are others that treat them as financings. Based in part upon this split — and, more importantly, the economic substance of repurchase agreements — the generally accepted legal view, at least in the US, is that they cannot safely be viewed as involving "true sales" of assets; they must instead be viewed as financings. US accounting principles generally follow this approach, with the result that assets "sold" under a repurchase agreement continue to be carried on the seller's balance sheet, with the seller also including offsetting entries for the cash received upon the sale (asset) and its repurchase obligation (liability).

In the early 2000s, however, Lehman developed an approach that it believed allowed it to characterize some of the agreements as sales rather than mere financings. The company enhanced the effect of this approach by using the proceeds it received under the repurchase agreements to reduce its debt. The net result of this, from an accounting standpoint, was that Lehman's leverage was reduced: the financial assets were removed from its balance sheet; it received an offsetting entry on account of the cash received but utilized that cash to reduce its debt; and it did not need to book an offsetting liability for its repurchase obligation. This became an especially handy tool as Lehman found itself under increasing pressure in 2007 and 2008 to reduce leverage.

Lehman's approach relied on certain technical aspects of FASB 140, the accounting standard that governed at the time. The strategy had two key elements. First, the "haircut" on the repo sale was increased to a level above prevailing market terms. For example, Lehman sold assets worth $105 in exchange for repo financing of only $100, whereas the market would have afforded $100 in financing for only $102 of those assets.

Second, the company needed a legal opinion that the transferred assets were presumptively beyond the control of its creditors, even in an insolvency proceeding. This necessitated, in other words, an opinion that the repurchase transactions constituted "true sales" of the assets, not mere financings, under applicable law.

According to the examiner appointed in Lehman's bankruptcy case to investigate its demise, Lehman was unable to find an American law firm to provide such an opinion under US law. It did, however, obtain such an opinion under UK law. Accordingly, in implementing these "repo 105" trades, all the transactions by any Lehman entity were funneled through its primary UK subsidiary.

While this approach may have been correct as a

technical accounting matter under FASB 140, Lehman implemented tens of billions of dollars of repo 105 trades just prior to the closing of its quarterly reporting periods in 2007 and 2008, the effect of which was to (temporarily) reduce its leverage on its quarterly balance sheets. But it did not disclose this approach in its quarterly reports — including the fact that in most instances, it incurred new debt days after the close of each reporting period, so it could then repurchase the "sold" assets and close out the repo 105 trades.

Former Lehman employees interviewed by the examiner admitted that repo 105 transactions had no economic substance and that they were designed solely as an accounting maneuver to allow the company to report lower leverage than was actually the case. Accordingly, and notwithstanding possible technical compliance with the accounting standards, the examiner concluded that Lehman's repo 105 strategy gave rise to colorable claims for breach of fiduciary duty and violations of securities disclosure laws by certain of Lehman's officers and other employees.

History repeats itself

One of the many unfortunate results has been that judges, regulators, investors and others may now have an unfairly jaundiced view of repurchase agreements, which are entirely legitimate financing techniques. Indeed, the SEC has announced it will conduct an inquiry into the use of the repo 105 structure by financial firms. This may become an example of history repeating itself: Enron's alleged abuse of off-balance sheet special-purpose securitization vehicles in the early 2000s led to an unfair perception of the structures. Such abuses — and the negative reactions of judges, investors and regulators — only make it harder and costlier for businesses to access the capital markets.

Boards and senior management would be well advised to consider these points as they assess existing and potential structured finance and related techniques that rely on the technical accounting treatment of repurchase agreements or other derivatives. In this regard, it is worth noting that while FASB 140 has been significantly revised, newly implemented FASBs 166 and 167 retain the same core concepts upon which Lehman relied in developing its repo 105 strategy.

US Bankruptcy Code safe harbors

Under the Bankruptcy Code, the commencement of insolvency proceedings generally stays most creditor collection efforts. The Code was significantly amended, however, most recently in 2005 and 2006, to afford "safe harbors" to numerous classes of derivatives agreements, including repurchase agreements, and securities, commodity, forward and swap contracts. In a nutshell, these safe harbors allow non-debtor counterparties to enforce bankruptcy-related defaults against bankrupt counterparties, including their contractual rights to terminate and close out the trades and liquidate their collateral.

These provisions, as they have been interpreted in Lehman and other recent bankruptcy cases, highlight that derivatives contracts may operate differently from what is expected; that they can reduce optionality; and that they can accelerate the course of events, necessitating rapid decision-making by boards and senior management.

For example, the 2005 revisions to the Bankruptcy Code define a qualifying, safe harbor repurchase agreement in very simple terms as a transfer of qualifying securities (including mortgage loans and related securities) with a simultaneous repurchase obligation. Significantly, the accounting and legal characterization of a repurchase agreement as either a financing or a sale was rendered irrelevant by the 2005 revisions. Indeed, the legislative history to the statute states that courts should no longer attempt to assess the economic substance of a transaction in order to determine whether a repurchase agreement qualifies for safe harbor treatment.

As a result of this change, agreements that may, on their face, not appear to qualify could in fact do so. For instance, many lenders modified their real estate lending forms post 2005 to comply with the safe harbors. However, these forms still "look" and "feel" more like secured loans than traditional repurchase agreements; indeed, they bear little resemblance to the forms of agreement developed by the Bond Market Association and other industry groups. Yet they are, in fact, safe harbor agreements.

The upshot is that those unfamiliar with the safe harbor provisions may not fully appreciate that their businesses are parties to agreements that could be closed out immediately when trouble hits; and that they will have little or no leverage, under the Bankruptcy Code or otherwise, for restructuring their affairs.

The 2005 revisions largely worked as anticipated when mortgage originators started filing for bankruptcy in early 2007 (since then, more than 150 have been forced into bankruptcy). These originators had sold large pools of their mortgages into securitization vehicles. Pending accumulation of pools sizable enough to securitize, the lenders financed the mortgages short-term through so-called "gestation" or "warehouse" repurchase agreement facilities. This is typical in the industry today.

But when financial trouble strikes a mortgage originator, there is little optionality available for it. Indeed, none of those that filed for bankruptcy were able to reorganize in any traditional sense of the word. Rather, their repurchase agreement buyers closed out their positions immediately, and the originators collapsed into bankruptcy court, where their only option was a very rapid sale of their servicing platforms.

Some entities in the mortgage securities business did not even have that option. For instance, funds sponsored by Bear Stearns and Carlyle Capital purchased mortgage-backed securities and financed them with qualifying, safe harbor repurchase agreements. Their business models were premised almost entirely on capturing an incremental interest differential between the interest paid on the securities and the financing charges under the repurchase agreements. When there were major market dislocations and their counterparties marked down the value of these securities and made margin calls, however, the funds did not have enough cash to meet the calls. In each instance their total asset positions — each in the tens of billions of dollars — were closed out and liquidated in a matter of days. The funds dissolved pursuant to offshore liquidation regimes.

Unexpected consequences

Even parties to more long-term supply agreements can be faced with unexpected results. At first blush, these may not appear to qualify as safe harbors. In fact, one bankruptcy court recently ruled that "ordinary supply agreements" do not, relying for its ruling on legislative history which says just that. However, based upon a very strict reading of the safe harbor statutes, the federal court of appeals reversed the bankruptcy court's ruling. The key takeaway for boards and senior management conducting a risk assessment of long-term supply agreements is that their company may have far greater or lesser rights — depending on which party is distressed and the economics of the agreement — than they might have anticipated in the event of trouble.

For instance, a supplier of a commodity under a long-term contract may believe that the contract constitutes a significant asset that it can retain if it

determines to restructure its affairs under the Bankruptcy Code. The reality, however, is that this may constitute either a forward or a swap contract under the very technical terms of the safe harbor statute. If so, then the agreement that would otherwise constitute a valuable asset may vanish in the event of the seller's bankruptcy, because the non-debtor buyer would be able to terminate the agreement upon a bankruptcy default. An in-court restructuring of the seller simply may not be a viable alternative in such circumstances.

Confusion reigns with CDOs

Yet another example of the somewhat unpredictable workings of the safe harbors is afforded by recent rulings in Lehman's bankruptcy proceeding. These rulings arose from an extraordinarily complex investment vehicle called a synthetic collateralized debt obligation (CDO) transaction. The key point here is that these structures included a swap agreement, along with an agreement between the swap counterparty and the holders of securities that established priorities with respect to collateral for both sets of obligations. The swap counterparty's rights were senior to those of the securities holders — except that in the event of a default by Lehman, that priority was to be inverted.

Litigation was commenced in both the US and UK courts regarding the enforceability of this provision in several transactions where Lehman entities were the debtor parties to the swap. The non-debtor counterparties argued, among other things, that the swap component meant the entire transaction was a qualifying safe harbor agreement and, hence, that the inversion of the parties' relative priorities upon a bankruptcy default was entirely proper and enforceable. Indeed, parties pointed out that billions of dollars of these structures had been implemented over the years — and that investors and rating agencies relied upon this priority inversion in assessing risk and rating the securities.

The matter was litigated first in the High Court of Justice in London, which ruled in favor of the non-debtor counterparties. The High Court's ruling was upheld by the Court of Appeal. Lehman's request for a hearing by the UK Supreme Court remains pending.

The very same matter was then litigated in the US bankruptcy court presiding over the US aspects of the proceedings — which ruled directly contrary to the UK courts. The confusion that now reigns is virtually unprecedented in the history of the bankruptcy system. Moreover, if the US ruling stands up on appeal, it may have implications outside the area of synthetic CDOs. As an example, the long-term supply agreements referred to above, and indeed many other commodity forward transactions, typically include provisions under which a defaulting party does not receive any value upon the termination of the contract. This type of "one-way payment" or "walk away" provision might be challenged under the same US Bankruptcy Code provisions that were at issue in the synthetic CDO cases.

The lesson for boards and senior management who engage in very complex structured finance transactions is clear: the mere fact that a structure has gained widespread industry acceptance and rating agency approval is no guarantee it will work as planned in the event of a meltdown — in other words, when the negotiated protection is needed most. Indeed, most of the indenture trustees involved in Lehman's synthetic CDO transactions simply froze after the bankruptcy — a result in no small part of a simple letter sent by Lehman representatives asserting that any effort by the trustees to close out the positions and liquidate the collateral would have exposed them to damages for intentional violation of the automatic stay. In this fashion, the "stay and delay" risk of bankruptcy that parties thought they had eliminated through these structures was made manifest.

Distressed CMBS-based structures

Additional derivative transactions that were, and will continue to be, negatively impacted by Lehman's collapse and the ensuing economic downturn are commercial mortgage-backed securities (CMBSs). Indeed an estimated $1.4 trillion of commercial real estate obligations are scheduled to mature between 2011 and 2014 and, accordingly, they will likely be part of a continuing wave of corporate defaults and derivatives-related litigation in years to come.

In a typical CMBS structure, an owner of income-producing real estate transfers it to a "bankruptcy remote" or "special purpose" vehicle (SPV) — an entity that exists purely to own the real estate, and whose charter provides that it may not voluntarily file for bankruptcy without the approval of an independent board member who must consider only the interests of the SPV and its creditors in reaching a decision.

Under this structure, a mortgage lender makes a loan to the SPV secured by the property, the proceeds of which are upstreamed to the vehicle's corporate parent. The lender then transfers the loan

to a trust, which in turn issues securities or certificates that are secured by the mortgage. As a consequence, the value of a CMBS is derivative of the underlying mortgage and property.

These structures are designed largely to defeat bankruptcy: the independent board member and related aspects of the structures make it more difficult for borrowers to avail themselves voluntarily of the bankruptcy laws. They also make it difficult for involuntary proceedings to be commenced. Even when these structures become the subject of bankruptcy proceedings, they may be very shortlived. The borrower is in effect a "single asset" borrower. If its only creditor is a recalcitrant lender, the borrower simply may have no realistic prospect of reorganizing, meaning that a bankruptcy court may be inclined to dismiss the case or, alternatively, modify the automatic stay to allow the lender to foreclose.

For real estate sponsors and their investment vehicles, including those structured as real estate investment trusts (REITs), the practical consequence is that when trouble hits, bankruptcy may not be a viable alternative, or at least not an alternative without significant execution risk and a potential for personal exposure.

To repeat, these structures were designed to defeat bankruptcy — and many of them may work to do so. On the other hand, bankruptcy can often be an effective tool for implementing a value-additive restructuring. Accordingly, the trade-off with these structures is that they may deprive stakeholders of a means of implementing a solution to financial distress.

Moreover, expectations can be thwarted in the opposite direction in the case of large, multi-property CMBS structures; arrangements that lenders and investors thought invulnerable to bankruptcy may actually be more susceptible to it. Examples are afforded by the General Growth Properties bankruptcy and the structures of numerous other REITs facing debt maturities in the coming years. In such structures, the enterprise may be comprised of hundreds of income-producing properties, each housed in its own SPV and some encumbered by securitized mortgage loans.

While each SPV in these corporate groups is ostensibly set up to be "bankruptcy remote" — including through the appointment of an independent board member — the reality is that the vehicles are economically interdependent. Generally, they benefit from a separate, affiliated management company that provides all the employees and services, along with a centralized cash management system through which intercompany loans are made and which allow some SPVs to finance the operations of other SPVs, for items such as tenant improvements.

Independent directors of these vehicles faced with a request by their corporate parents to vote for bankruptcy in the face of impending maturities may be much more inclined to do so in such circumstances — where piecemeal bankruptcies of some, but not all, of the affiliated SPVs may spell disaster for the group as a whole. Yet the boards and senior management of many CMBS lenders and investors seemed genuinely taken aback when General Growth filed for these very reasons, apparently having been under the mistaken impression that their borrowers simply could never do so.

As a result of General Growth's filing, some CMBS investors have focused on techniques for strengthening the "remoteness" of their borrowers. Ultimately, however, there is no way to make a structure "bankruptcy proof"; at best one can only reduce the odds, through creative structuring, of a borrower filing.

Triangular setoffs, suspension of payments, closeouts and related matters

Virtually all swaps are documented utilizing ISDA master agreement forms and related schedules, modified as appropriate to reflect the parties' particular arrangements. The enforceability of two common provisions in such agreements is now questionable in the light of developments in Lehman's bankruptcy proceeding and other cases.

The first provision relates to the ability of parties to set off obligations owing to one another. Obligations are "mutual" if they are due to and from persons in the same capacity, and it is widely understood that such a setoff provision is enforceable. However, many derivatives counter-parties modify the ISDA or enter into separate agreements to limit or dispense with the mutuality requirement, thereby allowing "triangular setoffs". Typically, this right permits affiliates of the non-defaulting party to set off against the defaulting party. This very common arrangement is driven by the need of many financial institutions to enter into derivatives through affiliates for regulatory capital and other reasons. To the extent feasible, the institutions want their counterparty exposure across such affiliates to be netted to a single number.

However, a pair of courts recently ruled that the Bankruptcy Code, which preserves parties' setoff rights, explicitly requires mutuality as a condition to an effective setoff. In particular, the Delaware bankruptcy court ruled — albeit in the non-derivatives context — that parties may not contract around the mutuality requirement by agreement to triangular setoffs among affiliates. While the ruling did not interpret the safe harbor provisions of the Bankruptcy Code, it called into question the enforceability of such arrangements with derivatives.

Even more recently, the bankruptcy court presiding over Lehman's liquidation held that a bank could not set off post-petition obligations it had to Lehman in connection with Lehman's post-petition transfers to deposit accounts maintained by the bank, against Lehman's pre-petition obligations to the bank as credit support provider under certain swap agreements. The bank had argued that mutuality was not required with safe harbor agreements because, among other things, the safe harbors were amended in 2006 to delete references to the word "mutual". The Lehman bankruptcy court was unpersuaded by this analysis, holding that the 2006 changes were designed to be technical and that, as a consequence, it was improper to construe this change as a sweeping change in the longstanding rule requiring mutuality as a condition of setoff.

The second provision of ISDA master agreements litigated in Lehman provides non-defaulting parties with the right either to terminate all transactions under the agreement or suspend current payments otherwise due to the defaulting party. Many of Lehman's counterparties, especially those that would have owed a net termination payment to the company, delayed sending a termination notice and/or suspended any current payments.

Lehman has made various efforts to force such counterparties to continue performing under the swap transactions, and to make any net termination payments due. In connection with a motion filed by Lehman to compel one counterparty to perform, the bankruptcy court ruled that although the safe harbor provisions protect counterparties' rights to end derivatives transactions, such rights may be limited in certain circumstances.

In particular, the court said that the counter-party's choice not to terminate the swaps for eight months after Lehman's bankruptcy — perhaps in the hope that favorable market movements would reduce any amount owed to the company — constituted inequitable conduct that constituted a waiver of the counterparty's termination right. Moreover, the court suggested that the payment suspension right in ISDA master agreements may be outside the safe harbors altogether and inconsistent with a debtor's general right under the Bankruptcy Code to compel counterparties to continue to perform under executory contracts, pending the debtor's determination whether to assume or reject.

The counterparty appealed the decision, but the parties ultimately settled. Others have challenged the substance of the bankruptcy court's ruling and its applicability. Accordingly, this area will likely generate significant and continuing disputes.

Taken by surprise

The Lehman bankruptcy has highlighted potential issues with related, seemingly routine aspects of derivatives trades. The first is that the process of properly closing out and valuing the transactions is more complex and less forgiving than many had realized. Although counterparties were clearly able to close out their derivatives positions based on Lehman's bankruptcy, there are many ongoing disputes relating to the timeliness and sufficiency of the termination-related notices, and the timeliness, substance and documentation of the related transaction valuations. Many counter-parties are learning that they will be required to pay more, or will receive allowed claims for less, than they had expected.

The second additional issue relates to the posting of excess collateral. Many derivatives transactions are collateralized, with one counter-party often being required to post to the other a set amount in excess of the current market exposure, in order to provide a cushion against adverse market movements. In Lehman, it has become clear, however, that the posting counterparty generally has only an unsecured claim for the return of collateral posted in excess of its actual obligation to Lehman. This result has surprised many counter-parties, and although a formal industry report addressing this issue is expected at some point, it may be a long time before widely accepted solutions to the problem emerge.

Conclusion

It is clear from Lehman's bankruptcy that the insolvency of a major derivatives counterparty has many unintended and unanticipated consequences. In some cases, expectations are undermined because structures do not work as generally understood; in others, ironically, they work so well that otherwise viable restructuring alternatives are useless. Indeed, the entire legal apparatus relating to derivatives, including derivatives in bankruptcy, is under consideration by Congress. It is too early to tell, however, in which direction Congress will turn, just as it is too early to tell how matters will ultimately play out in the courts.

These unpredictable outcomes in insolvency underscore the importance of the guiding principles to boards and senior managers in assessing their own businesses' derivatives positions and risks, including their determinations on whether to implement (overly) creative investment structures and vehicles and on how to report them to investors and regulators. The simple fact is that when the protection ostensibly afforded by such structures is needed most, it may not be there, or they may have unintended or unforeseeable consequences. Accordingly, close attention to the legal ramifications of these matters is critical.

The authors wish to thank Tom Kunz of Skadden's structured finance department for his helpful comments on this chapter.

20

Managing "fox in the henhouse" syndrome: Implementing effective internal controls

Van E Conway,
Founder and President, and
Kenneth J Malek,
Senior Managing Director,
Conway MacKenzie Inc

Across corporate America, executives and board members worry about the escalation of lawsuits against officers and directors. Do some actions attempt to charge us with a failure of 20:20 foresight whenever something goes wrong — be it with the overall economy or a business judgment or initiative that does not pan out? That obviously depends on the particular facts and circumstances. Corporate America breathed a collective sigh of relief in 2009 when Citigroup directors were not held liable for allegedly missing the "red flag" warning signals of the sub-prime meltdown.

Our firm is focused (both for our clients and ourselves) on maintaining and expanding market share and returning value to our owners, our stakeholders, our customers, our employees and our communities. We do not want a lawsuit distracting us from the task of managing the business until the economy really recovers for our clients. Nothing clouds short-term stock performance more than an action over corporate integrity.

At the end of the day, however, effective management is not about avoiding a lawsuit — or even avoiding liability on a lawsuit. Effective management is about sending a message that we are good corporate citizens, that we reward our employees for being good corporate citizens, that we do not cut corners — that we always ask for the order and we are tough competitors in our marketplace, but we will not compromise our integrity. No matter what. We will not do anything inappropriate to get the order. We will not do anything inappropriate to boost our stock price or our reported earnings or sales. It is an essential element of our culture — our corporate DNA. Behaving otherwise puts at risk all the value we have labored for years to create.

Controlling the culture

The larger the company, the bigger the rudder you need to steer the ship. By which I mean this: if our company has a lean management structure without a lot of layers — if operations are not spread all over the country or all over the world — then it is easy to control the corporate culture. If our company's growth is organic and we promote from within, it is also easy to control the culture. But if we are making strategic acquisitions, or looking to bring in new ideas by hiring executives from outside our industry, or recruiting management talent from competitors, then we have to do more than set aggressive goals that help to pressure them to achieve; we have to make sure that our culture, our systems and our procedures are so strong that no one cuts a corner.

Establishing the right culture is even harder when there are material overseas operations. It is not enough to make sure the management has the right work ethic and ability to produce; the message has to go out that while high performers will be rewarded, cutting corners will result in immediate termination. And the larger and more dispersed the organization, the harder we have to pull on the ship's helm.

The bone yards of corporate America are littered with the corpses of once-great companies where the executives themselves cut corners or failed to create the culture that would stop others doing the same. You know the names: Enron, WorldCom, Arthur Andersen, Refco. Some of these companies had outstanding brand value, respect in the business world, records of profitability, growth and contributions to the community, but they blew it. Sometimes the problem was in the highest executive ranks. Sometimes it was at the divisional level. In some of these situations, a significant portion of management knew that corners were being cut. A lot of people knew there was a fox in the henhouse. Systems, procedures and culture were either not in place or were there in name only.

There has to be a culture both of "fessing up" and of working harder than the next guy — of looking yourself in the mirror and saying that "I" played fairly and tried absolutely as hard as I could. I remember the story of Alberto Salazar, who ran the Boston Marathon with such intensity that he had to be given oxygen after winning. My son, a freshman at Wake Forest, is on the baseball team. After a double-header, I say: 'Son, how did you do?' He tells me he got two hits in four at bats in the second game. I say: 'What did you do that you don't want to tell me about in the first game?' He tells me he got a walk, grounded out and flied out. I tell him he has to work harder… that there is somebody trying harder than he is to earn his spot on the team. My son knows he has to tell me about both games and that I will not let him off the hook. This is about accountability to ourselves and to our stakeholders. I am my son's stakeholder because I pay his tuition and because he is my son.

The perils of pressure

There is so much pressure to perform in a distressed economy. Great swaths of corporate America have suffered declines of more than 30 per cent in top-line revenues. So the first things to go are the perks, travel and boondoggles. We cut the company cars and expense accounts. In private companies we cut the "cousins" off the payroll and cut the planes. When that is not enough, we cut advertising and promotion to the bare bones. We squeeze and drive efficiency in the supply chain. We improve plant efficiency, manufacturing processes and scrap. We grab the low-hanging fruit first, then figure out cost-benefit considerations for higher-hanging fruit. And when all of these are not enough, we have no choice but to start cutting payroll.

As the CEO of a turnaround consultant offering services such as interim executive management, I lose sleep every night about my client companies — about whether if I cut too deep, it will impair knowledge capital and the ability to ramp back up when consumer spending and demand start rebounding. I lose sleep about whether in cutting R&D and new product development to help meet bank covenants, I might also risk trashing long-term competitiveness. Idling physical plant capacity is a Hobson's choice (in this economy) — the chances of monetizing that capacity are slim at best, and if we do shut down, there are all the mothballing and security costs and environmental issues, plus the potential brand damage of not being seen as a good corporate citizen. It may be better to run plants on a negative-contribution basis, at least over the short term.

At my client companies, the employee and executive stock options are under water. The staff we have retained are loyal and worried about keeping their jobs. Everyone is working a lot harder to increase productivity. We have supervisory employees at the plants rolling up their sleeves and multi-tasking — serving production roles. They put themselves out to such an extent that I am concerned they are swinging for the fences when they need to focus on getting on base and basic play execution.

When the culture fails

When a company faces a crisis, the situation is ripe for someone to try to be the wrong kind of hero — one who cuts a corner and figures he or she and the company will not get caught.

Let us review a few sample cases. I am not an attorney but I do work with attorneys to help advise corporate directors facing difficult decisions, and these are cases I have learned about from very capable legal counsel.

As I mentioned earlier, *In re Citigroup Shareholders Derivative Litigation* was decided in 2009. This case concerned whether the directors were responsible for allowing the financial services conglomerate to expose itself to huge economic risks by continuing to invest in debt securities backed by sub-prime mortgages. During the period in which Citigroup was creating and syndicating these securities, it was reporting large front-end fee income. The court stated the directors' oversight duties and duty to monitor are ones of "supervision", but it also held that these are not duties that subject directors to personal liability for not adequately predicting the future or not adequately evaluating business risk.

The plaintiffs had alleged the existence of numerous "red flag" warning signals starting in

2005 that the directors had ignored. Regardless of the magnitude of Citigroup's huge losses from investments in securities tied to sub-prime mortgages, and the resulting ravaging of the company's stock price, the court tagged the directors with no personal liability. It held that the plaintiffs had to establish bad faith and that the directors knew that they were failing to discharge their fiduciary obligations or that they demonstrated a conscious disregard for their obligations by failing to act in the face of a known duty to act.

Another case, *In re American International Group Inc* (AIG), also addresses a duty to monitor standards. In *AIG*, the matter before the court was a motion by the defendants' counsel to dismiss the claim. The court allowed the claim to survive, stating that the complaint supported the assertion that top AIG executives were leading a "criminal organization" and that the pervasiveness and materiality of the alleged financial wrongdoing at AIG was extraordinary.

Another case, *Caremark International Inc Derivative Litigation*, is important because it addresses the directors' fiduciary duty of loyalty and, specifically, the requirement to monitor compliance and corporate integrity programs even if they have no evidence of suspicious circumstances.

Caremark was indicted on multiple felony counts for alleged kickbacks to healthcare providers that violated federal law. It settled the counts by agreeing to pay civil and criminal fines aggregating about $250 million. The directors were aware that some of the company's practices had been questionable, but they had taken steps to try and ensure there were no actual violations of law. These steps included Caremark issuing a guide to permissible relationships with doctors and hospitals; preparing an internal audit program for a comprehensive review of corporate integrity and compliance policies; and issuing an employee handbook and conducting employee training on compliance rules. Caremark's board had issued an ethics manual expressly prohibiting payments in exchange for referrals and requiring employees to report illegal activities to a hotline. The board had also employed a big accountancy firm as the company's outside auditor, which issued a report that there were no material weaknesses in Caremark's internal control system.

Caremark is often cited for the proposition that a failure to establish and monitor a corporate compliance program is a clear breach of the directors' duty of care and a possible breach of the duty of good

faith. That these violations occurred illustrates how vigilant corporate boards should be, whether or not they are aware of conduct that may be pushing the envelope... but especially when they are.

Asleep at the switch

Perhaps the most relevant case of all concerns the audit committee of a software firm that slid into bankruptcy amid claims of missing cash and inflated revenue claims. In *Lernout & Hauspie Securities Litigation*, the plaintiffs alleged that the audit committee was 'asleep at the switch, recklessly so, and failed to catch the massive fraud'. The court found that there was a strong inference of "scienter" (knowledge of wrongness or illegality) on the part of the committee, based on the following evidence:

• The company failed to implement the system of internal controls recommended by its outside auditor, KPMG.
• The audit committee disregarded KPMG's recommendation that it hire an internal auditor.
• The committee exercised no enhanced vigilance, despite its knowledge that the Securities and Exchange Commission (SEC) was investigating Lernout & Hauspie's accounting.
• Company management was issuing press releases, earnings forecasts and other financial information without any review by the audit committee — and the committee knew of such issuances.
• KPMG had reported to the audit committee at least nine instances of material transactions for which accounting was questionable.
• KPMG had communicated to the audit committee its inability to sign off on the 1999 audit, and had been unable to complete its review of a quarterly financial report due to unresolved revenue recognition and receivable collection issues.

The court held that, although KPMG had continued to issue "clean" audit opinions, it was the duty of the audit committee to 'guard the guardians'.

Spotting the warning signs

What are the red flags for which boards of directors should be watching? If results seem almost too good to be true, with consistent and growing profits, it is best to check them. Are the profits real or are they manufactured? If there is very rapid growth in the figures, the compliance and integrity programs, and the corporate culture, may be strained. Better check it.

Integrity programs can also come under strain

when a business faces economic hardship. There may be a back-room employee who wants to save the company by manipulating the numbers. At textile manufacturer Opelika, even though it was publicly held, a controller-level employee "borrowed" material payroll tax trust funds in a failed attempt to keep the business afloat. Instead, the illegal borrowing sank the company and tied up senior management and the board in years of litigation with the Internal Revenue Service.

Here are some other potential red flags. What if there is a record of reported strong profits but these are not manifested in net cash flow, and the company repeatedly goes to market for round after round of new debt and equity financing? What if the profits are derived from exceedingly complex financial transactions? Have management and the auditors adequately evaluated counterparty risk and concentrations of risk? What if the annual Form 10-K report is so complicated that it is hard to figure out how the company makes money? What if, like Caremark, management has a philosophy and culture of pushing the envelope?

Are there material off-balance sheet transactions? Are there material related-party transactions? Does the outside accountancy firm have the requisite knowledge and experience of the particular industry, or of complex concepts such as derivatives, hedges and commodity risk? Has the outside auditor expressed concerns regarding revenue recognition, the ability to realize the carrying value of assets or proper matching of revenues and expenses? Has it raised any issues on internal controls or corporate integrity? Have there been changes in accounting policies or accounting estimates? Are there transactions for which the economic substance or motivations are unclear? Have members of management engaged in large option transactions or otherwise monetized material portions of their stakes in the company?

These red flags are always obvious with 20:20 hindsight, but what boards of directors need is a culture that gives them 20:20 foresight.

Compliance and the law

Enacted in 2002 as a reaction to corporate and accounting scandals, the Sarbanes-Oxley Act (Sarbox) has been criticized by many for undermining American competitiveness by imposing costs of compliance that are not present in foreign markets. Others have maintained that the added comfort for investors is a major impetus to the continued dominance of American capital markets. Not surprisingly, after the market meltdown in September and October 2008, the critics have been silent.

In the new era of compliance and accountability, the primary functions of the audit committee are as follows: (i) to recommend the appointment of the outside accountants and review their findings on the financial reports of the corporation; (ii) to review the adequacy of the system of internal controls and of compliance with material policies and laws, including the corporation's code of ethics and conduct; and (iii) to provide a direct channel of communication to the board for the outside accountants and internal auditors and, when needed, finance officers, compliance officers and general counsel.

Part of the auditor's required role is to ensure that the audit committee is fully informed of any illegal acts that come to the auditor's attention, as well as any deficiencies in the design or operation of the corporation's internal controls that could affect the accuracy of the financial reporting.

For public reporting entities, SEC Rule 10A-3 requires that all members of an audit committee be independent — meaning that they must not otherwise be affiliated with the company and must accept no compensation from it beyond normal director fees. Rule 10A-3 also imposes the following responsibilities on the audit committees of public entities:

• They must be directly responsible for the retention, compensation and oversight of independent auditors.
• They must establish systems and procedures for the receipt and treatment of complaints on accounting, internal control and auditing irregularities, and of confidential, anonymous submissions from employees on questionable accounting or auditing matters.
• They must have the authority and ability to retain independent counsel and other advisors they deem appropriate for carrying out their responsibilities.
• They must have unimpeded access to appropriate funding to pay independent auditors, their own administrative expenses, and any legal counsel or other advisors that they decide to hire.

The New York Stock Exchange has also made changes to the rules governing audit committees. Approved by the SEC, the key rules are as follows:

• The audit committee must be comprised of at least three members, each of whom must either be financially literate at the time of the appointment or able to become financially literate within a short time. At least one member must have accounting or financial management expertise. Committee members should not generally serve on the audit committees of more than three public companies, and they must evaluate their other commitments to ensure they can meet the demanding responsibilities of the job.

• Each member must be independent. This is defined as the absence of any material relationship with the company — either directly or through indirect beneficial ownership, or as an officer of a company that has a direct or indirect material interest.

• The committee must have a written charter setting out its duties and responsibilities. The charter must require that, at least annually, the audit committee review the report by the independent auditor describing the auditor's internal quality controls, and any material issues raised by the most recent internal quality-controls review or peer review or by any inquiry or investigation by a governmental or professional authority within the preceding five years. The charter must also require that the committee review and discuss the company's annual audited financial statements and quarterly financial statements with management and with the independent auditor, including the MD&A, and must review and discuss the company's earnings press releases and earnings guidance provided to analysts and ratings agencies.

• The audit committee must discuss risk assessment and risk policies with management. It must also meet separately, on a periodic basis, with management, the internal auditors and the independent auditors, and must review any audit issues or difficulties and management's responses to them.

• The audit committee must set clear hiring policies for employees or former employees of the independent auditors.

• The audit committee must regularly report to the full board of directors.

• Each NYSE-listed company must have an internal audit function.

The COSO Framework

Sarbanes-Oxley has additional requirements relating to internal controls and codes of ethics. Under Sarbox Section 404, the annual Form 10-K report must state management's responsibilities for establishing and maintaining adequate internal control over financial reporting. The report must also identify the framework used by management to evaluate the effectiveness of the controls.

One example of this framework, which must be a publicly available standard, is provided by the Committee of Sponsoring Organizations (COSO). COSO is a voluntary body, established in the US, dedicated to providing guidance to executive management and governance entities on matters of internal control, enterprise risk management, organizational governance, business ethics, fraud and financial reporting. COSO has established a common internal control framework against which companies can benchmark their systems and procedures.

The COSO Framework is based on four key concepts. First, internal control is a process; it is a means to an end, not an end in itself. Second, internal control is affected by people; it is not merely policy, manuals and forms. Third, it can provide only reasonable assurance, not absolute assurance, to an entity's management and board. In the words of the *Lernout & Hauspie* court, everyone must view themselves as 'guarding the guardians'; it is everyone's job to keep the fox out of the henhouse, from the management down. Fourth, internal control is geared to the measurement and achievement of objectives in five separate but overlapping framework components.

COSO employs a capability maturity model to aid the assessment. Each organization determines which level of maturity is appropriate to support its business needs, priorities and availability of resources, with a rating of five representing the most mature systems: 0 = non-existent; 1 = initial/ad hoc; 2 = repeatable but intuitive; 3 = defined; 4 = managed and measurable; and 5 = optimized.

The "Control Environment" is the first of the five framework components. It sets the tone of the organization and provides the discipline and structure for all the other components of internal control. It is about integrity and ethical values, management's operating style, systems for delegation of authority, and the process for recruiting, managing and promoting the human capital of the organization.

"Risk Assessment" is the second of the five components. Risks are posed by both external and internal factors and must be assessed from the perspective of assigned objectives such as proper reporting of sales revenues.

The third framework component is "Control Activity" — the policies and procedures that help ensure management directives are carried out throughout the organization, at all levels. Examples include approvals, authorizations, verifications, reconciliations, reviews of operating performance, individual employee performance reviews, asset security measures, and segregation of functions (for example, treasury versus the finance department versus internal audit).

The fourth component is "Information and Communication". Information systems play a key role in the control framework, with reports addressing operational, financial and compliance-related matters. Formalized procedures should exist for employees to report possible fraud, and there should also be scope for effective communication with customers, suppliers, regulators and shareholders to ensure the organization has the capacity to recognize internal control issues that may be known to these external parties.

Lastly, internal control systems must be monitored, not just at discrete times but continuously. There must be a system to report upstream, for corrective action, any deficiencies and improvement opportunities discovered through monitoring activities.

Teaching to the test

Of course, some organizations think the internal control gurus are getting out of hand — that they are tying up companies in their shoe-strings and diverting management from creating value. For this reason, a lot of organizations are taking a "teaching to the test" approach to internal control, specifically designing a risk-and-control matrix that is tailored to the company's specific operations and expressly designed to satisfy Sarbox.

Under Section 404, for example, the Form 10-K report is required to include a statement of management's responsibilities for establishing and maintaining adequate internal control over financial reporting. The Form 10-K must also identify the framework used by management to evaluate the effectiveness of their company's system of internal control.

Relationships between audit committees and the CEO

The Audit Committee Leadership Network (ACLN) publishes periodic summaries of its meetings. The ACLN is comprised of the audit committee chairs of eight Fortune 100 companies and two representatives from a "Big Four" public accounting firm. Among the subjects they have discussed recently are the interaction of the CEO with the audit committee and the committee's role in helping to set the right tone at the top of the organization.

According to surveys conducted by the ACLN,

some CEOs attend audit committee meetings occasionally, some regularly, but in either case the committee chair must be sensitive to the ability of committee members to address concerns freely and frankly. The chair must take charge of the meeting and push back on the CEO if necessary. However, the involvement of CEOs in meetings can be a very positive factor as long as they regard culture-setting, and supporting the objectives of the audit committee, as an integral part of their job. The opposite, of course, may be true if the CEO views such activities as a necessary evil.

Members of the ACLN have used a number of terms to describe the optimal relationship between the CEO and the audit committee: 'Trust but verify' — President Reagan's dictum regarding Cold War negotiations with the Soviet Union; 'Cordial but somewhat distant'; 'Constructive skepticism'; and 'My CEO and I don't have a close personal relationship, but I know how he will react and he knows how I will react. It is valuable to me and to him.'

A number of audit committees, especially in the larger organizations, regularly interact with employees through site visits and by developing relationships with people who report to the CEO. There should be no wall between the audit committee and any part of the company.

Conclusion

Financial downturns put strain on the systems, procedures and culture essential for proper financial reporting and the avoidance of fraud. There is a lot of pressure to show improvement in results. There is a lot of pressure to meet bank financial covenants. There is pressure to avoid spending money on functions, such as internal control, that do not relate directly to reviving the revenue line and improving profitability.

The situation is ripe for another round of discoveries of material failures in internal control. We must be vigilant. We must continue to drive the culture to over-promise and over-deliver on both business results and corporate integrity. When the pool gets drained, you realize how many people have been swimming without clothes. When a company faces a crisis, that is when someone tries to be the wrong kind of hero — one who cuts a corner.

Without the right corporate culture, the most robust systems and procedures of internal control are no guarantee against the fox causing havoc in the henhouse. The culture has to report the approach of the fox. The culture has to bar the door. Integrity has to come first, ahead of performance.

21

Evaluating the balance sheet in a distressed environment: Differentiating strategic decision-making from desperation transactions

Walt Dlugolecki,
Executive Director,
and Ed Ordway,
Executive Director and
Managing Member,
**Capstone Advisory
Group LLC**

An economic downturn impacts virtually every business, large and small. For many, significant declines in volume trigger "desperate actions", such as layoffs, plant closures and other cash-conservation measures needed to adjust to the new, near-term reality of a minimum-growth economy.

It is against this backdrop that executive teams must re-examine the tools that they utilize to manage their businesses. After the downturn of 2007-09, the days of an economy fueled by "cheap and easy" credit and high-spending consumers are gone. When an economic storm subsides, it takes time.

So it is important that businesses have a process in place to ensure their operating activities are comfortably within their liquidity constraints. Such processes are truly put to the test in a distressed economic environment, when liquidity is strained not only by lower revenues and profits, but also by a tightening of credit policies and, therefore, the company's ability to borrow to fund its operations. It is not uncommon for management to focus too much on maximizing revenues, to the detriment of liquidity, working capital and the balance sheet; when sales volumes are down, that can be a route to financial distress.

To survive in the current economic climate, management must be proactive in implementing appropriate balance sheet management techniques to avoid having to resort to desperate actions to generate liquidity, and to avoid damaging their long-term viability. As noted by Paul Otellini, CEO of Intel: 'Having run a company through a major transition, it's a lot easier to change when you *can* than when you *have to.*'

The balance sheet management techniques discussed can and should be considered by management in good times as well as bad to maximize cash flow and return on assets and to minimize risk.

The use of analytics

Multiple techniques are available to management to evaluate their company's balance sheet, including benchmarking, ratio analysis and trend analysis. Benchmarking has long been used to measure a company's performance against its peers, and regular financial benchmarking can reveal ways of improving balance sheet management. The data is available to companies from industry groups, trade organizations and large accounting and financial consultancy firms, and key steps in the benchmarking process are as follows:

- Identifying criteria to measure.
- Selecting an appropriate comparison group.
- Establishing goals.
- Collecting data.
- Making comparisons.

• Analyzing the differences between company data and the comparison group.
• Developing initiatives to address weaknesses and to meet established goals.

Measurement criteria are as varied and numerous as the businesses that utilize this process, and include:

• Days' sales in accounts receivable.
• Inventory turns.
• Current ratio.
• Debt to assets.
• Return on assets.
• Asset turnover ratio.
• Return on equity.
• Debt to equity.

Although the comparison of financial ratios among peer group companies is a key element of the process, company-only analysis of liquidity, coverage and leverage ratios over a sustained period also can be a useful tool in measuring the effectiveness of balance sheet management techniques. It will provide an insight into whether or not the improvement initiatives are working.

The table shows the calculation of various liquidity, coverage and leverage ratios over a six-

year period at the homebuilder WCI Communities Inc. WCI was not able to react quickly enough to the 2007-09 economic downturn. With liquidity needs outstripping its ability to generate cash internally, and no outside and out-of-court sources of funding available, WCI entered into a Chapter 11 restructuring process on August 4, 2008 (it emerged from bankruptcy on September 2, 2009). A review of the changing ratios in the table reflects the negative impact on the business of the declining economy and the related real estate bust. Calculating and analyzing these measures on a regular basis can provide management with an early indication that corrective actions need to be taken to avoid more draconian measures down the road.

While ratios at a given point in time can be useful when compared to peer group company data and/or industry standards, analyzing them over a period (trend analysis) is also very useful. This helps identify both favorable and unfavorable trends, providing a basis on which to develop a plan for corrective action.

Improving working capital management
Many companies have substantial investments in working capital assets, primarily accounts receivable and inventories. In the case of receivables, a balance has to be found between overly aggressive collection and restrictive credit policies on one hand, and being too lax at the other extreme. The former will result in lost revenue and reduced profits, and the latter in increased bad debts and higher collection costs.

Accounts receivable are one of the two main components of the cash cycle (the difference between the time a company pays its vendors and the time it takes to collect from its customers). Any sustainable reduction in the collection period from customers translates into additional cash flow. In certain situations a company may choose to factor its receivables to accelerate the receipt of cash, though that option must be weighed against the cost of the factoring service.

Another step that certain companies can take is developing processes that better manage the frequency and volume of customer chargebacks, which can arise from incomplete or inaccurate shipments, a failure to follow delivery instructions, faulty products and merchandise returns. In many industries, customers are very aggressive in "taking" chargebacks and often do not follow procedures requiring authorization.

Mismanagement in this area can be very costly,

Ratio analysis

	Fiscal year					
Liquidity ratios	**2003**	**2004**	**2005**	**2006**	**2007**	**2008**
Current ratio	5.2x	8.7x	8.9x	17.6x	18.4x	4.3x
Quick ratio	1.7x	2.8x	3.5x	7.0x	4.3x	0.5x
Working capital/ total assets	70%	77%	77%	82%	80%	60%
Age of AR (AR days)	143.1	137.7	143.7	228.1	361.4	177.2
Inventory turnover	1.1x	1.1x	1.3x	0.9x	0.5x	0.4x
Age of inventory (inventory days)	347.6	338.0	289.7	396.7	776.6	890.2
Length of operating cycle	490.8	475.7	433.4	624.9	1138.0	1067.4
Coverage ratios	**2003**	**2004**	**2005**	**2006**	**2007**	**2008**
EBIT/ interest expense	5.7x	5.0x	10.1x	4.3x	n/a	n/a
EBITDA/ interest expense	6.1x	5.4x	10.7x	5.2x	n/a	n/a
(EBITDA-CapEx)/ interest expense	4.6x	4.4x	9.3x	4.0x	n/a	n/a
Leverage ratios	**2003**	**2004**	**2005**	**2006**	**2007**	**2008**
Debt/equity	112.1%	128.0%	127.8%	200.7%	458.0%	n/a
Debt/capital	52.9%	55.7%	55.7%	65.9%	81.1%	143.2%
Debt/EBITDA	4.0x	4.9x	3.5x	10.8x	n/a	n/a

Source: Capital IQ

and of course the converse is equally true: improving processes so they identify unauthorized chargebacks could be a source of liquidity.

Failure to adopt appropriate policies and procedures for accounts receivable can put a huge strain on liquidity, forcing a company to resort to drastic and potentially costly measures such as offering customer discounts for accelerated payments or settling disputed chargeback claims at deep discounts.

The second major component of working capital for many businesses is inventory, which again, if properly managed, could be a source of cash. "Best practice" techniques include the following:

• **Real-time updating of factory production plans**. This reduces the risks of under-production (missed sales) and over-stocking (excess, slow-moving inventory).
• **Stock-keeping unit (SKU) rationalization** — the elimination of low-margin and slow-moving products.
• **Attention to slow-moving and obsolete inventory**. This includes developing programs to avoid the creation of excess stock in the first place, early identification of excess levels, and disposing of such goods profitably.
• **Material requirements planning (MRP)**. Significant savings can be generated by refining procurement practices so that materials and services are ordered in the right quantity, at the right cost, and delivered at the right time.
• **Systems that allow monitoring of customer inventories**. Apparel and consumer products companies, in particular, are well served by being able to keep tabs on inventory movement at their retail customers. In this way they can plan production and replenishment.
• **State-of-the-art pick-and-pack systems**. Sophisticated warehouse systems reduce the risk of shipping errors and missing shipping windows, and help to optimize order fulfillment.
• **Shop-floor control systems**. High-quality systems reduce the work-in-process stage and improve production throughput.
• **Just-in-time purchasing and production systems** (JIT). If properly managed, JIT will keep inventory levels in all categories to a minimum.
• **Level-loading practices**. This practice can help to avoid spikes in inventory levels, overtime and other costs associated with the manufacture of seasonal products (lawn mowers, gas grills, etc).
• **Activity-based costing**. This analytical approach assigns costs to each product or service according to their actual consumption, providing a clearer picture of product profitability.
• **"Make versus buy" analysis** — a key exercise in determining whether products, or their components, should be outsourced to contract manufacturers.
• **Consignment purchasing**, which in effect provides for additional credit extension.
• **Hedging of raw material and energy costs**. This allows companies to manage the cost of otherwise volatile commodities.

One needs look no further than the retail industry to see the benefits of improved inventory management in the midst of an economic downturn. JCPenney, for instance, reduced inventories by around 17 per cent (more than $600 million) from 2007 to 2009, while the number of stores over the same period actually increased by 4 per cent.

Hedging has become a very popular tool, as many companies have been challenged by extremely volatile raw material and energy costs. While hedging programs can make a big difference here, it is imperative to develop policies that guard against inappropriate trading activities. This was amply demonstrated in the case of SemGroup, a $12 billion company engaged in transporting energy from wellhead to the wholesale market through a network of pipelines, terminals and storage tanks. The group's speculative energy trading through "naked options" transactions (positions in options at levels in excess of physical inventory levels), with no effective stop-loss limits, resulted in total trading losses in excess of $3 billion. SemGroup plunged into bankruptcy in July 2008.

Improper management of a company's inventories can result in excess capital being invested in materials, and sometimes the wrong materials, and becoming subject to price volatility and/or obsolescence. Given the constraints of warehouse space and the pressure of looming delivery dates, this can result in a company making ill-advised purchases at unfavorable prices or disposing of unneeded inventory at steeply discounted prices.

Managing relationships
Frequently, the ability of a company to exert pressure on its vendors for pricing and payment terms is directly related to its share of a vendor's overall volumes, but in some industries other factors may come into play. In pharmaceuticals, for example, FDA regulatory approvals limit the

manufacturer's ability to substitute ingredients/materials, and even the vendors themselves. We saw an example of this at a generic drugs company that was unable to complete a shipment until the bottle-cap supplier was paid.

Another example is the auto industry. As a result of sole sourcing arrangements, high tooling costs and long lead times, relationships in this sector tend to be symbiotic, with neither the vendor nor the customer being in a position to extricate itself. It has been quite common for an original equipment manufacturer (OEM) to grant a supplier sole-source status in return for lower pricing. And while in the short term this has made financial sense, it has also left OEMs hanging on the ability of their suppliers to produce and deliver on time. This risk became painfully evident in 2008 when OEMs needed to step in to support many liquidity-challenged parts suppliers.

In most large companies today, many functions are managed at division and headquarters level, rather than by the individual business units. While the centralization of these functions — billing, credit and collection, purchasing activities, vendor payments, risk management — is often considered an obvious efficiency step, in practice that is not always the case. In many businesses, distancing certain functions from the "line" operation results in operating inefficiencies. By being removed from certain activities, unit management can easily lose focus on how their actions affect the balance sheet of the group as a whole. Actions to readjust their sights include the imposition of an inter-company working capital or capital employed charge and the inclusion of such metrics in determining bonuses.

Optimization of property, plant, equipment

Capital-intensive businesses must have policies and procedures that ensure investment decisions on property, plant and equipment are based on detailed information that demonstrates there will be an acceptable return on the investment (ROI). In many industries, capital expenditure can be differentiated as being either of a maintenance nature or an investment/expansive nature. While both these categories can be curtailed or deferred over the short term, continued deferral of maintenance expenditures may eventually result in the need to spend more money on an "emergency" basis when equipment breaks.

Debt management

Management should continuously assess whether the company's debt levels are appropriate for its

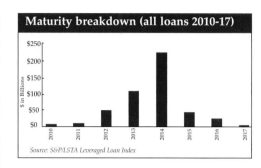

Maturity breakdown (all loans 2010-17)

Source: S&P/LSTA Leveraged Loan Index

needs and are within its servicing capability. A management team that does not pay close attention to this may find itself in the predicament of having to seek additional financing or a refinancing in a difficult credit environment. The results could be reduced credit, higher interest costs and additional covenant restrictions. Based on recent data, a significant maturity bubble is being created due to the high level of "amend and extend" activity over recent years, as reflected in the chart above.

Balance sheet strategies for the distressed company

Until now we have focused on techniques employed to avoid having to engage in desperate transactions in the future. But what if your business is already experiencing some level of distress? Is there nothing that can be done to avoid the worst outcomes?

Actually, there are, but first things first: most management teams have never had to lead a business through a period of distress. Of course, "distress" is a relative term, but basically it describes a situation where one or more of the following has happened or is predicted to happen: (1) liquidity is declining rapidly and may drop below acceptable levels; (2) defaults may occur under lending arrangements; (3) losses and erosion of creditworthiness in general affects the confidence of suppliers and may lead to the curtailment of credit extension; (4) the company's losses are expected to continue, such that a restructuring is considered necessary.

If a management team finds itself in distress, the actions to consider include engaging legal counsel and financial turnaround advisors with the skills and experience to identify possible courses of action and guide a company through its problems.

Before we delve into those "distress fixes", there are certain other steps that can be taken to improve the company's liquidity and strengthen its balance sheet:

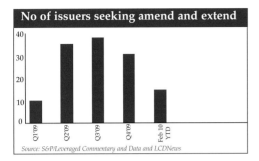

No of issuers seeking amend and extend

Source: S&P/Leveraged Commentary and Data and LCDNews

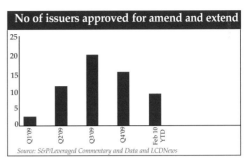

No of issuers approved for amend and extend

Source: S&P/Leveraged Commentary and Data and LCDNews

- Liquidate and/or discontinue unprofitable business activities.
- Downsize operations consistent with current and near-term volume/activity levels.
- Sell non-core assets.
- Sell or lease back facilities.
- Renegotiate terms with vendors.
- Renegotiate lease terms.

Non-core assets — whether individual assets such as machinery and production, or an entire business unit — can usually be sold or discontinued to generate liquidity without compromising the business. Additionally, liquidity "trapped" in long-term assets such as buildings and equipment can be freed up through sale/leaseback arrangements.

Whether these actions are strategic or desperate, though, depends on how quickly management pursues them once the signs of distress have been identified. Too slow and the process will be harder as pricing for distressed assets becomes more severe and the number of interested parties more limited.

The specter of a potential bankruptcy filing, which gives the company an economic means to reject real estate leases, may provide the leverage needed to renegotiate more favorable lease terms out-of-court. Depending on the nature of the relationship, the possibility of a bankruptcy may also allow the company to extract better terms from vendors, who would likely be substantially impaired in a filing. A case in point, again, is the auto industry: all of the "big three" manufacturers have routinely provided many of their seriously distressed parts suppliers with accelerated or even advance payments, to ensure an uninterrupted flow of components.

Obtaining additional equity capital
In those situations where the main equity participant is an equity sponsor, the company may

find it is willing to provide an additional infusion. In companies with a large number of investors, the same opportunity can be offered to equity holders through a rights offering, in which business benefits from the acquired liquidity and the investors avoid being diluted by new equity sources or from a conversion of debt to stock.

A number of other strategies are also available to distressed companies, including the following:

- "Amend and extend" defaulted or maturing debt arrangements.
- Refinancing with an asset-based loan.
- Refinancing with a high-yield debt offering.
- Distressed debt exchanges.

Amend and extend
Recently, many companies and their lenders have agreed to "amend and extend" credit arrangements, which are only feasible if the degree of distress is not severe. This has the obvious benefit to the company of not having to address a looming maturity of their financing arrangements in a tight credit environment. It also benefits the lender since the quid pro quo usually consists of improved pricing, fees, additional collateral and tighter covenants. Of course, the main assumption in such arrangements is that the extension will bridge the company to a time when economic conditions, and its financial performance, will be vastly better.

Some observers (analysts and the press) regard these transactions as simply delaying the day of reckoning for some companies, and they use the term "amending and pretending". Nevertheless, if the company can service the debt adequately, many lenders are willing to waive non-payment defaults and extend maturity. The two charts above show the number of companies seeking such amendments in 2009, and those that were actually successful in extending the maturity of their loans.

While loan modifications and extensions are by

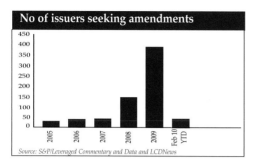

No of issuers seeking amendments

Source: S&P/Leveraged Commentary and Data and LCDNews

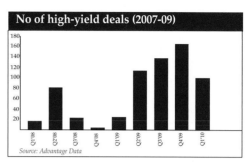

No of high-yield deals (2007-09)

Source: Advantage Data

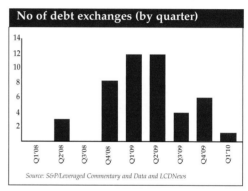

No of debt exchanges (by quarter)

Source: S&P/Leveraged Commentary and Data and LCDNews

no means new, the chart above shows that they rose to a dramatically higher level in 2009.

Refinancing with an asset-based loan
While not available to all businesses, those with substantial accounts receivable and inventory may be able to replace their existing revolver and pay down term loans by obtaining an asset-based credit facility. Even when credit is tight, companies with sufficient collateral have been able to find willing asset-based lenders.

Such lenders are somewhat indifferent to operating performance and covenants, although they will (almost) never lend beyond the liquidation value of the supporting collateral. Clearly there are pros and cons to such deals, the pro being the substantial relief of not needing to meet financial covenants, and the con being inflexibility about lending above the borrowing base.

Refinancing with a high-yield debt offering
For those companies defaulting or in danger of defaulting on their existing credit agreements, but having sufficient cash to service their debt, the high-yield market has proved to be fertile ground recently. However, while it has allowed many companies to obtain badly needed liquidity to finance operations or pay down maturing debt, it comes at a cost in the form of higher interest rates. Without a true turnaround of the business and/or a restructuring of the balance sheet, these companies run the risk that they will be unable to survive the eventual maturity of the new debt. The chart shown at the top right reflects the recent trends in new high-yield debt.

Distressed debt exchanges
Often, the capital structure of larger companies includes multiple levels of debt, the more junior of which may or may not be secured by the assets as collateral. Debt exchanges are sometimes used opportunistically by issuers not in financial distress to reduce their leverage at attractive valuations.

Recently, companies in distress have used the possibility of a bankruptcy filing as leverage against the holders of bond debt to "coerce" them into accepting, in exchange for their bonds, new securities at a discount to par but with an extended maturity and possibly a higher coupon. Why do holders of these securities willingly accept such arrangements? A June 3, 2009 article in *The Wall Street Journal* provides an insight: 'A new report from Moody's Investors Service... titled "Recoveries on Defaulted Debt in the Era of Black Swans", says that companies that have gone through distressed exchanges have a corporate recovery rate of 69.1 per cent, versus 50 per cent for the universe of defaulting companies over the last 20 years.' Simply put, history shows that a minor accomodation can avoid a possible business failure and the likelihood of a substantially lower recovery.

The next chart reflects the number of debt exchanges by quarter between 2008 and the start of 2010. Interestingly, there is an obvious inverse relationship between the level of high-yield activity and debt exchanges.

Bankruptcy as a strategic decision
Up until now we have discussed actions/techniques that can be employed by healthy companies to avoid becoming distressed,

and those steps that can be taken by companies in distress to avoid the ultimate desperate transaction — a freefall into bankruptcy. In certain circumstances, however, bankruptcy itself can be the preferred option. Some of the techniques discussed for distressed companies, particularly rights offerings and distressed debt exchanges, are frequently implemented as part of a "prearranged" or "prepackaged" filing.

In a prearranged bankruptcy, the company negotiates the key terms of the proposed restructuring with certain of the parties-in-interest prior to the actual filing. The prearranged bankruptcy has been employed recently by well-known companies including Atrium Companies Inc, Lear Corporation, Masonite Corporation, JL French Automotive Castings Inc and Chiquita Brands Inc.

The prepackaged bankruptcy takes this a step further, with the company negotiating, documenting and disclosing to its creditors its plan of reorganization, and obtaining the requisite consent — all prior to an actual filing. Both these forms of bankruptcy have the effect of lowering the costs normally associated with a Chapter 11.

Conclusion
While the US and global economies continue to recover from the 2007-09 recession, volatility remains significant with substantial fluctuations in the rate of consumer spending, asset values, and capital market availability. As important, unemployment remains stubbornly high. So businesses will be navigating a challenging economy for some time to come. In such an environment, management should continue to be proactive in managing their company's finances — from both an income statement and balance sheet perspective — utilizing the tools and techniques discussed here. This way they will give themselves the best chance of surviving the current distressed economy and positioning themselves to thrive when a more robust recovery arrives.

22

Refinancing the looming
"wall of debt" — boards beware

Jonathan Katz,
Co-Head of Restructuring
Investment Banking,
GCA Savvian
Advisors LLC

In the next several years, the "wall of debt" that was issued during the easy money/high valuation period from late 2005 through mid 2007 will be maturing. In the fall of 2009, that debt looked largely as though it could not be refinanced. The high-yield bond market was reopening but the senior loan market remained broken, and the fear that had forced capital under mattresses had yet to fully subside.

By mid 2010, things appeared radically different. The refinancing of senior debt by new high-yield issuances has topped up reinvestment baskets at the collateralized loan obligations (CLOs) that had otherwise been at death's door. The CLOs, together with other capital that was crowded out of asset-backed securities by the federal government's massive support for the mortgage market, have been clamoring for new senior loan originations in which they can put money to work.

Volatility now, volatility forever

The effect of all of this is that the wall of debt seems less intimidating, but still formidable. Our debt capital markets are huge, and when they are open they can process a lot of paper. That said, the clearest lesson I take from the credit crisis of 2008 (and the crises of 2001 and 1998) is that the efficiency of capital flows means market conditions can turn on a dime. Debt capital markets may have rebounded quickly but they have certainly not stabilized — easy capital one quarter, nothing available the next. It is an unstable and unpredictable system and will remain so unless the market is fundamentally rebuilt with strong governmental involvement and regulatory oversight (it will not be, by the way).

So where does that leave a leveraged borrower with a pending need for refinancing? It is hard to plan ahead when the appetite for leveraged loans swings so radically. You may be able to access more open markets, but for how long? If your company is underperforming, or simply too highly leveraged, you may think that waiting will allow you to turn the operational corner or lift valuation multiples.

Act now, go long

From where we sit, the extreme volatility of the markets offers only one answer: act now. Make hay while the sun still shines. The follow-up conclusion for underperforming companies is also simple: with markets in perpetual flux, lock in the longest maturities available to avoid subsequent disruption. The cost of refinancing now may seem high, the runway under your current facilities may look long enough, but an independent investment banking advisor can help you assess the cost of refinancing with long-dated paper in today's market against the potentially catastrophic costs of being frozen out of the market at some later date. Refinance from a position of strength, and let your independent advisor shop your deal among the leading agent banks for the best pricing, fees and terms.

The last ten years are littered with stories of management teams that failed to shore up their finances in the face of uncertain markets to the detriment of the businesses that they ran and their investors. Ford paid a fortune to raise long-term liquidity in anticipation of a challenging financial and operating environment. GM waited. Ford has bridged the gap, while GM is under new management (and ownership).

If there is a problem, get ahead of it

If you still cannot access the market today (too much leverage, too complex a story, too many other issuers, etc), it is better to know that now. The sooner you start thinking about strategic alternatives to a debt capital markets refinancing of outstanding indebtedness, the more options and time you will have in restructuring your balance sheet.

Maybe the capital markets will open further and allow you to refinance — maybe not. Bring that independent advisor back in as soon as it seems that you may not be able to refinance your debt, and you will optimize value across creditor and equity constituencies. You will give your investment bankers the luxury of time to conduct orderly processes to raise new capital or restructure existing debt through asset sales, rescue finance bridge facilities, exchange offers, consent solicitations, covenant relief negotiations and even prepackaged bankruptcies.

Fire sales and freefall bankruptcies in the face of debt that is coming due are the surest ways to destroy value. Get ahead of the problem as soon as you recognize you have one.

Capital markets update — volatility now, volatility forever

With $420 billion of leveraged loans coming due through 2014, there remains a wall of debt that will need to be refinanced. That said, as of early 2010, the debt capital markets had broadly reopened.

This reopening is concomitant with a broad (if weak) economic recovery powered by massive federal monetary and fiscal stimulus. Manufacturing is expanding, unemployment has stabilized at 9.7 per cent, and US factory orders continue to rise. The yield curve is rising and the spread between three-month T-bills and the 20-year bond stands at 449 basis points, all signaling an improving economy.

In 2009, borrowers refinanced and pushed out approximately 45 per cent (or almost $60 billion) of the debt that was coming due before the end of 2012, leaving only $70 billion outstanding. Three primary drivers have pushed demand for leveraged loan originations:

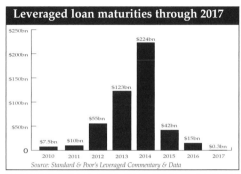

Leveraged loan maturities through 2017

Source: Standard & Poor's Leveraged Commentary & Data

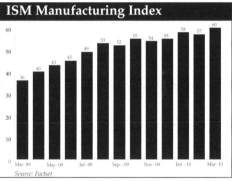

ISM Manufacturing Index

Source: Factset

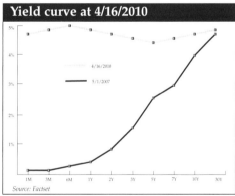

Yield curve at 4/16/2010

Source: Factset

• Investors have shaken off the fear of systemic collapse and begun again to seek yield.
• The federal stimulus programs in support of asset-backed securities have artificially forced down yields in those markets, forcing private investors to seek yield in other instruments (such as leveraged loans).
• Institutional non-bank lenders such as CLOs, which had represented approximately 40-60 per cent (depending on whom you ask) of the buy-side demand for new loans before the crisis, have re-emerged from the depths of the market meltdown

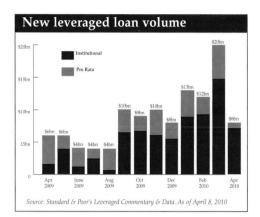

Source: Standard & Poor's Leveraged Commentary & Data. As of April 8, 2010

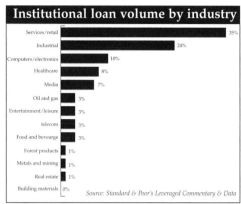

Source: Standard & Poor's Leveraged Commentary & Data

to resume their role in the loan origination market. This has been driven especially by the refinancing by a hot high-yield bond market of loans that the CLOs had held. Those refinancing proceeds are being reinvested in newly syndicated loans. In addition, for the first time since the crisis erupted in 2008 new CLO funds are being raised.

As demand for loan paper increases, the credit quality demanded of new issuers will drop. New leveraged loan volume has increased since the end of 2009.

Although investors will fight a rearguard challenge against aggressive loan terms and structures for companies that seek to borrow, highly leveraged underperformers across industrial sectors may soon have access to the loan market again on attractive terms.

This is all good news if you need to refinance your outstanding debt, as long as you are willing to go to the market soon.

I am not saying that the "easier money" loan market conditions will not last; I am just saying you do not want to bet your company that they will. As I have noted, above, the rebound in the debt capital markets' appetite for new paper is impressive, but it in no way signifies a stabilization of the availability of credit.

To the contrary, the quick snap back from 2009's moribund new issue market demonstrates the volatility of that market. The pendulum is swinging faster than ever.

Capital moves between asset classes with terrific speed, the economic recovery is jobless and (therefore, by definition) weak, and the federal intervention in the asset-backed markets will have to end at some point (unless the government is pursuing a policy of rampant inflation).

Act now, go long

In light of this volatility, if you have paper that will need to be refinanced before 2014 and your company has weak credit, you should be ready to go to market to raise new debt on a moment's notice. Further to that, to the degree the market is receptive to your new issue, you should not hesitate to sacrifice pricing for certainty (especially with respect to longer-dated maturity).

If the inability to refinance outstanding debt will cripple the ability of your business to operate, then hoping for even better conditions (be they macro or micro) to go to market at some future date represents a spectacular gamble. There are certainly costs to refinancing opportunistically and seeking longer maturities, but these must be weighed against the catastrophic cost to the business and its investor constituents of a failure to refinance debt that is coming due at some later date. If the market is open now, you must be prepared to act now.

This, of course, does not mean you have to borrow today. It means you have to be ready to borrow today. Which means you need strong independent advisors to work with you on a long-term basis — first, to help you put together the requisite materials and information to conduct a snapshot offering; second, to stay on top of capital markets conditions; third, to help you refinance from a position of strength when you decide to go to market.

Over-leveraged and underperforming borrowers will never be able to dictate market terms, but when I say refinancing from a position of strength, I really mean helping a borrower understand those elements of a refinancing facility that are most critical and, therefore, worthy of negotiating attention. Pricing, fees and other economic terms are all important, but there are certain provisions of every loan agreement that are relatively more important to your business.

Know your terms

Having a game plan before negotiating loan documentation can be a huge benefit. The key is focusing on those terms that will let you maintain sufficient operating flexibility in running your business. Debt incurrence buckets, reinvestment periods with respect to out-of-the-ordinary-course sale proceeds and similar restrictive covenants can be customized to reflect your company's anticipated operating activities. Lenders are usually more open to fine-tuning those elements than they tend to be on basic financial performance covenants if the borrower can explain why flexibility is needed.

If you are planning to divest a non-core operation and you hope to reinvest the proceeds of that sale in your business, be sure to have that explanation at hand when you negotiate your credit agreement with your agent bank. Specific anticipated transactions can usually be carved out of restrictive covenants, and the restrictions themselves can be loosened (with respect to dollar size of a bucket or timing limitations) in the face of a well-formulated business plan.

That said, you should expect to be competing for lender attention with many other prospective borrowers as the market works to absorb and refinance the wall of debt through 2014. So it is important to keep your eye on the critical terms that are basic to the operation of your business and, thus, worth paying for. The key term, as we have discussed, is maturity.

To the degree that the failure to raise new debt to make principal paydowns of existing loans comes at or near maturity, your business will have very few options other than a hasty freefall bankruptcy filing. There is no surer way to destroy capital than a bankruptcy in which the terms of restructuring have not been agreed to by the borrower and its critical creditors prior to the filing of the case. Your equity and junior debt capital investors will take massive hits to their positions, your senior lenders will drive the restructuring of your balance sheet, and significant fees and expenses will be paid to advisors of all of the creditor constituencies and be borne by the bankruptcy estate as a plan is slowly and painfully hashed out. Meanwhile, customer and vendor relationships will be strained, and the employees of your business will suffer substantial disruption to their lives. All this because you were unable to refinance existing debt.

That being said, you must also effectively forecast future working capital needs as the economy expands and raise debt and equity to meet your needs. If you fail to effectively plan, your company will face an unanticipated, and perhaps undesirable, need to sell, merge, reorganize, or worse yet, liquidate.

In an era of dramatic capital swings and unprecedented credit market volatility, then, it makes sense to limit your need to refinance to an absolute minimum. The longer the maturity of your next credit facility, the longer you will have before you will be faced with having to refinance that facility. Longer maturities equal longer life for companies that have substantial borrowing needs in uncertain markets. As such, you should understand the cost of stretching the maturity of a credit facility, and you should weigh that cost (likely to be a matter of basis points on the debt outstanding) against the probability of being frozen out of the credit markets in the future and the impact of that upon your business.

There was a piece I read a while back in the *Financial Times* on the negotiation of a rescue package for South Korea during the Asian currency crisis in the late 1990s. Bob Rubin, then of the US Treasury Department, was astounded that the South Koreans were dickering over a 25-basis-point cost in the package. Their entire financial system was at stake, and they were arguing over a quarter of a point in cost. He left the table.

The takeaway is simple: keep your eye on the big picture. In volatile markets, do not hesitate to sacrifice pricing for certainty.

If there is a problem, get ahead of it

Assume, at this point, that you have decided to take my advice. You will prepare to go to market to refinance your outstanding debt as soon as possible, and you will be willing to pay up for a longer-dated piece of paper. You get your ducks in a row, you know where you are willing to bend and where you feel you need to hold firm. You are ready to hit the market and lock in a new credit facility. What if the market remains closed to you? What if you cannot get traction with lenders because you are underperforming, or in an out-of-favor sector, or too leveraged, or simply crowded out by all the other issuers looking to raise money (there is a wall of debt out there that will need to be refinanced, remember)? What do you do if you go to market and you are denied?

Well, of course, that is bad news, but because it comes right away, it is the best way that you can get the bad news. The more time there is to come up with alternatives to refinancing your outstanding debt, the greater the range of options that you and your advisors will have for raising capital and/or restructuring your balance sheet without destroying the capital that has been invested in your business.

Explore the options

There is a series of actions that can be taken, first, to raise new capital through alternative means and, second, to restructure and reduce the debt currently on your balance sheet through negotiation with current lender groups. They all take time. So the more time you have before the repayment of a debt facility that cannot be refinanced comes due, the more alternative actions can be explored through orderly processes run by your advisors.

If you are unable to access the debt capital markets to refinance an existing facility, you can still explore the possibility of raising capital through "new money" sources such as minority equity investments by strategic or financial players, rescue finance facilities in the hybrid equity or mezzanine portion of the capital structure, or even new asset-based financings at the top of the capital structure (to the degree your existing lenders are willing to be primed by a new lender with respect to accounts receivable and inventory). The structuring, arrangement and marketing of any of these investments is time consuming and the money raised will come at a higher price than a traditional loan syndication or high-yield offering.

You may also consider raising capital by selling non-core assets and lines of business or entering into joint ventures by contributing assets in exchange for liquidity. Again, finding the right buyer at the right price for the assets you are willing to sell will take time. Attracting buy-side interest at an appropriate price will be as much a function of the sale process and how it is run as it is of the asset that is being sold. Without the time to conduct a proper process, you will be forced to take what is offered — and the offers in any fire sale will invariably be low.

Additionally, there are steps that you can take to restructure the debt currently on your balance sheet through negotiation with your existing creditors. If your debt is trading at a discount to the par value of the loan amount in the secondary market, there are a number of ways of buying back, exchanging and modifying the debt that might appeal to your lenders. If you are liquidity constrained, though, a direct purchase of debt in the secondary market is implausible, even if you can effect that purchase at a significant discount.

The better solution is often to exchange new debt with more appealing terms for the outstanding debt that is trading at a discount. Only those holders who consent to the exchange will get the new paper (and the associated fees), but if the offer is coupled with a consent solicitation to strip the old paper of restrictive covenants, you may incentivize some of the intransigent holders to play along with the exchange.

More broadly, though, the most popular and plausible solution to a pending default of a credit agreement is to negotiate a waiver, forbearance agreement or amendment to allow your company to continue to operate. The more complex and material the requested amendment, the more time will be needed to secure sufficient lender support (and the higher the requisite level of support will be as a percentage of the debt outstanding).

With respect to non-material events such as the breach of a performance covenant, the threshold of lender support to pass a waiver may be no more than 50 per cent. Should you wish to amend a credit agreement to extend maturity, alter amortization or change pricing, unanimous support is usually required. If you have sufficient time to do it, you could effectively refinance your debt through an amendment of your current credit facility that might extend the maturity of the debt while also easing and adjusting covenants to reflect the company's current operating environment and projected cash flows.

Prearranged and prepackaged bankruptcies

If you want to amend and extend your current facility but you cannot secure unanimous lender support, you may want to consider a prepackaged or prearranged bankruptcy, pursuant to which the borrower and the key lender constituents agree to the terms of a reorganization of the capital structure prior to the Chapter 11 filing. Bankruptcy is just a tool we use to help "right size" a capital structure to a borrower's current cash flow capacity. If used properly, it can be a cost-effective way to force dissenting members of a lender group to accept substantive revisions to their credit facility.

In bankruptcy court, the required level of lender support for material changes to a credit agreement is lowered from unanimity to half in number and two-thirds in amount. In a prearranged filing, you will have secured enough votes for the plan of reorganization before the filing is made, and the court will then simply have to bless the plan.

Prearranged/prepackaged filings thus have the

dual benefit of reducing the level of support needed from a creditor class to amend the terms of their credit facility, while keeping the length of the company's stay in bankruptcy (and the associated costs) to the absolute minimum. Moreover, court blessing for your plan of reorganization will eliminate material litigation risk.

Again, in each case, restructuring and recapitalizing a balance sheet is a time-consuming and complex process. The less time that you have to restructure, the more expensive it will be and the more value it will destroy. A leveraged company that may be frozen out of the debt capital markets needs to plan ahead.

Conclusion

The ever-more efficient movement of capital has created extreme volatility in the debt capital markets. They are open to many issuers as I write this article — which has made the prospect of refinancing the wall of debt coming due before 2014 much less intimidating. As such, and in light of the possibility that the markets may swing quickly shut again, you should be prepared to go to market now if you have a near- or medium-term debt maturity that will have to be refinanced.

In the case that the markets remain unreceptive to your issuance, it is better to know that sooner rather than later because the process of restructuring is time consuming (and value consuming if time is not available). In volatile markets, you borrow when you can for as long as you can — and as soon as you cannot borrow, you restructure.

23

A turnaround manager's risk-assessment imperatives for directors and officers

Lisa J Donahue,
Managing Director, and
Eva Anderson, Director,
AlixPartners LLP

Many in the US corporate world probably welcomed the close of the last decade. Along with the notorious financial scandals that bookended the decade (Enron and Madoff), the housing and commercial real estate bubbles, and the unprecedented job losses and credit contraction associated with the 2007-09 recession, *The Wall Street Journal* reported on December 20, 2009 that US stock performance had closed out the worst calendar decade since stock market data was first recorded in the 1920s.

If that was not enough of a challenge for corporate directors and officers, in the *annus horribilis* period ending September 30, 2009, the Administrative Office of the US Courts stated that 58,721 US business bankruptcies were recorded.

This represented an astonishing 63 per cent increase from the start of the decade and was more than 50 per cent higher than the comparable period in 2008. One would have to go back to 1997 to see the volume of business bankruptcy filings at levels above 50,000.

Among those thousands of filings in 2009, four of the top ten largest US bankruptcy filings commenced: CIT, Chrysler, General Motors and

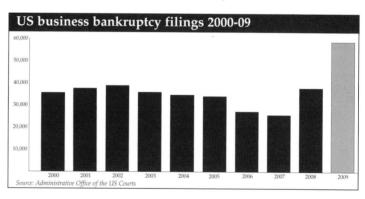

US business bankruptcy filings 2000-09

Source: Administrative Office of the US Courts

Thornburg Mortgage. During that period, the US government earned the distinction as the largest DIP financing provider. If a company was lucky enough not to be one of the filers, it might very well have been impacted by a supplier or customer that chose a bankruptcy path to restructure or even liquidate (as has been the case in the recent past with several high-profile and iconic brands such as Bear Stearns, Circuit City, Lehman Brothers, Linens 'n Things and Sharper Image).

In this context, the burden on the shoulders of corporate directors and officers feels like it has never been greater. How does one navigate in a distressed environment? Is any level of business risk acceptable, or is it time to batten down the hatches and simply aim for survival in challenging economic times?

Laying low is not an option

If only it were as simple as laying low for a few quarters. Unfortunately, such an approach presumes a company's directors and officers can control all the factors and forces impacting their businesses. The nature of today's global economy makes that presumption unrealistic, if indeed it were ever possible.

Energy, commodities and foreign currency exchange rates, for example, while all inputs that can be effectively hedged, are literally traded around the clock and around the globe, shifting risk and creating winners and losers with every trade. Relatively minor global events can cause significant disruptions to a company's near-term finances, while major international crises may virtually wipe out an otherwise stable business. A company may not sell a single product outside its US region, but its local utility and even its logistics providers buy power or fuel that is influenced by international factors. Its customers too may be owned by foreign companies whose purchasing decisions are directly influenced by exchange rates.

The global recession in 2007-09 showed corporate America just how fragile the safety net could be — that "too big to fail" was not quite absolute, but slightly more subjective when applied in the real world. In particular, the relatively easy access to credit experienced in the preceding five years masked trouble under the surface of many operating companies.

When consistent growth in the top line evaporated as consumers tightened their belts and corporations squeezed capital spending, rampant expense and overhead growth was often exposed and profits deteriorated. In addition, by removing the relatively automatic ability to refinance enormous short-term debt positions and investor appetites for risky, below-investment grade financial products, a much more Darwinian economic landscape has been created — one in which only the fittest companies survive.

Five key points for directors and officers

So what advice can we give to the directors and officers that find themselves and their companies negatively impacted in this environment and heading towards one or more of these serious scenarios in today's economic climate?

Based on our firm's experience in over 30 years of restructuring companies in a wide range of industries — during recessionary business cycles, rapid growth cycles, and other destabilizing market episodes — the advice can really be boiled down to

five key points that directors and officers need to think about in these situations.

With some practical nuances to each of these recommendations in light of the depth and breadth of this recession's impact, directors and officers need to think about the following questions:

How much cash do I have to work with and what is the near-term cash-flowing ability of my business? Does the amount of cash on hand give me enough time to execute on the turnaround?

Are the company and its current business plan viable? Is there a solid chance of restructuring the business given the industry's particular dynamics, prospects for the economy and customer base, competition, regulations, etc? Can my customers easily replace my product or service, or does the company have a unique value proposition?

Is the right management and board talent in place to lead the company through the crisis and/or restructuring process and beyond?

Does the company have the appropriate infrastructure in place to respond to the heightened sense of urgency that will be required in the crisis (such as fast and reliable financial/information systems and support, internal and external communications services and mission-consistent compensation structures)?

Does the business have the right capital structure in place to execute its future plans, including a turnaround phase, or will a waiver, forbearance agreement, debt restructuring or recapitalization be required?

Focus on liquidity

Easy credit during most of the last decade allowed many companies to decline into the financial equivalent of getting out of shape. With the prospect of having bankers line up and compete for each refinancing and generously sizing short-term credit lines, cash did not seem like an issue about which a company's directors and officers needed to be overly concerned.

The world changed in the global capital markets crisis.

If there are any major funding requirements coming due in the near term — such as seasonal inventory purchases, a note or bond maturity or coupon payment due on a company's debt, an earn-out payment to a seller following an acquisition, or even a lawsuit or arbitration settlement payment — a cash crisis is a more likely issue than ever before even in a recovering global economy, which still faces significant volatility.

Direct acknowledgment of the issue followed

by a rapid response by senior management is absolutely critical.

What will then most likely distinguish the outcome of these types of crises are: (i) how much cash is unencumbered and available in the company's bank accounts at that particular moment; (ii) how much cash is estimated to be generated (or burned) by business operations over the near term (next 13 weeks), as well as the next six- and 12-month periods; (iii) what other opportunities exist to generate quick and meaningful additional cash resources, such as through the sale of excess property, equipment or obsolete inventory, or potentially even through the sale of non-core businesses; and (iv) how flexible and accommodating a company's customers, suppliers and creditors are likely to be.

These questions about a company's cash position appear to be fundamental, yet surprisingly, many senior officers, including company treasurers, are unlikely to know the answers to all of the above with any precision. Board members might receive the typical package of financial statements — income statement, balance sheet and statement of cash flows. But even if these are received on a monthly basis, they are no adequate substitute for a direct-method cash-flow forecast.

In a crisis situation, cash reporting has to change immediately. If a company does not regularly monitor specific categories of receipts and disbursements and their relative flow on a daily and weekly basis, a process and a tool need to be established to provide reliable and accurate information about the cash position. This becomes increasingly critical the tighter cash is and the fewer days' "cash on hand" a company has to meet its obligations. Planning for specific large and routine outflows like payroll, benefits, rents, interest and raw material purchases, and more discretionary items like capital expenditures, along with anticipated collections on receivables and deposits, will provide vital insights into the peaks and valleys of the company's cash-flow needs over a compressed timeframe such as a 13-week or quarterly period.

Concurrently, the wallet and checkbook need to be tightly controlled by one point person, or a select group of senior managers, depending on the size and complexity of the operation. Directors and officers will either breathe a sigh of relief with the results of the near-term forecast and start working on the operational restructuring, or they will face yet another squall in the restructuring storm.

In particular, directors and officers need to be informed and engaged in situations where the financial distress borders the "zone of insolvency" and should also be aware that the exercise of their fiduciary duties is under a microscope. The duty of care and the duty of loyalty (and by extension, the duty of good faith) are guiding principles for directors' and officers' corporate behavior.

While specific legal advice should be sought by a company in this area, crossing over the gray line into the zone of insolvency generally means a company's debts may exceed the realizable value of its assets; that it may have difficulty paying its debts as they fall due; and that there may be insufficient capital to operate the business. A current balance sheet (as well as an approximation of the realizable value of the assets, as distinct from the book value), and a cash forecast will provide a point-in-time gauge, but officers and directors should err on the side of caution and be particularly aware of their actions and decisions when it is even a close call.

As a result of a series of recent Delaware Bankruptcy and Chancery Court rulings, the sense of blanket protection for directors and officers under the "business judgment" rule has been diminished somewhat, and directors and officers may be more exposed to allegations of breaches of fiduciary duty that could increase the risks of their own personal liability.

Engaging directors and officers in the necessary analysis, conclusions or scenarios around the liquidity situation, and having both groups actively participating in the evaluation of a range of options, is a helpful step in the process of exercising their fiduciary duties and moving a company forward through a restructuring. Glossing over, taking shortcuts or waiting too long to take decisive action to assess the severity of the situation is simply the wrong course.

Assessment of viability

The animal instinct of protecting one's young in times of crisis finds a parallel in the business world, often with disappointing or disastrous results. Directors and officers that hang on to a failing business or a particular subsidiary or strategy at all costs — adopting tunnel vision that does not recognize the signs of failure — perform a disservice to their shareholders and creditors. When senior management is on a path of borrowing to fund operating losses in the hope that growth in the top line or development of the "next big thing" will save them, the psychological investment may be too great to turn back without significant disruption.

The balance of power and healthy tension between executive management and company boards is exercised in these situations. Cold, hard objectivity is needed. Significant time, money and effort can be saved in the long run by determining relatively quickly whether there is a chance the business is viable and can be restructured, or if there is greater value to be obtained by pulling the plug on select pieces of the business — or on the entire operation.

The main task in the initial stages of the viability analysis is to break down each of the component business lines or units and assess them on the following bases: their cash-flow-generating or cash-burning prospects; their overall fit within the core business strategy; and their near-term and long-term prospects for success in the marketplace.

At this point, Voltaire's observation that 'the perfect is the enemy of the good' comes into play: the initial exercise is to triage to identify bleeding on the one hand and, on the other, to maintain the status quo at businesses that are performing well, so that efforts are accurately focused. That said, the more granularly the initial information can be analyzed from an operating unit perspective, the better, as consolidations can be created precisely to mask the underperformance of particular business units (or pet projects).

An independent perspective

Much of this analysis can be gleaned from an historical review of actual performance, supplemented by the current year's budget estimate, and then bootstrapped to the company's existing five-year business plan, if one exists. Chances are, however, that for many companies facing financial crisis, these prospective tools did not work well in practice, and in the midst of a crisis, recreating the analysis would appear to be a daunting and time-consuming task. Restructuring advisors are often brought in to assist management and the board with these fundamental analyses.

Furthermore, an independent third-party perspective is also often required by creditors who may feel that management's perspective is no longer credible. What directors and officers must understand is that even a high-level effort to project and document a base case of where the businesses appear to be heading at a given point in time is better than doing nothing. Effective internal financial planning and analysis functions may not save a company if events occur that are outside a

company's control. But their ability to develop alternate scenarios and build analyses quickly from a deep understanding of historical revenue and expense trends provides a solid foundation for evaluating the viability of a business, or particular components of the business, and useful, even though preliminary, enterprise valuations.

Depending on the initial viability assessment and how much time the company may have before an upcoming liquidity event, the initial base-case findings may serve as the basis for a company-wide performance improvement initiative, in particular with regard to those units that are in a gray area of viability. By evaluating areas such as product and customer profitability, the manufacturing plant footprint, employee and executive compensation and accountability models, as well as real estate or store portfolios, and then implementing the cost-reduction and revenue-enhancing initiatives identified, a company can potentially change the outlook for marginally performing businesses or units. This interim period may also present an opportune time to identify, market and sell non-core assets to generate additional cash and to allow management to focus more intently on the go-forward businesses.

Leadership

If directors and officers are facing a potential restructuring situation, they need to look carefully at the available talent pool from which the leaders of key elements of a restructuring will be drawn. The day-to-day requirements of running the business are ever present, but the responsibilities of successfully leading a company through the high-stakes environment of a restructuring are often themselves more than a full-time job. The rapid-fire analysis and decision-making, complex negotiations along multiple fronts with various creditor constituents, overall project management and co-ordination as well as leading the more technical aspects of a bankruptcy, if needed, are unlikely to be part of the average skillset of most corporate directors and officers.

While there may not be a typical restructuring situation, it has become more and more common for boards and senior management to appoint and empower an outsider as chief restructuring officer (CRO) to lead the charge. While an internal candidate might fill this position, sometimes the need for change is best met by retaining an outsider. But even with an outsider as CRO, it will not be business as usual within a company undergoing a restructuring. Additional executives and board directors will be drawn into the range of activities that constitute the restructuring process. Many will rise to the challenge, but because others may present a defensive posture that could obstruct progress, directors and officers should be prepared to make changes.

Restructurings will more often highlight talent deficiencies in companies that have grown rapidly via acquisition, than in those companies that have grown organically and at a slower pace. If companies are led by executives and board members who are skilled at acquiring businesses and motivated by getting the next deal done, the prevailing mindset may not serve so well when the business needs to be downsized and compensation is no longer correlated with transaction volume.

There are also often cultural challenges that surface in a restructuring. The additional workload required of many executives and staff as a result of the demands of a restructuring may be resented, when compounded with cost-saving efforts like the reduction or elimination of annual bonuses, elimination of 401k matches or mandatory furloughs. The "empty parking lot" syndrome, with a mad dash out of the parking lots at 5pm, is one symptom that will need to be addressed proactively by internal managers and human resources, and potentially through merit and performance-based incentives for key employees.

In contrast, an internal merger integration team (skilled in identifying synergies and cost savings, for example) can often be fruitfully redirected to identify and implement important performance improvement initiatives, taking a leadership role in the restructuring. Similarly, given the crucial importance of cash management and forecasting, company treasurers, accounts receivable and accounts payable managers are often in a position to rise to the occasion and take leadership roles.

In the case of directors, those serving on a board as representatives/partners of an equity sponsor may feel conflicted. In particular, when the initial analysis shows a significant reduction in enterprise value, or in a worst-case scenario, when residual equity value is questionable, there may be diminishing value to the equity fund in remaining on the board. Resignations may be the right course of action and board openings may present an opportunity to recruit talent that is valuable to the company while it navigates the restructuring. Independent board members often become key players in restructuring situations, fulfilling not only their traditional board duties but leveraging their independent perspective in interactions with important external constituents such as critical vendors, regulators and banking relationships.

Existing directors and officers will need to make candid assessments and take decisive action during the earliest stages of a crisis and identify the appropriate talent and critical roles. The sooner a viable and strategic restructuring team is in place, the sooner the process can move forward.

Corporate infrastructure

The corporate infrastructure in place at companies operating under normal conditions — including IT systems, financial reporting sub-systems, operational metrics and dashboards and compensation models — can be both a blessing and a curse when a company veers toward distress. Problems with a company's information systems are often one of the warning signals that should alert management and boards to perhaps more serious underlying problems confronting the company. Issues range from failing to integrate disparate accounting and reporting systems in acquired companies, leading to a reliance on high-level, manual or time-consuming consolidations, to operating with overly complex systems that are so customized that only a small number of internal staff will be adept at using them. These deep-seated problems can span both financial and operational areas, delaying the production of reliable and actionable information for senior management until it is too late.

Challenges identified

Highly decentralized organizations, especially those with layers of legacy corporate, tax and banking entities, often represent particularly challenging restructurings. Financial reporting timeframes are often compressed (particularly where cash reporting is concerned), with some simplification of the organization and reporting often required in order to convey the necessary information.

On the operational side, metrics and performance indicators that may have seemed perfectly logical when liquidity was not an issue may not only be irrelevant but could actually prove to be counterproductive during a crisis. An example might be an overly aggressive emphasis on meeting quarterly sales targets. If a particular customer or account were particularly unprofitable, increasing sales would actually undermine the company's restructuring progress.

Complex compensation models, as well as those that are geared largely towards senior executives, also need to be rethought during a restructuring. Some bonus and incentive plans have become highly contested issues in Chapter 11 cases since the bankruptcy laws changed in recent years. Employees of troubled companies, creditors and regulatory bodies will all be particularly sensitive to any suggestion that business failure is being rewarded. Company-wide milestone-based incentives, such as cash-generation or EBITDA targets, tend to draw a wider range of employees towards a common goal than do business-unit focused transactions or sales-based compensation models. That said, exceptions do exist — for example, in advertising sales or brokerage-based operations where employee compensation will often be predominantly commission-based.

While a crisis may seem like an inopportune time to start tweaking a company's standard reporting package, there may be no option but to do so. If companies are prepared to invest time in developing key metrics against which business units and their leaders will be held accountable, as well as measuring performance in an open and methodical way, they will send out the right messages about performance goals.

It is often helpful for senior leadership to establish smaller tactical teams during the restructuring to focus on specific tasks that are critical during the process (such as cash monitoring and forecasting, generating cash from non-operating sources such as asset sales and working capital improvements, identifying operational improvements and major operational issues and reducing corporate overhead). These smaller teams can become part of an executive leadership group that should meet and report regularly, with senior management, to report on progress, share successes and explain variances.

Communication is one area of corporate infrastructure that should not be cut back by directors and officers during a restructuring. Indeed, internal employee communications and external communications with groups as diverse as creditors, retirees, vendors, unions, landlords and local news organizations both have an essential role to play throughout the process.

In public companies especially, where internal and external counsel will usually be responsible for crafting carefully worded quarterly filings and interim reports, much of the content distributed in the public domain will be close to boilerplate, particularly where risk and forward-looking statements are concerned. While necessary, this can be counterproductive to the company's turnaround

mission if not supplemented by communications professionals who can shape the company's message. If this function is not adequately staffed within the company, or if the skillset is more geared towards marketing and publicity rather than crisis management, directors and officers should strongly consider retaining outside experts in this area. The communications function during a restructuring should be consolidated to ensure consistency of message and to co-ordinate the release of specific communications.

If a company does file for bankruptcy, communications also need to be highly co-ordinated with bankruptcy counsel and strategies and protocols developed for communicating with key constituencies.

Capital structure

Financial problems stemming from excess leverage seem to have dominated the news in recent years, with consumers and corporate America now reeling from the consequences of their previously unfettered access to low-cost capital. Almost everyone participated in this bonanza whilst it was in progress — from modest homeowners to the world's largest private equity funds. Few spotted the warning signs until it was too late.

Looking back, the beginning of the end of the leveraged buyout boom was probably marked by the Alliance Boots deal in Summer 2007. It was then that the underwriting banks failed to fully syndicate a large portion of the LBO transaction debt. But it is now clear that many of today's corporate directors and officers approved similar transactions, although each of these was unique in structure and circumstances. It is this uniqueness that means that now, in the harsh light of day, each company must navigate its own restructuring, developing its own solutions to its own capital structure problems.

That said, even though they are facing quite different circumstances, directors and officers can still find themselves in the same restructuring boat.

Consider the situation where a company's total leverage ratio is structurally appropriate based on its EBITDA performance and peer metrics, but a major debt maturity is approaching. With tough capital markets, and maybe an industry that is out of favor, the company is faced with limited or high-cost prospects for refinancing, and limited time to complete a transaction. Another company may have experienced plunging sales and profits, and the debt load is clearly no longer sustainable based on standard valuation and credit analyses. Clearly, though, the type and severity of the problem will affect the process and outcome of any restructuring, and the prospects for the former would certainly seem rosier than for the latter. Paying a higher interest rate or providing an additional collateral cushion for a loan, compared to a full-blown bankruptcy filing, are just a few extreme points on either end of the spectrum of capital structure solutions that companies might need to deploy.

Mapping out credit events

Directors and officers need to map out the major upcoming credit events on their corporate horizons (such as commercial paper rollovers, other maturing debt and covenant ratio step-downs) more carefully than ever before, as well as be proactive with regard to windows of opportunity for creative capital raising and refinancing. Using these analyses to validate a company's capital structure — its mix of short- and long-term debt, secured relative to unsecured, and debt v equity — or to identify alternative structures, is an important responsibility for directors and officers. Assuming a relatively stable business operation and enough time in advance of liquidity-driven capital events, the process should be much more controllable and provide a company with more latitude and options to consider.

When the crisis is sudden, or problems have not been acknowledged and the situation deteriorates, companies will obviously have fewer options to deal with capital structure problems. Making one more semi-annual coupon payment, or eking out an adjusted EBITDA calculation through generous add-back provisions, can sometimes buy three to six months, but may delay the inevitable for an overly-leveraged company in operational decline.

Using some of the forecasting tools mentioned, with credit/debt events clearly mapped, it should be apparent to directors and officers when one more payment might be possible, but the next two or three payments have no chance of being made. At this stage, the options should be evaluated in consultation with advisors and counsel and discussions with creditors carefully scripted.

A company's existing relationship with its major creditors is a starting point. If relationships are open and candid, they should continue in that vein. When there is distrust based on previous missteps, inserting an independent third-party advisor is one way of at least starting to repair the relationship. But this may not be enough. Depending on the scenario, it may also be important to make changes in either the director or officer ranks in order to reach a consensual

solution. Directors and officers need to be prepared for such responses, particularly when the required capital structure changes indicate there will be a significant shift in majority equity ownership as a result of the restructuring.

Other influences will be likely to affect the tone and course of a restructuring. Are the major creditors large banks, hedge funds or vulture investors, for example? Is the company amply secured or virtually underwater? And while these are not factors over which directors and officers will have any control, they will need to attempt to remain flexible and adaptable as new developments arise.

Conclusion

No company director or officer looks forward to guiding a company through a restructuring, unless they are brought in specifically to handle the challenge. But while it would appear to the senior leadership in a company that the restructuring process is a monumental distraction from running the underlying business, a restructuring can in fact provide a company with an opportunity to hit the restart button and craft a new organization with better prospects for the future.

Directors and officers facing a restructuring should do so with an optimistic, yet realistic approach. Based on our years of experience in such crises, early action can generally ameliorate the situation. While there will be plenty of pressure to point fingers and assign blame, and maybe even a few sacrificial lambs offered up along the way, a better approach for directors and officers is to remain focused on the process that lies ahead. The more rapidly this is embraced, and the more deeply involved the senior leadership becomes, the more successful the process will be.

While that will not guarantee success for the company across every measure targeted by the directors and officers, the process should provide enough transparency and thoughtful analysis to ensure that the outcome will be understood. In today's turbulent times, the difference between a successful restructuring and rapid liquidation still boils down to whether there is an underlying business that investors feel they can support financially and that offers the appropriate rewards relative to capital put at risk. It is critical that there should be raw data and back-story capable of supporting such an investment thesis. Equally, it is essential that the company's directors and officers should have full confidence in the plan that they are responsible for executing. Put bluntly, they need to be up for the challenge.

Restructuring Strategies in Distressed Situations

24

Negotiating with lenders: Forbearance, waivers, lender approval and the collective action conundrum

Howard Seife, Partner and Chairman of the Global Bankruptcy and Financial Restructuring Practice, and Andrew Rosenblatt, Partner, **Chadbourne & Parke LLP**

In the wake of the massive downturn in the global economy, more companies than at any time in recent memory have found themselves struggling financially. But while there has been an uptick in the number of formal bankruptcy cases being filed — under both Chapter 11 and Chapter 7 of the Bankruptcy Code — it is noteworthy that these have not kept pace with the spike in defaults.

Although corporate debt defaults have increased enormously compared to pre-financial crisis levels, total bankruptcy filings have only doubled, and stand just slightly above the 1980-2009 average.

Distressed companies are acting early

This gap in "expected filings" is explained, at least in part, by the fact that distressed businesses are increasingly identifying impending financial difficulties at a relatively early stage and taking action to avoid a non-negotiated, or "freefall", bankruptcy. In the current atmosphere of heightened competition and tight credit, they do not want the stigma and administrative costs associated with a formal filing. Companies that are

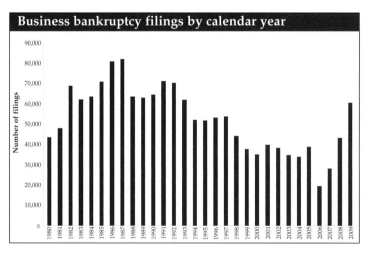

Business bankruptcy filings by calendar year

insolvent, or on the verge of becoming insolvent, are increasingly seeking to restructure their debt through either a consensual out-of-court process or a prepackaged bankruptcy. The number of businesses filing prepackaged cases more than doubled from 2008 to 2009.

The first step a company must take in either an out-of-court restructuring or a prepackaged bankruptcy is to buy time for all of the relevant parties to negotiate and develop a restructuring plan. Frequently, distressed businesses will find themselves in danger of defaulting on loan obligations by violating one or more of the financial covenants contained in the underlying loan agreements. As a result, they are often in the position of having to negotiate with their lenders for a waiver of certain defaults, or at least forbearance from enforcement of the contractual remedies.

Of course, lenders are rarely anxious to give up their valuable contractual rights, and businesses may literally have to buy the time they need to effect a restructuring. What follows is an overview of the process of negotiating waivers or forbearances, identifying some of the areas of contention that arise between lenders and borrowers and offering constructive solutions.

The parties

Negotiating a waiver of a financial covenant or other credit agreement provision will most often be a multilateral exercise. Obviously both the lender group and the company will be party to the discussions, but often a number of constituencies within the lender group will also play a large role in determining the fate of the negotiations.

First and foremost, most credit facilities are managed by an administrative agent, which is generally one of the institutions with a financial stake in the facility and very often will have been responsible for its origination and syndication. The agent is empowered by the lender group to act on their behalf with respect to the facility, although it cannot usually do anything "out of the ordinary course", such as granting a waiver, without the consent of "required lenders". Some credit agreements do grant agents the independence to take certain "out of the ordinary course" actions without the required consent, but agents almost universally refuse to do so in order to maintain good relations with their constituents and to avoid exposing themselves to potential liability.

Although the term "required lenders" is common to most credit agreements, its exact definition varies. It is relatively common for the term to mean any lenders holding, in aggregate, a majority of the total loan exposure under the facility. However, it is not unheard-of for the requisite percentage of total exposure to be two-thirds or even as high as 75 per cent. The breadth of lender support required for "out of the ordinary course" decisions is of course critical in the development of an appropriate negotiation strategy, particularly in cases where the interests of the various lenders are not perfectly aligned.

Certain loan provisions are viewed as nearly inviolable, and consequently most credit agreements require unanimous lender consent for modifying the principal amount of the loan,

waiving a payment, releasing any substantial collateral securing the loan or waiving a payment default. Businesses looking for such concessions should expect that they will face an uphill battle on these issues, and that even a single holdout may frustrate any out-of-court resolution.

Once waiver or restructuring negotiations begin, the lender group is likely to create a steering committee, comprised of the largest lenders, to work with the agent in negotiating on behalf of the entire group.

It will be critical for the borrower to establish a good working relationship with the steering committee, whose support will be vital in obtaining a waiver — particularly as the committee often constitutes "required lenders". If the credit facility has multiple tranches of debt, members of each tranche are likely to insist on adequate representation on the committee, and borrowers should be aware that members of the committee may not all have the same interests and goals.

Different types of lenders may have different risk tolerances and agendas driving their investment strategies. For example, some may have a "loan to own" strategy, in which case it is unlikely they will be interested in granting waivers on any terms — their explicit goal will be to assume control of the company. Other lenders, though, may be less interested in ownership and more willing to negotiate a consensual arrangement. Still others may specialize in investing in, or lending to, companies that are already distressed. Such lenders may be willing to grant a number of concessions as they will have purchased their share of the loan at a substantial discount.

Appreciating and exploiting these inter-creditor dynamics can help a borrower to negotiate a waiver successfully and, ultimately, restructure its debt.

Managers seeking to restructure should be aware of the interests of their own equity holders, who, particularly in privately held companies, are likely to seek an active role in the negotiation process.

A successful outcome often depends on managing the expectations of equity holders and understanding their restructuring objectives.

Navigating the terms of a credit document

In the event of a default, credit agreements typically provide lenders with a range of possible remedies. Some of these will be triggered automatically, while other, generally less serious, events of default trigger remedies only upon notice to the borrower at the request, or with the consent, of the required lenders.

Typical remedies include causing all

outstanding principal, interest and other obligations to become immediately due and payable ("acceleration"), and allowing the administrative agent to enforce liens and security interests against collateral ("foreclosure"). Common events of default include:

- The failure to make a payment when due under the credit agreement.
- A default under another loan agreement (a "cross-default").
- A breach of a financial covenant.
- A breach of representations, warranties or certifications of creditworthiness.
- A bankruptcy filing by the borrower or any subsidiary of the borrower, or the appointment of a receiver.
- A failure to discharge judgments or have them vacated.
- The occurrence of specified events under the Employee Retirement Income Security Act (ERISA).
- A change of control of the company.
- A failure to comply with the terms of the credit agreement.
- The termination or invalidation of loan guaranties.

The failure to make any scheduled payment and a filing for bankruptcy are generally regarded as the most serious events of default and usually trigger automatic payment acceleration.

Before seeking to negotiate the waiver of any loan requirements, a borrower must appreciate what defaults have occurred or are likely to occur in the immediate future. While a payment default is the most obvious (and perhaps the most serious) breach that might need to be waived, a struggling company will usually breach one or more of the various financial covenants contained in its loan agreements before it is in immediate danger of a payment default. Examples of financial covenants commonly included in credit facilities are:

- Leverage ratio limits (funded debt/EBITDA).
- Fixed-charge coverage requirements.
- Asset/liability ratio minimums.
- A net income floor.

These financial covenants are designed to act as early-warning signals that a borrower is becoming financially unsound. So, among companies seeking to buy time to carry out a restructuring, the most common focus of negotiations is for a temporary waiver that excuses compliance with one or more of the covenants.

Opening the talks

Successful negotiation requires convincing the lenders that it is in their own best interests to grant a waiver, which will probably entail demonstrating that they stand to lose money if the borrower is forced to declare bankruptcy or liquidate. Although credit agreements can and do vary, they tend to be fairly standard in terms of the requirements for waiving a breach or impending breach of a covenant. Typically, the consent of the required lenders will be needed — which could mean a borrower has to secure the support of anything from a bare majority to 75 per cent of the lenders by amount of their exposure. As discussed above, unanimous consent will be needed for waiving or altering payment amounts, changing the principal owed, or, critically, extending the maturity of a loan. Frequently, upon a default, credit agreements also provide for the potential for the acceleration of all payments. If acceleration occurs, borrowers seeking retroactive rather than prospective waivers may therefore face the difficult task of obtaining unanimous approval.

Success in gathering support may depend on the company's ability to present a credible work-out plan. If it cannot convince its lenders that they will be better off with a reorganization rather than a liquidation, then the game is up before it really begins. To this end, before contacting its lenders, the company should have a firm grasp of its financial condition and develop a three-month cash-flow projection that assumes the continuation of all current obligations. Critically, the plan should show that continued operation will not immediately erode the value of any collateral or prevent future payments to lenders. Developing this projection is likely to require the retention of financial professionals that specialize in restructuring distressed entities.

Once the cash-flow projection is in place, the company should contact the agent under its credit agreement, and perhaps its largest creditors individually, to set up a meeting to discuss possible solutions. It is best if this initial contact comes from either the company or its financial advisors, rather than the company's counsel (in-house or otherwise), because lenders typically respond better to hearing the first news of a problem from another business person. The company should set the meeting for a convenient but neutral location. If it has a significant number of out-of-state creditors, choosing a hotel or conference facility close to a major airport will help set the right tone for the negotiations.

As outlined above, the goal of the first creditors' meeting is to convince the required lenders that they will be better off if the business is reorganized, or at least that they will suffer no immediate harm by exploring this option. With this in mind, the company should be prepared to present not only the three-month cash-flow projection but its financial history and a preliminary liquidation analysis. The floor should then be opened to questions from the lenders, before the meeting is turned over to the company's counsel, who should present an overview of the options and request lender support for the waivers or forbearances.

Different relief options
Companies have distinct options when requesting relief from a financial covenant. They may elect to seek a waiver, under which agreement is reached to suspend compliance for a set period. For example, lenders might agree to waive the typical leverage-ratio covenant from May 1 of a given year through August 31 of the same year, so any violations that occur during this period will not trigger contractual remedies. Additionally, waivers may eliminate any covenant violations or defaults that have already occurred.

The company may also ask lenders to forbear from enforcing the remedies available following an event of default. The critical difference between forbearance and a waiver is that forbearance agreements do not eliminate any defaults that occur or may have already occurred. In fact, they expressly preserve all events of default. As a result, lenders may elect to exercise their remedies once the forbearance period has ended, unless an alternative arrangement has been reached. Another, often-overlooked, consequence is that the existence of a default under one loan document may trigger cross-default provisions in other agreements to which the company is a party. This issue may be particularly important if the borrower has foreign affiliates or subsidiaries. Indeed, foreign jurisdictions often impose more stringent duties on their officers and directors, which require them to commence bankruptcy proceedings under certain circumstances, including if their company is either balance-sheet insolvent or unable to pay its debts as they come due.

A default under a credit agreement that triggers a cross-default under a foreign entity's loan documents could give rise to liabilities that require foreign officers and directors to place their companies into bankruptcy. Moreover, many of these jurisdictions do not recognize the concept of a "debtor in possession" and require the appointment of an outside administrator for all bankrupt entities. Thus, a company that opts to pursue a forbearance rather than a waiver must perform sufficient due diligence to ensure it fully understands the implications of a default for its foreign subsidiaries and affiliates. Finally, with respect to forbearance, because the borrower has still technically defaulted on its obligations, lenders may be permitted to charge default-rate interest.

Another option for borrowers is to seek to amend the terms of the credit agreement itself to remove, limit or relax the problematic covenant. For example, a company might request a permanent modification of leverage-ratio requirements in order to allow it to maintain a heavier debt load without defaulting on its obligations. However, other than in the context of an overall restructuring, lenders tend not to favor amendments of this nature.

From the company's perspective, it might initially appear preferable to obtain a waiver rather than forbearance. Waivers do of course provide protections not afforded by forbearance agreements, but it is worth considering that lenders may demand a higher price for a waiver. Borrowers should consider whether, on the margin, it is worth the cost to get a waiver rather than forbearance. On the other hand, if the prospect of cross-defaults would needlessly complicate the lenders' own positions, they may be relatively inclined to grant a waiver instead of forbearance.

Key negotiating terms
Borrowers should remember that a waiver or forbearance is a stopgap measure designed to buy time. Unless the parties have agreed to an amendment of the credit agreement itself, any relief will come with a specific — and limited — lifespan, after which it will terminate and the normal compliance requirements will resume. Additionally, the agreement may provide for its early termination on a number of grounds, such as:

• The violation of any covenant or the occurrence of any event of default not specifically waived or the subject of a forbearance agreement.
• The breach of any of the representations and warranties made in connection with the waiver or forbearance.
• The failure to meet reorganization milestones (discussed below).

It is very rare that a significant waiver or forbearance is freely given. Lenders will demand a range of concessions to ensure their interests are adequately protected. First, the borrower will be required to disclose all outstanding defaults and, to avoid confusion or conflicts further down the road, these will be specifically listed in the waiver or forbearance agreement, which will also state that it is limited to the defaults listed. Generally, the agreement will also contain a clause stating that the lenders retain their rights to strict compliance with the loan documents.

The borrower should expect to pay a fee. While this may not be the case in particularly limited forbearances or waivers, in most cases there will be a fee of between 0.25 per cent and 1 per cent of the amount of the facility, based on the length and extent of the waiver or forbearance.

The borrower will typically be required to release any potential claims it may have against the lenders and reaffirm its obligations under the loan agreements. Guarantors will likely also have to reaffirm their obligations to avoid any argument that these have been eliminated as a result of the modification of the underlying obligations.

Lenders are almost certain to insist on new reporting and disclosure requirements as part of the consideration for a waiver. Generally, the borrower should be prepared to provide, on an ongoing basis, 13-week financial projections and cash-flow statements. The loan documents will be amended to reflect these new requirements, which often persist for the life of the loan rather than just during the waiver or forbearance period. Often, lenders also expect an "amendment fee" for any such changes, even where the actual amendment is designed to benefit the lenders.

The lenders will likely wish to retain restructuring specialists to analyze the borrower's finances. They will expect the borrower to bear the costs of these professionals.

To the extent that the loans are not already fully secured by liens on all of the borrower's assets (and often the assets of its subsidiaries), the lenders may request additional security. However, this may come under attack as a preference in the event that the borrower subsequently files for bankruptcy, if it is shown that the company was insolvent at the time the additional security interest was given. Courts have issued conflicting decisions as to whether granting a waiver or forbearance constitutes sufficient value to support granting a security interest. Borrowers should expect that lenders will seek to mitigate this risk and should be prepared to provide information that demonstrates solvency. Although this task is likely to be delegated to the borrower's financial advisors

initially, lenders may seek an independent solvency analysis if they perceive a significant risk of preference allegations. Again, the company will be expected to bear these costs.

Lenders may require an increase in the pricing of the loan to reflect the changed circumstances of the company. It is not uncommon for interest rates to be raised by 100 basis points or more, depending on the extent of the waiver requested and the overall financial health of the company. While borrowers may view this as a type of penalty, lenders merely see it as ensuring that price matches risk. Borrowers may be able to minimize upward repricing by presenting clear financial projections that chart a workable path back to stability.

Lenders will often condition the waiver on the borrower meeting "milestones" for the reorganization process. For example, the company could be required to produce a term sheet setting out restructuring terms within a specified timeframe. Failure to meet these milestones could result in termination of the waiver, either automatically or upon notice by the administrative agent. Essentially, the lenders will want to see concrete progress towards reorganization and will likely insist on a mechanism that allows them to act to prevent diminution in the value of their collateral if the borrower falls short.

The terms described above are only examples of what lender groups may request in exchange for a waiver or forbearance. The circumstances of individual borrowers and the make-up of their lender constituencies will determine what is sought in any particular case. While no borrower (distressed or otherwise) wants to part with more money, a properly structured waiver fee can actually be used to induce recalcitrant lenders to grant a waiver.

Dealing with holdout lenders

Precisely because syndicated credit facilities often bring together large groups of lenders with diverse interests, borrowers may occasionally find a waiver negotiation at an impasse due to the obstinacy of one or more holdout lenders. Credit agreements frequently contain provisions that create tension between individual lender and lender group rights. The very existence of the administrative agent suggests that credit agreements contemplate treating constituent lenders as a group, yet many actions under any given loan agreement require approval by each individual lender. Where individual and group interests conflict, a "collective action" problem may arise.

This occurs most often when a borrower seeks

a waiver that requires unanimous approval, as even a single lender can, at least temporarily, derail the process. However, even in instances where the loan documents require only majority or "required lenders" support for a waiver, dissenting creditors intent on exercising their rights have been known to bring suit to enforce alleged individual rights of action. These suits raise the question of whether the administrative agent, acting with the support of the contractually required number of lenders, has the authority to bind dissenters.

Courts have generally held that waivers granted by a contractually sufficient majority are effective to bind the minority and block individual suits, so long as the credit agreement in question unambiguously contemplates collective action. However, where the loan documents do not explicitly bar individual lender action, there is some risk that a waiver may prove ineffective. If dissenting creditors have not at some point given their consent to be bound by majority rule, borrowers may find that they are forced to negotiate individual settlements or are unable to obtain an effective waiver at all. The best protection against these suits is planning ahead: borrowers should ensure their credit agreements clearly contemplate collective action and contain prohibitions against individual lender action.

The good news is that even if dissenting creditors can block a waiver, loan documents almost invariably provide that most remedies — particularly taking action against collateral (including foreclosing on it) — require the blessing of the administrative agent and/or required lenders. A creditor in such a position will probably be able to make a lot of noise, but may have little recourse against the borrower outside of suing for any actual damages it may have suffered (in other words, its *pro rata* share of any unpaid amounts).

A borrower may even be able to turn collective action problems to its advantage to achieve a *de facto* forbearance with significantly less than majority support. For example, if a credit agreement states that the administrative agent may only foreclose on collateral with the support of the required lenders — and "required lenders" is defined as 67 per cent by amount of loan exposure — then a borrower will be able to block foreclosure as long as it manages to enlist the support of more than 33 per cent of the lenders.

Conclusion
After a recession, many companies find themselves in financial distress and face the prospect of

defaulting on financial covenants or even payment obligations under loan agreements. If not managed correctly, the process of dealing with lenders can sound the death knell for a defaulting borrower. Conversely, a borrower that manages the discussions well will give itself the best chance of reorganizing.

Officers and directors of troubled companies need to be prepared for the waiver and forbearance negotiations that represent the first and often the most critical juncture in the restructuring process. Here are some final takeaway points that should help set a borrower on the path to a successful negotiation:

• Know your credit agreement. It spells out the borrower's obligations as well as the lenders' rights and remedies. It is the starting point for all negotiations and will be the single most important document in the discussions.
• Know your lender constituency. A borrower that appreciates the goals of each of its lenders is a step ahead in crafting an incentive package that will bring everyone on board.
• Know what relief you want and what you are willing to pay for it. Lenders will inevitably have a number of asks in return for a waiver. Borrowers that are not surprised by these demands, and are prepared to provide a reasonable response, stand a much better chance of obtaining favorable terms.
• Have a plan of action. A borrower that can open negotiations by presenting a clear and credible plan for revitalizing the business is much more likely to convince lenders not to accelerate and foreclose.
• Preparation is key. While negotiating with lenders over the fate of a company can be a daunting prospect, an executive with clear goals and a credible plan stands a good chance of obtaining support.

The authors would like to thank Eric Daucher, an Associate in Chadbourne & Parke LLP's New York office, for his assistance in the preparation of this chapter. All financial data was drawn from Moody's Investors Service. See Moody's Investors Service, Special Comment: Corporate Default and Recovery Rates, 1920-2009, 1-3 (2010).

25

How distressed claims trading may impact your reorganization strategy

Edward S Weisfelner, Chair of the Bankruptcy and Corporate Restructuring Practice Group, **Brown Rudnick LLP**

The surging growth of the claims trading market, and the increasing influence exercised by hedge funds and private equity funds that purchase claims and interests, has revolutionized corporate restructurings.[1]

Claims trading has created a market-driven course of action, allowing the entry of sophisticated financial players that want to benefit from, participate in and control restructurings. It has significantly impacted the negotiating dynamics between the debtor and its creditors and equity holders.

Introduction

The reorganization process has benefited substantially from claims trading. Liquidity is added as banks, insurance companies, trade creditors and other financial institutions are given the opportunity to cash out and avoid the complications, delays and costs of participating in bankruptcy and restructuring cases. These liquidity benefits may flow through the entire financial system, as lending institutions are apt to provide increased capital to borrowers knowing that bankruptcy exit options exist if their loans sour. Moreover, claims trading gives financial entities seeking to invest in the debtor the opportunity to do so. Unlike banks and certain other financial institutions, hedge funds and private equity funds are permitted to receive, and often prefer, new equity in exchange for their debt claims. Often, these players are also willing to provide new cash to the restructuring.

These factors may benefit the debtor by increasing the reorganization options and allowing the enterprise to emerge from bankruptcy with less leverage. In addition, claims trading often narrows restructuring negotiations to a smaller band of sophisticated and well-funded players deeply aware of the law and market perceptions of value. These parties will often defend their views of value with their pocket-books, thus ensuring a much better Chapter 11 adjudication and final result, as debt placed in the hands of those who know what to do with it breeds informed conversation in and out of the court.

Nevertheless, it is important for the debtor to grasp the motivations of the claims purchasers so as to formulate a restructuring plan that benefits all its stakeholders, including the new participants.

While companies generally understand their relationships with their banks, bondholders and trade creditors outside bankruptcy, it is sometimes hard to determine the identity and motivations of the hedge funds and private equity funds purchasing claims and interests during times of distress. On a basic level, claims traders seek the same benefit as previous holders: generating a profitable return. However, while the traditional players typically benefit from a long-term, symbiotic relationship with the debtor, the claims purchaser may be motivated by short-term profits on trading or recovery spreads, or may be seeking an attractively priced takeover or ownership opportunity.

Often, debtors have little information about the identity and holdings of their claims' holders due to the intensity of claims trading. To assist themselves in negotiations, debtors may seek to obtain certain information about their active claimants through various disclosure requirements.

Claims trading also impacts the debtor in a number of other critical ways, including: (i) how it discloses public and non-public information in connection with bankruptcy negotiations; (ii) how it preserves negotiated deals; and (iii) how it preserves net operating losses and other tax advantages.

With a better understanding of the claims trading market and the motivations of its distressed investor claims holders, the debtor may be able to navigate the Chapter 11 restructuring process more effectively and formulate a plan that best satisfies the needs of its entire stakeholder constituency.

The bankruptcy claims trading market continues its dramatic growth

The trading of bankruptcy claims (the various interests against the debtor, whether secured or unsecured, including bank, bond and trade debt) takes place in a secondary market. Little disclosure is required and the market is, to a significant extent, unregulated.

Therefore, calculating its size is difficult, though it has generally been understood to be in the hundreds of billions of dollars, with the *LSTA Loan Market Chronicle* putting it at over $1 trillion. According to SecondMarket's 2009 Claims Trading Year in Review, an auction platform for "illiquid assets", the bankruptcy claims market is estimated to be worth $500 billion, of which nearly $300 billion consists of general unsecured claims. However, according to a recent article by Jonathan C Lipson, published in the *Boston University Law Review*, only a fraction of that market has traded historically, and has usually been concentrated in the largest bankruptcy cases.

But the growth has been dramatic and 2009 was one of the most active years in distressed claims trading history, due in large part to high US corporate default rates and numerous Chapter 11 filings. As the market has grown, so the influence of hedge funds and private equity funds has increased as well.

Distressed investors have various motivations that change the dynamic of restructuring negotiations

It is imperative that debtors understand what drives the professional distressed investor so they can negotiate and formulate a confirmable restructuring plan more effectively. These motivations may differ significantly from those of the more traditional financial interests.

Banks, bondholders and trade vendors

Prior to the explosion of the claims trading market, the debtor typically knew the identity and general motivations of its creditors, making it easier to negotiate a plan. Banks, bondholders (including insurance companies and other financial institutions) and trade vendors generally form long-term relationships with the company. The main concern of banks and bondholders is a return on principal and interest payments to compensate them for their investment and risk. In a restructuring, these institutions either want to be paid out in full or, if the bank debt or bond debt is reinstated, to receive an increased rate of interest and stronger covenant and default protections. Additionally, they are often prohibited from holding new equity in the reorganized debtor as a long-term investment, and may also conduct themselves to protect their reputation at the expense of short-term gains.

The principal concern of trade creditors is to preserve their relationships with the debtor and the rest of the industry. Thus, they may be willing to make certain financial concessions on their claims if it helps to promote competition, a successful restructuring and continuing trade relationships. They are also motivated to resolve, through the plan process, preference and other trade-specific liabilities, which less often pose risks for banks and bondholders.

Short-term profits on trading and recovery spreads

Distressed investor claim purchasers employ sophisticated financial analysis to buy at discounted trading prices (often significantly below par). They then hope to profit on the spread by either retrading the claims or receiving a bankruptcy recovery at a higher price.

Unlike the traditional bank, bondholder or trade claimant, this type of investor usually has no long-term interest in the debtor's reorganization, which may affect its voting and other behavior during the restructuring. Moreover, its appetite for recoveries often significantly differs from that of a par creditor. For instance, a distressed investor may accept a lower recovery as long as the process expedites the return on its investment, so it can make a quick gain and cash out.

The activity level of distressed investors often varies as well. Some will play a passive role in a case and hope to profit simply by buying low and waiting for a higher return. They often buy and aggregate smaller trade claims and hope for enhanced recoveries. Other distressed investors, however, may take an active role in the bankruptcy process, including engaging in substantial litigation and negotiations to increase recoveries. In any case, these investors may quickly trade in and out of the debtor's claims, as either their strategy or the market changes.

Takeover/ownership strategies

The distressed investor may also purchase larger claim stakes in the debtor to try to obtain ownership and/or control of the enterprise at an attractive price (often called the "loan to own" strategy).

In order to do this, it may try to determine the fulcrum security in the debtor's capital structure, meaning the debt or equity security that is likely to be converted to new, controlling equity in the reorganized company. This requires a thorough understanding of the capital structure and the likely treatment of the various tranches under the Bankruptcy Code's priority scheme. A distressed enterprise's capital structure may be comprised of: (i) secured bank debt (composed of multiple tiers such as first-lien debt, second-lien debt etc); (ii) unsecured bond debt (including senior and subordinated bond debt); (iii) general unsecured claims (including trade claims); and (iv) equity interests (preferred and common stock). The structure is often further complicated by guaranties and varying collateral packages.

Once the distressed investor has determined the fulcrum security, individually or as part of an *ad hoc* group, it will try to build a control position (two-thirds in value) or blocking position (one-third in value) in those claims. Often, it will buy in multiple tranches to hedge its takeover attempt. Unlike the build-up of equity interests, which must usually be disclosed under securities laws, there is generally no requirement to disclose the acquisitions of controlling and blocking debt positions.

A distressed investor pursuing this strategy may employ litigation and negotiation tactics to achieve its goal, and being paid cash on its claim may be the last thing that it wants.

Credit default protection and other motivations

While many distressed investors simply seek to profit on available spreads or to own the company, others may employ strategies that seem counter-intuitive or contrary to the restructuring goals of Chapter 11.

Synthetic credit default protections act as insurance where the seller takes on the risk of default while the holder/buyer retains ownership and control of the claim. By separating the risk from the underlying claim and assigning it to the seller, the holder's incentives change and it may be more apt to seek a default and deny covenant relief to trigger a "credit event", because the holder will be paid by the seller and can avoid the uncertainty and delay of working with a delinquent borrower. Such action may benefit the holder but be contrary to the best interests of the debtor and other creditors (including the seller of the credit default protection).

In addition, the distressed investor may be "net" short on the debtor, meaning that it profits if the debtor fails. It may acquire long debt or equity positions to influence the bankruptcy for the benefit of its "net" short strategy, even if that action harms the same long debt or equity position it has used to affect such a result.

Similarly, the distressed investor may buy claims in a debtor to further interests it has in a competitor or potential purchaser. These claims may be used to gain valuable information on the debtor's operations and assets, with the potential effect of interfering in the debtor's restructuring effort or forcing an attractive asset sale.

Alternatively, a blocking position (one-third in value) may be purchased to extract hostage value in the form of a direct buyout or a shift in plan distributions (also known as "greenmailing").

While it is difficult to know how often these strategies are used in practice, the debtor should be aware of these potential motivations during the bankruptcy process.

Different types of debts and interests

The different interests in a debtor have different implications for distressed investors, such as where they fall in the capital structure and the likelihood that the claim or interest will be the fulcrum security.

Bank debt. This is largely secured and has certain financial covenants, giving the holders the ability to exert greater leverage against the debtor. In addition, bank debt holders may seek additional leverage and influence by providing debtor in possession (DIP) financing during the case. Generally, they will also enjoy the advantage of having more information about the debtor. However, the enforceability of bank debt may be subject to attack if the bank has acted inappropriately to exert substantive control over the company to further its own interests prior to bankruptcy.

Bank debt syndications and participations allow the debt to be broken into pieces, traded and held by a larger number of entities — some of which would not otherwise qualify to own a beneficial interest. Thus, the debt has become fully accessible to distressed investors and the claims trading market.

In an economic downturn, bank debt holders are more often pushing for a low valuation in the bankruptcy proceedings and an equity return on the unsecured portion of their debt.

Bond debt. This is generally more liquid and has fewer risks because of the lack of previous substantive dealings between the debtor and bondholders. This debt is usually unsecured and is often attractive as the fulcrum security because it falls below the secured debt and is above or *pari passu* with general unsecured claims.

Trade debt. This generally has more counterparty risk and is often bought cheaply from creditors who prefer cash to riding out the bankruptcy process. Trade debt tends to be purchased by distressed investors hoping to profit from the spread, rather than to control the bankruptcy or seek a takeover of the debtor.

Old equity. This can be as attractive as the fulcrum security if the debtor is determined to be solvent. Distressed investors may be able to negotiate warrants or options if solvency is a genuine issue in a case. Equity can also be used to exert influence over management.

Negotiations complicated by continued trading and a changing creditor body

With bank debt syndications and participations, and the continuing explosion of claims trading, the debtor moves from negotiating with a single bank and set group of bond and trade creditors to a more fluid creditor body.

Moreover, as the claim holders change during the course of the case, the debtor may continually need to restart negotiations with the new entities and try to assess their motivations.

On the flipside, negotiations may become more streamlined if a distressed investor or group buys up large blocks of claims.

Distressed investors' conflicting positions in the capital structure

Distressed investors often purchase debt and equity interests in different levels of the capital structure to hedge their interests in the case. As a result, however, they may hold multiple, potentially adverse interests, making negotiations more difficult because the debtor may not know which interest the distressed investor is seeking to benefit.

Often, the distressed investor may hope to influence greater overall recoveries for all creditors and interest holders. For instance, if it is long in the bank debt, bond debt and equity, it may seek a valuation sufficient to keep them all in the money. But if the distressed investor is long in the bank debt and short on the bond debt and equity, it may seek a low valuation that leaves the last two out of the money, thus profiting on both its long and short positions.

How a debtor can obtain information about its active creditors

Although it outlines the procedures for claims trading and requires a transferee to file notice of transfer of a claim with the bankruptcy court, Bankruptcy Rule 3001(e) provides little, if any, teeth for required disclosure. In fact, 1991 revisions to Rule 3001(e) deleted any requirements that court filings reflect either the terms of a claims transfer or the consideration paid. Moreover, 3001(e) explicitly excludes publicly traded bond debt and has no practical application to bank debt, which is generally listed as a single claim held by the syndicate bank while the syndicated loans and participations continue to trade among distressed investors.

Bankruptcy Rule 2019(a), in contrast, offers an avenue for the debtor to seek certain disclosure from active creditors in its case. The rule provides that the verified statement of 'every entity or committee representing more than one creditor or equity security holder' must include 'the amounts of claims or interests owned by the entity, the members of the committee or the indenture trustee, the times when acquired, the amounts paid therefore, and any sales or other disposition thereof'.

Although *ad hoc* committees have not historically been required to disclose much in the way of detailed information about their members' investments, proposed amendments to Rule 2019 would broaden the requirement to apply to: (i) every entity, group, or committee that represents or consists of more than one creditor; and (ii), upon a motion of a party in interest or on the court's own motion, to any entity that seeks or opposes the granting of any relief. The proposed amendments would require all *ad hoc* committee members to disclose their holdings, dates of purchase, and, if directed by the court, the price paid for such holdings.

Running in parallel with the proposed amendments to Rule 2019 has been a recent decision by the Bankruptcy Court for the District of Delaware in *In re Washington Mutual Inc*, where it was held that because an *ad hoc* "group" of noteholders was in reality an *ad hoc* "committee", Rule 2019 required disclosure by each committee member. Furthermore, the court stated that such a group may owe "some obligation" to other members of the same class of creditors — even though the group was not purporting to represent those other creditors — and that this obligation may be fiduciary. Although the effect of *Washington Mutual* is unclear at this time, debtors may seek to rely on the decision, and the proposed amendments to extend the reach of Rule 2019, to force active claims traders to disclose not only their long positions but also their short and derivative positions.

Supporters of the proposed changes to Rule 2019 contend that such changes are necessary to provide a degree of transparency in bankruptcy proceedings, thereby giving debtors and judges a better understanding of the motives of creditors active in a case. However, opponents fear that the requirement to disclose confidential information on the holdings and dates of purchase will be inappropriately used as leverage by debtors, and will have a substantial impact on the willingness of hedge funds and other distressed investors to participate in a bankruptcy proceeding, thus tempering liquidity and hurting the reorganization efforts. Such opponents contend that a statement identifying the group participants and their aggregate holdings should be sufficient. Furthermore, although the proposed amendments to Rule 2019 do not require disclosure of a party's purchase price absent court order, information on the date of purchase may be equivalent to such disclosure, given the relative ease of determining the market price of bonds, syndicated loans or securities on any particular day.

For institutional investors, these disadvantages must be weighed against the benefits of acting as a member of an *ad hoc* committee, including the increased leverage that is gained in litigation and settlement negotiations, as well as a sharing of legal and financial advisory expenses. Debtors must also balance the benefits potentially available in seeking additional disclosures about active creditors and their holdings, against the cost to its restructuring

efforts and the potential loss from the process of a distressed investor's sophistication and liquidity.

Claims trading impacts a debtor's disclosure of material, non-public information

Banks traditionally maintain an open dialogue with a company about its current and future financial prospects, which includes the receipt of material, non-public information. In bankruptcy, it is usually necessary for the debtor to continue to share this information with the banks and also to provide it to certain other creditors so that plan negotiations are fully informed.

But the introduction of claims trading and active distressed investors to the bankruptcy process has made this more difficult. Because of the potential effect of insider trading laws, the general practice in bankruptcy cases is to provide material, non-public information only to parties willing to sign confidentiality agreements and to agree to restrictions on trading. Distressed investors, however, are typically hesitant about becoming restricted, or even hostile to the idea, because they desire to keep their positions liquid and to have the flexibility to trade in and out of the market.

In some instances, those investors that choose not to be constrained in this way end up negotiating in the dark, often resulting in lengthy, costly and unproductive negotiations and potentially avoidable litigation. Moreover, under certain circumstances, such negotiations may of themselves constitute the disclosure of material non-public information, which could lead to the imposition of the trading restrictions. In other cases, distressed investors have been permitted to receive material, non-public information and to continue trading, on the condition that they build "walls" within the firm to ensure the information is not shared with the side of the firm that continues to trade claims.

If the debtor is unable to share material non-public information with a key distressed investor, it may be forced to make public disclosures to allow the claims holder to understand the financial status of the business and negotiate accordingly. However, the company then runs the risk of disclosing competitive information and trade secrets.

In addition, questions arise over whether a distressed investor should be permitted to join an official committee of creditors, and whether it can participate effectively, if it will not agree to become restricted to receive material, non-public information. A distressed investor that holds claims and interests in various levels of the debtor's capital structure also raises conflict-of-interest concerns as to whether it will act to further the interests of unsecured creditors. For these reasons, a debtor should carefully consider whether it should object to a distressed investor's appointment to an official committee.

Lock-up agreements help preserve negotiated deals

The debtor may become concerned that upon striking a deal with one group of creditors, those creditors will sell out of their positions and the deal will disappear, leaving the debtor to begin talks again with a new group. The negotiated deal can be preserved by having the creditors enter into a lock-up or plan-support agreement, thus binding the distressed claims trader and any successor to the original deal. Such an agreement will either contain a provision that limits the ability of the claimants to continue trading, or require that they only sell their claims to purchasers who agree to be bound by the agreement.

The preservation of net operating losses and tax attributes

Trading in bankruptcy claims and interests can trigger "change in ownership" provisions that can have a substantially negative impact on the restructuring debtor's tax attributes.

Net operating losses (NOLs) can be a significant asset of a troubled company. NOLs are created when available deductions exceed income in a given tax year, which is often the case with a company entering bankruptcy. While NOLs can be carried back to offset taxable income during the previous two years, they can also be carried forward for 20 years to offset future taxable income, which can be particularly useful to a reorganized debtor exiting bankruptcy.

But generally, a debtor loses the ability to use its NOLs if a change of ownership occurs — as is common in a Chapter 11 restructuring as old equity interests are often extinguished and new equity is issued to creditors and/or old equity holders in exchange for their previous claims or interests against the debtor. Section 382(l)(5) of the Internal Revenue Code, however, provides a safe harbor for a change of ownership that occurs pursuant to a Chapter 11 plan of reorganization. This is provided that certain conditions are met, including that the historic shareholders and "qualified creditors" own at least 50 per cent of the value and voting power of the debtor after the ownership change. A qualified creditor is either: (i) an "old and cold" creditor, meaning a creditor that owned its claim for at least 18 months prior to commencement of the bankruptcy case; or (ii) a creditor that was always the beneficial owner of a claim that arose in the ordinary course of business (for example, trade debt arising from a business relationship with a supplier).

In addition, the tax regulations set out a *de minimus* rule that generally permits a presumption that the creditor is "old and cold" as long as it does not become a 5 per cent shareholder as a result of the restructuring.

The Second Circuit Court of Appeals held in *In re Prudential Lines* that NOLs are the property of the debtor's estate under Section 541 of the Bankruptcy Code and that the automatic stay provisions of Section 363(a)(3) of the Bankruptcy Code can be used to enjoin actions of others that would extinguish these positive tax attributes. Relying on this reasoning, bankruptcy courts regularly enter orders in connection with the debtor's first-day motions to prohibit or restrict claims and interests trading at various levels of the capital structure.

Some debtors, relying on the assumption that some unknown combination of old secured claims, unsecured claims and equity interests will be converted into new equity interests in the reorganized company, seek broad bars on claims trading as the only way to ensure protection of the NOLs. Bankruptcy courts may be wary of such requests if there is a suspicion that the debtor's intention is to: (i) lock in its current creditors for leverage; (ii) create a poison pill to entrench management; (iii) prevent influence by distressed investors; or (iv) unnecessarily chill trading in claims.

Despite these potentially nefarious objectives, however, most bankruptcy courts will enter claims trading orders to protect the NOLs, as long as they are tailored to protect the rights of parties to trade their claims and interests and to ensure liquidity in the restructuring process. For instance, appropriate procedures would grant the debtor some ability to monitor and object to trades that might result in a party acquiring claims that could result in ownership of 5 per cent or more of the reorganized debtor's stock. More recent trading orders have allowed liquidity in claims trading by allowing purchases of large positions in claims, with the requirement that some time prior to emergence, the debtor would evaluate whether such purchasers would need to "sell down" in order to qualify for more favorable tax rules.

Conclusion

The rise of claims trading in large restructuring and Chapter 11 cases is likely to continue. It provides substantial benefits for the restructuring process by increasing liquidity and flexibility and allowing the participation of well-funded, sophisticated financial players, which often ensures a better Chapter 11 adjudication and final result. Nevertheless, it is important for the debtor to understand the motivations of the distressed investor when negotiating and structuring its out-of-court restructuring or Chapter 11 plan of reorganization, to ensure the process leads to a deal or confirmation beneficial for all creditors and interest holders. Moreover, the debtor must be aware of the effects of claims trading on: (i) its disclosure of material, non-public information; (ii) the preservation of negotiated deals; and (iii) NOLs and other tax attributes.

Brown Rudnick Associates, Timothy J Durken and Patrick D Egan contributed to this article.

26

Evaluating strategic debt buybacks: How to pursue effective de-leveraging strategies

Dennis Dunne, Practice Leader in the Financial Restructuring Group and a member of the Global Executive Committee, Gregory Bray, Partner in the Global Financial Restructuring Group, and Robert Shenfeld, Senior Attorney in the Financial Restructuring Group.
Milbank, Tweed, Hadley & McCloy LLP

For a company facing financial challenges, the balance sheet restructuring glass is neither half full nor half empty; it is simply filled with opportunities. One of these is the strategic buyback or repayment of outstanding syndicated bank debt or debt securities at below par prices, through a process instituted by the issuer or an affiliate.

Debt buybacks are prevalent in times of economic turmoil. Discounts in the secondary market create enticing opportunities to de-leverage. Depending on the circumstances and an issuer's goals, the buyback program can be accomplished through a public tender offer or privately, in the form of negotiated transactions or open market purchases, otherwise known as "street sweeps".

The case for buybacks

Buybacks are appealing because they reduce leverage and lower interest expenses. When coupled with an exit consent, they can also amend restrictive and other covenants in underlying credit agreements or indentures. Ultimately, they can allow the issuer or private equity sponsor to amass a controlling position in a debt security that is now the fulcrum (the security that will not be paid in full because the enterprise value is sufficient to satisfy some but not all of the outstanding obligations of that security). Occasionally, the issuer can repurchase its equity in this way. Moreover, if the buyback program is initiated as part of an overall restructuring to rightsize the balance sheet through an out-of-court process, the issuer achieves a more realistic, and therefore sustainable, capital structure while instilling confidence in the market and in some cases preventing a Chapter 11 filing.

Debt buybacks are often preferable to an equity purchase for an issuer. If the business does not improve and Chapter 11 becomes necessary, equity is a lower priority for payment in bankruptcy. Moreover, if an issuer acquires its own equity, it is increasing leverage; with a debt buyback, it achieves the much-desired leverage reduction.

For the holder of the debt, buybacks tend to be more attractive than exchanges for equity, with the original purchasers of the debt generally being resistant to moving down the capital structure. In addition, equity exchanges often result in massive dilution, which may cause disquiet among shareholders and trigger further selling — which, in turn, can exacerbate an issuer's financial troubles. Moreover, most debt holders are wary of owning stock in a company facing economic or industry-wide challenges.

Ironically, in order to take advantage of steep discounts in debt, an issuer needs cash. Many investors have their own economic pressures, and the ability to monetize a distressed position may be a motivating factor upon which an issuer can capitalize. Cash is an exit and not a recommitment to the credit. It can be redeployed in other investments. It is a currency used to exploit deal fatigue among long-term creditors.

However, issuers facing economic hardship do not, as a general matter, have pools of spare cash to effect a buyback or debt repayment program. In those circumstances, they could consider debt exchanges. These can seem uncertain, especially in the current economic environment when debt holders are unlikely, without a strong enough financial incentive, to accept a transaction that will adversely affect their existing rights. But a compelling reason for an issuer to pursue the debt exchange, and for the holder to consent, is that the exchange will forestall a bankruptcy filing. The holders should prefer that an issuer remains in control of a restructuring process that can unfold out of court without the associated cost, uncertainty and delay.

If, however, a debt exchange is not possible, an issuer may seek an increased equity contribution from a private equity sponsor. Alternatively, if the affiliate is not willing to compound its equity investment but is intent on helping the issuer ride through the current economic downturn, it could pursue the de-leveraging program itself — especially if the secondary markets price the debt very low.

Below, we address the public and private options for de-leveraging, and outline the strategic decisions an issuer (or affiliate) might consider as it crafts and embarks on a debt buyback or repayment program.

Public tender offers

Here a company makes an offer to its debt holders to repurchase a predetermined amount of debt at a specific price for a set period. Tender offers may be the preferred method of deleveraging when an issuer wants to purchase a substantial percentage of its debt securities and to control the conditions precedent to the buyback. In addition, where there are covenants that restrict a repurchase of the debt, a tender offer can be coupled with a consent solicitation, which, if approved by the requisite number of debt holders, amends those covenants.

A tender offer has several benefits for an issuer:
• It provides broad access to the market and debt holders.
• It ensures equal treatment among the debt holders.
• It is particularly efficient if the debt is widely held.
• It may provide an issuer with advantages such as speed and efficiency over the course of a series of privately negotiated transactions, which in turn means that management spends less time being distracted from running the business.
• It allows structuring on price and conditions

(including, for example, a related consent solicitation to amend the terms of the securities, or a condition that the amount of debt tendered must satisfy the requirements for a vote in support of a reorganization plan in a Chapter 11 proceeding).
• It may alleviate shareholder pressure on the board of a company, with excess cash to de-leverage the capital structure.

A tender offer also carries burdens:
• It is subject to SEC rules, which add both disclosure requirements and costs.
• When there are relatively few debt holders, it may take longer to complete than a series of privately negotiated or open market purchases, because a tender offer must usually remain open for at least 20 business days.
• In some tender offers, there is a risk that the issuer might misjudge the market and overspend for the debt.
• The issuer may have reasons not to disseminate knowledge of the repurchase program.
• A rating agency may downgrade the issuer's credit status — regardless of its financial health — at the mere announcement or anticipation of a distressed buyback. (Ironically, once the buyback is completed, the untendered portion of a loan could be upgraded, due to the company's de-leveraged capital structure.)
• There is a risk that the issuer's conditions precedent for the tender offer might not be satisfied, requiring it to abandon a publicly disclosed program.
• There is a liability risk arising from claims of inadequate or inaccurate disclosure in the offering documents.
• It leads to higher transaction costs.

Public exchange offers

When there is insufficient cash to buy debt or to engage in private or open market purchases, an issuer in distress can pursue a debt exchange. Here an issuer trades debt for debt and the creditors absorb the impact of below-par prices, longer maturities, lower interest rates, or junior ranking in the capital structure.

An exchange offer, like a tender offer, can also be useful when the terms of the underlying agreement need to be amended to repurchase/exchange debt, and those changes would be so significant that the securities constitute a new issue. Examples of such changes are those in interest rates, maturity, subordination provisions, and terms related to collateral or relief from financial covenants.

The benefits and burdens of an exchange offer are similar to those of a tender offer. The principal beneficial difference is that an exchange allows the issuer to de-lever without using cash.

Privately negotiated or open market purchases of syndicated bank debt or bonds

These purchases are effective ways of de-leveraging the capital structure when an issuer is looking to buy a small percentage of securities, or when ownership of the securities is concentrated among very few holders. In this regard, the issuer can avoid the risks of a public transaction and still take advantage of distressed debt pricing.

The potential benefits of private transactions and open market purchases are as follows:
• They can provide greater flexibility in negotiating price and timing with the sellers.
• Under certain circumstances, these transactions may take place below the radar of secondary debt traders.
• They may be completed quickly, enabling the issuer to react to secondary market shifts without making a commitment to purchasing large quantities of debt or to long-term buyback programs.

However, there are also potential limitations and problems:
• They must remain small, one-off transactions, or they might fall foul of the SEC's prohibition on "creeping tender" offers.
• They can be distracting and time consuming for an issuer's management, as well as for restructuring advisors who are engaged in a broader balance sheet and/or operational restructuring.
• They may be difficult to achieve if the issuer is not aware of willing sellers.
• They may expose the issuer to allegations of unequal treatment of investors.
• There could be disclosure issues.
• A bond repurchase program may not give the issuer or the purchasing affiliate an advantage with a consent solicitation. (Since the provisions of the agreement or indenture governing the debt are likely to provide that bonds held by the issuer or affiliates are treated as not outstanding for purposes of determining whether requisite consents have been obtained, a buyback program may not affect the outcome of a consent solicitation. Ironically, by reducing the number of bonds deemed outstanding for purposes of a consent, a bond repurchase program could have the undesired effect of providing a few holders with extra leverage in a consent solicitation.)

Moreover, investors will in all likelihood base their decisions on an issuer's financial condition. They may want to form an ad hoc group and hire their own financial advisors and counsel at an issuer's expense. Providing the ad hoc group with financial information may also create the problem of restricting the holders from trading. As a result, an issuer will have to navigate the quandary of how much information it can divulge and the holders will accept.

Avoid the "creeping tender" offer

This offer refers to a privately negotiated or open market purchase of securities that should have been structured as a conventional tender offer, subject to SEC rules. If an issuer initiates a repurchase program that is later held to have been a non-compliant tender offer, it could face a variety of sanctions, including money damages, injunctive relief and enforcement actions by the SEC. Resulting entanglements with the commission could hit the value of the program and might also color public perceptions of the issuer (particularly relevant if other tranches of debt remain in the market). Since one of the critical advantages of a private transaction over a public tender or exchange offer is the ability to avoid SEC rules, it is imperative that any buyback program does not "look or walk" like a public offer.

While there is no bright-line test for whether, or under what conditions, privately negotiated or open market purchases of securities constitute a tender offer, courts tend to rely on certain signs. They look to whether: (1) the offers to purchase or the solicitation of offers to sell were disseminated in a widespread manner; (2) the purchase price offered represented a premium over the market; (3) there was a meaningful opportunity for negotiation of price and terms; (4) a substantial percentage of the bonds was solicited; (5) the offer was contingent on a minimum or maximum amount of bonds being tendered or purchased; (6) the offer was for limited duration; (7) the issuer may have pressured the holders; and (8) there were public announcements of the acquisition program, followed by a rapid accumulation of large amounts of the company's bonds.

Repurchase programs that are truly private transactions should not be carried out in ways that mimic the public option. For example, they should take place over a meaningful period. There should be no deadline for purchases. The pricing and terms should not be uniform and non-negotiable. Participation, where possible, should be limited to sophisticated institutional investors.

Buyback programs and the underlying agreements

The caveat to a debt buyback program is the need to understand the type of debt involved, and the terms and conditions of the underlying agreements governing that debt. These facts will control how (and if) an issuer or affiliate may repurchase debt. For example, syndicated loans are generally considered not to be securities. They are, therefore, not subject to the tender offer rules and 10b-5 disclosure obligations associated with securities. (Even though syndicated loans are typically not securities, bank regulations and common law fraud restrictions do apply.) Furthermore, contractual restrictions in the loan documents often impact a borrower's ability to repurchase its debt and may dictate the terms and conditions for buying discounted debt.

While agreements vary significantly, common issues include assignment restrictions, required consents, pro rata sharing or turnover provisions, and other contractual restrictions that control and limit the economic downside to the lenders or holders caused by a repayment prior to maturity.

By way of illustration, in a capital structure involving first and second lien loans, the first lien credit agreement is likely to place restrictions on: (1) the borrower's ability to prepay or repurchase its second lien loans; (2) the excess cash-flow sweep and obligations to prepay loans; and (3) the ability of an issuer or affiliate to participate in votes, including with respect to amendments or waivers of the credit agreement (presuming the issuer or affiliate is allowed to own loans in the first instance).

When formulating a bond repurchase program, an issuer must pay particular attention to the indenture and to the need for the indenture trustee to exercise its fiduciary duties on behalf of the bondholders. Among other duties, a distressed-debt trustee may be bound to seek par value. All covenants must be carefully examined before the program is commenced.

Aside from the contractual impediments, bear in mind that holders of debt (both originating banks and secondary market traders) normally have a set expectation on the return, especially when the loans are secured, and this is usually at or

near par. This mindset may affect the success of any buyback program. Distressed bank debt trades with the expectation that the buyer will achieve — either through a restructuring, bankruptcy or improvement in the issuer's performance — a recovery that exceeds the trader's discounted purchase price. It is not unusual for the trader to anticipate repayment at a considerable profit even if debt was acquired at a discounted price.

A discounted basis such as this cannot guarantee that a consensual buyback will be easier to achieve. Distressed bank debt traders are sophisticated institutions that do not fear a Chapter 11 filing by an issuer; some even relish bankruptcy as an opportunity to improve recovery. And since the fees and expenses of the lenders (for lawyers and financial advisors) are typically borne by the company, the economic imperative to avoid bankruptcy is not always present for bank debt traders. On occasion they seek to halt a program when they perceive the buybacks (and the resulting boost to reported earnings) as threatening other aspects of the capital structure — through breaches of covenants, say, or the attainment of targets that might force rifts among various classes of creditors in the capital structure.

Even in the absence of having to appease distressed bank debt traders, originating banks, funds or institutions also have expectations for par recovery. These expectations are often memorialized in the underlying credit agreements, which, without amendment, do not generally permit issuers to buy back debt at less than par.

Recently, we have noticed increased resistance to buybacks from loan participants. In particular, disputes over agents are emerging. Specifically, what actions can they take on their own authority and what actions require lender consent? Agents become frustrated and, as a result, intransigent. Attention should be paid to their contracted rights and duties.

SEC filing and disclosure obligations of public offers

If a buyback is carried out in a public forum, the issuer will be subject to all SEC filing obligations, including a report on Form 8-K and the general anti-fraud provisions of Rule 10b-5 of the Securities Exchange Act. Most importantly, it will have to consider with counsel whether it is in possession of material non-public information that needs to be disclosed to holders, or if the repurchases will have a material adverse effect on the business.

Disclosures can be made in a variety of ways,

including a press release or a Form 8-K report. Prior to making any purchases of its own debt securities, the issuer (or the purchasing affiliate) must analyze whether it is in possession of material non-public information that would prevent it from going to the market to repurchase bonds at below par prices.

SEC-reporting companies must also be careful not to have communications with holders that trigger Regulation FD. This prohibits disclosure of material non-public information to certain types of people unless a confidentiality agreement is in effect. In some circumstances, the mere fact that a repurchasing of bonds or loans is under way may itself be a material fact that triggers obligations under Regulation FD. Similarly, the possibility that the success or failure of the buyback program will impact the issue may constitute material non-public information.

Of course, not all debt repurchases will result in disclosure of material non-public information. Depending on the situation, and to be ultra safe, it may be prudent simply to disclose the initiation of the buyback program publicly. This may have positive and negative consequences, so the well-conceived strategy includes a careful analysis of the potential impact of disclosure on the market. The threshold inquiry is whether the fact that an issuer is formulating, or embarking on, a repurchase program is in itself material, non-public information. That said, each case is different. If it is determined that the program itself is material, non-public information, additional disclosure may be required to avoid falling foul of the reporting regulations.

If the effect of the repurchase program is not material either to an issuer's financial condition or to the trading market for its bonds, it may be that no prior disclosure of the commencement, pendency or conclusion of the program is required. If the trading price of the debt is sufficiently and consistently below par, an issuer may want to disclose the implementation of a general program of debt repurchase in its regular reporting. In a distressed economic environment, it will not come as a surprise to the market.

Possible tax consequences

An issuer's repurchase of its own debt at a discount could have tax implications in terms of cancellation of debt income (CODI) and a reduction in net operating losses. A repurchase can also have tax consequences for the exchanging holders.

Generally, the purchase by an issuer (or by a related party) of its outstanding debt securities at a discount gives rise to CODI to the issuer, which may also be the case in an exchange of debt for equity and, in certain instances, for new debt for the equity.

The amount of CODI is generally the difference between the principal amount of the debt repurchased (or its accreted value, if applicable) and the repurchase price. If debt is exchanged for equity or new debt, the price will generally be the fair market value of the equity or new debt. General tax principles require that CODI be included as taxable income of the issuer.

The Internal Revenue Code provides exceptions to this general rule in the case of CODI that occurs when the issuer is in bankruptcy or insolvent (but only up to the amount of the insolvency). Under these exceptions, an issuer that recognizes CODI does not pay tax on it but is instead required to reduce its tax attributes, including net operating losses, capital losses, credits and tax basis in assets.

Recent legislation generally allows an issuer recognizing CODI in connection with a reacquisition of debt in 2009 or 2010 to defer including it in income until 2014, at which time the issuer would include the CODI in taxable income ratably over a five-year period. This deferral rule could apply to all issuers, including those in bankruptcy or insolvency. But taxpayers must choose to apply the bankruptcy/insolvency exceptions to recognition of CODI or the deferral rules. They cannot apply both.

If the reacquisition is an exchange offer, there are tax considerations for the holders. For example, unless the exchange qualifies as a "reorganization" within the meaning of the tax law, holders of debt that receive new debt and/or equity for their debt will generally recognize a taxable gain or loss on the exchange.

The gain or loss will generally be equal to the difference between the value of the consideration received by the holder (other than interest and some consent payments) and the holder's adjusted tax basis in the debt surrendered. Consent payments may also be subject to taxation, potentially as ordinary income.

The taxation of consent payments will usually depend on the circumstances. Most likely, they will be treated either as additional consideration in exchange for the tendered debt — which means the payments will be taken into account in determining the gain or loss on the exchange — or as separate consideration in the nature of a fee for consenting to the proposed amendments.

Conclusion

The opportunity to buy back debt at large discounts and to adjust the capital structure to achieve greater balance requires a concerted effort by the board, management and restructuring counsel. An issuer has to present persuasive economic reasons for bondholders or lenders to sell back the debt at distressed prices. A properly orchestrated program that navigates the underlying agreements and other controlling documents — as well as SEC rules and regulations, tax laws and the Bankruptcy Code — can help an issuer or an affiliate to take advantage of distressed trading prices and propose a transaction that appeals to the holders and lenders. For an issuer facing economic challenges, a repurchase program can be an effective tool for exerting control over the restructuring process and/or profiting from below par debt pricing.

Being proactive is critical to the success of the program, as is timing the market. Wait too long, and if the debt trades up, the chances of a successful buyback program are reduced. Conversely, if the market further downgrades the debt or bankruptcy appears more imminent, such a development can be fatal. Allowing debt to trade at a steep discount, for a prolonged period, sends a negative message to the market.

While the initiation of a buyback program can alter such perceptions and send out a positive signal while an issuer restructures, if the message becomes too ingrained in investors' minds then it may be impossible to alter the march to bankruptcy.

Naturally, the challenges and hurdles are different for each issuer, but all the options outlined above form an overview that can be explored with your counsel as you embark on a program of debt repurchase and de-leveraging.

27

Leveraging exchange offers to maximize value in distressed situations

Timothy R Coleman,
Senior Managing Director and
Head of the Restructuring &
Reorganization Group
and member of the
Executive Committee,
Blackstone Group LP

'If I owe you a pound, I have a problem; but if I owe you a million, the problem is yours'
(John Maynard Keynes)

Whereas other restructuring cycles have been defined by industry downturns or specific companies with poor operating performance, the distinguishing feature of the most recent cycle has been one of good companies laid low by significant financial leverage. The balance sheet woes of many of these companies were exacerbated in late 2008 and early 2009 by the seizure of the credit markets, which eliminated refinancing opportunities and forced numerous businesses to seek Chapter 11 protection or pursue out-of-court restructurings. While bankruptcy can be a judicious option for companies looking for a fresh start and clean capital structure, it can be exceedingly expensive for equity holders, can reduce customer confidence in a business, and can often create administrative expenses that reduce value for all stakeholders.

Recently, a popular alternative for companies facing financial distress has been a type of out-of-court restructuring known as an exchange offer — a transaction by which a company swaps its outstanding debt for cash, equity or new debt. In the simplest example, a business may offer its debtholders the option to exchange a $100 debt claim for $30 of cash. If all the debtholders accept, the company will have reduced leverage by $100 while only giving away $30, thus creating $70 of value for the remaining stakeholders.

Why would debtholders accept less than 100 cents on the dollar for their claim? How does a company decide what form of currency — cash, equity or new debt – to put up in an exchange? Would debtholders want to hold out on accepting an offer if they thought the other creditors would be paid in full?

Exchange offer overview

If a company is over-levered with too much debt relative to cash flow, it has to divert a large portion of its operating income to servicing interest. In the most extreme cases, companies use all of the cash generated from operations, as well as in their bank accounts, to pay interest and principal. As a result, such companies are unable to reinvest in their businesses and/or meet future obligations as they come due. To reduce indebtedness, they can make an exchange offer — usually at a discount to the par amount of the claim.

From the company's perspective, a $1 debt claim is being traded in for less than 100 cents of another currency. From the point of view of debtholders, they are receiving a new currency that is potentially worth more than the ultimate recovery on their existing claim. Whether a given offer is acceptable depends on the debtholder's perception of the value of the existing debt, as compared to the value and form of the consideration offered in the exchange.

Cash is often the most attractive currency for debtholders in that they can monetize their claims immediately, as well as reduce their exposure to distressed credits — and that allows companies to give away the minimum value possible. Cash can be difficult to offer, however, given the precarious liquidity position of many distressed businesses.

Equity can be a more challenging currency for debtholders to accept in an exchange because, by exchanging their claim, they are in effect subordinating themselves to other debtholders who do not participate in the offer — as debt is senior to equity in a capital structure. Further, it can be difficult for debtholders to determine if equity in a distressed company is truly worth more than the value of the current debt claim — and, as a result, they often require a significant portion of the business's equity to provide a margin of safety in their equity valuation. From the company's perspective, this kind of offer conserves cash and allows for significant de-leveraging, but can be dilutive to existing shareholders.

The final form of consideration is new debt. If new debt is offered at a discount (for example, 70 cents of new debt for 100 cents of existing debt), it must usually be senior to the existing debt — with respect to security, structure or maturity — and have a higher coupon to be acceptable. A company may offer, for example, to exchange $100 of existing 10 per cent unsecured debt due in 2020 for $70 of 12 per cent secured debt due in 2019. By accepting, the debtholder will be obtaining a higher coupon (albeit less overall interest), additional security, and seniority over fellow debtholders who do not agree to the offer. The concern about this currency from the company's perspective is that it has less of an impact on reducing leverage and interest expense than exchanging for cash or equity. Trading $100 of debt for $70 of debt still leaves you with $70 of debt.

From the debtholder's point of view, it can be hard to judge if $70 of new debt is actually worth more than $100 of existing debt. If that existing debt trades at 50 per cent of par and the new debt is expected to trade at 100 per cent of par, the offer is clearly superior. But should the existing debt trade at 50 per cent of par and the new debt be expected to trade at 70 per cent of par, the situation is not so clear-cut. In reality, price does not equal value and should not be viewed as such.

Structuring an exchange offer

In structuring an exchange offer, advisors and company executives should keep three key questions in mind:

• Will the offer, if successfully executed, solve the company's financial issues? That is, will the company have adequate flexibility to manage its business and balance sheet going forward?

Debt-for-debt exchange

	Face amount	Trading price	Market value
Scenario 1			
Existing 10% unsecured debt	$100	50%	$50
New 12% secured debt	$70	100%	$70
Scenario 2			
Existing 10% unsecured debt	$100	50%	$50
New 12% secured debt	$70	70%	$49

• Does the company understand the motivations and needs of its debtholders, and does the exchange offer satisfy them?
• Does the offer minimize the possibility of significant holdouts?

Will the offer fix the company's financial issues?

The de-leveraging effect of an offer can improve a company's financial wherewithal by reducing annual interest expense, enhancing its ability to issue equity capital and potentially avoiding a covenant default or bankruptcy. However, it is essential that an exchange strikes the right balance. If too much cash is offered for outstanding debt, a company may simply run into another set of liquidity problems — defeating the point of the de-leveraging. If a company exchanges new debt for old debt, it may have to accept new restrictive covenants that hamper its ability to operate freely; target too little debt and leverage may not be reduced sufficiently to cure the financial distress.

A company and its advisors must therefore work hard on forecasting its financial statements under a wide range of operating scenarios and exchange-offer outcomes. It must be conservative and realistic in its projections and ensure that the exchange will not drain the company of the resources it needs to survive outside bankruptcy. The offer should be structured to show that, if successful, it will reduce leverage, create value for its stakeholders and enhance the company's ability to operate as a going concern. Just as there is no point patching the roof of a house with porous wood, it is not worth launching an exchange offer that will not improve the company's financial prospects.

Once management is satisfied that an exchange offer has the potential to fix the company's financial issues, it should turn its attention to making sure the offer is acceptable to its creditors.

Does the offer satisfy the needs of the debtholders?

By their nature, debtholders of distressed companies are a difficult lot to please. As the old adage goes: 'Running into debt isn't so bad. It's running into creditors that hurts.' This group, typically comprised of banks, hedge fund investors and large financial institutions, can have widely divergent interests yet share the belief that they should be paid in full before any junior stakeholders receive value. It is not uncommon for debtholders to reject proposals, even though it may be in their best economic interests to accept, because the proposals are deemed to be "unfair" for any number of reasons – the most common being that equity holders will receive some form of value while the senior debtholders are taking a haircut on their claims. This can have significant consequences for the outcome of an exchange offer, as you can see from the following example.

You are a debtholder with a $100 claim on Company X that is secured by all of the business' assets. Company X has run into difficulties and needs to undergo a restructuring because its business is now deemed to be worth only $80.

The management offers you the following deal: you can receive $60 cash to walk away from your claim, with the remaining $20 left for equity holders, or you can reject the offer and let the company file for bankruptcy. Do that and administrative costs and further business deterioration will decrease the total value of the company to $50. You will, however, receive all $50 of value because of the seniority of your claim. Do you take the $60, knowing that you are letting $20 go to equity holders, or do you wave the company down the road to bankruptcy and own 100 per cent of a $50 pie?

The decision is obvious in this example, but the complexities of valuing distressed securities and the uncertainty around the cost and outcome of bankruptcy proceedings make such decisions more difficult in the real world. There is no shortage of examples of debtholders refusing offers that appear to be in their best interest because they provide too much value to junior claimants. It is the role of the company's advisors and management to make sure the offer is structured in a way to be palatable to debtholders — even if the taste is a bit bitter.

A relatively new and more concerning reason for the rejection of seemingly attractive offers is the growing prominence of credit default swaps (CDS). A holder of CDS protection is paid upon a predefined triggering event, the most common being a default on a payment obligation. Consequently, debtholders with large CDS positions can have a greater economic interest in seeing an exchange offer fail and a company default on its debt. It is not possible to tell whether debtholders own CDS protection unless they provide the information themselves, and companies often have to launch offers without as much knowledge as they would like. Not surprisingly, the existence of large amounts of CDS on some corporate names has had a harmful impact on a number of exchange offers.

It is with these considerations in mind that management should try to evaluate the motivations of debtholders. Do they want to reduce their exposure to the company? Are they solely willing to hold debt or are they willing and able to own equity? Would they rather "kick the can down the road" through a debt-for-debt exchange that extends maturities, or do they want the company to confront its issues today and provide immediate value to its creditors? Are they "loan-to-own" lenders who would like to own a controlling position in the business or do they own CDS protection and have conflicting desires?

Management teams and advisors must try to answer these questions through market knowledge as they cannot easily communicate directly with public debtholders prior to the launch of an offer. While it will certainly not be possible to please everyone, the exchange does have to be tailored to be as palatable as possible to the majority of holders.

Yet even attractive offers can be unsuccessful if the debtholders are not encouraged, managed, even compelled into participating. To this end, companies can employ a number of techniques to minimize holdouts in an exchange.

Does the offer minimize the possibility of significant holdouts?

Unlike a bankruptcy, an exchange offer is only binding on those creditors who agree to participate. For some, the best outcome may be to hold on to their original debt while other creditors exchange and restore the company to good health. The incentive to reject the offer while hoping most of the other debtholders accept leads to what is known as the "holdout problem".

Take the example of Company Y, which has

$100 of cash, $200 of bonds and offers to tender for its bonds at 30 per cent of face value. If 80 per cent of the bondholders accept, the company will have paid $48 of cash to take out $160 face amount of the debt. It will be left with $52 of cash and $40 of bonds, and thus will have sufficient cash to pay the remaining bonds at par upon maturity. Realizing this, some of the more astute bondholders may well be likely to hold out from accepting the offer if they believe most of the other bondholders will participate. If too many of them were to draw the same conclusion, the offer would likely fail.

Much of the art of structuring exchange offers is about mitigating holdouts, through techniques ranging from setting minimum acceptance thresholds to implementing highly coercive measures. One approach is to give valuable protections to the bondholders who vote in favor of the exchange — for example, by issuing senior debt (potentially with collateral) in exchange for junior debt. In an offer where this strategy is employed, any bondholders who do not exchange would in effect be placed behind those who do.

Another technique used for mitigating holdouts is to strip away protections from non-consenting debtholders through the use of so-called "exit consents". Companies can ask those who plan on participating in the exchange to vote to eliminate covenants for their tranche just prior to their acceptance of the offer. Because most indentures only require a 50 per cent threshold for stripping covenants unrelated to payment terms, these debtholders can create a cost to "free riding" on their participation by leaving holdouts with reduced protections.

A more coercive tool for inducing bondholders to exchange is to couple the offering memorandum with a disclosure statement and a solicitation of votes for a prepackaged bankruptcy. Chapter 11 of the Bankruptcy Code permits a troubled company to solicit acceptances for a reorganization plan that can be implemented by class vote over the objection of holdouts. If the requisite votes are obtained, the company can file for and emerge from bankruptcy very quickly — sometimes in as little as 45 days. By threatening to file for bankruptcy if the exchange offer fails to meet the desired participation threshold, the economic incentives may shift because bondholders may be convinced they will be forced to accept the proposed economic terms in any event (through a bankruptcy).

A more subtly coercive technique is to offer different tranches of debt a pool of currency to fight over. The following example illustrates the point:

Company Z has $35 of cash and $100 of debt that is split into two tranches: $50 of secured bank debt and $50 of unsecured bonds. The company sets aside a fixed pool of currency for the offer — $20 of cash and $20 of new secured debt — and tells the two groups that they will each look to this same pool for currency in the exchange. The bank debt is offered $0.30 in cash and $0.30 in new debt for every $1.00 face amount, and the bonds are offered $0.20 in cash and $0.20 of new debt for every $1.00 face amount.

Further, the bank debtholders are given priority, meaning they will all be allowed to exchange before the first dollar of bond is allowed to participate. Thus, if 100 per cent of the bank debt participates in the exchange, those holders will receive $15 cash and $15 of new debt, with the remaining $5 of cash and $5 of new debt going to participating bondholders. If only 50 per cent of bank debtholders participate, $7.50 cash and $7.50 of new debt will go to them, while the remaining $12.50 cash and $12.50 of new debt will be available to participating bondholders.

Because senior debtholders, like the bank debt above, do not like to see valuable resources being paid to junior creditors, they are more likely to participate in the exchange when the alternative is cash and debt being provided to those junior stakeholders.

An important qualification with this approach is that the pool of currency must be large enough so that non-participants are unsure whether the company will have sufficient resources after the exchange to pay holdouts. In the example above, bank debtholders will compare the $20 of cash offered in the exchange to the $35 cash balance of Company Z and make a judgment call on whether the company would be able to pay at par if they held out.

Legal complexities

At this stage, it is important to note the legal restrictions that can prevent companies from offering certain currencies and implementing certain holdout structures. Credit agreements and indentures specify all the terms of specific tranches of debt, as well as the restrictions that companies have to abide by as a result of issuing those tranches. These documents often prohibit such actions as providing liens to junior debtholders, paying junior debtholders cash, issuing senior debt, paying debtholders on a non pro-rata basis and retiring debt at a discount. Executing a successful offer hinges on a company's ability to operate within this framework and to comply with securities laws and other legal requirements, which should be evaluated in detail prior to launching the exchange by a qualified law firm acting on the company's behalf.

Case Study: Ford Motor Company's exchange offer — March 2009

Background and capital structure
At the end of 2008, Ford Motor Company had approximately $26 billion of debt and $16 billion of automotive cash (excluding cash from its wholly owned finance subsidiary, Ford Motor Credit Company). According to the Barclays Capital Equity Research Report — published February 2, 2010 — Ford's cash position had been depleted by nearly $18 billion in 2008 due to a tough operating environment, retiree trust funding requirements and unfavorable working capital trends, and the company had justifiable concerns about its long-term ability to service debt. In addition to its balance sheet cash, Ford had a $10 billion undrawn secured revolver that its management had presciently obtained in a 2006 financing. (Ford drew its full revolver in Q1, 2009.)

The $26 billion of debt consisted of a $6.9 billion secured-term loan due in 2013, $0.5 billion of unsecured bonds due in 2010, $8.4 billion of unsecured bonds (comprised of more than 15 tranches due between 2018 and 2097), $4.9 billion of convertible notes and approximately $5 billion of other debt and preferred obligations. The term loan had liens on nearly all of the company's assets and thus had the right to receive the first $6.9 billion of proceeds from the monetization of those assets in a bankruptcy (or $6.9 billion of the first $16.9 billion if the revolver was drawn).

With a tumultuous year behind it and with the domestic automotive industry facing a bleak economic outlook, Ford's debt was trading at a significant discount to face value. On March 3, 2009 (the day before the exchange offer was launched), the company's term loan traded at around 31 per cent of par, bonds due in 2010 traded near 35 per cent of par, and all other bonds and converts traded around 20 per cent of par. These prices reflected not only an expectation of bankruptcy in the near future, but of a very low recovery for both secured and unsecured debtholders if a bankruptcy were to occur.

As Ford and its advisors examined the company's capital structure, it became clear that each tranche of debt had different holders, interests and concerns. It was determined that the term-loan class would want as little cash as possible to be paid

Ford capital structure: 12/31/2008			
	Face amount	3/4/2009 price	Market value
Secured debt			
Term loan	$6.9bn	31%	$2.1bn
Unsecured debt			
Bonds due 2010	$0.5bn	35%	$0.2bn
Bonds due 2018-97	$8.4bn	20%	$1.7bn
Convertible notes	$4.9bn	20%	$1.0bn
Other debt/ preferred	$5.0bn	20%	$1.0bn

to other debtholders, as it was senior in the event of a bankruptcy. The bonds due in 2010 would want the company to remain outside bankruptcy through at least June 2010, when the bonds matured and would potentially be paid in full. All other debtholders would want the company to maintain interest payments, in the hope it would turn things around and service debt through maturity. Many of Ford's debtholders, meanwhile, had large exposures to GM and Chrysler, which were going through even harder restructurings and were perceived to be even closer to bankruptcy.

It was against this backdrop that Ford had to make a decision about what to offer debtholders in exchange for their claims. Should it make an offer to holders of the term loan, the bonds, the converts, or all three? Should it put up cash, equity or new debt? What combination of currencies would have the greatest impact in reducing leverage and interest expense? Could it come up with a deal that would maintain sufficient liquidity, avoid breaching existing covenants and still be attractive to debtholders?

Determining holders' needs
To maximize potential debt reduction, Ford decided to propose exchange offers to all three of its main tranches. The term loan was owned primarily by large banks and hedge funds, which marked their positions to market. As the loan had recently traded as low as 30 per cent of face, the company felt that the holders might be willing to exchange their claim for cash offered at a premium to the market value of the loan, thus allowing the banks to take potentially large mark-to-market gains if they accepted. Further, the banks had significant exposure to other domestic auto manufacturers and were likely to have been given internal guidance to reduce their auto exposure. By offering cash instead of debt or equity,

therefore, Ford could enhance the possibility of these lenders accepting.

The $9 billion of bonds were owned by a mix of mutual funds, retail investors and hedge funds. Many of these funds were fixed-income funds and would likely be unable to accept equity. While the holders would have been amenable to owning secured debt in theory, the reality was that the existing term loan was trading at just 31 per cent of par, so every $100 of new secured debt provided to the bonds would be viewed as worth only $31. The practical implication of this was that Ford would have to issue too much new debt in a debt-for-debt exchange to make the offer worthwhile. By offering its bondholders cash at a premium to the market value of their debt claim (albeit at a steep discount to the face value of the claim), Ford could allow them to reduce their exposure to the auto industry and provide an attractive premium to the market's implied recovery value of the bonds.

The $4.9 billion of converts were owned by a concentrated group of hedge funds and proprietary trading desks that were identified as having a specialty in convertible arbitrage — a strategy by which an investor buys convertible notes and simultaneously shorts a company's stock in order to "lock in" the coupon on the note while eliminating equity risk. By offering equity and a small amount of cash, Ford could allow the convertible arbitrageurs to close out their short positions for free and pocket some cash to sweeten the deal. Given the significant redemptions that most hedge funds were facing at the time, letting them close out short positions for free while receiving some cash seemed an attractive proposition.

Minimizing holdouts

Although Ford and its advisors had a deep understanding of the holders and their needs, the success of its offer also partly hinged on its ability to minimize holdouts.

To this end the company employed two strategies to create tension between and within various tranches of debt. First, it set aside two pools of cash — one for the term loan and one for the bonds — and told each of the tranches that either of the pools could be upsized by the company if there was sufficient demand from holders. Thus, if the bank debt offer was undersubscribed and the bond offer oversubscribed, Ford could increase the cash offered to bondholders, and vice-versa. This was intended to incentivize participation as neither of the groups wanted extra resources paid to the other tranche.

Second, within the term loan tranche, the company established a Dutch auction for each lender to bid a price (inside a predetermined range) at which they would be willing to sell their portion of the loan. Ford said it would tender for the $500 million of term loan that bid the lowest price. Thus, if a given lender bid 45 per cent of face while $500 million worth of lenders bid at prices below 45 per cent, the first lender's holdings would not be tendered by Ford. Meanwhile, those who did not participate would be looking at a company with less cash.

The offer

On March 4, 2009, Ford and Ford Motor Credit Company (FMCC) put forward a series of exchange proposals. FMCC offered to use $1.3 billion of cash to tender for bonds at 30 per cent of par, representing a premium of ten points to the market value of the securities. Ford offered a 20-point premium to the holders of the bonds due in 2010 to recognize the near-term nature of their claims. It also announced a $500 million cash tender offer for Ford's term loan, with a price to be established through a Dutch auction in which lenders could submit bids to sell their positions for between 38 and 47 per cent of par.

The Ford offer

	Amount outstanding	3/4/2009 price	Premium offered[1]	Exchange price
$1.3bn tender offer for unsecured bonds				
9.50% Bonds due 2010	$0.5bn	35%	20%	55%
Other bonds due 2018-97	$8.4bn	20%	10%	30%
$500m tender offer for term loan				
Term loan	$6.9bn	31%	7%-15%	38%-47%
Exchange offer for convertible notes				
Convertible notes	$4.9bn	20%	8%	28%

Results of the Ford exchange offer

	Amount outstanding	3/4/09 price	Premium offered	Exchange price	Debt retired	$ of equity	Auto cash	FMCC cash	Total cash	Int expense reduction
Secured debt										
Term loan B	$6.9bn	31%	16%	47%	$2.2bn	—	—	$1.0bn	$1.0bn	$116m
Unsecured debentures										
9.50% Bonds due 2010	$0.5bn	35%	20%	55%	$156m	—	—	$86m	$86m	$15m
Other bonds due 2018-97	$8.4bn	20%	10%	30%	$3.2bn	—	—	$970m	$970m	$243m
Unsecured convertible debt										
Convertible notes	$4.9bn	20%	8%	28%	$4.3bn	$1.4bn	$344m	—	$344m	$183m
Total in exchange	**$20.7bn**				**$9.9bn**	**$1.4bn**	**$344m**	**$2.1bn**	**$2.4bn**	**$556m**

Ford also offered to exchange each dollar of its outstanding converts for a mix of eight cents in cash and about 20 cents of common stock (equivalent to the exact number of shares underlying each convertible note). As Ford's balance sheet was large enough that a fully subscribed offer would only need about 50 per cent of the total targeted debt to participate, the group decided a minimum acceptance threshold was not required. In doing so, it reduced the ability of a large group of holders to band together to hold out in an attempt to extract better terms. The table summarizes the offers made by Ford and FMCC.

Exchange offer results

Within weeks of launching the offers, Ford had received enough participation notices to count the exchanges as extremely successful. The term loan Dutch auction was heavily oversubscribed, with $2.2 billion of bids submitted throughout the preset range of prices. FMCC upsized its offer from $500 million to $1.0 billion of cash to purchase the entire $2.2 billion of term loan bid at a price of 47 per cent of par. The bond tender was also heavily subscribed, with $3.4 billion of bonds tendering for an aggregate purchase price of $1.1 billion. The convert exchange was perhaps the most successful, with 88 per cent of holders participating. In aggregate, Ford reduced total indebtedness by $9.9 billion and annual interest expense by $556 million, using $2.4 billion of cash and 468 million shares of common stock.

At the same time, the success of Ford's dramatic operational turnaround was becoming apparent. It restructured everything from its product line to its obligations on employee benefits, and the results have been recognized by consumers and market participants alike. From the first quarter of 2009 to the first quarter of 2010, Ford's sales increased by over 35 per cent, its stock price rose from $1.60 to above $13.00 per share, and its debt traded from the low 20s to par.

Conclusion

The frequency of exchange offers slowed towards the second half of 2009 as high-yield markets strengthened and the debt of most companies traded up. Despite the recent upsurge in market prices, exchange offers remain a useful tool for those companies with debt trading at significant discounts to par, looking to execute out-of-court restructurings. Management teams can utilize these offers to reduce leverage, increase financial flexibility and enhance their ability to issue equity capital over time.

The author would like to thank his research analyst, Michael Sperling, for his contributions to this chapter.

28

Building liquidity bridges through asset dispositions without bankruptcy

John E Luth, Chairman, President and CEO, Michael B Cox, Senior Managing Director, Global Head of Restructuring Advisory, and Lorie R Beers, Managing Director, Investment Banking and Financial Restructuring.

Seabury Group LLC

In the face of a liquidity crisis, companies often look to asset sales as a way of generating short-term cash. A well-planned, well-orchestrated asset sale program can provide much-needed relief to a liquidity-starved entity. By contrast, a poorly planned, "knee-jerk" reaction often ends up cannibalizing the business and pushing the company into a downward spiral toward bankruptcy or liquidation. In the latter instance, companies are often forced to sell off their "crown jewel" assets at a discount to provide liquidity, leaving less-attractive assets behind.

Overview

Generally, companies looking to sell assets as part of a liquidity program have three sale alternatives to consider:

- Non-core assets or divisions.
- Core assets or divisions.
- All or substantially all of the business either through an asset sale or a controlling stake in the entity.

In determining which of these is most likely to satisfy the company's requirements, it is vital to think of the future as well as the present. The most frequent mistake made by cash-starved enterprises is selling an asset at a discount, which can satisfy a short-term cash requirement but leave the company fundamentally unable to rehabilitate itself when it reaches the next liquidity hurdle. Sometimes "living to fight another day" is really just a stay of execution and it is important for any board of directors considering an asset sale to have undertaken a comprehensive analysis of the alternatives. Most companies are ill prepared for performing such an analysis on their own and require both the skillset and objectivity of an outside investment banker or financial advisor.

Additionally, when looking to asset sales to create a liquidity bridge, the company should evaluate the form of consideration offered by potential buyers. Non-cash bids for assets, even if at a higher face value, may not be as attractive if the need for liquidity is immediate. Conversely, a bid for an asset that provides payment over time in the form of a seller note may provide liquidity at a point in the future when the cash burn of the company is higher or its ordinary income is lower due to the cyclical nature of the business. The decision matrix on the following page illustrates the analysis that the company, together with its financial advisor, should undertake as it considers the alternatives.

Sale of non-core assets or divisions

This is often the first option a company will investigate as it looks to generate cash. If an asset or operating division is not integral to the enterprise, selling it will not generally disrupt the core business or substantially impact the operating metrics. That said, it is also likely to generate the smallest amount

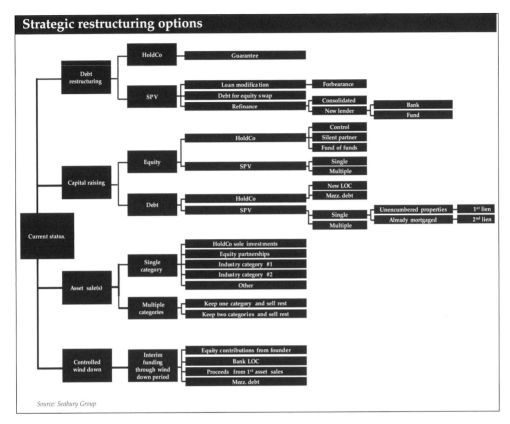

Source: Seabury Group

of liquidity. Often, these non-core assets are orphaned or capital starved and, as a rule, will yield a lower value in any sale process.

To maximize the value in an asset sale, it is fundamental that companies both (1) cast the net as wide as possible to potentially interested parties, and (2) run a robust, competitive process. Since the asset is non-core, concerns about strategic buyers are usually minimized and competition — involving financial as well as strategic parties — will create the best dynamic for achieving the highest possible price.

Case Study 1

A large public company (TCV) was a distributor of large-format televisions. It was the sole shareholder in a subsidiary, CVT — a distributor of cameras and camcorders throughout Asia, Europe, the United Kingdom and the United States. TCV had acquired CVT with a view to accessing its worldwide distribution channels, particularly in the UK and in continental Europe. As it turned out, TCV was never able to capture any synergies through CVT

and could not leverage those channels. TCV also had financial concerns of its own and, as a result, failed to focus on CVT and its capital needs.

CVT became an orphaned subsidiary, starved of capital and on the verge of insolvency. Although it had a good customer base and a recognizable trademark, it was forced into a program of recycling cash generated from sales to liberate product from its suppliers. TCV determined that CVT was non-core to its strategy going forward and elected to sell the subsidiary to generate much needed cash to service its senior debt.

Although the situation at CVT was bleak, the sale strategy was to market the company on a worldwide basis to both strategic and financial buyers. CVT's intellectual property, especially its valuable trademark, formed the cornerstone of the marketing effort, which yielded six potential bidders: three strategic and three financial. The contest ultimately narrowed to three and the winning bidder was a strategic competitor that highly valued CVT's intellectual property. As a result of this highly competitive process, the sale generated several times the value originally expected for this orphaned, non-core asset.

Case Study 2

A large airline (Air Group) was organized as a holding company with three subsidiaries: (i) mainline airline operations; (ii) in-house maintenance and repair operations (MRO); and (iii) a regional airline that provided a feeder service to the mainline operations. By having the second of these in-house, Air Group was able to control maintenance expenses for its own operations. In addition, MRO was generating cash flows through contracts with third parties.

Due to deteriorating macroeconomic conditions and diminishing demand for air travel, especially in the high-yield sector of business travel, Air Group's airline operating performance began to suffer. Dwindling profits turned into operating losses and this put a substantial strain on the company's ability to sustain its existing capital structure, which was heavily debt-laden as a result of the expansionary strategy employed in prior years. Air Group did not have any further debt capacity to shore up liquidity. In addition, the capital markets drought eliminated the option of raising unsecured debt. Equity investor appetite was also non-existent, given the high likelihood of bankruptcy.

In response to these circumstances, Air Group decided to pursue a divestiture of its MRO division. Even though this would result in the company giving up control over its maintenance costs, which would likely increase if outsourced, Air Group viewed this as the only viable option for boosting liquidity. It worked with its investment banker to position the division for sale and attract both strategic and financial buyers.

The eventual sale to a financial buyer generated the cash needed to pay off near-term debt, and provided the liquidity bridge that was so important during the macroeconomic downturn.

Case Study 3

A large international airline was faced with a deteriorating liquidity position and a credible threat of bankruptcy. In response, management embarked on a comprehensive restructuring plan, which had four central tenets: (i) Fly to Win; (ii) Fund the Future; (iii) Make Reliability a Reality; and (iv) Work Together. As part of Fund the Future, the airline concentrated on leveraging certain non-core assets. It closed a number of maintenance centers and outsourced long-term maintenance

contracts. It also sold five wide-body aircraft that were not considered core assets in the long-term restructuring plan. But perhaps the action with the most pronounced impact on its liquidity program was the company's agreement to sell its computer reservation system (CRS) platform to a leading strategic player in the space.

The airline transferred all its CRS assets and liabilities to the new owner and in exchange received consideration in cash and shares in the newly formed CRS entity. By making that sale, it avoided substantial near-term cash requirements for necessary investments in technology upgrades, lowered its own transaction processing costs, and added to its liquidity. The restructuring plan was a resounding success and resulted in the company posting the largest quarterly profit in its history.

Sale of core assets or divisions

The sale of core assets as a liquidity bridge is a struggle for any company. If an asset is central to operations, its sale may cannibalize the business and prevent further restructuring. On the other hand, if a valuable core asset can be hived off, that could make a big difference to liquidity and perhaps permit the company to acquire replacement assets in the future with a lower cost basis.

In many instances, a company with a strong aversion to bankruptcy (a family firm, for example) may, because of the reputational risk, elect to undertake the sale of a primary line of business to generate sufficient liquidity to pay creditors, either with or without a discount. The challenge in these instances is having the foresight to reshape the business going forward.

To determine which core asset or division is appropriate for this kind of sale, it is essential to determine the answers to several questions:

• How much liquidity will the sale raise?
• How much liquidity is necessary to satisfy the creditors and the needs of the company?
• Does the remaining business have sufficient debt capacity to support any shortfall?

This analysis should be run throughout the company to judge which assets will generate the optimal result. Ideally, this should be done dispassionately. Concerns about external factors, while relevant at the margins, may persuade the company to pursue a path that will not yield the best outcome and will frustrate its rehabilitation efforts.

Although it is still important to create a competitive dynamic and run a robust sale process, the importance of screening strategic buyers becomes a concern in sales of core assets. Because the company will continue to operate the remainder of its business after the transaction, disclosure of business practices and strategies must be judicious. Notwithstanding the need for liquidity, the company will have to make some judgment calls about allowing certain competitors into the process and about what information should be disclosed to those prospective buyers. Electronic data rooms make the segregation of information easy, but it is important to be mindful of protecting the same information in management meetings and due diligence as potential buyers move through the process.

Case Study 4

A commercial real estate development company (RDC) was in the business of buying raw land, developing a project, leasing that project and selling out of the asset. It operated four disparate business lines: commercial office, commercial retail, industrial and multi-family units. Typically, RDC would secure a construction mortgage on each property and that would be satisfied upon the sale of the asset.

As a result of the meltdown in both the real estate and credit markets, RDC found itself with an approaching liquidity crisis. Certain construction mortgages would be coming due and the lack of available credit rendered them virtually incapable of being refinanced. Likewise, sales of the projects (many of which were not yet tenanted) would be at values considerably lower than projected. RDC recognized that a piecemeal approach would leave it with a significant cash shortfall.

Although each of the four divisions was core to the company's overall operations, RDC concluded that the sale of two (commercial office and commercial real estate) would yield the most liquidity both to pay down its existing bank debt and to leave it well capitalized to survive the balance of the downturn in the real estate market — as well as to position it for growth in the future.

In some cases, certain assets are so vital to the overall business that companies cannot afford to sell them to generate liquidity. Often, the only viable option is to enter into a sale and leaseback transaction whereby the company monetizes any existing equity it has in the asset but also preserves its ability to continue utilizing the asset for a predetermined time through a lease arrangement.

This approach to boosting liquidity is common in the aviation and real estate industries.

Sale of all or substantially all of the business

This, again, is a bitter pill to swallow. The sale of all or substantially all of a business, either through an asset sale or a controlling stake in the entity, is often a last-resort strategy in creating a liquidity bridge to avoid bankruptcy. Indeed, in many instances, a company will seek to raise debt or equity capital and the process often morphs into this type of transaction.

When an enterprise elects to go down this route in the first instance, it is often because either (i) it has some interest that it is looking to protect (management, jobs, company reputation) and it believes this can be served through the sale; or (ii) it believes that no other alternative is workable as it seeks to avoid bankruptcy because of an external reason such as expense or delay.

In order to create maximum liquidity through the sale of substantially all of the business, it is again important to run a thorough and competitive process. As in the previous situations, casting the net wide and creating competition will serve to keep values high. In addition, if the company is under stress and absolutely must transact because of a lack of liquidity, it is critical to get the "story" right the first time. Crafting a compelling marketing piece is fundamental in attracting bids. Sophisticated financial buyers may be able to visualize the prospect represented by the transaction, but sophisticated strategic buyers may reject the proposed deal if they only see the stress and not the long-term opportunity.

Timing is also vital. When liquidity pressures loom, a company often attempts to compress the process, but remember that there is an inverse relationship between speed and value. You need to allow sufficient time for the process to yield the maximum number of bidders — and therefore the highest possible offer — and in over-emphasizing speed, you may sacrifice value because some bidders will opt out if they feel they cannot work to the schedule required. Getting the timing right is critical to achieving the goal of generating sufficient liquidity to avoid bankruptcy.

As with a core asset sale, it also important to be judicious about disclosure. Eliminating strategic bidders from the process is not advisable since, as a rule, they will generally pay more. That said, if the successful bidder turns out to be a financial buyer, it will ultimately compete against those same strategic parties. So you must be circumspect about the type and amount of information that is disclosed and at what points in the process.

Case Study 5

A family-owned, middle-market distributor of construction materials to local, regional and national homebuilders, FSO was a company whose business had been brought low by the collapse of the US housing market. In addition, its line of credit had matured and the lender would not extend new credit because the company was too heavily exposed to housing.

FSO did not want to file for bankruptcy, primarily because it wanted to: (i) avoid a loss of control over the process; (ii) avoid the expense associated with a Chapter 11; and (iii) avoid reputational risk in an industry dependent upon supplier/customer relationships. It elected to sell a controlling stake in its business in an effort to maintain jobs and the company's reputation, and, if possible, allow the family to retain a minority stake. Notwithstanding that, FSO faced an enormous and immediate liquidity crisis. Its senior lender had accelerated its loan and could commence sweeping the lock box, effectively leaving FSO without enough cash to operate the business.

FSO, together with its investment banker, formulated a process for a sale of the business. It worked out a schedule that it believed would generate sufficient liquidity for the bank within a reasonable time. It ran a competitive process in which several financial buyers and a select few strategic parties were introduced to the opportunity. Five financial buyers submitted indications of interest. Several of those insisted on a Chapter 11 proceeding to "cleanse" the assets.

By maintaining the competitive dynamic throughout the entire process, FSO was able to achieve nearly all of its goals. The winning bidder was an investor who let the family retain 25 per cent of the business, the banks received more than two-thirds of their principal while reinstating the balance, the employees kept their jobs and the company and family reputation was untarnished. All trade creditors were paid in full. Now, properly capitalized, the company is poised for growth and has been able to take advantage of some interesting opportunities because the market remains distressed.

Conclusion

The sale of assets has long been a mechanism for a company under liquidity stress to avoid a bankruptcy filing. It can, if properly executed, be a means to achieving a good result without the wholesale destruction of the company. There are, however, numerous critical analyses that must be undertaken and we stress that the involvement and advice of a qualified investment banker or financial advisor is critical to the success of any process. This, after all, has to be a bridge to liquidity — not a bridge to nowhere.

29

Alternatives to bankruptcy under federal and state law

Robert S Hertzberg,

Kay Standridge Kress,

Corporate Restructuring and

Bankruptcy Partners, and

Deborah Kovsky-Apap,

Corporate Restructuring and

Bankruptcy Associate,

Pepper Hamilton LLP

Distressed companies often assume that bankruptcy — either filed voluntarily by the debtor, or involuntarily by a group of creditors — is the only option. However, officers and directors might consider that a number of alternatives exist under both state and federal law that may result in greater flexibility and costs savings than liquidation in bankruptcy.

Foreclosure on real property

In general terms, foreclosure is the legal process by which a secured creditor takes title to and possession of collateral securing a defaulted loan. The specifics of foreclosure on real property are governed by state law, and vary significantly from state to state. If you need to foreclose on real property, or are contemplating making a loan secured by it, some key issues to consider include the following. Does the state where the property is located allow non-judicial foreclosures? Is it a "one action rule" state? Will the state permit you to pursue your deficiency claim if the collateral is not enough to satisfy your debt? Under the state's law, what is the effect of foreclosure on your ability to collect from third-party guarantors? What is the borrower's right of redemption after a foreclosure sale?

Judicial versus non-judicial foreclosure

Some states' laws provide only for foreclosure by judicial sale, while others provide only for non-judicial foreclosure. A number of states allow the creditor to choose between the two — though that choice may be circumscribed by a "one action rule", described below. Although there are benefits and drawbacks to each method, it is telling that in most of the states where creditors can choose their remedy, the vast majority of foreclosures are non-judicial — a process that is typically much faster. For example, in California, perhaps the nation's leader in real estate foreclosures, more than 95 per cent are non-judicial. In some instances, however, judicial foreclosure is the better — or the only — option.

Judicial foreclosure procedures

A judicial foreclosure is a lawsuit. The secured creditor sues the borrower and all other "necessary parties" — which may include the owner of the property if other than the borrower, anyone else liable for a deficiency judgment under the loan, and the holders of junior interests in the property — and records a *lis pendens* or similar notice against the property. The judicial foreclosure proceeds like any lawsuit, with service of the complaint, discovery, motion practice and trial. Once the creditor has obtained a judgment and order of foreclosure, the sale is conducted, typically by the sheriff or a court-appointed receiver or commissioner. The lender is entitled to protect its collateral from undervaluation at the foreclosure sale by credit bidding its debt.

If the sale proceeds are not sufficient to pay off the full debt, the lender can apply for a deficiency judgment, subject to certain restrictions. Some states have "anti-deficiency" statutes that prohibit a deficiency judgment on a purchase-money loan. (If the original purchase-money loan has been refinanced, it may or may not still qualify for protection, depending on what state you are in.) Additionally, many states limit the amount of the deficiency judgment to the difference between the mortgage debt and the fair value of the real estate, as determined by the court at a "fair-value hearing".

In a number of jurisdictions, the borrower may still exercise the right to redeem the property after a foreclosure sale. The redemption period and price varies from state to state, and may run as long as two years after the sale.

During that time, the borrower may remain in possession of the property. In states that provide for a redemption period, properties often sell at foreclosure sales at a significant discount (if at all) to compensate for the risk that the borrower may redeem the property.

Even after the redemption period has expired, the mortgagee cannot simply take possession of the property unless it has been abandoned (which in some jurisdictions may shorten the redemption period). If the borrower is still in possession, the mortgagee will have to initiate eviction proceedings, which can take up to 90 days depending on the particular state.

Length of the judicial foreclosure process
Judicial foreclosure provides the borrower with a forum not only to raise defenses but to assert counter-claims against the mortgagee — and, like any lawsuit, it can be time-consuming. Even an uncontested foreclosure, where the borrower fails to answer the complaint and the mortgagee is able to obtain a default judgment, can take six months. A vigorously contested judicial foreclosure may be drawn out for a year or more. Add this to the time for determination of fair value at a contested hearing, expiration of the redemption period and eviction of the borrower, and it may be several years before the mortgagee is able to take possession of the collateral.

Non-judicial foreclosure procedures
Foreclosures by power of sale, also called statutory or non-judicial foreclosures, are typically based on clauses in mortgages or deeds of trust that enable the mortgagee (or trustee, where the instrument is a deed of trust) to initiate a sale without resorting to the courts. The requirements for non-judicial foreclosure are established by state statutes and,

again, vary. In general, when a loan default occurs, the mortgagee is required to record a notice of default and notify the borrower about the default status. If the borrower does not cure the default within the specified statutory period, the mortgagee initiates the non-judicial foreclosure sale of the collateral by recording and publishing a notice of sale, posting that notice on the property itself and (usually) mailing it to the borrower. In some jurisdictions, a notice of default is not required; instead, the trustee can start directly with a notice of sale. In other jurisdictions, there is no requirement to inform the borrower directly of the notice of sale; the only requirement is publication.

The notice of sale sets the foreclosure sale date, which cannot be until the expiration of a set statutory period that varies from state to state. After the legally required notice period expires, a public auction will be held and the property will go to the highest bidder. As with a judicial foreclosure, the mortgagee will be able to credit bid its indebtedness and thus prevent undervaluation of the collateral.

Typically, any winning offer other than a credit bid must be paid in cash or cash-equivalent at or promptly after the auction. Following a foreclosure by power of sale, the borrower has no right of redemption; the sale is final.

Length of the non-judicial foreclosure process
The biggest advantage of non-judicial foreclosures is their relative speed and efficiency. In many states, they can be completed in as little as two to four months, though the process may take considerably longer if the borrower contests the action in court and seeks a delay of the sale. Nonetheless, most non-judicial foreclosures move much faster than judicial ones, particularly when the lack of a redemption period is factored in.

Considering deficiency claims in choosing a method of foreclosure
The primary reason for choosing a judicial foreclosure is that this is the only way of obtaining a deficiency judgment. If the mortgagee chooses a non-judicial foreclosure, its recovery will be limited to the value of the collateral.

Thus, if the mortgagee believes the property securing its loan is worth less than the amount owed, *and* the borrower has significant other assets that could be collected, *and* the loan is a recourse loan, it may be worth the time, expense and uncertainties of the judicial foreclosure process to obtain a deficiency judgment against the borrower.

What is a "one action rule" and why is it important?

A handful of states, most notably California, have what is known as a "one form of action rule". This requires the mortgagee to foreclose on the collateral property, taking either the judicial or non-judicial route, before seeking to recover the debt from the borrower by any other means. In short, if real estate is taken as collateral for a loan, and the collateral is in a one-action-rule state, the mortgagee *must* foreclose on the real estate security first. (An exception: if the mortgagee is a junior lien holder and the collateral is fully encumbered by senior liens, it will not be forced to go through the futility of foreclosure.) Furthermore, only one "action" may be brought against the borrower and must be used as the primary source of repayment when collecting the loan.

The one-action rule has been subject to particularly broad interpretation in California, and the consequences for failing to adhere strictly to the rule are severe. In *Security Pacific National Bank v Wozab*, a secured creditor set off approximately $3,000 in the borrower's accounts in partial satisfaction of a $1 million debt, without first foreclosing on the real property securing the debt. The California Supreme Court held that even though the creditor's exercise of its equitable right of setoff was not an "action", it nonetheless violated the one-action rule's requirement for relying on the security before trying to enforce a debt. As a result, for setting off just $3,000, the creditor lost its security for the remaining $997,000 owed by the debtor.

The moral of this cautionary tale is that it is critically important that a creditor seeks legal counsel before taking any action against a borrower, lest the creditor find itself deprived of its security altogether.

Effect of foreclosure on third-party guaranties

Generally, if a guarantor is a co-obligor on a note secured by real property, it is entitled to the same protections under anti-deficiency and one-action rules as the borrower. In a one-action-rule state, the mortgagee would be forced to pursue such a guarantor through a judicial foreclosure. On the other hand, if the guarantor is a person or entity who is not the borrower, and the guaranty contains the appropriate statutory waivers for that jurisdiction, the mortgagee should have the right to foreclose judicially or non-judicially on the property, and then pursue the guarantor — even in a one-action-rule state. Because the waiver and

other requirements for guaranties vary so widely, it is important for a creditor to understand the particular requirements of the state in which it is lending before the guaranty is executed.

Assignment for the benefit of creditors

Like foreclosure, an assignment for the benefit of creditors (ABC) is a creature of state law. ABCs have long been popular in a few states, most notably California and Illinois, but they are beginning to gain traction in other states as a less expensive alternative to bankruptcy.

What is an ABC?

An ABC conveys all property, legal and equitable rights of the assignor to the assignee, for the purpose of liquidating the assets and distributing them to creditors according to the priorities established by applicable law (usually the same order of priorities set forth in Chapter 7 of the Bankruptcy Code). Except in rare circumstances, where the assignee operates the business for a short period pending liquidation, an assignment ends all ordinary business operations. Thus, there is no ability to reorganize in an ABC.

Selection of the assignee

Unlike in Chapter 7, the party making an ABC gets to choose the assignee who will liquidate its assets. If you are the secured lender or a major creditor, you should seek to have input in this important decision, as well as in negotiations with the proposed assignee regarding his fees and expenses, and any discussions about what is likely to happen during the assignment. The assignee will act in a fiduciary capacity for the benefit of all creditors, and should be experienced in liquidating assets and selling businesses in the assignor's particular industry or field.

Formation of an ABC

Companies cannot be compelled to make an assignment; there is no state-law equivalent of an involuntary bankruptcy. However, companies can be encouraged to do so when it is in the best interests of their major creditor constituencies.

As a formal matter, creditor consent is not required for making an ABC, but rather is presumed. In practice, however, since any secured creditor can unwind an ABC by foreclosing on its collateral, most companies will seek the consent and co-operation of their lenders.

Some states require a court filing to initiate or complete an ABC, while in other jurisdictions a written instrument is sufficient. A short time after the ABC is made, the assignor must typically provide the assignee with a list of all creditors, an inventory, and the description, location and value of all property and rights assigned. For his part, the assignee must post a bond in excess of the value of the property.

Effect of an ABC

By accepting the assignment and taking possession, the assignee becomes the trustee for both the assignor and the creditors, with the duty to administer the trust property so as to pay creditors, and then to account to the assignor for the surplus, if any. Acceptance creates an "estate" that remains subject to all secured and unsecured claims.

It is important to note that because an assignee has the rights of a lien creditor under the Uniform Commercial Code (a version of which has been enacted in all 50 states), the rights of holders of unperfected security interests are subordinate to those of an assignee. The assignee takes the assignor's property subject to all existing liens and interests.

From a creditor's perspective, an ABC generally involves little more than submitting a proof of claim form to the assignee by the stated deadline, and then waiting for distribution of the dividend, if any.

ABCs compared with Chapter 7 or liquidating Chapter 11

Unlike a bankruptcy, an ABC does not impose an automatic stay of all actions. In practice, however, creditors are prevented from executing on the assignor's assets because those assets have been moved out of their reach by operation of the assignment. Also, unlike a liquidating Chapter 11, the assignor does not receive a discharge in an ABC but rather remains liable to creditors for any deficiencies.

All states have enacted some form of the Uniform Fraudulent Conveyances Act or the Uniform Fraudulent Transfers Act. Under these state laws, assignees can pursue actions to avoid and claw back fraudulent transfers, just as a trustee could do in bankruptcy. However, only some states have enacted statutes that allow an assignee to avoid and recover preferential transfers.

ABCs may be more attractive to creditors because they do not provide certain protections that debtors would otherwise enjoy in bankruptcy. For example, unlike a bankruptcy trustee or debtor in possession, an assignee cannot sell assets free and clear of interests, or assume and assign

executory contracts, without creditor consent. The Bankruptcy Code largely invalidates contractual *ipso facto* clauses, but those clauses remain in full force and effect in an ABC, allowing creditors to declare a default based on the assignment itself. The Bankruptcy Code caps landlords' damages for breaches of real property leases, but no such limitation exists in an ABC.

An ABC may also be a preferable alternative to bankruptcy simply because it is likely to be much faster and cheaper. An ABC avoids the need to file multiple motions and seek approval of the bankruptcy court throughout the process, and to pay the fees of numerous professionals. Accordingly, creditors may often obtain a better recovery than through bankruptcy proceedings. On the other hand, those proceedings take place under the watchful eye of the bankruptcy court and with full notice to all creditors and parties in interest. In an ABC, they may or may not receive similar notice.

Federal receiverships

Secured creditors may, upon default by a borrower, exercise a variety of remedies to enforce their interests. An under-utilized remedy, however, is offered by federal receiverships, which may be the quickest and most cost-effective method of gaining control over the collateral.

Foreclosure actions are generally brought in the county in which the property is located, while state receivership actions relate to property in that state. So these remedies present logistical issues when the collateral is in multiple locations. By comparison, federal receivership actions may be commenced in any district in which the federal court has jurisdiction. Generally, they are better able to achieve uniform results and are less costly than a foreclosure action or state receivership. Additionally, unlike foreclosures or most assignments for the benefit of creditors, a federal receivership may maintain the value of the collateral as it will allow the business to continue to operate. The receiver will preserve and protect the collateral as well as the financial integrity of the business as a going concern.

Appointment of a receiver

A federal court must have jurisdiction in order to be able to appoint a receiver. For example, the courts have "federal question" jurisdiction to appoint SEC receivers because those cases arise out of the violation of federal laws. By contrast, because a secured party's enforcement of its rights is not usually based upon a federal question, diversity of citizenship between the parties and a minimum amount in controversy exceeding $75,000 must exist in order to invoke the jurisdiction of a federal district court. Once this is established, the federal district court has ancillary jurisdiction to appoint a receiver, as well as ancillary subject matter jurisdiction over every suit the receiver subsequently brings in the appointing court to execute his duties.

Procedurally, to have a receiver appointed, the secured creditor will first file suit against the borrower for breach of contract. In some jurisdictions, depending upon state law, the complaint will include a count for foreclosure. Then the secured creditor will file a motion to appoint a receiver, supported by an affidavit alleging the basis for the relief requested.

The decision as to whether a receiver should be appointed is made by federal standards and resolved by federal law. In their determinations, courts typically weigh factors such as the plaintiff's probable success in the underlying complaint, any fraudulent conduct on the part of the defendant, and any imminent danger that the property may be lost, concealed, injured, diminished in value or squandered.

Once appointed, the receiver is required to post a bond, after which he is vested with complete control of all property of the defendant, personal and real, wherever situated, with the right to take possession. A receiver must, within ten days of entry of the appointment order, file a copy of the complaint and the appointment order in each district in which property is located. If he fails to do so, he may be divested of control over the property in those districts. However, the receiver does not need to be separately "appointed" in each district; simply filing the copy of the complaint and order is sufficient. Thus, maintaining legal control over all property, wherever located, is relatively straightforward.

Role of the receiver

On appointment, the receiver becomes an officer of the court, managing and operating the property according to the laws of the state where the property is located. In addition, the receiver may be sued with respect to any acts taken, or transactions engaged in, while carrying on the business. However, an action by a third party to gain possession of property held by the receiver can only proceed at the discretion of the court appointing the receiver.

The court has broad powers and wide discretion to determine appropriate relief in an equity receivership. These powers enable the court to effectively supervise a receivership and protect the interests of its beneficiaries. As courts of equity, the federal courts have authority in appropriate circumstances to impose broad stays of all actions against the entities in receivership, except by leave of the receivership court. There is no inherent legal limitation on the amount of control that a receiver may wield over the entity and/or the collateral over which he was appointed. The receiver's powers are delineated by the appointment order.

Sales of assets by a receiver

These sales are governed by statute. Additionally, the power of sale is within the scope of a receiver's complete control over receivership assets — a concept firmly rooted in the common law of equity receiverships. The statutory provisions governing the sale of assets are very specific in certain respects (such as notice provisions and appraisals), but vague in terms of the procedures to be employed in the sales, thereby allowing for flexibility and creativity. In addition, under federal law there is no right of redemption from judicial sales. As in a non-judicial foreclosure, the sale is final when made.

The sale of real property by a receiver may be through a public or a private sale. A public sale must occur in the district where the receiver was appointed, unless the court specifically orders that it take place in another district. In addition, the terms and conditions will be as directed by the court. Notice of a public sale must be approved by the court and published at least once a week for four weeks prior to the sale — in at least one newspaper in general circulation in the county, state or judicial district where the property is located.

A private sale may occur if the court determines that it is in the best interest of the estate. As with a public sale, the terms and conditions will be as directed by the court. In a private sale, however, the court must appoint three disinterested appraisers to appraise each parcel of property. The originally proposed offer will not be confirmed by the court unless the sale price is two-thirds of the appraised value, or unless another offer of at least 10 per cent over the original offer is received. Notice of the private sale must also be approved by the court and published in a newspaper of general circulation at least ten days prior to the hearing on the confirmation of the sale.

The sale of personal property is governed by the same rules as that for the sale of real property, unless the court orders otherwise.

Courts are generally liberal with respect to receivership sales. A judicial sale that complies with the procedural requirements will not be denied confirmation or be set aside based on the price unless that price is 'so gross as to shock the conscience of the court' — and even then, most courts will require additional circumstances indicating unfairness such as chilled bidding. In one case, the Court of Appeals for the Third Circuit upheld the expedited sale of corporate property that did *not* comply with the statutory procedures regarding appraisals and certain notice provisions, because of the extraordinary circumstances of the case and the dire financial condition of the corporation.

Interplay between bankruptcy and federal receiverships

At the commencement of a bankruptcy case, the bankruptcy court has exclusive jurisdiction over the property of the estate, and the automatic stay provisions prevent the continuation of receivership proceedings and action by the district court. In other words, if you have a receiver appointed and other creditors then file an involuntary bankruptcy petition against the debtor, bankruptcy law will trump federal receivership law. You will not necessarily lose the benefits of your receivership, however; you can file a motion asking the bankruptcy court to abstain from the case and, after weighing the equities, the court may allow the receivership to proceed instead of the bankruptcy.

The various legal and practical differences between receiverships and bankruptcy proceedings may be significant in certain situations. Some district courts, for example, have enacted local rules specifically pertaining to receiverships, and those should be reviewed. Meanwhile, receivership proceedings are often referred by busy district judges to magistrates. This presents the issue of the parties' willingness to consent to a magistrate judge hearing the case and order entry of judgment, or merely making recommendations to the district judge.

The receiver's ability to pursue certain causes of action on behalf of the estate also needs to be considered. There is no authority for a receiver to avoid and recover preferential transfers. Nor is there statutory authority to employ the "strong arm" powers of Section 544 of the Bankruptcy Code to avoid unperfected liens. Equity receivers do, however, have standing to assert fraudulent conveyance theories to recover property for the estate.

In addition, a receiver may be able to bring certain actions against third parties that a bankruptcy trustee, debtor in possession or committee cannot bring successfully because of defenses that may be asserted against them. For example, courts have refused to apply the *in pari delicto* defense to bar a receiver from asserting fraudulent conveyance claims against third parties who had received funds from the receivership entities. Under the *in pari delicto* defense, the court will not allow a party to seek damages from the other side if that party's own conduct was wrongful. The rationale is that the appointment of the receiver removes the wrongdoer from control and sufficiently changes the equities such that the *in pari delicto* doctrine "loses its sting". By contrast, courts have held that bankruptcy trustees (and other bankruptcy estate representatives) are subject to the *in pari delicto* defense.

On a practical level, another difference between receiverships and bankruptcy proceedings is in the nature of the courts themselves. District court judges tend to be far less experienced than bankruptcy judges in dealing with sales and other estate administration matters. They are often receptive to suggestions as to procedures to be employed on these issues. The district courts often rely on analogous provisions of the Bankruptcy Code and rules for guidance where appropriate, although they are not bound to follow them. In addition, a district court presiding over a receivership is less likely to share the view of many bankruptcy courts that it should not permit a case to go forward (or authorize a sale) if the sole beneficiaries are the secured creditors.

Conclusion

While officers and directors may assume that bankruptcy is the only available option in times of economic distress, other, sometimes more advantageous alternatives exist under state and federal law. We have discussed three of those alternatives — foreclosure, assignments for the benefit of creditors, and federal receiverships — in some detail. Before deciding to file for bankruptcy, officers and directors of distressed companies should consider these and other alternatives as they may result in greater flexibility and cost savings than a conventional liquidation in bankruptcy.

30

The race to the starting line: Developing prepackaged and prenegotiated reorganization plans to maximize value

James HM Sprayregen,
Restructuring Partner,
Richard M Cieri,
Restructuring Partner,
David R Seligman,
Restructuring Partner,
Chad J Husnick,
Restructuring Associate, and
Jeffrey D Pawlitz,
Restructuring Associate.
Kirkland & Ellis LLP

As any good athletics coach will tell you, rarely is a race simply about running as fast as you can. Instead, it involves strategy, pacing, self-analysis, keeping an eye on the other runners, knowing when to separate from the pack and when to sprint for the finish. The same is true in a Chapter 11 case. But there is one critical difference: the runner looks forward to the race and the opportunity to shine on the track; a company never looks forward to the Chapter 11 process and wants to complete it as soon as possible. It can be an expensive distraction, cause disruption to the business and lead to the loss of customers and key employees. Chapter 11 is one big obstacle race.

It is often said that filing for bankruptcy is not an end in itself; rather, it is only the start of a long race. So before the company lines up in the starting blocks, it should think about what kind of Chapter 11 case is appropriate. The traditional approach is where the company files for bankruptcy, often due to events like a liquidity crisis or debt acceleration, and then uses the breathing space afforded by the automatic stay to figure out its next steps and to begin developing its business and restructuring plans. Because a company often starts a traditional Chapter 11 without a predetermined means to an agreed-upon end, these cases tend to be long, complex and costly.

But not all Chapter 11 restructurings have to be drawn-out. Prepackaged and prenegotiated restructurings substantially shorten the length of Chapter 11 cases and, more importantly, mitigate "event risk". In both cases, the material terms of the plan and possibly the plan itself are negotiated prior to commencing Chapter 11. As a result, the company's stay in Chapter 11 is generally much shorter, less expensive and less contentious, as well as offering a greater degree of certainty about the outcome.

Prepackaged and prenegotiated restructurings: an overview

In a traditional Chapter 11, a company files for bankruptcy without a consensual restructuring plan in place. It may have engaged some of its key stakeholders in reorganization discussions, but these talks may well be placed on the back burner as the company takes advantage of the automatic stay to make the transition to Chapter 11, to stabilize its operations, and to communicate with its employees, customers and business partners. Only after the company has made a soft landing into Chapter 11 does it shift its attention towards working with its constituencies to develop business and restructuring plans that will form the basis of a reorganization. A traditional Chapter 11 case lasts six months at least and has gone on for many years in some cases. Indeed, this can be a very long race.

In contrast, in a prepackaged or prenegotiated bankruptcy, a company can complete the in-court portion of its restructuring much more quickly, between 45 and 120 days after the filing.

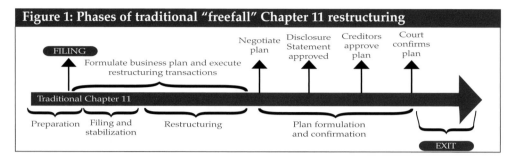

Figure 1: Phases of traditional "freefall" Chapter 11 restructuring

The prepackaged restructuring: the 100-meter dash

In a prepackaged case, the company develops its business plan, negotiates a plan of reorganization and supporting documents, and solicits the approval of its creditors — all prior to the company's bankruptcy filing. Only after the company has received the requisite votes in favor of its plan does it commence bankruptcy to effect the terms of that strategy.

As in a traditional bankruptcy, the company will still need to make the transition into Chapter 11, usually by obtaining standard "first-day relief" from the bankruptcy court. In addition, it will likely file its plan of reorganization and supporting documents, as well as a voting report, on the first day of its case and request that the court set a combined hearing to approve the disclosure statement and other solicitation materials and to confirm the plan. The combined hearing is unique to prepackaged bankruptcies; in prenegotiated and traditional Chapter 11 filings, a hearing is held to approve the disclosure statement, then solicitation occurs, and, finally, a second hearing is held to confirm the plan.

In prepackaged cases, the combined disclosure statement and plan confirmation hearing takes place approximately 30 days after the filing, and the company emerges from bankruptcy upon expiration of the two-week appeal period. In other words, a company can come out of a prepackaged bankruptcy in 45 to 60 days.

As discussed below, prepackaged plans usually focus on balance sheet restructurings of "funded debt" claims, rather than operational restructurings. Therefore, they provide for claims held by the company's trade vendors, customers, lessors, contractual counterparties and the like, so these groups can "ride through" the bankruptcy unimpaired. As such, it is common practice to obtain first-day relief from the bankruptcy court authorizing (but not directing) a debtor company to continue to pay pre-petition unsecured trade claims as they come due in the ordinary course of business.

The prenegotiated restructuring: the 400-meter race

This approach is best thought of as a hybrid between a prepackaged and a traditional Chapter 11 restructuring. The company will have engaged in some level of negotiation over the terms of a plan of reorganization with some of its constituents, and will often have received a form of support such as a "lock-up" agreement. This usually includes a detailed sheet containing the material terms of a restructuring that will be implemented through a confirmed Chapter 11 plan. Unlike a prepackaged case (but like a traditional Chapter 11), however, formal solicitation of votes to accept or reject the

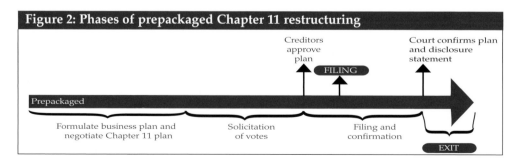

Figure 2: Phases of prepackaged Chapter 11 restructuring

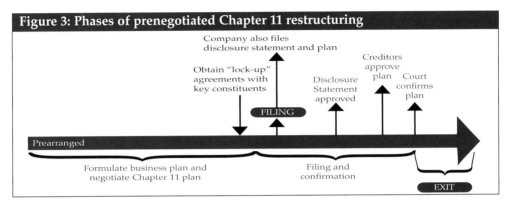

Figure 3: Phases of prenegotiated Chapter 11 restructuring

plan, and possibly negotiation of some of the details, are completed only after the bankruptcy case commences.

The solicitation of votes in favor of a prenegotiated restructuring is substantially similar to that in a traditional Chapter 11; the timing is the only difference. Because negotiations are substantially completed pre-petition, and because general support agreements have already been obtained, a company may file its plan and disclosure statement shortly after commencement of its Chapter 11 case.

The company will then seek approval of the solicitation documents within the first 30 to 45 days, before beginning solicitation of creditor votes and, finally, seeking confirmation of the plan of reorganization. In contrast, in a traditional Chapter 11, it is normally some time before a company is in a position to formulate, negotiate and file a plan of reorganization.

Compared to a prepackaged restructuring, however, a company will spend more time in Chapter 11 because solicitation is completed during the bankruptcy case in a prenegotiated restructuring. The in-court process may take 100 to 120 days before a plan is confirmed and consummated. It is still a quick race but not a sprint.

The benefits of prepackaged and prenegotiated restructurings

In the right circumstances, a company can realize real benefits with a prepackaged or prenegotiated bankruptcy, as compared to a traditional Chapter 11 case. First and most importantly, these approaches usually have substantially less impact on a company's operations than traditional filings, mainly because the company is in Chapter 11 for a much shorter time.

Second, the transition into Chapter 11 can be smoother because the company has had the chance to conduct significant planning in advance of the filing. For example, prepackaged cases often contemplate the continued payment of all trade debt in the ordinary course because a plan has already been accepted by a company's major creditors, or at least those creditors have committed to supporting it. This continued payment of trade debt is more controversial in prenegotiated restructurings — because the plan has not actually been solicited and accepted at the time Chapter 11 begins — but the trend now is towards allowing similar relief in these cases.

Third, because the company has already reached some form of agreement with its major constituencies, it can convey a positive message to interested parties. A company can stress to employees, vendors and customers that the bankruptcy will be brief and that operations will continue as normal. This is particularly true of prepackaged restructurings, where the company has already received the votes of acceptance needed to effect its plan of reorganization.

Fourth, the early planning necessary in prepackaged or prenegotiated cases can be useful in avoiding an in-court Chapter 11 process in its entirety. Sometimes, a company's efforts to reach out to its stakeholders and negotiate a restructuring can concentrate minds: it is not out of the ordinary for stakeholders to realize that they can accomplish almost all of their restructuring goals without having to resort to Chapter 11.

An out-of-court restructuring, however, cannot always be achieved, thus entailing the parallel track of an in-court filing on a contingency basis. For example, an out-of-court restructuring can only be imposed on those creditors who agree to the treatment; "holdouts" and "free riders" will reject it in the hope of being bought out or having their claims carved out from any creditor compromise. (To incentivize the first creditors to approve the out-of-court plan without fear of "free riders", out-of-court restructurings often require a threshold acceptance percentage by creditors, often 90 to 95 per cent.)

But this "holdout" problem is, to all intents and purposes, a non-issue if a bankruptcy case is consensual and a debtor can impose (or "cram down") a certain treatment on dissenting creditors so long as at least two thirds in amount of the creditor class and more than one half in number vote to accept that treatment. By pursuing a prepackaged plan in parallel with the out-of-court solicitation, a company can utilize the bankruptcy forum as a backstop in the event that the requisite threshold of acceptances is not reached. Moreover, because the plan of reorganization itself can often serve as the operational document for both the in-court and out-of-court reorganization, and the corresponding documents also are substantially similar (a Form S-1 in the out-of-court and a disclosure statement in the in-court restructuring), a company can effect the dual solicitation without substantially increased costs or efforts.

Understanding when a prepackaged or prenegotiated plan is a viable option

So why not pursue a prepackaged restructuring all the time? In some circumstances, it simply may not be the best restructuring option. As discussed above, a great deal of the work is front-loaded, which involves developing a new business plan, negotiating with stakeholders, drafting reorganization documents and soliciting acceptance. In advance of a liquidity crisis, or another event that would necessitate a bankruptcy filing, there just may not be the time for a prepackaged or prenegotiated filing. For example, a company seeking to restructure public securities must comply with applicable non-bankruptcy securities law in connection with a pre-petition solicitation. Often, compliance in this area (perhaps requiring that the company registers the securities with the SEC) can substantially increase the time, cost and effort of completing solicitation, negating the benefits of a prepackaged restructuring.

The composition of the creditor base is also a factor. Prepackaged and prenegotiated restructurings depend upon a company's ability to reach a negotiated agreement with a body of creditors, and where that base is widely disbursed it can be hard to reach a consensus. Not only may

there be substantive differences of opinion on how the company should be restructured, but the mere negotiation process without the backdrop of a Chapter 11 may be impossible. This is particularly so where certain creditors may not want access to material, non-public information about the company (a prerequisite to agreeing to a compromise) and, thus, be restricted from trading in its securities.

When a business considers pre-filing negotiations with a body of creditors, it should also take into account its tolerance for the public disclosure of its restructuring efforts. For example, it may have to reveal that it is contemplating a bankruptcy (albeit a prenegotiated one), which can cause trade vendors to tighten credit and, potentially, drive a company towards the traditional Chapter 11 case that it was trying to avoid.

Another consideration in prepackaged and prenegotiated cases is whether a company should pursue a simple balance sheet restructuring (of its funded debt claims), or a more comprehensive operational restructuring. For example, the Bankruptcy Code allows a company, among other things, to reject executory contracts (both the company and the counterparty have material unperformed obligations) and unexpired leases, terminate pension plans and modify retiree benefits, and sell non-core assets free and clear of liens. Even the debtor's ability to reject executory contracts under the Bankruptcy Code, for example, is a useful tool in encouraging a counterparty to renegotiate the terms of the agreement during the bankruptcy.

Utilizing these provisions, however, takes time. For example, the Bankruptcy Code requires a company to engage in meaningful and often lengthy discussions with counterparties prior even to beginning the drawn-out process of restructuring pension and labor liabilities in a bankruptcy. And the more provisions that a company seeks to use, the longer it is likely to stay in bankruptcy.

Moreover, many of the restructuring tools available under the Bankruptcy Code are marginalized in a prepackaged and prenegotiated restructuring. For example, where general unsecured claims ride through unimpaired under these plans of reorganization, the ability to reject executory contracts will provide little or no practical benefit because the contract counterparty will be entitled to 100 per cent recovery on any claim under the plan. That said, the Bankruptcy

Code does offer real value by capping any damages that arise from the rejection of unexpired leases and employment agreements.

Steps to carrying out a prepackaged or prenegotiated plan

Early planning is essential given the volume of work that must be completed pre-petition. And all the while, the company must also engage in the standard first-day preparations, including determining which entities will file for Chapter 11, along with the pleadings needed to ensure a smooth transition into Chapter 11.

Given all this, a company should retain highly qualified restructuring professionals during the early stages of the restructuring process. Although the thought of incurring additional professional fees at a time when solvency hangs in the balance can be daunting, the preparation should result in material savings down the line and a more favorable outcome. Moreover, retention of advisors will help directors and officers to satisfy their fiduciary duties in the run-up to a restructuring and protect them from liability for difficult decisions.

The first task of the restructuring team is to develop a timeline for filing. This should note any problem areas that may require the company's creditor constituencies to waive a default or amend an agreement to avoid a default. The restructuring team should understand any trigger defaults under the company's funded debt documents, real property leases and major trade contracts, as well as any grace periods or cross-defaults. It will often be able to negotiate an amendment of facilities with creditors, or forbearance from exercising remedies.

The next stage is to develop a thorough decision-making process. This will serve to create a good record and protect against liability for restructuring-related decisions in a market where creditors are increasingly looking to second-guess directors and officers with the benefit of hindsight. In prepackaged and prenegotiated restructurings, establishing the process early is vital. Many of the major decisions will have been made by the company prior to filing, and, as such, it will not have the benefit of public records and bankruptcy court approval.

Once the restructuring professionals have been retained and the timeline and decision-making process has been determined, the company must develop a business plan and start negotiating with creditor constituencies on the treatment of their respective claims. This process is intense and, as discussed earlier, is what sets prepackaged and prenegotiated cases apart from traditional Chapter 11 ones because of the amount of work that must be done pre-petition.

The restructuring team should also determine whether to use any of the tools in the Bankruptcy Code to carry out operational restructuring initiatives. Again, this can be time-intensive. For example, if the company would prefer to reject certain leases or contracts during the bankruptcy case, it will have to prepare schedules of assets and liabilities and establish a bar date by which claims must be filed against the company. This process, if not adequately prepared early on, can delay confirmation and consummation of a plan of reorganization.

Moreover, the restructuring team must consider some important corporate governance issues. The company has to select the directors and officers for the reorganized company, structure an equity incentive plan and ensure adequate insurance for them, and provide closure for the existing directors and officers, which may include obtaining a separate insurance policy.

Finally, to the extent certain creditors stand to take full or partial control of the reorganized company, all operational restructuring decisions should be vetted by those constituencies ahead of time.

Conclusion

A Chapter 11 restructuring is normally a once in a corporate-lifetime experience. So the company must develop a vision of its reorganized self to understand the type of restructuring required and whether an accelerated process is appropriate and achievable. Prepackaged and prenegotiated bankruptcies provide the acceleration and, although only suitable in some circumstances, they can maximize value for a company and minimize the effects of a bankruptcy on its operations.

31

Managing traditional Chapter 11 reorganizations: A primer for directors and officers on bankruptcy fundamentals

John C DiDonato and
Daniel P Wikel,
Managing Directors
in the Restructuring and
Turnaround Practice,
Huron Consulting Group

There are typically many reasons or circumstances that may cause a company to be in a distressed or stressed situation, including industry and/or economic influences, internal company issues or a one-time, unfortunate event. Specifically, a company may have expanded its operations too quickly or beyond its true core competencies. As a result, the company may become over-leveraged due to underperformance in the marketplace, or it may experience a decrease in enterprise value. In many cases, both outcomes will occur. In any event, as directors and officers manage through a distressed situation, it is likely over time that they will exhaust "out of court" restructuring options such as asset or business sales, amending their credit facilities and seeking replacement or bridging capital to improve the company's liquidity position and "weather the storm". At this point, the only option may be to file for bankruptcy protection.

Sometimes the best weapon, and strongest negotiation tactic with creditor constituents, is to play the "bankruptcy card". Most parties are aware that filing for protection affords companies "time out" from their creditors and the precious time to regroup, restructure and perhaps emerge a stronger organization with an adequate capital structure, workforce and market footprint.

However, the company cannot simply use the bankruptcy card in its strategic negotiations without being fully prepared actually to file for bankruptcy protection. Directors and officers need to understand the benefits and costs of a traditional Chapter 11 reorganization in order to maximize the restructuring objectives. As such, it is vital that a company pursues parallel paths, one that incorporates its out-of-court restructuring efforts and one that provides for a properly planned bankruptcy filing, as a contingency, as early as possible.

Parallel paths: out-of-court restructuring and Chapter 11 planning
A company needs to prepare in a number of ways if it is to "ease seamlessly" into bankruptcy protection. Contingency planning will prioritize additional cost-cutting and cash-conservation opportunities, minimize the administrative cost of filing, and shorten the time in Chapter 11.

It has been our experience that a delay in contingency planning or a filing, when there is an imminent need for one, reduces the chance of a successful restructuring. Such delays can make it hard to achieve the right inventory levels to maintain the company's operations, while unclear communications may impact key relationships with customers, vendors and employees, and lead to the loss of important leverage in negotiating post-petition financing. Moreover, directors and officers must be sensitive to their own duties to all stakeholders when a company finds itself in the zone of insolvency.

During the flurry of airline bankruptcy filings in the early and mid 2000s,

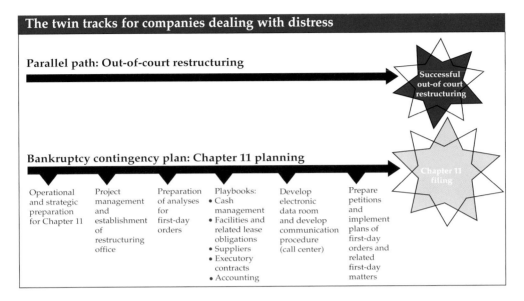

The twin tracks for companies dealing with distress

Parallel path: Out-of-court restructuring

Successful out-of court restructuring

Bankruptcy contingency plan: Chapter 11 planning

Chapter 11 filing

| Operational and strategic preparation for Chapter 11 | Project management and establishment of restructuring office | Preparation of analyses for first-day orders | Playbooks: • Cash management • Facilities and related lease obligations • Suppliers • Executory contracts • Accounting | Develop electronic data room and develop communication procedure (call center) | Prepare petitions and implement plans of first-day orders and related first-day matters |

companies were very focused on a seamless entry into Chapter 11, so as not to disrupt flights, crew schedules and airport operations, and to maintain the confidence of customers. This was achieved through diligent preparation, the implementation of detailed plans or "playbooks", and strong leadership. From an operational perspective, and from the point of view of customers and suppliers, the initial filings were non-events and resulted in minimal disruptions.

Pre-petition bankruptcy contingency planning

In preparing for a Chapter 11 bankruptcy filing, the management team, with guidance from its directors and officers, must develop a comprehensive plan with a specific endgame in mind. During this planning period, everything will seem to be moving more quickly than usual, as there are many initiatives and out-of-court outcomes that could ultimately divert a filing. As the organization is often working long hours and resources are stretched, it is important to remain steady and give the appearance of being in control — both internally to the employees and externally to the company's many stakeholders. The following are some of the important steps that we recommend companies take during the pre-petition planning process:

• Identify a core team of talented and hard-working company personnel across all functions (key departments and business operations) who

will co-ordinate the planning for a Chapter 11 reorganization.
• Consider creating a restructuring office within the organization in order to centralize communications and manage restructuring and bankruptcy-related work.
• Consider choosing an executive to manage and be accountable for the restructuring office.
• Plan for stakeholder communications, including customers and suppliers.
• Obtain debtor in possession (DIP) financing to sustain the restructuring efforts.
• As expensive as they may be, hire seasoned and experienced professionals as early in the process as possible for their expertise in both the out-of-court and bankruptcy contingency planning.
Bankruptcy cases are legally driven and it is important to have an experienced legal team in place. Interview and select this firm carefully, seeking input, where appropriate, from creditors, lenders and other parties that will be impacted by a Chapter 11 filing. Also consider engaging investment bankers, who can assist in securing DIP financing, preparing for the sale of a business to raise liquidity, and providing any valuations in the early part of the case. Additionally, financial advisors can be effective in restructuring and bankruptcy activities.
• Begin to identify the appropriate legal entities that will file for relief under Chapter 11 and prepare the necessary petitions for each debtor entity for submission to the court.

• Identify the major and critical goods and service providers and manage these relationships closely, as they are typically very active in bankruptcy cases.
• Draft first-day motions, which will allow relief from the automatic stay.

First-day motions

On the petition date, a debtor will file a variety of motions with the court. These set out policies, procedures and other administrative matters for the case, as well as requesting court approval for the payment of certain pre-petition claims, including the following:

• **Cash management.** This motion, if granted, will allow the debtor to maintain the existing system of cash management (bank accounts, check stock, etc).
• **Wages and benefits.** Generally, this will ensure that all employees continue to receive uninterrupted compensation and benefits.
• **Critical trade vendors.** This will allow the debtor to pay pre-petition debts to certain essential trade creditors. Such motions will need to demonstrate that the creditor is the sole provider of a good or service and finding a replacement would be prohibitively difficult or expensive. It will also have to be shown that losing the supplier's business would significantly, and potentially irreparably, impair the debtor's ability to conduct operations.

Recently, there has been a trend towards disallowing the concept of critical vendors. In those situations, it is vital to communicate early and often with any goods and service providers on which the company is dependent.
• **Foreign vendors.** The debtor may seek authorization to pay pre-petition obligations in foreign jurisdictions to prevent disruptions of its business.

If the court grants these motions, the debtor will have the latitude to pay pre-petition obligations in the ordinary course that are critical to operating the company. The most obvious example of a first-day motion is allowing the company to pay wages and employee benefits earned prior to the petition date. Depending on the type of company, additional motions may include customer programs, such as discounts, retention of bankruptcy professionals, continued use of ordinary-course professionals, utilities and joint-case administration (when multiple legal entities are filed).

The traditional Chapter 11 bankruptcy filing

Chapter 11 of the Bankruptcy Code is a protective mechanism whereby a company receives temporary relief from the collection efforts of goods and services providers and other creditors so that it can undergo a financial reorganization. A company in Chapter 11 operates as a debtor in possession of the assets, with existing management typically remaining in control of day-to-day operations. Additional financing is almost always arranged by the company in order to meet current and future obligations.

Unlike a Chapter 7 bankruptcy, where the debtor must liquidate its assets and discontinue its operations, Chapter 11 enables a company to continue operating while it reorganizes its debt obligations and operations.

It is important to note that day-to-day decisions are still made by management while key decisions are generally made by the board of directors. However, an important regulation in Chapter 11 is that actions outside the ordinary course of business must be approved by the bankruptcy court, with appropriate notice given to all parties.

The purpose of a traditional Chapter 11 reorganization is to give the company temporary relief from its creditor constituents and time to establish a plan of reorganization.

Chapter 11 bankruptcy protection can also be used to restructure the finances of an otherwise solidly performing operating company that is simply over-leveraged and has critical cash-flow problems. This may have been caused by an over-recapitalization, an untimely or poor acquisition, or a litigation event. A few recent examples are Anchor Fluid Drilling, Charter Communications, CIT and General Growth Properties.

Companies have also used Chapter 11 as a means to protect themselves from massive product liability claims. Quigley Company, Solutia and USG Corporation, among others, filed Chapter 11 bankruptcy proceedings for this reason. In many of these cases, not only have mass tort claims against the company been resolved inside the bankruptcy court forum, but also claims against the directors and officers.

Alternatively, Chapter 11 bankruptcy protection can be used for an operational transformation or as a vehicle to sell assets or businesses that might otherwise be difficult to market because of liabilities that are either unknown or hard to quantify. The steel industry provided an example of the elimination of excess capacity when the operations of Acme, Bethlehem,

LTV and Weirton, and other selected assets, were consolidated into the International Steel Group.

Furthermore, legacy costs related to collective bargaining agreements, pension plans and retirement benefits, as well as complex corporate governance, can be reduced, simplified or eliminated — as seen in Bethlehem Steel, Chrysler, Delta Airlines, General Motors, LTV, Mirant, National Steel, Northwest Airlines and United Airlines.

The ultimate objective of the Chapter 11 reorganization is to seek court and creditor approval for the company's plan of reorganization and associated disclosure statement, so it can emerge a stronger and more competitive enterprise. This is achieved by executing the restructuring objectives and developing a feasible business plan and capital structure around those objectives.

This is not always straightforward, as many factors and predicted outcomes can change or simply not occur as expected during the case. For example, in many of the major airline, steel, chemical, automotive and transportation cases, there were several collective bargaining agreements that needed to be negotiated and finalized before emergence. As with any moving target, not all cost-saving and work-rule goals and timelines were achieved. In several of the airline cases, the business model was impacted by 9/11, the SARS breakout, the entrance of new competitors in certain markets (low-cost carriers) and continued pricing pressure during the case, volatile oil prices and limited access to the credit markets.

As a result, the business plan was continuously recalibrated and vetted by all creditor constituents and the capital structure requirements had to be adjusted accordingly. Moreover, this process required tactical negotiation skills and continuous adaptation to input from customers, employees, company advisors and stakeholders — all taking place under the supervision of the court.

Technical terms

We commonly hear from directors and officers who are going through the process for the first time that one of the more difficult parts of filing for bankruptcy is unfamiliarity with the terminology involved. The following are some of the key terms and definitions used in bankruptcy proceedings (*a comprehensive list can be found at www.uscourts.gov/ bankruptcycourts/bankruptcybasics/glossary*):

- **Absolute Priority Rule.** In the liquidation of a company, this rule states that secured debtholders must be paid in full before holders of unsecured

debt, who in turn have precedence over shareholders.
- **Automatic Stay.** This provides for a period in which all judgments, collection activities, foreclosures, lawsuits, garnishments and repossessions of property are suspended, as of the date of filing. They cannot be pursued by the creditors on any debt or claim that arose before the filing of the bankruptcy petition, unless and until special permission is received from the bankruptcy court by way of a motion.

The automatic stay gives the debtor protection from its creditors, subject to the oversight of the bankruptcy judge, and brings all of the debtor's assets and creditors into the same forum, the bankruptcy court, where the rights of all concerned can be balanced.

The automatic stay does not stop the following: criminal proceedings; actions for a family support order or the modification of such an order; actions to collect support from property that is not property of the estate; a tax audit, demand for tax returns or assessment of tax (collection of tax is still stayed; the tax authorities, to their chagrin, are subject to the stay, just like other creditors).

The automatic stay remains in effect until a judge lifts it at the request of a creditor, the debtor gets a discharge, or the item of property is no longer property of the estate.
- **Confirmation hearing.** The debtor must attend this hearing before the judge, wherein all oral and/or written objections to the plan are addressed and the bankruptcy judge either approves or denies the debtor's plan of reorganization or repayment.
- **Discharge.** This is an order of the court releasing the debtor from personal liability for certain debts. It stops the creditors from taking any action against the debtor, or its unsecured and/or non-exempt property, to collect the debt.

The trustee or a creditor may object to the discharge within 60 days following the first meeting of creditors. Under normal circumstances, if no objections are filed, the court will grant a discharge after the 60 days have expired. If a debtor is denied a discharge, it will continue to owe the debts as if the bankruptcy had not been filed.

Examples of reasons for a denial of discharge are as follows: fraud, concealment of assets, false information and/or statements, refusal to obey court orders, intentional injury or damage to others, embezzlement, larceny, theft, government and criminal fines, and debts not listed in the bankruptcy petition.

While a discharge will eliminate the debtor's

personal liability for a debt, a co-debtor who does not file for bankruptcy will remain fully liable. Furthermore, mortgages and certain other liens pass through bankruptcy and remain valid and enforceable post-bankruptcy.

•   **Meeting of creditors (also known as a "341 Meeting", based on US Bankruptcy Code 11 USC Section 341).** The debtor must attend this meeting, at which a trustee and creditors ask questions under oath regarding the debtor's finances. The debtor must respond in good faith. This meeting generally occurs one month after the initial filing of a Chapter 7, Chapter 11, or Chapter 13 (individual debt adjustment) bankruptcy petition.

In a bankruptcy, the parties that often have the most to lose and the least leverage in protecting their interests are the unsecured creditors. Understanding that, Congress incorporated into the Bankruptcy Code a mandate in Section 1102(a)(1) for the establishment of a committee representative of this creditor class.

Committee members are appointed by the United States Trustee and usually selected based on answers to a questionnaire sent to the 20 largest unsecured creditors. The law does not set the number of participants, but committees typically consist of three to nine members.

•   **Petition.** This is the legal instrument filed with the bankruptcy court that initiates a bankruptcy proceeding. A company may file its petition in the jurisdiction (i) where it is incorporated; (ii) where it has had a residence, principal place of business or principal assets for at least 180 days; or (iii) where a bankruptcy case of an affiliate is pending. In certain circumstances, an entity's creditors may file a bankruptcy petition for the entity. This is referred to as an involuntary petition.

•   **Plan of reorganization.** A debtor's detailed description of how the debtor proposes to pay creditors' claims over a fixed period of time. The debtor has 120 days to file a plan, otherwise known as the "period of exclusivity".

•   **Preference or preferential debt payment.** This is a payment, made to a creditor in the 90-day period before a debtor files bankruptcy (or within one year if the creditor was an insider), that gives the creditor more than it would receive in a Chapter 7 case.

•   **Priority.** This is the Bankruptcy Code's statutory ranking of unsecured claims, which determines the order in which they will be paid if there is not enough money to pay all unsecured claims in full. For example, under the Bankruptcy Code's priority scheme, money owed to the case trustee or for pre-petition alimony and/or child support must be paid in full before any general unsecured debt (for example, trade or credit card debt).

•   **Secured claim.** The creditor has a lien or mortgage on the debtor's collateral.

•   **Trustee.** This is a representative appointed by the court to examine the assets of the debtor for the benefit of payment to creditors.

•   **Unsecured claim.** The creditor has no collateral to secure its claims.

Sequence of events in a traditional Chapter 11 reorganization

Once a company files for bankruptcy protection, it becomes a debtor or debtor in possession and an automatic stay immediately goes into effect. The bankruptcy court provides notices to all creditors advising of the filing and a "341 meeting". The US Trustee conducts the meeting. The US Trustee is assigned to review the petition and oversee the case and related reporting requirements, as well as conduct due diligence.

While the company is executing its restructuring objectives, the secured creditors, unsecured creditors, other stakeholders and the management negotiate the final form of the plan of reorganization. Once this is accomplished, the company files the final plan and associated disclosure statement with the court. These documents must provide the "adequate information" needed by creditors to make an evaluation and vote on the plan. If a minimum number of acceptances is achieved among the company's creditor classes, the debtor will solicit court approval for the plan.

Shortly after this, the company will emerge from Chapter 11 as a reorganized company, its pre-petition debt officially discharged and a new debt and equity structure in place.

Coping with the challenges of Chapter 11

Managing a company through a Chapter 11 restructuring can be very challenging. Initially, the process means more work for what will already be a stressed organization, requiring extra effort to manage key customer and supplier relationships, the creditor committees, lenders and the media.

After the first-day motions are approved, they need to be implemented swiftly and accurately to maximize the benefits of Chapter 11. Additionally, several reporting requirements and information requests need to be satisfied during the case. For larger organizations, managing all this under the umbrella of a restructuring office will ensure compliance and adherence to deadlines, while keeping the professional fees in check. The

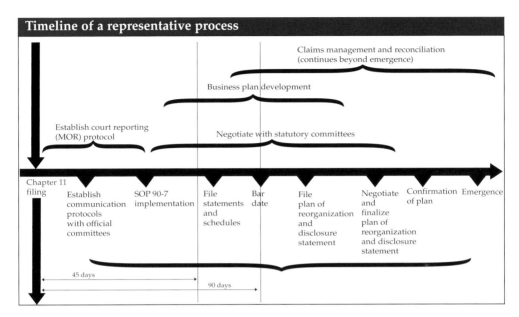

Timeline of a representative process

following are a few examples of key Chapter 11 concepts and workstreams.

Pre-petition versus post-petition

At the time of a Chapter 11 filing, two periods are established: pre- and post-petition. Assuming a filing date of 12/31/09, these periods are as follows:

• **Pre-petition** consists of all activities and obligations incurred through the close of business on 12/30/09.
• **Post-petition** consists of all activities and obligations incurred from 12/31/09 until the company emerges from bankruptcy.

Pre-petition invoices or obligations are generally "frozen". As of the petition date, the company is given relief from these payments and they cannot be paid without court approval or until the company emerges from Chapter 11.

Post-petition invoice or obligation payments will be made in accordance with historical or established payment terms. Goods and service providers typically receive limited protection in the form of elevated priority if the case is converted to a Chapter 7 (liquidation).

Post-petition supplier management

After a Chapter 11 filing, the company will need to preserve liquidity by negotiating aggressively for post-petition trade credit with its suppliers. At this stage, the debtor may well experience product and service "hostage" situations that threaten operational performance, a high volume of supplier calls, and suppliers seeking to cut trade credit dramatically and perhaps requesting critical payments. A structured communications program needs to be developed to ensure that accurate information is provided to suppliers in a timely way and their questions and concerns are answered.

The benefits of a well thought-out supplier management plan include the preservation of working capital, avoidance of delays or stoppages in products or services, and the prevention or limitation of post-petition price increases.

Rejection or assumption of contracts or leases

One of the rights afforded to debtors under the Bankruptcy Code is the ability to reject unfavorable executory contracts — where some or all of the obligations of each party have not yet been completed — and unexpired leases. Particular points to note are as follows:

• Executory contracts or leases may be viewed as unfavorable if the amounts being paid by the debtor are above market rates or if the property being leased is no longer used.
• In some cases, longstanding purchase orders have been interpreted as representing executory contracts.
• Termination clauses relating to a company's

insolvency, financial condition or filing for bankruptcy are effectively rendered unenforceable under the Bankruptcy Code. Contractual provisions prohibiting assumption or assignment by the debtor or trustee are also invalidated.

• When an executory contract or unexpired lease is rejected, a pre-petition unsecured claim for damages is created.

• Damages associated with the rejection of an unexpired real estate lease are limited to the larger amount of one year's rent or the rent for 15 per cent of the remaining term. Should the remaining term exceed 20 years, an outside limit of three years' rent becomes effective.

• Executory contracts and unexpired leases that are not rejected must be assumed, often with more favorable terms, by the debtor, in which case the following conditions must be fulfilled: (i) curing any monetary default or provide assurance of prompt cure; (ii) paying or assuring payment for actual pecuniary damage; and (iii) giving adequate assurance of future performance.

Liquidation analysis

In all plans of reorganization, recovery under the plan must be compared to any value that creditors would receive under a hypothetical Chapter 7 liquidation. The plan cannot be confirmed if liquidation would yield a greater return.

The company will need to prepare a liquidation model that values its assets and potential creditor payouts under both liquidation and reorganization scenarios. In this analysis, the proceeds from a hypothetical liquidation are then used to pay down claims according to the absolute priority rule, with any surplus funds staying with the debtor, which is very rare.

This analysis is often used to negotiate consideration with the various constituencies to show the downside versus a plan of reorganization.

Bankruptcy reporting requirements

The Schedule of Assets and Liabilities (SOAL) and Statement of Financial Affairs (SOFA) represent a one-time reporting event early in the case. Typically, they are filed by legal entity, which can cause challenges in the finance and accounting area as traditional GAAP or internal reports are not by legal entity.

Monthly Operating Reports (MORs) are to be filed within 15 days of each month-end. The US Trustee requires that the debtor prepare certain monthly financial reports for each debtor entity. These may include the following:

• Balance sheet and income statement.
• Statement of cash receipts and disbursements.
• Statement of aged receivables and statement of aged payables, including activity.
• Tax receipts and proof of insurance coverage (including director and officer insurance).

In addition to the reporting requirements established by the courts, the lending group and creditor constituents will require the debtor to provide weekly reporting packs that may include updated 13-week cash-flow projections, reconciliation of bank accounts, and "flash reports" that highlight and explain any variances between the projected financial and operational performance and actual results.

Conclusion

Managing a traditional Chapter 11 reorganization requires hard work, communication and negotiation skills, and a willingness to work with trusted advisors. Although we have highlighted many of the benefits and examples, there is definitely a cost benefit to filing for bankruptcy protection, and it requires steadfast execution of both the pre-petition planning and post-petition workstreams. As we have discussed, the likelihood of a successful reorganization improves when you understand the entire Chapter 11 process and ensure the process leads to the endgame objective for your company.

Of course, this does not come without costs, such as the stresses imposed upon all the relationships in the capital structure, supplier and customer relations and employee morale — and perhaps a large price tag for professional services. But ultimately the bankruptcy process — although problematic, complex and carrying high transaction costs — can preserve and restore enterprise value.

32

Asset dispositions in Chapter 11: Whether to sell through Section 363 or a plan of reorganization

Corinne Ball, Partner and
Leader of the Global
Restructuring Practice,
Jones Day

Virtually every Chapter 11 debtor faces a change in control of its business that will be effected through a sale or a reorganization plan. Most debtors, however, do not have sufficient value to pay all claims in full, so at least some creditors are likely to suffer a loss. Under most Chapter 11 plans, pre-petition equity is likely to be diluted, if not extinguished and replaced, with equity issued to creditors or "new money" investors. A sale — which can be effected through a plan sale or independently under Section 363 of the Bankruptcy Code — can provide for the transfer of the going concern to a buyer, leaving the distribution of the proceeds to be accomplished under a Chapter 11 plan. The buyer may be independent but may also be the holder of claims, particularly secured ones, against the company. Of course, the debtor can pursue its restructuring through a series of sales of excess or non-core assets under Section 363, leaving the core business to be reorganized under Chapter 11.

Introduction

Using Section 363 enables the Chapter 11 debtor and the buyer to separate the sale of assets and assignment of contracts from the distribution of proceeds and the realization of losses. A Section 363 sale can only be initiated by a debtor and requires approval by the court after notice and hearing. A plan sale can only be effected following a class vote of the creditors solicited upon a court-approved disclosure statement with adequate information to enable them to make a reasonably informed judgment about the Chapter 11 plan. It must be demonstrated that at least one class has accepted the plan and that each creditor will receive more than they would in liquidation, and there must be safeguards such as protection for any dissenting classes. The voting threshold is acceptance of the plan by creditors representing two-thirds in amount, and a majority in number, of all claims in the class.

The determination to sell all or a portion of its business is driven by the debtor's duty to maximize values for the creditors and its estate. Often, debtors cannot reorganize their operations on a standalone basis because they need new capital, and that can be hard to raise if the company has little or nothing in the way of unencumbered assets and faces a senior secured lender or a syndicate and, perhaps, some junior secured lenders. Moreover, these lenders may impose severe restrictions upon a debtor's access to cash to fund continued business operations, in turn placing time constraints on the process to find an investor or buyer.

There are factors that point to a going concern sale and others pointing to investment under a reorganization plan. Some key elements to consider are:

- The time and cash needed to operate through a plan, versus the time and cash requirements for a sale process, which is shorter.
- Whether existing creditors, especially secured ones, will decide to exit or to stay and provide the necessary capital infusion.
- Whether the debtor's revenue and operating cost structure is strong

enough to survive aspects of the plan process such as environmental obligations, collective bargaining agreements, pension and other legacy obligations, material executory contracts and leases requiring immediate attention. On the other hand, some of the debtor's assets or operations — intellectual property licenses, joint ventures or other complex structures — may be better addressed through a plan of reorganization.

• The tax attributes — because preservation of these and avoidance of transfer taxes usually favor a plan approach.

• The effect that offshore, non-debtor subsidiary or affiliate operations may have on a sale or plan, which includes assessing their ongoing capital needs. The key will be to examine how the subsidiary or affiliate's value is best maximized.

• Is the whole of the business worth more than the sum of the parts?

The debtor must consider all these factors to determine whether a standalone plan is a realistic option. If it is decided that a sale is a better alternative, then it must be demonstrated that this will provide more value than a liquidation or standalone plan. Actions undertaken by a Chapter 11 debtor prior to commencing its case, if sufficiently rigorous, will show it is discharging its duty to maximize the value of the estate for creditors and shareholders — and justify the preliminary selection of a buyer prior to any court-supervised process. In any such selection, however, the buyer ought to anticipate that it will be subjected to some kind of auction — which, at a minimum, will serve as a public "post market" check on the sale process.

Once the debtor has concluded that new capital is only available through a sale transaction, the question becomes which course of action will best achieve the objective of maximizing value while still complying with the Bankruptcy Code. That is, should the debtor conduct a Section 363 sale or a plan sale?

Section 363 sales

A sale pursuant to Section 363(b) of the Bankruptcy Code permits the debtor to sell assets outside the ordinary course of business. Before this can occur, notice is given to the creditors and a hearing is held to assess whether the debtor has taken the necessary measures to ensure the assets are being sold to the bidder with the highest and best offer. "Highest and best", however, does not necessarily mean the highest price. In many instances, the sale can be structured as "free and clear" of all liens,

claims, encumbrances and interests under Section 363(f) of the Bankruptcy Code. Historically, qualifications for "free and clear" sales have been based upon: (i) consent from the lienholder under Section 363(f)(2); (ii) selling at a price reflecting market value under 363(f)(3); (iii) an interest being the subject of a bona fide dispute under 363(f)(4); and (iv) the ability to compel an entity with an interest to accept a money satisfaction under Section 363(f)(5).

The court in *Clear Channel Outdoor Inc v Knupfer* raised an issue with sales at market value and essentially limited free and clear sales to the rare situation in which the sale price exceeds the stated amount of debt secured rather than the majority view that getting a market value price meets the free and clear requirements. Even in that jurisdiction, the utility of Section 363 free and clear sales is still recognized even if a lienholder objects to the sale by relying upon Section 363(f).

Courts also rely upon consent under the emerging "collective action" doctrine based upon the contracts governing secured lending syndicates, as was the case in *In re Chrysler*. In that circumstance, although a syndicate may have numerous lenders, courts have construed the contracts for loan and security agreements as authorizing the syndicate's agent, post default, to act upon the instruction of a specified percentage of the lenders in exercising remedies, including assenting to Section 363 sales. In *Chrysler*, some minority lenders attempted to object to a free and clear sale. However, they could not prevail where the contracts allowed the agent, following such collective instruction, to consent to the free and clear sale.

Unless a court orders otherwise, lienholders are permitted to credit bid for a debtor's assets at Section 363 sales, which means they may bid up to the nominal amount of their lien and offset their claim against the purchase price. Credit bidding allows lienholders to protect themselves if they determine that the price offered is less than the collateral value. This is also an area where the collective action doctrine has been recognized, with courts permitting credit bidding by an agent despite the existence of dissenting members in the secured lending syndicate. The continuing vitality of the collective action doctrine will, of course, be subject to the terms of the contracts governing syndicates.

A Section 363 sale is not intended to supplant a reorganization because, upon completion, the liens on the debtor's assets attach to the sale proceeds and remain with the estate for distribution to creditors pursuant to the plan of reorganization that will be filed after the Section 363 sale has concluded. Additionally, the plan of reorganization is not supplanted because it will still govern the disposal of the assets that were not purchased through the Section 363 sale.

Disposing of essentially all a debtor's assets pursuant to Section 363 may open the debtor to attack on the grounds that the sale is a *sub rosa* plan that impermissibly disenfranchises creditors. The objectors argue the sale: (i) supplants and essentially determines the provisions of a plan; (ii) provides for the distribution of estate property to creditors outside a plan; and (iii) implements an irreversible decision — to sell all or substantially all of the assets — that should be subject to creditor approval rather than that of the bankruptcy court. A Section 363 sale can raise concerns when a management team — put in place by, and potentially answering to, "out of the money" equity — comes to the bankruptcy court with a buyer in hand seeking an expedited sale, potentially placing a substantial burden on the bankruptcy judge to approve a sale over creditor objections. Those concerns must be addressed by a clear demonstration that the debtor's sale decision is the product of a diligent management discharging its duty to maximize value for the creditors.

Such demonstration should include extraordinary efforts to inform the judge and the creditors of the facts that have led the debtor to determine that a sale is the best course of action available. This will entail a well-prepared process in which bidders can obtain diligence materials and participate in a sale process, creating a level playing field for other potential buyers. The sale process should also include reasonable access to both key management and other witnesses who can testify in support of the sale and the circumstances leading to it, with expert reports and any liquidation analyses being made available. Ideally, the buyer should also be available to testify and explain the terms of the deal, including any deadlines.

In all, the record before the bankruptcy court should establish that the debtor's decision to pursue a sale outside a plan of reorganization is justified by the specific facts and circumstances. For example, a debtor could show its assets are rapidly deteriorating in value and it has no source of cash for continuing operations beyond the sale process timeframe. If cash resources are limited, it is incumbent on the debtor to conduct a realistic process that maximizes value. Simply operating until a debtor runs out of cash in an attempt to get

to a plan confirmation is not an adequate or responsible reaction. On the contrary, companies in this position may have to move decisively towards a sale process. Recent examples of Section 363 sales of substantially all of a debtor's assets under very urgent conditions are *Bethlehem, Chrysler, General Motors, Lehman Brothers* and *Metaldyne*.

A Section 363 sale typically involves the following steps.

Notice

Under bankruptcy rules 6004 and 2002(a)(2), at least 21 days' notice is required, though it may be possible to shorten this period if there is just cause. Moreover, local rules must also be met, particularly with sale motions brought in the very early stages of a case. Lastly, timeframes for sales are very dependent upon any additional steps that may be appropriate to ensure the debtor is satisfying its duty to maximize values. The sale motion will seek not only approval of the sale itself, but also of the auction process and bidding procedures.

Selection of a stalking-horse bidder

The debtor and its financial advisors market the business and negotiate the terms of a purchase agreement with a potential buyer, the idea being that this initial bid will put a floor under the offers made at an auction. This process may occur before a bankruptcy filing is even contemplated, or it may come after the filing. If a purchase agreement is negotiated in advance, the buyer will often require that the business file for bankruptcy protection. A stalking-horse bidder, however, is not required for a Section 363 sale and a debtor will occasionally conduct "naked auctions", though this may be perceived as a sign of a failed marketing process and may have the unintended result of discouraging bids and suppressing the value of the assets.

Bidding procedures

The bidding procedures determine, among other things, who can participate in the auction and on what terms, how competing bids will be assessed and the ramifications for the debtor of selecting a bidder other than the stalking horse. The following terms are often included in these procedures: (i) a definition of who is a qualified bidder; (ii) a bid deadline and proposed auction date; (iii) overbid requirements; (iv) minimum bid requirements; (v) criteria for determining which bid is the highest and best; (vi) an expense reimbursement and break-up fee for the stalking horse if its bid is topped; and (vii) auction rules.

Objections to bidding procedures may allege that the proposed sale is improper, the timeline is too short, the buyer is acting in bad faith because insiders are involved with the stalking horse's bid, or that the proposed procedures inappropriately favor the stalking horse and will, therefore, chill the bidding in the auction process. Typically, the stalking horse's purchase agreement will provide that it can be terminated by the buyer if the bidding procedures are not timely approved by the bankruptcy court. If a buyer seriously wants break-up fees, it is also critical that the purchase agreement provides that court approval of the fees is a condition to the effectiveness of the buyer's obligations.

Sale hearing

After the auction is concluded, the debtor presents the successful bid to the bankruptcy court for approval. If the judge determines that the process has been conducted in a fair manner and obtained the highest and best offer for the debtor's assets, an order will be issued approving the sale and conveying the assets to the buyer free and clear of any liens. "Highest and best" is broadly defined to include considerations such as certainty and speed of closing, the liquidity of the offer and, potentially, other intangible economic benefits to the estate. A bankruptcy court will typically defer to the debtor's discretion in choosing the successful bidder, especially if the key creditors support the decision.

Stay of the sale order and statutory "mootness"

Unless a stay of the sale order is obtained, Section 363(m) provides that 'the reversal or modification on appeal of the authorization of a sale under [Section 363(b)] does not affect the validity of the sale' to a "good faith" purchaser. This provision means that there is no appellate jurisdiction for an "unstayed" sale order, except to examine the buyer's good faith.

Recently, in *In re Westpoint Stevens*, the Court of Appeals for the Second Circuit unequivocally held that under Section 363(m), in the absence of a stay, it lacked appellate jurisdiction to review the entire sale order — not just the actual transaction. The Court of Appeals was clear that Section 363(m) protects the sale and the sale order provisions, including all the terms and conditions of the sale, from appeal once the sale closes. To give objectors time to get a stay pending appeal, the bankruptcy rules provide that authorization for a sale under Section 363 is stayed for 14 days unless the court orders otherwise.

Often the buyer will insist that a debtor, as part of its sale motion, seek a waiver or shortening of the stay provided by Bankruptcy Rule 6004(h) so it can proceed promptly to closing the sale and more quickly attain the protection of Section 363(m).

Overview of asset sales via a plan of reorganization

A bankruptcy case is brought to its conclusion by the confirmation of a plan of liquidation or a plan of reorganization. The former provides for the distribution of assets to creditors, while the ultimate goal of the latter is the reorganization of the debtor as a new entity, with a new capital structure and, likely, new owners. A plan of reorganization may result in the entity obtaining exit financing and issuing new debt and equity securities to creditors or new investors in exchange for their claims, cash or other considerations.

A plan must first be accepted by at least one class of impaired creditors, following solicitation with a court-approved disclosure statement, before moving on to a bankruptcy court hearing where approval will be granted after the plan proponents establish that the plan meets confirmation requirements including: that it is feasible; that the value to be distributed to each creditor is greater than what they would receive in a liquidation; and that there are other, adequate safeguards such as protection for dissenting classes of impaired creditors.

A plan of reorganization could be used to effect a sale of all or parts of a debtor's business in a variety of ways:

• It could provide that a designated buyer would purchase assets in exchange for cash, the assumption of specified liabilities or some other consideration, which would then be distributed to the creditors.
• It could provide that the debtor would issue new equity and perhaps new debt to creditors in satisfaction of their claims. By converting the pre-petition debt and other liabilities into equity, the debtor is in effect selling the businesses to the creditors.
• The plan could provide that "new money" investors (which may include existing creditors) contribute cash or other consideration in exchange for some or all of the reorganized debtor's equity. The proceeds are then distributed to creditors.

The plan confirmation process can be very long and cumbersome, mainly because a plan of reorganization disposes of all claims against the estate, which provides ample opportunities for creditor disputes. Generally, a plan involves the following steps:

Formulation

During its exclusive period, which may last as long as 18 months from the bankruptcy filing date, only the debtor may propose a plan of reorganization. A plan premised upon a sale is often a product of negotiation between the debtor, representatives of creditors whose claims will likely be impaired, and "new money" investors who may also be the "buyer".

This process typically involves a great deal of valuation work that will be used to justify the adequacy of the consideration paid under the sale, as well as the treatment of various creditors' claims. If the plan contemplates "new money" investments or commitments of support from existing creditors, agreements governing those matters will be negotiated on a parallel track.

Once the plan is finalized, it is filed with the bankruptcy court, and in order to provide assurance that the plan is feasible, there may also be provisions for exit financing or acquisition financing for the buyer.

Preparing the disclosure statement

The Bankruptcy Code requires that votes in favor of a plan be solicited by a debtor using a disclosure statement, which not only describes the treatment of creditors but also assesses analyses supporting the feasibility of the plan and the related valuations. A minimum 28-day notice period for the hearing on the adequacy of the disclosure statement is required under Bankruptcy Rule 3017.

Hearing to approve disclosure statement

The bankruptcy court hearing often provides an opportunity for dissenters to voice their concerns about the plan sale by challenging the contents of the disclosure statement, which is mailed, together with ballots, to the debtor's creditors. The solicitation period is rarely shorter than 30 days and often much longer.

Confirmation hearing

Once the voting is complete, the bankruptcy court will hold an evidentiary hearing to determine whether the plan should be confirmed and implemented (assuming acceptance by the requisite number of votes in at least one class of impaired creditors). Again there is an opportunity for creditors or equity to be heard in opposition or support. If there is a dissenting class, the plan

proponents have extra burdens to establish that the plan does not unfairly discriminate against the dissenting class and is fair and equal.

Stay of confirmation order and equitable mootness

Under bankruptcy rules, the confirmation order is stayed for 14 days unless the court orders otherwise. Again, once a plan is consummated, including closing on any sale, mootness will attach if the actions taken cannot be undone. Generally, equitable mootness prevents effective appeal of confirmation orders unless a stay pending appeal is obtained, which may require the posting of a sizable bond in accordance with Bankruptcy Rule 8005. Thus, parties will often move quickly to consummate a plan — even to the extent of seeking a waiver or shortening of the 14-day stay imposed under Bankruptcy Rule 3020. Buyers should bear in mind, however, that equitable mootness is not nearly as broad or protective as the statutory mootness mandated for 363 sales.

Because a plan of reorganization involves multiple hearings at which every creditor of the estate may raise issues, the time required for a plan sale is impossible to predict with any degree of accuracy, particularly if the secured lenders vote to reject the plan. However, debtors can proceed with confirmation by seeking to "cram down" the plan and related sale over the objection of the secured lenders, and to this end most debtors rely upon Section 1129(b)(2)(a)(ii), which permits a cramdown through a free and clear sale of the secured lenders' collateral at an auction subject to their right to credit bid.

If the buyer is resistant to an auction and, in particular, credit bidding, the Court of Appeals for the Third Circuit recently held — in *In re Philadelphia Newspapers* — that this is not the exclusive means of confirming a plan over the objections of secured lenders. *Philadelphia Newspapers* stands for the proposition that the debtor may seek to confirm a plan premised upon a free and clear sale of assets by establishing that it provides dissenting lenders with the "indubitable equivalent" of their collateral. In *Philadelphia Newspapers*, the debtor is going forward with its confirmation hearing to establish that its dissenting lenders are receiving the indubitable equivalent of their claims through a plan premised upon a free and clear sale at an auction where credit bidding is not permitted.

A plan sale, even under the most perfect circumstances, might be completed up to 90 days after the filing of the plan. The process can be shortened with a "prepackaged" or "preapproved" reorganization where the plan has been fully negotiated, documented and accepted by the requisite creditors before the debtor even files for bankruptcy protection. These approaches will likely take around 45 days from the date of the petition because the confirmation hearing requires at least 28 days' notice and the confirmation order is stayed for 14 days.

Recent examples of plan sales include *Lear Corporation, Magna Entertainment Corp* and *Solutia*. Interestingly, in *Delphi*, a proposed plan sale that was not going to be subject to auction and credit bidding was modified following objections from secured lenders. Ultimately, these lenders mounted a successful credit bid for the auto parts maker.

Common benefits of plan sales and Section 363 sales

Both plan and Section 363 sales offer a number of benefits to debtors:

• Assets can be acquired selectively and transferred to the buyer free and clear of liens and unwanted liabilities.

• Contracts can be assumed (in most cases regardless of anti-assignment provisions) selectively. Undesirable contracts are rejected and become unsecured claims against the debtor's estate. Notably, the prospect of rejection often motivates contract counterparties to agree to modifications.

• A sale is supervised and approved by the bankruptcy court, and debtors and asset purchasers can rely upon the integrity of the process, which provides a forum and rules for resolving disputes and assessing competing bids. In this way, the debtor's board and management are protected from creditor and shareholder claims concerning breach of fiduciary duty, fraudulent conveyance and the like.

• Consideration for either a plan or Section 363 sale can be cash (as was the case in *Chrysler*), securities (*Westpoint Stevens*), credit bidding (*Delphi* and *Metaldyne*) or any combination of these. So long as the purchaser is providing the debtor with the highest and best value for the assets, particularly where the assets are subject to multiple levels of liens, the bankruptcy court should approve the transaction.

Advantages of a Section 363 sale

When comparing a Section 363 sale to a plan sale, however, a Section 363 sale offers significant advantages from a buyer's perspective over a plan sale and, in most cases, a Section 363 sale will be the preferred method for buying a debtor's assets during the bankruptcy proceeding. These advantages include:

• **Speed**. A Section 363 sale can be accomplished in as few as 30 days, while a plan sale can take months. In most cases this is reason enough to go down the 363 route, assuming the bankruptcy judge can be convinced that circumstances justify this course, which should be a safe assumption if the debtor desires to sell a discrete business that could not be classified as substantially all its assets. If, however, the intention is to sell substantially all the assets and the debtor cannot make a convincing case that the value will dissipate if a lengthy process is required, the debtor may be forced to conduct a plan sale.

• **Control**. Although the bankruptcy court will always play a supervisory role and will scrutinize the process in hindsight, the debtor has great latitude to run the Section 363 sale as it deems appropriate. For example, it can entertain bids for different configurations of assets and liabilities, it can combine bids, it can prescribe rules limiting the types of consideration that may be offered, it can dictate timing and can abandon the process entirely. Plan sales do not offer the same degree of control and flexibility because they are very complex and, by their nature, require creditor participation. The debtor may also lose control of this process because, once its exclusivity period expires, creditors have the authority to propose a plan of reorganization or liquidation and solicit support for it.

• **Competition**. Section 363 sales are designed to foster competition for assets. While plan sales can be structured to include a competitive process, transactions typically take place in the context of a sometimes contentious resolution of multiple creditor claims and disputes. The barriers to effective competition are high because proposals need to provide a solution for all creditor constituents. In contrast, all a bidder needs to do to compete in a Section 363 sale is to comply with the bidding procedures order, which usually requires the bidder to sign a confidentiality agreement, provide evidence of the wherewithal to purchase the assets, and appear at the auction.

• **Simplicity**. In a Section 363 sale, the main focus of the court is on being satisfied that the process used to market and auction the debtor's assets has been designed and implemented so as to obtain the highest and best offer. This is a relatively simple goal to achieve and, once the sale order is entered, the buyer can purchase the assets, rely upon the sale order and walk away. A Section 363 sale is much more straightforward than a plan sale because it separates the purchase and transfer of the assets from the distribution of the proceeds. In contrast, a plan sale can become bogged down in issues that are essentially unrelated to the sale of the assets — the resolution of claims of unsecured or trade creditors, state, local and federal government entities, and expensive and expansive litigation. As a result, purchasers will often have to consider buying out creditor constituencies that may have the power to hold up confirmation.

• **Maximization of value**. In most cases, these Section 363 advantages permit buyers to pay more for the assets than would be the case in a plan sale. But so long as the debtor is able to show there is no realistic alternative that would provide greater value, a bankruptcy court should approve the sale.

• **Certainty of closing**. As a corollary to the timing and complexity differences, a Section 363 sale presents less execution risk for a debtor than a plan sale. Section 363 agreements typically contain limited representations and warranties, simplified closing conditions and virtually no post-closing exposure. As a result, once the sale order is entered, the transaction should close quickly and easily.

Are there advantages to plan sales?

The plan sale is, of course, the default option for debtors when a Section 363 sale cannot be justified because of the nature of the assets to be sold or other compelling circumstances.

In addition, plan sales are always more appropriate when the sale of a debtor's business is part of an overall reorganization — in other words, the byproduct of a reorganization rather than its objective.

A plan sale may also be preferable where the restructuring calls for a distribution of debt and equity to the creditors or those that have provided new capital. In that circumstance, a Section 363 sale may not be an appropriate method for reorganizing the debtor, either because the business is too large to be auctioned effectively or because a buyer is neither interested in nor would be able to finance a purchase of the entire business.

In such cases, the best way to maximize recovery for creditors may simply be to transfer the debtor's business to its creditors and capital providers through a plan sale.

Given recent developments, a plan sale may

also be preferable for a buyer that does not want to be subject to an auction process or credit bidding.

And under a plan, of course, there may be far more flexibility in respect of preservation of tax attributes and avoiding transfer taxes. This was demonstrated by *Charter Communications*, and the continuing role of its controlling shareholder, where creditors essentially took over that company through a plan that, by retaining an equity role for its controlling shareholder, also preserved substantial and valuable attributes.

Conclusion

Whether to dispose of assets through a Section 363 sale or a plan of reorganization is a complicated decision that requires officers and directors to weigh the pros and cons of each against the company's individualized restructuring objectives. Directors and officers should obtain the advice of expert restructuring professionals to assess the available alternatives and formulate a sales transaction that is tailored to the unique set of facts and circumstances faced by their particular companies.

33

How, why and when creditors may credit bid their debt for your company

Keith A Simon, Partner and member of the Finance Department and Insolvency Practice Group,

Latham & Watkins LLP

When a company is trying to restructure its debt and maintain its "going concern" value for the benefit of creditors, one approach very often pursued is a sale of substantially all of its assets. In Chapter 11 cases, this process is almost always conducted pursuant to Section 363 of the Bankruptcy Code as opposed to a plan of reorganization. Applicable case law is very clear that directors and officers of the selling company have a fiduciary duty to obtain the highest or otherwise best offer for its assets for the benefit of its estate and creditors.

If the potential bidders are offering to conduct the transaction in cash, the analysis is not usually too difficult: the winning bidder should be the one who will pay the highest net purchase price for the assets. There may of course be other factors to consider, such as the amount and scope of assumed liabilities and the speed and certainty of closing the sale, but ultimately this will be a straightforward cash transaction.

In many cases, however, one or more of the potential bidders will be holders of secured debt of the selling company. Accordingly, they will make an offer comprised partly of cash and partly a "credit bid" of their debt. To add to the complexity of this type of transaction, the bidder may merely be one lender in a syndicate or perhaps a newly created limited liability company that is wholly owned by a subset of lenders in the syndicate. In such situations, can these lenders still credit bid their secured claims? What happens if other members of the syndicate refuse to participate? How are these "non-credit bidding lenders" treated? Furthermore, what if the interests and liens that secure such claims are held by a collateral agent for the benefit of the whole syndicate? Can an individual lender credit bid at all?

The basics of credit bidding

What exactly are credit bids and why are they permitted?
Section 363(k) of the Bankruptcy Code states the following:

> 'At a sale... of property that is subject to a lien that secures an allowed claim, unless the court for cause orders otherwise, the holder of such claim may bid at such sale, and, if the holder of such claim purchases such property, such holder may offset such claim against the purchase price of such property.'

In answering 'what is a credit bid?', the key phrase is 'may offset such claim against the purchase price'. At its core, Section 363(k) is merely a setoff mechanism, designed to create efficiency. For example, assume a company is selling a widget that is subject to a lien securing $100 owed to a single lender. After conducting an open auction pursuant to Section 363, the company determines that the secured lender has made the highest and best offer for the widget at a proposed purchase price of $115. The parties could complete the sale as follows: (i) the lender pays the company $115 for the widget; (ii) the company transfers the widget to the lender; (iii) the company transfers $100 of the $115 purchase price back to the lender as proceeds of its collateral (the widget); and (iv) the lender reduces its outstanding secured claim against the company to $0.00 since it has been paid $100. Thus, in the end, the secured lender receives the widget and reduces its claim, and the company keeps the excess $15. Looked at this way, it is clearly much more efficient for the lender to structure its offer as a credit bid and to pay only the $15 excess to the company.

Such an arrangement also provides a secured lender with protection against attempts to sell its collateral too cheaply. Thus, if it believes that its collateral is worth more than the proposed purchase price, it may credit bid its debt and take title to the property. Moreover, applicable case law is generally clear that a secured lender may credit bid the entire face amount of its allowed claim and that its bid is neither limited by the alleged economic value of its collateral nor by the amount that it may have paid to acquire the claim.

The power of a credit bid is magnified if the secured claim was purchased at a discount, because the lender can still credit bid a full dollar's worth of the debt even if less than a dollar was paid to acquire it. For example, assume the lender described above had bought its $100 claim for only 25 cents on the dollar ($25 in the aggregate): the $115 purchase price offered by the lender would really only cost it $40 in the aggregate (the $25 paid to acquire the $100 claim, plus the $15 excess). Alternatively, if a third party purchased the widget for $115 in cash, then the company would transfer $100 to the lender as proceeds — with the lender earning a 300 per cent return on its investment (the $100 less the $25 paid to acquire the claim).

Who can make a credit bid?

The illustrations above represent the most straightforward type of credit bid transaction because there is only one lender holding both the claim and the lien securing the claim. In syndicated transactions, however, while each lender has a claim against the assets of a company, the lien is almost always held by a collateral agent for the benefit of all members of the syndicate. Does this mean that only the agent can make a credit bid? The answer is no: each lender can still make a credit bid in the amount of secured debt that it holds. This comes directly from Section 363(k) and its statement that 'the holder of such claim may bid at such sale' and 'such holder may offset such claim against the purchase price of such property'. The

only reference to the lien is in the introductory phrase — 'at a sale of property that is subject to a lien that secures an allowed claim'. This merely establishes when a credit bid may be made; it does not impose restrictions on who can make it.

Thus, the Bankruptcy Code makes it clear that the holder of a claim can credit bid for its collateral so long as (i) such claim is 'allowed' and (ii) the property being sold is 'subject to a lien'.

This leads to the next question: if the right to credit bid belongs to each individual secured lender, can the collateral agent ever make a credit bid on behalf of the lending syndicate? The answer is yes —but not because of Section 363(k). Rather, the agent may have been authorized by the lenders to make a credit bid as part of the collateral documents to which they are all bound. This is discussed more fully later.

What is the general treatment for the "non-credit bidding" lenders?

The above analysis shows that each lender in a syndicate is able to make a credit bid. But what happens to the claims held by members of the syndicate that are not part of the credit bid?

The answer is that each must receive the same net paydown of debt as the credit bidding lender. This conclusion is not contained in Section 363(k) but is dictated by the terms of the credit agreement to which all lenders are bound. Specifically, in syndicated transactions, it is almost universal for the lenders to agree to "*pro rata* treatment" of their debt obligations. Two samples of this *pro rata* sharing language are provided below:

> **Sharing of payments by lenders**. 'If any Lender shall, by exercising any right of *setoff* or counterclaim or otherwise, obtain payment in respect of any principal of or interest on any of the Loans made by it resulting in such Lender's receiving payment of a proportion of the aggregate amount of such Loans and accrued interest thereon greater than its Pro Rata Share thereof as provided herein, then the Lender receiving such greater proportion shall (a) notify the Administrative Agent of such fact, and (b) purchase (for cash at face value) participations in the Loans of the other Lenders, or make such other adjustments as shall be equitable, so that the benefit of all such payments shall be shared by the Lenders ratably in accordance with their respective Pro Rata Share.'

Sharing of payments. 'Any Lender exercising a right to *setoff* shall purchase for cash (and the other Lenders shall sell) interests in each of such other Lender's Pro Rata Share of the Obligations as would be necessary to cause all Lenders to share the amount so set off with each other Lender in accordance with their respective Pro Rata Shares.'

For instance, assume a company owes $300 in the aggregate, and $100 individually, to three lenders. The $300 claim is secured by a lien on the sole asset of the company (the universal widget), with the lien being held by a collateral agent. If the lenders are bound by the *pro rata* sharing requirements, and if the company sells its widget for $99 in a cash transaction, each lender will receive a $33 paydown of its secured claim and will have a remaining deficiency claim of $67 against the borrower.

Because of the *pro rata* sharing requirement, the $99 of widget proceeds is divided evenly among the three lenders — $33 for each. Since each lender holds a claim for $100, the remaining deficiency claim for each lender is $67 ($100 claim less the $33 paydown).

By agreeing to such *pro rata* treatment in advance, each lender will be more motivated to maximize the return on the loan obligations as a whole, as opposed to only focusing on its individual return. This helps minimize the "race to the courthouse" risk and the pursuit of individual self-help remedies by any single lender to the detriment of the lenders as a group.

But what if the winning bidder here is Lender A in a credit bid transaction for $99? To comply with the *pro rata* sharing requirement, it must do the following: (i) pay $66 in cash to the company (which in turn will distribute $33 each to Lender B and Lender C as the proceeds of the widget); and (ii) credit bid $33 of its secured claim.

Thus, in the end, each lender will receive the same $33 paydown and have the same $67 deficiency claim.

The result is the same as compared to if Lender A just buys the widget for $99 in cash. In that case, the company will again distribute $33 to each lender — and it is inefficient for Lender A to pay $99 just to receive $33 back; it should simply offset such amounts via a credit bid and make a net payment of $66 to the company for the benefit of Lender B and Lender C.

Why would Lender A purchase the widget at all if it has to pay its *pro rata* share to its fellow lenders? The answer is that it must believe the widget is undervalued by the $99 sale price and could be sold for more in the future. In that eventuality, it will be able to keep the excess profit for itself as the *pro rata* requirement has already been satisfied by the $33 paydowns; Lender B and Lender C cannot share in the upside potential of their former collateral because any excess amounts received by Lender A are not on account of its secured claim. Rather, Lender A is being compensated for the risk of taking ownership of the collateral — a risk that Lender B and Lender C are not taking by being "cashed out" as part of the purchase by Lender A.

As another example, what if the winning bidder is a newly formed limited liability company (Newco) owned equally by Lender A and Lender B? In that case, to comply with the *pro rata* sharing requirement, Newco must do the following: (i) pay $33 cash to the company (which in turn will distribute the $33 to Lender C as the proceeds of the widget); and (ii) credit bid $66 on behalf of both Lender A and Lender B. Thus, in the end, each lender will receive a $33 paydown of its applicable secured claim and have a remaining deficiency claim of $67 against the borrower. This is the same result that would occur if Newco just paid $99 in cash for the widget, with $33 being distributed to each lender as the proceeds.

Due to the *pro rata* requirement, Lender A could not merely credit bid $99 of its secured claim. That would result in a 99 per cent recovery to itself and a 0 per cent recovery to Lender B and Lender C. Lender A could make this offer if, and only if, it also paid $198 in cash to the company (which, in turn, would distribute $99 to both Lender B and Lender C as the proceeds of the widget). Likewise, Newco could not merely credit bid $99 of the aggregate secured claims of Lender A and Lender B; that would result in a 49.5 per cent recovery for them and a 0 per cent recovery for Lender C. Newco could only credit bid $99 if it also paid $49.50 in cash to the company (which would distribute such amount to Lender C as the proceeds).

In summary, each lender can credit bid up to the amount of its applicable secured claim as long as sufficient cash is also provided so that each non-credit bidding lender in the syndicate receives the same net paydown of debt as the credit bidding lender. In such a situation, the company and all the lenders are receiving the same treatment that would apply if the winning bidder were making an all-cash offer.

Minority members of a lending syndicate — "drag-along" versus "cashout"?

In many circumstances, the usefulness of a credit bid can be significantly diminished (or perhaps even eliminated) by the requirement to pay cash to the non-credit bidding lenders — for example, if the transaction described above required a $33 million payment to each lender, as opposed to only $33. Does this mean that the non-credit bidding lenders are *always* entitled to a cash payment?

The answer is no — they may already have waived their right to this as part of the collateral documents to which the collateral agent and all lenders are bound, and likewise agreed to be "dragged along" with the majority lenders in a credit bid. While the "cashout" and "drag-along" determination will ultimately depend on the specific language in the documents (which will necessarily differ from case to case), most courts that have dealt with this issue have found that the agent can credit bid 100 per cent of the secured claims with the written direction of the "required lenders", which is normally those holding more than 50 per cent of the outstanding principal amount of the applicable loan obligations (the "majority lenders").

For example, many collateral documents contain language similar to the following with respect to the exercise of remedies by the collateral agent:

> **Code and Other Remedies**. 'If an Event of Default shall occur and be continuing, *the Collateral Agent, on behalf of the other Secured Parties, may exercise*, in addition to all other rights and remedies granted to them in this Agreement and in any other instrument or agreement securing, evidencing or relating to the Obligations, *all rights and remedies of a secured party under the Uniform Commercial Code or any other applicable law*. Without limiting the generality of the foregoing, *the Collateral Agent may* in such circumstances forthwith collect, receive, appropriate and *realize upon the Collateral*, or any part thereof, and/or may forthwith sell, lease, license, sublicense, assign, give option or options to purchase, or otherwise dispose of and deliver the Collateral or any part thereof (or contract to do any of the foregoing), in one or more parcels at public or private sale or sales, at any exchange, broker's board or office of the Collateral Agent or any Secured Party or elsewhere upon such

terms and conditions as it may deem advisable and at such prices as it may deem best, *for cash or on credit* or for future delivery without assumption of any credit risk. The *Collateral Agent or any Secured Party shall have the right upon any such public sale or sales*, and, to the extent permitted by law, upon any such private sale or sales, *to purchase the whole or any part of the Collateral so sold*.'

Bankruptcy courts have generally found this to mean that the minority lenders have previously delegated their right to credit bid to the agent (acting on the direction of the majority lenders). Specifically, the courts have found that the minority lenders have already authorized the collateral agent, on their behalf, to exercise 'all rights and remedies of a secured party under the Uniform Commercial Code or any applicable law', and that 'any applicable law' includes the Bankruptcy Code in general, and Section 363(k) in particular.

Two additional issues are very important here. First, determining that the agent can credit bid 100 per cent of the secured claims does not necessarily mean it is the highest or otherwise best offer for the company. Likewise, to the extent that the credit bidding lenders seek to acquire assets that are not part of their collateral, they must provide value for the unencumbered assets over and above their credit bid. This consideration could take the form of cash or assumed liabilities. Otherwise, they are basically acquiring the unencumbered assets for free, and it could be argued that the company should just abandon the encumbered assets to them and sell the unencumbered assets for cash to the higher and best bidder.

Second, there has yet to be a reported case on credit bidding by lender groups that has actually determined the treatment required for non-credit bidding lenders. The courts have not addressed, for example, whether they are required to receive any kind of cash payment or could instead be forced to accept equity in Newco or to enter into a shareholder agreement governing the Newco. In fact, various bankruptcy courts have expressly reserved the claims and causes of action of the non-credit bidding lenders against the collateral agent and majority lenders with respect to their treatment. Such claims and actions, to the extent filed, would presumably occur in state court since they are intra-lender disputes that do not involve the company or property of the bankruptcy estates.

Given this threat of prolonged litigation, even though the disputes would be between and among the lenders themselves, it is appropriate for companies to take these matters into account when determining which bid is the highest or otherwise best offer — to the extent the litigation risk could delay the closing of the proposed sale.

Conclusion

A credit bid is designed to create efficiency in asset sales. A secured lender is given credit for its outstanding secured claim and only pays the net difference, if any, to the company. The right to credit bid belongs to each individual lender but, pursuant to the applicable collateral documents, such right may have been previously assigned to a collateral agent for the benefit of all lenders.

The officers and directors of the selling company need to understand the issues so they can select the offer that maximizes the value of their company's assets.

The opinions expressed here are solely the opinions of the author and not of Latham & Watkins LLP or any client of Latham & Watkins LLP.

Special Focus Forum

34

The busted spinoff: lessons for directors

Todd R Snyder, Managing Director in Restructuring and Reorganization and Global Co-Head of the Automotive Sector, and Vik Jindal, Associate, **Rothschild Inc**

Corporate transactions, particularly mergers, acquisitions and restructurings, highlight the critical role served by individual directors (and, collectively, boards of directors) during times of substantial corporate change. One such form of transaction is the corporate spinoff which, by its unique nature, has periodically led to substantial failure and consequent legal challenge. Here, we examine the corporate spinoff to identify certain lessons and basic principles for application in the everyday life of directors.

Although there can be any number of permutations, for our purposes, a spinoff is broadly defined as a transaction in which a publicly traded corporate parent ("ParentCo") distributes pro rata ownership in a subsidiary, in whole or in part, to its shareholders in the form of a dividend, thereby creating a new, separately governed, publicly traded corporation of the former wholly-owned subsidiary ("SpinCo"). After the distribution, SpinCo is no longer a subsidiary of ParentCo and ParentCo's stockholders hold both the stock of ParentCo and the stock of SpinCo. Our definition takes account of the fact that spinoffs can be structured in a variety of ways including partial divestiture of ParentCo's ownership stake, or an IPO/spinoff structure where shares are sold, at some point, to new shareholders and not fully distributed to ParentCo shareholders.

Spinoffs or similar transactions add complexity and challenges to the usual array of fiduciary duties borne by directors. We can examine these complexities as a means of highlighting more standard directorial roles and responsibilities and as a means of shining some light on best practices in more ordinary circumstances.

Phases in the life of a spinoff

From a directorial point of view, the spinoff transaction can be viewed in three distinct phases, each bearing its own cautionary message about process, motivation/incentives, and likely challenges/outcomes. We propose the following three distinct phases in the life of a spinoff:

- Phase 1: Pre-transaction, or conceptualization and negotiation, phase.
- Phase 2: Post-transaction operations phase.
- Phase 3: Renegotiation or reorganization phase (to the extent necessary).

Each phase has its own dynamics that can be separately examined and evaluated. The pre-transaction phase is defined as the time when a subsidiary is first internally identified as a potential spinoff candidate up to the time at which a spinoff transaction occurs. Often, during the conceptualization and negotiation phase, business units, specified assets and identified liabilities are moved around the corporate chart to set the stage for a subsequent transaction. Accordingly, it is frequently not the case that a spinoff is of an entity that long pre-existed the transaction. Similarly, it is not uncommon to spin off disparate holdings that may have had no historic relationship. During this phase, the subsidiary is evaluated by both management and the board as a potential candidate for spinoff, as is the transaction's ability to achieve potential corporate goals such as creating "pure play" securities, separating certain businesses from unrelated risks, releasing shareholder value, and creating investor liquidity.

The appropriateness of a transaction, from an operational, governance and corporate finance/valuation perspective is determined following a rigorous analysis that is typically aided at various stages by investment bankers and lawyers. It is also at this point that the terms of a relationship between ParentCo and the prospective SpinCo are determined. Following the completion of the evaluation period, whether months or years, a decision is made regarding the feasibility and suitability of a spinoff transaction. During the first phase, ParentCo's board of directors has all of the decision-making authority and responsibility.

Once a spinoff transaction has occurred, the newly formed SpinCo enters the next phase of its corporate life, the post-transaction operations phase. During this second phase, SpinCo operates as a standalone company governed by its new board and officers whose obligations run only to SpinCo owners. The relationship between ParentCo and SpinCo, either implicitly stated or governed by executed documents, is adhered to and the business operates as an independent entity with its own governing body, separate management team and financial and operational controls.

As SpinCo's board and officers have been selected by ParentCo's board and likely worked for ParentCo pre-spin, the operating and cultural distinction between the two companies is sometimes harder to achieve than the purely formal one. It is frequently true that certain of SpinCo's directors and officers will come from the ranks of former ParentCo directors and officers. As such, the sudden (and perhaps somewhat wrenching) shift in duties frequently takes hold much more gradually than a single transaction closing date would imply. Both sets of directors and officers continue to play golf in the same clubs, frequent the same restaurants and socialize in the same circles. The historic relationships, communication, and human desire to fill expected roles come into play in subtle but meaningful ways.

Because of the fact that, during the conceptualization and negotiation phase, ParentCo's directors and officers do not necessarily have a true negotiating counterparty as they try to decide which assets and liabilities will comprise SpinCo, SpinCo is often overburdened with liabilities that ParentCo seeks to shed and under-endowed with cash-flowing businesses and valuable assets that ParentCo declines to bestow. As a result, not infrequently, a spinoff, either immediately, or more often after several years operating as an independent entity, finds that it cannot go forward in its current standalone state. This could be due to a variety of factors relating to its initial formation and/or market conditions, including ParentCo/SpinCo go-forward operational relationship issues, capital structure issues and issues arising from the structural changes as a result of the spinoff itself. In this third renegotiation/reorganization phase, SpinCo goes through a process of restructuring to alleviate these burdens, either through negotiations with ParentCo, capital providers, or other parties in interest.

The path through the phases for each potential spinoff candidate is different. Some subsidiaries never make it out of the first phase. The potential transaction is discussed and evaluated and, for a variety of reasons, the decision not to proceed is made by ParentCo somewhere along the way. Some subsidiaries successfully transition from the first to the second phase and then operate on a standalone basis in this post-transaction phase. Many spinoffs succeed as conceived and never enter into the third phase. However, some spinoffs do find themselves in a situation that necessitates a restructuring in the third phase.

Evaluating the three spinoff phases

The transition from one phase to another is typified by significant change in the structure of that subsidiary (or former subsidiary in the case of spun-off entities). Thus, in order to properly evaluate the three phases of a spinoff, directors and officers of both ParentCo and SpinCo should consider the following characteristics at each phase, as they relate to questions of enterprise risk and valuation from the perspective of the parties to whom those directors and officers owe their respective (and shifting) duties:

• What are the assets and liabilities of SpinCo? (And consequently, what are the remaining assets and liabilities of ParentCo?)
• What are the operating relationships and dependencies between SpinCo and ParentCo?
• What are the governance inter-relationships and dependencies between SpinCo and ParentCo?

The following provides some commentary on the driving issues and primary considerations in each of the three phases we have outlined above using these three important metrics. Although we are applying this evaluation structure to spinoffs in particular, this rubric can serve to delineate a consistent assessment framework for most transactional decisions encountered by directors.

Phase 1: Pre-transaction, or conceptualization and negotiation, phase

What are the assets and liabilities of SpinCo?

Prior to consummation of the spinoff transaction, at the genesis of the notion to undergo a distribution, ParentCo's directors and officers are well advised to spend ample time clearly defining the purposes and goals of the transaction, using this clear logic as a touchstone for each subsequent analysis. ParentCo must then clearly define which entity it is evaluating for spinoff, as well as the assets and liabilities that are associated with that business.

Some subsidiaries enter this process as very distinct from their corporate parents. They have separate managers, separate financial statements and sometimes even a separate financing structure. This parent/subsidiary structure is exemplified by Warren Buffett's Berkshire Hathaway, where the parent, with a staff of approximately 20, leaves the subsidiaries and their managers with a great deal of management autonomy. These subsidiaries simply report to Mr Buffett and send excess cash to the corporate parent for his subsequent reallocation.

This is highlighted in Berkshire's 2009 Annual Chairman's Letter, which states: 'We tend to let our many subsidiaries operate on their own, without our supervising and monitoring them to any degree... With our acquisition of BNSF, we now have 257,000 employees and hundreds of different operating units. We hope to have many more of each. But we will never allow Berkshire to become some monolith overrun with committees, budget presentations and multiple layers of management. Instead, we plan to operate as a collection of separately-managed medium-sized and large businesses, most of whose decision-making occurs at the operating level. Charlie [Munger, Vice Chairman] and I will limit ourselves to allocating capital, controlling enterprise risk, choosing managers and setting their compensation.'

The allocation process in focus

However, unlike the case of Berkshire Hathaway, it is often true that ParentCo has not previously examined the separation of assets and liabilities of the potential SpinCo. Quite frankly, there may have been no need to expend the effort required to do so. Most often, a subsidiary is formed, not with the intention of creating an entity for future divesture, but rather as a permanent part of the whole enterprise that may tend to evolve more organically. In those cases, the subsidiary is simply an operating business without any obviously differentiated liabilities beyond typical operating liabilities (eg accounts payable, payroll etc) — and sometimes those do not even reside at the subsidiary level. The material liabilities (debt, litigation, contractual obligations) are often in the name of ParentCo.

From this point, what occurs is the allocation of assets and liabilities between ParentCo and SpinCo. Not unlike preparation for a divorce, this allocation process can often be a contentious one and the likely result is that things will never be quite the same again once parties start down this path. Who owns what asset? Does this factory belong to ParentCo or SpinCo? How does the manager of the factory feel about the entity to which they have been allocated? As one can imagine, the internal politics of this process can be harrowing. Interestingly, managers of subsidiaries being evaluated for spinoff have anecdotally reported that as the pre-transaction phase progresses, and the separation procedures are put into place, there is an alienation process that occurs between ParentCo and those individuals associated with the subsidiary as managers are increasingly treated like outsiders.

Understanding the purpose of the spinoff

Complicating matters, the allocation of assets and liabilities between ParentCo and SpinCo must take into account the specific agenda of ParentCo, its managers and its board of directors. Every spinoff has a reason for happening — a *raison d'être*. In other words, ParentCo had a specific goal in mind when determining whether or not to spin off one of its businesses. Those goals are always focused on the needs of ParentCo and its owners, not SpinCo.

There are numerous possible reasons why a company may spin off one of its subsidiaries. For example, one reason may be to reverse a previous acquisition and diversification strategy that went poorly, with ParentCo seeking to refocus on its core business, a category to which SpinCo does not belong. Another motivation could be an adverse regulatory ruling that forces ParentCo to spin off one of its subsidiaries involuntarily. Sometimes,

ParentCo sees a net shareholder benefit because the separate entities will be valued higher than the entity taken as a whole — a notion known as "reverse synergy". Often, a conglomerate may be valued at a discount to the separate values that the market would attribute to each of its individual "pure play", faster-growth or higher-return businesses that make up the component parts of the conglomerate.

Kerr-McGee and Tronox
Sometimes, the goal of a spinoff is to create a net benefit to ParentCo at the cost of SpinCo. This desire can be realized in the allocation of assets and liabilities between ParentCo and SpinCo. For example, in 2005, Kerr-McGee Corporation, an oil and gas concern, commenced the distribution of its smaller titanium dioxide business to a new entity called Tronox Inc. Although the litigation is still pending, it has been alleged that Kerr-McGee (since acquired by Anadarko Petroleum) spun off Tronox and, in doing so, transferred a significant portion of Kerr McGee's legacy liabilities to Tronox in order to successfully rid the parent of those liabilities — perhaps in anticipation of selling the business more easily. In fact, it is alleged that Kerr-McGee only spun off the Tronox subsidiary after determining there was no willing buyer of the chemical business in the face of significant legacy liabilities that would be allocated to Tronox. According to court documents, one prospective buyer even referred to the situation as "criminal".

Tronox filed for bankruptcy, in large part because of the onerous costs associated with those transferred liabilities, many of which were not created as a result of Tronox's own operations, and the resulting inaccessibility of the capital markets. In the case of Tronox, it appears that ParentCo may have tried to allocate its problem liabilities to SpinCo in order to ringfence ParentCo to shield it from future obligation.

The spinoff was followed in quick succession by a sale of ParentCo to Anadarko Petroleum, which, it was asserted, was free from SpinCo's liabilities. This sale transaction, it is believed, was made possible by the distribution of legacy liabilities to SpinCo.

Monsanto and Solutia
Similarly, in the matter of Solutia Inc, Monsanto Company went through a series of transactions that effected its conversion from a century-old chemical company to a new technology bio- and life-sciences business that is today a leader in engineered crop seed and farming nutrients. To get to this state, Monsanto spun off major arms of its business together with the assets, liabilities, and contingencies built up over those one hundred years of chemical manufacturing. As a result, from the broadest perspective, a large, global company's significant liabilities for pension, other post-employment benefits (OPEB), tort damages, litigation, environmental remediation, and certain funded debt were distributed to a smaller, more narrow, less diversified business (ie SpinCo). In many cases, the liabilities pertained to businesses SpinCo never operated, businesses that even ParentCo had exited years before.

The logic asserted seemed to be that ParentCo was "giving" SpinCo certain lines of business with all of each business line's assets and liabilities. That argument has momentary appeal if you are negotiating with yourself, in your own conference room, with your own bankers and lawyers, and no real counterparty who, at that moment, is not employed by you. Were it otherwise, the counterparty might have pointed out that all of the value created by ParentCo's creation of the legacy liabilities over the years has already been enjoyed by ParentCo. ParentCo's distributing of the legacy liabilities, having enjoyed the corresponding value creation years ago, is not compelling logic. Furthermore, without the hope of creating any value from the operations of long-closed business lines whose liabilities ParentCo wishes to allocate to SpinCo, there is a real risk — all too frequently realized, as in the cases of Tronox and Solutia — that legacy liabilities will mount over time while current business lines cycle with the markets.

Asking the right questions
On its face, this should give directors of spinoffs pause for thought. It demonstrates the potential intent on the part of some corporate parents to perform a spinoff for the sole benefit of one party, to the potential detriment of the other — often referred to as a "GoodCo-BadCo" structure.

The spinoff is structured without consideration being given to SpinCo's ability to pay its obligations as they come due. Or perhaps, motivated as it is, ParentCo has not adequately scenario-tested the new SpinCo structure for negative market cycles. At the very least, it demonstrates that directors of spinoffs must examine the history behind the initial logic and purpose of the parent's decision to spin off one of its subsidiaries when determining its asset and liability allocation. Directors must ask themselves,

'What accommodations were made to magnify the benefit to one party at the expense of the other?' The answer to this question is one of the most important that the spinoff director faces, as such issues tend to be the most highly contentious should they be raised later — for example, at the time of a subsequent restructuring.

Challenges at the conceptualization/negotiation phase

The allocation of assets and liabilities between ParentCo and SpinCo during the conceptualization and negotiation phase can be particularly difficult. This is due to a number of factors, including the motivations of ParentCo (as mentioned above), as well as the status relationship that exists between ParentCo's directors and officers on the one hand and soon to be SpinCo directors and officers on the other.

As soon as they have been identified for the SpinCo role, SpinCo's directors and officers become branded as "other" and their motivations become suspect, as if they were true negotiating counterparties. And yet, they are not. Prior to the closing of the spinoff transaction, even though identified as potential SpinCo directors and officers, such individuals still have the reporting lines and responsibilities they always had at ParentCo — not to mention the same professional, social and peer pressures discussed above. The "negotiation" that takes place between ParentCo and SpinCo often exists in name only. ParentCo dictates a result. It will be the rare SpinCo director or officer who will have the intestinal fortitude to look the ParentCo's "gift horse" in the mouth and require "more." Remember, there usually is a ParentCo employee being offered the CEO position of his or her own public company. It will be hard, if not impossible, to demand more from the CEO of ParentCo. Additionally, ParentCo will have lawyers, bankers and other advisors working to structure the deal. SpinCo, on the other hand, will likely be the passive, unrepresented and unadvised recipient of the result.

Consequently, the allocation of assets and liabilities in the pre-transaction phase is a serious matter with long-term implications that must be carefully considered and evaluated for fairness and appropriateness.

SCA and XL Capital

An illustration of this point, and a demonstration of the potential unintended consequences of ParentCo's ability to dictate a structure to SpinCo, arises from the spinoff of Security Capital Assurance (SCA and now known as Syncora Capital) from XL Capital Corp. Because of the statutory capital requirements and the rating agency capital requirements necessary to achieve a commercially desirable high investment grade rating for SpinCo (SCA), ParentCo (XL Capital) was compelled to contemplate capital contributions as part of the spinoff. To minimize the immediate cost to ParentCo of such a contribution, XL Capital contributed an "excess of loss" treaty, a guaranty against losses in pre-spin financial guaranty contracts that were distributed in the spinoff to SCA. The face amount or par value of the liabilities guaranteed was about $100 billion. This excess of loss treaty was treated by the insurance regulator and the rating agencies as a contribution of capital. But when, in 2007 to 2009, the housing market imploded, that guaranty threatened to take ParentCo down the same restructuring path that had to be traveled by SpinCo.

For its own purposes, ParentCo initially contributed what it likely considered to be less value to SpinCo. However, to XL Capital's dismay, that guaranty was eventually commuted/settled for a payment of close to $2 billion to SCA.

What are the operating relationships and dependencies between SpinCo and ParentCo?

Similar to the discussion above regarding asset and liability allocation, the determination of the interdependency between ParentCo and SpinCo is, in most cases, dictated by ParentCo. Even if the nature of the relationship is understood, many SpinCo companies have not previously completed the necessary legwork, or have not had the freedom to understand and address the economic relationship between subsidiary and parent. On a basic level, this is an exercise in transfer pricing (allocation of profits between entities if one entity supplies another within the same corporate structure), corporate overhead allocation, and other similar issues. On a deeper level, evaluating the relationship between the parent and subsidiary is a matter of determining who has the leverage in the relationship. For example, SpinCo could be the sole supplier of the raw or intermediate materials for ParentCo, or vice versa. These dynamics play a huge role in pre-transaction structuring and evaluation of the spinoff.

More real-world examples

In the cases of both Visteon's spinoff from Ford and Delphi's spinoff from General Motors, both companies were formerly auto-parts supplier subsidiaries or divisions of their original equipment manufacturer corporate parents. Although both were prominent auto-parts suppliers, they had very heavy concentrations of business with their respective parents. (Given the competitive nature of the auto-industry, it is not hard to imagine that Toyota or Honda would be leery of having either GM or Ford as their parts supplier.) Thus, in part, the decision to spin off the subsidiaries was made so that the suppliers could diversify their customer bases and theoretically create significant additional value by appreciating unrealized operating leverage as they generated incremental sales using the same level of overhead and R&D.

Interestingly, however, both Ford and GM remained somewhat dependent for parts on their former supplier subsidiaries. Thus, similar to the situation described in XL Capital / SCA, it is not always the ParentCo that has the consistent leverage in the ParentCo-SpinCo relationship, particularly when and if SpinCo fails.

The case of Monsanto/Solutia presents an interesting contra-example. Although Monsanto spun off its chemical businesses to Solutia, it retained some of the operations that provided critical feedstock in certain markets. As a result, because there was no economically viable substitute for the Monsanto input, Monsanto retained significant negotiating leverage throughout Solutia's reorganization. In the auto-parts supply companies (Delphi and Visteon), this dynamic resulted in a standoff. Whereas Monsanto had the global strength and diversification to simply shut off supply to Solutia if it chose to do so, ParentCo auto-manufacturers (GM and Ford) needed SpinCo auto-parts to keep their own assembly lines running. Conversely, ParentCo auto-manufacturers were the SpinCo auto-parts supply companies' major customers for finished parts and the basis for future business plan projections.

Often, the drafting of these go-forward operating procedures is further complicated by other factors. For example, the pre-transaction structure in the case of the auto-manufacturers and their auto-parts supplier subsidiaries was complicated by the fact that ParentCo and SpinCo have the same employee bases and the same unions. One can imagine the goal of the unions is to protect their constituents such that they are allocated to the entity with the best pension and OPEB paying resources and the best long-term, collectively-bargained contract, whether it be ParentCo or SpinCo. This dynamic, which limits

flexibility with regard to structuring a spinoff transaction, led to some very contorted employee "leasing" arrangements.

Focusing on economic relationships

It is for these reasons that, as the spinoff is being considered and the terms of separation drafted, economic relationships and guarantees must be well established during the pre-transaction phase. The last thing ParentCo wants is the ability of SpinCo to hold it hostage for better terms or vice versa. Thus, to the extent necessary, one often sees long-term governing principles and operating procedures put in place during the pre-transaction phase. Determining whether these forward-looking operating provisions will stand up to the pressure of a subsequent restructuring is often what a "busted spinoff" reorganization is all about. Again, this process, like the asset and liability allocation, requires great care.

What are the governance inter-relationships and dependencies between SpinCo and ParentCo?

Ironically, the pre-transaction governance procedure, one of the most important areas of the ParentCo/SpinCo process, is also the least transparent and well established. In short, proper governance is virtually non-existent at the subsidiary level prior to the spinoff. More often than not, there is no separate board at the subsidiary level as there is simply no need for such a redundancy in most corporations. The management and board of directors of ParentCo determine the needs of the entire enterprise.

Often, when a spinoff is being considered, the board of directors at ParentCo will form separate special committees of independent ParentCo directors in order to determine the appropriateness of the spinoff. However, this procedure is fraught with conflicts of interest. After all, a board member of ParentCo, whether independent or not, is charged with looking out for the best interests of ParentCo, no matter what "committee" he or she serves.

Stakeholder incentives

With such a one-sided governance procedure, it is not difficult to see how lopsided negotiations can occur. Every stakeholder or party in interest has some incentive to push even an unfair transaction forward. The management and board of directors of ParentCo, those with the best information, are eager for the parent to thrive and create excess value for ParentCo's shareholders. In fact, case law suggests that ParentCo and its directors generally do not owe any fiduciary duties to the prospective shareholders of SpinCo after ParentCo declares its intention to spin off the subsidiary, as was illustrated in the case of *Anadarko Petroleum Corporation v Panhandle Eastern Corporation*. While making its decision, ParentCo's board must fulfill its fiduciary duties of good faith, loyalty and due care in designing and effectuating the transaction. If the board satisfies these requirements, the case law suggests it will likely be protected under the business judgment rule.

Similarly, the shareholders of ParentCo, although usually not armed with the information to have sufficient input, are expected to benefit from ParentCo board's decision and so are likely to have a bias akin to the management and board of ParentCo. Thus, they too would be eager to extricate ParentCo from growing liabilities and distracting non-core businesses.

The current management of the subsidiary, and likely future management of SpinCo, who, one would think, would be the most vocal protester against a structure that is burdensome to SpinCo, in fact embrace the anticipated spinoff structure for several reasons. First and foremost, prior to the spinoff, they are typically still employees of ParentCo. Thus, they are not likely to disagree with the wishes of their employer. Second, these internal managers are likely top contenders for the job as management of the new publicly traded corporation. They know that if they raise a fuss over the proposed structure of the spinoff, they may be viewed as potentially unco-operative SpinCo managers, and ParentCo may look elsewhere for new management of SpinCo. These powerful incentives lead the future managers of the spinoff to accept the logic of the contemplated spinoff with very little dissent. Ultimately, the flaw in the process here is that there is no party that operates on an arm's-length basis prior to effecting the transaction.

Market reaction

Even the markets themselves are eager recipients of spinoffs. Despite the troublesome burdens bestowed upon the spun-off entities, these spinoffs continue to trade with significant market capitalizations. For example, both Tronox and Solutia had large market capitalizations post-spinoff despite being burdened by onerous legacy liabilities. This is due to the fact that the markets often know little about the growing liability and off-balance sheet contingencies, and as such, cannot value SpinCo appropriately. Also, miraculous as it seems, ParentCos seem frequently to execute spinoff transactions into markets where SpinCo's liabilities may be understated (or contingencies misunderstood), while the value the market places on SpinCo's business lines may be at a cyclical (or worse, a secular) high. That is not to say that some evidence of growing liabilities or contingencies is not discernable in all of the voluminous paper that a public spinoff creates. It is merely true that it is very difficult to find and, once found, harder to understand.

Irrespective of robust post-spinoff trading values, directors should evaluate spinoff decisions against reasonable downside scenarios, not merely against current market expectations — which frequently misperceive contingent SpinCo exposure. In other words, directors should make decisions based on the reality of the situation as they know it to be, not upon public misperception of the value of SpinCo. Just as in the case of the failed pre-spinoff auction of Tronox, the markets were willing takers of the spinoff despite more knowledgeable buyers with better information rebuffing the subsidiary as a potential takeover target.

Once the three characteristics of the pre-transaction phase have been thoroughly reviewed and the transaction appropriately structured, the determination is made and the transaction is either consummated or not. If the transaction is completed, SpinCo moves to the second phase.

Phase 2: Post-transaction operations phase

What are the assets and liabilities of SpinCo?

Once an entity has closed the spinoff transaction, and SpinCo has become a separate, publicly traded corporation, the assets and liabilities are structured as agreed in the separation agreement between ParentCo and SpinCo.

One of the new realities is that as a newly formed public company, SpinCo, and its managers, are now likely confronted with a host of issues for the first time. These include dealing with public shareholders, employing market-based financing, and managing relationships with banks and other capital providers. Specifically, managing the "right side" of the balance sheet is a wholly new endeavor for management — often warranting the introduction of new managers experienced in dealing with public company issues.

Also, to the extent that ParentCo has saddled

SpinCo with new liabilities (eg through a special one-time dividend to ParentCo pre-spinoff, or a liability transfer to SpinCo's balance sheet upon separation), SpinCo must now manage its cash flow to deal with this new cash use. To the extent that SpinCo is unable to do so, it may be forced to move to the third phase.

What are the operating relationships and dependencies between SpinCo and ParentCo?

Here, again, SpinCo is now managing under the new reality of its legal separation from ParentCo. SpinCo, in many ways, must now fend for itself where it had not needed to before.

One of the major, wrenching changes post-spinoff is the status change in the relationship between managers from the two companies. Prior to the distribution, SpinCo business line managers could expect flexibility and co-operation from ParentCo managers in areas such as raw material supply, management of various contingent liabilities including safety and environmental, the office of the general counsel, the regulatory affairs unit and the public relations department. Post-distribution, over time, and sometimes instantaneously, these same functional areas of ParentCo become hostile counterparties to SpinCo.

Unless explicitly agreed to, SpinCo can no longer depend on the negotiating strength, operating flexibility or financial wherewithal of ParentCo to provide a backstop in case of performance issues suffered at SpinCo. Prior to the spinoff, SpinCo was simply a smaller entity within a much larger organization, often trading under the name of ParentCo, rather than under its own name. In many instances, prior to the spinoff, ParentCo is the counterparty to third-party business agreements. In cases where SpinCo is the counterparty, agreements may have come with the implicit performance guarantee of ParentCo.

This market unfamiliarity with a standalone SpinCo creates a host of new issues. Without the credit guarantee of ParentCo, implicit or explicit, counterparties to agreements with SpinCo have less assurance SpinCo will be able to perform on the terms of those agreements. Among other things, this could result in trade creditors putting SpinCo on shorter credit terms as a standalone entity than SpinCo had enjoyed under the ParentCo umbrella, crimping cash flow. Ultimately, the separation from ParentCo forces SpinCo to evolve and change the way in which it does business, for better or worse. Successful spinoffs manage this transition well. Unsuccessful spinoffs do not.

Looking at separation agreements

In tandem with this new operating environment, SpinCo may be party to separation agreements that are disadvantageous to SpinCo *vis à vis* ParentCo. Ultimately, as mentioned previously, given the lack of unbiased stakeholders looking out for the best interests of SpinCo in the structuring and negotiating of the spinoff transaction, and ParentCo's reasonable discretion and authority to set the terms of the separation with SpinCo, it is not unthinkable that ParentCo will receive some go-forward economic benefit from SpinCo through these contractual arrangements, sometimes at the expense of SpinCo's competitiveness.

For example, a parent may spin off a subsidiary with an agreement for the subsidiary to purchase supplies from the parent at above market prices. With this type of agreement, ParentCo has effectively created a de facto way for pre-tax excess cash flows to be distributed to ParentCo from SpinCo post-separation — to the detriment of SpinCo's competitiveness. This is especially true if the agreement prevents SpinCo from doing business with other companies with manifestly better pricing in the marketplace.

Conversely, an enlightened and forward-thinking ParentCo may agree to provide support to SpinCo in the form of below-market pricing for specified goods and services. The usual thinking is that SpinCo will be weaned off ParentCo support over time as SpinCo settles into independent existence and as market trends or subsequent financing or asset sales permit. In the context of a Phase 3 restructuring, this support may shift the negotiating leverage in unexpected ways, with SpinCo's failure to perform on its contractual obligations sometimes being deemed to excuse ParentCo from its continuing subsidy.

Material separation agreement support

The case of XL Capital and the spinoff of its subsidiary, SCA, presents an example of material separation agreement support running from the ParentCo to the SpinCo. Here, the ParentCo-SpinCo operating relationship was of paramount importance to SpinCo's ability to achieve a high investment-grade rating in Phase 2 and, subsequently, in Phase 3. In this case, the contractual operating relationship took the form of a guarantee that, at the time of the spinoff, was considered by ParentCo to be of negligible economic value, but allowed SCA to continue to operate. SCA, formerly named XL Capital Assurance (XLCA), was the financial guarantee subsidiary of insurance company XL Capital. In other words, SCA was in the business of writing insurance on financial contracts and products such as residential mortgage-backed securities (RMBSs).

At the time of the spinoff, SCA needed substantial capital to maintain its AAA rating from the rating agencies, an assumed prerequisite for a financial guarantee insurance provider to write new insurance contracts. XL Capital was reluctant to provide SCA with the capital necessary to operate with an AAA rating. Instead, it determined that the best, cheapest, and most efficient way to provide capital support to SCA was to provide an "excess of loss" treaty for all financial guarantee business written by XLCA prior to the spinoff.

At the time, it was viewed that the capital support of the parent, XL Capital, with all of its financial resources, would be sufficient to provide counterparties to the insurance contracts with confidence that SCA would have the financial resources to cover its obligations as they came due.

Ultimately, this agreement allowed SCA to operate as a smaller, perhaps more capital efficient player in an industry characterized by few players with dominant market shares. Later, when the financial crisis struck in 2007, this contractual relationship provided a significant benefit to SCA during its subsequent restructuring.

What are the governance inter-relationships and dependencies between SpinCo and ParentCo?

During the post-transaction phase, many board members of SpinCo are likely to have been chosen by ParentCo. Sometimes they can even be former managers or directors of ParentCo. This can create a lingering and largely unseen bias towards operating SpinCo for ParentCo's benefit. This bias is appreciably felt by SpinCo and its directors and officers, but not often (in our experience, never) reciprocated by ParentCo. The bias is only magnified when ParentCo retains some ownership in SpinCo and has contractual rights to appoint members to SpinCo's board until certain ownership thresholds are breached, as occurred in XL Capital/SCA.

The need for vigilance

This lingering and likely hidden bias seldom manifests itself in decisions facing the typical board. However, this tendency of board members toward perspectives born of legacy relationships only reinforces the notion that an independent board member must remain particularly vigilant

when matters pertaining to ParentCo-SpinCo relations are brought before the board. In those instances, independent board members must remain vigilant by seeking a fair and equitable outcome for SpinCo. The demands of corporate governance can be particularly problematic during times of great stress on ParentCo-SpinCo relations — for example, whenever SpinCo is forced to renegotiate or restructure a material operating or contractual arrangement with ParentCo.

Phase 3: Renegotiation or reorganization

What are the assets and liabilities of SpinCo?

For many of the reasons above, it is not unusual for SpinCos to reach a point when failed structuring or market changes mean they can no longer meet their obligations when due. This can result from a variety of factors including an over-leveraged capital structure, a change in business operations, material changes in market valuations or availability of capital, or a shift in contractual arrangements between ParentCo and SpinCo that is too onerous for SpinCo to maintain profitability. Although situations vary, there will often be some component of the renegotiation and reorganization phase that requires the former ParentCo to come to the table, often bringing with it significant value.

A ParentCo guarantee can be a valuable asset to SpinCo

We have discussed how XL Capital spun off SCA with a form of guarantee that allowed SCA to achieve an AAA rating and operate as if the company were independently well capitalized. At the time, the financial collapse of 2007 to 2009 had not yet occurred. In fact, financial guarantee and/or credit default swap loss expectations at SCA were modest and financial guarantee insurance had been an historically steady business of premiums earned, modest losses and a high, predictable return on equity. In all likelihood, when XL Capital provided the excess of loss treaty, it believed this guarantee was materially risk-free. XL Capital probably believed providing this guarantee to be a method by which it could capitalize SCA to achieve a high rating at minimal expense, with a guarantee that would never be called upon.

Although that is what XL may have thought, as the financial crisis unfolded it became clear that SCA would deplete its capital base due to insurance contracts written against poorly performing RMBSs, collateralized debt obligations (CDOs), and asset-backed securities (ABSs). The guarantees provided by XL Capital to SCA forced them to the negotiating table with SCA to provide additional support in exchange for the release of that guarantee.

Ultimately, an agreement between XL Capital and SCA provided for the termination, commutation or elimination of certain guarantees and other contractual arrangements between SCA and XL Capital in exchange for a cash payment by XL Capital and other concessions to SCA approximating $2 billion. As a result of the commutation, XL Capital no longer had the right to vote, nominate directors to SCA's board of directors or any other extraordinary rights.

The structure of the post-spinoff relationship of SCA and its former parent, XL Capital, provided SCA with a benefit that the directors of the spinoff sought to capitalize when negotiating with XL Capital. More to the point, although the operating agreement was thought to be risk-free, it ultimately became a significant asset of SCA and provided SCA with the capital needed to restructure.

Obligations of support

As shown above, ParentCo's obligation of support can be an asset to a SpinCo in need of restructuring. But not all these obligations are contractually designated. In some instances, the support of the parent is explicit and enforceable (eg SCA and Delphi). In cases where it is not, participants in SpinCo's capital structure will often seek to realize value through restructuring-related litigation.

Even the prospect of this litigation, which may be costly and potentially damaging from a reputational standpoint, may bring ParentCo to the table before an in-court restructuring is initiated or litigation proceedings commence — as was the case, to some degree, with Solutia. There, the parent, Monsanto, provided some significant, although ultimately inadequate, support to resuscitate the struggling Solutia.

This support was largely in the form of advance payment for future deliveries and support for the ongoing environmental and tort litigation processes. When this support proved to be inadequate, Solutia filed for bankruptcy and Monsanto found itself providing additional capital to support the ultimately successful restructuring of Solutia.

Piercing the corporate veil through fraudulent conveyance law

Some SpinCos are rebuffed by their former parents when in search of capital support (or they are given inadequate support when it is sought), whether before or after a restructuring is initiated. Very often in these cases, creditors of SpinCo look to fraudulent conveyance law to pierce the corporate veil created by ParentCo's careful structuring and contractual indemnification provisions included in separation agreements. In the pursuit of compensation for an alleged fraudulent transfer, SpinCo or its stakeholders (creditors, shareholders etc) may pursue claims based on an assertion of actual or constructive fraud in order to reclaim value from ParentCo (under Bankruptcy Code Section 548 (a)(1)(A), actual fraud is defined as a transfer made "with actual intent to hinder, delay, or defraud" creditors. The sweep of this provision is considerably broader than the common law concept of actual fraud.) It is worth examining Section 548(a)(1)(B), the section of the US Bankruptcy Code dealing with fraudulent transfers and obligations, to better understand the "look back" powers of spinoff entities under these circumstances.

Section 548(a)(1)(B) of the US Bankruptcy Code reads as follows:

'(a) (1) The trustee may avoid any transfer (including any transfer to or for the benefit of an insider under an employment contract) of an interest of the debtor in property, or any obligation (including any obligation to or for the benefit of an insider under an employment contract) incurred by the debtor, that was made or incurred on or within two years before the date of the filing of the petition, if the debtor voluntarily or involuntarily

(B)(i) received less than a reasonably equivalent value in exchange for such transfer or obligation; and

(ii)(I) was insolvent on the date that such transfer was made or such obligation was incurred, or became insolvent as a result of such transfer or obligation;

(II) was engaged in business or a transaction, or was about to engage in business or a transaction, for which any property remaining with the debtor was an unreasonably small capital;

(III) intended to incur, or believed that the debtor would incur, debts that would be beyond the debtor's ability to pay as such debts matured ; or

(IV) made such transfer to or for the benefit

of an insider, or incurred such obligation to or for the benefit of an insider, under an employment contract and not in the ordinary course of business.'

Passing the tests

As stated in Section 548 above, there are several "tests" that must be passed in order to avoid a transfer under the fraudulent conveyance section of the Bankruptcy Code. First and foremost, the transfer must have occurred within a two-year window of the date of bankruptcy filing. It should be noted, however, that Section 548(e)(1)(d) states that actual intent gives rise to a much longer look-back period. Avoidance actions can also be brought under Section 544(b). This provides that the trustee may avoid a transfer 'that is voidable under applicable law by a creditor holding an unsecured claim'. This means that the trustee may look to non-bankruptcy law (usually "state" law) and deploy any avoiding power that he finds there (a right of action under state fraudulent transfer law, the UFTA or UFCA). This also means that a trustee can pursue remedies that a creditor could have pursued against other claimants to the debtor's property had there been no bankruptcy case. Most often, this is particularly useful to the trustee (or debtor) because of the longer reach-back period available under state law (usually two to six years, depending on the state).

Next, the debtor (in this case, SpinCo) must have received less than "reasonably equivalent value" in the transfer. Although the term "reasonably equivalent value" is not defined by the Bankruptcy Code, the courts will examine relevant facts to determine whether the transaction conferred value reasonably equivalent to the realizable commercial value of the assets transferred. Additionally, the transfer must be found to have occurred at a time when the debtor was, or by virtue of the transfer was rendered, insolvent.

There are three forms of insolvency: (i) the debtor's liabilities exceeded its assets (legal or balance sheet insolvency); (ii) the debtor was operating or about to operate without reasonably sufficient capital; or (iii) the debtor intended to incur, or believed that it would incur, debts that would be beyond its ability to pay as such debts matured (equitable insolvency).

If one or more of these tests are met, the debtor may be able to pursue a case of fraudulent conveyance and seek for SpinCo a reallocation of assets and liabilities with ParentCo.

It is important for the directors of SpinCo to keep such fraudulent conveyance limitations in mind when determining the appropriate course of action to take and their leverage against the actions of a parent.

The case against Kerr-McGee

For example, in the case of Tronox, as stated earlier, Tronox alleges that its former parent, Kerr-McGee (later acquired by Anadarko Petroleum), spun off Tronox and loaded the company with significant legacy liabilities (actual and contingent environmental liabilities, tort, retiree and other liabilities), grossly undercapitalized Tronox without sufficient assets to pay its debts, and forced Tronox to provide indemnities to Kerr-McGee — all in order for the owners and executives of Kerr-McGee to obtain windfall profits through dividends and a subsequent sale of the now "cleansed" company. Given the circumstances around the case, it is possible that either litigation or settlement proceeds from Kerr-McGee (now Anadarko Petroleum) will provide a significant portion of the recovery to stakeholders. In fact, a key source of value being distributed in the Tronox restructuring is the interest in Tronox's litigation case against Kerr-McGee and Anadarko — despite the contingent nature of the litigation's value at this time.

Given the possibility of significant value being available to distribute to stakeholders through actions to avoid fraudulent transfers, directors should weigh the value of such a proceeding and any potential upside (and downside) with regard to the pursuit and ultimate distribution of that value and the long-term effect on the ParentCo/SpinCo relationship. Notably, this dynamic clearly illustrates the point that the relationship between ParentCo and SpinCo often turns from a liability at the initiation of the spinoff to an asset once a restructuring commences.

What are the operating relationships and dependencies between SpinCo and ParentCo?

During the restructuring phase, it is not unusual for the relationship between ParentCo and SpinCo to become highly strained. This can be due to a variety of factors, but is often due to the fact that SpinCo is either no longer fulfilling a prior obligation under an operating agreement, is seeking financial remuneration from ParentCo over fraudulent transfer-type accusations, or because actions are being taken by participants in SpinCo's capital structure who claim derivative standing.

Ultimately, such a contentious relationship is, to some extent, unavoidable under the circumstances. This is especially true in cases where there is an absolute separation of ParentCo and SpinCo without any post-transaction operating agreements.

GM and Delphi

Often, however, this relationship must remain productive, even in the restructuring phase. In the case of Delphi, for example, Delphi continued to remain one of General Motor's largest suppliers — even years after its spinoff. As such, the relationship required a significant balancing act by Delphi, its management and its board (not to mention the US taxpayer, who ultimately footed the bill) as it entered the restructuring phase. On the one hand, Delphi was looking for adequate compensation on account of performance guarantees by General Motors. On the other, it was eager to keep the relationship productive.

It is worth noting that this desire to keep the relationship cordial was both from a business and personnel standpoint. The business issues are obvious. Delphi was one of GM's largest suppliers, shared an employee base, and had go-forward contracts that were highly valuable. From a personnel perspective, it is worth noting that many employees at Delphi remained from the days when Delphi was still a subsidiary of GM. As a result, there was a highly integrated personal bond between GM and Delphi employees. This should not be understated.

Overall, it is true to say that both parties benefit from far greater value if the right balance can be achieved. In the case of Tronox, however, with distinct businesses from its former parent and no go-forward operating linkages with either Kerr-McGee or Anadarko Petroleum, the relationship is clearly one of a strictly legal nature. As a result, it is significantly less flexible and amicable.

What are the governance interrelationships and dependencies between SpinCo and ParentCo?

Generally, if the directors of the spinoff can maintain good relations with the parent, the restructuring process can become less painful for both parties. It is important, however, to remain vigilant with respect to the biases of other directors. Given the former relationship with ParentCo, some SpinCo directors may ultimately have de facto and sometimes almost invisible conflicting interests in the outcome from ParentCo's perspective. Sometimes these directors may not be cognizant of these subtle tugs on historical allegiances.

Conclusion

The spinoff transaction offers a useful lens for directors and officers to consider their company's and their own motivations and incentives. Material changes in job title from ParentCo director to SpinCo director demand parallel adjustments in analytic and management disciplines. These shifts will not always be easy or readily apparent. But the exercise and sometimes the sacrifice called for by the potential of a busted spinoff cannot and should not be overlooked by directors and officers — for they do so at the peril of a failed company and a range of expensive and frustrated expectations.

35

Recovering fraudulent transfers made in business transactions

Albert Togut, Senior Partner, and
Neil Berger, Partner,
Togut, Segal & Segal LLP

Companies in distress are often pressured by creditors to make payments that would otherwise be resisted and that are regretted after they are made. Commonly, the pressure is applied when companies are already insolvent, but sometimes they become insolvent as a result of the payments. Unknown to most management teams is that there are opportunities to recover assets and cash transferred in this way, and to avoid burdensome obligations. These payments may be undone after the fact.

State law and the United States Bankruptcy Code contain "strong arm" powers to avoid or undo fraudulent conveyances, and these can restore liquidity and facilitate business restructurings. The purpose of these statutes is to protect against the improper depletion of a distressed business's assets, and while they are usually used by debtors, they can also be employed by creditors who are prejudiced by the debtor's payments.

What follows is a summary of the significant aspects, purpose, origin, substance and procedures of fraudulent conveyance laws, along with illustrations of the part played by avoidance in business transactions and restructurings.

The purpose of fraudulent transfer laws

These laws were designed to preserve and recover a debtor's assets for the benefit of creditors by allowing certain transactions to be unwound. Consider this example. Company A raises $1 billion in a bond issuance. Shortly thereafter, creditors of Company B, an insolvent subsidiary of Company A, demand that Company A satisfy their claims, totalling $500 million, and execute guaranties of their claims against Company B. As a result of the payment of Company B's obligations and the execution of the guaranty, Company A becomes insolvent and unable to make scheduled interest payments to its own bondholders. Using state law and the "strong arm" provisions of the Bankruptcy Code, Company A may recover the $500 million transferred to the creditors of Company B and set aside the guaranty that it was pressured to undertake.

Although undoing transactions after the fact may seem unfair to the non-debtor transferee party, fraudulent transfer laws are designed to promote equality of treatment of creditors, as well as sound debtor/creditor relations, and to deter attempts to transfer assets that would otherwise be available to pay valid creditor claims. In essence, the management has the ability to say "no" when an improper payment is demanded.

Consider the following examples of common business transactions that are subject to avoidance as fraudulent conveyances:

• The redemption of worthless stock by officers of a corporation has been found to be a fraudulent transfer because it fails the "reasonably equivalent value" requirement. When worthless stock is redeemed, the corporation is not receiving any consideration, whether or not the stock would have value for another purchaser. When the solvency of a company is in doubt, a board of directors can refuse a demand for stock redemption.

• A shareholder plan to liquidate a corporation and distribute assets among the investors before the corporation satisfies its tax obligations is subject to attack. Transfers of assets to shareholders are fraudulent if non-insider claims are not first met.

• Payments to employees for covenants not to compete have been held to be fraudulent conveyances.

• Trustees have used strong-arm powers to sue and set aside the transfer of customer lists to an affiliate corporation.

• The transfer of a valuable asset to an affiliate in exchange for a long-term note may be fraudulent if the transfer was made to hinder or delay efforts by creditors to collect a claim against the transferor.

The history of fraudulent transfer laws

Despite their frequent application in modern bankruptcies and distressed transactions, these laws predate the American bankruptcy system and have their origins in British law. Beginning in 1570, the Statute of 13 Elizabeth has served as the model for all modern American fraudulent transfer rules. The Statute of 13 Elizabeth 'was aimed at a practice by which overburdened debtors placed their assets in friendly hands, thereby frustrating creditors' attempts to satisfy their claims against the debtor'. (*Mellon Bank NA v Metro Communications Inc, 945 F2d 635, 644-45 [3rd Cir 1991]; 13 Eliz, ch 5 [1571].*) Following the enactment of 13 Elizabeth, English courts declared that its primary purpose was to provide protection against debtor actions that would defraud creditors of their lawful debts.

In 1918, the Uniform Fraudulent Conveyance Act (UFCA) was promulgated. This codified 13 Elizabeth but also expanded the scope of voidable transfers to those that were constructively, rather than actually, fraudulent. Many states, including New York, adopted the UFCA. In New York, every conveyance that is made without consideration when the person making the conveyance is a defendant in an action for money damages, or a judgment in such action has been docketed against the transferor, is deemed fraudulent as to existing creditors, without regard to the actual intent of the transferee, if that judgment goes unpaid.

The federal fraudulent conveyance law is set out in Section 548 of the Bankruptcy Code. This enables a Chapter 11 debtor in possession or a trustee in bankruptcy to avoid transfers that were made and/or obligations that were incurred by the debtor if certain financial tests are met and if

constructive or actual intent to hinder, delay or defraud creditors is established. The timeframe covered by Section 548 is the two-year period before the bankruptcy filing date.

Section 548 is derived from the UFCA and resembles it closely enough that case law under one statute is usually applicable to the other. Like the UFCA, the Bankruptcy Code classifies fraudulent transfers as actually fraudulent (in other words, made with intent to hinder, delay or defraud) or constructively fraudulent (made at a time when the debtor is financially troubled or unsound, and without adequate consideration).

In addition to the measures in Section 548, Section 544(b) of the Bankruptcy Code provides the debtor in possession and a bankruptcy trustee with whatever avoiding powers an unsecured creditor with an allowable claim might have had under applicable state or federal law to avoid transfers by the debtor prior to the bankruptcy filing. What this means in practice is that they may assert fraudulent conveyance causes of action under state laws, some of which contain a longer retrospective period.

In 1984, a Uniform Fraudulent Transfer Act (UFTA) was approved by the National Conference of Commissioners on Uniform State Laws to replace the UFCA. To date, an overwhelming majority of states, and the District of Columbia, have adopted the UFTA, which borrowed heavily from the Bankruptcy Code and contains important changes from the UFCA. These include: provisions that make transfers to insiders voidable ("insiders" includes officers, directors, shareholders and persons in control); enhancement of creditors' remedies against transferees; the inclusion of a uniform statute of limitations; a new, more objective definition of "insolvency" than the definition in the Bankruptcy Code; the elimination of the "good faith" requirement in the UFCA's definition of "fair consideration"; the enumeration of certain "badges of fraud" (discussed below); the omission of a provision directed specifically at transfers or obligations of insolvent partnership debtors; and certain new defenses for recipients of fraudulent transfers who find themselves defendants. In New York, the timeframe for the "look back" is six years; in other words, the attack on the transfer can be made up to six years after the transfer.

Despite their similarities, federal and state fraudulent conveyance laws are grounded in different philosophies. Section 548 is designed to protect against the depletion of the bankruptcy estate. This is in contrast to the purpose of state laws, which seek to prevent transfers that place the debtor's property beyond the reach of creditors who are entitled to realize returns from that property. Under state law, the fraudulent conveyance action belongs to creditors; under the Bankruptcy Code, that right belongs to the debtor and/or the trustee. The Bankruptcy Code allows these parties to utilize both state and federal laws.

Rules for avoiding fraudulent transfers under the Bankruptcy Code

Not all of the debtor's past transactions may be avoided under Section 548. As noted, only those transfers that occurred within a two-year period before the filing can be challenged.

Consider this example. In November 2000, Company A transferred a valuable and exclusive distribution contract to a third party for less than adequate consideration. It was insolvent at the time of the transfer or was rendered insolvent as a result of the transfer.

On December 2, 2002, Company A filed a Chapter 11 bankruptcy petition. It would not be able to recover the transfer of the distribution contract under Section 548 of the Bankruptcy Code because, despite being a fraudulent conveyance (a transfer for less than "reasonably equivalent value" while Company A was insolvent), the transaction occurred more than two years prior to the filing.

However, Section 544 of the code would allow Company A to use state law to step into the shoes of a creditor that existed when the contract was transferred and avoid the conveyance to Company B. Presuming New York law governs in this scenario, Company A could reach back six years before its bankruptcy filing to avoid transfers. Significantly, Company A can recover either the distribution contract or the cash value of it at the time of the transfer.

The party seeking to avoid a fraudulent transfer must demonstrate that the debtor had actual or constructive intent at the time it made the transfer. Actual fraud can be proved by showing that: (i) the debtor transferred property or incurred an obligation; (ii) the debtor had an interest in the property in question; and (iii) the transfer was made or the obligation incurred with actual intent to hinder, delay or defraud creditors. The action must be brought on behalf of the creditors of the debtor.

While actual fraud is difficult to establish, a number of "badges of fraud" have been identified by courts since the Statute of 13 Elizabeth: (i) a transfer of all the debtor's property; (ii) retention of possession of property by the debtor, when title

exists in another entity; (iii) a level of secrecy in the transfer; (iv) the existence of a trust between the debtor and the person to whom the property is conveyed; (v) the transfer of the property while a suit against the debtor is pending; (vi) the instrument effecting the transfer suspiciously states that it is bona fide; (vii) inadequate consideration in exchange for the transfer; and (viii) gifts to affiliates, insiders and family members.

Courts have held that the fraudulent nature of a transfer may be inferred from relationships among parties and the secrecy of a sale. Other badges of fraud include hasty, unusual transactions out of the company's ordinary course of business; and the use of "dummies", "straw men" or fictitious parties. Transfers made when an adverse judgment is imminent or on the eve of a bankruptcy filing are highly scrutinized.

Transfers can also be avoided where there is constructive fraud. Under Section 548, this can be established by evidence that:

- The transfer of the debtor's interest in property, or the incurrence of any obligation, was made or incurred by the debtor within two years prior to bankruptcy.
- The debtor received less than the reasonably equivalent value in exchange.
- The debtor was insolvent when the transfer was made or the obligation was incurred, or became insolvent because of the transfer or obligation.
- The debtor was engaged in business or a transaction, or was about to do so, for which any property remaining with the debtor was unreasonably small capital.
- The debtor intended to incur, or believed that it would incur, debts beyond its ability to pay as they matured.

Now assume that Company A guarantees the obligations of a supplier of Company B at a time when Company A is insolvent or when the obligations of the supplier, when added to the obligations of the debtor, are beyond the debtor's ability to pay. If Company A receives consideration that has a value worth less than the amount of the obligations covered by the guaranty, the guaranty can be avoided.

The debtor in possession or the trustee is also able to avoid a fraudulent transfer under state law pursuant to Section 544, which gives the debtor "strong arm" powers and avoidance rights of unsecured creditors.

Insolvency and reasonably equivalent value

The two most commonly litigated issues in fraudulent conveyance disputes are whether the debtor was insolvent at the time of the transfer and whether it received less than reasonably equivalent value in exchange. Ordinarily, the party that seeks to avoid the transfer or an obligation bears the burden on both of these issues, and often they must be established by experts. In certain instances, usually involving transfers among corporate affiliates and insiders, the transferee will bear the burden of adequacy of consideration, which is fact-intensive and turns, in large part, on business judgment and valuation.

Courts use different standards to determine solvency, which can make it more difficult for management to judge whether precautions should be taken when planning a business transaction or whether to attack a pre-petition transaction.

Section 101(32)(A) of the Bankruptcy Code defines insolvency as a 'financial condition such that the sum of such entity's debts is greater than all of such entity's property, at a fair valuation'. Some courts will make a solvency determination according to a measure of the company's balance sheet, after making necessary adjustments to asset valuations and debt obligations. Other courts examine the company's discounted cash flow. A small number have also considered a business's generally accepted accounting principles (GAAP) income statement.

Under the discounted cash-flow test, the value of the company is equal to the discounted value of its future profit stream, rather than the value demonstrated by its balance sheet. In one case, the bankruptcy court held that a debtor company was insolvent at the time of the challenged transfer because a financial statement covering that period indicated the business had a net worth of a negative $4 million.

Under a balance-sheet test, insolvency exists when the value of the transferor's assets is less than its liabilities. Courts generally apply a two-step analysis to see if the company was insolvent under this test. First, the court determines whether it is proper to value the company's assets on a going concern or liquidation basis. Second, it will conduct its own fair valuation and assign a value to the assets and liabilities to see if the debts exceed the assets. Under a going concern analysis, the company's assets will be valued according to what could be realized from a sale of the property within a reasonable period. In a liquidation analysis, the assets are valued at what they would generate in a distressed sale; this solvency standard is appropriate if liquidation was imminent or the company was "on its deathbed" when the challenged transfer was made and valuation as a going concern is impossible. The liquidation value will almost always be less than the going concern value.

GAAP income statements are often used by management as a decision tool and have in some instances been used by courts to determine whether a company was insolvent at the time of a transfer. Following an acquisition, GAAP requires assets (excluding goodwill) to be valued at the lesser of their fair market value or the purchase price. Therefore, if the GAAP value of assets exceeds liabilities at the time of the transfer, the company may be determined to have been solvent for fraudulent transfer analysis purposes.

Obtaining a solvency opinion before the transaction is executed is one of the tools that can help to protect a transaction from future attack as a fraudulent transfer. A solvency opinion is a third-party expert's opinion concerning the transferor's financial condition at the time and its ability to remain solvent after the transaction.

Another commonly litigated issue is whether the debtor received reasonably equivalent value in exchange for the transfer. In the sale of an asset, this test calls for a comparison of the consideration received by the company and the value of that asset. Nowhere, however, does the Bankruptcy Code define "reasonably equivalent" or "reasonably equivalent value".

Courts generally use a two-step approach. The first inquiry is whether what the debtor received constituted "value" at all. The second step is whether the value was "reasonably equivalent" to what the debtor transferred. Courts may also evaluate whether an indirect economic benefit to the transferring entity constitutes reasonably equivalent value. In that instance, courts will consider whether the transaction conferred a realizable commercial value on the transferor that was reasonably equivalent to the commercial value of the assets, so that the debtor's value before and after the transfer is at least the same. Just as an expert's opinion is helpful on the financial condition of the transferor, an appraisal of the property transferred is desirable.

"Value" is an important concept in conveyance law because only transfers for less than reasonably equivalent value may be attacked as fraudulent under the circumstances described above. In general, value may consist of property or the satisfaction or securing of a present or antecedent debt. Therefore, an insolvent debtor receives value by paying an old debt; accordingly, the good-faith payment of a debt, even if it is old, is not a fraudulent conveyance because the value in the exchange is the cancellation of the debt. The payment may prefer one creditor over others but it is not a fraudulent conveyance.

Avoidance of fraudulent transfers in common business transactions

It is necessary to begin a lawsuit to avoid a fraudulent conveyance. In the context of a Chapter 11 restructuring, an adversary proceeding must be commenced not later than two years after the start of the bankruptcy case (which is different from the two-year "look back" period under Section 548). A complaint must be filed and served upon the transferee. If actual fraud is asserted, the complaint must plead that specifically; constructive fraud requires fewer specifics.

Fraudulent conveyance adversary proceedings can be lengthy and involve extensive discovery. The issues of solvency and adequacy of consideration are the most contentious. Discovery, such as demands for documents and interrogatories, is likely, and deposition testimony of management should be anticipated. Expert witnesses may be necessary to establish solvency or insolvency and value based on, among other things, demand, market conditions and the financial status of the transferring entity. Few, if any, fraudulent conveyance disputes are resolved on motions for summary judgment when issues of solvency and reasonably equivalent value are in dispute; those are ordinarily subject to factual disputes that must be resolved by the court after a trial.

Transactions that can be challenged as fraudulent, and how to prevent them

Mergers and acquisitions
Transfers that occur in the context of M&As are often subject to attack. The adequacy of the consideration in exchange for the transaction should be examined carefully and steps can be taken to avoid a challenge, including:

- Obtain a third-party valuation report of the asset that is to be acquired or divested.
- Obtain a fairness opinion.
- Solicit and entertain competitive bids using fair-bidding procedures.

- Document internal approval procedures and revisions.
- Comply with applicable SEC and other reporting obligations.

Transactions carried out with these safeguards in place are difficult to attack because an open process in a competitive market is the best indicator of value. But it is also important to identify and disclose any conflicts of interest in an M&A transaction. For example, if directors or officers have a management role or an equity interest that could be enhanced, or if they can receive any part of the purchase price, this should be disclosed and they should abstain from any vote on the transaction. If a company has its own conflicts-of-interest processes, each step should be taken and documented.

Dividends
Under certain circumstances, stock dividends may be recoverable as fraudulent conveyances. Even if a dividend is authorized under state law, it may be avoidable under bankruptcy law. For example, Delaware General Corporation Law permits payment of dividends to the extent of a company's "surplus" or "net profits" from the current or preceding year, but it does not prescribe a solvency test. Under New York Business Corporation Law, dividends may be paid only to the extent of a surplus.

Dividends are the means by which a corporation distributes its profits to its shareholders; they are not the means by which a corporation satisfies a present or antecedent debt. The decline in the company's assets at the time of a payment means it did not receive reasonably equivalent value for the dividend. When a corporation pays dividends, it converts its assets to cash and so reduces the amount of assets available to senior creditors.

If dividends are made while the corporation is insolvent or becomes insolvent as a result of the payments, they will be avoided as fraudulent conveyances. Under this construct, bankruptcy courts regularly hold that insolvent corporations are required to pay creditors before they may pay their shareholders, who have to return dividends made by insolvent businesses.

It is also worth noting that the Bankruptcy Code contains what is usually referred to as the absolute priority rule, which requires that all senior classes of creditors be paid in full before equity (the shareholders) can receive anything.

Departure payments

Another area to be considered is separation payments made by financially distressed corporations to former employees, officers and directors. The Fifth Circuit Court of Appeals recently held that departure payments can constitute fraudulent transfers within the meaning of the Bankruptcy Code. In that case, the corporation's former CEO negotiated a $3 million payment in exchange for his resignation and promises not to sue. Seven months after the CEO's departure, the company began a Chapter 11 bankruptcy case. A liquidation trust was established as part of the plan of reorganization, and the liquidating trustee commenced an adversary proceeding to avoid the payment as a fraudulent transfer.

The central issue was whether the CEO's departure and the releases that he executed in favor of the corporation could constitute reasonably equivalent value in exchange for the payment he received. The court concluded that from the standpoint of the creditors, the releases received were not "adequate consideration" and the departure payment was ordered to be returned to the corporation.

Private equity transactions and leveraged buyouts

These are transactions in which a company (the "target") is acquired using borrowed money, the repayment of which is secured by liens against the assets of the target. The borrowed money is used to purchase the equity interest in the target from its prior owners.

In a leveraged buyout (LBO), the assets are used as collateral to finance the change in ownership of the company for the benefit of shareholders. This structure is not always in the best interests of, or for the benefit of, the target itself or its creditors, because the target may become highly leveraged and hopelessly unable to satisfy its current debt. This is especially true if it is insolvent or in the zone of insolvency at the time of the LBO.

In the late 1980s and early 1990s, LBO transactions often failed because the targets carried too much debt after the buyout — the "over-leveraged" buyout. Those deals frequently ended in the bankruptcy courts with litigation against old equity. Usually, a trustee or debtor in possession of the failed LBO would bring a fraudulent transfer action to (i) recover the payments made to "cash out" the target's former shareholders, and/or (ii)

invalidate the liens granted to the third-party lenders as security for financing the LBO. The basis of the action would be that the LBO resulted in the target not receiving reasonably equivalent value because all that had transpired in the transaction was a change in ownership and a newly created or increased secured debt obligation for the target. The new debt on the balance sheet constrained its ability to obtain credit and impaired its ability to satisfy debts as they came due.

During the 2000s, investment funds rebranded LBOs as private equity transactions. The substance of the deals, however, has been no different, often with the same debt burdens after the transaction.

When economic conditions soured later in the decade, many forecasts and business models were found wanting in their projections of revenues that would support the debt burden taken on by the target to implement the private equity deal. It is now expected there will be a new wave of private equity deals in bankruptcy; this, in turn, could lead to a new round of fraudulent transfer litigation.

When considering a private equity transaction, management should be mindful of, among other things:

- The debt burden that the target will be asked to carry after completion of the LBO.
- The accuracy of the projections of the target's ability to service that debt.
- The jurisdiction in which the target may have to seek Chapter 11 protection if the LBO is over-leveraged and fails.
- The source of the payment to old equity.

Conclusion

Avoidance of fraudulent conveyances can be used to enhance a company through the recovery of assets and cash, and the elimination of burdensome obligations. However, those same avoidance powers can be used by creditors to interrupt carefully planned deals and restructurings, which, on the surface, appear appropriate. Careful consideration should be given to the financial health of the company when a transaction is about to be executed, the proposed consideration to be received, the relationship between the company and the counterparty to the transaction, and the existence of creditors at that time.

When a business enterprise is financially distressed, all of its transactions, especially those that are out of the ordinary course of its business or that take place under unusual circumstances, will be closely scrutinized.

36

Evaluating executive compensation "best practices" in the post-recession world

Linda E Rappaport, Practice Group Leader of the Executive Compensation and Employee Benefits/Private Clients Group, Douglas P Bartner, Partner in the Bankruptcy and Reorganisation Group, James L Garrity, Partner in the Bankruptcy and Reorganisation Group, and Amy Beth Gitlitz, Associate in the Executive Compensation and Employee Benefits Group.

Shearman & Sterling LLP

The extraordinary failures in financial services companies and government intervention in private industries arising from the economic crisis of 2007-09, as well as the continuing turmoil in the global financial markets, have subjected executive compensation practices to extraordinary scrutiny. While initially focused on the financial industry, criticism has now trickled down to virtually all public companies. Shareholder advocates, legislators, the Internal Revenue Service (IRS), the Department of Treasury, and the Securities and Exchange Commission (SEC) have all turned their attention to executive pay, including the special corporate governance provisions of the Dodd-Frank Act. Except in the case of financial institutions participating in the Troubled Asset Relief Program (TARP), the goals of these parties have not generally been to dictate or cap compensation but rather to inform and empower investors by:

• Enhancing compensation disclosure.
• Providing shareholders with an opportunity to voice their opinions on compensation.
• Regulating the management of risk in compensation decision-making.
• Regulating the manner in which compensation is determined.

The buzzword is "risk". There is a widely held belief that certain compensation structures contributed to the financial crisis through incentivizing "excessive risk-taking" by executives. In determining pay as we emerge from this period, directors must consider the specific risks that their companies face and whether pay packages incentivize executives to take actions that threaten the value of the company.

In this context, pay should be viewed as part of more general strategic planning. While risk for financial services companies has attracted the bulk of the attention to date, the interaction between risk and compensation requires further exploration as it varies from industry to industry and market to market. There is no one-size-fits-all approach.

Given that profit-making activities generally involve some risk, the directors must work out how much the company is willing to take in order to maximize shareholder value, and determine the appropriate pay structure to meet this goal. They and their advisors must balance possible regulatory and legislative developments and shareholder views with the ultimate goal of executive compensation — that is, to attract, retain, motivate and incentivize qualified individuals who will contribute to the long-term success of the company.

In today's context of shifting, and sometimes competing, regulatory concerns, this is not an easy task. Directors interested in pursuing executive compensation best practices should incorporate at least the following considerations into their review of existing compensation programs:

• Refocusing the programs to ensure "pay for performance".

- Adoption of hold-through or hold-until-retirement share ownership guidelines.
- Implementation of clawback policies.
- Examination of "golden parachutes".
- Reconsideration of executive perquisites.

Directors should also be cognizant of issues surrounding the compensation committee and its decision-making process and the use of independent compensation consultants. Moreover, boards of directors of distressed businesses need to be familiar with limits on executive compensation imposed by the US Bankruptcy Code.

Refocusing incentive compensation programs

It is broadly agreed that a significant portion of compensation should be tied to performance to encourage long-term value creation. Implementing this principle in a manner that accounts for a company's risk horizons requires a nuanced approach that takes into account the specifics of an organization and its retention needs. The following are current approaches being considered by public companies.

- **Rebalance performance metrics**. Boards should review the performance metrics used for short- and long-term incentive programs and consider a combination of financial-based targets, qualitative performance measures and individual qualitative metrics to ensure profitability and attainment of strategic objectives, as well as appropriate risk management. A diversified mix of financial targets reduces the risk that a single measure drives a majority of the payout, thereby causing an executive to be too focused on a narrow measure of performance. Importantly, incentives based on "soft" goals, such as organizational objectives or leadership, play a key role in influencing executive behavior more broadly. Goals should also be tailored for individual executives, which may require varied mixes and weightings of bonus opportunities.
- **Ensure sufficient fixed compensation**. One lesson taken by the financial services industry from the recession to help guard against possible excessive risk-taking is the need to restore some balance between performance incentives and sufficient fixed cash compensation to meet an executive's basic financial needs.
- **Reconsider the time horizons of incentives**. Goal setting is proving difficult for some industries in the financial downturn. Consequently, a number of companies have adopted quarterly or semi-annual time horizons for their short-term incentive programs, allowing for clearer lines of sight for executives and more precise target setting. At the other end of the spectrum, some companies are putting a greater emphasis on long-term value creation, with incentive schemes to match. Once again, the mix of short- versus long-term in the compensation mix will be dictated by business demands and industry sectors.
- **Equity compensation**. Equity awards continue to be a central component of remuneration. Currently, full-value awards (for example, restricted stock and restricted stock units) play a predominant role, with options taking a back seat, most likely due to the perception that they do not sufficiently align the interests of employees with those of shareholders. Companies will continue to weigh the appropriate mix as the economic environment faced by their industry develops.
- **Utilize balanced vesting schedules**. The balance between performance-based and time-based vesting is being reconsidered, with an emphasis on the former at senior employee levels. In addition, many companies are re-examining the length of vesting cycles, often choosing longer timeframes. Also being re-evaluated is the extent to which accelerated vesting upon termination of employment or a change in control is appropriate.
- **Retain discretion on payouts**. The design of an incentive plan should permit companies to retain a certain level of discretion over levels of payouts, so as to: (i) guard against unintended consequences of financial results; (ii) allow for adjustment for unexpected events or circumstances; and (iii) permit adjustment in the event of issues concerning performance or quality of earnings. Given the focus on the management of risk-taking behavior, reserving the right in bonus plans to recalculate incentives can be an important tool. For executives whose compensation is subject to the deductibility limits of Section 162(m) of the Internal Revenue Code, however, directors may exercise discretion only to decrease amounts generated by payout formulas if deductibility is to be preserved.

Adoption of hold-through or hold-until-retirement stock ownership guidelines

Long-term stock ownership fosters alignment of executives' interests with those of shareholders, as a substantial portion of an executive's net worth is comprised of company stock.

For many businesses, ownership guidelines require that executives hold (i) a fixed number of shares or (ii) shares with a value equal to a multiple of base salary, and that they achieve the relevant level of ownership within a specified period (generally five years after the executive becomes subject to the guidelines). As the size of annual equity awards has increased over time, however, it has become much easier for executives to meet these guidelines and they have come under scrutiny by investors.

An alternative approach is to adopt retention-based guidelines that would require executives to hold a percentage of "profit shares" acquired under equity grants for a specified period. The term "profit shares" refers to the shares that remain after payment of taxes and, if applicable, the stock option exercise price. The number of shares an executive must own under a retention-based guideline is not fixed; it increases incrementally as executives receive new equity grants. This provides a means of accumulating significant stockholdings over the course of their careers and addresses investor concerns that stock ownership guidelines have not kept pace with the higher level of grants. Retention-based policies also emphasize long-term performance as executives will not be permitted to benefit from short-term fluctuations in share prices.

There are two common structures for retention-based guidelines: (i) hold until retirement, which requires the executives to hold a portion of their profit shares until a termination of employment; and (ii) hold through retirement, which stipulates holding some of the shares for a specified period following termination (generally, one to two years).

It is important to note that the guidelines are holding, not vesting, requirements. Executives are not at risk of forfeiting the shares after other vesting requirements have been satisfied. Companies considering implementing retention-based guidelines will need to consider and make design decisions with respect to: (i) how deeply within the executive ranks to apply the requirements; (ii) the percentage of profit shares it will require executives to retain (many institutional shareholders recommend 75 per cent); and (iii) the consequences of a failure to comply.

Hold-until or hold-through-retirement programs have garnered significant momentum with institutional shareholders. Nevertheless, their design should be approached with caution. Hold-until-retirement requirements, for example, may perversely give key executives, particularly those with large accumulations of stock, an incentive to leave the company early in order to be able to realize value from their stockholdings and avoid the risk of price fluctuations. In part for this reason,

guidelines requiring executives to hold a significant proportion of their equity for one to two years following separation from service with the company are gaining traction, sometimes coupled with provisions allowing for some diversification of the investment in limited circumstances such as attainment of age or tenure thresholds.

Implementation of clawback policies

Clawback refers to the company's recovery of compensation from an employee based on a specific type of triggering event. It may be a forfeiture of a future or unvested award, or a recouping of compensation already paid to the employee. The concept is not new. Equity compensation arrangements at many public companies have historically included so-called "bad actor" clawback provisions that discourage executives from violating restrictive covenants (such as non-competition and confidentiality provisions) or engaging in misconduct (such as misappropriating company assets, or engaging in unethical conduct, illegal acts or similar malfeasance). In recent years, however, companies have also been implementing clawback policies designed to recover incentive payouts in the event of financial errors or restatements.

Section 304 of the Sarbanes-Oxley Act of 2002 provides for the recoupment of certain incentive payments to either the chief executive officer or chief financial officer of a public company, in the event that the business is required to prepare an accounting restatement due to material non-compliance with financial reporting requirements as a result of misconduct. Unfortunately, Section 304 is vague and the SEC has been reluctant to use it as an enforcement tool.

More recently, there has been a string of regulations and proposed regulations mandating the adoption of clawback policies, particularly clawback provisions included in the Dodd-Frank Act. Companies receiving assistance under TARP have been required to implement the policies to recover compensation paid to senior executives. Shareholder advocates have also initiated campaigns requesting that businesses adopt the policies. In recent years, many companies have voluntarily done so, to reinforce their commitment to sound governance. When considering the implementation of a compensation clawback policy, there are several common design features that come into play:

• **Covered individuals**. A threshold issue in implementing a clawback policy is determining which employees will be subject to recoupment. This category should be broad enough to cover those who influence decision-making on critical business issues such as long-term planning, corporate strategy and risk management. Many policies do not differentiate between current and former employees, and this is particularly common with clawbacks triggered by the restatement of financials where accounting irregularities may come to light after individuals have left the company. Common groupings include the named executive officers in the proxy statement, or all executive officers. Some companies subject a wider group of senior managers, or even all employees who participate in an incentive program, to the clawback policy.

• **Appropriate triggering events**. A major consideration in selecting clawback triggers has been whether the executive must be culpable in order to warrant recoupment. If so, what level of responsibility should be the standard? Must there be fraud, misconduct, negligence or willful acts? The board should also consider how it will assess the requisite level of conduct or knowledge in the event of a potential triggering event. The following are common approaches:

(1) Recoupment only where there is a trigger relating to financial performance (regardless of whether there is any culpability on the part of an individual). For example, (i) when there is a misstatement of the company's financial statements; (ii) incentive compensation was paid based on materially inaccurate performance metrics or other criteria; and/or (iii) there is a restatement of financials (whether voluntary or required).

(2) Recoupment if the individual engaged in fraud, misconduct or other acts that caused one of the above events to occur.

(3) Recoupment if the individual engaged in fraud or misconduct or any other activity "detrimental to the company". This includes activities not related to the company's financials, such as a violation of a non-compete, non-solicitation or confidentiality obligation.

• **Covered compensation**. Clawback policies can be designed for any type of compensation but are most likely to cover cash or equity performance-based pay. Some companies have adopted provisions that apply to recouping gains from selling stock, when the price of the stock was affected by improper accounting. Generally, clawback provisions may cover forfeiture of unpaid compensation (for example, unexercised stock options or unvested equity awards), or obligate an

individual to disgorge compensation previously received, or both. Salary is not typically subject to a clawback policy, often due to state wage laws.

• **Duration of clawback rights**. Consideration should be given as to whether the clawback should be limited to compensation that is paid within a specific period (for example, 24 to 48 months) prior to the discovery of the triggering event.

• **Application**. Policies are often drafted to allow for discretion on the part of the administering body in determining whether or not to apply the clawback.

• **Enforceability**. As with all contracts, companies must ensure that their clawback policies will ultimately be enforced if challenged. It may be necessary to consider whether an existing plan or agreement permits a unilateral amendment to add a clawback provision, or whether employee consent is necessary. When implementing new awards or pay programs, the policy should require, as a condition to the receipt of the compensation, that the employee agrees to be subject to it. International and state laws should be reviewed, as in certain instances clawbacks may be unenforceable.

Examination of golden parachutes

Traditionally, golden parachutes such as severance and change-in-control benefits were intended to provide executives with a level of security so that they could focus on the needs of the company and its shareholders.

Today, as many executives have accumulated significant wealth from equity grants and long-term incentive programs, these benefits have come under increased scrutiny from regulators and shareholders, who question whether they continue to enhance long-term value as they guarantee substantial benefits regardless of company performance. There are several current initiatives aimed at limiting severance and change-in-control benefits:

• TARP recipients are expressly prohibited (during the period in which they participate in the program) from making any golden parachute payments to their ten most highly compensated employees.

• Several legislative proposals would require a shareholder vote on all change-in-control payments at the time of the transaction.

• Institutional shareholders have commenced campaigns seeking limits on severance and supplemental retirement plans, and elimination of change-in-control gross-ups. Similarly, many shareholder advocates and proxy advisory firms consistently note that they take severance and change-in-control arrangements into consideration when evaluating compensation programs and making voting recommendations.

Many directors are under pressure to justify decisions to enter into or renew golden parachute agreements. Against this backdrop, boards are re-examining these benefits to determine (i) whether they are necessary and appropriate considering both the company's circumstances and those of the individual executive, and (ii) whether they continue to align the interests of executives and shareholders.

In conducting their analysis, directors should regularly take into account the full value that an executive would receive as a result of a departure or change in control — often referred to as the "walk-away" number. This includes a review of:

- The actual payments that are made upon a triggering event.
- The executive's total "wealth accumulation" under outstanding and previously granted equity and incentive awards.
- The executive's pension, supplemental retirement and deferred compensation benefits.

Institutional investors and shareholder advocates encourage the full disclosure of walk-away numbers in proxy statements. To this point, the SEC has noted that the Compensation Discussion and Analysis section of a proxy should address whether these benefits are aligned with shareholders' interests and truly incentivize performance.

Severance considerations

Sunset provisions. Severance arrangements are often entered into upon commencement of employment to address competitive concerns and provide a level of protection to individuals taking a "risk" by switching employers. But while such protection may make sense initially, it may no longer be appropriate once an executive has been employed for a certain period. Boards may consider phasing out the arrangements with existing executives and including a "sunset provision" in new contracts, limiting the time during which severance protection will apply.

Reduced severance for failed performance. Many shareholder advocates criticize agreements that pay full benefits to an executive whose employment is terminated for poor performance that does not fit within the definition of "cause". Some boards are

considering whether a reduced severance benefit in these circumstances might be appropriate.

Change-in-control considerations. Arrangements that provide enhanced severance in the event of a change in control have recently come under increased scrutiny. Three areas, in particular, are being examined.

- First, while change-in-control agreements have often provided severance equal to three years worth of salary and bonus, particularly for the chief executive officer, there have recently been attempts to bring this down to two years, especially with new agreements.
- Second, "single trigger" agreements are increasingly falling out of favor. These provide for severance solely upon a change of control (the single trigger), without no-cause termination or resignation for good reason (the second trigger).
- Third, shareholder advocates and many legislators have voiced their opposition to Internal Revenue Code Section 280G tax gross-ups, which provide a "make whole" payment to executives who become subject to the 20 per cent excise tax levied on change-in-control payments, as defined under 280G. Boards are paying particular attention to these provisions.

Reconsideration of executive perquisites

This remains a hot-button issue. The case against perquisites has been made by the SEC, shareholder advocates, proxy advisory firms and the media. The general view is that executives should be responsible for their personal expenses, as is the case for other employees. Of particular concern are tax gross-ups provided with respect to perquisites. In response to these criticisms, many public companies have already begun to limit their use of perquisites and this trend is expected to increase in the immediate future. Directors should review whether they align with long-term shareholder value.

The compensation committee

Various laws and regulations require that most US public companies maintain a compensation committee composed of directors who meet prescribed standards of independence.

Given the complexities and importance of compensation design, the committees increasingly seek the support of counsel and independent consultants who can assist in a rigorous analysis of decisions. Consultants can also be invaluable in keeping committees abreast of developing trends and practices. To stay apprised of the company's risk tolerance and philosophy and to ensure that these elements are reflected in compensation practices, committee members are increasingly consulting both members of the management team (such as legal, audit and risk officers) and the board's audit and risk management committees.

Ultimately, given the SEC's focus on transparency of process, and investors' concern about paying for performance, compensation committees are very mindful of their accountability.

Use of independent compensation consultants

The SEC, the Treasury and Congress have each focused on the use of compensation consultants who provide a broad array of services (for example, actuarial, tax and risk management) to a company in addition to advising on pay. There is concern that these consultants will be more likely to recommend higher compensation for executives in order to keep their other, non compensation-related, engagements. To begin addressing these concerns, the SEC amended the proxy disclosure rules in December 2009 to increase disclosure on compensation consultant independence.

Aware of the need for unbiased and informed advice, it is common practice for compensation committees to control the hiring and termination of consultants, as well as their work flows and assignments. To be effective, a compensation consultant should be answerable solely to the board. A collaborative relationship with management need not undercut the independent relationship so long as the ultimate line of responsibility is clear and care is taken to uphold transparency.

Compensation limitations for companies in Chapter 11

Companies facing a possible Chapter 11 filing should bear in mind the limitations of the Bankruptcy Code in respect of certain types of compensation payment. Arrangements entered into before the company makes a Chapter 11 filing will be subject to these restrictions if they are assumed or maintained in the bankruptcy case. In certain circumstances, furthermore, the trustee may avoid executive compensation payments made in the two years before the bankruptcy filing as fraudulent transfers.

- **Retention payments**. Payments made for the purpose of inducing an insider to remain employed by the Chapter 11 debtor must (i) be necessary because these individuals have a competing job offer at the same or greater rate of compensation;

(ii) be for services provided by the insider that are essential to the survival of the business; and (iii) be within certain monetary limits.

- **Severance payments**. Payments for severance by Chapter 11 debtors to insiders must (i) be part of a program that is generally applicable to full-time employees; and (ii) be within certain monetary limits.

- **Payments outside the ordinary course**. Compensation payments by Chapter 11 debtors that are not severance or retention payments may still be prohibited if they are outside the ordinary course, or not justified by the facts and circumstances of the case. This last requirement has been interpreted to mean the payment is permissible if it is a fair and reasonable exercise of the company's business judgment. In this regard, the process followed in the implementation of the compensation program will be particularly important. Note that these restrictions do not just apply to payments to insiders.

Because of the limits imposed on retention payments, companies in Chapter 11 typically structure non-ordinary-course executive bonuses as incentive plans. To pass scrutiny, the payment must not be available to the executive simply for remaining employed at the company, but rather be contingent on achieving certain performance targets. These targets should not be so artificially low so as to guarantee the payments will be made.

Note that compensation payments made by non-debtor parents, subsidiaries and affiliates will not be subject to the three restrictions listed above.

Laying the groundwork now

The numerous issues that must be taken into account in setting executive pay have significantly increased the burden on directors in the post-recession era. Boards must be proactive in implementing compensation reforms as appropriate for their companies. Shareholders are increasingly seeking a seat at the table in compensation discussions and, with the likely effectiveness of "say on pay" by the 2011 proxy season and with the inclusion of "say on pay" provisions in the Dodd-Frank Act, they will have a stronger voice.

It is important to lay the groundwork now to demonstrate to shareholders that the board is listening to, and acting on, their concerns. At the same time, directors cannot forget that the ultimate goal of an executive compensation program is to attract, retain, motivate and incentivize qualified individuals and to reward those who contribute to the long-term success of the company.

37

Managing global companies: Cross-border issues

Antonio M Alvarez III,
Managing Director, Europe,
and Jeffery Stegenga,
Managing Director, North
America Restructuring,
Alvarez & Marsal

Trouble, like water, has no natural fixed borders. Nor, as we have seen in the recent global financial crisis, is there a single magic way to stem the tide. Moreover, while we live and operate businesses in a global community, this community continues to have disparate factions that behave differently, as evidenced by the sovereign debt and related economic crises ongoing in Dubai, Greece, Portugal and Spain, among others. In the face of fierce recessionary headwinds, directors and officers of multinational businesses have been forced to battle distress on several fronts, navigating complex and varying rules, regulations and protocols. And, in many cases, they have lacked the experience necessary to execute successful financial and operational turnarounds in a rapidly changing global climate.

Having led the way in numerous cross-border restructurings, including Lehman Brothers, Visteon Corporation and Chesapeake Corporation, we have experienced first-hand the issues increasingly faced by global management teams and developed strategies to deal with them in a way that preserves value for stakeholders and mitigates risk.

Boards of directors: management duties and related issues

Being a board member or manager of a distressed multinational company can resemble the opening scene of an Indiana Jones movie, with Dr Jones narrowly avoiding danger through a combination of archaeological knowledge (fact base) and savvy reactivity (good judgment). As a company enters the zone of insolvency — a state defined differently in different countries — the duties of directors and officers often shift dramatically. Understanding these changes and how they differ from one jurisdiction to the other is critical for corporate directors when charting the right course for the company and in reducing the risk of personal liability. Because actions taken on behalf of troubled businesses typically come under heavy scrutiny and are often reviewed with hindsight, it is important to keep calm and have experienced, local legal counsel in place sooner rather than later.

In the US and Canada, the concepts and laws governing corporate renewal are relatively well known and allow management and boards reasonable flexibility in exercising business judgment on operations and activities within their own legal borders. When a company approaches the zone of insolvency, directors and officers have to maximize enterprise value for the "entire community of interests". In most cases, they are not subject to personal liability for pre-bankruptcy actions unless they breach fiduciary duties by committing fraud or securities law violations, or support other business-related activities that willfully benefit one interest over another.

In the UK, however, once a company enters the zone of insolvency, its officers and directors must focus on maximizing value for creditors. Moreover, management can be held personally liable for misfeasance (even unintentional mistakes), fraudulent trading or wrongful trading (continuing business operations while knowing that liquidation is unavoidable). They can also be held criminally liable for fraud and misconduct (ie unethical behavior).

It is even more precarious in other European countries, such as Germany, France and Italy, where directors and officers can also face personal consequences, including criminal liability, if they do not file for bankruptcy when insolvency triggers have been pulled.

While specific triggers are defined by each country, they generally relate to the company's liquidity position and ability to pay debts on time. This environment can result in bankruptcy filings that allow for the self-serving objective of protecting directors, but may not be in the best interests of creditors.

Herein lies the big management quandary: distressed multinationals operating in cross-border distressed company jurisdictions must deal with complex and often-diverging legal, practical and personal interests.

Cash management issues

In any distressed situation, whether US or non-US, cash is king. Proper cash oversight and management is essential. In cross-border restructurings, cash pooling and cash repatriation are typically quite challenging issues.

Cash pooling

Cash pooling is employed by many global companies and is an effective way of managing cash across many entities, particularly when these entities have varying cash-flows. Instead of a typical inter-company loan system, the structure has one central unit (typically a US parent company) that manages liquidity for a group of subsidiaries or units acting as both borrowers and lenders to the pool.

While there are numerous benefits to cash pooling when a company is performing well, the system can create several pitfalls if there is financial uncertainty. For example, what happens if a large net borrower from the cash pool fails? Who covers the shortfall? In addition, significant costs may be associated with supporting the pool structure, and direct cash infusions from the US parent may be necessary to address any of the following problems:

- A collective pool deficit.
- Conservative cash generators unwilling to support the pool fully.
- A shortfall in reserve or escrow funds to backstop revolving credit facilities or enforce guarantees.

Nonetheless, even with these potential challenges, our experience has shown that the efficiency benefits of cash pooling in a distressed situation generally outweigh the negatives — that is, as long as some or all of the entities within the pool have value worth preserving.

European credit insurers/trade insurers

Across Europe — since there is little in the way of in-court debtor in possession (DIP) rescue financing — suppliers must often write off receivables in the wake of a customer's filing. As a result, trade credit insurance is widely used by suppliers to protect against loss. However, because companies have no relationship with their suppliers' credit insurers and, therefore, have no real insight into the situation, the insurers will often reduce or cancel cover on any future shipments if they sense even moderate risk. This, in turn, can lead to a run on a company's liquidity within a 60-day cycle as suppliers, no longer covered by insurance, go into conserve-and-protect mode.

Clear dialogue and reporting are essential between the company and the credit insurers. Other strategies can include increasing the US parent's DIP financing package to include funding for certain foreign operations to reassure the credit insurers, increasing cash pool resources or securing a letter of credit to backstop the insurer.

Cash repatriation

If entities that generate cash exist outside a pooling system, managers in distressed situations must see how best to repatriate money for the benefit of the global restructuring. International boards will typically challenge existing policies on the basis of local solvency and attempt to slow down outflows to North American or other cash-strapped countries. Another concern is tax treatment: strategies to share liquidity efficiently — in other words, avoid local-country dividend taxation — will require discrete analysis.

Companies must not underestimate the negative impact of a US bankruptcy filing (particularly one with no prenegotiated outcome) on their ability to repatriate cash from non-filers. That makes proper planning essential, including determining the appropriate size of the DIP financing facility.

Local bilateral debt

However sophisticated the finance and treasury team, and however comprehensive its syndicated debt and cash management facilities, the parochial nature of European domestic markets means there will usually be at least one entity that sits outside the norm, clinging on to a local, bilateral facility. Local banks, perhaps more accommodating in good times, quickly seek to frustrate when fearful of being relegated to a bit-part role in a large syndicate's aims. Where covenants have not been brought into line with the syndicated facilities, every advantage will be taken in an amendment request. This means it is no longer a majority vote, but a majority vote plus the bilateral lender's 100 per cent consent.

The size of the issue will depend on the importance of the local entity — what assets it owns, profits and cash generated, key employees, its customers, suppliers and contracts. Subject to these factors, the support of the bilateral lender will be important and can be best achieved through good stakeholder management. More information and more frequent updates can avoid onerous conditions such as a demand for extra collateral and cancelled headroom. In the absence of this, it may draw conclusions that are darker than the truth.

Moreover, a bilateral lender's refusal to co-operate is highly effective, but only for as long as the borrowing entity is key to the corporate group. Otherwise, a local subsidiary insolvency, or the threat of it, can be the key leverage point. Of course, sometimes the only solution is for the syndicate to take the lender out entirely, even if it means doing so at par.

If a bilateral lender is oblivious to the looming crisis, which is rare but has happened, then one strategy is to let sleeping dogs lie. It will need care and the same information that is being provided to the large syndicates if and when it wakes up.

Debt capacity/plan considerations

As discussed, cash-repatriation issues can pose a liquidity challenge for the global enterprise. However, in thinking through such issues at the onset of a case, it is also appropriate to fast-forward to related issues that may arise during the confirmation process in Chapter 11, where debt-capacity analyses will be run using global post-confirmation cash-flows.

This analysis will likely be from a consolidated viewpoint, making an assumption that all cash is fungible and accessible when clearly it is not; it might be blocked by local directors worried about their duties, or simply not be available due to tax inefficiency. As near-term post-petition liquidity stabilizes, senior management should not lose sight of the post-confirmation issue of "trapped" cash on

the level of/location of debt obligations that can be serviced.

Inter-company issues and simultaneous insolvency procedures

Most major enterprises operate as one organization but have affiliates in several foreign jurisdictions that are established for operational, legal, accounting, regulatory and/or tax reasons. While this can be a benefit during healthy times, it can create a mismatch between legal entities, assets and resources in distressed situations.

Added to that, management often lacks the experience and tools to deal with these situations, sometimes leading to hasty, knee-jerk decisions that can jeopardize the viability of the entire group. For example, bankruptcy filings by individual units or subsidiaries can result in entity interests taking precedence over group interests, with the organization being splintered into as many separate units as there are separate bankruptcy proceedings.

To minimize the risk of one panicky affiliate bringing down the entire operation, it is essential to plan and implement a co-ordinated approach, involving close communication among management groups, local expertise and advice from restructuring professionals (both legal and financial).

Lehman Brothers offers a case study in navigating international insolvency protocols. Once the fourth-largest investment bank — with operations in over 40 countries, and more than 900 operating entities and 3,500 legal entities — Lehman operated as a global group with a cash management system, organizational structure, product lines and operating platforms to match. As such, there were cross-border and cross-entity interdependencies. The 2008 bankruptcy filing of the parent company, Lehman Brothers Holdings Inc, resulted in more than 80 separate proceedings in numerous jurisdictions, with each entity seeking to maximize its value by challenging other entity claims and enforcing its own claims on the global parent and its former siblings.

The situation underscored the need for an international bankruptcy charter that would ensure maximum creditor recoveries through fair-dealing rules among administrators and co-ordinated proceedings across multiple jurisdictions.

To manage these issues effectively, Lehman implemented a multi-party, cross-border insolvency protocol. While this code, which seeks to minimize costs and maximize fair recoveries for all creditors through information sharing and co-ordination, is non-binding (at the time of writing), it has been formally endorsed by more than ten jurisdictions and informally adhered to by at least a dozen more.

Until a formal international bankruptcy charter is adopted and/or the filing of a global enterprise is preceded by significant pre-planning, the protocol will help bankruptcy administrators to adopt a more co-ordinated approach across jurisdictions.

It cannot be underscored enough that in a distressed multinational business, senior management must plan, communicate and understand cash movements in a bid to stop the group disintegrating into individual local units.

European workers: union issues

A multinational chieftain based in the US once mentioned that laying off Europeans was like watching *A Nightmare on Elm Street*. But while negotiating a reduction in force (commonly called "social plan") in Europe is more difficult and expensive than in the US, it does not have to be a nightmare.

Most European jurisdictions have a collective dismissal process whenever more than ten to 20 positions need to be eliminated. The UK's collective consultation process is generally the quickest, easiest and least costly. On the Continent, the process generally takes from six to 12 months and redundancy costs amount to 12 to 18 months of salary.

To be successful, management must build a realistic and justifiable case for the plan. In France, for instance, profit improvement is not a legally acceptable justification; only financial distress, or the jeopardizing of a company's livelihood if it does not act, are acceptable. In most jurisdictions, all other cost-reduction measures must be implemented before a layoff plan is proposed. Finally, management must adhere to legal procedures such as notice of meetings and minimum delays between different steps in the process, or the negotiations could be voided for non-compliance.

It is easier to lay off workers in a distressed environment since the reason is clear. But it also requires planning and good local interlocutors.

One of our clients found itself dealing with social unrest when it tried to close its cash-intensive French factory. Strikes ensued, bonfires were lit and the non-French general manager of the factory was taken hostage — the usual stuff. The company resolved this catastrophe only when it dispatched experienced advisors resident in the region. The union bosses just wanted someone to speak in their language.

UK pensions

Some multinational manufacturers have shifted plants out of the UK to lower-cost Eastern European countries, and one side-effect has been the issue of managing any under-funded pension liabilities that may be tied to stranded UK employees. The British Pensions Regulator (the equivalent of the Pension Benefit Guaranty Corporation) has become more active in recent cases in pursuing recovery options, although its ability to do so is unproven.

Any management team contemplating an operational move out of the UK should, where appropriate, analyze the ability of the Pensions Regulator to "reach" beyond the British entity, as well as the outcomes of any recent efforts to do so.

International tax issues

In distressed environments, tax strategies are often overlooked in favor of short-term survival and cash. Yet they can be a source of "new" money for troubled businesses. Although tax-efficient repatriation and good use of net operating losses (NOLs) are key considerations, attention also needs to be given to transfer pricing, the global impact of loss planning, and potential "holiday" relief on VAT and other indirect taxes.

Repatriation

Avoiding withholding taxes on the repatriation of earnings, simplifying the corporate structure to avoid unnecessary tax, and finding overpayments of income and sales tax from prior years are just a few of the many ways in which debtors can enhance their value.

Net operating losses

There are numerous caveats — such as NOL transferability limitations when selling subsidiaries, or the inability to shield withholding tax payments — that could leave the taxpayer facing a large bill. Specifically, bankrupt entities must take care to marry tax and business planning, as any debt forgiveness or change in ownership can reduce the value of the losses. Troubled companies might also find opportunities to mitigate tax liabilities, such as using NOLs to offset built-in gains on the sale of appreciated assets, or preserving the NOLs to offset post-bankruptcy profits.

Tax holidays — VAT and payroll

Many European tax authorities allow for short holidays if a distressed corporation can show deferment will help the business survive in the long term. With payroll taxes and VAT due monthly in Europe, this can give a huge boost to cash-strapped companies.

Transfer pricing

Reorganizing, eliminating, moving or consolidating operations in distressed situations can have direct transfer-pricing implications. Ownership and other changes present opportunities to hit the "reset" button for tax planning and make savings through moving intangible property or sources of borrowed money.

Disclosure/confidentiality

Transparency and openness are essential in distressed or restructuring companies, to maintain or rebuild management credibility with stakeholders. Sometimes, this is the driving force behind hiring turnaround professionals, who can challenge operating assumptions and strategic initiatives, work to maximize liquidity, and provide full disclosure through a comprehensive communications program that includes employees, customers, suppliers, lenders, shareholders and, if appropriate, regulators.

But it is not always that simple. In certain cases, restructuring negotiations with one group of lenders can trigger defaults on leases or other debt instruments that, if foreclosed or enforced, could sink the local business. This, in turn, can have a domino effect on other parts of the business. In addition, certain countries have reporting requirements for M&A transactions or restructuring discussions, so the plans could be seen by the company's unions. Finally, with the advent of the digital age, companies must make sure when disseminating information that it does not "leak" into the hands of competitors. All these aspects need to be brought to bear in developing the crisis communication strategy.

Country overview

To best understand the challenges faced by directors and officers of global companies, one need only compare the insolvency systems in various non-US jurisdictions with the US system that is more well known to US-based officers and directors.

Canada

Commercial insolvency proceedings in Canada involve two primary federal statutes: the Companies' Creditors Arrangement Act (CCAA) and the Bankruptcy and Insolvency Act (BIA). The CCAA is commonly used for restructuring medium to large-sized companies, while the BIA is utilized for bankruptcies (liquidations), interim receiverships and smaller restructurings.

Proceedings under the CCAA are ordinarily initiated by an application by the debtor company, which must be insolvent and have at least C$5 million in liabilities. There is no automatic stay on filing; rather, the Court can grant a stay on all proceedings against the debtor company at the time of the initial hearing. Initial stays may not exceed 30 days but can be extended through subsequent applications.

A unique aspect of insolvency law in Canada is that, as part of the initial court application, the debtor company proposes a firm to act as CCAA Monitor in the proceedings. The Monitor must have a Canadian bankruptcy trustee license, must consent to act and may not be the debtor company's auditor. The Monitor is an officer of the court, acts independently of all parties, and reports to the court on all matters of interest, including the fairness of the process, the progress of the restructuring, compliance with legislation and cash-flow/operating updates.

One of the most important decisions in the restructuring of any global entity is what, if any, procedure needs to be undertaken in each individual country to best protect the value of the organization. In large North American cases, companies often need to file under both CCAA and Chapter 11; where appropriate, a cross-border protocol and joint hearings can be part of the procedure. If Canada is not the "centre of main interest", it is often still necessary to file the Canadian company under the CCAA (for example, where DIP financing is required to maintain the liquidity needed to operate the business). There is also provision under the CCAA for a foreign recognition order, similar to Chapter 15 proceedings in the US.

France

There are two out-of-court and three in-court restructuring proceedings in France. The former comprise *mandat ad hoc* and *conciliation*, with both being confidential and entailing a court-appointed agent to organize informal negotiations between the company and its major creditors. While there are differences between the two procedures, including timeframes and money privileges, both open the door for companies to seek government assistance to reduce immediate cash needs. Out-of-court proceedings are only binding if all parties of interest sign an agreement prior to their conclusion.

If they are unsuccessful, the company will usually move to in-court proceedings, which comprise *sauvegarde* (safeguard), *redressement judiciaire* (reorganization) and *liquidation judiciaire*. Prior to 1996, when the *sauvegarde* process was introduced, over 95 per cent of cases of involuntary proceedings resulted in liquidation.

While it is commonly perceived that *sauvegarde* is intended to be similar to Chapter 11, the main practical benefits are the French equivalent of the automatic stay and the ability to cram down minority creditors. In addition, and unlike Chapter 11, creditor classes are based on debt nature, not the economic priority of the capital structure. The court is also appointed with certain extraordinary powers, including the ability to reinstate antecedent debt with a ten-year maturity if a business cannot come to terms with its creditors. To date, companies that have successfully applied the *sauvegarde* proceedings — which are public — tend to be ones that have debt principally at the holding company rather than operating level, or those with a prearranged/pre-voted agreement in place, increasing the odds of an expedient process and successful cram-down of minority creditors.

The evolution of restructuring proceedings and the growing sophistication of the creditor community have had pros and cons for private equity sponsors and international parent companies. Recently, creditors have been more prone to sit at the table and negotiate with the company and its shareholders, and recent deals have tended to be more consensual rather than resulting in liquidation. While the system remains generally very protective of shareholders, creditors have also become more willing to consider debt-for-equity swaps — a strategy employed at record pace in 2009.

Germany

The fundamental purpose of the German Insolvency Code is to satisfy the company's creditors, in priority of claim, through an insolvency dividend. The primary focus is on creditors' rights, rather than on rehabilitating distressed companies or maximizing enterprise value.

The process is legally (not commercially) driven, with a court-appointed insolvency administrator, and incentive fees are tied to the proceeds paid to creditors.

In general, the creditors are broken down into classes and a majority (by value and number voting

per class) approves the plans. Voters are directed by the insolvency administrator either to sell the company as a going concern, liquidate assets or reorganize the estate pursuant to a plan. Under the law, it is possible to reject onerous contracts such as leases and supply agreements, and a court can cram down a majority vote on reorganization on dissenting creditors, though it cannot extinguish fully the rights of shareholders without their consent. In addition, while there is no concept of a "prepackaged" insolvency, quick asset sales are possible to save a rapidly deteriorating or illiquid business. It is also permissible, but very rare, for a debtor to choose to execute a "self-administered" insolvency, led by company management rather than an insolvency administrator, with the goal of a standalone plan of reorganization.

The German insolvency process has several other unique characteristics, including the potential for board members to face criminal liability. Also, while there is no provision for third-party DIP financing, there is one for a government subsidy of the wages of German employees during the 90-day "preliminary" insolvency proceedings. Along those lines, pensions not fully repaid or assumed by an acquirer of the ongoing business, or assets that are fully assumed by a government-backed pension insurance scheme, become unsecured claims against the estate. In addition, there is no concept of a corporate "group" and each entity has its own proceeding. Finally, judges and administrators are loath to allow any cash or value to escape the insolvent estate, so it is difficult for a German-based multinational to support foreign subsidiaries.

Italy

Restructuring businesses based in Italy remains extremely challenging as a result of: a lack of in-court DIP financing; liquidity defaults that force bankruptcy filings; the complexity and cost of shedding labor; and the fact that an Italian entity cannot operate legally, even on a temporary basis, with a negative net worth.

That said, Italian bankruptcy laws offer several tools for reorganizing either in or out of court. In *concordato preventivo*, a court-supervised process, the debtor company makes a proposal that becomes binding if it is approved by creditors representing the majority of the debts. The process is often used to sell or transfer certain assets representing a going concern, similar to a prepackaged Section 363 sale under Chapter 11.

Additionally, the "Prodi" and "Marzano" laws, enacted in the wake of the 2003 *Parmalat* case and available for qualifying large companies, allow a special administrator with wide powers to be appointed to lead the restructuring. The administrator seeks a buyer for the going concern, or part thereof, with the interests of employees and creditors being the main priority.

Finally, there are ordinary out-of-court or in-court restructuring frameworks (articles 67 and 182 of bankruptcy law) whereby the restructuring plan is vetted by an independent expert (an accountant or lawyer). Per article 67, the plan must foresee the full repayment of outstanding obligations, though the due date may be rescheduled. Under article 182, the plan may include the need for creditors to take writeoffs, subject to their agreement.

UK

The merits of the British insolvency system are heavily debated. The availability of out-of-court restructuring procedures in the UK is seen as a positive, although there are strong arguments that they should be strengthened with binding moratoriums while the details of the restructuring are being discussed. In the absence of these, companies have to secure standstills and forbearance agreements with creditors to allow time to formulate and negotiate a plan.

The UK insolvency and restructuring regime offers three principal routes for distressed entities: liquidation, administration and the consensual out-of-court (but legally binding) procedures of a company voluntary arrangement (CVA) and scheme of arrangement. The right for certain creditors (typically lending banks) to appoint a receiver still exists, but the circumstances in which such a right can be exercised were curtailed under the Enterprise Act 2002.

Other key issues are the absence of super-priority DIP financing and the ability to cram down classes of creditors who are "out of the money". A CVA requires the approval of 75 per cent (in value) of the creditors and a scheme of arrangement requires 75 per cent (in value and number) of each class of creditor. In both of these voting procedures, it is irrelevant whether creditors are out of the money, as each class must approve the plan and cram-downs can only happen within classes of creditors. However, a cram-down can happen if the court is persuaded that creditors with no monetary interest in the process will undermine a restructuring to the unfair detriment of the other creditors.

Forum shopping

While venue shopping has become common within the US, as companies seek to file in jurisdictions with a history of favorable legal rulings on those issues, the differences in bankruptcy laws and practices between US states are nowhere near as varied and complicated as those between one country and another. Certain nations are more "debtor friendly" and others more "creditor friendly". Certain bankruptcy regimes have features that allow for quicker asset dispositions or the ability to cram down minority creditors seeking to block a restructuring plan and hold out for more value.

A European directive clearly states that the country in which a company's main interests reside (headquarters, treasury operations, etc) should be where the bankruptcy proceedings take place. However, there have been several examples of a company's center of operations being shifted from one country to another in order to carry out the desired restructuring approach. For example, several German companies have effectively avoided the country's courts by moving operations to the UK and carrying out a prepackaged reorganization via a scheme of arrangement.

Conclusion

While there are common themes in any cross-border restructuring, each battle will be different given the mix of operating issues, structural considerations (legal, capital and tax), human dynamics and individual motivations that make managing a global turnaround both challenging and exciting. The importance of early intervention and planning in managing the restructuring process and stopping it from spiraling out of control cannot be underscored enough. This approach will increase the chances of keeping the company intact and moving forward, which typically provides the greatest preservation of value.

We would like to thank the following A&M professionals who contributed to this chapter: Adriano Bianchi (Italy), Peter Briggs (Germany), Neil Christie (local bilateral debt), Nate Arnett (cash pooling), Mike Corner-Jones (European credit insurers), Daniel Ehrmann (inter-company issues and international protocols), Paul Kinrade (UK pensions), Helen Lee (France), Bob Lowe (international tax), Merryck Lowe (UK pensions), Doug McIntosh (Canada), Scott Pinfield (UK), Douglas Rosefsky (France) and Stefaan Vansteenkiste (European workers).

38

Preserving global enterprise value: Managing international subsidiaries and affiliates through cross-border reorganizations

Simon Freakley,

Managing Partner, Europe,

and Joff Mitchell,

Managing Partner, United States,

Zolfo Cooper

Directors and officers of a US-based corporation are likely to face important challenges in guiding a global business through a period during which its domestic entities will have filed for Chapter 11 under the US Bankruptcy Code and certain of its overseas entities may also have entered into an insolvency procedure. Fortunately, these challenges are manageable provided that senior management and the board of directors focus on certain key practical issues as they consider and prepare for a filing.

We will address the international impact of the Chapter 11 filing, which management will need to consider when continuing to run the global corporation on a "business as usual" basis.

We will also explore the implications of overseas filings in more detail and draw on our direct experience of advising US corporations with operations in Europe and within NAFTA. However, the issues raised will be relevant in other jurisdictions, such as Asia and Central and South America, taking into account differences in national legislation and solvency requirements, potential government intervention and local customs.

The underlying assumption in this chapter is that the key objective is for the corporation to emerge largely intact from any in-court restructuring process, with minimum disruption to the operations of the business during the filing period. But necessary operational and financial restructuring steps can effectively be carried out, with the filing offering umbrella protection.

Corporate structure

The legal entity structures of most global corporations are driven by a combination of acquisition history and a desire to maximize the impact of tax-efficient strategies. The internal reporting structure and the outside world — customers and vendors — usually pay little attention to this legal structure, and finance teams generally only focus on it when asked to do so by auditors. However, in a bankruptcy, it will be critical. The key challenge is to maintain the integrity and operational capability of global businesses, product groups and supply chains within a legal structure. "Fault lines" are likely to emerge along the divisions between filed and non-filed entities, and potentially between filed entities in differing jurisdictions. Liquidity management, ongoing funding and jurisdictional processes are key areas around which these fault lines will develop.

Communication

Insolvency/bankruptcy outside the US has far more stigma attached to it than a Chapter 11 filing, which is seen as a rehabilitation tool and a debtor in possession (DIP) process. Chapter 11 allows existing management to continue to run the business, albeit with far greater scrutiny and input from all stakeholders.

Certain other jurisdictions are slowly beginning to introduce DIP insolvency procedures — for example, the Companies' Creditors Arrangement Act (CCAA) process in Canada and self-administration in Germany — but insolvency remains a major perception issue and has important implications, internally and externally, for the corporation's international communication strategy.

The development and execution of a comprehensive communications plan prior to filing in the US is crucial to the overall success of the restructuring. Failure here can derail the whole process before it even starts.

In addition to the regular dialogue with financial creditors, communication plans will need to be developed for the following key stakeholders:

• Overseas management, some of whom will have strict local legal obligations and personal liability issues.
• Employees.
• Major customers and vendors (management visits to key players is recommended).

It is important not to implement a communication plan too far in advance of the Chapter 11 filing as this may lead to unnecessary rumors that could unsettle stakeholders and ultimately lead to loss of customers, vendors tightening credit limits and employees losing focus on their day-to-day responsibilities.

However, early internal communication at the executive level is desirable, but confidentiality constraints should also be appreciated. Well-timed communication can also avoid uncertainty developing into problems with employees, customers and potentially the media in host countries of international operations.

Retaining a professional communications advisor with the required international experience and resource base to help develop the plan and manage the flow of information throughout the Chapter 11 process is strongly recommended. Without such assistance, demands on management's time will be so great that it is unlikely they will be able to devote sufficient time to running the day-to-day operations of the business.

Liquidity and financing through Chapter 11

The first priority in preparing for a bankruptcy filing is to manage the global deployment of the corporation's available cash and credit lines.

Undrawn credit will evaporate instantaneously and most other international funding arrangements, not directly impacted by the filing, will most likely be withdrawn or accelerated.

It is imperative that the organization produces detailed, rolling 13-week cash-flow projections by jurisdiction, and that these are then consolidated into a centralized cash-flow forecast. At the very least, this will be needed to support the use of cash collateral when continuing to trade the business and will also form the basis of a DIP facility should additional funding be necessary during the filing. Understanding where cash resides will also be important in determining the extent of any repatriation issues.

It is not unusual for companies to draw down their revolving credit facility prior to filing, in order to ensure they have sufficient liquidity to navigate the Chapter 11 process. Such proceeds, together with existing cash-on-hand balances and a DIP loan, usually provide the funding needs for all Chapter 11 filings.

Demonstrating that the company has sufficient liquidity to trade will be a key disclosure in the communication plan and it should also be a way of allaying any fears among employees, customers and vendors with regard to a bankruptcy filing.

Securing a DIP loan is not without its challenges. These facilities are usually granted a "priming lien" over existing assets, meaning that they rank ahead of all other secured debt in a waterfall analysis. Such a concept rarely exists in non-US jurisdictions. These loans are usually subject to comprehensive credit agreements and tight covenants based on a detailed DIP forecast produced by the company and its advisors. However, with multi-jurisdictional operations, the lenders will likely want to understand several key issues:

Whether the overseas operations are cash-flow positive or a cash drain

The availability of DIP funds for non-US companies outside the Chapter 11 filing may be key and will require persuasive argument based on the maintenance of enterprise value of global businesses or divisions (or potentially through the releasing of security or liens). Even if it can be demonstrated that companies in overseas jurisdictions are standalone cash positive/solvent, the availability of DIP funding may be critical in reassuring local suppliers and lenders, maintaining established credit arrangements and coping with local needs.

The financial performance and solvency position of international subsidiaries

These units are often thinly capitalized and dependent on intra-group funding from the parent corporation, from intermediate holding companies, or simply from cash-rich sister companies. Local funding will typically be backed by a parent guaranty. Within this structure, subsidiaries can continue to trade — even though, if viewed as independent operations, they might fail either or both of the cash-flow and balance sheet tests of solvency laid down in their local jurisdictions.

Following a Chapter 11 filing at corporate level, international subsidiaries will typically need to be able to "stand on their own feet". In addition to the funding consequences of this, these businesses will also need to be able to pass local tests of solvency.

How inter-company balances and flows operate

This will be crucial as stakeholders will want to establish that such transactions are "arm's length". Corporate funding arrangements will be global, complex and typically involve some combination of overseas debt issue and guaranties/security pledges from international subsidiaries. These arrangements may trigger a series of local filings as a consequence of a Chapter 11 bankruptcy filing by the parent company. In a consensual restructuring, it may be possible to amend critical guaranty and security provisions in facility agreements prior to filing to avoid such automatic triggers.

The corporation will need to develop a full matrix of inter-company cash flows and balances, both trading and financing, and engage financial advisors to carry out the detailed contingency planning necessary to determine the following on a jurisdiction-by-jurisdiction basis:

- The likely solvency.
- The options for curing any potential insolvency.
- Local insolvency filing options.
- The "center of main interest" (COMI) of the business and options for moving this (see below).
- The extent to which there are unencumbered assets that can be used to secure financing should it be necessary.

In addition to the information requirements for lenders, management may consider:

- Diverting operational cash receipts to any non-collateralized bank accounts. This may be legally challenging in certain jurisdictions but is a required preparatory step, for example, under German law.

- So far as practically possible, locating all free cash balances in non-filing companies (assuming the filing companies will be covered by cash collateral or DIP funding). Management, however, will have to be careful not to trap excess cash in companies at risk of local filings or in companies likely to be impacted by foreign exchange convertibility or transfer restrictions.
- Within legal/confidentiality constraints, holding talks with potential or current lenders to international companies outside the proposed filing group, in order to secure post-filing credit facilities on acceptable terms. This can be challenging, particularly if there is only limited availability of free collateral.
- Reviewing controls and authorization limits on discretionary spending.
- Moving the COMI of a critical intermediate holding company, with loan utilization or guaranty obligations, to the US. This can have the benefit of gaining the protection of the Chapter 11 filing for this entity, while mitigating the risk of a local insolvency filing.

Operational issues

To achieve a successful restructuring in a timely manner, a cohesive approach is imperative. It is not unusual for incentive programs to be put in place for key management across some or all jurisdictions to ensure that focus is maintained.

Such incentive plans are usually linked to targets around cash-flow generation and/or the amount of time the company is in bankruptcy. Ultimately, stakeholders will need to sign off on these programs, but they are widely recognized as providing additional certainty in a Chapter 11 process. The basis of retention agreements may differ in jurisdictions outside the umbrella of a Chapter 11 filing; in Europe, for example, a retention program does not by law have to be incentive based. However, most have incentive elements built into them.

Global corporations generally operate complex supply-chain arrangements that, in all probability, will involve multiple jurisdictions, often including Mexico, China or Eastern Europe. Many US manufacturing corporations, for example, have operations in Canada and Mexico operating as separate legal entities, or maquiladoras, which will be impacted by a US filing. The maintenance of these arrangements post-filing will have a major impact on customer service levels and potentially dictate the value of the businesses individually and the corporation overall. It is therefore in the interests of all parties, including the corporation's lenders and other major creditor groups, to maintain these supply chains despite the obvious challenges, which may include:

• Credit limits from key suppliers and credit insurers being reduced or eliminated.
• Certain vendors reducing terms or even insisting on cash in advance.
• Goods trapped in filed entities under "retention of title" or "reservation of title" clauses. Such clauses are more prevalent in overseas jurisdictions (the UK, for example), as critical vendor or Section 503(b)(9) status under the Bankruptcy Code can often alleviate such a problem in the US. Arrangements are frequently put into place to pay trade creditors (often in full) in order to maintain the operations of the business while lenders and other financial stakeholders agree on the restructuring plan. In certain cases, ransom demands from international suppliers may be expected.
• Inability to settle pre-petition inter-company debts, and potential subordination and setoff issues.
• Restricted raw material and component supplies, freight service disruption, manufacturing capacity constraints and interrupted investment programs.

Certain pre-filing actions may be undertaken to mitigate such circumstances. These include:

• The building of "buffer stock" at critical points downstream in the supply chain.
• Speaking confidentially, if possible, to major customers and critical vendors at a senior level (there are certainly good precedents on the customer side in the automotive industry). They can help plan for potential bottlenecks and will themselves build buffer stock.
• Seeking to avoid unplanned international primary or secondary insolvency filings.

Other stakeholders

Joint ventures (JVs) may get caught up in insolvency filings and therefore their management and funding will need to be carefully considered. The first consideration will be the JV agreement itself. Such agreements often contain bankruptcy-triggered default and cross-default provisions. Strategic JVs, very important to the operational and supply chain structure of global product groups, would need to be confidentially consulted in advance of an insolvency filing to secure the waiver or renegotiation of such default clauses.

Funding of JVs may be dependent on equity injections or debt guaranties from the partners. Payment under such guaranties may not be possible post-filing and equity funding could be practically impossible (although there have been examples of investment funding for joint ventures being provided under DIP lines within preset limits). It will be important to establish independent local funding arrangements and dividend policies with JV partners in preparation for a group filing.

Insolvency filings raise critical issues for labor unions and other employee representatives. In many jurisdictions, contracts previously agreed upon with unions may be set aside or renegotiated within a filing; a successful operational restructuring may depend on this. Moreover, unions may be pivotal in representing employee or retiree claims in the bankruptcy estate.

In many European jurisdictions, organized labor has an important role to play in approving planned restructuring initiatives, as well as extensive consultation rights in many areas.

Pension arrangements and funding issues play a pivotal role in many cross-border insolvency filings. It is important to understand the arrangements in each jurisdiction, their funding position and the extent to which they are reliant on a corporate-level guaranty that may cover the funding obligations of a foreign subsidiary. An insolvency filing at corporate level will remove this guaranty or covenant and may trigger a deficit funding claim at the local level. This may, in turn, threaten the solvency of the subsidiary or national holding company involved.

Recognizing value

When planning for a filing, it is important to recognize where the value of the corporation resides — in other words, which operations/divisions are generating positive EBITDA/free cash flow after taking into account inter-company transactions and an appropriate allocation of corporate overhead/service costs.

This has implications for funding the Chapter 11 process when considering unencumbered assets and exiting bankruptcy as it relates to revised or new credit agreements. Other areas that can affect value include:

• **Customer ownership**. This has assumed particular significance with the move in many industries to sourcing from low-cost countries in Eastern Europe, Central and South America, and Asia. In such supply chains, the ownership of the customer contract and associated goodwill should be clearly established. Such ownership can determine both control and profit margin, and ensuring that it resides in the critical company may protect enterprise value in key subsidiaries.

• **Intellectual property**. Customer goodwill, patents, registered trademarks and designs, brands, websites and domain names, know-how and key employees all form part of the intellectual property (IP) of the corporation. The development, ownership and use of this IP will be located in different legal entities. It is important that the contingency planning work for an insolvency filing ensures that ownership and the rights to utilize IP are clear and appropriately protected. In particular, a check should be carried out on intra-group licensing arrangements to ensure that these are formally documented, are in line with current trading arrangements, and reflect the use of the corporation's brands and proprietary technology by its subsidiaries, associates and JVs.

• **IT systems**. Like IP, these are often developed, owned and utilized within different legal entities. A filing could potentially impede free access to group systems by decentralized operating units. It is, therefore, important to check that IT systems will be available and supported post-filing. This requires that license agreements are in place, are paid up to date and that funding will be available to maintain critical centralized or locally concentrated support functions.

Directors' liability and responsibility

In the group structure of a global business, product-line management reporting frequently cuts across jurisdictional and corporate entity boundaries. In an insolvency filing, even when localized in one jurisdiction, individual legal entity and national holding company responsibilities and accountabilities will tend to assume much greater importance. Local directors of international subsidiaries are likely to be very concerned about the potential for being held personally liable. Senior management in filed entities may have to cede their executive authority to court-appointed insolvency administrators or trustees, and will in any event have duties to assist the appointed insolvency practitioner.

These changes may override any established reporting relationships within global product groups. New protocols, potentially court-sponsored, may be needed to regulate group management and trading relationships, especially in multi-jurisdictional filings.

There is a considerable risk that directors of international subsidiaries, mindful of their local legal responsibilities and unfamiliar with, and perhaps mistrustful of, the Chapter 11 process, will seek local insolvency protection unless their concerns and personal legal risks are thoroughly addressed prior to any filing.

It is therefore vital that corporate management communicate as openly (and as early) as possible with international management, who should ideally be provided with legal advice from a party familiar with multi-jurisdictional procedures. This addresses the risk that they will obtain conflicting advice from a local lawyer who, unfamiliar with international insolvency procedures, may offer advice that favors the low-risk local strategy — which could be, "when in doubt, file".

The receipt of such advice will practically create the obligation to act accordingly, if only to protect the management from legal exposure to civil action or even (for example in Germany) criminal prosecution. In anticipation of this, it may be necessary to change the constitution of local boards prior to a Chapter 11 filing to reduce this risk.

Directors are personally liable and can subsequently be disqualified from acting as directors in certain overseas jurisdictions if they do not fully meet their legal responsibilities — hence the importance of solvency tests in each country. These tests are: balance sheet (does the company have sufficient assets to meet its liabilities?); and cash flow (is the company able to pay its debts as they fall due?).

The first of these may include potential and contingent liabilities as well as those accounted for on the current balance sheet. The value of assets will be critically impacted by whether or not this test is carried out on a going concern basis. In a "break-up" scenario, value is likely to be significantly impaired.

The cash-flow test will look to the future but not beyond one or two years in any jurisdiction.

If intermediate holding companies/ subsidiaries or associate companies cannot meet these tests, directors may have to file for insolvency protection in the local jurisdiction.

Directors' powers cease in certain jurisdictions on the commencement of an insolvency process, and responsibility passes to the practitioner, whose duty is to maximize recoveries for creditors of the companies to which he has been appointed. Directors still have a duty to assist the insolvency practitioner in any way required.

Local filings of international subsidiaries

Unco-ordinated local filings can have chaotic consequences for international groups. Insolvency administrators or trustees in individual jurisdictions will have obligations principally to creditors of the filed company and other local stakeholders, and will have no interest or legal freedom to put the interests of the global group or the corporation above their own fiduciary duties. If this is not handled carefully, a global supply chain working on a "just in time" basis can collapse in days.

Local filings may be unavoidable but various actions can be taken to control and mitigate the associated risks. Practically, if there has been a US filing and the goal is to preserve the international footprint, multiple filings in other jurisdictions will not be the optimum approach and need to be avoided. This may be easier said than done and will require open dialogue with local management and may entail funding from the parent company if solvency on a cash-flow basis is a potential concern.

Although DIP filing options now exist in Canada and certain European jurisdictions, a co-ordinated approach requires a single umbrella filing.

It is also worth understanding and considering European Union (EU) legislation. This permits the filing for insolvency of corporate entities and groups in an EU jurisdiction where the center of main interest lies. A company's COMI does not have to be where its principal operations or registered offices are located; it can be moved. And moving the COMI of a holding company or key subsidiaries can maximize control of the European group if an EU jurisdiction is chosen that can work in a complementary way with the Chapter 11 process.

The additional advantage of establishing a European group COMI is that a single insolvency administrator can take an overall view of the European group and thereby better ensure the maintenance of its enterprise value as an integrated operation. However, there are limitations:

• Local creditors in an individual jurisdiction may act to protect their rights to local assets through a secondary filing in that jurisdiction. Any secondary filings need to be carefully planned and choreographed to ensure the stability of the European operations.
• Establishing or relocating a COMI outside a company's current country of registration is not straightforward. Careful planning is required, involving communication with third parties.

Relocating the COMI of key European companies can be challenging if time is of the essence.
• In certain continental European jurisdictions, there is a high level of sensitivity to the potential erosion of the rights of local stakeholders (not just creditors but also customers, employees etc). This may include the deterioration in status of various claimant classes, how inter-company liabilities are treated (subordinated or not) and how the netting off of debtor and creditor balances will work. This has to be anticipated and planned for so that those stakeholder concerns are addressed and managed as part of a successful COMI strategy.

Exit from bankruptcy

Assuming that the objective of restructuring is for the group to emerge from Chapter 11 bankruptcy largely intact, a quick exit is preferred, and that can be achieved through familiarity with some of the key concepts included in the company's plan of reorganization (POR) and disclosure statement. The POR, which is filed with the bankruptcy court, describes the process by which the corporation will change structurally and financially in order to remain in business. The disclosure statement provides the information needed by the creditors in deciding whether or not to vote in favor of the plan.

Generally, Chapter 11 provides for an exclusivity period during which the debtor can develop and propose a POR. The exclusivity period is initially 120 days and can be extended with court approval. Insolvency filings in most continental European jurisdictions are typically of a similar length to a Chapter 11 filing, although tactics and strategy will ultimately determine duration. In the UK, administrations may be shorter as they are often a prelude to the sale of the business or assets. If there are insolvency proceedings under way in a number of jurisdictions, a simultaneous exit from bankruptcy/insolvency will be desirable. This can be challenging but is certainly possible.

In a Chapter 11, the POR can include "cramdown" provisions that force certain classes of creditors to accept the plan once approved by two-thirds in value and one-half in number of creditors voting. However, non-US filings will likely differ in this regard. The UK, for instance, has limited ability to "cram down" dissenting classes of creditors.

Prepackaged and prearranged filings — in which the results of the POR are known, having been negotiated before the filing — will speed up the process and should permit an exit within one to six months. This eases the challenge of maintaining the global business and keeping its underlying value intact. Prepackaged deals also exist in Europe but are generally used as a way to sell assets quickly, free and clear of all liabilities.

The disclosure statement will require a credible five-year business plan, which will need to be prepared on a "bottom up", company-by-company basis. The same plan is normally utilized to provide a valuation of the global operation, which forms the basis for determining the company's enterprise value upon emergence and the attendant fair-value adjustments required pursuant to the application of the Financial Accounting Standard Board's SOP 90-7.

Finally, even with the global entity's exit from Chapter 11 and any non-US filing(s), there are usually residual claims that need to be addressed, resulting from the rejection of executory contracts, litigation, or creditor claims that have been compromised. For emerged entities under a Chapter 11 process, the resolution of these claims is usually managed either by separate staff or an allocation of the ongoing resources of the global entity, and funded through plan assets. Claims resolution usually rests with the insolvency practitioner for non-US filings and would be funded through the residual assets of the filed entity.

Choosing the professional team

A bankruptcy filing is usually a complicated and specialized process, especially if there are international implications. Not only is there a need to engage US advisors but also international legal and financial professionals. When considering the appointment of advisors, it is essential that the selected firms have cross-border experience in the critical jurisdictions. This is not only because of their local knowledge but their ability to step into the operation of the entity should local management not be prepared to continue. This will save time and, ultimately, cost.

39

Delicate state: Selection of the post-bankruptcy board

Julie H Daum, Co-Leader of the North American Boards & CEO Succession Practice at **Spencer Stuart**, the executive search firm, and Bettina M Whyte, Chairman of the Advisory Board, **Bridge Associates LLC**

A company still reeling from bankruptcy needs the right board to get back on its feet. A company emerging from bankruptcy is not unlike someone who has suffered a heart attack. The individual may be on the mend, may even be back at work, but there are still a number of precautions and different stratagems that must be followed to ensure survival and a return to peak health. For a company on the mend, to extend the metaphor just a little, a board of directors is somewhat akin to a team of doctors in whose care the patient's future rests. The need will be for directors who are often specialists in areas that will be critical to a turnaround — who have the judgment and expertise needed, and the time to devote.

The recruiting challenge

Recruiting good directors has become more difficult for all companies, but in the case of a post-bankruptcy board there are distinct challenges. Before even dealing with the issue of whom to recruit, there is a major hurdle to get over — namely, how to shift the focus of the group choosing the new directors away from each constituent's narrow personal interest to the broader perspective of serving the company's best interests.

This is not your normal selection committee. Most often, the people choosing the next board will be the lenders — the bondholders who have purchased at par; the debt traders who may have purchased at prices in the teens; and even the trade creditors. These are the groups that will initially own the new equity of the emerging company, and they often have diverging, even conflicting, goals.

For example, the traditional bank lender may want to continue to advance money to the post-bankruptcy entity, but on a very tight leash, so it may be looking for significant input into the operations of the company. The trade vendors will want a company that has substantial liquidity and room for aggressive growth so that, post-bankruptcy, it can buy goods and services at an expanding rate. The bondholders, especially those who have bought in at low prices, have a very short-term perspective: their goal will be to have debt and equity that will trade at par upon emergence from bankruptcy, enabling them to sell out of their positions within a very short time. Indeed, many of the debt holders may trade out of their positions during the board selection process. And, if there is a private equity or hedge fund that holds a large position, they will require representation on the board.

These differing agendas can make the creation of a board that will help the emerging company succeed and serve everyone's interests — creditors, management, employees and current and future investors — a daunting task.

A process that builds consensus

While it is not possible for all constituents' interests to be represented on the board, it is important that each party — secured and unsecured creditors, equity holders and, to some extent, management — is given some involvement in designing a selection process that is fair to everyone.

Most groups find it useful to have a subcommittee, or a selection committee, charged with handling all aspects of the process. This body should set criteria, review prospects and interview all the candidates. In order to bring credibility and integrity to a complex, often divisive situation, there is a strong argument for engaging a third party, such as a search firm, to organize the process and identify board candidates. To add to the case for this approach, it is not uncommon for members of the original subcommittee to trade out of their debt during the process, which may entail the selection of new members. A search firm, therefore, can bring a degree of stability and continuity.

While existing management may have a role in this process, it is unusual for any of them to sit on the selection committee. Obviously, one of the first duties of the board in these situations is to reach an objective judgment on whether the emerging company has the right management team, including the CEO, to effect a transformation in fortunes. If existing management participates in the selection procedure, there is a natural tendency to choose individuals who will be sympathetic to their own positions and beliefs, which may not be in the company's best interests.

For similar reasons, current board members are not generally considered for the new board. And, if they are, it is usually only one person, on the grounds that he or she can bring continuity.

It is also important not to leave the recruitment of the new board to the last minute, as often happens when those involved in the bankruptcy are exerting all of their efforts to negotiating a consensual plan of reorganization. However, it is preferable to have three months to select the new board, for getting this right will be fundamental to the future success of the company. At a minimum, the selection committee should answer these questions before starting the recruitment process:

• What are the most critical issues that will confront the company over the next one, two, and three to five years?
• What qualifications will be needed in new directors to match the challenges facing the company?
• How will prospective directors be identified and evaluated?
• Will there be a split between the role of the CEO and that of the chairman?
• What about term limits?

Building consensus on critical issues such as these forms the underpinning of the selection model. We have seen what happens when those charged with building a board do not rely on a strong and impartial process. Those who have served on these boards tell us that directors maintain a primary identification with the interests of the particular constituent group that placed them in their positions. As a result, it becomes difficult for the board to move forward and make unified, unbiased decisions.

In addition, if each of the constituents recommends one or two directors who represent the constituent's standpoint, there is a risk that the board will be filled with an overwhelming number of financial people, and too few with industry and operating experience.

Balance on the board

Building a board from the ground up, once a fair process is in place and ground rules have been established, means assessing what the board and company will need to accomplish over the next one, three, five years, and what complementary skills will be required in individual directors to succeed in this mission. While the task of recruiting multiple directors may be challenging, handpicking directors with the right skills and track records can represent one of the best strategic opportunities a company will ever have.

Although each company will have specific requirements for its directors based on its own needs, there are a few general categories of experience and skills that will be useful in most situations.

For instance, the board of a business that has gone through Chapter 11 should have one, and preferably more, individuals with a financial background. Often, one of these people will have a strong grounding in the public markets, while the other may be a retired CFO in a listed company or an individual who was a senior partner in a major audit firm and can therefore chair the audit committee.

In addition, it is helpful to have an executive with hands-on experience in the specific industry. This person will bring knowledge of the strengths and weaknesses of the company, and its competitors, and will have a view on the challenges facing the whole sector in the future. Also important is a director who has been through a reorganization and will quickly detect any cracks in the emerging company's armour and recommend solutions. Besides executives who have successfully led a company through troubled times, this role is often filled by someone from the crisis-management industry.

An outside CEO's viewpoint and skills are indispensable to the mix. Though there may be a shortage of chief executives to take on these assignments, there is no substitute for someone who has day-to-day operating and strategic experience in the hot seat, and who knows first-hand what it takes to get and keep a company going and deal with all of the constituent groups. This can be particularly important if a new CEO is going to be chosen to lead the post-bankruptcy company; if that person is inexperienced in the role, the outside CEO can help mentor them. He or she will also bring integrity to the board.

It is also wise to have a director who lends instant credibility to the board. For example, it might be very helpful for an international construction company that focuses on government contracting to appoint a retired high-ranking military person with influence "on the Hill". Likewise, if the company is recovering from a financial crisis or scandal, then finding an individual whose name stands for honesty and integrity is important. This person can help allay the concerns of analysts, investors and even customers who may be reluctant to do business with a company that has been in trouble. Such a director will be an ambassador to the world outside the company as it makes its comeback.

The crucial role of chairman

Increasingly, across all boardrooms, the roles of the CEO and chairman are held by different individuals. But the split is particularly important in companies emerging from bankruptcy.

First, because the board will likely be comprised of a new group of directors, the chances are they will have never worked together before, so there will be no established modus operandi. This makes an independent chairman who brings leadership and direction an essential element.

Second, one of the board's first tasks is often to determine if the existing CEO should remain or a new one be recruited; an independent chairman is in the best position to lead this process. In some cases, when the board decides to look outside, the chairman will also be called upon to step into the role of interim CEO until the new chief executive is in place. If this eventuality is a possibility, that should be a consideration when choosing the chairman, as he or she will need the leadership skills, ability and time to take on this position.

A third reason for splitting the roles is that a new CEO will have his or her hands full learning the business and running the company. Adding the responsibility of chairing the board is an unnecessary and distracting burden at a critical point in the company's life.

Leadership comes through over time, but to ensure a fast and productive start, it is advisable to appoint an outside chairman before the first board meeting. Often during the recruitment process, the selection committee gains a sense of the best person to fill this role based on the individual's temperament and the dynamics of the new board that spring from its other members. Because it is the chairman, rather than the CEO, who will run meetings and control the agenda, he or she will shape the priorities and ensure the critical issues are being fully addressed. Having a pre-selected professional who knows the ins and outs of running a board and establishing committees, and is committed to the company's success, is a huge advantage. It is also imperative that the new chairman has the time to commit to the task.

As a further note, it is not recommended that the board go the route of appointing a lead director. While he or she may be an objective outsider, such an individual will not have the clout and authority of a chairman.

A time for term limits

A post-bankruptcy board has a particular mission and directors are chosen for specific experience and skills that may or may not be essential once the company moves out of reorganization and on to the next stage. Just as corporate turnaround specialists may initially be important assets on a board, they are often replaced with another sort of leader after the crisis has passed. And while the practice of annual elections of all board members has become more prominent, it is not necessarily advisable when a company is newly out of bankruptcy and is just beginning to come together and function.

Neither is it uncommon for various board members to be assigned different terms, in the expectation that some changes will be required over time. This gives the board flexibility and the option of replacing directors when terms expire in order to gain the skills needed for the next phase of the company's development.

An investment in time

Ask people who have served in a company emerging from Chapter 11 and they will all agree on one thing: this is not your average board assignment and it takes a great deal of dedication to do the job well. Most individuals who are interested in working with a company coming out of a bankruptcy do not accept a board seat because they need something more to do or they want the extra income. Rather, they see it as an opportunity to recreate a company that has been through troubled waters and now needs to find the bridge to success and value.

From the viewpoint of the CEO, an active, involved group of directors is a critical resource. Directors in a post-bankruptcy company must understand upfront the demands that will be made on their time, because they will be far more involved than the average board member. They will be more drawn in than is typical in overseeing the operations of the business, as well as formulating the new strategy of the company. Additionally, they will be required to formulate new board and committee charters and other forms of best practices in governance.

As a result, their commitment means not only regular board meetings, as often as monthly, but more frequent committee meetings and calls with the CEO on an ad hoc basis. No "yes" men or women need apply.

As a picture of the type of director who serves on a post-bankruptcy board emerges, it is little wonder that retired CEOs and other retirees who have held executive management positions in publicly held companies are in demand for these boards. Not only do they possess a wealth of useful knowledge and operational experience, they also have the time to commit to the task.

Compensating fairly

When determining how to remunerate directors who sign on to a post-bankruptcy board, the time commitment must be kept in mind. Directors on these boards are actually paid on par with their counterparts elsewhere. However, they are interested in participating in the upside if the company does well.

So as an added incentive and as recognition of their efforts, board members generally also receive shares in the emerging company, which stand to become very profitable. Because of the greater time and expanded duties, the non-executive chairman often receives a larger percentage of shares and/or additional cash compensation.

In summary

Before the board is assembled, and well before the challenge of confronting pressing business and strategic questions, several other issues must be addressed and resolved by those given the task of building a board of directors:

• **Will the CEO stay or go?** As we alluded to earlier, those charged with getting the company back on solid footing — namely the new board — will have to examine the root of the troubles. Was the CEO part and parcel of the company's woes, or can those woes be attributed to factors beyond his or her control? Even if the latter is true, the board may decide that starting afresh, with a new board and ultimately a new CEO, will aid recovery, particularly if the company's name, and by association the CEO's name, is tarnished in the industry.

• **Solidifying the team**. Most boards have a culture and style. Over time, board members develop strong working relationships and often social bonds. It is a very different story when a group of newly elected directors is thrown together and must immediately get down to serious business without the luxury of first establishing a rapport. A pre-selected chairman will be able to take an active role in unifying the group and establishing a constructive plan of action. Well in advance of the first board meeting, all new members should receive extensive information on the background of the company, including a history of its troubles, and just as important, they should meet socially to get to know one another. It is also best practice for the outside board members to meet in executive session as part of every regular board meeting.

• **Be mindful of key criteria**. Keep important selection criteria at the front of your mind when building the board. Finding the right mix of executives will be important to the board's success, ensuring, for example, that the board is weighted in terms of hands-on operating experience rather than merely financial and banking executives. There are people who are really interested in these board assignments, but it is vital to identify those who will add the most value.

The common goal

The right board is critical to a company emerging from bankruptcy, with each director selected to contribute carefully identified skills. Despite the tensions and often competing interests of creditors charged with assembling a post-bankruptcy board, implementing a fair process can allow a disparate group to come together and work towards the success of a company in which they all have a stake.

Specialized Restructuring Resources in Distressed Situations

40

Why turnaround professionals are indispensable to directors and officers

Gerald P Buccino,

Founder and CEO,

Buccino & Associates Inc

Much has been written about the fiduciary duties of directors and officers during a corporation's periods of solvency, insolvency and that debatable period known as the "zone" or "vicinity" of insolvency. Yet, the subject remains the central issue of many restructuring cases and most litigation claims pursued by disaffected creditors and/or shareholders.

I have advised many directors and officers over the past 30 years, but I have also sat where you sit — as a CEO and director of public reporting entities employing many thousands of employees and responsible to complex constituency groups. Aside from the legal definitions of duties, I have often found that if directors and officers act in the best interests of the corporation and not themselves — if they ask the difficult questions, hire the appropriate professionals and demand the data needed to make the best decision — then they will have acted in good faith, demonstrating independence, care and loyalty to the corporation.

But aside from all the resources available to a board, what perspective can a turnaround professional bring to the discussion? And why should our opinions be solicited? What business environments do we normally work in that allow us to be both analytical and intuitive? And how can we assist the director and officer in avoiding the zone of insolvency?

How to avoid the zone

An experienced turnaround professional can contribute by recognizing the warning signs of financial distress. These will be flashing red long before a business reaches the zone — an area commonly defined as where the fair market value of the company's assets is exceeded by that of its liabilities; or where it is unable to pay its fixed obligations as they fall due in the ordinary course of running the business; or where the company has insufficient capital to finance future operations.

The ability to read these signs quickly and clearly will determine the success or failure of an enterprise.

Turnaround professionals are often retained just prior to the zone, or, at times, when the company is already in it. As a result of our many experiences, we have become adept at spotting the warning signs and acting with a sense of urgency, often protecting directors and officers from the pitfalls of operating within the zone of insolvency.

The value in retaining a turnaround professional early

While the idea may seem self-serving, directors and officers will never need outside advice more than in an economically distressed business climate. Even when they believe they have reviewed all the options in making a critical decision, the input of turnaround professionals is essential in such a highly litigious environment.

I am often asked the following questions by directors who want to pinpoint the signs of business distress:

- Where can I find these warning signs?
- Which should I see first?
- How could I have seen them sooner?

In reality, these signs are not always found in historical financial statements and it is not easy for outside directors to make the necessary observations when they only meet four times a year in the boardroom. But those on the inside live among them on a daily basis and the critical issue is to identify them long before distress has a chance to overtake the company. I am often retained after some of the threats have become all too apparent, although little has been done to address and reverse them.

The big three warning signs: customers, creditors and employees

The signs are present from one to three years before a company reaches the insolvency stage, so there is plenty of time to address them and avoid the zone. But, they are not all evident from the company's financial statements, which is why it can make sense for the board to keep an ear to the ground by meeting at some of the group's operating locations. It can even be a good idea for outside directors, without attempting to manage the business, to talk to one of the company's big customers. To give a concrete example of this, I currently serve on the Board of Regents of a major university, and our policy is that one of our Regents should always be a recent graduate, so we can better understand what students (our customers) want. Of course it is not usually practical to have a customer on a corporate board, but their input (unfiltered) is very important — as are the views of suppliers and employees.

In a distressed business and legal environment, directors cannot just show up for a meeting in a nice setting, take input only from management and believe that they are finished with their duties until the next meeting. None of this is intended to pit outside directors against management, but one phrase sums up how they might approach their responsibilities: 'When you think you've done enough, do a little more.'

The internal reasons

There are many warning signs of corporate distress that arise from the internal workings and philosophy of a business.

The following are some of the more common ones that I have witnessed in working with hundreds of clients.

- **Over-expansion** — the need to grow larger at any cost by expanding through acquisition into areas offering little synergy and where the business itself offers inadequate industry knowledge.
- **Inadequate business planning or none at all** — the idea that each year will be successful without the benefit of a budget or a bottom-up plan. One of the worst strategies seen in troubled companies is the "waterfall approach", where everything begins with an expected sales volume requiring additional overheads to achieve a growth number that often does not occur. In the meantime, management has invested in fixed infrastructure to achieve that unrealistic sales level. This is one of the most common signs.
- **Failure to change a strategy that is not achieving the desired results**. There are times when a board must insist that management change a course or be changed themselves. Turnaround professionals, by our nature, are change agents — or, at a minimum, advisors who can help a management team and a board to see things differently.
- **Poor asset management**. Whether a division, product or working capital, poor management of line activities results in excess or obsolete inventories and aged receivables. This sign should be seen early.
- **Overdependence on one client**. When a customer accounts for 25 per cent of a company's annual volumes, a warning sign is flashing and management must implement appropriate incentives to diversify the customer base. Apart from the obvious risk of being overexposed to the whims and business fortunes of a single client, there is also the question of negotiating power. For example, big retailers have been known to lure a supplier into plant expansion to handle increased volume — and then position themselves to set the terms and conditions going forward. At this stage, it is too late for the supplier to reduce its dependence on the customer as it has made the investment and needs the volume to absorb this increased overhead. To avoid this kind of vulnerability, boards should ensure they receive an analysis of customer volume and related accounts.
- **Poor pricing policies**. Either a company does not know the true costs of delivering its product or service and so cannot make a profit, or, as is customary, pricing is being driven by market forces and the company cannot compete. I strongly recommend that management assemble a pricing committee with input from marketing, sales, finance, purchasing and production. This will

provide an insight into all the factors that must be considered when setting a policy.

• **Excessive leverage or funded debt**. This is usually due to poor operating results, excessive expansion without planned returns on investment, or an overpriced acquisition.

• **Extended vendor payables**. If vendor credit terms are 30 days and the company is beyond 60 days, there is a cash-flow issue that must be addressed quickly.

• **Labor issues**. Long before a threat of disruption and strike action, there will be warning signs such as increased employee grievances, absenteeism, reduced productivity and quality-control issues. While outside directors are not in a position to spot such problems, they can ensure that management pays attention to its workers.

• **Poor internal controls, poor accounting systems and a management team that cannot operate in a leveraged environment**. Although management may be well versed in the company's industry, a highly leveraged business with limited resources provides a different challenge.

A common theme here is that all these problems can be avoided. They are the result of a management philosophy and, unfortunately, a board cannot see these signs in a current quarterly report. The warning signs will, though, be evident to a turnaround professional as we see them far too often. If they are addressed early enough, then the company can steer clear both of the zone of insolvency and the attendant risks for directors and officers.

The external reasons

External threats to a company are often more difficult to navigate, but a good management team and a well-informed board can deal with them successfully. Here is a selection of the possible issues.

• Competitive changes, including offshore companies that can operate at lower labor rates.
• Economic factors, including recession, excessive inflation or deflation, interest rates and currency movements.
• Technology changes moving at warp speed.
• Social changes, including consumer lifestyles and attitudes, and "green" issues.
• Government constraints, including tax rates, legislation, cap and trade issues, and product safety.

These signs will not be unique to any one company. The director and officer cannot claim that the environment in which they operate is outside their control. After all, a competitor will be in the same situation. I have often been told by new clients that their problems all began with an economic downturn. But my take is this: 'Recessions do not cause business failures — they identify them.'

The turnaround professional offers a different perspective to the board of a company facing the zone. In addition to being an independent third-party assessor of unfiltered facts, we import a sense of urgency to the boardroom — a sense that "business as usual is over" and that change must be implemented soon. While much of what we do is reactive to a distressed situation, we not only have the experience to identify the warning signs but also to deal with them in a rational way, prioritizing the remedial steps. Knowing what to do is important — but knowing what to do first is more important.

None of this implies that a board should hand over all responsibilities to a turnaround professional, for it still has fiduciary duties. But the retention itself does at least represent a "good faith" effort to exercise that duty of care.

Assisting directors and officers while the company is in the zone

It is not uncommon for the turnaround professional to meet the board for the first time when the company is either in or very near the zone of insolvency. By its nature, the zone is a difficult environment to define and is often determined after the fact, but directors and officers must protect themselves from those who will pursue claims against them should the company either fail or, at the very least, return less than was expected to its constituencies. The threat of litigation to recover even unwarranted amounts can be personally very expensive.

In this environment, directors and officers need to act with caution and with the guidance of outside professionals. The steps they take at this stage will almost certainly be reviewed should the company seek to restructure in Chapter 11 or, worse, liquidate.

How can the turnaround professional assist at this stage? What value do we bring?

The roles of a turnaround professional

The assessor or independent third party

Having reviewed the warning signs above, it is likely the company is now losing market share and key employees, and likely suffering from negative cash-flow. Secured creditors are lowering lines of credit, or worse, the company is in default and an amendment to the loan agreement is required to assure funding needs. Vendors are refusing to ship without cash on delivery or cash in advance, or worse, they are threatening litigation to collect. The business is at crisis stage and remedial action is required, and so the first task of the turnaround professional — the independent third party — is to provide an "unfiltered" report of the facts.

Based on these findings, several options might be available for addressing the situation. Given that the company is now in the zone, it is important to understand all its obligations, including those on the balance sheet (secured and unsecured creditors) as well as operating leases and other executory contracts that might be "off balance sheet". I also like to provide the board with a "hypothetical liquidation analysis" to highlight the priority of claims and any negotiating leverage the business might have with each group, and to outline the possibility of de-leveraging the company without a judicial process.

The assessment should include the turnaround steps that can be taken to improve both operating results and cash-flow. At this point, the board should insist that the business is managed on a "cash basis", because while profits are important, it is cash profits that will be pivotal in rehabilitating the company. It is a turnaround professional's mantra that cash measures reality while accrual accounting often reflects judgment bias, and as part of this, directors and officers will need reliable and meaningful short-term cash projections so they can examine all the options for improving the business and maximizing value for stakeholders.

The assessment becomes the document on which directors and officers can rely in making the difficult decisions. It should be presented at a formal board meeting and include a discussion and conclusion on the viability of the company, because, even in the zone, options are available for rehabilitation.

The advisor

Once the assessment is presented and the board accepts a strategy, the turnaround professional should become a trusted advisor. In addition, I always insist that outside counsel be present for all discussions on the best course of action, because it is not unusual to recommend steps that are beyond the ordinary course. The best advice here is that any decision must be driven by stakeholder value, whether it is the elimination of a product line, the

sale of an operating division, a reduction in staff or any other steps that appear out of the ordinary but are in the best interests of the company — in other words, a fiduciary duty. Together with outside counsel, the experienced turnaround professional is well qualified to provide the board with the necessary guidance to maximize the company's value for its stakeholders.

At times, it is necessary to examine the Chapter 11 options as a means of rehabilitating and reorganizing the business. The turnaround professional understands the post-petition process and often assists in the preparation for the filing. Statistics support the contention that the most successful Chapter 11 outcomes are those that have been carefully planned. Here, it is important to understand future financing needs and whether debtor in possession (DIP) financing is available — and, if not, how long the company can operate on a cash collateral basis without diminishing its asset value and so risking liquidation. The turnaround professional can negotiate the DIP and be a key witness in convincing the court on this matter.

If the lender group is demanding liens on the company's assets or, if already secured, is seeking additional collateral, directors and officers must understand the consequences and impact on other stakeholders. The turnaround professional can advise on the solvency/insolvency status or, if retained after liens have been granted, assess actions to "lift" them if they were granted within the preference period.

The chief restructuring officer

If it is deemed appropriate, the turnaround professional is the ideal candidate to assume this position. While management might still oversee the daily business operations, the chief restructuring officer (CRO) will be the interface with the board, the stakeholders and the bankruptcy court. Should the company sell all or some of its assets, the CRO will play a key role in negotiating the terms and conditions to maximize value for all the constituencies, so acting as a buffer for the board in meeting its fiduciary duties.

If it becomes necessary to replace top management, the CRO can step seamlessly into the CEO role. I once made this transition at a public company when our assessment uncovered a significant accounting fraud that placed the entire board at risk. Together with outside counsel, we discussed and advised on the options, and ultimately this client was successfully reorganized in Chapter 11 and the board did not face litigation.

The communicator

Directors and officers require someone with an independent and credible voice to speak to them, and so do the stakeholders. In a distressed situation, communication with all interested parties is essential to promote co-operation. In this respect, the turnaround professional should be supplying independent and reliable business and financial data to everyone, including the official creditors' committee and the court in a Chapter 11 setting.

The negotiator

I cannot imagine a situation where the turnaround professional is not part of the negotiating team when it comes to a restructuring of the company's obligations. Given our roles as assessors and advisors to the board, we become a natural conduit for all parties. This is the main reason why directors and officers must retain a firm or individual that has no interest in investing in the company; the conclusions reached by the board will be viewed as tainted should it transpire that its advisors are not independent third parties.

I have negotiated on many issues for boards. In pre-petition or non-judicial settings, I have talked to labor, landlords and customers. Turnaround professionals are best placed to manage these affairs should the board become uneasy with management's direction.

In Chapter 11 settings, I have found myself negotiating the terms and conditions for the retention of key employees on behalf of the board, and presenting these issues to the creditors' committee, trustee and the court. Independence is essential in obtaining bankruptcy court approval.

The witness

During the course of a Chapter 11 proceeding, court testimony on myriad issues will be required. While others might be called upon to give opinions on selected matters, the turnaround professional has the standing to discuss many business and financial issues, including the necessity of actions to be taken that are not considered ordinary business activities. These issues might include the termination of a business segment; the need to sell selected assets and to obtain reasonable recoveries for those assets; litigation issues that arise in Chapter 11; and, ultimately, the feasibility or reasonableness of your company's plan to exit the bankruptcy proceeding.

Should directors or officers find themselves having to defend their prior actions, the turnaround professional can be a valuable resource in presenting their efforts to carry out their fiduciary duties.

Conclusion

I have studied the reasons for business distress and failure for a generation, and I have learned and documented that companies do not fail overnight but over a three-year period. Even more important, however, is that the rate of failure is not linear but exponential. By year three, a company is failing at a rate far faster than in years one or two — which is why a board can benefit from seeking the advice of an experienced turnaround professional early, as the first warning signs appear.

We do not replace lawyers or outside accountants, but rather instill a sense of urgency in spotting the warning signs and influencing "change management". We are no longer viewed only as crisis managers — arriving when it is too late — but as professionals who can move from analysis to conclusion quickly and thoroughly enough to avoid the zone of insolvency, preserve value and eliminate the risk of litigation against directors and officers.

41

Effective communications in the distressed world: The role of a strategic communications adviser

Michael S Sitrick,
Chairman and CEO,
Sitrick Brincko Group

As is often the case, the general counsel of a defense company contemplating a debt restructuring sent a letter to bondholders outlining the company's proposal. The letter included all of the standard cautionary legalese, but went one step further. It definitively stated that unless the bondholders agreed to the terms outlined in the letter, the company was in such dire straits that it would have no choice but to file Chapter 11.

'You didn't send this letter out like that, did you?' I asked. 'You really should have couched it and said the company has no choice but to consider a number of options, one of which is filing for protection under Chapter 11.'

'Why?' he asked.

'Because when the media gets hold of this letter, and the headline reads "Agree to restructuring or it's Chapter 11", your customers, vendors and employees will all panic.'

'That's not going to happen,' he said.

'Why not?' I asked.

'Because all of the letters are numbered and confidential.'

I wanted to say, 'You're joking, aren't you?' But of course I did not. I did not know him that well at this point.

'Well maybe your bondholders are different from others I have worked with — and I am hoping that I am wrong — but I am betting that *The Wall Street Journal, New York Times, Financial Times* or some other media outlet has a copy of your letter.'

'You are wrong,' he stated. 'Each of the recipients signed confidentiality agreements.'

I looked at his outside bankruptcy counsel who was sitting next to me, and he just shrugged his shoulders.

'As I said, I hope I am wrong,' I responded. 'Talk to you tomorrow.' Or so I thought as I left for the airport.

When I got into my office that night, there was a call from the client. '*The Wall Street Journal* has a copy of the letter,' the general counsel said. 'They are going to run a story tomorrow. This is a complete disaster. Unless it says that any filing would include a provision for payment in full to our vendors, we will be cut off and likely be forced out of business within weeks.'

I immediately called the reporter and asked where he was on the story.

'We need to include two statements,' I said — 'one that says a filing is but one of several options being considered, and another that says any filing would provide for payment in full to the vendors.'

The reporter said he was sorry, but that information was not in the document he had read — and besides, he had already submitted the story to his editor.

I then called his editor's editor, who I knew, and told him that if they published their story without these two facts, they would be making news — not reporting it. I was telling him on the record that a filing was just one of the options and that, should it occur, vendors would be paid in full.

He agreed to include that statement, and the crisis was averted.

Why would a firm in Chapter 11 need PR?

Having been involved in this area for nearly 30 years, it continues to amaze me that one of the first questions I am asked when I meet with executives or a company's board of directors is: 'Why would a distressed company need public relations counsel? The last thing we want is to generate press coverage.'

Well, you might have been able to keep the negotiations or the state of a company secret 25 years ago, but not today.

If you are running a public company or a company with public debt, there are the SEC filings. Even if your business is not prominent enough for coverage in one of the major news outlets — Bloomberg, *The Wall Street Journal, Financial Times* or *New York Times* — the local media will likely see the statements made in your public filing if you are a major employer in any city.

'Well, who cares if *The Des Moines Register* publishes it?' is sometimes the reply. Again, welcome to the 21st century. Not only do the media that cover your company have it on Google alert, but in all likelihood your vendors, customers and many of your employees do, too. You might as well send out a blast email.

And then there is always, 'We'll just let the facts speak for themselves.' Are you sure you want a reporter interpreting the information in your public filings — or worse yet, going to some pundit for comment or clarification?

'No comment' can be a terminal mistake

One of the most common reactions to a media inquiry among companies trying to keep a low profile is to say nothing. A reporter calls and says, 'I have heard that you have hired bankruptcy counsel, and I wanted to chat with you about that and some other things I have heard.'

The company's response is often: 'I'm sorry, but we have no comment.'

That can be a critical mistake. We always advise our clients at least to find out what the reporter wants and make an informed decision before they decide not to comment. At the very least, having been forewarned, the company can prepare for what is coming. And there is always the possibility that the information they have will change your mind, especially if it is untrue.

This is not just a theoretical statement. This has happened when we have been called in to counsel a company, and even after the fact.

Take the case of the communications executive of a major publicly traded retailer who got just such a call from a reporter at *The Wall Street Journal*.

The reporter wanted the executive's reaction to some comments he had heard that vendors were no longer willing to ship goods on credit but rather were demanding cash upfront, or at least on delivery, because of concerns they had about the company's financial viability.

It will come as no surprise to anyone with knowledge of business that rumors like this can send struggling companies over the edge. Few companies, least of all a retailer, have enough cash on hand to pay for merchandise before it is delivered.

But this particular rumor was not only dangerous, it was false. Although the company did have financial problems, its vendors were still shipping on normal terms.

The executive was thus understandably outraged and brusquely dismissed the reporter's inquiry as nonsense. 'I won't even dignify that with a response,' he snapped, 'except to say that it is patently untrue.' Then he hung up.

The next day a story appeared in *The Wall Street Journal* recounting the rumors the reporter had heard, backed up by quotes from three of the company's vendors, all of whom said they would no longer ship merchandise to the chain without payment in advance. The executive's one-sentence denial was also included in the story.

As it happened, the three vendors quoted in the article were not representative of the chain's more than 10,000 suppliers. The reason they had stopped shipping merchandise was that they had been "cut off" — the result of a dispute with the chain over the quality and timely delivery of some previously contracted goods.

Nonetheless, once reported by the *Journal*, their comments set off what we refer to as a vendor stampede. Suppliers who had previously shipped goods on normal credit terms suddenly began to get nervous that they were in the minority — so nervous that many of them simply pulled the plug. The chain's headquarters was flooded with calls. 'Look, I believe in you guys,' company executives were told over and over again, 'but I can't afford to be the only vendor still shipping on terms. After all, if something were to happen to you, I'd be badly hurt. I'm sorry, but I have to protect my interests. I still want to do business with you, but it will have to be on a COD or cash-upfront basis.'

Over the next few weeks, the situation continued to worsen — until finally what the

Journal reported became reality. The company's vendors stopped shipping on any terms other than upfront or on delivery. Eventually it had no choice but to file for Chapter 11. It did not survive long enough to emerge.

How then should that retail chain executive have handled the call from the *Journal* reporter?

Instead of merely saying 'That's ridiculous' when asked about vendors refusing to ship, he should first have asked how many vendors the reporter had spoken with and who they were.

While it is true that reporters often balk at identifying their sources, in this case he probably would have told the executive, since he wound up quoting them by name in his story. In any event, he almost certainly would not have objected to letting the executive know how many he had interviewed.

Let us say all the reporter was willing to reveal was that he had spoken to roughly half a dozen vendors. Our response would have been: 'Come on, we have more than 10,000 vendors who sell to us. Are the people you spoke with major suppliers? We buy more than $1 billion worth of goods and services every year. Ask your sources how much business they do with us. What makes you think they represent our typical vendor?'

Assuming that was not enough to get him to drop the story — and, frankly, we would be surprised if it was — we would have gotten the company to assemble a list of names and phone numbers of 50 or 100, maybe even 200, of its most enthusiastic vendors. We would then have given those names to the reporter and suggested he call any or all of them.

Had the reporter revealed the identities of the unhappy vendors he had interviewed, we would have quickly ferreted out the details of each of their problems. In this particular case, it turned out that the outstanding balance for the three vendors combined was less than $100,000 (out of the more than $1 billion the company purchased annually), and that in two of the three cases the payment had been held up because the vendors had shipped inferior goods. Oh, and the third case involved disputed payments of less than $10,000.

If, after being informed of all this, the reporter had still insisted on proceeding with the story, we would have asked if he had called any of the vendors on the list we gave him.

'Look,' we would have told him, 'you have three vendors who say they are not willing to ship. We gave you the names of 100 who said they are. It is only fair that if you print this story, you quote some of the vendors who are more representative of what is going on at the company.'

We would also have pointed out that publishing a story based on the negative comments of just a few vendors out of more than 10,000 is both irresponsible and damaging, not only to the company and its employees, but to its vendors.

We would then have gone off the record and informed the reporter that the company was very concerned that even though it was not true its vendors had stopped shipping, an article in *The Wall Street Journal* saying otherwise could make it a reality.

Having actually been involved in such conversations more times than I would like to remember, and knowing the reporter who happened to make this inquiry, I can say with confidence that at the very least he would have phoned some of the other vendors for comment — with the result that his information would have been balanced and accurate. Indeed, there is a very good chance the story would have been killed.

There is more to communications than the media

Properly handling strategic communications for a restructuring involves a great deal more than just working with the media. It entails strategy and preparation of communications for all of the company's constituents. It requires an understanding of both traditional and digital media, including Facebook, YouTube, Twitter and the like. It takes a grasp of the nuances of the process so that you can react quickly to any problem that arises — whether that is a labor issue, or a customer, vendor or creditor crisis, or being able to get to the right editor on a Sunday night to correct or provide information that is sufficient to kill a story.

Equally important is being able to co-operate closely with the other professionals in developing and implementing actions to bring a successful conclusion to the process. It is critical that all elements are consistent and work together, because a company can tell its constituents that everything is fine but if the next day a national newspaper publishes an article stating that the company is headed for liquidation, then, true or not, the effect will be devastating. Who do you think they will believe?

As I have said since the day I started the firm: this is not an area for beginners or on-the-job training. You are betting your company on this process.

Some 28-year-old may seem perfectly capable until a news agency is about to run a damaging story with facts you dispute and you need to get to a top editor at 8.00 pm on a Friday, or you have a major labor issue that requires communications expertise as part of the solution. Hopefully, you will only go through this process once, and you want to make sure you do it right.

But communication is not just about damage limitation. In the right circumstances it can, among other things, "encourage" a reticent lender to renew a loan; set the stage to put a filing in its proper perspective; or convince a lender to stick with its commitment to provide exit financing after it has reneged on the deal.

Encouraging a lender to reconsider the provision of financing

Late one Friday evening — the time it usually happens in these situations — we received a call from a lawyer in Denver with whom we had worked on a previous case.

'We need your help in providing damage control,' the attorney said, skipping the niceties. 'We're going to liquidate the Purgatory Ski Resort, and in the process, devastate the town of Durango, Colorado.'

'Why are you liquidating?' I asked

'The bank refuses to extend our client's line of credit,' he answered.

'Why — is the resort bleeding red ink?'

'No, it's moderately profitable.'

'Then why won't they extend the line?'

'Because the bank was sold to an out-of-state bank that has no interest in continuing to participate in the ski business,' he said.

'How recently was the sale?' I asked.

'Within the past three or four weeks.'

'I don't believe you are going to have to close the resort,' I responded.

'Why? Do you know something about Colorado law that we don't?'

'No,' I said, 'but you tell me what the governor of Colorado is going to say when asked by *The Denver Post* whether, when he approved the sale, he bothered to ask if the bank intended to continue to support businesses within the state — let alone its most important industry? Was he aware that one of their first acts was going to devastate an entire town of 2,500 people? What do you think the state banking commissioner is going to say?'

There was dead silence at the other end of the line.

'How soon can you guys get here?' the lawyer asked eventually.

'Tomorrow morning,' I replied. 'But if you're in

agreement, I would like to tee this up with *The Denver Post* as soon as possible.'

'We would certainly like to see if we can convince the bank Monday morning that this [extending credit] is the right thing to do,' he responded.

'That's okay,' I said, 'but please don't tell them what we are contemplating because it will take away the element of surprise.'

I added that we could have the conversation with *The Denver Post*'s business editor off the record, with the understanding that if the bank agreed to extend the line of credit on Monday, it would be as if our conversation with him had never happened.

The lawyer gave us the go-ahead. I then called the business editor, who I knew well.

'Henry,' I said, 'I have a story that will knock your socks off. But before I say another word, here's the deal. My client still thinks there is a chance he will be able to negotiate his way out of this. So I will give you the information on the condition that (a) it is off the record until I say otherwise; and (b) that if he is successful in his negotiations, what I am about to tell you cannot appear in any form or fashion in your newspaper.

'Oh, and one more thing: I am going to give the story to you exclusively, but in return I want major play,' I stated.

'Okay on the first two points,' he replied, 'and if it's as good as you say, you've got a deal on the last point as well.'

After I told him the story, he said: 'I hope your client isn't successful in his negotiations. This is a fabulous story.'

Well, the client saw the bank on Monday morning. The meeting lasted three hours, at the end of which the bank told him to take a hike.

After some preparatory work with the client and his lawyers, we called the reporter to whom the editor had assigned the story in mid-afternoon. Unfortunately, by the time we had finished, it was too late for her to get anyone at the bank. She put a call into the governor's office and to the office of the banking commissioner, both of whom promised they would get back to her.

On Tuesday morning, the story appeared on the front page of the business section of *The Denver Post*, and all hell broke loose. When they spoke to the reporter, the governor and state banking regulator called the bank's actions outrageous. A Senator called for an investigation. The bank issued a statement from its out-of-state headquarters that there had to be some misunderstanding.

There was another story on Wednesday (we

wanted to keep them under what we call the "wheel of pain"). By Friday, our client had not only had its credit line reinstated but increased and the interest rate reduced, saving millions a year.

Setting the stage

In the weeks leading up to a possible Chapter 11 filing, an airline client of ours was very concerned that if a filing occurred, it could be extremely harmful, maybe even terminal, to its business. Management was worried that the media would slam it, and that its constituents would think the airline was headed for liquidation.

We felt it was critical to get out in front of this story — to "educate" the media. In order to accomplish this, we arranged a series of off-the-record meetings between the company's CEO and top reporters and editors. We explained the situation the airline was in, the options it had and that, yes, Chapter 11 was one of them. Then we explained the advantages if this proved to be the best option.

Some weeks later, when the airline filed Chapter 11, the media played back what we had told them during our meetings. Their stories explained not only why the filing was necessary but why it was the right way to go, replete with the benefits Chapter 11 provided. As a result, it was business as usual for the airline. It emerged from Chapter 11 a successful company and continued to operate in this way until 9/11 and the fuel crisis hit.

Encouraging lenders to keep their word on exit financing

When a major Midwest manufacturer filed Chapter 11, management knew it needed to make significant operational changes to adjust to current market demand. What it did not expect was that the necessary move to shutter facilities, consolidate delivery routes and improve operational flexibility was going to be stalled by more than 500 separate collective bargaining agreements with four unions covering approximately 29,000 hourly workers.

When a new management team was brought in, it quickly determined that a more customer-focused and streamlined business model was needed if the company was to survive. However, in order to accomplish this objective, it also recognized that it would have to gain employee support — against a backdrop of contentious union relationships, a decentralized workforce with no company-wide communications in place, and a demoralized staff base with a strong distrust of management.

Working with the company's legal counsel and its senior management, executives from our firm created and implemented a six-month campaign called 'You Decide'. This included a comprehensive employee outreach program and management participation at the local level that encouraged employees to speak directly to union leaders, telling them they wanted to keep their jobs and were willing to fight the union to do it. We also worked with local media to ensure the story was being accurately told.

Some time later, as the company was preparing to emerge from Chapter 11 after successfully dealing with all of these issues, another major problem arose. On New Year's Eve, while vacationing in Mexico, I received a call from the company's outside bankruptcy counsel. I was told that one of the lenders who had committed to provide the exit financing was backing out. Lender liability counsel had been retained, but by the time the litigation wound through the courts, the company would be liquidated and 29,000 employees would have lost their jobs.

'Didn't this lender get TARP assistance?' I asked. 'Wasn't the idea behind providing this assistance that lenders would lend?'

'Not TARP, but another form of government aid called the Temporary Liquidity Guarantee Program,' one of my partners, who was on the call, responded.

'Then I think we need to shine the light of day on them,' I said. 'We should go to the unions, the Senate Banking Committee, local Congressmen and Senators and union leadership. There are 29,000 jobs at stake here, and most of these people will not be able to find other jobs. Oh, and I think the media would be very interested in this story as well.'

That is exactly what we did. The lender received letters and/or calls from the two most senior US Senators on the banking committee asking why, after the United States government had guaranteed hundreds of millions of dollars on its balance sheet, it was reneging on a commitment to provide $125 million of very low-risk exit financing. Union leaders weighed in strongly, generating more political pressure; they got letters and calls from numerous members of Congress and other Senators. An article appeared in *The Wall Street Journal* highlighting the fact that financial institutions in receipt of government aid were not in fact lending — mentioning this lender by name.

Just to prove that miracles do happen, the lender changed its mind, and the manufacturer got its exit financing.

With not a minute to spare, the company emerged from Chapter 11 with leaner operations, a working relationship with its unions and a focused direction for rebuilding its business.

Conclusion

Directors and officers generally pose two questions. The first is, 'Can't internal communications staff handle this?' To which our general response is, 'Can your internal legal staff handle it?' And the second is, 'What role will our internal people play?' That is up to management and the staff members themselves. Sometimes the company wants its own communications people to concentrate on what they had been doing before. Other times they want them to be involved in the process. In that case, they work right alongside the outside communications advisor as an integrated team.

While by no means complete, we see the primary goals of restructuring communications as being to:

- Help maintain stability and preserve the value of assets in periods of financial volatility and change.
- Create communications, both traditional and digital, that advance the company's business goals and align with its legal strategy.
- Maintain the confidence of all stakeholders while the company explores strategic alternatives to resolve its financial and organizational issues.
- Manage expectations and calm uncertainties with direct, targeted communications, using the media judiciously and conveying messages that resonate.
- Provide communications counsel and assist in the development and implementation of those programs, working side by side with staff and advisors who are charged with the tasks of business development, investor relations, franchise relations and other key functions.
- Make sure the media tells the client's story, factually and fairly.
- Work with management, and its advisors to ensure a successful outcome to the process.

This really is a "bet your company" situation. It is not a job for beginners.

42

How a claims agent can maximize value and speed successful outcomes in Chapter 11 reorganizations

Daniel C McElhinney,

Executive Director,

Epiq Bankruptcy Solutions LLC, and

Lorenzo Mendizabal,

Managing Director,

Epiq Systems

For a company on the brink of a Chapter 11 filing, the goals are pretty simple: (1) enter bankruptcy; (2) survive; and (3) emerge from bankruptcy as quickly as possible. A full-service claims agent can help a company achieve these goals by focusing their talent and technology on the often complex administrative aspects of a Chapter 11 case.

The services provided can vary from straightforward tasks such as managing claims processing and noticing, to more complex projects such as developing an online claim form in order to streamline the bar date process. Regardless of the size or complexity of the case, the agent will be critical to the debtor company's success in mounting a speedy exit from Chapter 11.

Because officers and directors are not always familiar with the services, products and benefits a claims agent can provide, we will discuss each of these in turn, with an emphasis on how they can drive value for a debtor company before, during and even after a Chapter 11.

What does a claims agent do anyway?

To answer this question, we must first explain how an agent becomes involved in a Chapter 11 case. Normally, a debtor company is required by local bankruptcy rules to retain a claims agent where the anticipated number of creditors exceeds a few hundred. These rules acknowledge that the clerk's offices of many bankruptcy courts are not equipped, staffed or funded to fully manage the claims processing requirements of cases beyond a certain size.

Unlike the debtor company's legal and financial advisers, who are retained as "professional persons" pursuant to Section 327(a) of the Bankruptcy Code, the claims agent is engaged pursuant to 28 USC Section 156(c), a non-Bankruptcy Code provision governing the outsourcing of administrative services otherwise provided by the clerk's office. The debtor's estate has to pay for those services, although despite the statutory basis for retaining the claims firm, it can quickly become an important part of the debtor's restructuring team.

The term "claims agent" does not adequately capture all of the services provided. Clearly, the management and maintenance of proofs of claim asserted against the debtor company are the core tasks, but the industry has evolved over the past 20 years to a point where it performs a far more diverse set of tasks. Among these are:

- Creating and hosting interactive restructuring websites.
- Providing data mining, preservation, cleansing and review services.
- Assisting with creditor communication, including establishment of a call center.
- Assisting in preparing the creditor matrix and schedules of assets and liabilities.
- Compiling documents for, and hosting, a virtual data room.
- Planning and placing notices for publication domestically and globally.
- Providing bondholder identification services.

• Co-ordinating balloting and tabulation, including to holders of public debt securities.
• Co-ordinating disbursements of cash and securities.

As expectations of a claims agent's services have grown, so too has the need for more specialized expertise. In the last five years in particular, there has been a noticeable increase in the number of bankruptcy attorneys and restructuring advisors joining agents and forming "consulting" groups. The need for experience in the legal and financial complexities of Chapter 11 has only served to increase the involvement of, and reliance upon, claims agents in the administrative areas of a case.

It has also helped to change the general perception of the firms. Once thought capable only of managing primarily ministerial tasks (claims intake, data entry, basic noticing), they are now seen as experienced administrators capable of advising on, and managing, the often complex aspects of large Chapter 11 cases.

It also helps that they have evolved beyond their initial form. Ten years ago, claims agents were privately owned, independent companies with little obvious investment in the development of new technology. Today, the leaders in the industry are part of larger, publicly traded firms where technology is a key component of the business plan.

As an example, the two leading claims agents, Epiq and KCC, are owned by public high-tech companies that provide services and solutions internationally in a variety of industries.

The capacity, leverage and expertise available to agents that are part of well-capitalized groups cannot be underestimated, particularly given the increasingly global scope of Chapter 11 cases.

How does a claims agent drive value?

In the current economic cycle, more debtor companies are seeking to shorten their time in Chapter 11 by commencing prepackaged or prearranged cases. Others are filing and immediately proposing to sell nearly all of their assets via a Bankruptcy Code Section 363 sale. In each of these scenarios, the desire is to have the debtor company (in its current corporate form or via acquisition by another) emerge from Chapter 11 in as short a time as 30 days. The speed of these cases crystallizes the value of a full-service claims agent.

Data collection

The likelihood of success in an accelerated Chapter 11 case can hinge on the debtor company's ability to collect all of the right data prior to or immediately after filing. In a traditional Chapter 11 case, there is time to supplement or amend the company's creditor matrix or its schedules of assets and liabilities should new data be discovered. This is not true in an accelerated case.

For example, in situations where the debtor in possession has only 45 days to obtain court approval of the sale, finding out 30 days after filing that certain creditors did not receive the sale notice because their information was maintained in a long-forgotten database will not just delay the sale, it may kill it.

Similarly, the information provided in the debtor company's schedules and statement of financial affairs takes on a greater importance when creditors and an official creditors' committee are being asked to evaluate an accelerated sale. A material change to the schedules after they are filed will put immense pressure on the process and, again, jeopardize the sale. Given the absence of any margin for error, it is crucial for the debtor company to have the appropriate assistance at every level of the process.

A full-service claims agent will be able to help formulate and implement the data-collection process. The firm can work with the company and its advisers to identify the general types of creditors that should be captured. If on-site, the agent also can provide data systems and preservation specialists to assist the company's employees in creating queries that will capture the necessary data, and ensure that none of this is inadvertently deleted.

In many cases, the debtor company's leases and contracts are not maintained in a central location, and even less often are they maintained electronically. The claims agent can assist in the collection, data entry and scanning of contracts and leases, which can then be maintained on CD or in a virtual data room (see discussion below). Once gathered, the agent will often have technology that can be used to assimilate all of the creditor information into the correct format for filing with the bankruptcy court.

Data gathering on this scale is not usually straightforward. Every debtor company is different, and so questions inevitably arise as to whether certain information belongs in a particular schedule or as an answer to a question about a financial statement. An agent can help the debtor company and its advisors address these issues by drawing on its experience from other cases.

Just as important, the agent will have

technology tailored specifically to the creation of schedules. These applications are frequently used to consolidate disparate data points across many different debtors and then to produce all of the data by debtor in the proper bankruptcy form for filing with the court.

Interactive websites

A standard part of every new Chapter 11 case is the creation of a restructuring website through which the debtor company can disseminate information and notices. The separation of this site from the debtor company's existing corporate/sales website is intentional, as most businesses in this position prefer not to muddle positive messages with bankruptcy information. In addition to the content and key documents identified by the debtor company, clients and the general public receive automatic updates as to what is filed on the bankruptcy court docket at no cost. The restructuring website also includes "Contact us" information allowing creditors to submit questions.

Certain claims agents have the technical capacity and technology infrastructure to develop and host customized online claim-filing. Doing so increases efficiency and reduces the costs of managing the claim-filing process. Specifically, charges associated with the intake of physical claims, scanning, data entry, quality-control review and physical storage are all eliminated through the use of online claim filing. Having the data in an immediately available format speeds its transfer to the debtor company and its advisers, who can then begin claim reconciliation that much earlier. In cases with a large number of international creditors, utilizing a claim-filing site will reduce costs and administrative hurdles unique to non-US creditors.

Virtual data rooms

Virtual data rooms (VDRs) are web-based document-storage sites created to disseminate information simultaneously and confidentially to multiple users. Aside from being a valuable repository for contracts and leases, one of the most common applications of a VDR comes in a sale of substantially all of the debtor company's assets. When a sale is planned for early on in the case, establishing a due-diligence room with all of the company's key financial data is one of the first steps in the process.

Full-service claims agents not only provide VDRs, they also offer full management of the rooms. In certain cases, this will mean going on-site to multiple locations to pull and scan hard-copy versions of key contracts and leases for uploading to the data room. After this, the agent will work with the debtor company's advisors to identify and categorize the files.

Perhaps the most important task, however, is ensuring that permissions to the site are set correctly. The worst case is that a prospective bidder, particularly one that may also be a competitor, inadvertently gains access to confidential information.

Virtual data rooms are also valuable when gathering data for use in preparing first-day motions. In years past, key data collected from the company would be emailed, or copied and circulated in paper form, to those involved in the drafting of these motions. Recipients could include the client, financial advisor and one or more law firms. With a VDR, the information can be loaded into a secure, centralized platform that can be accessed by all the debtor company's advisors, resulting in a higher degree of confidentiality and efficiency in the critical days leading up to a Chapter 11 filing.

Call centers

How well a debtor company manages communications with customers, employees, vendors and others at the point of entering Chapter 11 can materially affect its ability to reorganize successfully. Managing this part of the process well usually results in the public having a clear understanding of the reasons for filing and the debtor company's plan for exiting Chapter 11, thereby limiting any negative impact on performance, customer orders and vendor issues. Manage it poorly (or not at all) and what could result is an avalanche of angry customers and confused and frustrated vendors. In light of all this, debtor companies, big and small , are utilizing call centers to help address questions from their various constituencies at the beginning of the case, as well as at other key points.

A claims agent can help in establishing a call center and provide model scripting and other communications assistance. Such facilities are capable of providing recorded messaging and live operators in multiple languages. Messaging can be used to direct different customers to information that pertains to them specifically, resulting in a better experience for the caller and, therefore, better value for the debtor company.

Additionally, having a call center in place at the time of the filing will save employees and advisors from being inundated with hundreds if not thousands of calls. The cost savings and increased productivity that result are hard to quantify, although they do tend to have a favorable impact on a case.

Expert services

When a claims agent firm has experienced restructuring professionals on its staff, the conversations with the debtor company and its legal and financial advisors are more informed and valuable. There is no gap in understanding as to the way ahead. In many areas, in fact, claims agents are active participants in discussions over how best to advance the administrative process.

In many prearranged cases, the debtor company files a plan and disclosure statement with the Chapter 11 petition and seeks to confirm the plan in four to six months. Unlike in prepackaged cases, which immediately move towards a confirmation hearing within 30 days, many of the usual milestones of a Chapter 11 case must occur in a prearranged case before a hearing can be held. Thus, schedules and statements must be filed, a Section 341 meeting held, a bar date set, a disclosure statement hearing held, and solicitation and tabulation of votes on the plan must take place, all within a much shorter timeframe than in a usual case.

As the entity distributing the various all-creditor notices, processing the proofs of claim received, and co-ordinating the solicitation and tabulation of ballots on the plan, among many other tasks, the claims agent must be consulted to determine if the proposed timeline can be achieved. The restructuring professionals on staff at full-service agents, calling on their detailed knowledge of the local and bankruptcy rules, as well as their experience in handling expedited matters in many other cases, are uniquely qualified to inform the debtor company and its advisors on what is possible.

Another example of the value provided by a claims agent is in the area of public securities solicitation. This is a very specialized discipline and one that requires professionals who can speak the language of Chapter 11 while also conversing fluently with Wall Street back-offices and depositories.

Conclusion

The debtor company, which is to say its officers and directors, in consultation with legal and financial advisors, will usually have a clear idea of the legal,

operational and financial path to a successful Chapter 11 restructuring. Officers and directors could risk significant delay and, potentially, jeopardize the restructuring if the administrative aspects of the process are not considered. It is in this area that the claims agent can make a difference in a successful reorganization.

43

Evaluating and monetizing assets: The role of the independent asset advisory firm in corporate decision-making

Jeffrey W Linstrom,
Managing Director,
**Hilco Recovery
Strategies LLC**,
Jeffrey B Hecktman,
President and CEO, and
Richard L Kaye,
Executive Vice President,
Hilco Trading LLC

You are the CEO of a company that has just been informed by its banks that all future financing must be supported by adequate collateral. You need to borrow $50 million over the next three months. Who can tell you if the value of your collateral will be sufficient to meet your needs?

You are the CFO of a company involved in a restructuring and your lenders are demanding that you sell assets to generate cash to pay down debt and generate liquidity. Your company owns a major office building that it can sell, and the board is asking for your recommendation as to whether an offer on the table of $100 million is the best it will get in a reasonable timeframe. Who can help you with this decision?

The answer to both questions is an asset advisory firm.

Overview of asset advisory firms

Many officers and directors would have little reason to know there are firms that specialize in the valuation and monetization of virtually all assets on a balance sheet. They will be aware that investment banks and accounting firms provide valuations for healthy businesses in certain circumstances, or advise on the fairness of a financial transaction. But, what these organizations typically do not do is value specific assets, particularly in the context of distressed transactions.

Hired by the various parties involved in a financial restructuring, asset advisory firms have developed an expertise in determining the value of machinery and equipment, inventory, real estate, accounts receivable and intellectual property. They make these assessments under a range of different valuation scenarios, from forced liquidation to fair market value. The best of the advisory firms will also be adept at realizing the worth of the assets and turning them into cash. They routinely "trade" in the assets, selling them for a client on a brokerage basis or for their own account.

Financing transactions and the role of an asset advisor

For many companies in financial distress, the hardest task can be obtaining and maintaining adequate working capital. This financing often takes the shape of secured bank debt or "asset-based lending" — which, as the name suggests, refers to funding provided by banks and finance companies according to the value of a borrower's assets. So, the role of the advisor here is to determine what those assets are worth.

Asset-based lending

These loans can come in many different forms. Depending on the borrower's collateral base, a lender may extend a revolving loan and sometimes a term loan as well. Revolvers are typically secured by accounts receivable and inventory, and the principal outstanding fluctuates according to working capital assets and collections. The credit agreement governing the revolving loan will provide for a "borrowing base" that uses advance rates on accounts receivable and inventory to establish the borrowing limit. For example, an advance rate on receivables will be a specified percentage of the face amount of "eligible" accounts — perhaps 50 per cent. The rate on inventory will be a percentage — perhaps 65 per cent — of the net orderly liquidation value (NOLV) of "eligible" inventory.

What qualifies as "eligible" will be laid out in the credit agreement with the asset-based lender. Ineligible accounts receivable and inventory will not be counted in the borrowing base and these can include accounts of affiliated entities, those that are past due, accounts with too much "concentration" (too large an amount owing from one debtor), and those that are subject to litigation. "Ineligible" inventory will include damaged, defective or obsolete finished goods, work in process and supplies, and inventory covered by a document of title (for example, warehouse receipt or bill of lading). Specific categories of inventory identified as problematic by the asset advisory firm will also be ineligible.

Term loans are for a fixed principal amount with a specified maturity date, and they are usually secured by fixed assets. The principal tends to be a specified percentage of the NOLV of those assets — for example, real estate, machinery and equipment, and intellectual property. This brings us to the role of advisors in the financing transaction because they will determine this value — as they will the NOLV of the inventory on which the amount of borrowing available under a revolving loan will turn.

The advisor's assessment, therefore, is vital: the higher the appraised asset value, the greater the potential boost to the company's liquidity. Consequently, an officer or director of a company receiving an asset-based loan must understand the critical role played by an asset advisory firm and how to work with them to benefit the business.

Who picks the firms to perform the appraisals?

Lenders subject to the Financial Institutions Reform, Recovery and Enforcement Act (FIRREA) must be the ones retaining the appraisal firm if a valuation is needed for a borrower's real estate. But, there is no similar legal requirement for inventory, intellectual property or machinery and equipment, and so a borrower who has enough negotiating leverage with its lender may be able to choose the advisor. And, if that company is fortunate enough to have a number of asset-based lenders competing to provide financing, it should be able to pick one firm to be used by all of them. Indeed, it is important that the different lenders

issue proposals on an "apples to apples" basis where the assets to be evaluated are defined by the borrower and the selected advisor's appraisal report is the single one used by all parties. This provides clarity in the sense that one lender may propose an advance rate on eligible inventory of 85 per cent and another may offer 80 per cent, and it is clear which offer provides more liquidity because the NOLVs are the same.

How do you pick the right firm?

The first step for a borrower is to consult its other professional advisers — for example, lawyers, turnaround professionals and investment bankers. They will know the top firms in the area and suggest one or two. What qualities should directors and officers be looking for? First, the firm should have expertise in all the relevant asset classes. If you need both inventory and intellectual property appraised, do they have practices in both areas? Second, ask the firm if it has experience in your industry; a key component in understanding the value of assets is how they are used in your sector. Third, an advisor with actual buying and selling experience in the relevant assets will have a far superior perspective on value than one that only carries out appraisals. Fourth, confirm that the appraisal firm you wish to retain is on the lender's approved list.

Finally, although this may sound self-serving, do not base your choice on the lowest price quote. Saving thousands of dollars by picking the cheapest provider is penny wise and pound foolish if their value opinion is too low.

How do the advisors perform their appraisals?

The appraiser and the party that has engaged it (lender or borrower) will enter into a retention agreement that outlines the following: the assets to be appraised; the valuation standard to be employed (fair market value, NOLV, forced liquidation value) and a definition of that value; the scope of work to be undertaken (site visits, management interviews, desktop valuation); and the delivery date for the written report. The schedule should build in enough time for the user of the appraisal to review and understand it before the financing transaction is due to close.

The next step will be a written request from the appraiser setting out the due diligence information it needs from the borrower to perform its analysis. Once these details have been provided, the appraiser will schedule site visits to assess real estate, machinery and equipment, and inventory, with factors taken into account here including any unusual features of a building and the age of the machines. For intellectual property appraisals, interviews with management will be conducted to understand licensing arrangements, among other issues.

The appraiser will then review all this information, search its own valuation database for comparisons with similar assets and conduct market research (such as recent real estate transfers in the local market). The final step is the written report setting out the valuation opinion and the underlying analysis.

Look for an USPAP-compliant appraisal

The Uniform Standards of Professional Appraisal Practice (USPAP) is the generally accepted code for this sector in North America and applies to all types of appraisal service. Standards addressing ethical and performance obligations are included for real estate, personal property, business and mass appraisal.

Nearly all asset-based and real estate lenders require compliance with USPAP. They may also require that appraisers be certified by one or more industry bodies, such as the Association of Machinery and Equipment Appraisers (AMEA), the American Society of Appraisers (ASA) or the Master Appraisal Institute (MAI).

What role should an officer play in the process?

First, understand the important role the appraiser will play and share this perspective with the management team that will work with the firm.

Second, timing is often critical in financing deals, so make sure the appraisal timeline meets that schedule and that you have adequate management resources dedicated to getting the information to the asset advisor on deadline.

Third, ensure that your side of the story is told in the way you want it to be told when an appraiser is being interviewed by management. What explains recent sales trends? Why have you changed your inventory mix from a year ago and what does it mean for near-term performance?

Ask the appraiser what key metrics it will concentrate on and address each of them. Encourage the firm to follow up with you personally on any outstanding questions. Never assume that, just because you know why certain negative trends are not a major issue, the appraiser will reach the same conclusions.

What if you think the values are too low?

The appraisal report has been issued and you think it undervalues your inventory. What can you do? Sometimes nothing; once the report is out, it may be too late to change the appraiser's perspective. But, other times, you may be able to suggest factors that the firm has not taken into consideration. Another strategy is to ask for a second opinion, although you will need to check with your lender on how this might be treated; if it will not be used to increase your borrowing base, it may not be worth the cost and effort.

Monetizing assets: the advisory role

Let us go back to the opening example of the CFO who has been asked to advise the board on whether a $100 million offer for an excess office building is a good deal. In a financial restructuring, the sale of assets takes on considerations and dimensions that do not normally exist. In this case, the CFO knows that the disposal of the building must be accomplished in six months to be of any benefit. An asset advisory firm is hired on the recommendation of another outside professional service provider and the first assignment set by the CFO is to assess if the board should proceed with that $100 million deal, or whether it should seek a better offer even though the clock is already ticking down to when the deal must close.

The real estate arm of the asset group performs its valuation analysis and explores other potential deals that could be closed in six months. It concludes that $100 million is fair value for the sale of the building in its current unused state. However, the firm also advises that the building could be sold for a materially higher value in six months if a tenant can be found and a lease signed. Further, it believes it can find a tenant and a buyer within that timeframe. The CFO advises the board to reject the $100 million offer, to hire the firm to find a tenant and then to market the building. The company's lenders had been pushing for a quick sale at $100 million, but they back off, respecting the opinion of the asset advisor, whom they know well. Five months later, a tenant is secured on favorable lease terms and a buyer agrees to a cash price of $140 million. The deal closes within the schedule.

In this example, the asset advisory firm has played the role of an independent expert on to which the board and the lenders could shift responsibility for the outcome. Without that external perspective, the lenders would have been reluctant to accept any suggestion from the company that it could secure a better deal; by this point in the relationship, they have grown suspicious of the company's own view of the value of its own assets. The entry of a third party changes the picture because the lenders know that the asset advisor would not jeopardize its reputation, and thus future assignments, just to support its client's view. In addition, the company and its board have insulated themselves from the fallout if events prove that wrong decisions have been taken; they could hardly be blamed for relying on an expert in the field. In other words, one of the key services provided by an asset advisory firm in a restructuring is protection.

Asset advisory firms can do much more in a restructuring than sell assets for a fee. In many circumstances, they are asked to put capital at risk to guarantee a specific outcome. We discuss below how this works with various asset classes.

Monetizing assets: the investment role

Let us assume a manufacturing group has a plant that is idle and not part of a restructuring plan. It believes at least $20 million worth of assets is tied up in the plant and that some portion of this value is needed immediately to meet upcoming liquidity needs. The company's law firm suggests hiring specialists to monetize the assets under a structure that gets the company cash before the plant is sold. The industrial arm of an asset advisory group is hired.

The firm performs due diligence and concludes the plant can be sold for $20 million over 18 months. The carrying cost of the plant (basic maintenance, taxes) over that time is $3 million. The firm proposes a sale approach known as "guaranteed recovery", under which it offers the company an upfront payment (the guarantee) of $12 million and an upside sharing payment of 50 per cent of the amount collected, net of carrying costs, over $12 million. The deal is accepted, the $12 million is paid and the asset advisor is given exclusivity on the sale of the plant.

Some 14 months later, the sale has been completed. The gross recovery amount is $21 million. At this point, the $12 million upfront guarantee payment is deducted from gross proceeds, as is $3.25 million, representing the asset advisor's carrying costs plus its cost of capital. Therefore, the net upside to be shared is $5.75 million. Based on that 50 per cent formula, the company receives another $2.875 million

In this example, the asset advisory firm has provided the company with vital liquidity in a much shorter time than it would otherwise have taken to sell the asset. Lenders, typically, would be unwilling to provide such liquidity because they do not like to make advances against assets that are not part of a "go forward" operating plan.

Asset advisors can also play a critical role in monetizing retail inventory in restructuring transactions. Let us assume a department store chain has ten branches that have been unprofitable for the past 18 months, with no reasonable prospect of that changing in the foreseeable future. The stores have an aggregate cost inventory of $40 million. The retailer decides to close all ten and, initially, plans to use its own people to run the process. However, the company's financial turnaround consultants say management time would be better spent focusing on the "go forward" stores that need significant improvements to meet the company's business plan. It also suggests hiring an asset advisor with expertise in retail store closings.

The selected firm begins its work by performing due diligence on what could be achieved on a net recovery basis through closing sales. It concludes that this will be a certain percentage of inventory cost. It proposes to conduct the sales at the ten stores and guarantees a net recovery to the company that is paid upfront after the inventory is counted by a specialist firm. It is surprising to the retailer that the guaranteed recovery is higher than it expected to achieve on its own. The advisor firm is given the assignment and brings in its staff to conduct the sale utilizing the company's store associates. The upfront payment provides liquidity for the retailer at the beginning of the sale process, rather than it having to wait for the final outcome ten weeks later.

Two important points about restructuring transactions are made here. First, the retailer was able to advance its own business plan because management could focus on the "go forward" stores. Second, by using an asset advisory firm specializing in store closing sales, the retailer achieved a better monetization result while the upfront payment improved its near-term liquidity.

Other roles of asset advisors in restructurings

Continuing with the example of the retailer, some of the stores that have a future may nevertheless be only marginally profitable because of above-market lease terms. If those leases could be restructured to lower the costs, the stores would be clearly profitable due to the extra cash-flow. Certain asset advisory firms have practices that specialize in renegotiating leases with landlords.

Although the retailer may have its own real estate group, the specialized expertise of the asset advisor will almost always achieve better results. This stems from several factors. First, the advisory firm will know what terms are being achieved in similar situations. Second, it understands how to use the specifics of a financial restructuring to deliver a story to the landlords that will motivate them to do a deal. In a similar situation, the retailer's own staff would be reluctant to play up a difficult financial condition with the landlords after years of playing up its financial strengths to drive the best lease terms.

Conclusion

For the officer or director of a company engaged in a financial restructuring, asset advisory firms can play a vital role. They can determine the value of your collateral to provide you vital asset-based financing. They can find the best way to monetize assets, often providing liquidity through an upfront investment. Ultimately, they can allow you to concentrate on your own job.

Closing Reflections

44

Does reorganization need reform? Time for a new look at Chapter 11

Robert J Keach, Co-Chair of the Business Restructuring and Insolvency Practice Group, Bernstein Shur, writing on behalf of the **American Bankruptcy Institute**

After over 30 years, does Chapter 11 need reform? Ironically, at a time when other countries have just started to borrow Chapter 11's best elements for their own insolvency regimes, the statute is undergoing a period of re-examination in its country of origin. Recent events — perhaps reaching a nadir with the Chrysler and General Motors cases — have many calling for a fundamental re-examination of the system of corporate restructuring in the United States.

Chapter 11 — the "orthodox" model

The "orthodox" model for a Chapter 11 — ushered in by the 1978 Bankruptcy Code — involved a debtor voluntarily seeking relief, largely to address balance sheet issues and often short-term or one-time operational disruptions (mass tort litigation, product issues, accidents, natural disasters etc). Under the central feature of the Code, the debtor and its existing management remained in possession of the debtor's assets and in control of its reorganization, albeit under court supervision. The debtor in possession (DIP) would negotiate with its existing lender (or a new DIP lender or even several potential DIP lenders in the recent 'golden age' of liquidity) for DIP financing.

Once the business was stabilized, the debtor would negotiate its plan of reorganization with its various creditor constituencies, including a creditors' committee of trade creditors and bondholders, most of whom held their claims and had a long-term interest in the debtor's survival, either because they wanted a customer to sell to or simply because their best hope for a decent return on their claims lay in the debtor's recovery and survival.

Debt was often exchanged for equity, but existing equity often kept a small piece of the action as well. A plan was developed, sent to all creditors and voted on by creditor classes. Rarely, cramdown (confirmation over objection) occurred. Cases often took years, with little pressure to emerge from the protective cocoon of Chapter 11 until all of the balance sheet and operational issues were resolved. There were some sales of all of the assets — Section 363 sales — but they were by no means the norm. The principles of creditor democracy, equality of distribution among like creditors, absolute priority and fundamental fairness — along with a fresh start for the debtor — were paramount.

Restructuring in a changing world

The 1978 version of Chapter 11 was seen — and often criticized by creditor groups — as "debtor friendly" or, at least, as reorganization friendly. The degree to which it succeeded in saving businesses, as well as the jobs they provided, was often debated. But, in the case of the larger firms, it largely met the announced goals of its originators. Or at least, it did for a time.

The world of credit — and restructuring — has changed a lot since 1978. Secured credit appears at multiple levels of the balance sheet, with first lien, mezzanine and third lien debt. Debtors now often arrive at Chapter 11's door seriously over-leveraged, with little or, often, no equity in their assets after payment of the secured claims. The situation where there is value to distribute to even priority creditors, such as employees, is increasingly rare. Indeed, many cases — even very large cases — flirt with administrative insolvency from their earliest stages, meaning that, without a "gift" from the secured lenders, the costs of the Chapter 11 case itself cannot be met.

An efficiently functioning market for distressed debt, even for small unsecured claims in middle-market Chapter 11 cases, steadily emerged. Creditors no longer needed to wait for a distribution from the estate if they wanted a return on their claims; they could simply sell them, albeit at a discount, to a willing claims trader.

The face of lenders changed, too. Many (most) loans are not made by "traditional" lenders (the banks), but rather by private equity funds, hedge funds and others — when they are made at all. The new class of lenders often had very high expectations for rate of return, and very little patience for an underperforming borrower. Unlike their state- and federally-regulated predecessors, the new lenders were also willing, and sometimes anxious, to take over a struggling borrower entity.

Changes to the Bankruptcy Code

The Bankruptcy Code has also changed over time, as various special-interest groups gained advantages. Prior to 2005, there was little in the way of comprehensive reform, but rather a series of incremental changes. The 2005 legislation (known as BAPCPA) introduced what many consider to be the most devastating changes to the cause of traditional restructuring — changes that others defended as a necessary tilt towards the rights of creditors. Landlords obtained shorter maximum periods to assume or reject leases. New administrative expense categories were created, including for suppliers. And utilities obtained increased rights, which further stressed liquidity.

Swaps, repurchase agreements and forward contracts and other derivatives, which previously had some limited protection, were essentially carved out of the Code, with counterparties allowed to terminate the contracts free of the automatic stay and insulated from avoidance action risk. The definition of those contracts and instruments included within the category of the exempted derivatives was broadened widely in 2005. In sub-prime mortgage company cases like New Century and American Home Mortgage, the bulk of the assets left the bankruptcy estate within days of filing — possessed and either retained or sold by warehouse lenders, the counterparties under master repos and similar constructs.

In response, transactional lawyers and their counterparty clients also began adjusting to the breadth of the derivative safe harbors — recasting loans as master repurchase agreements and supply contracts as forward contracts. The new, expanded provisions were being used, arguably, not just to protect the functioning of public markets — their original announced purpose — but rather to "bankruptcy proof" otherwise routine secured lending and commodity supply arrangements.

Labor made some legislative gains in the 2005 amendments, particularly in the area of limiting retention bonuses and executive compensation. Retention pay programs were sharply curtailed, if not virtually outlawed, especially for senior executives. But for the most part, labor contended that the changes to Chapter 11 operated to the detriment of workers.

Financing and sales

Through case law development and practice, DIP financing got more onerous, with lenders obtaining more control. Case law had previously prohibited, or at least severely curtailed, the practice of cross-collateralizing pre-petition secured debt with new post-petition assets. However, this practice, perfected in a DIP financing structure known as a "roll-up", became commonplace (in a roll-up, the DIP financing "pays off" the pre-petition loan, while the entire balance of the "new" financing, which often involves minimal new money, is secured by a first-position lien in all pre- and post-petition assets). Lenders also sought and obtained broad releases, which were also limited under prior case law. More critically, Chapter 11 cases began to look like streamlined foreclosures, as DIP financing deals added tight deadlines by which the debtor's assets needed to be sold or the financing would end.

Sales — very quick sales — became the norm for highly and over-leveraged debtors arriving in Chapter 11. Sales of substantially all of the debtor's assets, free and clear of liens, were completed, often within 30-60 days of the filing of the case, if not a shorter period, with the buyer sometimes being the hedge or private equity fund that was the pre-petition and DIP financing lender.

These so-called "loan to own" deals became more and more common, while also attracting increasing scrutiny.

In the quick sales transactions, collective

bargaining agreements were often rejected. In a number of cases, the sales price was less than the secured debt. Debate raged over whether the lender should carve out money for the junior classes of debt, sometimes derisively referred to as the secured party's "tip" for use of the bankruptcy system to foreclose on collateral.

Chrysler and General Motors

Then came the Chrysler and General Motors cases. In both, the US and Canadian governments were pre-petition lenders and the DIP financing sources. The central assets of two of the world's largest automakers were sold, within a couple of months of the case filings, in each case to a "new" company largely owned by the governments and by labor union affiliates, the latter having earned stock in the new entity by virtue of agreeing to new, company-friendly collective bargaining agreements and pension arrangements. Many dealer agreements were rejected to devastating effect, closing down a number of Main Street businesses. Tort claimants — the alleged victims of accidents caused by allegedly defective vehicles — were largely left to recover from the unsold residual assets, as were other classes of unsecured and under-secured debt, although there were variations between the two cases in this respect. Both were essentially large loan-to-own cases, the US government standing in the role usually occupied by a hedge fund or bank lender.

Commentators — and others — rushed to declare a possible new era for restructurings, while at the same time pleading that the automaker cases be treated as "one-offs" and a product of unique government intervention necessary to save the struggling, and critical, US auto industry.

While Section 363 sales of all or substantially all of the debtor's assets were, as noted above, nothing new, many saw Chrysler and GM in particular as having cast aside the concepts of creditor democracy, equality of distribution, absolute priority and fairness. They contended that Chrysler and GM had the potential to usher in what may be called the "sale model of reorganization".

In that model, arguably, creditors participate in the reorganization based upon what the purchaser sees as their capacity to contribute to the survival, indeed success, of the new post-Chapter 11 enterprise.

Those that do not are left to divide up the residual assets. Defenders of the Chrysler/GM results declare them nothing new or radical, but simply large Section 363 sales of the typical variety.

Addressing the questions

Questions abound. Is Chapter 11's demise greatly exaggerated? Is the market — and the creativity of the practitioners — outrunning the legislation? Is it simply time for a reset, a re-examination of the Code after 30-plus years in light of these developments? Should we save "orthodox" Chapter 11, and could we if we wanted to? What should the "new" Chapter 11 look like? Back to the future (save bootstrap reorganization) or brave new world (sale model)?

The American Bankruptcy Institute (ABI) joined the examination of these issues through a symposium entitled "Chapter 11 at the Crossroads: Does Reorganization Need Reform?" on November 16-17, 2009 at the Georgetown University Law Center, Washington, DC.

At this event, the ABI invited some of the finest minds in the insolvency community — academics, practitioners, and jurists — to participate in a discussion of eight, distinct Chapter 11 reform topics. The questions that were discussed highlight the scope of the issues requiring discussion and consensus:

A re-examination of the original 1978 code: strengths, weaknesses and what amendments may have done to the balance of the "original" code

This segment of the symposium examined the structure and philosophy of the original Bankruptcy Code and studied whether or not they remain viable and functional in light of the changes to secured lending and the credit and distressed debt and asset markets. The panel also looked into whether or not the numerous creditor-friendly amendments to the code destroyed or (as creditors would argue) restored its balance. Were the amendments a necessary response to an overly debtor-friendly regime, or overkill, leaving the statute unable to achieve its goals? Is it as simple as going backwards, or is more comprehensive reform required?

Legislative impediments: should the BAPCPA changes be rolled back?

This panel discussion focused on four specific changes made by the 2005 amendments. First, Section 503(b)(9), which created an administrative claim for suppliers that had shipped goods within 20 days of the petition date. Critics of the provision claim it has contributed to administrative insolvency and made it more difficult to reorganize. Proponents defend it as a much-needed protection for suppliers, especially when state-law reclamation rights are often rendered worthless by blanket liens in inventory and receivables held by asset-based lenders.

Second, the changes limiting the maximum time period for the debtor to decide to assume or reject commercial real property leases.

Critics allege that this provision has almost single-handedly killed retail reorganizations, and point to cases like Circuit City as evidence of same; lenders are alleged to have reacted to the possible early loss of leases by compelling early liquidations. Defenders of the change argue that it brought needed balance to the statute, since the prior provisions often lead to courts extending the time to assume or reject leases for years, leaving landlords in limbo.

Third, the panel looked at the cap on the debtor's exclusive period to file a plan of reorganization. Are creditors now better able to "wait out" the debtor, leading to more liquidations?

Fourth, the provisions outlawing key employee retention plans were examined. Have the provisions helped thwart reorganizations by making debtors powerless to retain critical management personnel or were they a much-needed change, merely preventing insiders from enriching themselves at the expense of other creditor constituencies despite no demonstrable retentive purpose or effect?

Do the provisions regarding forward contracts, swaps, repurchase agreements and other derivatives need reform?

This panel focused on the so-called "safe harbor" provisions. These allow non-debtor counterparties to forward contracts, swaps, repurchase agreements and other like contracts to terminate the contracts and liquidate the underlying assets without first obtaining relief from the automatic stay in bankruptcy. They also largely insulate such counterparties from any risk that the exercise of remedies, pre- or post-bankruptcy, will be subject to avoidance by the debtor, a trustee or a creditors' committee. Critics contend that, especially after the 2005 changes, these safe harbors extend to far too many transactions, many of which have no connection to public markets, resulting in the bankruptcy estate being deprived of valuable assets at the outset of the case, with little or no ability to insure that the value of such assets is maximized. Proponents contend that the provisions are essential to the smooth functioning of the markets in such instruments.

Labor issues: would reform of Code provisions and related federal law regarding employee and labor claims and actions in Chapter 11 help or hurt reorganizations?

This panel focused discussion on proposed changes to the Bankruptcy Code set forth in HR 3652 (also known as the Conyers Bill, after its sponsor) and sought by labor unions. (Labor has since introduced similar legislation.) Among the many labor-friendly aspects of the Conyers Bill, the legislation would make it much more difficult to reject collective bargaining agreements under Section 1113 of the Bankruptcy Code. The Conyers Bill would amend Section 363 to provide that courts, in approving sales, would be required to consider the extent to which the bidder has offered to maintain existing jobs, preserve retiree benefits and assume defined benefit pension plans in determining the "highest and best" bid. It would also create a $20,000 per retiree surcharge on sale proceeds in certain sales.

The proposed changes include the ability to surcharge secured party collateral for payment of wages and benefits. The standards for confirming a plan would be amended to require consideration of whether the plan proponent made every reasonable effort to maintain jobs and mitigate losses to employees and retirees, and would require — in the context of competing plans — confirmation of the most labor-friendly plan. The Conyers Bill would also place several additional limits on executive bonuses and executive compensation in Chapter 11 cases.

Critics contend that the changes would make reorganization far less likely. Labor contends that the changes are essential to ensure that employees are not left empty-handed under modern restructuring regimes and structures.

Financing and cash collateral: too much control to the lenders (and what can we do about it anyway)?

This portion of the symposium examined whether pre-petition and DIP lenders are acquiring far too much control via DIP financing agreements, and whether, if so, the cause of such control lies in changes to secured lending generally or a more liberal approach to such control by the Chapter 11 constituencies. Possible statutory changes to ban such provisions were considered. Critics of the "modern" DIP lending agreements contend they have too often turned Chapter 11 into a foreclosure mechanism. Lenders contend that the provisions are necessary given the typical balance sheet of the modern candidates for Chapter 11 relief.

Who should run the Chapter 11 process?

This discussion focused attention on the continuing viability of the debtor in possession/creditors' committee structure for reorganization. Should the management that brought the company to Chapter 11 stay in place to guide the restructuring? What skills does that management bring to the table if the company is going to be sold in any event? Given that claims are often traded — with the "trade creditors" exiting the case early via the sale of their claims to distressed debt traders — does the creditors' committee still work as an ally of, and also a check and balance to, the debtor in possession? Should the US look at Canadian and European regimes and more often employ an independent third party to monitor, if not administer, the Chapter 11 case?

The present and future of the "one size fits all" approach of current Chapter 11: do we need a Chapter for the "too big to fail"?

While proponents of Chapter 11 reorganization maintain that it should have continued to be the nearly exclusive venue for restructuring "too big to fail" entities like Chrysler, CIT, GM and Lehman Brothers, Congress recently rejected this view when it adopted the Dodd-Frank Act. The Act includes provisions that create "resolution authority", the ability of the government to take over and restructure, sell or merge large non-bank institutions, the failure of which poses "systemic risk". The closest model to this new resolution authority is the federal bank receivership, under which the FDIC seizes control of troubled banks and often merges them with, or at least transfers deposits and other key assets to, healthy banks.

The sale model of reorganization after Chrysler, GM and Lehman: Evolution or demise of Chapter 11?

Finally, this panel examined whether or not the auto cases really do portend a new model for restructurings, one that uses Section 363 not only to sell assets but to accomplish restructurings using a buyer controlled by some, but not all creditor elements of the existing debtor. The panel considered whether or not this model is fair, or whether it is unduly prejudicial to excluded creditor groups and abandons long-held principles of creditor democracy, absolute priority and like treatment of similarly situated creditors.

The discussion also focused on legislation proposed by some commentators that would limit the use of Section 363 sales of substantially all of the assets of the debtor and/or would import into that process elements of disclosure, creditor democracy and fair and equitable treatment that are now mandated in connection with the confirmation of Chapter 11 plans.

The symposium was not a mere academic exercise. As noted, bills have previously been introduced in the US Congress on a host of proposed labor and employment reforms to Chapter 11, as well as to repeal the BAPCPA provisions affecting business reorganizations. The reintroduction of those efforts is expected.

Conclusion

While the crowded legislative calendar likely prevents bankruptcy reform legislation from being adopted in the current Congress, the press for Chapter 11 reforms will not go away, fueled by a possible flood of new Chapter 11 cases to come, as the Great Recession continues to leave its wake. The list of parties claiming to be "losers" under the current insolvency regime could grow, followed by requests for legislative redress.

Moreover, this debate is set to continue for some time. Indeed, in this respect, the years following the recession of 2007-09 could be as historic as the recession itself. Examination of the Bankruptcy Code, as it now functions, could bring a call for fundamental changes to the insolvency regime, whether change comes merely in the form of a "back to the future" approach that restores what so many saw as the perfect balance of the 1978 Code, or in amendments that accept that the sale is the dominant model and attempt to soften the blow of such transactions.

If 2005 swung the pendulum toward creditors' interests, will the next round of legislative changes portend a return swing toward debtor rehabilitation? Regardless of the approach, and the precise timing of reform, the basic blueprint of US restructuring is likely to look different before too long.

45

Find it, face it, fix it: How to protect your company from the boom and bust cycle

Leonard J Kennedy, retired General Counsel, Corporate Secretary and Chief Government Affairs Officer, Sprint Nextel Corporation

In any capitalist economy, it is common for businesses to fail, even during the best of times. Over the last several years, we have seen a steady parade of failing businesses, including some that had always seemed woven into the American fabric — in industries like automobiles, airlines, housing, as well as financial services.

At first glance — but only at first glance — that just looks like the nature of competitive, capitalist economies, characterized by what the famous Harvard economist, Joseph Schumpeter, called "creative destruction". Schumpeter celebrated the ways in which new enterprises rise from the ashes of the "creatively destroyed" older enterprises, the new ones embedding and embodying the lessons learned from the ones that fell by the wayside. And, so the theory goes, that is ultimately to the benefit of ordinary citizens and consumers who get better products and services at more favorable prices.

That is the theory — the way capitalism looks in conceptual models and in the pristine pages of academic textbooks. But, of course, that is not at all what we see in the turmoil unleashed by the economic downturn. Rather than "creative destruction" at the level of the giant players on Wall Street, we have instead seen the emergence of a new and entirely unwelcome phenomenon: corporations that are declared "too big to fail". That just means we taxpayers get to prop them up with our money.

Meanwhile, ordinary citizens, rather than being the beneficiaries of creative destruction, are instead victims of the cruel destruction caused by high rates of long-term unemployment and the anxiety it causes.

As President George W Bush said: 'Wall Street got drunk and the rest of us got the hangover.'

What makes all this particularly distressing is that many leaders in both the private and the public sectors seem not to have assimilated the lessons from the recent turmoil. Not to learn lessons from the recent economic misery is to invite its return. As farmers point out: 'There's no wisdom in the second kick of a mule.'

And we cannot afford a second kick of the mule.

Find it, face it, fix it

The chairman of JP Morgan Chase, Jamie Dimon, recently wrote in his letter to the bank's shareholders: 'If we are to deal properly with this crisis moving forward, we must be brutally honest and have a full understanding of what caused it in the first place.'

Dimon is certainly right. This crisis has revealed a catastrophic failure of business judgment, corporate governance and regulatory oversight. Consequently, it will not be easy to follow his advice. It is simple, but it is not easy. When we were in grade school we all learned the "Three Rs": readin', writin' and 'rithmetic.

Today I submit that as a society, as leaders in government and in business, we need to learn the "Three Fs": find it, face it, fix it.

Find the problem. Face the problem. Fix the problem. Simple. But not easy. Because finding, facing and fixing problems means we have to put aside our very natural tendency to deny, delay and divert ourselves from the necessity to make big changes in our patterns and practices.

For example, even though the recent crisis has shown in sharp relief the failures of the regulatory system to prevent the debacle, some market fundamentalists have already started to claim that the crisis is now behind us and that no new regulations are needed. If we were to follow their ideologically skewed advice, we would quickly experience the full force of the second kick of a mule.

And, of course, that sort of denial is not confined just to one group of Americans. The humor newspaper called *The Onion* probably had it right recently when it ran a fake headline: 'Polls Show That Most Americans Pray For a New Bubble'.

Running a global economy as a continuously looping roller-coaster ride — rising with bubbles, falling with busts — is no way to ensure security, whether economic security, political security or military security. Instead, we have to come up with an adequate and serious diagnosis as to how we got in this mess, how we get out, and how we erect barriers to ever falling into it again. We have to get beyond boom and bust, guided by the three Fs.

How did we get into this mess?
We start by finding how we got into this problem in the first place. As you know, the list of "suspects" is long and broad. Many point to the usual business cycle. Others cite the fancy derivatives that Wall Street cooked up in recent years, including mortgage-backed securities, collateralized debt obligations and credit-default swaps. Many others cite Alan Greenspan, the former head of the Federal Reserve, saying his very loose monetary policy kept interest rates unrealistically low for too long. Others point to the rating agencies that were too often guilty of malfeasance or at least misfeasance.

Some take a wide-angle lens perspective and point to the global imbalance between countries with negative balance of trade numbers — like the United States — and those with positive balances, like China, Germany and Japan. And, as I have already suggested, we were certainly not well served by the crushing hand of outdated ideologies that held policymakers in their spell for too long. Certainly we have all learned about the predatory lending practices that put people into homes they could not afford and rating agencies that were

asleep at the switch. All of those problems were exacerbated by the rise of a huge "shadow banking" structure beyond the reach of any regulatory regimes whatsoever.

Finally, library shelves groan these days with the weight of new books that chronicle distracted, irresponsible and sometimes corrupt senior managements and boards of directors. Far too often, companies and banks made their toxic contributions to the economy by taking extremely unsound risks.

That is the partial list of suspects. If you were to ask me who is the real culprit, my answer would be — as in Agatha Christie's famous novel, *Murder on the Orient Express* — they all worked together. But certainly the most toxic collaboration was the huge leverage combined with a system that encouraged absurd risks.

The prevailing ideological perspective of the time had long since become a set of blinders that hid reality from the vision of government and business people alike. As Greenspan said in public testimony: 'Those of us who looked to the self-interest of lending institutions to protect shareholders' equity, myself especially, are in a state of shocked disbelief…' He went on to say that the radical free market, with limited regulation, that he had followed for 40 years was wrong.

Who makes the decisions?
Note Greenspan's assertion that he thought the self-interest of the lending institutions would protect shareholders. The problem with this formulation is that it skirts over the question of who makes the decisions at those large financial concerns. In fact, it seems to suggest that they are made by some abstract legal entity called the "corporation". To be sure, there is such a thing as a "legal corporation" that is more than just the employees, the shareholders and the executives. But it is not this abstract legal entity that makes the decisions about how to operate or how to invest shareholders' money; these decisions are made by the senior management. In theory, they are done so with the over-arching guidance of the directors, who are stand-ins for the investors who actually own the corporation. However, aligning the interests of boards and managements with those of shareholders has been a vexing challenge ever since corporations were first designed.

Key to understanding how ineffective officers and directors can destroy business value is understanding that the decisions they made were too often formulated in a thick tangle of interconnected structures that motivated and rewarded exactly the wrong decisions.

It was a thicket comprised of loose regulations, fancy and sophisticated new derivatives like mortgage-backed securities and credit-default swaps, and the rise of the shadow banking system. All of these, in combination with other factors, led to an economic and financial disaster because the entire system had been hollowed out at its core. What should have been soundly secured by a rock-solid core fashioned from legal, institutional, personal and fiduciary responsibility instead became an empty game of grab by those at the top of the pyramid.

By personal responsibility, I mean a system in which the central players and decision-makers do not just know that they, along with their enterprise, will gain from their wise decisions; they also know that if they make the wrong decision — one that does not help secure and advance their shareholders' interests — they will personally suffer the consequences.

At the same time, the executives and traders in many of those financial institutions were paid their salaries and their bonuses at the point when they originated loans, rather than later on when it could be determined whether or not the loan was really going to be paid back.

Trillions of dollars' worth of sub-prime mortgage loans were originated and packaged together, sliced and diced into a broad array of slivers, and sold to investors. Then those investors resold them up the line to other investors and on and on all over the globe. It was a hot potato with a constantly reconstituted forwarding address. When it started to burn whoever it ended up with, it was far removed from the hand of the loan's originator.

The development of securitization techniques served a purpose: the financing of risky business activity. In the climate that prevailed, irresponsible risk-taking was not limited to corporate executives; many homebuyers of all economic classes took out mortgage loans far beyond their means, counting on the rising tide of house prices to cover their risky bets.

Of course, the real estate tide did not keep rising, and when it began to recede, it left a lot of homeowners exposed. When the tide goes out, as Warren Buffett has observed, you can see who has been swimming without a bathing suit.

To some extent, of course, that ebb and flow of the economy is just the usual business cycle. And, since the Great Depression, economists and policy makers have found a handful of tools to moderate both the severity and the length of these cycles. As the Nobel Prize-winning economist Robert Solow recently wrote: 'A modern capitalist economy with a modern financial system can probably adapt to modest shocks — positive or negative — with just a little help from monetary policy and mostly automatic fiscal stabilizers,' like higher unemployment insurance and lower taxes. But, Solow continued, if that system is hit with large shocks — and he cites all the culprits on our list — then much more difficult economic problems can follow, starting with incredibly high levels of speculative leverage.

Leverage examined

So let us look briefly at what we mean by leverage. Start with some numbers. If I have $100 and decide to invest in a venture that might earn 10 per cent interest, at the end of the year I will have $110 if the investment performs as advertised. Should the investment earn no interest, I will still have the original hundred bucks.

But suppose I can borrow $900 at, say, 5 per cent interest to add to my $100? Then I will have $1,000 to invest at a potential 10 per cent return. In that case my "leverage" is 10 to 1 because I have invested $10 for every $1 that I put up myself. If that 10 per cent interest rate proves true for my investment then at the end of the year I will have $1,100. From that sum, I subtract the $900 I borrowed and the $45 I paid in interest — $900 at 5 per cent. I am left with net earnings of $55 on my initial hundred bucks. That is a 55 per cent return on investment.

Not bad! And, when you start adding zeroes to those numbers, and when you can leverage your investment at a ratio of 30 to 1 or more, it is not hard to understand why a bunch of bright folk on Wall Street — the "traders" — started looking for ways to go after those kinds of returns. They were also busy inventing all sorts of clever new instruments to do it — the famous derivatives.

But suppose the investments in our hypothetical case do not work out, and they earn no interest at all. Again, if I just put in the $100 of my own money, I still have my $100. But here is a key point: if I have made the 10 to 1 leveraged investment, and it earns no interest, then I still have to pay back the $900 I borrowed plus the $45 in interest I paid, leaving me with only $55 of my original $100.

The point is that by borrowing to invest — by leveraging — I greatly increase both the upside potential and the downside risk.

As you may know, the British do not use the metaphor of leverage to talk about this investment strategy; they say "gearing". A bicyclist can keep exploiting a higher gear the longer he has the wind at his back. The traders on Wall Street could keep reaching for greater and greater financial gearing that would yield bigger and bigger returns, as long as they felt the wind at their back. The wind at the back for the traders on Wall Street was constantly rising house prices and historically low interest rates.

A bicyclist with a good tailwind and a favorable slope might conclude, after a number of miles, that the road ahead will continue the same way — until he turns a sharp corner and suddenly faces a steep hill and a strong headwind. The cyclist falls slowly but inevitably to the ground. If he is part of a tightly packed group, one cycle going down brings down dozens of others.

Our financial institutions were no less tightly inter-connected. When one went down, the others crashed, too. Think of Lehman Brothers or Bear Stearns.

So here is a rough and ready answer to the question, 'What happened?' The normal business cycle met up with abnormal levels of gearing or leveraging in pursuit of short-term growth, excessive fees and over-investment in real estate. The result: a huge and cascading financial crash.

Confronting the problem

Having found the problem, our next task is to face the problem — to face it in all its aspects without blinking, and without trying to escape backwards into the shibboleths and ideologies that got us here in the first place. As our case is new, as President Lincoln once put it, we must think anew.

When we are talking about the huge leverage, or gearing, that traders found so compelling and irresistible, the question naturally arises, where were the regulators?

It is clear that regulation was ineffective; a liquidity-inspired shadow banking system emerged outside the watchdogs' purview. This was partly because of the sway of an ideology that the best market was an entirely unfettered and unregulated market. And, rigid ideologies hold the greatest sway. Greenspan put the point with admirable clarity when he said he was shocked that the ideology he had been relying on for 40 years turned out to be wrong.

Greenspan was shocked. The economy was electrocuted.

Clearly, regulations need to be revamped and extended to cover new phenomena like shadow banking enterprises. Once the rules are in place, we have to make sure that the regulators responsible for enforcing them do so in a vigorous, fair and transparent way, unimpeded by old ideologies.

But, even if we have all the necessary regulations in place, the actual day-by-day decisions that determine our national economic health will still rest in the hands of the same people who have always wielded the influence — those who manage businesses and corporations.

We have talked about bicycles and bicycle crashes. Let us shift our transportation metaphor and think of the national economy as a car that has gone off the road and landed in a ditch. The federal government has moved in huge machinery to pull it up and set it back on the road. But, that will do little long-term good if the same drivers, and the same driving habits, get behind the wheel once again.

Fixing the problem

We have so far focused on finding and facing the problem. Now we need to find the ways to fix it.

It is exactly for this reason that we must take a long, hard look at the pivotal players on the entire economic scene — corporations and the people who lead them. The history. The structure. The governance.

Herman Wouk, the author and chronicler of World War II, once famously observed that the Navy was an organization designed by geniuses to be operated by idiots. But the reality of the American economic system is that it needs not only genius in its design; it also has to be operated by people of energy, insight and integrity. However bright those leaders are, they will not always be right. For that reason, we have to build in checks and balances in the executive suites.

Let us go back to that group of bright Wall Street professionals — the traders — looking for more and more opportunities to use greater and greater leverage to bring in bigger and bigger returns for their employers. And, not coincidentally, bigger and bigger bonuses for themselves.

At the same time, there is another group of professionals in those same institutions. Their goal is constantly to assess and control that risk — to counterbalance what can become the unwarranted exuberance of the traders. But as Richard Posner pointed out in a recent book, *A Failure of Capitalism: The Crisis of '08 and the Descent into Depression*: 'Risk management, unlike trading, is generally not treated as a profit center in a firm because it is difficult to attribute profits to risk managers... Hence a financial firm will tend to give more weight to the views of successful traders than to those of risk managers.'

So who will curb the over-arching and sometimes dangerous exuberance of traders — or, indeed, of top-level managements in any corporations, whether they are in the financial sector or elsewhere?

Well, a first candidate is the board of directors. In theory — at the level of ideas — that is what they do. But as the poet TS Eliot wrote: 'Between the idea and the reality... falls the shadow.' A good place to start analyzing the recent global economic catastrophe is by looking at the shadow falling between the idea of the way in which the business operates, and the somewhat less appetizing reality of how it has been conducted of late.

Here is the idea, and it is a pretty simple one. The modern corporation's governing structure is established by laws and state charters. These do not specify what the corporation does — what it makes, what it designs, or what service it provides. What they do specify is how the responsibility for the use of investors' capital is to be recognized and protected. Put simply, investors' capital is at least implicitly to be used to maximize profits.

The board of directors is responsible for making sure that these profits accrue to the investors. In that sense, it is basically the stand-in for the investors, the owners of the corporation. It has a fiduciary responsibility to ensure that the interests of the owners are protected.

To fulfill those responsibilities, the board chooses, evaluates and constantly monitors information that is material to the corporation's performance, very much including the decisions and actions of the management.

Focusing on reality

That is the idea. Now let us look at some recent realities — and we can find several grim snapshots of reality in the ways in which the personality traits of various senior bank board members contributed, however indirectly, to the demise of some of Wall Street's most venerable financial institutions during the throes of the recent banking crisis.

Between the idea and the reality falls the shadow.

And, what an economic and financial shadow we have been experiencing since the financial crisis broke. It has been an incredibly dark shadow, blacking out the sun of consumer confidence,

freezing lending, darkening prospects for future generations, and basically doing to the economy what a cloud of locusts does to a wheat field.

It is worth a brief look back to see how corporate governance has evolved. In the decades after the laws setting up corporations were passed, there was a growing split between the executive management of the large public companies and the increasingly diverse group of shareholders — the owners. In other words, the links between the management and the ownership of corporations were becoming increasingly attenuated.

As Adolf Berle and Gardiner Means famously pointed out in their 1932 book *The Modern Corporation and Private Property*: 'The rise of the modern corporation has brought a concentration of economic power which can compete on equal terms with the modern state — economic power versus political power, each strong in its own field. The state seeks in some aspects to regulate the corporation, while the corporation, steadily becoming more powerful, makes every effort to avoid such regulation.'

What Berle and Means observed almost 80 years ago is, of course, even more accurate today. Despite a lot of discussion and insightful analysis, the realities of how boards govern, and how executives manage, have not evolved to address the complex corporate organizations operating in a global economy.

The change agenda

The list of changes needed is long. First on that list has to be the abandonment of the "growth at any cost" mindset. That means jettisoning the incentive structures for CEOs and management which too often reward taking huge, but unjustified, risks to get growth; these result in big bonus payouts for executives when they are successful, but they carry little or no personal penalty for the executives if the efforts go bad.

Second on the list has to be repudiation of complex, risky and poorly understood financial engineering in all its forms — especially when those risks are grounded on mathematical assumptions that are simply false. Third, there must be adoption of an operating view that is long-term and balanced; and fourth, there must be the placing of shareholder interests above those of management. Fifth must come rejection of speculative, "bet the company" pursuits that are poorly understood, poorly supervised and do not promise outsized rewards from risk.

Too often, boards and managements have

chosen procedural niceties and a checklist mentality instead of fulfilling their fiduciary duties. These approaches may satisfy legal requirements, but they utterly fail in answering critical questions, such as: whether to proceed with a difficult merger; whether the disclosed business objectives make sense in light of industry and capital market conditions; whether stock buyback or dividend payment policies are justified; and whether the operations of the business are satisfactory.

In short, this style of corporate governance is the equivalent of trying to ensure airline safety by requiring pilots to complete a checklist while they are speeding toward take-off in a 747 — without any detailed prior specifications on aircraft construction, airworthiness, crew training or any of the other ways in which flying safety is "built in".

Several years ago, there was global concern among aviation experts about the large number of plane crashes involving Korean Airlines. In fact, the authorities in Canada came very close to denying Korean aviation the right to fly through their air space. What was the problem? After a lot of analysis, it was discovered that the problem was rooted in the cockpit conversations — not what was said but what was not said. With two or three professionals in the cockpit, one of them will see something in the instruments or out of the window that suggests a danger not seen by the others. But in a very hierarchical system, and that description fits the old Korean cockpit, the junior officers would not feel they had the license to express their concerns to the captain — with tragic results.

The solution was to institute a "culture shift" so that everyone in the cockpit, whatever their rank, felt empowered to speak up. With that change, Korean Airlines became as safe as US airlines.

We need a culture change in US business, too.

A cultural shift

In fixing the problem, the solution is simple. But it is not easy. We need a profound cultural shift, one in which board members and executives are empowered to — and do — speak up when they see something amiss in the strategy or tactics of the senior management or the apparent success of the business. We need a cultural change in which the purpose of the corporation is not to enrich or flatter the senior executives, but to fulfill a dual responsibility: to meet the long-term interests of shareholders and other stakeholders, and at the same time, to contribute to the reputation of an American free market system that has made our economy the strongest in the world.

We need, in short, a new beginning. We need a new beginning centered on boards of directors who understand, and hold the management team accountable for, the business, its operating and capital plans, strategy and risks. Focused enterprise management is the key to success in business and the heart of good corporate governance. And we must recognize that corporate governance, because of its excessively procedural focus and too limited an enterprise management role, has so far failed to ensure wise management, resulting in corporate failures.

A new beginning will also require an independent board operations and capital budget committee that focuses on strategy and execution to reduce management incentives for self-interest and the appetite for risk and short-term decision-making at the expense of fiduciary duties and shareholder interests.

For that new beginning we also need a reform in business management that might be thought of as an "enhanced stress test", similar to what the Treasury Department carried out for troubled American financial institutions.

The version I propose would not just run several computerized economic and monetary scenarios to assess how well a balance sheet would hold up; it would subject any consequential executive decisions for the enterprise to a thorough-going appraisal and critique instituted by the board to look at the possible risks, dangers and outcomes.

Management and boards must embrace a culture of "closing the loop". They must find the problem; face the problem and fix the problem.

Implementation of this recommendation would result in drastic improvements in corporate decision-making. For example, "bet the company" decisions like mergers, acquisitions, divestitures and dramatic changes in strategy would be subjected to an intense devil's advocate analysis — if need be, under the supervision of an independent board committee.

Alternatively, a public company board might be required to form a strategy/operations committee to ensure a full understanding of the prospects of the business. This method would ensure the board and management were singing off the same hymn sheet in their understanding of the business, and that this understanding was reflected in public disclosures and that executive compensation was reasonable in light of performance and the challenges facing the business.

Conclusion

There are a number of reasons for the current financial condition, and we should recognize that putting our economic house on a stronger foundation will also require a lot of ideas, a lot of reforms, and a lot of cultural transformations. A few have been outlined here. But, as we go along, I am sure we will find other changes to make our system strong and less vulnerable to the "out of control decisions" by a few that can devastate so many.

If officers and directors are serious, sober and straightforward, they can, indeed, learn the best lessons from this recent catastrophe. They can do it by finding, facing and fixing the problems. And avoiding another kick of the mule.

Notes and References

Navigating Today's Environment: Notes and references

Chapter 3. From hangover to recovery? The thoughts of a turnaround lender

(1) Federal Housing Finance Agency, Housing Price Index, December 2009. Cashouts as a percentage of mortgage refinancing ranged between 60 per cent and 70 per cent in the 2005-2007 period, up from the 35 per cent to 45 per cent range during the 2002-2005 period.

(2) 'Bernanke offers broad definition of systemic risk' — *Wall Street Journal* blog, November 2009. Federal Reserve chairman Ben Bernanke said "systemic risk" can be broadly defined, including unsafe amounts of leveraging by banks, gaps in regulatory oversight and the possibility that the failure of a large interconnected firm could lead to a breakdown in the wider financial system.

(3) 'Federal government faces balloon in debt payments' — *New York Times*, November 22, 2009, section A, page 1.

(4) 'More homeowners fall behind on mortgages' — *Wall Street Journal*, November 20, 2009.

(5) *Ibid.*

(6) Ed McKelvy, 'US recovery: Why V is unlikely' — Goldman Sachs Global Economics Commodities and Strategy Research, *US Economics Analyst*, issue no: 09/19, May 15, 2009.

(7) 'Existing Home Sales: November Report' — Real Estate abc.com, October 30, 2009.

(8) 'The downside of a loan pickup' — WSJ.com, November 12, 2009.

(9) 'Moody's predicts default rate slowdown' — *Financial Times*, August 20, 2009.

(10) 'Lending declines as bank jitters persist' — *Wall Street Journal*, November 25, 2009, section A, page 10.

(11) David L Johnson, 'The changing shape of a distressed financing: trends driving the evolution of a market' — *Journal of Private Equity*, vol. 12, number 3, summer 2009.

Chapter 7. Avoiding Chapter 22: Why post-emergence liquidity, profitability and leverage make all the difference

Reference works

Alderson, Michael, and Brian L Betker, 1999. 'Assessing Postbankruptcy Performance: An Analysis of Reorganized Firms' Cash Flows'. Financial Management 28:68.

Altman, Edward I, 1983, 1993. *Corporate Financial Distress and Bankruptcy*. 1st and 2nd editions. John Wiley, NY.

Altman, Edward I, 1968. 'Financial Ratios, Discriminant Analysis and the Prediction of Corporate Bankruptcy'. *Journal of Finance*. 33: 189.

Altman, Edward I, 2005. 'An Emerging Market Credit Scoring System for Corporate Bonds'. *Emerging Markets Review*. 6. 311-323.

Altman, Edward I, John Hartzell and Matthew Peck. 1995. 'Emerging Markets Corporate Bonds: A Scoring System'. Salomon Brothers. *The Future of Emerging Market Flows*. 1997. Ed by R Levich. Klumer. Holland.

Altman, Edward I, and Edith Hotchkiss. 2006. *Corporate Financial Distress & Bankruptcy*. 3rd edition. John Wiley, Hoboken. NJ.

Altman, Edward I, and Brenda Karlin. 2010. 'Defaults and Returns in the High Yield Bond Market: The Year 2009 in Review and Outlook'. NYU Salomon Center Report. February.

Dahiya, Sandeep, Kose John, Manju Puri, and Gabriel Ramirez. 2003. 'Debtor-in-Possession Financing and Bankruptcy Resolution: Empirical

Evidence *Journal of Financial Economics* 69. 1: 259.

Eberhart, Allan, Reena Aggarwal, and Edward Altman. 1999. 'The Equity Performance of Firms Emerging from Bankruptcy'. *Journal of Finance* 54: 1855.

Evans, John, S Luo and N Nagarajan. 2008. 'Bankruptcy, CEO Retention and the Evolution of Contractual Practices'. Working Paper, Katz School of Business, University of Pittsburgh.

Gilson, Stuart. 1997. 'Transactions Costs and Capital Structure Choice: Evidence from Financially Distressed Firms'. *Journal of Finance* 52: 161.

Goyal, Amit, Matthias Kahl, and Walter N Torous. 2003. 'The Long-Run Stock Performance of Financially Distressed Firms: An Empirical Investigation'. Working Paper. Emory University and UCLA.

Heron, Randall, Erik Lie and Kimberly Rodgers. 2006. 'Financial Restructuring in Fresh Start Chapter 11 Reorganizations'. Working Paper. University of Indiana.

Hotchkiss, Edith S. 1992. 'Investment Decisions under Chapter 11 Bankruptcy'. PhD dissertation. New York University.

Hotchkiss, Edith S. 1995. 'Postbankruptcy Performance and Management Turnover'. *Journal of Finance* 50: 3.

Hotchkiss, Edith S, and Robert Mooradian. 1997. 'Vulture Investors and the Market for Control of Distressed Firms'. *Journal of Financial Economics*. 43: 401.

Hotchkiss, Edith S, and Robert Mooradian. 1998. 'Acquisitions as a Means of Restructuring Firms in Chapter 11'. *Journal of Financial Intermediation*. 7: 240.

Hotchkiss, Edith S, and Robert Mooradian. 2004. 'Post-Bankruptcy Performance: Evidence from 25 Years of Chapter 11'. Working Paper. Boston College and Northeastern University.

Lee, J Thomas and John Cunney, 2004. 'The Chapter After Chapter 11'. New York. JPMorgan.

LoPucki, Lynn M, and William C Whitford. 1993. 'Patterns in the Bankruptcy Reorganization of Large, Publicly Held Companies'. *Cornell Law Review*. 78: 597.

Maksimovic, Vojislav, and Gordon Phillips. 1998. 'Asset Efficiency and Reallocation Decisions of Bankrupt Firms'. *Journal of Finance.* 53: 1495.

McHugh, Christopher and Kerry Mastroianni, Editors. *The Bankruptcy Yearbook and Almanac*. New Generation Research. Boston. MA 2008.

McHugh, Christopher, Allen Michel, and Israel Shaked. 1998. 'After Bankruptcy: Can Ugly Ducklings Turn into Swans?' *Financial Analysts Journal*. 54. 3:31.

Rattanaruengyot, Thongchai. 2007. 'The Nature of Companies Who Filed Chapter 22 and 33'. Honors thesis, NYU Stern Undegraduate College.

Chapter 14. White-collar crime: The law enforcement agenda

(1) In 2009, the SEC announced it had filed complaints in four separate sub-prime cases against nine executives and one company, in connection with fraudulent accounting practices and misleading disclosures. In 2008, it filed complaints against the two Bear Stearns hedge fund managers acquitted in the Cioffi case, five mortgage brokers charged with fraud in connection with a sub-prime loan refinancing scheme, and two Credit Suisse bankers who failed to disclose they were selling auction rate securities backed by collateralized debt obligations. The DOJ also indicted the Credit Suisse bankers in September 2008.

(2) Insider trading cases have been of particular interest to law enforcement in recent years. The SEC brought approximately 60 enforcement actions related to insider trading in both 2008 and 2009, up from an average of 46 cases for the previous four years. And the scope of cases and breadth of investigation tactics are expanding concomitantly. A growing number of cases involve private equity and hedge fund managers, who have traditionally eluded the government's reach due to regulatory voids in those industries. The director of enforcement has said that the SEC is 'committed to pulling back the curtain on hedge fund operations' by increasing scrutiny of trading activity. Robert

Khuzami, remarks at press conference (October 16, 2009) (available at http://www.sec.gov/news/speech/2009/spch101609rk.htm).

Accordingly, in 2009, dozens of individuals were charged in connection with illegal trading activity at several hedge fund groups. One trader was charged in the first-ever case involving credit default swaps, which were instrumental in the 2008 financial meltdown and, specifically, the AIG bailout. Meanwhile, in November 2009, the DOJ revealed that it had relied extensively on secret surveillance to bring down an insider trading scheme.

In *United States v Rajaratnam*, the FBI infiltrated a ring of attorneys and hedge fund managers engaged in insider trading by intercepting telephone calls and text messages, logging telephone calls made and received by the defendants, and wiring informants. While wiretaps are more commonly associated with street crime, *Rajaratnam* may signal that more aggressive investigative techniques become prevalent in the white-collar context.

(3) The government's heightened interest in cross-border conduct, and recent success in obtaining settlements in the hundreds of millions of dollars, does not end with the FCPA enforcement agenda. For example, UBS has been entangled with the Internal Revenue Service and DOJ since 2008 over allegations that the bank helped wealthy, tax-evading Americans hide assets in secret offshore bank accounts. In February 2009, UBS entered into a Deferred Prosecution Agreement with the department and agreed to pay $780 million in penalties. See press release, DOJ: 'UBS enters into Deferred Prosecution Agreement' (February 18, 2009) (available at http://www.justice.gov/opa/pr/2009/February/09-tax-136.html).

Additionally, in December 2009, the Department of the Treasury's Office of Foreign Assets Control announced a $217 million settlement with Lloyds TSB bank, which was accused of intentionally deleting information about US sanctioned parties in wire transfer instructions routed through third-party banks in the US. The bank also paid the DOJ $350 million as part of a DPA. See press release, Department of the Treasury: 'US Treasury Department announces settlement with Lloyds TSB Bank PLC' (December 22, 2009) (available at http://www./treas.gov/press/releases/tg458.htm).

Similarly, the DOJ and Manhattan District Attorney's Office announced a $536 million settlement with Credit Suisse in December 2009, in connection with allegations that the bank illegally funneled money through US banks on behalf of clients subject to US sanctions, intentionally concealed the Iranian origin of $1.1 billion of payments, and secretly executed trades for sanctioned Libyan and Sudanese clients. See press release, New York County District Attorney's Office (December 16, 2009) (available at http://manhattanda.org/whatsnew/press/2009-12-16.shtml).

(4) See Bruce A Green, 'Regulating Federal Prosecutors: Let There Be Light', 118 *Yale LJ* Pocket Part 156, 157 (2009).

(5) See Ellen S Podgor, Department of Justice Guidelines: Balancing 'Discretionary Justice', 13 Cornell JL & Pub. Políy 167, 189-194 (2004).

(6) See Bruce A Green, 'Regulating Federal Prosecutors: Let There Be Light', 118 *Yale LJ* Pocket Part 156 (2009).

(7) *Id.*

Chapter 25. How distressed claims trading may impact your reorganization strategy

(1) The author reviewed and relied on commentary discussing the motivations of distressed investor claims traders in the following articles: Adam J Levitin, 'Bankruptcy Markets: Making Sense of Claims Trading', 4 Brook. J Corp Fin & Com. L 67 (2009); Jonathan C Lipson, 'The Shadow Bankruptcy System', 89 BUL Rev 1609 (2009); and Douglas G Baird and Robert K Rasmussen, 'Antibankruptcy', 119 *YLJ* 648 (2010).

Chapter 27. Leveraging exchange offers to maximize value in distressed situations

(1) Premium included a three-point "early acceptance premium" for holders who agreed to exchange within 15 days of receiving the offer.

Profiles

Navigating Today's Environment: Consulting Editor's profile

John Wm. ("Jack") Butler, Jr
Partner and Co-Practice Leader
Skadden, Arps, Slate, Meagher & Flom LLP
155 North Wacker Drive, Chicago, Illinois, USA
Tel +1 312 407 0730
Fax +1 312 407 8501
Web www.skadden.com

Email
Jack.Butler@skadden.com

Jack Butler co-leads Skadden, Arps' global Corporate Restructuring Practice where he focuses primarily on advising companies and investors with respect to complex business reorganizations, troubled-company M&A, debt restructurings and financing matters, including cross-border transactions and advising officers and directors on corporate governance and fiduciary duty matters.

He has assisted many global businesses restructure outside the US, execute cross-border financing and privatization transactions, and divest various business lines and entities. His representative engagements include transformational restructurings in the airline, automotive, energy, healthcare, manufacturing, media and telecommunications, retail and utilities industries. Mr Butler also participates regularly in *pro bono* legal programs, including acting as a guardian *ad litem* in contested guardianship cases in Cook County, Illinois.

Mr Butler was named one of the decade's most influential lawyers by *The National Law Journal* in March 2010, and is one of two practicing lawyers and ten inductees in the inaugural class of the *Turnaround, Restructuring and Distressed Investing Industry Hall of Fame*. He was one of *The American Lawyers'* Dealmakers of the Year in 2010 and 2004, and also received the *ILO Client Choice Award 2010* based on client nominations for excellent client care and quality of services rendered. In 2008, Mr Butler received the *Ellis Island Medal of Honor*, which is awarded to Americans who exemplify outstanding qualities in both their personal and professional lives, while continuing to preserve the richness of their particular heritage.

Mr Butler has been regularly recognized as a "leading lawyer" by *Chambers Global*; *Chambers USA*; *The International Who's Who of Business Lawyers*; *Who's Who Legal USA*; *Who's Who Illinois*; *The Best Lawyers in America*; Euromoney and Legal Media Group's *Expert Guide to the World's Leading Insolvency and Restructuring Lawyers*; *IFLR 1000*; *Global Counsel (PLC Which Lawyer?)*; and *The Lawdragon 500: Leading Lawyers in America*. He has also been included regularly in the *K&A Restructuring Register*, the peer group listing of the top restructuring attorneys and financial advisors in the United States, and *Turnarounds & Workouts'* ranking of the outstanding restructuring lawyers in America.

In addition to his consulting editor responsibilities for *Navigating Today's Environment: The Directors' and Officers' Guide To Restructuring*, Mr Butler has published frequently on corporate governance best practices, including, most recently, *Preserving State Corporate Governance Law in Chapter 11: Maximizing Value Through Traditional Fiduciaries* (18 Am Bankr Inst L Rev. 337 [2010]) and *Corporate Governance of Troubled Companies and the Role of Restructuring Counsel* (63 Bus Law 855 [2008]).

Mr Butler served as Chairman of the Turnaround Management Association for two years in 1996 and 1997, and is a fellow in the American College of Bankruptcy and International Insolvency Institute. A past director of the American Bankruptcy Institute, he founded INSOL's Group of 36 and has served many other industry organizations, including the American Board of Certification, Commercial Finance Association Education Foundation and the New York Institute of Credit.

Navigating Today's Environment: Contributor profiles

AlixPartners LLP

40 West 57th Street, New York, NY 10019
Tel +1 212 490 2500 **Fax** +1 212 490 1344
Web www.alixpartners.com

Eva Anderson

Director
Email eanderson@alixpartners.com
Eva Anderson has more than 15 years of investment banking, business operations and management consulting experience concentrated in regulated industries such as energy and healthcare. She joined AlixPartners from the Corporate Advisory and Restructuring Group at Kroll Zolfo Cooper, where she was a director involved in a range of bankruptcy and out-of-court turnaround and restructuring assignments. She served as an associate director of restructuring in the Enron bankruptcy reorganization for over three years, focused on the resolution of Enron's complex off-balance sheet financing structures.

Previously, Ms Anderson was a Vice President at Morgan Stanley and served as the Senior Director for Capital Finance for the New York City Health and Hospitals Corporation.

Lisa J Donahue

Managing Director
Email ldonahue@alixpartners.com
Lisa Donahue co-heads the Turnaround and Restructuring Practice. She specializes in financial and operational reorganizations — an expertise that led to her being named one of New York's "Forty Under Forty" by Crain's New York Business in 2002, "Outstanding Young Turnaround Manager" by *Turnarounds & Workouts* in 2001, and in May 2007, International Women's Insolvency & Restructuring Confederation (IWIRC) "Woman of the year". Her most recent role was serving as the Chief Restructuring Officer of SemGroup LP from July 2008 to December 2009.

Ms Donahue has extensive experience in cash management and cost reduction, negotiation, situational analysis, and debt restructuring for both domestic and international organizations. Her engagements have been in the manufacturing, distributing, professional services, energy, apparel, and retail industries. Over the years, Ms Donahue has been successful as both an interim executive and as a financial advisor. She is currently a board member for InMotion Inc, a New York-based, non-profit organization that provides assistance to victims of domestic abuse.

She is a former director of the Turnaround Management Association and is a member of the International Women's Insolvency and Restructuring Confederation and the Association for Corporate Growth, and she sits on the New York Advisory Board for the American Bankruptcy Institute.

Alvarez & Marsal

6th Floor, 600 Lexington Avenue, New York, NY 10022
Tel +1 212 759 4433 **Fax** +1 212 759 5532
Web www.alvarezandmarsal.com

Antonio M Alvarez III

Managing Director, Europe
Email talvarezIII@alvarezandmarsal.com
Antonio Alvarez III, a Managing Director with Alvarez & Marsal, has built and led the A&M Europe practice since 2001. Mr Alvarez has played an integral role in several high-profile turnarounds and performance improvement projects over the last decade, and brings more than 20 years' experience serving public and privately owned companies. He has led several complex pan-European engagements, and has worked in every major country in Europe, including the UK, Germany, France, Belgium, Netherlands, Italy, Switzerland, Finland, Sweden and Estonia.

Jeffery Stegenga

Managing Director, North America
Email jstegenga@alvarezandmarsal.com
Jeffery Stegenga is a Managing Director with Alvarez & Marsal and leads the restructuring group for A&M's Central Region, which includes offices in Detroit, Chicago, Houston and Dallas. He also chairs the firm's Executive Committee for North American Restructuring. Mr Stegenga is nationally regarded as a specialist in out-of-court restructuring

and bankruptcy consulting. Over the last decade, he has worked almost exclusively on large, complex, company-side engagements.

American Bankruptcy Institute

44 Canal Center Plaza, Suite 400, Alexandria, Virginia 22314
Tel +1 703 739 0800 Fax +1 703 739 1060
Web www.abiworld.org

Robert J Keach

President
Email rkeach@bernsteinshur.com
Robert J Keach, a shareholder at Bernstein, Shur, Sawyer & Nelson, practices in the area of bankruptcy, reorganization and work-outs. Mr Keach's practice focuses on the representation of various parties in work-outs and bankruptcy cases, including debtors, creditors, creditors' committees, lessors and third parties acquiring troubled companies and/or their assets.

Mr Keach has appeared before the bankruptcy courts in the Districts of Maine, Massachusetts, New Hampshire, Delaware, the Northern District of California and the Eastern District of New York. He has also appeared as a panelist on national bankruptcy, lender liability and creditors' rights programs, and is the author of several articles on bankruptcy and creditors' rights. Mr Keach is admitted to practice in Maine and Massachusetts.

Professional affiliations: American Bankruptcy Institute (President); American Bar Association, Section on Business, Banking and Corporations, Section on Real Estate, Probate and Trust Law (Committee on Enforcement of Creditors' Rights) and Section on Litigation; Certified — Business Bankruptcy Law — American Board of Certification (ABC).

Baker & McKenzie LLP

One Prudential Plaza, Suite 3500, 130 East Randolph Drive, Chicago, Illinois 60601
Tel +1 312 861 8000 Fax +1 312 861 2899
Web www.bakermckenzie.com

Michael F DeFranco

Partner
Email Michael.DeFranco@bakermckenzie.com
Michael DeFranco advises clients on transactional matters, including mergers and acquisitions, securities law compliance, corporate governance issues and disclosure concerns. His extensive experience includes representing multinational companies in both public and private acquisitions and divestitures. He represents buyers, sellers and their financial advisors in a wide variety of transactions and strategic alliances. Mr DeFranco also advises public companies on compliance issues related to Sarbanes-Oxley matters, and NYSE and Nasdaq listing standards.

David F Heroy

Partner
Email David.Heroy@bakermckenzie.com
David Heroy has played a leading role in many of the US's major corporate restructurings and bankruptcies of the past 25 years. He served as lead counsel for official committees of creditors and equity security holders in numerous high-profile mega-cases, as well as for owners or purchasers of distressed assets.

Mr Heroy is also well known for lecturing and writing on related issues for organizations such as the Practicing Law Institute, the Wharton Restructuring Conference, the Japan American Business Conference, the State-Owned Asset Supervision and Administration Commission in China and the Yale Law School. He is a member of the Global Steering Committee for the firm's Global Restructuring, Reorganization and Insolvency Practice Group.

The Blackstone Group LP

345 Park Avenue, New York, NY 10154
Tel +1 212 583 5352 Fax +1 212 583 5707
Web www.Blackstone.com

Timothy R Coleman

Senior Managing Director
Email Coleman@blackstone.com
Timothy Coleman is a Senior Managing Director, Co-Head of the Restructuring and Reorganization Group and a member of Blackstone's Executive Committee. Since joining Blackstone in 1992, Mr Coleman has worked on a variety of restructuring and reorganization assignments for companies, creditor groups, special committees of corporate boards, corporate parents of troubled companies and acquirers of distressed assets.

Mr Coleman's notable assignments include Adelphia, AT&T, Bear Stearns Asset Management, Cable & Wireless Holdings, Credit-Based Asset Servicing and Securitization (C-BASS) LLC, Criimi Mae, Delta Air Lines, Ermis Maritime Shipping, Financial Guaranty Insurance Company, FLAG

Telecom, Ford Motor Company, Geneva Steel Company, Guangdong Enterprises, Harrah's Jazz Company, JPS Textile Group Inc, Koll Real Estate, Mirant Corp, MoneyGram International Inc, RCN, RH Macy & Co, Stratosphere Corporation, Williams Communications, Xerox Corporation and XL Capital.

The International Financing Review has recognized Mr Coleman's efforts in leading the "Restructuring of the Year" for the past two years for C-BASS (2008) and Ford Motor Company (2009).

Bridge Associates LLC
483 Sharon Station Road, Amenia, New York, NY 12501
Tel +1 212 207 4710 **Fax** +1 845 373 7897
Web www.bridgeassociatesllc.com

Bettina M Whyte
Chairman
Email bwhyte@bridgellc.com
Bettina Whyte is a nationally recognized leader in the financial and operational restructuring industry. Until October 2007, Ms Whyte was a Managing Director of MBIA Insurance (NYSE), where she founded and headed the Special Situations Group, a unit of in-house specialists who worked with bond issuers experiencing operational or financial problems. Prior to joining MBIA, she was a Managing Director of AlixPartners.

Ms Whyte has served as an interim CEO, COO and Chief Restructuring Officer of numerous large public and private companies. She has been active in a broad range of industries, including airlines, oil and gas, commodity trading, retail, food services, transportation, distribution, manufacturing, telecommunications, healthcare, professional services, entertainment and financial services.

She is currently the Chairman of Bridge Associates LLC's Advisory Board, a premier crisis-management and restructuring firm. Ms Whyte also serves on the board of directors of AGL Resources (NYSE), where she is a member of the Finance and Risk Management Committee and chairs the Compensation and Management Development Committee; of Rock-Tenn Company (NYSE), where she serves on the Audit and Compensations Committees; and of Amerisure Insurance, a mutual insurance company, where she chairs the Audit Committee and sits on the Investment and Acquisition Committee. She is also on the Business Advisory Board of Solera Capital, a private equity firm. Ms Whyte is a past President of

the American Bankruptcy Institute and a Fellow of the American College of Bankruptcy.

Brown Rudnick LLP
Seven Times Square, New York, NY 10036
Tel +1 212 209 4900 **Fax** +1 212 209 4801
Web www.brownrudnick.com

Edward S Weisfelner
Chair
Email eweisfelner@brownrudnick.com
Edward S Weisfelner is the head of Brown Rudnick's Bankruptcy and Corporate Restructuring Practice Group. He has over 28 years' experience representing official and ad hoc creditors' and equity holders' committees, individual creditors, indenture trustees, equity holders, and other parties in many of the nation's largest in-court and out-of-court restructurings. Mr Weisfelner also regularly represents buyers of assets and claims in Chapter 11 proceedings and has served as a court-appointed mediator and examiner.

Mr Weisfelner is a five-time recipient of the "Outstanding Restructuring Lawyers" award from *Turnarounds & Workouts*, most recently in 2009. He was included as one of only 67 nationally recognized restructuring attorneys in the tenth edition of The K&A Restructuring Register, a peer group listing selected by an advisory board of financial advisors, lawyers and private practitioners. He is also recognized by *Chambers USA: America's Leading Lawyers for Business* in the area of bankruptcy law. Mr Weisfelner is a member of the American Bankruptcy Institute, the New York and American Bar Associations and the Turnaround Management Association.

Buccino & Associates Inc
200 West Madison St., Suite 2620, Chicago, Illinois 60606
Tel +1 312 629 1200 **Fax** +1 312 284 5626
Web www.buccinoassociates.com

Gerald P Buccino
Chairman and CEO
Email jerryb@buccinoassociates.com
Gerald (Jerry) Buccino is the Founder of the firm and resides in both the Chicago and New York City offices. He and his firm have assisted over 1,000 clients in its 30-year history and he is considered one of the founders of the Turnaround Management Association, where he served as

national Chairman in 1991 and 1992. Mr Buccino is considered one of the "Deans" of the turnaround industry and has consulted with CEOs and boards of directors on turnaround strategies to improve profitability, cash flow and enterprise value. His business experience and comprehensive understanding of the turnaround process has led to an array of successful business turnarounds and reorganizations for clients in the United States and abroad.

Mr Buccino has been an expert witness on corporate governance issues in a number of landmark cases and has lectured extensively and published many articles on the turnaround process and the related corporate governance duties and responsibilities.

Cadwalader, Wickersham & Taft LLP
700 Sixth Street, NW Washington, DC 20001
Tel +1 202 862 2475 Fax +1 202 862 2400
Web www.cadwalader.com

John J Rapisardi
Co-Chairman
Email John.Rapisardi@cwt.com
John Rapisardi, Co-Chairman of Cadwalader's Financial Restructuring Department, has more than 27 years' domestic and international restructuring experience across a variety of industries. He recently served as outside counsel to the United States Department of Treasury and the Presidential Auto Task Force with respect to the restructuring of Chrysler, General Motors and Delphi, and represented the government in the restructuring of CIT, the distressed bank holding company. After law school, he served as a law clerk for the Chief Bankruptcy Judge of the Southern District of New York.

Capstone Advisory Group LLC
Park 80 West, 250 Pehle Avenue, Suite 105, Saddle Brook, NJ 07663
Tel +1 201 587 7100 Fax +1 201 587 7102
Web www.capstoneag.com

Walt Dlugolecki
Executive Director
Email wdlugolecki@capstoneag.com
Walt Dlugolecki is an Executive Director in the firm's New Jersey office and his background includes financial and management consulting, and over 20 years of manufacturing plant management and corporate and financial management. Over the past 14 years he has provided restructuring advisory services to creditors, equity holders and companies in troubled situations including bankruptcy.

Mr Dlugolecki's industry experience includes manufacturing, real estate, consumer products, metals, distribution, apparel, food, auto, aerospace and retail. Prior to joining Capstone, Mr Dlugolecki was a Managing Director at the Policano and Manzo legacy practice of FTI Consulting from 1999 to January 2004. Prior to joining Policano and Manzo, he held controllership and chief financial officer positions primarily in middle-market companies.

Mr Dlugolecki is a member of the American Institute of Certified Public Accountants, the American Bankruptcy Institute, the Association of Insolvency and Restructuring Advisors and the Institute of Management Accountants.

Edwin N Ordway Jr
Executive Director
Email eordway@capstoneag.com
Edwin Ordway is an Executive Director and managing member in the firm's New Jersey office and he specializes in providing financial restructuring advisory and investigative services to companies, creditors, equity holders and third-party purchasers in the work-out and financial communities.

Prior to co-founding Capstone, Mr Ordway was a Senior Managing Director at the Policano and Manzo legacy practice at FTI Consulting for 14 years, most recently as co-leader of FTI's National Restructuring Practice. Previously, he spent five years as Chief Operating Officer of Knickerbocker Associates, a real estate development and investment company.

Mr Ordway is a member of the American Institute of Certified Public Accountants, the Association of Insolvency and Restructuring Advisors and the New Jersey State Society of Certified Public Accountants.

Chadbourne & Parke LLP
30 Rockefeller Plaza, New York, NY 10112
Tel +1 212 408 5100 Fax +1 212 541 5369
Web www.chadbourne.com

Andrew Rosenblatt
Partner
Email arosenblatt@chadbourne.com
Andrew Rosenblatt is a Partner in Chadbourne & Parke LLP's New York office and has over 12 years' experience in the area of bankruptcy and corporate

restructuring. Mr Rosenblatt has represented debtors in Chapter 11, borrowers and lenders in out-of-court restructurings, secured and unsecured lenders in Chapter 11 cases and foreign representatives in cross-border ancillary proceedings.

Howard Seife
Partner
Email hseife@chadbourne.com
Howard Seife is a Partner in Chadbourne & Parke LLP's New York office and chairs the firm's Global Bankruptcy and Financial Restructuring Practice. Mr Seife recently represented the ad hoc committee of counterparties in the successful restructuring of the monoline insurance company ACA Financial Guaranty. He has built his reputation on representing financial institutions, and creditors' committees, in some of the largest and most complex Chapter 11s, such as Lehman Brothers, Enron, Spiegel Inc/Eddie Bauer, Parmalat and Refco.

Mr Seife is also a leader in the area of cross-border insolvencies, having commenced, in the first major test of Chapter 15, a case in New York for the Russian receiver of Yukos Oil. His role as a leader in the innovative use of ancillary bankruptcy proceedings was recently recognized by *The Deal*'s Bankruptcy Insider, describing him as the 'top-ranked US lawyer to foreign debtors'.

Conway MacKenzie Inc
401 South Old Woodward Avenue, Birmingham, MI 48009
Tel +1 248 433 3100 **Fax** +1 248 433 3143
Web www.c-m-d.com

Van E Conway
Chief Executive
Email VConway@c-m-d.com
Van Conway is nationally recognized in the fields of insolvency/bankruptcy; financing, reorganization and management of troubled companies; mergers and acquisitions; debt restructuring; and litigation support. He has provided advisory services to underperforming businesses and related parties for nearly 30 years and is a certified turnaround professional, certified insolvency and restructuring advisor and certified in distressed business valuation.

Mr Conway has been engaged as a turnaround consultant and financial advisor for clients in various industries, including: automotive, manufacturing, steel, service, transportation, distribution and contracting. As a financial advisor, he has worked closely with debtors, lenders and creditor committees in out-of-court or Chapter 11 restructurings and has provided consulting services in turnaround, profit enhancement and cost-reduction strategies.

In the area of litigation support services, Mr Conway is qualified to provide expert testimony on lost profits, economic damages, business valuation and related matters. As a certified public accountant and certified fraud examiner, he also offers assistance with fraud-related issues, including detection, investigation and quantification.

As one of the founders of Conway MacKenzie, he has been with the firm since its inception in 1987. Previously, he was a Partner at Deloitte & Touche where he specialized in insolvency, litigation, and mergers and acquisitions. Mr Conway is a member of the Turnaround Management Association as well as numerous other professional organizations.

Conway MacKenzie Inc
303 W Madison St, Suite 1600, Chicago, IL 60606
Tel +1 312 220 0100 **Fax** +1 312 220 0101
Web www.c-m-d.com

Kenneth J Malek
Senior Managing Director
Email KMalek@c-m-d.com
Ken Malek brings to Conway MacKenzie over 30 years' experience in assisting companies undergoing transition, underperformance and distress, including turnaround, financial and accounting advisory, mergers and acquisitions, valuation and expert testimony. He has been engaged as an advisor in a number of industries, including: airline/travel and leisure, financial services, manufacturing, real estate, construction, retail, steel, technology and telecommunications. As a financial and turnaround advisor, Mr Malek has worked with borrowers, lenders, debtors in possession, creditors' committees, trustees and equity holders, in out-of-court restructurings and turnarounds and in Chapter 11 restructurings.

Mr Malek has served as examiner and testified as an expert on valuation and bankruptcy matters in the US district courts of Delaware, Illinois and Texas, in the US bankruptcy courts of Illinois, Indiana, Louisiana, Michigan and Virginia, in the US Court of Federal Claims and in arbitration proceedings. The matters on which he has been engaged as an expert include: business viability and Chapter 11 confirmation standards; valuation, bankruptcy recovery actions, solvency and insolvency; economic damages, causation, and mitigation of damages; fraud, Ponzi schemes, tracing of funds, and forensic investigations; accounting methods and standards; professional practice standards; substantive consolidation, recharacterization and equitable subordination; and wrongful takings issues pursuant to the US Supreme Court's Penn Central standards.

Mr Malek is a Fellow of the American College of Bankruptcy and is Past President and remains a member of the Board of Directors of the Association of Insolvency and Restructuring Advisors. He is also a member of the Turnaround Management Association and the American Bankruptcy Institute.

Epiq
90 Park Avenue, 8th Floor, New York, NY 10016
Tel +1 212 225 9200 Fax +1212 225 9201
Web www.epiqsystems.com

Daniel C McElhinney
Executive Director
Email dmcelhinney@epiqsystems.com
Dan McElhinney is Executive Director of the claims administration business, where he oversees the day-to-day operations of the business unit. He brings seven years of experience in the practice of law in the business reorganization and restructuring department of Willkie Farr & Gallagher LLP. He has overseen cases such as Lehman Brothers, AMPEX, Tribune Company and Nortel.

Lorenzo Mendizabal
Managing Director
Email lmendizabal@epiqsystems.com
As the Managing Director of the bankruptcy services segments at Epiq, Lorenzo Mendizabal oversees the development and tailoring of the products and services that the firm provides to its bankruptcy clients. As the former President of the Trumbull Group, he oversaw and managed cases such as K-Mart, Armstrong, Safety-Kleen and Mid-Valley (Halliburton), Pittsburgh Corning and Quigley (Pfizer), Trump Hotels and Casino, Stone and Webster and many others.

Evercore Partners Inc
55 East 52nd Street, New York, NY 10055
Tel +1 212.857 3100 Fax +1 212.857 3101
Web www.evercore.com

William Repko
Senior Managing Director
Email Repko@Evercore.com
Bill Repko is a Senior Managing Director and Co-Head of Evercore Partners' Debt Capital Markets and Restructuring Group.

Prior to joining Evercore, Mr Repko served as Chairman and Head of the Restructuring Group at JP Morgan, where he focused on providing comprehensive solutions to clients' liquidity and reorganization challenges. He joined Manufacturers Hanover Trust in 1973, which, after a series of mergers, became part of JPMorgan Chase. After joining the bank's Special Loan Group in 1981, Mr Repko was responsible for its exposure in International Harvester and Allis Chalmers, among others. In 1988 he was given responsibility for the bank's Alternative Investment Management group, which sought to convert the bank's sovereign debt to less developed countries into equity stakes in companies in those countries. He retired from the firm in 2005 as Chairman of the Restructuring Group, which he formed in 1992. Mr Repko was one of the initial inductees in the Turnaround Management Association's Hall of Fame.

FTI Consulting Inc
250 Pehle Avenue, Suite 305, Saddle Brook, NJ 07663
Tel: +1 201 843 4900 Fax: +1 201 843 8044
Web www.fticonsulting.com

Dominic DiNapoli
Executive Vice President
Email dominic.dinapoli@fticonsulting.com
Dominic DiNapoli is Executive Vice President and Chief Operating Officer of FTI Consulting, a publicly traded, $2.2 billion global business advisory firm. He is responsible for the day-to-day operations of the company's five business segments, which have more than 3,500 employees across 23 countries.

In addition to his operational role, he oversees the strategic direction of FTI and is the driving force behind key initiatives designed to promote integration and cross-selling across business segments. He developed the Industry Solutions program which organizes FTI professionals around important industries, offering clients a multidisciplinary approach. Mr DiNapoli also chairs the Global Expansion Committee, a cross-segment, multinational group of FTI professionals responsible for developing the operational infrastructure to better serve clients on a global scale.

Prior to his appointment to COO, Mr DiNapoli was Senior Managing Director and Co-Leader of the FTI Restructuring segment and was appointed to work with executive management to evaluate and implement FTI acquisitions. During that time he led the acquisition of the KPMG dispute advisory services practice. Today the FTI Corporate Finance/Restructuring segment contributes more than $500 million in annual revenue to the firm.

Previously, Mr DiNapoli was the managing partner of PricewaterhouseCoopers LLP's US Business Recovery Services (BRS) practice. As Managing Partner, he initiated the discussion that led to the acquisition of the BRS practice by FTI.

FTI Consulting Inc
3 Times Square, 9th Floor, New York, NY 10036
Tel: +1 212 247 1010 **Fax:** +1 212 841 9350
Web www.fticonsulting.com

Randall S Eisenberg
Senior Managing Director
Email Randall.Eisenberg@FTIConsulting.com
Randall Eisenberg, a Senior Managing Director in FTI's Corporate Finance practice, is Co-Practice Leader of FTI's services for underperforming companies. He has extensive experience advising senior management, boards of directors and equity sponsors on how to revitalize companies that are stagnant, underperforming or in crisis. Mr Eisenberg has led many high-profile national and international assignments across a multitude of industries.

He is a past chairman of the Turnaround Management Association, a past president of the Association of Certified Turnaround Professionals, and a Fellow in both the American College of Bankruptcy and International Insolvency Institute.

Adrian Frankum
Senior Managing Director
Email adrian.frankum@fticonsulting.com
Adrian Frankum is a Senior Managing Director in FTI's Corporate Finance Practice and has more than 15 years' experience in advising companies, boards of directors and creditors on strategic, operational

and financial issues in a number of companies and jurisdictions. He has served as a leader in many high-profile corporate restructurings, garnering extensive experience in a variety of industries, including: automotive, telecommunications, chemicals and manufacturing.

Mr Frankum is a board member of the Turnaround Management Association.

FTI Consulting Inc
227 West Monroe Street, Suite 900, Chicago, Illinois 60606
Tel: +1 312 759 8100 **Fax:** +1 312 759 8119
Web www.fticonsulting.com

Armen Emrikian
Managing Director
Email armen.emrikian@fticonsulting.com
Armen Emrikian is a Managing Director in FTI's Corporate Finance Practice. He has extensive experience in advising debtors, creditors and equity holders in financially distressed situations (both in and out of court). Mr Emrikian has advised in restructurings in a variety of industries, including: automotive, telecommunications, retail and general manufacturing. Mr Emrikian is a certified insolvency and restructuring advisor and is a member of the Turnaround Management Association.

FTI Consulting Inc
1101 K Street, NW, Suite B100, Washington, DC, 20005
Tel: +1 202 312 9100 **Fax:** +1 202 312 9101
Web www.fticonsulting.com

DeLain E Gray
Senior Managing Director
Email DeLain.Gray@FTIConsulting.com
DeLain Gray, Senior Managing Director and Practice Leader of the FTI Consulting Corporate Finance Practice, has served as auditor, consultant and advisor to companies in numerous industries for more than 30 years. He has extensive experience representing both creditors and debtors in formal bankruptcy and out-of-court restructurings. That experience encompasses a wide variety of industries, ranging from companies in charter aircraft operations to retail, textile manufacturing, waste management, high technology, healthcare, telecommunications and leasing/financial services.

Mr Gray is a member of the American Institute of Certified Public Accountants, the Missouri Society of Certified Public Accountants, the Association of Insolvency and Restructuring Advisors and the Turnaround Management Association.

FTI Consulting Inc
1201 W. Peachtree Street, NW, Suite 500, Atlanta, GA 30309
Tel: +1 404 460 6200 **Fax:** +1 404 460 6299
Web www.fticonsulting.com

James Guglielmo
Managing Director
Email jim.guglielmo@fticonsulting.com
James Guglielmo is a Managing Director in FTI's Corporate Finance Practice and is based in Atlanta, Georgia. Mr Guglielmo has extensive experience providing a wide array of financial advisory services to both debtors and creditors in reorganization and bankruptcy matters. He has served as an advisor to companies and boards of directors, as well as to secured lenders and unsecured creditor committees. He specializes in enhancing value in underperforming businesses and distressed lending situations. Mr Guglielmo is a certified insolvency and restructuring advisor and a member of the Turnaround Management Association and the Association of Insolvency and Restructuring Advisors.

GCA Savvian Advisors LLC
1330 Avenue of the Americas, 28th Floor, New York, NY 10019
Tel +1 212 999 7090 **Fax** +1 212 999 7073
Web www.gcasavvian.com

Jonathan Katz
Managing Director
Email jkatz@gcasavvian.com
Jonathan Katz is the Co-Head of Restructuring Investment Banking at GCA Savvian. Prior to joining GCA Savvian, Mr Katz ran two funds that invested in distressed assets, first as Founding Partner of JP Morgan Special Situations Investing and then as founder of Panagos Katz Situational Investing.

Mr Katz initially practiced law at Seward & Kissel and subsequently trained in corporate finance and restructuring at JP Morgan.

Greenberg Traurig
77 West Wacker Drive, Suite 3100, Chicago, Illinois 60601
Tel +1 312 456 8400 **Fax** +1 312 456 8435
Web www.gtlaw.com

Keith J Shapiro
Co-Managing Shareholder
Email shapirok@gtlaw.com
Keith Shapiro is Co-Chair of Greenberg Traurig's Business Reorganization and Bankruptcy Practice. He has more than 25 years' experience and appears worldwide in corporate restructuring matters and work-outs representing troubled companies, financial institutions, creditors' committees, and hedge and private equity funds. Mr Shapiro was co-editor-in-chief of Wiley's annual *Bankruptcy Law Update* and was the lead author of the American Bankruptcy Institute's *Health Care Insolvency Manual*.

A leader in the restructuring community, Mr Shapiro is a member of the International Board of Directors of the Turnaround Management Association and a Fellow of the American College of Bankruptcy. He was previously Chairman of the Board and President of the American Bankruptcy Institute, and a member of the Board of Directors of INSOL International.

Hilco
5 Revere Drive, Suite 206, Northbrook, Illinois 60062
Tel +1 847 509 1100 **Fax** +1 847 509 1150
Web www.hilcotrading.com

Jeffrey B Hecktman
Chairman and CEO, Hilco Trading LLC
Email jhecktman@hilcotrading.com
Jeffrey Hecktman is a pioneer in the asset repositioning business sector in North America and Europe. He founded Hilco in 1987 to conduct business asset liquidations. Today, under his guidance, Hilco has expanded its services to include asset appraisals, acquisition and disposition services, specialized debt and equity financing, investment banking and retail consulting. Over the course of his career, Mr Hecktman has structured and directed thousands of transactions valued in the billions of dollars.

Mr Hecktman is an active member of the National Retail Federation, the Commercial Finance Association, the Turnaround Management Association and the American Bankruptcy Institute.

Richard L Kaye

Executive Vice President, Hilco Trading LLC
Email rkaye@hilcotrading.com
As Chief Marketing Officer for Hilco's global enterprise, Mr Kaye brings nearly 40 years of corporate marketing and business administration experience to the organization. After graduation, he spent five years in the corporate world developing marketing strategies and leading in the execution of ensuing marketing initiatives. Then, in 1972, Mr Kaye founded Kaye & Company Inc, which spawned three organizations, including a strategic marketing consultancy, an advertising agency and a public relations firm. Kaye & Company went on to become one of the Chicago area's most respected business-to-business strategic and operations marketing services firms.

Following a brief retirement, during which he consulted for Hilco, Mr Kaye joined Hilco full-time to lead its marketing efforts.

Jeffrey W Linstrom

Managing Director, Hilco Recovery Strategies LLC
Email jlinstrom@hilcotrading.com
At Hilco, Jeff Linstrom has served as both General Counsel and an Executive Vice President of the holding company. He was instrumental in helping Hilco build its business platform and has structured and executed on hundreds of distressed asset transactions.

Mr Linstrom has nearly 25 years' experience in corporate reorganizations, bankruptcies, work-outs and lending transactions.

Prior to joining Hilco in 2000, he was a partner in the Jones Day law firm and counsel at Skadden, Arps. Over the course of his law practice career, Mr Linstrom has served as counsel to debtors, secured lenders and creditors' committees in some of the largest and most complex reorganization cases in the US, including Federated Department Stores, Mercury Finance Corporation, Montgomery Wards, Morrison Knudsen Corporation, Philip Services Corporation, the Singer Company NV and USG Corporation. He has also represented both lenders and borrowers in numerous financing transactions and work-outs.

Huron Consulting Group

1120 Avenue of the Americas, 8th Floor, New York, NY 10036
Tel +1 212 785 1900 **Fax** +1 212 785 1313
Web www.huronconsultinggroup.com

John C DiDonato

Managing Director
Email jdidonato@huronconsultinggroup.com
John DiDonato has more than 20 years' experience in reorganization, restructuring, capital raising, buy and sell side advisory, and merger integration. He provides guidance to financially challenged entities proceeding through both out-of-court and court-supervised restructurings. Mr DiDonato has extensive experience servicing debtors with complex capital structures. Throughout his crisis-management career, he has raised replacement and exit financing in excess of $1 billion.

He has served in excess of 100 debtors, functioning for many as chief restructuring strategist. His expertise encompasses a wide range of industries, including automotive; aerospace; engineering and construction; metals; equipment leasing; logistics; distribution; and retail.

Mr DiDonato serves as the Practice Leader and Managing Director of the Restructuring and Turnaround Practice of Huron Consulting Group. Prior to joining Huron, Mr DiDonato was President of Glass & Associates Inc. He is a certified turnaround professional and certified managerial accountant, and a member of the Turnaround Management Association.

Huron Consulting Group

550 W Van Buren Street, Chicago, Illinois 60607
Tel +1 312 583 8700 **Fax** +1 312 583 8701
Web www.huronconsultinggroup.com

Daniel P Wikel

Managing Director
Email dwikel@huronconsultinggroup.com
Daniel Wikel advises clients on corporate turnarounds and restructurings, lender work-out situations, and raising capital. He has significant experience managing large bankruptcy cases and related matters. His operational expertise spans the areas of strategic planning, investment analysis, operational process and identifying cost improvements.

Prior to joining Huron, Mr Wikel was a Director in Arthur Andersen's Corporate Restructuring Practice. Prior to joining the restructuring consulting group, he was involved in the Zenith

Electronics Corporation turnaround and bankruptcy as the Director of Planning and Analysis. He also held various financial positions with the Tenneco Inc organization and began his career with KPMG in the audit practice.

Mr Wikel has served as a financial advisor to a number of companies in various industries, including: aerospace/airline; transportation; consumer products; modular homebuilding; packaging and forest products; general C&I manufacturing.

Representative examples of his engagement experience include: acting as Huron's leading financial advisor in the UAL Corporation & United Airlines bankruptcy case, working closely with the company's investment bankers and attorneys. In addition to assisting on bankruptcy preparations, first-day orders, and DIP and exit financing, Mr Wikel managed several aspects of the bankruptcy process on a day-to-day basis and was a participating member of the company's restructuring office. Since emerging from bankruptcy protection, the airline has been given a number of awards, including the Turnaround Management Association's Turnaround of the Year Award.

Mr Wikel also served as the Chief Restructuring Officer for United Fixtures Corporation Interlake (UFCI), a $300 million designer and manufacturer of heavy-duty steel storage and display racks to targeted markets throughout the US, Canada and Mexico, stabilizing and selling the business to a strategic buyer via a Section 363 auction.

Mr Wikel is a certified public accountant, a certified insolvency and restructuring advisor, and an officer of the Turnaround Management Association and member of the Association of Insolvency and Restructuring Advisors.

Jones Day
222 East 41st Street, New York, NY 10017
Tel +1 212 326 7844 **Fax** +1 212 755 7306
Web www.jonesday.com

Corinne Ball
Partner
Email cball@jonesday.com
Corinne Ball has 30 years' experience in business finance and restructuring, with a focus on complex corporate reorganizations and distressed acquisitions, both court-supervised and extra-judicial, including matters involving multi-jurisdictional and cross-border enterprises. She is Co-Head of the New York office's Business

Restructuring & Reorganization Practice and leader of the firm's Global Restructuring Practice.

She led a team of attorneys representing Chrysler LLC in connection with its successful Chapter 11 reorganization, which won the Investment Dealers' Digest Deal of the Year award for 2009. She has also orchestrated many other complex reorganizations and has counseled lenders and bondholders in numerous restructurings.

She won the Turnaround Management Association's International Turnaround Company of the Year award, and was named Dealmaker of the Year by *The American Lawyer* and one of "The Decade's Most Influential Lawyers" by *The National Law Journal*. She is a director of the American College of Bankruptcy and the American Bankruptcy Institute.

Leonard J Kennedy
6500 Broxburn Dr, Bethesda, MD 20817
Tel +1 202 438 6038 **Fax** +1 301.320.9044
Email lenkennedy@gmail.com
Len Kennedy has more that 30 years' experience as a lawyer, government official and businessman in regulation, financing, restructuring and strategy development for telecommunications, information and media businesses. In addition, he advises and consults with communications firms and professionals.

Mr Kennedy served as General Counsel, Corporate Secretary and Chief Government Affairs Officer for Sprint Nextel, a Fortune 50 company serving 50 million customers, through 2008. He exercised day-to-day supervisory responsibility and operational management authority over the legal affairs of the company and provided legal advice to the board and senior management. In this capacity, he oversaw all the legal, governance, compliance and external affairs of the company, including supervising and negotiating multibillion-dollar mergers and acquisitions.

From 2001 to 2005, Mr Kennedy served as Senior Vice President and General Counsel of Nextel Communications, a Fortune 250 company. He restructured and closely aligned the legal department with Nextel's business units and senior management to realize the company's strategic initiatives, reduce its business risks and protect its business interests. Mr Kennedy also played a pivotal role in major merger initiatives and areas such as debt restructuring, corporate governance, government affairs, marketing and outsourcing.

Prior to joining Nextel in January 2001, Mr

Kennedy was a member of Dow, Lohnes & Albertson PLLC, a leading media and communications law firm, advising clients on telecommunications law, regulation and policy, and investment matters affecting wireless, wired and internet communications services.

From 1990 to 1991, Mr Kennedy served as senior legal advisor at the Federal Communications Commission to Commissioner Ervin S Duggan. He also served as senior legal advisor to Commissioner Patricia Diaz Dennis from 1986 to1988.

Kirkland & Ellis LLP

601 Lexington Avenue, New York, NY 10022
Tel +1 212 446 4800 **Fax** +1 212 446 4900
Web www.kirkland.com

Richard M Cieri
Partner
Email richard.cieri@kirkland.com
Richard Cieri is a Restructuring Partner in the New York office of Kirkland & Ellis LLP. He is an internationally recognized authority on domestic and cross-border restructurings, and in corporate governance and director and officer fiduciary duty matters (including "deepening insolvency"). He is best known for representing financially challenged companies, debtors and boards of directors. Mr Cieri has also been recognized as one of the country's outstanding restructuring lawyers by numerous publications in which clients have complimented his leadership on some of the largest Chapter 11 and business restructuring matters in the country. In April 2009, Mr Cieri was selected as one of the "Dealmakers of the Year" by *The American Lawyer*.

Kirkland & Ellis LLP

300 North LaSalle Street, Chicago, IL 60654
Tel +1 312 862 2000 **Fax** +1 312 862 2200

Chad J Husnick
Associate
Email chad.husnick@kirkland.com
Chad Husnick is a Restructuring Associate in the Chicago office of Kirkland & Ellis LLP. He concentrates his practice in all aspects of corporate restructuring, bankruptcy and insolvency proceedings, and has extensive experience assisting clients with understanding, addressing and, where necessary, litigating the complex issues associated with restructuring "legacy liabilities" such as labor costs, pension liabilities and retiree medical liabilities. Mr Husnick's experience includes both in- and out-of-court restructuring and contingency planning. He has represented his clients in a plethora of bankruptcy litigation matters, including contested confirmation hearings, turnover actions, proceedings to enforce the automatic stay and claims adjudication.

In addition to his experience with Chapter 11 restructuring, Mr Husnick has represented his clients in various out-of-court restructuring and contingency planning transactions. Specifically, he has counseled clients on addressing the fraudulent transfer and preference risks associated with complex, multibillion-dollar merger and acquisition transactions.

Mr Husnick has represented distressed companies in various aspects of their financial and operational restructuring and contingency planning.

Jeffrey D Pawlitz
Associate
Email jeffrey.pawlitz@kirkland.com
Jeffrey Pawlitz is a Restructuring Associate in the Chicago office of Kirkland & Ellis LLP. He focuses his practice on all aspects of corporate restructuring, bankruptcy and insolvency proceedings.

Mr Pawlitz has navigated a number of clients through in- and out-of-court restructurings, and has represented clients seeking to purchase estate assets through a Chapter 11 proceeding.

David R Seligman
Partner
Email david.seligman@kirkland.com
David Seligman is a Restructuring Partner in the Chicago office of Kirkland & Ellis LLP. He concentrates his practice in all aspects of corporate restructuring, bankruptcy and insolvency proceedings, both in the US and in connection with complex cross-border insolvencies. He focuses on representing large publicly held corporations and privately held portfolio companies in restructuring matters both in and out of court, as well buyers in large bankruptcy asset sales.

Mr Seligman has also represented trustees and creditors' committees in all types of bankruptcy proceedings.

James HM Sprayregen
Partner
Email james.sprayregen@kirkland.com
James HM Sprayregen is a Restructuring Partner in the Chicago and New York offices of Kirkland &

Ellis LLP. Mr Sprayregen is recognized as one of the country's outstanding restructuring lawyers. He has extensive experience representing major US and international companies in and out of court, as well as buyers and sellers of assets in distressed situations. He also has extensive experience advising boards of directors, and generally representing domestic and international debtors and creditors in work-out, insolvency, restructuring and bankruptcy matters. He has handled matters for clients in industries as varied as manufacturing, technology, transportation, energy, media and real estate.

In March 2010, Mr Sprayregen was selected by *The National Law Journal* as one of 'The Decade's Most Influential Lawyers'.

Mr Sprayregen returned to Kirkland & Ellis in December 2008. He rejoined the firm after nearly three years with Goldman Sachs, where he was Co-Head of its Restructuring Group and advised clients in restructuring and distressed situations.

Prior to joining Goldman Sachs, he spent 16 years at Kirkland & Ellis, where he led bankruptcy cases for United Airlines and Conseco, among many others.

Latham & Watkins LLP
885 Third Avenue, New York, NY 10022
Tel +1 212 906 1200 **Fax** +1 212 751 4864
Web www.lw.com

Keith A Simon
Partner
Email keith.simon@lw.com
Keith Simon is a partner in the New York office of Latham & Watkins and a member of the firm's Finance Department and Insolvency Practice Group. He is currently serving on the firm's Bankruptcy Advisory Committee and the New York City Bar Committee on Bankruptcy & Corporate Reorganization.

Mr Simon has experience in a variety of insolvency matters on behalf of secured lenders, debtors, unsecured creditors, contract parties and liquidators in bankruptcy proceedings and out-of-court work-outs. Mr Simon also has extensive out-of-court work-out experience representing secured lenders in comprehensive restructuring transactions and Article 9 foreclosures.

Mesirow Financial Consulting LLC
353 North Clark Street, Chicago, Illinois 60654
Tel +1 312 595 6000 **Fax** +1 312 595 4246
Web www.mesirowfinancial.com

Thomas J Allison
Executive Vice President and Senior Managing Director
Email tallison@mesirowfinancial.com
Thomas Allison is one of the foremost professionals in the restructuring and turnaround field, with over 30 years' experience. He has been managing complex turnaround situations since 1979 and has been an advisor on major reorganizations and insolvencies throughout the US. Mr Allison is a member of the Executive Leadership team and is responsible for Mesirow Financial Consulting's interim management and debtor restructuring capabilities on a national basis. He was previously a partner at Arthur Andersen and served as the national restructuring practice leader at Huron Consulting.

Mr Allison's industry expertise includes mortgages, airlines, transportation, retail, consumer products, general manufacturing, importing, distribution, high technology, healthcare, food, paper and packaging. He has served as chairman, CEO and chief restructuring officer for several companies, and is currently serving as chief executive officer of a care retirement operator.

Mr Allison is a member, director and past chairman of the Turnaround Management Association, and a founder and former chairman of the Association for Certified Turnaround Professionals. He has testified on modifications to bankruptcy law and served as an advisor to President Clinton's Economic Council (Bankruptcy Working Group).

Melissa Kibler Knoll
Senior Managing Director
Email mknoll@mesirowfinancial.com
Melissa Kibler Knoll has over 20 years' experience providing financial advisory services to companies, unsecured creditors, secured lenders, and other parties in bankruptcies, restructurings, turnarounds and related litigation. Ms Knoll's experience includes addressing various financial, accounting, valuation, operational, liquidity and leverage issues in Chapter 11s, out-of-court work-outs, receiverships/ trusteeships and other forums. Ms Knoll has also provided a variety of litigation support, expert testimony and forensic accounting services in avoidance actions and other commercial litigation matters.

Her industry experience includes retail, energy, steel, automotive, distribution, manufacturing, healthcare, financial services, telecommunications and natural resources.

Ms Knoll was previously a partner in KPMG's Corporate Recovery Practice, after starting her career at Price Waterhouse. She is President of the American Bankruptcy Institute and is a Fellow of the American College of Bankruptcy. She is also a member of the Turnaround Management Association.

Mesirow Financial Consulting LLC

666 Third Avenue, 21st Floor, New York, NY 10017
Tel +1 212 808 8330 Fax +1 212 682 5015
Web www.mesirowfinancial.com

Ralph S Tuliano

President and Executive Managing Director
Email rtuliano@mesirowfinancial.com
Ralph Tuliano is President and Executive Managing Director of Mesirow Financial Consulting LLC, and is based in New York. He serves as a member of the Mesirow Financial Board of Directors and Executive Committee.

Mr Tuliano has over 20 years' experience providing restructuring, litigation support, valuation, forensic accounting and related services on a variety of assignments. He has advised debtors, secured lenders and unsecured creditors' committees in the context of out-of-court restructurings and Chapter 11 bankruptcy proceedings. In addition, Mr Tuliano has provided consulting services and damages assessments on a variety of complex commercial litigation matters, including breach of contract, securities fraud, intellectual property and fraudulent conveyance assignments.

He has been qualified as an expert and rendered deposition and trial testimony on numerous occasions. His experience includes retail, healthcare, manufacturing, energy, telecoms, technology, natural resources and other industries.

Mr Tuliano was formerly the National Partner-in-Charge of KPMG LLP's US Corporate Recovery Practice.

Milbank, Tweed, Hadley & McCloy LLP

601 South Figueroa Street, 30th Floor, Los Angeles, CA 90017
Tel +1 213 892 4000 Fax +1 213 629 5063
Web www.milbank.com

Gregory Bray

Partner
Email gbray@milbank.com
Gregory Bray is a Partner in the Global Financial Restructuring Group at Milbank, Tweed, Hadley & McCloy LLP. He has specialized in bankruptcy, creditors' rights, complex corporate work-outs and lending for more than 25 years.

He has a diverse national practice and has been involved in out-of-court restructurings and bankruptcies in a wide variety of industries, including automotive, media, construction, retail, apparel, healthcare, oil and gas, telecommunications, project finance, energy, sub-prime lending and leasing, franchises, manufacturing and high technology.

Mr Bray regularly represents hedge funds, private equity funds, money center banks, financial institutions, lender syndicates comprised of first- and second-lien lenders, trustees and receivers, creditors' committees and equity securities holders. He frequently advises funds making control investments in, and potential purchases of, financially distressed companies, both in and out of court.

Mr Bray also advises lenders in the structuring and documentation of high-risk loans and DIP loans, and the board of directors of public companies in financial distress with respect to corporate governance and fiduciary duty issues.

Robert Shenfeld

Senior Attorney
Email rshenfeld@milbank.com
Robert Shenfeld is a Senior Attorney in the Financial Restructuring Group and is based in the firm's Los Angeles office.

Mr Shenfeld has extensive experience in corporate reorganization both in and out of bankruptcy, bankruptcy-related litigation and providing strategic advice in connection with maximizing the value of distressed debt. He represents a wide range of clients in insolvency situations, including secured and unsecured creditors, official and unofficial creditors' committees, debtors, financial institutions, hedge funds and indenture trustees.

Milbank, Tweed, Hadley & McCloy LLP
One Chase Manhattan Plaza, New York, NY 10005
Tel +1 212 530 5000 **Fax** +1 212 530 5219
Web www.milbank.com

Dennis Dunne
Practice Leader
Email ddunne@milbank.com
Dennis Dunne is the Practice Group Leader in Milbank's Financial Restructuring Group and one of the members of the firm's Global Executive Committee. He has extensive experience in representing debtors and creditors in reorganization cases and out-of-court work-outs, including exchange and tender offers, as well as acquirors of financially distressed companies.

His engagements have ranged across a wide array of industries, including automotive, airline, apparel, cable and broadcasting, chemical, construction, gambling, healthcare, housing development manufacturing, pharmaceutical, project finance, retail, shipping, telecoms and textile. Mr Dunne has played a leadership role in these matters, frequently as counsel to the company or official and unofficial committees representing key creditor constituencies, such as bondholders, agents for lender syndicates and large debt or equity holders.

Mr Dunne has also regularly represented private equity funds, hedge funds and other financial institutions acquiring control positions in financially distressed companies, both in and out of court. He has also assisted prospective providers of high-risk and DIP financing in structuring, documenting and obtaining approval for such loans, and regularly advised boards of directors of public companies on corporate governance and fiduciary duty matters in the restructuring context. In all such matters, he has drawn upon his board experience across several disciplines to craft practical solutions and build the consensus required to implement these solutions.

Miller Buckfire & Co
153 East 53rd Street, 22nd Floor, New York, NY 10022
Tel +1 212 895 1800 **Fax** +1 212 895 1853
Web www.millerbuckfire.com

Henry S Miller
Chairman
Email henry.miller@millerbuckfire.com
Henry Miller is Chairman and Co-Founder of Miller Buckfire, an independent and privately owned investment bank. Over the course of his career, Mr Miller has represented debtors, creditors and other constituents in numerous out-of-court and Chapter 11 matters. These have included extremely complex reorganizations where the services provided involved raising "rescue" financing, strategic assignments and divestiture of substantial assets or businesses of the affected enterprises.

Prior to founding Miller Buckfire, Mr Miller was Vice Chairman and Managing Director at Dresdner Kleinwort Wasserstein, where he served as the global head of the firm's Financial Restructuring Group.

Before that, he was Managing Director and head of the Restructuring Group at Salomon Brothers. Mr Miller is a former trustee of the Turnaround Management Association and was recently inducted into the TMA Hall of Fame.

Pepper Hamilton LLP
Suite 3600, 100 Renaissance Center, Detroit, Michigan 48243
Tel +1 313 259 7110 **Fax** +1 313 259 7926
Web www.pepperlaw.com

Robert S Hertzberg
Partner
Email hertzbergr@pepperlaw.com
Robert Hertzberg is a Partner with Pepper Hamilton LLP, resident in the Detroit and New York offices. He is Co-Chair of the firm's Corporate Restructuring and Bankruptcy Practice Group.

Mr Hertzberg, an accomplished bankruptcy lawyer and fellow of the American College of Bankruptcy, has been practicing almost exclusively in the bankruptcy and restructuring field for more than 29 years, representing secured lenders, debtors, debtors-in-possession, trustees, creditors and creditors' committees.

He is a past president of INSOL International (2003-05), the leading international organization of bankruptcy professionals. He also was a member of the board of INSOL International from 1997 to 2006, and is currently chairman of INSOL's Technical Electronic Newsletter Editorial Board.

Mr Hertzberg is also active in many other professional organizations, including the International Bar Association, the Turnaround Management Association, the Commercial Law League of America (past chairman of the Bankruptcy Section) and the American Bankruptcy Institute (past chairman of the Central States Workshop program).

Deborah Kovsky-Apap
Associate
Email kovskyd@pepperlaw.com
Deborah Kovsky-Apap is an Associate in the Corporate Restructuring and Bankruptcy Practice Group of Pepper Hamilton LLP, resident in the Detroit office. She focuses her practice on bankruptcy and insolvency, out-of-court work-outs, and commercial and securities litigation.

Ms Kovsky-Apap is Chair of the Michigan Network of the International Women's Insolvency and Restructuring Confederation and is a member of the American Bankruptcy Institute. Prior to joining Pepper Hamilton, she was an Associate at Wilmer Cutler Pickering Hale and Dorr LLP in New York.

Kay Standridge Kress
Partner
Email kressk@pepperlaw.com
Kay Standridge Kress is a corporate restructuring and bankruptcy partner in the Detroit Office of Pepper Hamilton LLP. She concentrates her practice in corporate restructuring, insolvency and bankruptcy matters and has over 20 years' experience in representing debtors, creditors' committees, secured creditors, trustees and individual creditors and parties in interest, both as lead counsel and as co-counsel in out-of-court work-outs and in bankruptcy courts in the Eastern District of Michigan, the Western District of Michigan, the District of Delaware, the Southern District of New York and in other bankruptcy courts in the US.

Ms Kress has extensive experience representing secured creditors in federal receivership actions. She is a Fellow in the American College of Bankruptcy.

Pine Brook Road Partners LLC
One Grand Central Place, 60 East 42nd Street, 50th Floor, New York, NY 10165
Tel +1 212 847 4348; **Fax** +1 212 847 4395

Lawrence A Marsiello
Special Advisor
Email lmarsiello@pinebrookpartners.com
Lawrence Marsiello serves as a Special Advisor to New York based private equity firm Pine Brook Road Partners. He focuses upon the financial services segments including specialty finance companies as well as commercial banks. Mr Marsiello also serves as an advisor and consultant to financial institutions on strategic and credit-risk management. He has more than 35 years' experience in credit risk, including lending, investing, portfolio management, syndications and business development. He is the former Vice Chairman and Chief Lending Officer of CIT Group, a global finance company that provides financial products and advisory services to more than one million customers in over 50 countries.

Mr Marsiello is a member of the Turnaround Management Association and was elected to its Hall of Fame in 2008.

Rothschild Inc
1251 Avenue of the Americas, 51st floor, New York, NY 10020
Tel +1 212 403 3500 **Fax** +1 212 403 3501
Web www.rothschild.com

Todd R Snyder
Managing Director
Email todd.snyder@rothschild.com
Todd Snyder is a Managing Director of Rothschild Inc, a leading international investment banking and financial advisory firm.

Mr Snyder has been an advisor to companies in restructurings and reorganizations for 22 years. He has been instrumental in a diverse selection of complex transactions including restructurings, reorganizations, financings, work-outs, exchange offers, mergers, divestitures and management-led buyouts. He has advised companies in a range of industries. Mr Snyder has also advised two Administrations with respect to the reorganization of the automobile industry (including General Motors, Chrysler and Adam Opel), and is a Global Co-Head of Rothschild's Automotive Industry Sector.

Named "2009 Rainmaker of the Year" by *Institutional Investor*, he is an adjunct professor at New York University Law School, New York University Leonard N Stern School of Business and speaks frequently on reorganization-related topics. Before joining Rothschild, he was a Managing Director in the Restructuring and Reorganization group at Peter J Solomon Company. Prior to that, he was a Managing Director at KPMG Peat Marwick in the Corporate Recovery Group. Mr Snyder also ran his own advisory and investment firm, Hesperus Advisors, specializing in recapitalizations and work-outs.

Seabury Group LLC
1350 Avenue of the Americas, 25th Floor, New York, NY 10019
Tel +1 212 284 1133 **Fax** +1 212 284 1144
Web www.seaburygroup.com

Lorie R Beers
Managing Director
Email lbeers@seaburygroup.com
Lorie R Beers is the Managing Director, Investment Banking and Restructuring, with responsibility for Seabury's restructuring practices for all industry segments outside the aviation and aerospace sectors.

A recognized financial industry leader, Ms Beers has more than 20 years of corporate restructuring and insolvency experience representing companies on distressed M&A transactions, refinancing, recapitalizations and debt renegotiations. Ms Beers is familiar with a wide range of industries and has driven both in-court and out-of-court restructuring successes, and is credited with developing the Complex Financial Restructuring Program for the American Bankruptcy Institute (ABI).

Prior to joining Seabury, Ms Beers was Managing Director for KPMG's Special Situations Advisory Group in New York. Her previous experience also includes working with the investment bank of Gordian Group LLC, as well as being a partner in the bankruptcy and insolvency practice at Kasowitz, Benson, Torres & Friedman LLP. Ms Beers sits on the board of directors of the ABI and is Co-Chair of its Investment Banking Committee. She is also a member of the Turnaround Management Association.

Michael B Cox
Senior Managing Director
Email mcox@seaburygroup.com
Mike Cox joined Seabury in 1998 and today is the Global Head of Restructuring Advisory. He has over 25 years of airline and aviation-related experience and has advised numerous airline clients on a variety of projects, including treasury, corporate finance and airline restructuring. His engagements have included leading numerous successful restructuring efforts around the world, including Air Canada, Frontier Airlines, Northwest Airlines, South African Airways and US Airways .

Prior to joining Seabury, Mr Cox was a Director at Price Waterhouse LLP, where he led the aviation consulting/restructuring group. He also worked for Continental Airlines, where he served in a variety of financial positions including Vice President and Treasurer. At Continental, Mr Cox initiated and structured numerous financings to increase cash reserves and finance fleet acquisitions.

John E Luth
Chairman, President and CEO
Email jluth@seaburygroup.com
John Luth is the Founding Partner and Chief Executive of Seabury Group and has senior account responsibility for corporate transformations, equity placements, corporate finance and M&A advisory engagements. At Seabury, he has led deal teams that have executed successful equity placements for clients in aviation, logistics, media and travel technology.

Mr Luth has led many highly successful restructurings, including financings and restructurings for Air Canada, America West Airlines, Continental Airlines Inc, NWA and US Airways Group.

Mr Luth was previously Senior Vice President, Finance & CFO of Continental Airlines. He also served as Vice President, Syndications with Manufacturers Hanover Trust Company and worked for the corporate finance division of Exxon Corporation in New York.

Shearman & Sterling LLP
599 Lexington Avenue, New York, NY 10022
Tel +1 212 848 4000 **Fax** +1 212 848 7179
Web www.shearman.com

Douglas P Bartner
Partner
Email dbartner@shearman.com
Douglas Bartner is a Partner in Shearman & Sterling LLP's Bankruptcy & Reorganization Group. He regularly represents debtors and creditors and acquirors of assets in Chapter 11 bankruptcies and out-of-court restructurings. Mr Bartner joined the firm in 1982 and became a partner in 1991. Mr Bartner is a member of the Committee on Commercial Bankruptcy of the New York County Lawyers' Association, a member of INSOL International, and a member of the American Bankruptcy Institute.

James L Garrity, Jr
Partner
Email jgarrity@shearman.com
James Garrity is a partner in Shearman & Sterling LLP's Bankruptcy & Reorganization Group. His practice focuses on representing debtors, creditors and court-appointed fiduciaries in Chapter 11 and

cross-border cases. Mr Garrity is a certified mediator for the United States Bankruptcy Court for the Southern District of New York. He has mediated disputes in adversary proceedings in complex bankruptcy cases in New York and Delaware.

Before joining Shearman & Sterling, he served as a judge in the United States Bankruptcy Court for the Southern District of New York. Prior to his appointment to the bench, he was an Assistant United States Attorney in the Civil Division for the Southern District of New York, where he served as Chief of the Tax Unit.

Mr Garrity is a Fellow in the American College of Bankruptcy and the American Bar Foundation, a Director of the International Insolvency Institute, a member of INSOL International, and both an Adjunct Professor of Bankruptcy Law and a member of the Advisory Board at St John's University Masters in Bankruptcy Law Program.

Amy Beth Gitlitz
Associate
Email agitlitz@shearman.com

Amy Beth Gitlitz is an Associate in the Executive Compensation & Employee Benefits Group in New York. Her practice focuses on all aspects of executive compensation, including securities, tax and employment laws and regulatory compliance. She has experience in the design and implementation of a wide variety of executive compensation programs for US and non-US public and private corporations, including cash and equity-based incentive compensation plans, deferred compensation programs and employee stock purchase plans.

Ms Gitlitz also has experience in the negotiation of senior executive employment, change-in-control and termination agreements on behalf of both corporations and executives.

She is involved with the firm's corporate governance practice area and has been the Senior Compensation Attorney for the annual Shearman & Sterling Corporate Governance and Executive Compensation Survey since its inception in 2004.

Ms Gitlitz has been at the firm since 1997.

Linda E Rappaport
Partner
Email lrappaport@shearman.com

Linda Rappaport is Practice Group Leader of the Executive Compensation & Employee Benefits/ Private Clients Group. Her practice focuses on all aspects of executive compensation and benefits,

including corporate, securities and tax laws, and the Employee Retirement Income Security Act (ERISA). She has extensive experience in the design and implementation of executive incentive programs, including equity-based plans, retirement and welfare plans, and the negotiation and preparation of employment contracts and severance arrangements, with particular emphasis on the financial services and entertainment industries.

Ms Rappaport's experience includes the representation of global, US and non-US companies and their boards of directors and compensation committees in corporate governance, CEO succession, public disclosure and executive compensation matters. Ms Rappaport has broad experience in compensation and benefits issues associated with corporate acquisitions, divestitures, public offerings, restructurings and bankruptcies, and in all aspects of employment law, including discrimination in the employment relationship. She has a special focus on the design and documentation of carried interest and co-investment programs for executives managing investment funds.

Sidley Austin LLP
One South Dearborn Street, Chicago, Illinois 60603
Tel +1 312 853 7000 **Fax** +1 312 853 7036
Web www.sidley.com

Jessica CK Boelter
Associate
Email jboelter@sidley.com

Jessica Boelter is an Associate in Sidley Austin LLP's Corporate Reorganization and Bankruptcy Group. Ms Boelter advises clients in a wide variety of complex in-court and out-of-court restructuring matters. She has represented debtors in possession, secured creditors, unsecured creditors, equity holders and other interested parties in Chapter 11 reorganizations, bankruptcy asset sales, debt-for-equity exchanges and work-outs.

James F Conlan
Co-Chairman
Email jconlan@sidley.com

James Conlan is Co-Chairman of Sidley Austin LLP's firm-wide Corporate Reorganization and Bankruptcy Group. Mr Conlan is a member of the firm's Executive Committee. He has advised numerous domestic and international clients on all aspects of restructurings.

Mr Conlan was selected by *Turnarounds & Workouts* for its 2009 list of the top dozen outstanding restructuring lawyers in America. He is regularly listed as a leader in the corporate restructuring field by various industry and legal publications, including *Chambers USA: America's Leading Lawyers for Business* and the *International Who's Who of Business Lawyers*. Mr Conlan is also widely recognized as a leader in large-scale cross-border restructuring and insolvency, having led some of the largest cross-border restructuring matters.

Sitrick Brincko Group

1840 Century Park East, Suite 800, Los Angeles, CA 90067
Tel +1 310 788 2850 **Fax** +1 310 788 2855

Michael S Sitrick

Chairman and CEO
Email Mike_Sitrick@sitrick.com
A nationally recognized expert in the strategic use of communications, Michael Sitrick has been the subject of numerous articles and profiles focusing on the results he has achieved for clients. *Los Angeles* magazine wrote: 'Sitrick is a pure product of the 24-hour news cycle, of a culture dominated and defined by newspapers, magazines, TV, radio, the internet, of the never-ending noise streaming into our lives. Beyond his aggressiveness, beyond his toughness, what distinguishes Sitrick is his ability to play the media to his clients' advantage.'

Since founding Sitrick and Company, he has provided advice and counsel to more than 1,000 companies, including some of the nation's largest corporations and highest-profile individuals — on both routine and extremely sensitive matters. Matters with which he has been involved pretty much span the spectrum. While many of his cases dominate the headlines, perhaps even most telling are the cases that are never heard about — where Mr Sitrick and his firm are brought in to keep their clients out of the press, a much more difficult task. Virtually since its inception, the firm has been ranked either the number one or the number two strategic public relations firm in the US by *Inside PR* magazine.

Prior to forming the firm, Mr Sitrick was Senior Vice President, Communications for Wickes Companies Inc. A member of the senior management group, he was the architect of Wickes' Chapter 11 communications programs. Mr Sitrick serves on the board of directors of the Turnaround Management Association and the Jewish Television Network, and is a member of the Advisory Board of The 1939 Club, the largest Holocaust Survivors organization in the US.

Skadden, Arps, Slate, Meagher & Flom LLP

155 N Wacker Drive, Chicago, Illinois 60606
Tel +1 312 407 0700 **Fax** +1 312 407 0411
Web www.skadden.com

John Wm ("Jack") Butler, Jr

Partner and Co-Practice Leader
Email jack.butler@skadden.com
Jack Butler co-leads Skadden, Arps' global Corporate Restructuring Practice where he focuses primarily on advising companies and investors with respect to complex business reorganizations, troubled-company M&A, debt restructurings and financing matters, including cross-border transactions and advising officers and directors on corporate governance and fiduciary duty matters. He has assisted many global businesses restructure outside the US, execute cross-border financing and privatization transactions, and divest various business lines and entities.

Mr Butler was named one of the decade's most influential lawyers by *The National Law Journal* in March 2010, and is one of two practicing lawyers and ten inductees in the inaugural class of the Turnaround, Restructuring and Distressed Investing Industry Hall of Fame. He was one of The American Lawyers' Dealmakers of the Year in 2010 and 2004, and also received the ILO Client Choice Award 2010 based on client nominations for excellent client care and quality of services rendered.

Mr Butler served as Chairman of the Turnaround Management Association for two years in 1996 and 1997, and is a fellow in the American College of Bankruptcy and International Insolvency Institute. A past director of the American Bankruptcy Institute, he founded INSOL's Group of 36 and has served many other industry organizations, including the American Board of Certification, Commercial Finance Association Education Foundation and the New York Institute of Credit.

J Eric Ivester

Partner
Email eric.ivester@skadden.com
Eric Ivester represents clients in business reorganizations, acquisitions and divestitures. He has represented debtors, creditors, investors, sellers, purchasers and other financial advisors in all stages

of complex restructuring transactions, from Chapter 11 reorganizations to out-of-court negotiations, work-outs and divestitures. Mr Ivester has a wide range of engagements in middle-market, large-cap and cross-border transactions, including in both the manufacturing and retail sectors.

The Turnaround Management Association recognized Mr Ivester for his work on the Interstate Bakeries Chapter 11, naming it the "Large Company Transaction of the Year" at its 2009 Transaction of the Year Awards. In February 2009, Mr Ivester was named "Dealmaker of the Week" by *The Am Law Daily* for his work on the same case. He has been repeatedly selected for inclusion in *Chambers USA* and *The Best Lawyers in America*.

Skadden, Arps, Slate, Meagher & Flom LLP
Four Times Square, New York, NY 10036
Tel +1 212 735 3000 **Fax** +1 212 735 2000
Web www.skadden.com

Peter Allan Atkins
Partner
Email peter.atkins @skadden.com
Peter Atkins is an internationally recognized attorney involved in Skadden's corporate and securities practices, with extensive experience in the M&A and corporate governance fields. He has represented acquirors (US and non-US), targets and investment banks in many mergers, acquisitions, takeovers (negotiated and contested), leveraged buyouts, spin-offs and joint ventures. He also counsels clients on corporate, securities and business-related matters, including directors' duties, disclosure, corporate compliance and internal investigations. Advice often is provided to boards, independent directors and special committees in crisis situations and where satisfaction of their fiduciary duties is subject to particular scrutiny. Mr Atkins has had substantial transactional involvement in numerous industries, including airline, defense and aerospace, energy, financial institutions, forest products, healthcare, information technology, insurance, media and telecommunications, retail and utilities.

Mr Atkins writes and lectures on corporate and securities topics, including mergers and acquisitions and corporate governance. He serves on the Board of Advisors of Harvard Law School's Forum on Corporate Governance and Financial Regulation. Mr Atkins has been recognized as a "leading lawyer" by *Chambers Global*; *Chambers USA*; *The International Who's Who of Corporate Governance Lawyers*; *PLC Which Lawyer? Yearbook*; and *The Best Lawyers in America*.

John K Carroll
Partner
Email john.carroll@skadden.com
John Carroll is a partner in Skadden, Arps, Slate, Meagher & Flom LLP's White Collar Crime and Regulatory Enforcement Group. He represents institutional and individual clients in complex civil disputes and domestic and multinational criminal and regulatory investigations relating to alleged financial fraud, corrupt payments, online gaming and other matters.

Mr Carroll formerly served as the chief of the Securities and Commodities Fraud Task Force in the Southern District of New York. He also was a member of the US Attorney General's Economic Crimes Council and the Department of Justice's Securities and Commodities Fraud Working Group.

Mark A McDermott
Partner
Email mark.mcdermott@skadden.com
Mark McDermott represents public and private corporations and their principal stakeholders in troubled company M&A, restructuring and financing transactions. He has represented corporations in out-of-court restructurings, prepackaged and prearranged Chapter 11 cases, and traditional Chapter 11 cases. He also has represented bank groups, bondholders, financial institutions, investment funds, equity holders and real estate developers in all types of distressed investments.

Mr McDermott advises businesses and investment vehicles in non-distressed transactions, including M&A, spinoff and structured finance transactions. He counsels clients on the bankruptcy aspects of derivatives and similar structured financial products. He has also represented troubled companies, or their stakeholders, facing government investigations and mass tort liability.

Mr McDermott has advised clients in numerous industries, including consumer products, energy, entertainment, finance, healthcare, homebuilding, manufacturing, oil and gas, real estate and real estate finance (including CMBS), retail, technology, telecommunications and transportation.

John W Osborn
Partner
Email john.osborn@skadden.com
John Osborn is head of Skadden's Derivative Financial Products Group. He has a very broad

practice in both over-the-counter derivatives transactions and in capital markets transactions with derivatives elements. His practice in both of these areas involves co-ordination with numerous offices and areas of expertise within the firm and has a strong focus on new product structuring and development.

Mr Osborn's OTC derivatives practice has involved the full range of transaction types, including various forms and combinations of forward contracts, swaps, options and hybrid, structured and credit-linked notes. These transactions have involved numerous reference instruments, including not only equity, debt and other securities, but also interest rates and currencies, term and revolving bank loans, various commodities, and defaults and other credit-related attributes. He has represented numerous dealers and a broad spectrum of end-users, including issuers, with a focus on accelerated share purchase and hedging programs, as well as other corporates and private funds.

In his capital markets practice, Mr Osborn has worked on diverse public and private convertible and exchangeable securities offerings and related OTC derivative transactions, including call spreads and share lending and forward agreements. He has also worked on numerous equity security units transactions, as well as on various structured debt securities offerings and complex cross-border financings. He has represented underwriters and placement agents as well as numerous issuers.

Skadden, Arps, Slate, Meagher & Flom LLP
300 South Grand Avenue, Suite 3400, Los Angeles, California 90071
Tel +1 213 687 5000 Fax +1 213 687 5600
Web www.skadden.com

Richard Marmaro
Partner
Email richard.marmaro@skadden.com
Richard Marmaro is the head of Skadden's West Coast SEC Enforcement and White Collar Criminal Defense Practice. He has successfully defended individuals and corporations, both nationally and internationally, in all phases of complex civil, criminal and regulatory matters, including those involving allegations of insider trading, accounting and disclosure irregularities, stock options backdating, market manipulation, financial frauds and wrongful termination.

Prior to entering private practice, Mr Marmaro

served as a law clerk to a federal judge in the Southern District of New York and as an assistant United States Attorney in the Central District of California, where he was an Assistant Chief of the Criminal Division.

Spencer Stuart
277 Park Avenue, 32nd Floor, New York, NY 10172
Tel +1 212 336 0200 Fax +1 212 336 0296
Web www.spencerstuart.com

Julie H Daum
Co-Leader of the North American Boards and CEO Succession Practice
Email jdaum@spencerstuart.com
Julie Daum is the practice leader for the North American Board and CEO Succession Practice of Spencer Stuart, the leading executive search firm. She consults with corporate boards, working with companies of all sizes from the Fortune 10 to pre-IPO companies, and has worked on over 450 director assignments. She serves on the board of directors of Spencer Stuart, Women's Refugee Commission, Citymeals on Wheels, the James Beard Foundation and SmileTrain.

Ms Daum is also involved in the organization of the Northwestern Conference on Corporate Governance and was the founder of the Wharton/Spencer Stuart Directors' Institute. Prior to joining Spencer Stuart, she was the Executive Director of the corporate board resource at Catalyst. She managed all board of directors' activities and worked with companies to identify qualified women for their board. Ms Daum began her career as a consultant with McKinsey & Company in Los Angeles.

Stern School of Business
NYU Stern, Henry Kaufman Management Center, 44 West Fourth Street, New York, NY 10012
Tel +1 212 998 0100
Web www.stern.nyu.edu

Edward Altman
Email ealtman@stern.nyu.edu
Edward Altman is the Max L Heine Professor of Finance at the Stern School of Business, New York University, and Director of the Credit and Fixed Income Research Program at the NYU Salomon Center.

Dr Altman has an international reputation as an expert on corporate bankruptcy, high-yield bonds, distressed debt and credit risk analysis. He was named Laureate 1984 by the Hautes Etudes Commerciales Foundation in Paris for his accumulated works on corporate-distress prediction models and procedures for financial rehabilitation, and awarded the Graham & Dodd Scroll for 1985 by the Financial Analysts Federation for his work on default rates and high-yield corporate debt.

He was inducted into the Fixed Income Analysts Society Hall of Fame in 2001 and elected President of the Financial Management Association (2003) and a Fellow of the FMA in 2004. He was among the inaugural inductees into the Turnaround Management Association's Hall of Fame in 2008.

Dr Altman is an advisor to many financial institutions, including Concordia Advisors, Paulson and Company, Investcorp and RiskMetrics (MSCI), and was an investment advisor to the New York State Common Retirement Fund, as well as on the boards of the Franklin Mutual Series Funds and Automated Trading Desk. He is also Chairman of the Academic Advisory Council of the Turnaround Management Association.

Togut, Segal & Segal LLP
One Penn Plaza, Suite 3335, New York, NY 10119
Tel +1 212 594 5000 Fax +1 212 967 4258

Neil Berger
Partner
Email neilberger@teamtogut.com
Neil Berger is Partner of Togut, Segal & Segal LLP, where he practices restructuring and insolvency law. For the past 25 years, he has specialized in the representation of the interests of Chapter 11 debtors, creditors, creditor committees, and Chapter 11, Chapter 7 and post-confirmation trustees.

A significant portion of Mr Berger's practice includes the representation of parties in fraudulent conveyance and preferential transfer litigation. Among other representations concerning avoidance litigation, Togut, Segal & Segal LLP has or currently serves as plaintiff's counsel in: Collins & Aikman, Delphi Corporation, Enron Corp and SemCrude. Mr Berger was named as a New York Super Lawyer for 2009 and 2010.

Albert Togut
Senior Partner
Email altogut@teamtogut.com
For the past 35 years, Albert Togut has specialized in bankruptcy law to the exclusion of all other areas of practice. His firm is debtor's counsel in some of the largest and highest-profile Chapter 11 cases.

Mr Togut has served as Trustee in several thousand bankruptcy cases, under Chapter 11 and Chapter 7 of the Bankruptcy Code, including the largest Chapter 7 case ever filed — the $4 billion Refco LLC (registered commodities broker) estate — and Anthracite Capital, a specialty finance company that invested in commercial real estate assets in an investment pool having an aggregate face (or par) amount exceeding $19.5 billion. For 30 years, he has been an active member of the trustee panel maintained by the Southern District of New York.

Mr Togut is a Fellow of the American College of Bankruptcy and a member of its Second Circuit admissions screening committee, a Fellow of the International Insolvency Institute, and a Director of the American Bankruptcy Institute. He was named as a New York Super Lawyer for 2007, 2008, 2009 and 2010.

Turnaround Management Association
150 South Wacker Drive, Suite 900, Chicago, Illinois 60606
Tel +1 312 578 6900 Fax +1 312 578 8336
Web www.turnaround.org

Duffield Meyercord
Partner, Carl Marks Advisory Group LLC
Email dmeyercord@carlmarks.com
Duff Meyercord serves as Partner of Carl Marks Advisory Group LLC and Carl Marks Healthcare Partners LLC. He has more than 30 years' experience in directing strategic projects and providing operational advisory services to numerous businesses in a range of industries. These services include restructuring, turnarounds, M&A advisory, lender communications, due diligence, valuation, cash monitoring, and serving in interim management positions.

Before joining Carl Marks, Mr Meyercord was President and founder of Meyercord Advisors, where he provided advisory services to businesses. Concurrently, he was Managing Director and founder of Venturetech Management Inc, a venture capital fund.

Mr Meyercord launched his career with McLean Industries, which maintained equity positions in land development, manufacturing, shipping and technology companies. He spearheaded the firm's Corporate Development, Strategic Planning, and M&A functions, often serving as CEO or sitting on the board of many McLean-owned companies.

Weil, Gotshal & Manges LLP
767 Fifth Avenue, New York, NY 10153
Tel +1 212 310 8000 Fax +1 212 310 8007
Web www.weil.com

Harvey R Miller
Senior Partner
Email harvey.miller@weil.com
Harvey R Miller is a Senior Partner in the New York-based international law firm of Weil, Gotshal & Manges LLP, where he had been a member of the Management Committee for over 25 years and created and developed the firm's Business Finance & Restructuring Department, specializing in reorganizing distressed business entities and representing creditors, investors and purchasers of distressed businesses and assets. From September 2002 to March 2007, he was a Managing Director and Vice Chairman of Greenhill & Co LLC, an international investment banking firm.

Other posts: Adjunct Associate Professor of Law, 1974-76, and Adjunct Professor of Law, 1976 to present, New York University Law School; Visiting Lecturer, Yale Law School, 1983-84; Lecturer in Law, 2000 to present, Columbia University School of Law; Member, Board of Visitors, Columbia University School of Law through 2002; Member, Dean's Council, Columbia University School of Law, 2003 to present; Member, National Bankruptcy Conference; Fellow, American College of Bankruptcy; Fellow of the American Bar Foundation.

WL Ross & Co LLC
1166 Avenue of the Americas, 27th Fl, New York, NY 10036
Tel +1 212 826 1100 Fax +1 212 317 4891
Web www.wlross.com

Wilbur L Ross
CEO
Email wlross@wlross.com
Wilbur Ross, CEO of WL Ross & Co LLC, may be one of the best-known private equity investors in the US. His private equity funds bought Bethlehem Steel and several other bankrupt producers and revitalized them into the largest US producer, before merging them into Mittal Steel for $4.5 billion. Mr Ross remains a Director of what is now ArcelorMittal, the world's largest steel company. He also created and chairs International Coal Group; International Textile Group, the most global American company in that industry; and International Auto Components Group, a $4.5 billion producer of instrument panels

and other interior components, operating in 17 countries; Compagnie Européenne de Wagons Sarl, the largest rail car leasing company in Europe; and American Home Mortgage Servicing Inc, the second-largest servicer of sub-prime mortgages. He is a member of the boards of Assured Guaranty and Greenbrier Companies, both NYSE-listed.

Mr Ross was Executive Managing Director of Rothschild Inc for 24 years before acquiring its private equity partnerships in 2000. He is a board member of the Whitney Museum of American Art, Japan Society, Yale University School of Management, Partnership for New York City, Harvard Business School Club of New York, the Committee on Capital Markets Regulation, the Harvard Committee on University Resources, BritishAmerican Business, the Blenheim American Foundation, and the Chairman's Council of the US/India Business Council. President Kim Dae-jung awarded him a medal for his assistance in Korea's financial crisis, President Clinton appointed him to the Board of the US-Russia Investment Fund, and he served as Privatization Advisor to New York City Mayor Rudy Giuliani. Mr Ross is the only person elected both to the Private Equity Hall of Fame and the Turnaround Management Association Hall of Fame.

Zolfo Cooper
Grace Building, 1114 Avenue of the Americas, 41st Floor, New York, NY 10036
Tel +1 212 561 4060 Fax +1 212 213 1749
Web www.zolfocooper.com
Simon Freakley, Joff Mitchell
Managing Partners
Emails sfreakley@zolfocooper.eu, jmitchell@zolfocooper.com
Simon Freakley and Joff Mitchell are (respectively) the Managing Partners of the European and US practices of Zolfo Cooper, a leading independent global corporate advisory and restructuring firm.

Specializing in corporate advisory and restructuring work for over 25 years, combining his skills of business turnaround, strategic consulting and mediation, Mr Freakley has led many large and high-profile assignments, including cross-border restructurings for US and European stakeholders.

Mr Mitchell has been an operating executive and turnaround specialist for over 25 years, providing leadership to companies and stakeholders facing operational and financial challenges. Assignments include serving as CEO and Chairman of a multibillion-dollar energy company, leading the restructuring of a financial services operation, and advising the board of a publicly held giftware company.

Navigating Today's Environment: Sponsor profiles

The American Bankruptcy Institute

The American Bankruptcy Institute (ABI) is pleased to be associated with *Navigating Today's Environment: The Directors' and Officers' Guide to Restructuring*. The timeliness, scope and quality of the content make it an excellent resource for ABI members, and for any practitioner interested in a field guide to today's complex restructuring landscape.

The ABI's membership consists of nearly 13,000 insolvency professionals in the United States and more than 30 other nations. ABI members come from all insolvency disciplines, including attorneys, lenders, judges, accountants, financial advisors, restructuring officers, appraisers, investment bankers, academics, turnaround specialists and others representing both debtors and creditors in commercial and consumer cases.

The multi-disciplinary scope of our membership creates a diverse environment in which to advance our education and research mission, while providing robust opportunities for networking and business development. More than 20 committees, including our International Committee, provide an easy way to access the latest developments in the field and advance professional development.

Founded in 1982, the ABI is the leading provider of continuing legal education programs in the United States and Europe. The two dozen-plus US programs each year are complemented by cross-border conferences in venues such as Frankfurt (2009), London (2010) and Dublin (2011). Live programs cover cutting-edge topics in both commercial and consumer bankruptcy. They feature a variety of formats, including interactive workshops.

ABI publications include the monthly *ABI Journal* and the semi-annual *ABI Law Review*. The *Journal* contains regular columns on developments in Europe, Latin America and elsewhere. The ABI also adds several new books per year to its growing catalogue of publications. Included among these is a recently updated primer on the EU Regulation on Insolvency Proceedings, written by Professor Bob Wessels.

The ABI is also the largest US member of INSOL International, the federation of international insolvency organizations. Our joint website, www.GlobalINSOLvency.org, provides news and a rich trove of country-specific information. Members can receive daily news via email. We continually seek out opportunities to partner with worldwide organizations and publications of excellence.

We trust you will find this Guide to be a rich resource that you will turn to frequently, and that will encourage you to become active in the ABI.

Critical thinking at the critical time.™

FTI Consulting Inc

FTI Consulting Inc exists to help companies and their stakeholders protect and enhance enterprise value in an increasingly complex economic, legal and regulatory environment. We deliver a unique breadth of expertise and thought leadership across the globe.

From restructuring to "e-discovery" experts and strategic communication specialists, from former chief executives to Nobel Laureate economists, FTI Consulting is a leader and innovator in driving solutions to many of the most complex business challenges of our time. United by a culture of urgency, we provide deep expertise in five core segments:

Corporate finance/restructuring

FTI is the leading provider of turnaround, performance improvement, financial and operational restructuring services. Our professionals address the full spectrum of challenges faced by companies, boards, private equity sponsors, creditor constituencies and other parties-in-interest. Our corporate finance/ restructuring team also provides transaction-related services to both buyers and sellers of businesses.

Economic consulting

We are one of the world's leaders in economic consulting, providing law firms, corporations and government clients with clear analysis of complex economic issues for use in legal and regulatory proceedings, strategic decisions and public policy debates. The economic consulting segment includes Nobel Laureates and top-ranked anti-trust economists.

Forensic and litigation consulting

FTI is a leading global provider of strategic solutions for law firms and corporations facing complex disputes and investigations. Our team of experienced advisors provides a complete range of services throughout the dispute, investigation and litigation life cycle. The forensic and litigation consulting segment has the greatest international reach in its field.

Strategic communications

Our global strategic communications segment, FD, is one of the world's most sought-after business and financial communications consultancies. FD has helped many of the world's leading organizations harness the power of communications to solve critical business problems. The segment, the largest of its kind in the world, was recognized as the Asia Pacific Public Relations Firm of the Year in 2008.

Technology

FTI Technology provides software, services and consulting that empower corporations and their law firms to secure the best-possible results for legal or regulatory matters — without disrupting their core business.

Rothschild Inc

Rothschild is a worldwide financial advisory firm that is family controlled and independent. Its businesses include investment banking, merchant banking and wealth management.

In the area of global financial advice, Rothschild provides impartial, expert advisory and execution services to corporations, governments, institutions and individuals. Senior bankers lead every assignment from start to finish, so all clients benefit from the collective intellectual capital, specialist expertise and wealth of experience. With 1,000 bankers based in 40 countries around the world, Rothschild's scale, reach and local knowledge enable it to develop relationships and deliver effective solutions to support its clients wherever their business takes them.

Rothschild provides a wide range of advisory services to its clients, including advice on mergers and acquisitions, privatizations, valuations, strategic advice and financing advice, relating to debt, equity and restructuring solutions in both domestic and cross-border situations. The Rothschild approach is characterized by combining in-depth global industry knowledge with a detailed understanding of local markets.

Rothschild places a strong emphasis on developing trusted long-term relationships with clients, and a significant proportion of its revenue is from repeat business, evidencing the strength of the firm's relationship- driven approach, free from potential conflicts.

As a firm that focuses exclusively on providing clients with advice, rather than financial products or capital, Rothschild organizes its business around five key tenets:

Advisory only

As an advisory-only firm that does not trade, underwrite, or provide research or capital, Rothschild places the client first and its actions are driven by discretion and integrity. Nothing gets in the way of providing impartial advice for each and every client.

Scale and experience

Rothschild advises on many industries' most complex transformational assignments. The firm applies its full intellectual capital to each client's needs, and is insightful and innovative in delivering the best solutions. Rothschild's creative approach is dedicated to providing clear value added, utilizing, as needed, specialists with in-depth experience on industry and balance sheet issues.

On the ground worldwide

Rothschild bankers are based around the world and are committed to exceptional, focused, hands-on service that delivers the full benefit of the firm's global network and deep local and industry sector knowledge.

Long-term perspective

As a family-controlled business, Rothschild is unconstrained by short-term thinking and quarterly reporting. It can take a long-term view to deliver each client's interests.

Trusted and independent

Rothschild bankers appreciate that long-lasting relationships depend upon the quality and integrity of their advice. The scale of the business means that Rothschild is not dependent on any one client.

Globally, Rothschild completes more transactions than other advisors, while remaining only as good as its last assignment. This has been true for more than 200 years, and is why Rothschild is the leader in financial advice, worldwide.

Skadden, Arps, Slate, Meagher & Flom LLP & Affiliates

Skadden, Arps, Slate, Meagher & Flom LLP

With approximately 2,000 attorneys in 24 offices on five continents, Skadden, Arps, Slate, Meagher & Flom LLP and affiliates serve clients in every major financial center. Our strategically positioned US and international locations allow us proximity to our clients and their operations and ensure a seamless and unified approach at all times.

For more than 60 years, Skadden has provided legal services to the corporate, industrial, financial and governmental communities around the world in a wide variety of high-profile transactions, regulatory matters, and litigation and controversy issues. Our clients range from a variety of small, start-up companies to a substantial number of the 500 largest US corporations and many of the leading global companies.

We have represented numerous governments, many of the largest banks — including virtually all of the leading investment banks — and major insurance and financial services companies.

Corporate Restructuring Practice

The global Corporate Restructuring Group at Skadden works to provide innovative, practical legal solutions to clients involved in distressed company situations. Our goal is to give effective and expedient responses, which allow clients to minimize costs, enhance value and properly position themselves for the future. Skadden's experience across a variety of industries and with all types of restructurings, combined with our international reach, wide-ranging practice capabilities and dedication to client service, allows us to address clients' needs in any restructuring situation.

We represent troubled companies, their boards, management, owners, creditors and investors, handling restructurings in and out of court, financial recapitalizations, business reorganizations and liquidations. The group draws on the firm's experience in M&A, banking and capital market transactions to develop innovative strategies for clients. Our lawyers also advise on insolvency issues in corporate and financing transactions and on all aspects of distressed debt trading and securities issues.

Approximately 100 attorneys from other departments within the firm, such as tax, banking, corporate, litigation, real estate, securities, and mergers and acquisitions, regularly work on restructuring and bankruptcy matters; the seamless integration of Skadden's restructuring practice in our offices in Europe and Asia allows us to address clients' needs in the context of insolvency and bankruptcy regimes around the world.

Our business-oriented focus has led to innovative and economically efficient strategies for our clients, including debt and equity exchange offers, purchases and sales of distressed assets, prepackaged and prenegotiated bankruptcies.

We help clients to minimize the time spent in Chapter 11, and our experience in high-stakes, troubled company disputes includes expedited litigation.

Additionally, a substantial aspect of our practice focuses on avoiding or mitigating the adverse effects of liquidity or other crises through contingency planning and helping companies overcome the inertia of a downward spiral while they still have alternatives to bankruptcy.

Turnaround Management Association®
Dedicated to Corporate Renewal

The Turnaround Management Association

The Turnaround Management Association is the only international non-profit association dedicated to corporate renewal and turnaround management. Its international headquarters is in Chicago.

Established in 1988, the TMA has more than 9,000 members in 46 chapters, including 32 in North America, and one each in Australia, Brazil, the Czech Republic, Finland, France, Germany, Italy, Japan, the Netherlands, Southern Africa, Spain, Sweden, Taiwan and the UK, with a chapter in formation in Hong Kong/China.

TMA members are a professional community of turnaround and corporate renewal professionals who share a common interest in strengthening the economy through the restoration of corporate value. They include:

- 45 per cent — turnaround practitioners who consult with or participate in helping troubled companies in the recovery process, including interim corporate managers, financial and operating advisors and accountants.
- 15 per cent — lenders and bankers/work-out officers.
- 14 per cent — attorneys.
- 10 per cent — investors, including equity investors, investment bankers and venture capitalists.
- 16 per cent — other related professionals, including receivers, appraisers, trustees, auctioneers/liquidators, factors, academics, government/judges.

All TMA members must sign a Code of Ethics each year specifying high standards of professionalism, integrity and competence. The TMA's Certified Turnaround Professional (CTP) program recognizes professional excellence and provides an objective measure of expertise related to work-outs, restructurings and corporate renewal. Applicants for certification must meet stringent standards of education, experience and professional conduct, pass a comprehensive examination and maintain the credential through continuing education credits.

TMAssist is a public service program originally formed to aid businesses affected by the 2005 Gulf Coast hurricanes through workshop presentations and educational materials. In 2008, 75 volunteers helped plant irises in New Orleans City Park to revitalize the lagoon as part of the TMA's 20th Anniversary Celebration.

The Journal of Corporate Renewal, TMA Annual Report and website (www.turnaround.org) are the TMA's principal publications and media outlets.

The 2010 TMA International meetings include the Distressed Investing Conference in Las Vegas, January 27-29; the Spring Conference in New York, April 20-22; and the Annual Convention in Orlando, October 6-8. TMA chapters will also hold several regional conferences in 2010.

Since 1993, the TMA has recognized outstanding achievements by chapters and individual members at its Annual Convention. The Turnaround of the Year Awards began in 1996; the Carl Marks Student Paper Competition in 2003; the Butler-Cooley Excellence in Teaching Awards in 2004; and in 2005, the Transaction of the Year Awards. The TMA established the Turnaround Management, Restructuring and Distressed Investing Industry Hall of Fame in 2008 and inducted 10 icons at the TMA 20th Anniversary Celebration.

The TMA's principal spokespersons for the corporate renewal industry are 2010 Chairman Patrick C Lagrange, Managing Director at Carl Marks Advisory Group LLC in New York City, and 2010 President Lisa M Poulin, Managing Partner with CRG Partners Group's Bethesda, Maryland office.

For more information or to request an interview, contact Public Relations Manager Michele Drayton at +1 312 242 6044, or mdrayton@turnaround.org.